Treat this book with care and respect.

*It should become part of your personal
and professional library. It will
serve you well at any number
of points during your
professional career.*

 W9-AUO-683

Management & Organization

3d Edition

Henry L. Sisk

Professor of Business Administration
North Texas State University

Published by

G42 **SOUTH-WESTERN PUBLISHING CO.**

CINCINNATI   WEST CHICAGO, ILL.   DALLAS   PELHAM MANOR, N.Y.   PALO ALTO, CALIF.

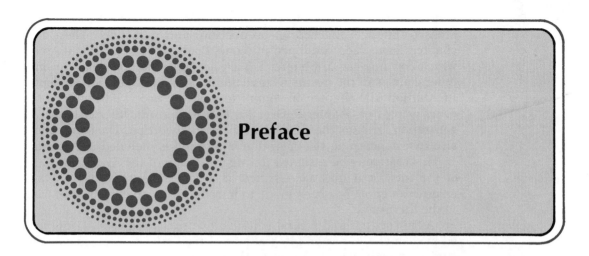

Preface

Several assumptions are implicit to the writing of a textbook about management. First, it is assumed that there are aspects of the practice of management that can be taught to others. Such a statement runs counter to the belief that managers are born or that experience is the only teacher; yet the belief that managers can be taught minimizes in no way the value of experience and practice in the development of managerial skills and insights. It is believed, however, that those who enter managerial positions with knowledge and concepts gained from a formal study of management require less time to develop an acceptable level of managerial performance than those who have not studied management as a discipline. Second, it is assumed that management is best defined as a process of coordinating all the resources of an organization in order to achieve organizational objectives. The definition of management as a process permits the description and analysis of that process, thus making it possible to develop and organize the concepts and techniques of management in a systematic way. Third, there is the implied assumption that the management process is present in and necessary to all formal organizations — business, governmental, educational, social, religious, and charitable — if they are to achieve their respective organizational objectives effectively. Because of the universality of management and the consequent demand for managers, the study of management fulfills an important educational need.

This book is intended for use in the introductory management course in four-year colleges and universities and in those community colleges offering either a mid-management curriculum or the introductory management course. The book may also be used in management development programs offered by companies and by governmental agencies.

One of the major objectives of this third edition has been to reduce the overall length of the book without sacrificing content. The second edition contained two chapters concerning planning for the functional areas of finance, marketing, production, and personnel. These two chapters have been combined into one, Planning for Functional Areas, which now appears as Chapter 5. They are introductory in nature since other courses in the business curriculum cover these subjects in depth. In addition, the chapter on committees of the second edition now appears as part of Chapter 9, Organization Structure. Otherwise, the organization remains the same as in the second edition. The comprehensive case concerning the operation of a motel is included in Appendix B. This case may be assigned to integrate each of the five major parts of the text, or it may be assigned as a comprehensive case. In each chapter an effort has been made to introduce new materials appearing in the literature.

As in the first and second editions, two case problems are presented in each chapter as an integral part of the text. These cases offer the student an opportunity to relate the material in the text to an actual situation. The cases are also helpful in securing maximum student participation in class. Each chapter begins with an opening case problem that describes a business situation. In most of the chapters the case is referred to in the text material, thereby utilizing the case as a practical example to make the discussion in the text more meaningful. Generally the closing case for each chapter draws upon concepts presented in the latter part of the chapter for its solution. The case is related to the text by means of a bridge paragraph at the end of the chapter.

Many persons contribute to the writing of a book; however, for a third edition there is a special debt of gratitude to the professors and students who have written to the publisher and to the author. Many of their comments have been incorporated in this edition, and it is hoped that the feedback provided by professors and students will continue during the current edition. A special note of thanks is due Mr. M. W. Isbell, Chairman of Ramada Inns, Inc., for his cooperation and interest in the development of the comprehensive case. In addition to the many colleagues in other institutions who have read portions of the revised manuscript, the author wishes to thank Professor Elvis Stephens, Chairman of the Department of Personnel and Industrial Relations at North Texas State University, for providing the teaching schedule necessary for the author to have the time to complete this work. Mrs. Joy Bellomy has contributed very much through her help in the literature search, revision and development of case problems, and editing the revised manuscript.

Henry L. Sisk

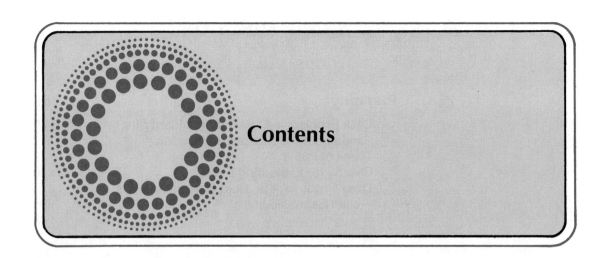

Contents

PART TWO ● THE PLANNING FUNCTION

PART THREE ● THE ORGANIZING FUNCTION

PART FOUR ● THE LEADERSHIP FUNCTION

PART FIVE ● THE CONTROL FUNCTION

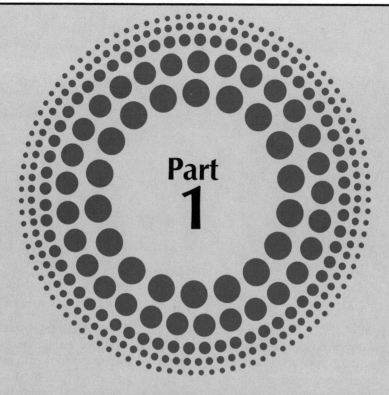

Part
1

Introduction

What do you think of when you hear or read the word *management*? Do you think of management as a group, as a profession, as a science, or as an art? How widespread is management and when is it needed? What does a manager do? These are the questions that form the framework of the discussion concerning the nature of management. From the discussion a definition of management as a telic, or purposeful, process is developed. One of the approaches, the modern or systems approach, to the study of management is introduced briefly. Though systems theory is introduced in the first chapter and referred to throughout the text, the approach used in this book is best described as eclectic; that is, information is drawn from a broad range of sources so that the differing needs and interests of students may be met.

As part of the introduction to any field of study a brief statement of the historical development of that field is helpful. In Chapter 2 the development of management concepts is traced. From time to time different aspects of management have been emphasized. First there is an emphasis upon production, not surprising when one considers the industrial revolution and the need to know how to best utilize mass production facilities. Then the emphasis shifts to the administration of the entire enterprise. Some refer to an emphasis on one aspect of management in preference to another as a school of management. The emphasis upon production and administration is often referred to as the classical school. Another area of emphasis is human relations. There are so many schools or approaches to the study of management that they have been termed a jungle and their proponents have been accused of engaging in inky warfare. Some of the brush in this jungle is cut away and an integrative view is presented.

The introduction closes with a discussion of two subjects that may seem, at first glance, unrelated. These topics are objectives and ethics. Objectives are goals, and form the basis of an approach to management best described as management by objectives. As managers do those things necessary to achieve objectives they interact with other people and the interaction is often described as being either ethical or unethical in nature. Personal values are one of the major determinants of ethical behavior. The personal value systems of managers and the problem areas requiring ethical judgments are discussed.

Chapter 1

Management Defined

Case Problem 1-A
WHO IS "MANAGEMENT"?

As he entered the conference room, Mr. Martin, division manager of a gas utility company serving 200 communities, noted that all the members of his staff were present for the special meeting called for the purpose of organizing a management club. Seated at the table were the division accounting supervisor, the supervisor of engineering, the construction superintendent, the sales manager, the employee relations manager, and the division home economist.

Mr. Martin opened the meeting with a brief review of some previous discussions that had taken place regarding the formation of a management club. He continued, "As you may remember, four suggestions have been made as criteria for membership in the club. These are: first, all people whose names appear on the division organization chart, including district office supervisory personnel; second, all employees with supervisory responsibility; third, all persons exempt from the overtime provisions of the Wage and Hour Law; or, finally, everyone whose earnings are over $125 a week."

Mr. Harmon, engineering supervisor, immediately voiced his doubts as to the value of such a club. "I'm not sure that the men working under me have the time or the inclination to participate in a management club. It seems to me that it is important to determine first of all the purpose for having this sort of organization and the possible benefits that might be gained from it."

"John, let's get to that in just a minute," Mr. Martin replied. "First, I'd like to hear what some of you think about the criteria that have been suggested for membership."

The employee relations manager, Mrs. Ross, said, "Well, I can foresee some difficulties arising if we use earnings of $125 a week as a criterion. All of us know that we have people in some departments who earn that much money each week simply because of length of service. For instance, two of the clerks in our customer service department who have been with us for 20 years are earning more than $125 a week. Yet they have no managerial responsibilities. What do we do about them?"

Mr. Walker, sales manager for the division, stated that he agreed with both Mr. Harmon and Mrs. Ross. "Frankly, my district sales supervisors have more than they can do now, without getting involved in a management club. And, as Mrs. Ross pointed out, even though they would most certainly qualify for membership if the criterion is earnings of $125 a week, many of them don't supervise any other employees. In addition, the situation is further complicated because some of these people are on commission and their total earnings vary from month to month."

"I was going to suggest that we say 'salary' rather than 'earnings'," Mr. Fowler, the accounting supervisor, said. "However, the budget director would fall in that category and he doesn't supervise other people."

Miss Carter, the home economist, commented, "Yes, I would qualify for membership under those conditions, too, though my responsibilities are professional rather than managerial."

"And in the engineering department the situation is just the reverse," remarked Mr. Harmon. "Some of the engineers, who are also professionals, do have people working for them."

Mr. Perez, the construction superintendent, asked, "Well, who would qualify if we follow the suggestion of having as members all whose names appear on the organization chart?"

Mr. Martin replied, "That would include any person who is exempt from overtime pay. Some of you may remember that that was the qualifying factor considered when we made up the organization chart last year."

Noting that there were few positive suggestions being offered, Mr. Martin said, "At any rate, possibly the best way to decide this matter will be to have Mrs. Ross prepare a summary recommendation for our regular staff meeting next week, taking into consideration the questions each of you mentioned today. Mrs. Ross, I suggest that you begin with a statement of the purpose or objectives of such an organization, that is, whether we will be getting together to solve some of the problems that we share as managers, or to improve the flow of information through the division, or even for purely social reasons. And include recommendations for a name for the club and who will be eligible for membership."

1. Assume that you are in the position of Mrs. Ross, employee relations supervisor. Write a brief memo to Mr. Martin as requested.
2. Of the possible objectives stated for the management club, which do you believe are the more important ones? Justify your selection of the important objectives.
3. *Research Assignment.* Mr. Martin indicated that if an employee did not receive overtime pay for extra hours worked, he was eligible for inclusion on the company organization chart. Such employees are normally termed *exempt*, since they are exempt from the overtime provisions of the Fair Labor Standards Act, commonly called the Wage and Hour Law. Consult your nearest wage and hour office, either in person or by letter, and review those publications which discuss the basis for exemption. Discuss briefly whether exemption from overtime payment serves as a valid criterion for membership in a management club.

Seemingly, each person has different ideas concerning the meaning of the term "management." Some use the word "management" as a collective noun and refer to management as a certain group within an organization. Others define management as a process calling for the performance of specific functions, and there are those who view management as a profession, a science, or an art. Management is also regarded as an academic discipline and field of study. Each of these concepts of management reflects a different aspect of the nature of management. Serious study of management requires a relatively precise definition, and as a means of developing such a definition, let us examine more closely the nature of management.

THE NATURE OF MANAGEMENT

It is said that the lead sentence of a news story should answer the following questions: who, what, when, where, why, and how? These are questions that must also be answered so that a precise definition of management can be developed. In Case Problem 1-A, one question to be resolved is the *who* of management: Who is considered a member of management? However, before the *who* of management can be determined, it is necessary to know *what* management does, *how* it is done, *when* management becomes necessary, *where* management is found, and *why* management is necessary. These key questions form the broad organizational outline of the first part of this chapter.

The Need for Management

Our discussion of the need for management answers the question: *Why* is management necessary? *Management is responsible for the success or failure of the business.* The need for management is succinctly stated in the phrase, "to run the business," or within the context of Case Problem 1-B, "to mind the store."[1]

The statement that management is needed to direct the affairs of a business tells *why* management is needed, but does not indicate *when* and *where*. Whenever and wherever a group is formed having stated objectives, management is needed to direct and coordinate those efforts. Group action often requires that the members of a group subordinate their individual desires to attain the group goal. Effective group action requires a management to provide leadership in order to attain stated objectives.

The Functions of Management

An analysis of the functions of management tells us *what* management does. Also, an analysis of the functions of management provides the first step in the development of a precise definition of the word "management."

When studying management as an academic discipline, it is necessary to consider management as a *process*. When management is regarded as a process, it can be analyzed and described in terms of several major functions. In discussing the process of management, it is convenient, and even necessary, to describe and study each function of the process separately. As a result, it may seem that the management process is a series of discrete functions. Nothing could be further from

---

[1]An interesting account of another outstanding retail organization, Neiman-Marcus of Dallas, is Stanley Marcus, *Minding the Store*, A Memoir (Boston: Little, Brown & Co., 1974).

the truth. In practice, a manager may, and often does, perform simultaneously, or at least as a part of a continuum, all of the following four functions: planning, organizing, leading, and controlling.

Planning. When management is reviewed as a process, planning is the first function performed. Once objectives are determined, the means necessary to achieve the stated objectives are presented as plans. An organization's plans determine the course it takes and provide a basis for estimating the degree of probable success it will have in fulfilling its objectives. Plans are prepared for activities that require many years to complete; they are also necessary for short-term projects. Examples of long-range planning are found in product development programs and in the plans that guide the financing of a company. At the other end of the time scale, a production supervisor plans the output of a department for a period of one day or week. Each of these examples represents an extreme in the time span covered by the planning process, and each is necessary for the achievement of stated company objectives.

Organizing. In order to carry out plans, it is necessary to create an organization. It is a function of management to determine the type of organization required to execute stated plans. The kind of organization that is developed determines to a large extent whether or not the plans are fulfilled. In turn, the objectives of an enterprise and the plans required to meet these objectives have a direct bearing upon the characteristics and structure of the organization. A company whose objective is to provide food and shelter to the traveling public requires an entirely different organization than a firm whose objective is to transmit natural gas through a pipeline.

Leading. The third function of management — leading — has been termed motivating, directing, guiding, stimulating, and actuating. Although each of these words has a different connotation, any one of these terms indicates clearly that this function of management is concerned with the human factors of an organization. It is as a result of the efforts of each member of an organization that goals are attained; hence, a major function of the management process is to lead the organization so that objectives may be achieved.

Controlling. The last phase of the management process is the control function. The control function measures present performance against standards of performance. As a result of that comparison, it can be determined whether or not corrective action is needed to bring present performance in line with the expected performance expressed as standards. The control function is exercised continuously, and, although related to the functions of organizing and directing, it is more closely associated with the planning function. The corrective action of control almost invariably calls for a restatement of plans. As a result, many students of the management process consider the planning and control functions as part of a continuous cycle of planning-control-planning.

The analysis of the functions of management as a process not only answers the question concerning what management does, it also tells us *how* stated goals are achieved.

Management as a Group

One of the questions asked at the beginning of the chapter is whether or not management may be regarded as a group of people — the *who* of management. To some it is unfortunate that the word management is used as a collective noun to designate a group of managers instead of limiting the use of the word to describe the specific processes of planning, organizing, leading, and controlling. Nonetheless, reference to management as a group is deeply imbedded in our everyday language, and clarification of who is normally considered a member of management is needed.

Managers are those persons in an organization who accomplish their work primarily by directing the work of others. Some of the managers in Case Problem 1-A are seeking an answer to the question: Who is eligible to join the management club? Stated another way, who are the persons performing any or all of the functions of planning, organizing, leading, and controlling?

In a typical corporation there are a board of directors, a president, a group of vice-presidents or major executives, managers of divisions or departments, and supervisors of specific areas or functions who report to the manager of that department. Reporting to a departmental supervisor are workers whose function is the performance of specific duties assigned by the supervisor. There is general agreement that those who direct the work of others are a part of management. In addition, there are some who do not direct the work of others, yet participate in planning, organizing, or controlling. These people are usually referred to as staff specialists, rather than managers, and are also considered a part of management. Those who perform relatively specific and routine duties under the direction of a manager or a staff specialist are called operative personnel and are not classed as a part of management.

As a rule, the distribution of a manager's time spent in planning, organizing, leading, or controlling is a function of the level of that person's position in the organization. The major executives of a company devote much of their time to planning and organizing. They are charged with policy making, a form of planning, and they must also determine the organization necessary to execute these policies. On the other hand, a departmental supervisor directs the operative personnel in one department and is responsible for the amount and quality of work produced. Consequently, a large portion of the supervisor's time is spent in leading and controlling the efforts of subordinates.

Is Management a Profession?

The question is often asked: Is management a profession? If a profession is defined as an occupation that serves others, it is possible to consider management a profession. However, if a profession is defined as a vocation requiring licensing and graduate study, such as medicine and law, then management is not a profession. There are certain characteristics implied when considering management a profession that are worth discussing.

There is a body of knowledge that is peculiar to the study of management. Over the years certain concepts of management have been developed, and there is a vast amount of technical information related to the management of specialized areas such as production, sales, finance, and personnel. Thus, in respect to specialized knowledge, management is a technical field that requires mastery. One of the reasons for studying an introductory course in management is to become acquainted with some of this information. However, neither a license nor a degree is required in order to practice as a manager. The absence of formal licensing and educational requirements is essentially sound because it places the emphasis where it belongs: on performance rather than on academic training. Although academic training is to be highly regarded, access to the field of management should not be limited only to those who have completed a prescribed course of study. Nonetheless, a trained manager usually performs better than an untrained one, particularly in today's complex industrial society.

Is Management a Science or an Art?

A discussion of management as a science or an art seldom resolves the question conclusively to anyone's satisfaction. However, since the question is raised frequently in management literature, it is well to establish a point of reference so that students may answer the question to their own satisfaction.

Historically, scientific management is defined as management that uses the methods of science in making its decisions and evaluating its subsequent courses of action. Every effort is made to obtain complete, valid, reliable information pertinent to the problem under consideration before a decision is made. Under these conditions the decision is consistent with and derived from the obtained information, and subsequent courses of action are subject to rigorous control procedure as a further check upon the correctness of the original decision. The antithesis of the scientific approach is management that operates "by the seat of its pants." It is an approach to management that places emphasis upon sources of information such as personal experiences, intuition, and hunches, all of which have unknown validity.

The art of management refers specifically to the practice of management. There are many phases of business operations that are not readily amenable to rigorous examination and control. Consequently, information developed in these fields is less precise than information obtained by means of the scientific method. As a result, a greater emphasis is placed upon the individual manager's past experience and judgment than is placed upon knowledge resulting from a technical course of study, such as engineering or accounting. The solutions to problems involving human relations call upon skills developed primarily through experience. When these skills are practiced smoothly and successfully by a manager, they are often regarded as an art; yet in their development and acquisition, they differ only in degree, not in kind, from skills and knowledge acquired through the more critical methods of science.

A Definition of Management

A precise definition of management is needed as a basis for our study of the principles of management. There are three parts to a definition of management as a process: first, the coordination of resources; second, the performance of managerial functions as a means of achieving coordination; and, third, establishing the purpose of the management process. Each part is discussed separately.

1. The first aspect of a definition of management is coordination. The manager of an enterprise coordinates the resources of the organization, namely, money, materials, and men.

   In a business enterprise, and for that matter in most organized groups, a prime requirement is money. There is seldom an organization without some measure of capital, a requisite for fraternal, social, and religious groups as well as for business organizations. Materials include the physical properties of a business, such as production equipment, plant facilities, and inventories. The people who are members of the organization are the third element. These three elements form a convenient mnemonic device: the three M's of management — money, materials, and men. And, although an oversimplification, this device is an aid in remembering the coordinative aspect of management.

2. The coordination of the resources of an organization is achieved by means of the managerial functions of planning, organizing, leading, and controlling.

3. A definition of management as the coordination of resources through the utilization of the functions of the management process is not complete. Management is a telic, or purposive, process; it is directed toward the attainment of stated goals or objectives. Without an objective, there is no goal to reach nor can there be a path to follow. The concept of goal orientation and the subsequent statement of that goal as an objective provide the purposive characteristic of management.

From the above discussion a definition of management may be stated: *Management is the coordination of all resources through the processes of planning, organizing, leading, and controlling in order to attain stated objectives.*

The Universality of Management

The definition of management as a purposive, coordinative process is universal in its application to all forms of group endeavor. It is not confined to business enterprises alone, but is applicable whenever people attempt to reach a stated goal through group efforts. The concept of universality of management is also applicable to all levels of managers within an organization and is not confined to the top echelon. Every manager and every staff specialist of an organization participates in the coordination of resources and the exercise of one or all of the managerial functions, and all are working to achieve the stated objectives.

ABOUT THIS BOOK

An introductory course to the study of management is by nature a survey course, drawing data and observations from many sources and disciplines. Thus, some may term the approach of this book eclectic. At the same time, the approach is integrative and may be classed as a modern approach in that both behavioral and systems concepts are utilized in the analysis of certain aspects of the process of management. The student might at this time read Chapter 21, A Summing Up, which integrates the functions of the management process and discusses in detail the behavioral aspects of management as well as the systems concept. A brief epilogue defines the relationship between the introductory course and the study of management in relation to other courses studied in the business curriculum.

Although the concepts of management are applicable to the management of religious, social, charitable, and educational groups, our primary concern is with the management of business enterprises in a political climate relatively free of governmental controls. Consequently, the illustrative material of the text and the case problems are based upon situations that occur in business organizations. Each chapter of this book, except the last one, begins and ends with a case problem, a descriptive statement of a business situation.

Case problems portray an incident or a brief series of related incidents, in contrast to the comprehensive case or case study that generally describes most of the events that occur in a company or other form of organization over a relatively long period of time. The difference between a case problem and a comprehensive case is one of degree, not of kind. Case problems are used as an integral part of this textbook for two reasons. First, case problems make the text more meaningful; and second, they provide a means of improving one's ability to solve business problems.

Case problems make the information presented in the text more meaningful by relating that information to a specific business situation. As a result, the student has at hand an example that shows how the concepts of the text can be transformed from an abstract statement to a practical situation. The abstract concepts of management are more readily remembered when they are described in the context of an easily remembered business experience. Case problems also make the text more meaningful by offering an opportunity to apply management concepts and principles as tools in the solution of specific business problems — another method of facilitating learning. In addition, case problems simulate a real business situation and provide the basis for improving one's skill in problem solving — a requisite for the successful manager. Thus it is necessary to learn how to analyze a case problem.

THE ANALYSIS OF CASE PROBLEMS

Although there is no one way of analyzing a case problem, the following suggestions have proven to be of value in developing skill in the analysis of cases. Before reading the case in its entirety, note the title of the chapter and the title of the case. The title of the chapter tells you what the chapter is about. For example, the title of Chapter 1, "Management Defined," should convey to you that the chapter deals with the definition of management. Similarly, the title of Chapter 2, "Development of Management Concepts," lets you know that the chapter is concerned with the historical development of management. Since the case problems in this textbook are an integral part of the chapter in which they appear, identifying the subject matter of the chapter often reveals the central theme of the case.

Second, the title of the case itself is of significance. Unlike many case problems, the name of the company in which the incidents described occurred is seldom used as the title of the case. Instead, the title is a descriptive phrase related to the central theme of the case. Thus, the title of Case Problem 1-A, Who is "Management"?, informs you immediately that the problem is one of defining management.

Reading the Case

After noting the clues offered by the titles of the chapter and the case, read the problems at the end of the case so you will know what is expected. Then read the entire case rapidly to gain a first impression of the total situation. Next, a careful reading and a detailed analysis are necessary.

Knowledge of the structure of case problems is helpful in the detailed analysis of the case. Usually the first and second paragraphs are a statement of the setting in which the incidents described in the case occur. In these paragraphs the central characters of the case are introduced, the name of the company is given, and if relevant the product or services and the geographical location are mentioned. Information required for the definition and solution of the problem is presented in differing ways. Sometimes data is presented in the form of exhibits at the end of the case. Exhibits may be financial statements, organization charts, tables, or similar summaries designed to present a large amount of information in concise form. However, in most of the case problems the relevant facts of the situation are presented in the form of discussions among the central characters of the case. Thus, the titles of the people described are significant since the title of the position one holds in a company indicates the role that may be expected. For instance, the title of president or general manager indicates that the major functions, and consequently the role that may be expected, are those of planning and coordinating. On the other hand, a title that designates a person as being in charge of one of the functional areas, such as finance, sales, production, or personnel, indicates that that person is responsible for a given function and may be expected to have that specific function as a major concern — sometimes to the detriment of other functions and to the achievement of overall organizational objectives.

There will be times, even after having read the case thoroughly, when you will say that more information is needed to define the problem and develop a solution. Admittedly, limitations of time and space require that the situation be described in broad strokes and rarely does a student reading a case have the same information possessed by a manager of a company. Yet every effort has been made to provide all the information needed for the definition and solution of the problem. All too often the criticism that a case does not contain sufficient information may become an automatic excuse for not coming to grips with the problem. It must be remembered that in practice executives rarely have all the information that they would like to have prior to making a decision, but the exigencies of the situation require a decision despite the incompleteness of the information upon which that decision is based.

Analyzing the Case

The following specific steps aid in the systematic analysis of a case.

1. State the Problem. After reading the case thoroughly and studying the problems at the end of the case, write a statement of the problem — what is the case about, what is there to be done, what action has to be taken, or what questions have to be answered. It may be necessary to state several problems; and, if this is required, you must then decide which of the problems is the most important. For example, in the last paragraph of Case Problem 1-A a request is made of the employee relations manager that she prepare a report indicating the name of the proposed management club, a definition of who is eligible to join the club, and a statement of the objectives of the club. Thus, there are three problems: title, membership, and purpose. Which of these is the most important? In this instance the last item is the most significant since the objectives, or the purpose, of a club may well determine the title and the membership of the club. The right answer to the wrong problem is of little value.

2. Collect Data. In most instances the data required for the definition and solution of the problem is contained in the case. Marginal notes and underlining are helpful in identifying and summarizing relevant data. Occasionally it may be necessary to prepare a summary on a separate sheet of paper.

3. Analyze Data. In order to analyze and evaluate effectively the data presented in the case, the data must be arranged in a systematic manner. Figure 12-3, Checklist of Organizational Effectiveness (page 268), and the accompanying discussion, "Evaluating Organizational Effectiveness," (pages 267 to 272), present one way of arranging such information. Read this section of the text *now*. Even though you are not expected to be thoroughly familiar with all the terms and concepts used in the discussion, there is much that you can understand and apply. Note that many problems can be categorized within one of eight problem areas, ranging from overall planning to provisions for control. Reviewing the checklist on the left-hand side of Figure 12-3, provides a quick way of identifying problem areas.

4. Formulate Tentative Solutions. It is well to develop the habit of regarding initial solutions as tentative. By so doing the danger of assuming a rigid position is minimized and at the same time the door is left open for other, and sometimes better, solutions. In Case Problem 1-A there are four possible solutions in regard to membership — all employees whose names appear on the published organization chart, all who have supervisory responsibility, all exempt personnel, and all who have earnings greater than $125 per week. The range of objectives and the proposed names of the club should also be regarded as tentative. All tentative solutions should be given due consideration.

5. Select a Recommended Solution. From the list of tentative solutions, a single solution has to be selected. The final solution should offer the best answer to the problem as stated in Step No. 1, and it should be based upon the data collected in Step No. 2. However, of greatest importance in the selection of a recommended solution is the extent to which that solution is capable of execution. Ultimately solutions to business problems require the commitment of company resources if they are to be executed.

Preparing Written Reports

When a student prepares a written report for a case problem, the report should be regarded as a project assigned by an employer rather than a class assignment. As a task to be performed as part of your job, the report will have its effect upon pay and advancement within the company. The mechanical aspects of the report — spelling, punctuation, neatness, and grammatical style — should be above reproach; yet the format of the report may vary considerably. It may take the form of a memo as requested in Case Problem 1-A. If so, the memo should indicate clearly the person to whom it is directed, its origin (including the name and title of the author of the memo), and the subject of the report. The body of the report is then presented in narrative form. When reports exceed one or two pages in length, it is well to present the conclusions or recommendations on the first page, with the body of the report containing the substantiating data from which the conclusions were drawn.

Case Problem 1-B affords an opportunity to apply the techniques of analysis described above. The company described in the case, Sears, is one familiar to everyone. Sears has had an excellent management for many years; yet there is an apparent need for a change in sales policies. Unlike most cases there is very little hindsight to be drawn upon; instead, you are asked to look into the future with the management of Sears.

Case Problem 1-B
SEARS

After decades of dominance, Sears, Roebuck and Co. is now just one of the boys. At least that's what Wall Street seems to be saying. For the first time in memory, Sears' stock is selling at a lower multiple of earnings than two of its chief competitors'. Sears has dropped from around $105 to $55 since last summer. Some $7.7 billion in market value has evaporated, and the Sears shares and other assets in Sears' famed profit-sharing plan have dropped in value by about one half, to $2 billion. Sears' earnings multiple has shrunk from 23 to 13. Archrival J. C. Penney sells at 14 times earnings: Kresge at 19 times.

Suddenly, the heat is on Sears from all directions:

Sales are poor. For at least a year now the $12-billion retailer has posted merely around

the same growth as the average Main Street merchant, roughly 8%. And that's no real growth at all, because most of the 8% represents higher prices.

The Allstate Group is as flat as a punctured tire. The multibillion-dollar insurance subsidiary — which earns more than J. C. Penney and provides 30% of Sears' $680-million profit — is trapped in a bad insurance underwriting cycle that is bound to get worse before it gets better.

Earnings are down. Without the usual good hand from Allstate, Sears' earnings fell nearly 9% in the last quarter, ended July 31.

High And Mighty

Is the stock market right? Has Sears lost its edge? It's too early to tell. But don't jump to conclusions. The old champion is still very tough and surprisingly agile.

High up in Chicago's new 110-story Sears Tower, the world's tallest building, Chairman Arthur Wood bristles at any suggestion that

Frank Lalli and Judith Koblentz, "Sears," *Forbes*, Vol. 114, No. 7 (October 1, 1974), pp. 28–30, 35. Senior Editor Frank Lalli and Reporter Judith Koblentz report on the views of Sears, Roebuck's management concerning the company's future.

Sears is slipping: "Sears' growth combined with Allstate will enable us to grow at the same pace as we have in the last ten years, around 8% a year compounded." But he left the clear impression that the 8% figure is a minimum target. One telling sign: FORBES has learned that management asked each national merchandising manager to "promise" to increase sales by 15% during the rest of the year.

Says Wood, a bushy-browed, 61-year-old lawyer who is the first Sears chairman not to come up through the stores: "We are not *about* to do something now. We *are* doing it. We are going after the business."

To meet Wood's minimum 8% goal, the $12-billion behemoth will have to add a profitable $1 billion in sales a year. A skeptical competitor says: "I keep asking myself: 'What is Sears' next growth kicker?' I can't think of anything."

Certainly it isn't going to be easy. All of yesterday's kickers are about depleted, at least for the time being. The prime example is Allstate. By expanding aggressively into life insurance and financial services, the once-tiny auto insurer founded by Sears in 1931 has roughly quadrupled its profit since 1965, to $200 million a year, and doubled its share of Sears' total net earnings to 30%.

Two major segments — life insurance and investment income — are still growing at around 18% to 20% a year. But two others that provided 24% of the Allstate Group's 1973 net profits — insurance underwriting and stock market capital gains — are sinking out of sight. Inflation, heavy storm damage and accelerating auto accidents (compared with last winter's energy crisis lows) are threatening to make the next 12 months about the worst in underwriting history. "And some state insurance commissioners," adds Allstate Chairman Archie Boe incredulously, "are still talking about *cutting* rates." Allstate's underwriting could slip into the red early next year. As for capital gains, Boe says, in effect, that Allstate doesn't have any left. What it has is around $300 million in unrealized capital losses.

As a result, this year and next, Allstate's profits will increase only modestly, if at all.

Sears' growth kicker, if it can develop one, will have to come from its retail side. But how?

A catalog boom? No chance. The low-profit operation, which started with Richard Sears' and Alvah Roebuck's 98-cent watches in the 1890's, has contributed a flat 20% to 25% of sales since the fifties. Furthermore, Penney's and Montgomery Ward's "wish-books" are becoming truly competitive. Penney's Chairman Donald Seibert told FORBES: "Our catalog operation in the first half was up 19%." Sears' was up an estimated 9%.

A major store expansion? That's out of the question. Sears has already blanketed the country with 100 million square feet of store space, compared with only 45 million for Penney and 26 million for Ward. Roughly half of the 4 million square feet Sears builds each year replaces existing stores. Although the company denies it, a rival retail vice president says: "Sears, Roebuck is developing sites that it used to reject five years ago." At the same time, Penney, Ward, Kresge and other retailers are growing by building — and by moving into regions that Sears once had to itself.

If you can't increase selling space, the logical alternative is to increase the value of the stuff you sell. And that is exactly how Sears' stores have been growing since the late sixties. Through extensive television advertising (of around $50 million a year), the company has promoted its house brands as name brands, expanded its high-profit software sales and quietly boosted markups. The strategy was a natural for a society that was becoming steadily more affluent — until double-digit inflation struck.

At first, by capitalizing on its quality suppliers and its old unquestioned reputation for fair-priced merchandise, Sears' trade-up strategy scored big with Cling Alon hosiery, the DieHard battery and other top-of-the-line winners. But Sears didn't confine the fatter markups to special products. Soon all prices were creeping up, and whole segments of lower-priced markets — once the company's meat — were surrendered to discounters and other competitors.

Imagine McDonald's introducing a sirloin steak, raising the price of its Big Mac and withdrawing its plain hamburger. That was Sears' growth strategy, namely, to "trade up America," as some insiders put it. A former Sears merchandising man says: "There was constant pressure from upstairs to increase markups, even by one-tenth of 1%."

Several people think that as time went on Senior Vice President for Merchandising James Button, who was passed up for president in 1972, went overboard. "He's like that," says a Sears supplier. "He gets fixations. A few years ago he met Tito. The next thing you knew, he sent every merchandising manager to Yugoslavia to look for goods to buy. I laugh just thinking about it."

Today Sears' house brands are at least as expensive as such national brands as Maytag and General Electric in clothes washers, Sylvania and Magnavox in TVs and Firestone and Uniroyal in radial tires. Sears' markup is now roughly 44% *vs.* 32% for Kresge and 50% for a prestige department store like Federated's Bloomingdale's in New York. But also, Sears is being forced to pass on the soaring manufacturing costs of its captive suppliers, such as Kellwood Co. and Warwick Electronics.

No matter what's to blame, the net effect of the higher prices is the same. Competitors are rejoicing as more shoppers stop assuming that Sears' prices are the "best" for the value received. Sears' strongest lines are durable goods like appliances and furniture (some 65% of sales). But even they aren't immune. A retail trade editor, who asked that his name be withheld, says: "Traditionally, when Sears walked into a market, most of the appliance retailers caved in. But there have been men, like Mel Landou in Miami and Sol Polk in Chicago, who have tackled Sears head on and built up $50-million to $100-million businesses."

A woman shopping with her three sons in Sears' Danbury, Conn., store summed up the company's problem this way: "An average-income family can't afford to shop here anymore."

Comments like that threaten Sears' carefully nurtured image as "the family store." So does the trouble the company has been having recently with the Government. The Federal Government, which is already investigating Sears' equal employment record, has just accused the company of deceptive "bait and switch" selling tactics. The Federal Trade Commission alleges, for instance, that Sears baited shoppers with ads for $58 sewing machines; then the stores' commission salesmen tried to switch them to more costly models.

"Ridiculous . . . ludicrous," fumes Sears' normally reserved chairman. He vows to "vigorously oppose" the FTC (though Sears did agree to a Wisconsin state consent decree over similar charges two years ago). But in a sense, it is a losing fight. Whether ultimately proved or not, the FTC accusation itself is a severe blow to a company that was built on fair practices.

Down the Up Escalator

The image worries aside, Sears' basic pricing problem suggests its solution. As the old saying goes — what goes up, must come down. By going too far to "trade up America," Sears has created a potentially golden opportunity to "trade down with America." And that, to oversimplify it, will be Sears' basic growth strategy for the foreseeable future. "You will see Sears," says Chairman Woods, "in a new economic framework."

Sears has moved toward this new strategy very slowly. As early as last summer, while inflation picked consumers' pockets, Penney, Ward and others cut prices and beat the promotional drum. Discounter Jerry (What's-the-story?) Rosenberg, who manages to display his hairy belly while hawking appliances on New York TV, says: "I saw the trend to low prices, and I'm not even a high school dropout. I'm a high school throwout."

But Sears sat tight. It didn't do anything special last year, except to decorate its year-end earnings with a plush layer of accounting changes.

Sears says it wasn't caught off base last year; it was just characteristically cautious. As Public Relations Vice President William McCurdy likes to say: "This company wears a belt and suspenders." That way, Sears never gets caught with its pants down. But last year, perhaps, it couldn't get its pants off.

Like most managements, the top men at Sears were more hopeful about the economy than they should have been. Company economist Jay Levine warned them that the economy would soften — and with it retail sales. But he also predicted that interest rates would begin to drop as the year went on — and would stay down. In *fact,* interest rates kept going up and, in the end, cut about 30 cents a share from Sears' profit, reducing it to $4.33.

As 1974 wore on, it became obvious that things were getting worse, not better. Allstate had to pay three times its normal storm-damage claims. Sears had to absorb additional inventories and interest costs to bail out wobbly suppliers. One of them, Whirlpool, was hit by a 19-week strike. And a cool summer froze Sears' profitable air-conditioner sales.

The result: The unthinkable happened. Sears' second-quarter earnings declined 9% on a modest 5.7% sales increase, compared with the like period last year. In all, first-half earnings were down roughly 1%. No disaster. But Sears did lose face. Management moved to adapt to the tougher times.

In late August Chairman Wood emerged from his dugout swinging what he described as a new, aggressive price-promotion plan. He immediately made a hit before 100 security analysts summoned to the Sears Tower by stating: "We'll make life interesting for our competitors."

The company is vague about its new strategy. But clearly, it is not another routine sales effort; prices will be included in national ads. Nor is it a radical departure; Sears has opened some 150 Budget Shops selling low-priced women's clothes in the last two years. Instead, it can be viewed as a companywide rededication to the basic penny-conscious merchandising that made Sears successful in the first place. General Robert Wood (no kin to the present chairman), who ran the company from 1928 to 1954, once summed up Sears' early success this way: "If there was any mistake we didn't make, I don't know it. But we did have values."

"The policy for the next 12 months," explains a Sears supplier, "is to get the customer back, get sales up and get market share up. There is no pressure to increase markups."

The goal is to strike a sales balance between, say, a middle-of-the line appliance promoted at 10% to 15% off, and a higher profit dress. Hopefully, the customer buys both, giving Sears its same old profit margin on increased sales. And even if the shopper takes only the item at 10% off, Sears can fall back on a cushion that most competitors lack. Partly because of its huge purchasing power, Sears is able to "overbill." That is, its 500 merchandise buyers slap roughly an extra 3% margin on top of the *supplier's* price, and then they add on the normal store markup.

And if the new price level still isn't low enough to attract customers? "Then it will go where it will," says Senior Vice President Button.

President A. Dean Swift says flatly that, if necessary, Sears will cut its profit margins to stimulate sales. "We are merchants," says the plainspoken Swift, who began as a Sears salesman in Highland Park, Ill. 34 years ago. "We aren't going to ruin anyone. We aren't going to undercut anyone. But we are going to compete."

In a sense, the more Sears cuts margins, the stronger its competitive position would be. Sears has a special advantage — the thickest profit margins in retailing. It nets 5½ cents on each sales dollar, compared to 4 cents for Federated Department Stores, 3 cents for Penney and Kresge and 2 cents for Ward. Sears can afford to take less; the others aren't so fortunate.

"Sears' promotion battle plan," says Mesirow & Co.'s savvy John Landschulz with a chuckle, "is at least as sophisticated as the plans for the Normandy invasion."

It's too early to know if Sears' invasion of lower pricing will turn the tide — as Normandy did. A possible weak point is its 12,000 suppliers. If the recession riddles them, Sears will have to carry them despite the cost. Comptroller Jack Kincannon says: "We would do anything possible to help them." But assuming that isn't too bloody a burden and Allstate is permitted to raise rates and the economy eventually rebounds, a penny-sharp Sears could once again establish its industry preeminence over the next year or two.

Who would Sears hurt? Just about everybody. First hit would be the general merchandisers whose prices are generally a notch or so under Sears', such as Penney, Ward, W.T. Grant and an array of local appliance dealers. As Sears comes down the price ladder, it is going to step on them. That collision, in turn, could set off a chain reaction as any number of the middle-range merchandisers scramble farther down the ladder to avoid Sears and smack into Kresge and even the bottom-rung discounters. With competition intensified and the economy weak, a retail shakeout would seem almost inevitable. Already, Drexel Burnham's retail analyst, Jeffrey Feiner, estimates that $4 billion to $5 billion worth of retail sales is "in weak hands."

So Sears' new thrust is good news for consumers, but bad news for its rival retailers.

Will Sears make it? Without dropping his poker-face mask, Chairman Wood lets an edge creep into his voice when he says: "We will be in business a long time." Sears surely will.

PROBLEMS

1. What factors, external and internal, caused the decline in sales and earnings of Sears? Of these two sets of factors, which are within the control of the Sears management?
2. Evaluate the basic strategy to be used by Sears as a means of recovering its position of dominance over its competitors. What inherent strengths or weaknesses in the Sears organization will aid or make more difficult the company's effort to regain its position of leadership?
3. What factors made it possible for Sears to gradually upgrade its merchandise and raise its price structure?

CHAPTER QUESTIONS FOR STUDY AND DISCUSSION

1. Briefly answer the questions who, what, when, where, why, and how as they relate to the study of management.
2. Is it possible for a manager to be at the same time highly skilled in scientific management and also an excellent practitioner in the art of management? Give an example.
3. What are the four major functions of management? Which of these functions, in your opinion, is the most important in each of the following types of business: an oil pipeline transmission company, a door-to-door sales organization such as the Fuller Brush Company, a large retail discount store, and a complex multiproduct company such as General Motors?
4. Is management still responsible for the success or failure of a business when economic fluctuations or changes in the political environment affect an entire industry? Why or why not?
5. Do you agree with the statement made in the text that it would be undesirable to require a prescribed course of study as a requisite for a management position? Why?
6. What is meant by the phrase "universality of management"?
7. What is the definition of management given in the text? What are the three major factors included in the definition of management? Develop a series of definitions using only two factors for each definition. Evaluate each definition thus developed in respect to its completeness.

Chapter 2
Development of Management Concepts

Case Problem 2-A
SYMPTOMS OR CAUSES?

It was six o'clock in the evening on the last Friday in April as Marsh Saunders sat at his desk organizing the impressions he had gained during his first month as plant manager for Excellent Foods, Inc. Though he had been a plant manager for Excellent Foods for more than five years, this was the first time he had managed a can manufacturing plant for the company; his previous experience had been in food processing plants. He jotted down a list of his major observations on a sheet of paper. Following each "symptom" he listed possible causes. The following is a copy of his notes with the "causes" in italics.

1. Production — in all operating departments — assembly, shipping, lithography, and press room — operating in the red as measured by engineered standards. Losses range from −20% to −5%; average monthly loss for plant is −15%.
   Machines not properly maintained. Personnel not capable, need more training. Applies to all four departments.

2. Labor relations — poor.
   Every effort to increase efficiency called for a speedup. Too many grievances; 150 last year. (Is this the cause of Symptom No. 1, or is it the result of poor performance?)

3. Quality — very poor, many complaints.
   Operating personnel and supervisors don't seem to care. Improperly maintained and poorly adjusted equipment.

4. Housekeeping — lousy.
   Entire plant dirty with nothing ever in its right place. Machine shop has no idea of spare parts inventory.

5. Quality of supervision — probably technically competent as they all came up from the ranks. Seem to be beat down, no spirit, poor human relations in all departments.
   Do not consider themselves a part of the management team. Afraid to do anything, seem fearful of losing job. Would a guarantee of no personnel changes for six months be a good move?

6. Manager's staff — all heads of staff departments (industrial, engineering, personnel, purchasing, quality control, production control, and accounting) have been in their respective jobs for at least three years. No one willing to exercise authority or take responsibility — all seem mediocre in ability.
   Is poor performance of this group due to lack of native ability or would additional training help? Should training be in respective technical fields or general management? Though mediocre, these people know the organization.

7. Low morale at all levels from the hourly production workers, through the clerical help, to supervision and staff.
   The plant seems to lack a common purpose or goal. An esprit de corps is completely lacking.

As he looked at this list, Mr. Saunders wondered if Symptom No. 7, poor morale, should not be listed as the number one problem in place of low production. He knew that the list was incomplete and that another 10 to 15 items could be added without much difficulty. He also knew that before he could start the much needed management training program he envisioned, he would have to group his problems, or symptoms, into several major areas.

1. Assume that you are Mr. Saunders. How would you group the seven symptoms so that a training program could be directed toward three major subject matter areas?

2. Do you think that the words "symptoms" and "causes" are better choices than "problems" and "solutions"? Why?
3. In his notes on the probable causes for Symptoms No. 2 and No. 5, Mr. Saunders raised several questions. How would you answer these questions?
4. Which of the approaches to management offers the greatest value to the solution of the problems faced by Mr. Saunders?

As you read this chapter, you will discover that the problems confronting Mr. Saunders are neither new nor unique to his plant; they are as old as management itself.

There is considerable evidence that effective management of complex social groups has existed for well over 6,000 years. The early civilizations of the Egyptians, the Greeks, and the Roman Empire could not have existed for centuries had there not been well-developed administrative organizations and procedures. Even before these civilizations, there is reason to believe that considerable thought and effort had been expended on studying and formulating the management process.

One of the earliest analytical statements of management concepts appears in the Bible, Exodus 18:13-26. This passage tells how Jethro, Moses' father-in-law, observed Moses spending an entire day listening to the complaints and problems of his people. Following this observation, Jethro told Moses that what he was doing was too much for one man and suggested specific steps that should be taken to relieve him of his burden. His first recommendation was that "ordinances and laws" should be taught to the people. The modern counterpart of this advice is an organization's policy statement. Secondly, he recommended that leaders be selected and assigned "to be rulers of thousands, and rulers of hundreds, and rulers of fifties, and rulers of ten." The process of appointing leaders, each of whom is responsible for a given number of subordinates, is referred to as delegation of authority. Jethro's third point, that these rulers should administer all routine matters and should bring to Moses only the important questions, forms the basis for a well-known control procedure. This procedure of attending to the exception that does not conform to expected results is known as the *principle of the exception* and is discussed in Chapter 18.

The recounting of Jethro's advice to Moses illustrates that interest in management as a process existed in antiquity. However, the systematic study and development of the formal literature of management appears at a much later date. Most students of management recognize three phases in the development of management thought. First there is the classical approach, which includes an emphasis on the production processes and the administrative processes within organizations. Second, there are those who emphasize the importance of establishing sound practices of human relations as a means of improving the management process. Those who stress the importance of human relations are concerned with the human element in management. It is a convincing point of view for there are many instances where improved relationships between management and the workers and among the workers themselves have solved the problems of a particular company. Finally, there are several contemporary approaches to the study of management that emphasize either the social system, the decision-making process, the application of quantitative methods, or the systems approach to the study of management. These may be grouped together as modern approaches to the study of management.

Since the classical approach to the study of management emphasizes both production and administration each topic is treated separately. This discussion is followed by a review of some of the major findings in the human relations approach. Finally, an analysis of the modern approaches to the study of management is presented.

THE EMPHASIS UPON PRODUCTION

The industrial revolution, with its development and utilization of semiautomatic and automatic machinery, made possible the mass production of goods and also created the modern industrial organization. These new organizations with their vast potential for production were little understood and the need for knowledge about the management of such organizations soon became apparent. It is not surprising that the first approach to the study of management emphasized the dominant characteristics of these new industrial organizations — production. The contributions of Charles Babbage and Frederick Winslow Taylor, two pioneers in the study of the production function, are examined.

Charles Babbage

Charles Babbage laid the groundwork for much of the work that later became known as "scientific management." A project which he worked on throughout his life and, unfortunately, was never successful in fully developing was the "Difference Engine," an invention considered to be the forerunner of our modern data processing equipment. His interest in production problems resulted in two contributions that are as valid today as when they were first presented. The first contribution stresses the importance of dividing and assigning labor on the basis of skill. The second provides a means of determining the feasibility of replacing manual operations with automatic machinery.

Division of Labor. In 1832, in his "On the Economy of Machinery and Manufactures,"[1] Babbage presented a keen analysis of the alternative methods then available in making pins. In his analysis of making pins by hand, he offers convincing and complete data showing that a division of labor on the basis of skill is an economic necessity. He cites as advantages of dividing labor by its level of skill the fact that the learning time is reduced, since any one worker has to learn only one skill rather than all. Secondly, in the actual process of manufacturing, there is a saving because less time is lost as the result of changing from one set of skills to another. Babbage also points out that a high degree of precision can be acquired by each worker, for the worker is learning only one task and repeating it many times. In addition, since the job is broken down into its component parts on a basis of the skills required, there is the obvious possibility of developing specialized tools and equipment to further aid the process. All of these observations result in the conclusion that dividing a job into its component levels of skill enables the manufacturer to acquire and pay for only the exact amount of skill required for each operation.

Manual vs. Automatic Operations. Following his discussion on the art of making pins by hand, Babbage then mentions briefly a new (remember, 1832) American process of making pins by machine. He suggests several questions, the answers to which determine whether or not the introduction of machine methods is desirable:

1. To what defects pins so made (i.e., by machine) are liable?
2. What advantages they possess over those made in the usual way?
3. What is the prime cost of a machine for making them?
4. What is the expense of keeping it in repair?
5. What is the expense of moving it and attending to it?[2]

These questions are as important today as they were when originally asked by Babbage almost 150 years ago in that they raise questions concerning quality, the original cost of the machine, and the cost of operation including labor and maintenance. Much of management's effort is directed toward obtaining an answer to these questions.

Frederick Winslow Taylor

By far the ablest exponent of the probing, analytical attitude expressed by Babbage was Frederick Winslow Taylor, commonly regarded as the father of scientific management. A strike at a navy arsenal against the Taylor System led to a Congressional investigation of "the

---

[1]Charles Babbage, *On the Economy of Machinery and Manufactures* (Philadelphia: Carey and Lea, 1832), Chap. 17, pp. 121–140, "On the Division of Labour," reprinted in Harwood F. Merrill (ed.), *Classics in Management* (New York: American Management Association, 1960), pp. 29–44.
[2]*Ibid.*, p. 43.

Taylor and Other Systems of Shop Management" in 1912. The hearings afforded Taylor an opportunity to present his views regarding the concept of scientific management, the term he and his associates adopted before the hearings began to refer to the Taylor system.

Taylor opened his testimony with a statement that eliminated many misconceptions concerning scientific management.[3] In part he said that scientific management is not merely cost-keeping systems, time studies, functional foremanship, new schemes for paying men, or efficiency systems. He emphasized that while these devices in whole or in part are not scientific management they are useful adjuncts to scientific management as well as to other systems of management.

Scientific Management — A Mental Revolution. Taylor, after stating what scientific management was not, went on to state clearly the main characteristic of scientific management. To him, "a complete mental revolution" was necessary for scientific management to come into being. Further, and this is important because it points up the fact that Taylor was far more than a capable technician, this mental revolution must occur in the *worker's* mind as well as in the mind of management. Taylor's analysis of industrial problems existing between management and labor concluded that, to a large extent, it was an argument over the division of the surplus created by industry. Indeed, this still remains one of the major issues in current collective bargaining. The first part of the mental revolution, according to Taylor, is that both parties stop quarreling about how the surplus should be divided and unite to increase the size of the surplus so that the need for hair-splitting in this area becomes less acute.

The second phase of the mental revolution is that the scientific method must be the sole basis for obtaining information to determine the proper procedure to be used in performance of each job and to establish the proper level of output per man-hour. It is the second phase of scientific management that has caused most of the criticism of the Taylor system. The reason is that the application of the scientific method requires so much detailed work and time that the original goal of increasing the surplus is never realized. An example of the extensive work necessary in some areas to determine the scientific basis for the performance of an operation is found in the series of experiments conducted by Taylor extending over a 26-year period to determine the best methods of machining or cutting metals. In the process, high-speed tool steels were developed, and the science of cutting metals was

---

[3]Merrill, *op. cit.*, p. 77. The statement concerning scientific management is based upon testimony of Frederick W. Taylor at hearings before the Special Committee of the House of Representatives to Investigate the Taylor and Other Systems of Shop Management, January 25, 1912, p. 1387. For a review of Taylor's work, which is highly critical in nature, the following is recommended: Charles D. Wrege and Amedeo G. Perroni, "Taylor's Pig-Tale: A Historical Analysis of Frederick W. Taylor's Pig-Iron Experiments," *Academy of Management Journal*, Vol. 17, No. 1 (March, 1974), pp. 6–27.

broken down into 12 interrelated variables. These interrelationships were expressed mathematically by formulas, and slide rules were developed so that the optimum conditions for any given task could be computed. It is no wonder that a person becoming immersed in the mathematical analysis of production problems loses sight of the first great mental revolution required; namely, a change in attitude.

The Need for Scientific Management. Scientific management was developed to solve two major problems: to increase the output of the average worker and to improve the efficiency of management. To a degree, increasing the productivity of the average worker is the same problem that challenged Elton Mayo, an able exponent of the human relations approach, at a later date. But the approaches used by each of these men were different. Mayo sought the answer in terms of the social forces that affect the worker as a member of a group while Taylor considered each worker as a separate economic man motivated by financial needs.

Taylor believed that the basis of a worker's tendency to restrict output was fear of displacement, not too unlike the fear expressed in some quarters today in regard to automation. He suggested two methods of minimizing the fear of displacement expressed by the workers. One approach was to educate the workers to understand that their economic salvation lay in producing more at a lower cost. The other method was to prove to the workers the effectiveness of this argument by placing them on a piecework system and thereby permitting them to earn more.

Taylor's Principles of Management. The second major problem, improving the efficiency of management, was to be solved through the application of Taylor's four principles of management. The first of these principles urged a gathering, analysis, and codification of all "rule-of-thumb" data existing in the business. The second principle urged careful selection and a thorough study of workers so that they may be developed to their maximum capabilities. Third, was the persuasive principle of educating, or more properly "inspiring," people to use the scientific principles derived from the careful analysis of all data and methods used in each job. Lastly, Taylor urged that management organize in such a manner that it could properly manage and carry out its duties.

THE EMPHASIS UPON ADMINISTRATION

The second of the classical approaches to the study of management emphasizes the administrative aspects of management. The emphasis is on an overall approach to the problems of management.

The task of management has been summarized in a single word, *coordination*, by Mary Parker Follett; but in order to understand this concept it is necessary to know what is being coordinated and to review suggestions as to how coordination can best be accomplished.[4]

Fayol's Principles of Management

Henri Fayol, a French engineer and geologist, was the first to state a series of principles of management that provide guideposts for successful management coordination. Concurrent with Taylor's study of management through a detailed analysis of the individual worker, Fayol, manager of a large French mining and metallurgical company, analyzed the problems of top management. He modestly believed that his success was not due to any personal characteristics of leadership, but was the result of applying a set of general administrative principles that could be isolated and taught to others. In *General and Industrial Management*, Fayol presents 14 principles of management.[5]

Five of Fayol's 14 principles are concerned primarily with the improvement of human relations. One of his principles emphasizes production efficiency, and the remaining eight are directed toward administration of the organization.

Principles Emphasizing Human Relations

The five principles applicable to problems in the field of human relations are: subordination of individual interest to the general interest, equity, stability of tenure of personnel, initiative, and esprit de corps. In discussing subordination of individual interest to the general interest, Fayol states that individuals and small groups within the overall organization should make their needs secondary to those of the firm. He also emphasizes that it is necessary for the firm to place its interests second to those of the society in which it operates. Recognition of the fact that the administrator of an organization is dealing with a number of groups, in contrast to a number of individuals, is fundamentally the same group concept of Elton Mayo. Fayol suggests that subordination of interest can be achieved by close supervision, good examples of subordination of personal interest by supervisors, and making agreements with various employees and groups of employees as fair as possible.

When discussing equity, he defines what is meant by fair agreements. Equity is composed of two ingredients — kindliness and justice. The equal application of policies and practices to all groups and individuals within an organization is certainly a concept difficult to

---

[4]Mary Parker Follett, *Freedom and Coordination* (London: Management Publications Trust, 1949), reprinted in Merrill, *op. cit.*, pp. 337–352.

[5]Henri Fayol, *General and Industrial Management* (London: Sir Isaac Pitman and Sons, 1949), pp. 19–42, reprinted in Merrill, *op. cit.*, pp. 217–241. The copyright date, 1949, is the date of the English translation. Fayol's "General Principles of Management" first appeared in 1916 in an industrial association bulletin published in France.

quarrel with, yet also difficult to apply at all times. Fayol applies the concept of desirability of stability of tenure to all levels of the organization. The production worker must have some feeling of security in order to learn his job so that he may perform it well, and he must also have some feeling of psychological security.

Stability of tenure for top management is necessary, for it takes time to get to know the organization, its problems, and its personnel. Fayol even suggests that it might be better for a concern to have a mediocre manager with long tenure rather than have a succession of brilliant managers. In this connection, the following interesting question is raised: Is the poor performance of a company that is experiencing a high turnover of managerial personnel the result of the turnover; or, is the poor performance of managerial personnel the cause of the turnover? It is a question that plagues many companies today, and they are no nearer the answer than was Fayol.

To Fayol, participation in the solution of problems is represented by the principle of initiative. The principle is with us today and is illustrated by the efforts of companies to establish suggestion systems at all levels of the organization so that the ideas and energies of all workers may be tapped in the solution of common problems. Effective employee suggestion programs utilize the principle of initiative, for they enable an employee to see his ideas carried through to a successful conclusion.

In his last principle, esprit de corps, Fayol states his belief that in union there is strength and warns against a system of divide and conquer in an organization. While dividing and conquering may be a good way of eliminating the opposition, it does not work within a single group such as a business organization. The manager's task is not to eliminate the opposition, but rather to unify all divergent groups and individuals.

Production Efficiency

The first of Fayol's principles, division of work, is similar to the thesis that Charles Babbage presented in "On the Division of Labour."[6] Fayol offers the same reasons for dividing work and creating groups of specialists. He mentions the resulting increased skill, the reduction in learning time, and the increased efficiency that results from not having to change from one task to another. But he goes further than Babbage and applies the principle of the division of work to all levels of management, not limiting its application to the hourly worker. Also, the first principle is an expression of the same interest shown by Babbage and Taylor; namely, an emphasis upon the production process with a desire to increase efficiency. It is the only

---

[6]Babbage, *loc. cit.*

one of his 14 principles which can be classed as solely emphasizing production. However, there are two principles of such breadth that production processes are included in their application: remuneration and order. These are discussed later.

Principles Emphasizing Administration

The remaining principles are new in concept, for they deal with the problems of top management — administration and organization. Fayol's principle of authority is the first of this group. Authority is defined as the right to give orders and is discussed with its corollary, responsibility. The granting of authority to a manager implies that in accepting that authority, he has also accepted responsibility. It is organizationally unsound and inefficient to assign responsibility without, at the same time, granting authority commensurate to this responsibility. Fayol recognized that authority is misused and suggests that preventing the abuse of authority is dependent upon the integrity of the individual having authority.[7]

Discipline is regarded as the respect shown by all members of the organization toward the written agreements, or policies, governing their conduct in the firm. Fayol proposes that good discipline be achieved by having all agreements between the company and the employees presented as clearly and as fairly as possible, that all supervisors throughout the organization be thoroughly capable, and that if the need for penalties or discipline arises, such penalties should be as fair as possible.

The principles of unity of command and unity of direction are similar and closely related. Yet there is sufficient difference in their purposes so that two separate principles are warranted. The first of these, unity of command, states that orders should originate from one source only. Thus, subordinates are assured that only one superior in the organization can give them orders. Unity of direction is not directed toward the individual, but refers to the plan or work activities of the group and emphasizes that for one plan there should be one head or director. Thus, these two principles complement each other; the former assures the employee that there will be only one superior, and the latter assures organizational effectiveness in that for every group of workers carrying out a plan, there shall be only one director.

These principles of organization — authority, discipline, unity of command, and unity of direction — leave little room for deviation or individual choice. Because of their nature they appear to be an "all or none" proposition. However, not all of Fayol's principles dealing with organization are as rigid, as illustrated by his principles concerning centralization and the scalar chain or line of authority. The scalar

---

[7]The problem of integrity is discussed in Chapter 3, "Objectives and Ethics."

chain principle urges that definite lines of authority be established from the bottom of an organization to its very top in such a manner that the exact lines of authority relationships between the successive levels of management are unmistakably clear. When it becomes necessary for individuals in different sections of the organization to work directly with each other in order to attain speed of action, the formal chain of command should be short-circuited, provided all people concerned are properly informed.

The same type of flexibility is evident in determining the optimum degree of centralization in an organization. In general, those actions that tend to reduce the authority and responsibility of subordinates and place more in the hands of a superior may be considered as actions which lead to a greater degree of centralization of authority, while those acts that increase responsibility and authority at lower levels result in what is termed a greater degree of decentralization of authority. With the concept of varying degrees of centralization of authority, there is no recommended absolute level of centralization or decentralization. The desired level or degree is dependent upon the situation and includes such factors as the nature of the organization, the problem of the department at hand, and the capabilities of the subordinates in question.

The remaining two principles describe operating procedures of such breadth that they are difficult to classify within the framework of either human relations, production, or administration. These principles, remuneration and order, encompass all three areas. Since they are expressed as problems of top management rather than problems in human relations or the improvement of production, the principles of remuneration and order are considered among those principles contributing to the administrative efforts of management. One of these, the principle of remuneration, starts with the assumption that the wages paid to personnel should be based upon concepts of equity and should be satisfactory both to the employee and the company. The various methods of paying hourly employees are listed, and Fayol shows that he was thoroughly familiar with the piecework system advocated by Taylor. He also mentions the problems involved in profit-sharing plans and bonuses, not only for hourly workers, but for all members of the organization. Again, Fayol develops a flexible conclusion that the method of payment selected should be the one that works best for the particular situation, and the definition of "best" should include the point of view of all interested parties.

The other principle, also broad in scope, is that of order. At first glance, the meaning of order may seem to be the same as Taylor's admonition that the placement of materials and tools should be the result of a methods study to assure efficient production. Fayol's principle does include the concept, "A place for everything and everything in its place." However, it means much more than the neat arrangement of physical materials of an organization. Fayol's idea of order also applies to the human element of the organization. An application of this principle is the organization chart, a device which literally shows the place of every person in the organization and the relationships of each to the other. In addition to knowing personnel as they appear on the organization chart, Fayol recommended they be considered human resources with different capabilities and desires.

Figure 2-1 presents the principles of both Taylor and Fayol and summarizes the two approaches to the study of management normally considered as classical in nature.

TAYLOR'S PRINCIPLES OF SCIENTIFIC MANAGEMENT

1. Management must gather, analyze, and codify all existing rule-of-thumb data pertaining to the business in order to develop a science.

2. Workers must be carefully selected and thoroughly studied so that each one may be developed to maximum capabilities.

3. Workers must be inspired or trained to use the scientific methods developed as the result of analyzing and codifying rule-of-thumb data.

4. Management must organize in such a manner that it can properly manage and carry out its duties.

FAYOL'S PRINCIPLES OF MANAGEMENT

Human Relations

Subordination of individual interest to the general interest	Stability of tenure of personnel
	Initiative
Equity	Esprit de corps

Production Efficiency

Division of work

Administration

Figure 2-1 PRINCIPLES OF THE CLASSICAL APPROACH

Authority	Centralization
Discipline	Scalar chain (line of authority)
Unity of command	Remuneration
Unity of direction	Order

THE EMPHASIS UPON HUMAN RELATIONS

The works of two proponents of the human relations school are reviewed briefly. The first statement, expressed by Robert Owen, appeared in 1828 and is regarded as one of the first formal writings in the field of management. Although he is considered a proponent of the human relations approach to management, Owen's views are now regarded as highly paternalistic in nature. Secondly, a brief view of the work of Elton Mayo, who is considered the founder of the human relations approach to management, is presented.

Robert Owen

Robert Owen, a successful textile mill manager in Scotland from 1800 to 1828, made some remarkable observations concerning the factors which influenced the productivity of the personnel in his plants. He referred to his employees as "vital machines," and in describing how they should be regarded and treated, he compared the importance and nature of "vital machines" with the "inanimate machines" of the factory. A summary of his position was presented in "An Address: To the Superintendents of Manufactures, and to those Individuals generally, who, by giving Employment to an aggregated Population, may easily adopt the means to form the Sentiments and Manners of such a Population." The date of publication of this address was 1813, and in some ways it foreshadows the conclusions of the famous Hawthorne Studies of Mayo which were not undertaken until more than a century later.[8]

Owen stated that it was generally accepted that mechanical equipment kept in a state of good repair more than paid for itself by its increased productivity and longer life. Reasoning by analogy, he concluded that if this were true for the "inanimate machines," it should also be true for the "vital machines." He applied this conclusion to his own plants in New Lanark, Scotland, and claimed that as a result of attention to his personnel, he was receiving more than a 50 percent return on any money so spent.

George Elton Mayo

Closely related to the work of Owen, though separated by slightly more than 100 years, are the efforts of George Elton Mayo and his team of Harvard researchers. Mayo was born and educated in Australia, came to the United States in 1922, and was first associated with the University of Pennsylvania. In 1926, he joined the faculty of Harvard University, where he remained until his retirement in 1947. One of his early studies, completed while he was at Pennsylvania, illustrates clearly the results that may be expected by following Owen's admonition "to treat it (the vital machine) with kindness, that its mental movements might not experience too much irritating friction." Appropriately, the title given to this work is "The First Inquiry."[9]

---

[8]Robert Owen, *A New View of Society* (1st American ed. from the 3d London ed.; New York: E. Bliss & F. White, 1825), pp. 57–62, reprinted in Merrill, *op. cit.*, pp. 21–25.

[9]Elton Mayo, *The Social Problems of an Industrial Civilization* (Boston: Division of Research, Graduate School of Business Administration, Harvard University, 1945). Portions of this work and the Hawthorne Studies are reprinted in Merrill, *op. cit.*, pp. 407–436.

"The First Inquiry." Mayo and his group were asked to solve an industrial problem, the symptoms of which were an excessive turnover of employees in a certain department of a Philadelphia textile mill. The department in question was that of the mule-spinners, whose annual turnover rate was nearly 250 percent while that of other departments in the mill was between 5 and 6 percent. Several consulting firms, then called efficiency engineers, had previously worked on the problem and, among other things, had established a financial incentive plan. The reasoning behind this approach assumed that people are economic animals, and, as such, they will respond to financial incentives or rewards. However, this was not the case, for not once had the workers in the department produced enough to earn the rewards of the financial incentive plan. The morale of the department was low. There were many complaints of foot trouble, neuritis, and other miscellaneous aches and pains. The employees were working five 10-hour days each week with the day being broken only by a 45-minute lunch period at the end of the first five hours. There were no rest periods during the day, and since the workers were on their feet continually, there was reason to believe that fatigue might be playing an important part in creating their general feelings of depression.

The experiment began with the introduction of rest periods for some of the workers in the mule-spinner's department. But rest alone was not the only changed condition in the experiment. The problem had been discussed with all employees in the department, and, as a result, they were made to feel a part of the whole program. In addition, these workers were fondly attached to the manager of the plant, a colonel with whom many had served in World War I. They were confident that if the rest periods worked for the experimental group, about one third of the workers, all of them would soon have rest periods because of the essential fairness of "the Colonel."

The results of the experiment were almost immediate, not only for the third who received the rest periods, but also for the two thirds who served as the control group and did not receive rest periods but who had taken part in discussing the problem. For the first time since the installation of the incentive bonus plan by the efficiency engineers, the mule-spinners earned incentive pay. This continued for a period of four and one-half months, until February 15, 1923. Then, within a period of seven days the entire department had returned to their initial pessimism and production dropped to its former low level.

What had happened? Nothing that had not happened thousands of times in industrial plants prior to this experiment and thousands of times since this study. There was a sudden demand for the product of the textile mill, and, as a result, the supervisor in the department simply ordered the abandonment of all rest periods. The results were immediate and nearly disastrous. The sequel to this supervisor's ill-advised, albeit typical, act is often overlooked. The Colonel, the one man in whom the workers had complete personal confidence, took immediate charge. He reinstated the four rest periods and guaranteed that every employee would have two 10-minute rest periods in the morning and two in the afternoon. Practically everyone, except the Colonel himself, doubted that this loss of 40 minutes a day per man could be made up since the machines could not be speeded up. However, the Colonel was right. During the month of April the workers made a bonus, and the rate of production continued to climb until the efficiency figures were well above 85 percent, a considerable change from the March low of 70 percent. In addition to reestablishing the rest periods in a manner which had left no doubt in anyone's mind as to what management believed, the Colonel had done something else of great significance. He had delegated responsibility to the workers themselves. Each group of three employees was to determine the exact time when the group would take its individual rest periods, but each knew that, without fail, the group would receive four such periods a day. Thus, a guaranteed policy of management and the fact that the workers themselves were to participate to some extent in the decisions involved had turned the tide.

The Hawthorne Studies. Shortly after completing his work, "The First Inquiry," Mayo joined the faculty of Harvard University where, as head of the Industrial Research Department, he led a series of pioneering studies at the Hawthorne plant of the Western Electric Company.[10] Initially, the purpose of the study was to determine the effect of illumination upon the output of workers; however, at a later date, the studies sought to determine methods of establishing teamwork and continuing cooperation in industrial groups.

In the illumination study, workers were divided into two groups — an experimental group and a control group. Lighting conditions for the experimental group were varied from 24 to 46 to 70 footcandles in intensity while the lighting of the control group remained constant. As expected, the output of the experimental group increased with each increase in light intensity, but the performance of the control group was not expected. Their production increased at about the same rate as the production of the experimental group. Later, the light of the

---

[10]There have been several major books published by Mayo and his coworkers describing the extensive work completed at Western Electric. Among them are:

Elton Mayo, *The Human Problems of an Industrial Civilization* (Boston: Division of Research, Harvard Business School; 2d ed.; New York: Macmillan Co., 1946).

F. J. Roethlisberger and W. J. Dickson, *Management and the Worker* (Cambridge: Harvard University Press, 1939, 10th printing, 1950).

F. J. Roethlisberger, *Management and Morale* (Cambridge: Harvard University Press, 1942).

F. J. Roethlisberger, *Man-in-Organization* (Cambridge: Belknap Press of Harvard University Press, 1968). This book is a series of essays by F. J. Roethlisberger, several of which are concerned with Elton Mayo and the Hawthorne studies.

experimental group was reduced from 10 to 3 footcandles. Again, the output of the experimental group continued to increase, and so did the output of the control group. Finally, a decline in productivity of the experimental group did occur, but only when the intensity of light was low enough to approach the level of moonlight. Clearly, something other than illumination was the cause of changes in productivity.

Similar results were obtained in the relay assembly test room experiment, only this time the variable was the amount of rest, rather than lighting, to determine the effects of fatigue on productivity. First, normal production was established, then rest periods of varying lengths and frequency were introduced. Production increased with the increase in frequency and length of rest periods. Finally, in Period XII of the experiments, it was decided to return to the original conditions: no formal rest periods, no lunches, and a full 48-hour week. The return to the original conditions did not result in the expected drop in production; instead, production stayed at its usual high level.

The Hawthorne Effect. The Hawthorne Studies show quite clearly that factors other than working conditions and the physiological state of the worker have a marked influence on productivity. These factors are recognized as social and psychological in nature. The workers of these studies were the subjects of experiments of interest to the managers of the plant and to their immediate supervisors. Further, the workers knew that they were participating in experiments that were of interest to management. They responded to this interest, a social force, rather than to the experimentally induced changes in the external physical environment. This phenomenon of responding to the social and psychological aspects of the situation on the part of individuals participating as subjects of the experiment has come to be known as the *Hawthorne Effect*. Because of this phenomenon it is sometimes very difficult to determine whether the subjects of an experimental study are responding to the environmental factor that is being varied by the experimenter or whether they are responding to the knowledge that they are the subjects and participants of an experiment.

The Hawthorne Effect is demonstrated quite clearly in the results of Period XII of the studies concerned with the effect of fatigue. As a result many consider this study a turning point in our understanding of human relations because the importance of attitudes toward work, toward management, and toward the work group is recognized as vitally significant.

Conclusions

Several conclusions from Owen and Mayo can be drawn at this time. First, people are essentially social beings, not economic, and should be regarded as such. Second, as social beings they are members of a group; therefore, it is the group that should be approached to participate in discussing problems and in determining the solution. There is a third conclusion to be drawn from a study of these two works. Mayo touches on this point only lightly and Owen not at all, although in the case of the latter it might have been considered immodest if he had. In both instances, the men running the company (Owen in New Lanark, Scotland, the "Colonel" in Philadelphia) were leaders and were even perceived as such by the employees. Both were men who "knew" when they were right, and both were sincere in their desire to do the best that they could for the physical well-being of their employees. However, these attributes on their part were not sufficient without a reciprocal feeling on the part of the employees. In each instance, the employees had strong feelings of confidence regarding the ability and sincerity of their leader. Therefore, it is clear that for any successful program in human relations there must be a leader with ability and sincerity, and these traits must be recognized by the employees.

MODERN APPROACHES TO THE STUDY OF MANAGEMENT

In addition to the approaches to the study of management that emphasize production, administration, and human relations, there are other areas that have been stressed in the development of management concepts. Indeed, there have been so many ideas concerning the central problems of management that one writer has referred to "The Management Theory Jungle"[11] and another writer has called the sometimes vituperative statements of the proponents of the various management schools a form of "inky warfare."[12] Let us examine this "jungle" so that we might obtain a broader view of management concepts. Also, though not fully developed, there is the beginning of an integrative point of view in management theory. The diverse theories or schools of management are presented as the "jungle," which is followed by an integrative point of view.

The Jungle

Professor Harold Koontz in his now famous article, "The Management Theory Jungle," describes briefly six major schools of management. He groups Taylor and Fayol together and refers to their approach as the "management process" school. The work of those who emphasize human relations is recognized separately as the "human behavior school." In addition he recognizes four other schools or theories of management: the empirical school, the social systems school, the decision theory school, and the mathematical school.[13]

---

[11]Harold Koontz, "The Management Theory Jungle," *Academy of Management Journal,* Vol. 4, No. 4 (December, 1961), pp. 174–188.
[12]Lyndall F. Urwick, "The Tactics of Jungle Warfare," *Academy of Management Journal,* Vol. 6, No. 4 (December, 1963), pp. 316–329.
[13]The discussion that follows is based on Koontz, *op. cit.*

The Empirical School. The empirical school studies management through an analysis of the experience of successful managers. The purpose is to permit the formation of generalizations concerning the nature of management. An example of this approach is found in Ernest Dale's *The Great Organizers*, a review of the operations of such companies as Du Pont, General Motors, National Steel, and Westinghouse Electric Corporation as seen through the eyes of the chief executive of each of these organizations.[14]

In a sense this approach to management is saying, "Let us look at several successful operations, their chief executives, and how they did it, and as a result we will be able to transfer this information to another situation." To a degree the empirical school of management is closely related to the management process school of Taylor and Fayol. Each of these men was a highly successful manager in his own right and much of the writings of each is a distillation and reporting of his own experience as a manager, while Dale's work is a reporting of the experience of others. Thus the two approaches are closely related, the difference lying in who is doing the reporting, with both schools hoping to derive a set of concepts or principles to serve as the basis for managing organizations.

The Social Systems School. Closely related to but distinct from the behavioral school is the social systems school. The behavioral school has its origin in the work of academicians, such as Mayo, but the social systems school is attributed to Chester Barnard, formerly president of the New Jersey Bell Telephone Company. It has been said that Barnard writes "with authority about authority" and perhaps he should, having been president of a major corporation. Yet Barnard viewed the organization primarily as a social system.[15]

One of the major contributions of this point of view is recognition of the importance of the informal organization and its impact upon the formal organization as portrayed by the organization chart. Another contribution concerns the nature of authority. The management process school views authority as being derived from ownership and flowing downward throughout the organization; however, Barnard sees authority as originating in the extent to which it is accepted by members of the organization. This view concerning the origin of authority, known as *subordinate acceptance*, is discussed and reconciled with the institutional view of authority of the management process school in Chapter 10.

---

[14]Ernest Dale, *The Great Organizers* (New York: McGraw-Hill Book Co., 1960). In addition to the experiences of the "organizers" of each of these four companies, Professor Dale examines concepts of organizational theory in the first chapter and in the concluding chapter discusses the accountability of management.

[15]Chester Barnard, *The Functions of the Executive* (Cambridge: Harvard University Press, 1938).

The Decision Theory School. The decision theory school is concerned with the making of a choice, or decision, between one or more alternatives and considers decision making as one of the primary activities of management. Decision theory is not as narrow as it might seem at first glance; instead, it can and does study not only the decision but also the decision-making process and the behavioral aspects of the decision maker.

The Mathematical School. Intertwined with the decision theory school is that group referred to as the mathematical school. The relationship between these two schools is very close because many of the decisions made by management may be expressed as mathematical models and subsequently solved by mathematical processes. In earlier years, the mathematical approach has been called operations research or operations analysis, but presently the term *management science* seems to predominate. Significantly the emergence of mathematics to a dominant position among the approaches to the study of management has coincided with the development of the high-speed electronic computer, thereby permitting the management scientist to construct mathematical models containing as many as one thousand simultaneous equations.[16]

An Integrative View

The divergence of opinion concerning the central issue of management is reminiscent of the three blind men, each of whom described in turn an elephant as a rope (the one who touched the tail), a snake (the one who found the trunk), and a tree stump (the one who touched a leg). The question arises whether there is a sighted one amongst us who can describe management in its entirety rather than describing a single aspect of the process. There are those who believe that there is such a theoretical framework available at the present time; however, there are discrepancies concerning the details of this framework. Professor Scott has supplied us with a fine summary of an integrative approach to the study of management that is generally referred to as *modern* organization theory.[17] Scott has noted that modern approaches

---

[16]A discussion of management science for the student interested in learning more about this field may be found in Harvey M. Wagner, *Principles of Operations Research with Applications to Managerial Decisions* (2d ed.; Englewood Cliffs: Prentice-Hall, 1975). Note that the title shows the close relationship between the mathematical and the decision theory approach to the study of management.

[17]William G. Scott, "Organization Theory: Overview and an Appraisal," *Academy of Management Journal,* Vol. 4, No. 1 (April, 1961), pp. 7–26. Professor Scott reviews briefly earlier theories of management and classifies them as the classical doctrine. The human relations movement is classified as neoclassical theory of organization. However, the major portion of the article is devoted to modern organization theory. The discussion that follows is based upon this article.

to the study of management have one thing in common — the utilization of the systems concept as a means of describing the total organization rather than emphasizing a specific function such as decision making (the decision theory school) or an elaboration of a method (the mathematical school) to solve organizational problems. The following questions are asked in the systems approach to understanding the management of organizations:

1. What are the strategic parts of the system?
2. What is the nature of their mutual dependency?
3. What are the main processes in the system which link the parts together and facilitate their adjustments to each other?
4. What are the goals sought by systems?[18]

The Parts of the System. The individual is the fundamental unit of the organizational system. The individual is considered in terms of personality, defining personality as the sum total of one's experiences and abilities. One of the significant aspects of the individual's personality is that it sets forth one's expectations as an individual and as a member of the organization.

The second part of an organization is the arrangement of the individuals and the functions they perform into what is termed the *formal* organization, often portrayed — albeit inadequately — by the formal organization chart. A fundamental question arises at this point: to what extent are these two parts of the organization in conflict? Some students of management believe that the extent of the conflict is considerable; that is, the demands of the formal organization are contrary to the nature of its individual members.[19]

The third part of the organizational system is known as the *informal* organization. The informal organization, not shown on the official organization chart, is composed of informal groups that arise out of the work situations. Sometimes the informal groups develop as a means of completing the assigned work of the formal organization. When this happens the goals of the two groups are frequently in accord; however, there are instances where the expectations of the formal organization are in conflict with the desires of the informal organization. When this happens the individual is frequently torn between the conflicting demands of the formal and informal organization.

The fourth part of the organization derives from the study of social processes and consequent recognition of the demands of both the

---

[18]*Ibid.*, p. 16. In a more recent article, Dr. Scott indicates the forces that are from outside the organization rather than those forces from within the organization. It complements his 1961 article. William G. Scott, "Organization Theory: A Reassessment," *Academy of Management Journal*, Vol. 17, No. 2 (June, 1974), pp. 242–254.

[19]Chris Argyris, *Personality and Organization* (New York: Harper & Brothers, 1957). Of a special interest in regard to the question raised above are Chapters 2, 3, and 7.

formal and informal organization. One of the demands of the organization, formal or informal, is that individuals assume a *role* — prescribed and expected patterns of behavior — that is a result of their position and function in the organization. A specific concept of role that has developed is that of the role at the interface, the demands that are made of the person who is figuratively in the middle and must bring together two segments, or interfaces, of the organization.[20]

Finally, the last part of the system is the *physical setting* within which the individual or the group performs its respective duties. It is a setting that is not limited to the physical factors and working conditions such as those investigated by the Hawthorne illumination studies. Instead, it is a concept that seeks the optimum relationship between man and his environment and attempts to allocate the resources and capabilities of man so that they mesh effectively with those of the physical settings of his environment. This method of viewing man in relation to his environment is described as a *man-machine-system*, a concept that strives to optimize the capabilities and performance of both man and the machine.

In summary, the individual, the fundamental building block of the organization, is a member of and is influenced by the formal organization. The requirements of the formal organization determine the composition and nature of work groups. The work groups in turn may form the basis for the informal organization, which is composed of individuals who are simultaneously members of the formal and the informal organization. Both the formal and the informal organization have goals that do not necessarily coincide. In addition, the goals of the formal and the informal organization are related to the expectations and goals of the individual. Also, there is the role that is demanded of the individual as a member of the formal organization and the role demanded as a member of the informal organization. Finally, there is the realization that all organizational functions occur within a physical setting that evolves beyond the man-machine-system concept to a man-organization-system concept.

The Linking Processes. It is easy to state that the parts of the organization are interrelated, simply because they appear to be so. However, the student of organizational theory must do more than make the statement; the ways in which the processes link the various parts of the organization must be designated and described. One of the linking processes is the *role*, or actions, performed by the individual member of the organization which serves as a means of relating to other people and to other groups in the organization. *Communication* is another means of linking the parts of the organization. The term communication includes not only verbal expressions, both written and oral, but also all information needed for effective operation of the organization.

---

[20]For a discussion of the role at the interface see Chapter 13, p. 308.

When communication is used in this sense, the organization is viewed as a total "information system." Thus there is concern for the flow of information from one subsystem to another subsystem so that the parts are linked together. Closely related to the concept of an organization as an information system is the concept of *balance* or homeostasis. This concept, sometimes referred to as a steady state, is one of the fundamental aspects of systems theory; that is, there is a normal state for the system and when the system is out of balance there is a tendency for it to return to its normal homeostatic state. Another linking process is *decision making*. The process of making decisions may be used to change the direction or goal of the organization, or the decision may be designed so that it restores balance to the system.

Organizational Goals. Scott has stated that the "organization has three goals which may be intermeshed or may be independent ends in themselves. They are growth, stability, and interaction."[21] He points out that the last goal refers to those organizations which exist primarily as vehicles that permit their members to interact with other members — for example, professional societies and certain social organizations. In setting the goals of organizations, it is necessary not only to seek a balance between potentially conflicting organizational goals, but also to relate these goals to those of the individual and to the goals of the informal organization. Thus the problem of establishing congruent goals for all components of an organization becomes highly critical.

The Next Development

It has been suggested by several people, among them Professor William C. Frederick, that the next step in the study of management is the development of a general systems theory.[22] His reason for making this statement is that a review of the development of management concepts indicates that five components of a potential general theory of management have been developed. In discussing these components, Frederick first points out that the classical management of Fayol and Taylor resulted in the establishment of management principles, including a delineation of the functions and processes of management. The human relations school, a second component, stresses that the formal organization is at the same time a human and social organization and as such should serve these purposes as well as fulfilling purely economic ends. The third component is the contribution made by the

---

[21]Scott, "Organization Theory: Overview and an Appraisal," p. 20.

[22]William C. Frederick, "The Next Development in Management Science: A General Theory," *Academy of Management Journal*, Vol. 6, No. 3 (September, 1963), pp. 212–219. The discussion that follows is based upon the five major components of a general theory of management as described by Professor Frederick.

decision theory school, including mathematical approaches to management processes, and recognition that decision making performs a linking function in the organization. The fourth factor is the behavioral sciences. Though quite similar to the human relations school and in the opinion of some an extension of the work of Mayo, this group stresses that individuals may be regarded as systems and function within larger social systems. Finally, the fifth component is value theory, a means of establishing the social responsibility of organizations and managements and placing in perspective the diverse contributions of the classical, human relations, decision theory, and behavioral approaches to the study of management.[23]

The conclusion is inescapable. Modern approaches to the study of management or organizations are pointing toward the development of what will someday be a general systems theory of organizations and their management. The next theory of organization will stress the systems concept. Such a theory is presented in Chapter 8, "Organization Theory," as a first step in the development of a general systems theory of organization.

In Case Problem 2-B, a modern counterpart of making pins by hand is described. The solution of the decision to be made by this management rests not only upon the work of Charles Babbage, but also upon the fundamental concepts developed by Taylor, Fayol, and Mayo.

Case Problem 2-B

ELIMINATING AN ASSEMBLY LINE

Plasco Incorporated is a company that molds and manufactures plastic products. Some of the molded parts are sold to other firms for use in their finished products; however, the company also manufactures and distributes several completed products that require the assembly of molded parts as well as the molding process itself. One such product is a hand-actuated lever-type pump spray used with window cleaners, detergents, and similar products normally packaged in a plastic bottle, also produced by Plasco.

The lever-type pump consists of 15 plastic parts, a steel pin to hold the lever in place, and a plastic hose which extends into the container holding the liquid to be sprayed. Present production methods utilize an assembly line operating two shifts to assemble the product. There are five workers (semiskilled) engaged in the assembly of subassemblies. The

---

[23]A similar point of view has been expressed by Professor William T. Greenwood who notes that there are eleven existing management theory concepts that can be reduced to four concurrently and sequentially developing ones. He also states that the evolutionary developments in management theory indicate that a future "general theory" probably can result from an analysis and synthesis within the present decade by utilizing the management process theory as a comparative base. William T. Greenwood, "Future Management Theory: A 'Comparative' Evolution to a General Theory," *Academy of Management Journal*, Vol. 17, No. 3 (September, 1974), pp. 503–513.

final assembly line consists of 20 to 25 workers, dependent upon attendance, who are seated on either side of a moving assembly conveyor belt. One inspector is assigned to each shift. There is also a supervisor who oversees the assembly operation and performs coordinative functions with the molding department to assure that the necessary parts for the product are available for the assembly area. The total annual cost of the assembly operation for direct wages and fringe benefits for both shifts is approximately $300,000 per year.

Recently the president of Plasco has had several discussions with a designer and builder of special machinery. The engineering design company has built several similar products and has presented a firm offer to Plasco to build a machine that will perform all subassemblies and final assemblies. The price of the machine installed is $300,000. Plasco estimates that the payback period for the machine will be approximately one year since it equals the annual amount spent for total wages for the manual assembly operation.

The manufacturer of the proposed machine has indicated that there is need for at least two highly skilled mechanics, one for each shift, to be trained by the manufacturer to maintain the equipment. Further, a high degree of uniformity of component parts is required since nonstandard parts are automatically rejected. However, such parts are not necessarily scrapped since a rework department of four or five employees may be established to salvage an estimated 75 percent of the rejections by means of hand assembly. It is expected that the two inspectors and approximately 60 subassemblers and final assembly

employees will be eliminated. Two operators, in all probability former assembly line employees, are required for each shift to fill the hoppers at each station so that continuous production may be maintained. Maintenance costs on the new equipment are expected to be minimal though slightly higher than the maintenance costs of the present assembly line; however, these costs should be offset in part because of the reduced number of defective assemblies. No significant change in total units assembled per shift is anticipated.

It is expected that approximately six to eight months production experience may be required before all minor difficulties normally encountered with complex automatic equipment that performs humanlike motions are eliminated. Even so, it is estimated that the payback period, based upon savings in wages, will range between the 12 months suggested by the manufacturer of the automatic assembler and a maximum of 18 months assuming the greatest number of problems.

PROBLEMS

1. Which of the questions raised by Charles Babbage are applicable to the situation described above?
2. What is your answer to each of Babbage's five questions?
3. What are the social implications of displacing approximately 55 to 60 workers? Is your answer dependent upon the level of unemployment in the area?
4. To what extent do the principles of Taylor and Fayol and the observations of Mayo contribute to the decision to be made by the Plasco management?

CHAPTER QUESTIONS FOR STUDY AND DISCUSSION

1. What basic management concepts are illustrated in the recounting of the passage from the Bible concerning Moses and Jethro?
2. What advantages did Babbage see in the division of labor on the basis of skill?

3. Scientific management principles were developed to solve two major problems. What are these two problems? In what way or ways did the approach of Elton Mayo to solving these problems differ from that of Frederick Taylor?

4. What was the initial purpose of Mayo's Hawthorne Studies? What areas or problems did the studies later consider? Briefly discuss the phenomenon known as the Hawthorne Effect.

5. What major conclusions can be drawn from the work of Owen and Mayo?

6. In what respect does Fayol's concept of the division of work differ from Babbage's concept in "On the Division of Labour"?

7. Why is it unsound for a manager to approach an organization with a "divide and conquer" philosophy?

8. Differentiate between Fayol's principles of unity of command and unity of direction.

9. Is there "one best way" in the application of the management process in view of modern organization theory? Explain.

10. What is the meaning of the term "centralization" according to Fayol?

11. What are the six major schools of management described by Professor Koontz in his article, "The Management Theory Jungle?"

Chapter 3

Objectives and Ethics

CONSUMERISM

The development of objectives for an organization is of primary importance since it determines the direction, or goals, of the company. An account of one company's efforts to respond to the growing consumer demand for better quality products and services (the so-called "wave of consumerism") is described in an article by Esther Peterson, consumer adviser to the president of Giant Food Inc., a 102-store food retailer based in Washington, D.C.[1]

In 1970, Giant Food Inc. decided to make a determined effort to meet the growing dissatisfaction of consumers with the services and products offered to them. To aid this effort, Giant enlisted the services of Mrs. Esther Peterson. Her experience as special assistant for consumer affairs to President Lyndon Johnson together with her service for many years as assistant secretary of labor made her eminently qualified to assist Giant in its efforts to respond to consumer complaints. Mrs. Peterson accepted the company's offer after she was assured that she would be free to speak out according to her convictions, that

she would have a voice at the highest levels of the company in decision making, and that the company would make a commitment to some of the programs that Mrs. Peterson believed to be of value in giving consumer advocates the recognition they seek.

It had been Mrs. Peterson's observation from her experience in consumer affairs that businesses typically progress through five distinct steps in their reaction to the complaints of consumers.

1. When charged by consumer groups, deny everything.
2. If denial does not work, discredit the person or organization making the charge.
3. When consumers are ignored and seek aid through legislative action, oppose such action.
4. If legislative action is passed, weaken it by preventing its implementation or securing an administrator who would not be overenthusiastic in administering the law.
5. Take positive action to solve the problems raised by consumer groups: consider the charges seriously, give consumer representatives a fair hearing; and finally, take constructive action to meet consumer complaints.

---

[1]This case problem is based on Esther Peterson, "Consumerism as a Retailer's Asset," *Harvard Business Review,* Vol. 52, No. 3 (May–June, 1974, pp. 91–101.

When Mrs. Peterson accepted her position with Giant Food, the company had reached the fifth stage of reacting to consumerism — doing something constructive to solve the problem. Hiring Mrs. Peterson was the beginning of Giant's successful effort to meet the issues raised by consumer groups.

Mrs. Peterson's initial efforts were directed toward bridging the communications gap existing between Giant's executives and consumer representatives. She began a series of discussions with the company's Consumer Action Task Force, chaired by the assistant to the president, and including the vice-presidents of store operations, advertising and sales promotion, purchasing, manufacturing, warehousing, and distribution. These discussions resulted in a more favorable attitude on the part of company executives toward consumer advocates. At the same time Mrs. Peterson met with consumer representatives to explain what she was trying to do and to ask for their help. These meetings resulted in the formation of a number of advisory committees in such areas as the environment, nutrition, and drugs.

To implement Giant's consumer program, the task force members unanimously agreed to adopt the format set out in President Kennedy's Consumer Bill of Rights. These rights are "the right to safety, the right to be informed, the right to be heard, and the right to choose." The task force added two rights not included in Kennedy's Consumer Bill of Rights — the right to redress and the right to service. The action taken in adopting the above-mentioned rights serves an extremely important function in that it establishes objectives and a means of implementing these objectives concerning consumer demands. For example, the right to safety and its subsidiary concern with such areas as chemical additives in foods and the ecological effects of chemicals in laundry products led to the establishment of a Quality Assurance and Sanitation Department. Its primary duties are to develop product specifications, maintain surveillance over food products in the company's own laboratories, set sanitation policies, and oversee enforcement through its inspection program.

The company's commitment to the consumers' right to be informed is achieved through better labeling that provides complete and accurate information; through institutional advertisements emphasizing Giant's consumer programs; and through comments on issues affecting consumers and the food industry. Also, Giant Food's commitments to these goals are seen in its practices of unit pricing, open dating, nutritional labeling, percentage of ingredient labeling, and completely frank advertising.

Mrs. Peterson emphasizes the importance of continuing communications between the company and consumer representatives. She believes that such open communication is the foundation of Giant's consumer program. The results of these exchanges are evidenced in Giant's more recent concern in the areas of toy safety, care labeling, guarantees, flammability, and sizing of clothing.

The consumers' right to choose seems almost inherent in the nature of the food retailing industry with its huge variety of merchandise. However, trade-offs must sometimes be made between the desires of customers, stimulated perhaps by advertising, and the potential hazards of certain products such as fruit-scented cleaning products or foods which contain additives. The consumers' right to redress is perhaps the least difficult goal to achieve by establishing a policy of an unconditional money-back guarantee for all products purchased.

Mrs. Peterson concludes that the Giant Food management has no regrets about its consumer program. She states, "What seemed to some people to be a highly suspect and risky alliance has turned out to be a breakthrough for consumers as well as a great competitive asset for the company. Furthermore, in these times of shortages of goods and inflation of prices, Giant's forthrightness with the public has earned the company a sympathetic ear for its side of the story."[2] She further comments that the basic principles of good operation — clean stores, good merchandise, and efficient management — are

_____
[2]*Ibid*., p. 101.

not enough for the successful operation of a retail food organization today because consumers expect a part in the decision-making process that affects them. Apparently, Giant has been successful in offering them a role in this area.

---PROBLEMS---

1. Are the objectives of Giant Food in regard to its relations with consumer groups external or internal in nature?

2. Should groups who are not employees or shareholders of the organization have a part in the decision-making process as it affects them as customers?

3. Would your answer to the above question be the same for other industries; for example, heavy machinery, suppliers to industrial firms, and service organizations such as management consultant firms and certified public accounting firms?

4. If more companies took the position that Giant Food has taken, would there be more or less government regulation of industry? Why?

In Chapter 1, management is defined as the coordination of all resources through the processes of planning, organizing, leading, and controlling in order to attain stated objectives. The determination of the objectives of a firm defines the framework within which the management processes take place. The methods used to attain these objectives inevitably affect various groups of people and reflect the ethical standards of the organization. This chapter discusses organizational objectives and reviews some of the problems encountered in analyzing and establishing ethical standards for formal organizations.

MANAGEMENT BY OBJECTIVES

The setting of objectives, the utilization of these objectives in the management process, and the measurement of both individual and organizational performance against these objectives is known as *management by objectives* (MBO). Further, MBO implies that objectives are set jointly, or participatively, by superior and subordinate and that the subordinate's performance is appraised in terms of the degree of attainment of such objectives.[3]

In order to understand the fundamentals of MBO, it is necessary to define an objective and state its significance in concise form. Values generally attributed to objectives are discussed. Then, types of objectives and methods of stating objectives are examined. Finally, a brief evaluation of MBO as an approach to the management of organizations is presented.

Definition

Managing a firm without stated objectives is as frustrating and meaningless as sailing a ship without a destination. For management

---

[3]See Chapter 12, pp. 278–282.

there is no direction to its efforts or effective coordination of resources until there is a stated purpose or goal. Thus, an *objective* may be defined as *the end point or goal toward which management directs its efforts.* The statement of an objective is in effect a statement of purpose, which, when applied to a business organization, becomes the statement of that firm's reason for existing. In order to gain maximum effectiveness from a statement of objectives, an organization must state its objectives prior to initiating the management processes of planning, organizing, leading, and controlling. Stating an objective may require considerable research, yet it is not a part of the planning process. The planning process is put into effect, along with the other three management processes, to achieve stated objectives.

Principle of the Objective

The requirement that the objective should be predetermined is considered of such significance that it is referred to by many as the *Principle of the Objective.* The principle of the objective is stated concisely by John F. Mee: *"Before initiating any course of action, the objectives in view must be clearly determined, understood, and stated."*[4]

The principle of the objective stresses the outstanding characteristic of an objective. This characteristic is that an objective is *predetermined,* an act which thereby sets it apart from the processes utilized in reaching the objective. A second characteristic of an objective is that it is stated. Generally, stating an objective implies that the statement be in written form. Companies that are reluctant or unable to state their objectives in writing reflect either an inability to reach accord on their goals or a fear of criticism that might be engendered by such a statement. The third characteristic of an objective expresses a duality that, on the surface, appears to be contradictory. An objective should be well within the reach of the organization, yet difficult to attain. If an objective is not attainable, it will be disregarded. When this happens, there is no goal. At the same time, an objective must be sufficiently difficult so that it presents a challenge to everyone concerned; otherwise, its potential as an incentive is not realized. The poet Robert Browning expresses the conflicting duality of an objective well in the following lines:

> Ah, but a man's reach should exceed his grasp,
> Or what's a heaven for?[5]

Value of Objectives

There are four outstanding benefits that result from a statement of objectives. Stated objectives fulfill a need for direction and also serve

---

[4]John F. Mee, "Management Philosophy for Professional Executives," *Business Horizons* (December, 1956), pp. 5–11.

[5]*Andrea del Sarto*, lines 97–98.

as motivators for the personnel of an entire organization. In addition, objectives contribute to the management process and form the basis for a sound management philosophy. These four benefits, especially the contribution of objectives in forming management philosophy, make it possible to adopt management by objectives as a basic approach to the management of organizations.

Objectives Provide Direction. The primary need for objectives is implied in the definition of an objective as an end point or goal toward which management directs its efforts. That need is the need for direction and is felt throughout the entire organization. Not only should there be a statement of objectives for the company as a whole, but there should also be a statement for each organizational unit of the company. Each unit of the business should have its own related objectives so that its efforts may be coordinated and unified toward a common goal.

Objectives Serve as Motivators. Ideally, objectives serve as motivators in addition to providing direction. Examples of the motivating value of an objective are the monetary rewards used in industry. Incentive plans for hourly workers assume, to some degree, that one of the objectives of a worker is to earn more money. When this assumption is true, it follows that the creation of a situation making it possible for a worker to increase earnings motivates the worker toward achieving that immediate goal or objective. The desire for economic gain underlies the concept of behavior held by Taylor and others who have installed incentive plans. The creation of corporate profit is often stated as one of the major objectives of business; however, a subtle problem of differentiation exists in determining whether profit is in fact a goal or whether it is primarily a motivator of managers.

Objectives Contribute to the Management Process. The third value to be gained from a statement of objectives is that such a statement makes a significant contribution to the management process. Clearly understood and realistic objectives form a basis for the control process, the measurement of the firm's present position in relation to its desired goal. Objectives are important in that they influence the size and characteristics of an organization and affect the type of leadership required; however, the closest relationship is between objectives and the processes of planning and control. Plans are formulated in order to reach specific goals, and the control process measures the extent to which these plans are achieved. Neither is possible without a prior statement of objectives.

Objectives Are the Basis for a Management Philosophy. Lastly, the statement of objectives forms the basis for a management philosophy. It makes possible the creation of a management by objective rather than management in response to "crash programs" and "special drives." When objectives are not formally stated, the solutions of immediate emergencies are dignified as objectives, and, as such, they become a series of short-term projects that lack cohesiveness and are frequently contradictory in purpose. Crisis management makes it virtually impossible to achieve Fayol's esprit de corps, or singleness of purpose, for the simple reason that there are no cohesive objectives. The organization is continually shifting its attentions and efforts in first one direction and then another, with no opportunity to achieve a goal or objective that would result in a feeling of singleness of purpose.

Types of Objectives

There is no single objective for a business organization. Some objectives are primarily of interest to people and organizations not a part of the organization itself. Others are of special concern to those who are members of or owners of the firm. It is not a question of determining which objectives are more important — those external to the firm or those internal to the firm — instead, it is a problem of determining how to fulfill each set of objectives to the maximum degree.

External Objectives. The executives of Giant Food realize that service to its customers is a necessity if the firm is to continue to grow and to make a profit. Their problem is not unique for those firms engaged in selling directly to the public. To ignore the charges of consumers or to deny such charges is failure to recognize that there is a current wave of consumerism, based not only upon the formation of formal consumer groups, but also upon the failure of business organizations to recognize that service to consumers is a necessary objective of a firm if that firm is to continue to exist. No organization can exist unless a portion of the public becomes its customers and buys its service or its product. Unless a product or service is comparable in respect to price, quality, and utility to that of competing products or services, it will not be purchased in sufficient quantities to generate a profit large enough to permit staying in business. Inviting consumer groups to participate in decision making, normally regarded as a purely internal function, is one way of assuring a market for the firm's products or services. The desire to make a profit and the hope of sharing that profit motivate all employees, particularly managers; but in order to create profit, an organization must serve a customer. Thus, a primary objective of any organization is a service objective — to serve the needs of a customer.

There are many types of businesses that are prohibited by law. For example, most states prohibit gambling. There are also restrictive federal laws, such as the antitrust laws. Consequently, the objectives of an organization must be in accord with the wishes of society or that organization is not permitted to continue operation. Thus, the values of society as reflected by its laws and regulations and the acceptance of a firm's product or a service by customers are external objectives that must be recognized and met if that organization is to continue.

Internal Objectives. The two objectives of service to a customer and service to society are objectives *external* to the firm. At the same time these objectives are being fulfilled, an organization is interested in satisfying certain objectives that are of particular interest to the firm itself. These objectives are *internal*. The first of the internal objectives is the overall position of a firm in relation to its competitors. A company may desire to be the largest, to be the most profitable, to show the greatest growth, or to produce the greatest number of new products.

Secondly, there are objectives related to employee groups. The firm may be desirous of attracting and holding the finest type employee possible; or depending upon the nature of the business and the objectives of its management, it may seek an employee with minimal qualifications. In addition, various employee groups may have subobjectives of their own. An example of this is the desire for wages and fringe benefits as expressed by unions.

A third group of objectives is directed toward satisfying the stockholders. These objectives are considered internal since stockholders are a part of the firm and are not necessarily the customers nor representatives of the society that sanctions the firm. Stockholder-related objectives usually define profit as a goal so that the stockholders may receive a return on their investment in the firm. Profits are also necessary to provide funds that permit the attainment of the first of the internal objectives, the desired relative position of the company with respect to its competitors.

In summary, the objectives of a firm are classed as external and internal. External objectives are service objectives. Business firms, if they are to survive, must provide a product or a service that is acceptable to customers and sanctioned by society. Internal objectives define the position of a firm in respect to its competitors and state specific goals for employee groups. There are also internal objectives directed toward satisfying stockholders. Profit, the lifeblood of a business firm, functions as both an objective and a motive; but profit is not possible unless the customers are satisfied and unless the objectives of the firm are sanctioned by society.

Statement of Objectives

So that objectives may be meaningful and perform the dual role of goal and motivator, they must be stated in a manner that is easily understood. Since there are external and internal objectives which may be in conflict with each other, it is highly unlikely that a satisfactory statement of goals can be accomplished by setting one single objective. Therefore, objectives must be stated for each of several areas of performance. Peter Drucker suggests that objectives be stated for each of the following eight areas of accomplishment:

1. Market standing
2. Innovation
3. Productivity
4. Physical and financial resources
5. Profitability
6. Manager performance and development
7. Worker performance and attitude
8. Public responsibility[6]

Objectives for the first five areas are susceptible to quantitative measurement and statement and may be expressed as a numerical value. For example, market standing may be expressed as a rank position in the industry or may be stated in terms of specific dollar volume of sales. Innovation, or technological development, is also susceptible to quantitative measurement and expression. Productivity may be expressed in terms of total units or in a manner that measures the efficiency of the production process, such as units per man-hour or units per dollar of capital expenditure. Physical and financial resources and profitability may also be expressed in dollars. These are the traditional measures of the growth and well-being of a firm, but unless these objectives are properly supported by stated objectives in the last three areas — manager performance and development, worker performance and attitude, and public responsibility — they become meaningless and the entire structure of objectives will collapse like a house of cards.

It may be argued that the last three objectives relating to the performance of management, the workers, and the meeting of public responsibilities are not objectives but in reality a statement of policy; that is, a broad framework within which the organization operates. Be that as it may, an organization is composed of people, and unless plans are made for the perpetuation of the organization and its improvement as a functioning unit, the organization will not be capable of maintaining or advancing its position in respect to market position, technological development, physical resources, and profitability. It is also necessary that broad social responsibilities be recognized and stated as objectives since society sanctions, or permits, business to exist.

Evaluation of MBO

More than 20 years have passed since the publication of Peter Drucker's *The Practice of Management*, the forerunner of present-day

---

[6]Peter F. Drucker, *The Practice of Management* (New York: Harper & Brothers, 1954). These eight areas for which objectives should be set are of significance not only in the setting of objectives but also in determining the areas for which controls must be provided. Seven of these areas appear in Chapter 18 as those areas needing controls.

MBO.[7] Yet surprisingly little objective research has been conducted to support the reported strengths of MBO and to point out its limitations. Nonetheless, there are indications of positive results when MBO is used as an underlying approach to management. At the same time, there are indications that MBO is not a panacea for all organizations or all management problems.

If a statement of objectives is to provide direction for an organization, it must provide realistic attainable goals for the organization itself. Organizational goals are usually formulated by the highest echelon of management and the board of directors. Then and only then can goals be set for the managers of each succeeding lower level of management. Some companies have extended the process of goal setting to hourly production and clerical workers. The dangers inherent in the goal-setting process are that the objectives may be unrealistic and unattainable. Or, they may be too simplistic as the result of failing to recognize that there are multiple objectives. Finally, there may be a tendency for written statements to become cast in concrete; thereby making it impossible to maintain the necessary flexibility to meet internal changes within the organization and the external changes of the environment.

One of the attributes frequently ascribed to MBO is that it motivates subordinates as the result of setting clear objectives and then appraising subordinates in terms of the results obtained as opposed to rating them on a series of vague and meaningless personality traits. Motivation occurs only if there has been a truly participative setting of goals by superiors and subordinates. In addition, there must be a continuing feedback to subordinates, hopefully positive in nature, so that their desire to achieve the jointly set goals is reinforced. If there is inadequate feedback or if the feedback is negative, the value of goal setting as a motivator is correspondingly decreased.

Perhaps the greatest effect that MBO has upon the management processes is its effect upon planning. Plans must be developed that serve as a blueprint for action directed toward the attainment of objectives. Such plans must be objective and offer a degree of structure to the organization and its members, yet retain the element of flexibility. They must also contribute to the economic well being of the organization (see Chapter 4, Planning). MBO has its effect upon the organization since it requires an organization capable of meeting stated objectives. Lastly, the control process cannot be ignored since it provides the feedback necessary to assess one's position relative to the attainment of objectives.

MBO as the cornerstone of a management philosophy requires that all managerial personnel be trained in the processes of participative goal setting. Second, training is required in the means of appraising

---

[7]Ibid.

the performance of subordinates. MBO requires an openness and communication between superior and subordinate not usually found in most organizations. There must be a shift in management style for most organizations so that the superior becomes supportive in nature rather than directive or authoritarian. Unless the style of the superior is supportive, feedback from subordinates concerning their attainment of objectives will be severely limited and sometimes distorted and inaccurate. Finally, it must be recognized that participative approaches do not solve all problems, nor are participative approaches appropriate for all organizations.[8]

ETHICS

Once the objectives of a firm have been established, and assuming that these objectives are sanctioned by society, the manner in which objectives are achieved falls within the province of ethics. The word, ethics, as it is used today, comes from the Greek root, *ethos*, and in its original form referred to habitual practices and customs. At a later date the concept of character became a part of its meaning. *Ethics* is defined as the study of conduct between individuals — what are the standards governing their interrelationships? The problem of ethics is concerned with the behavior of individuals; therefore, such terms as "business ethics," "corporate ethics," and "corporate morality" become vague and meaningless. Furthermore, a person's impression of the state of "business ethics" is actually a judgment of the behavior of individuals employed in the business community. A business firm may have policies that govern to some extent the conduct of its executives, but the firm itself is a legal entity, not an individual. Thus, a firm is incapable of personal interrelationships that characterize individuals.

A second concept implied in the definition of ethics is that the word clearly indicates a desirable standard of performance as demonstrated by the existence and use of the word *unethical*, which denotes behavior that does not meet desired standards.

The Nature of Ethical Problems

There are two approaches to the determination of ethical standards. First, there are writings that record examples of behavior so

---

[8]For similar evaluations of MBO, the following sources are recommended: David R. Hampton, "The Planning-Motivation Dilemma," *Business Horizons*, Vol. 16, No. 3 (June, 1973), pp. 79–87; Bruce D. Jamieson, "Behavioral Problems With Management by Objectives," *Academy of Management Journal*, Vol. 16, No. 3 (September, 1973), pp. 496–505; Dale D. McConkey, "MBO — Twenty Years Later, Where Do We Stand?" *Business Horizons*, Vol. 16, No. 4 (August, 1973), pp. 25–36; William E. Reif and Gerald Bassford, "What MBO Really Is," *Business Horizons*, Vol. 16, No. 3 (June, 1973), pp. 23–30; Henry L. Tosi and Stephen J. Carroll, "Managerial Reaction to Management by Objectives," *Academy of Management Journal*, Vol. 11, No. 4 (December, 1968), pp. 415–426; Donald D. White, "Factors Affecting Employee Attitudes Toward the Installation of a New Management System," *Academy of Management Journal*, Vol. 16, No. 4 (December, 1973), pp. 636–646.

that they may be classified and synthesized. This method provides a series of philosophical essays as guides. Second, several empirical studies analyze current ethical practices and values of American business executives. Both approaches are examined and recommendations are made to describe how an individual firm can aid in establishing the ethical standards desired for its management.

No two writers have described the questions of ethics for business people in exactly the same way. However, analysis of the literature results in at least three distinct problem areas:

1. Problems related to the making of decisions that are based on personal values rather than upon factual data.
2. Problems that are best described as a conflict of interest within the individual which arise because the individual is simultaneously a member of several groups that often have conflicting goals.
3. Interpersonal relationships; that is, relationships with other individuals or groups of individuals.

Problems Relating to Decision Making. Not all decisions resolve into ethical problems. Some questions are neatly solved by the application of an impersonal mathematical formula. Examples are plentiful and can be found in all areas of business and at all levels within the organization. The production foreman decides which machine will be used in making a certain part after analyzing the relative merits of the machines with respect to availability, cost, quality, and amount of time the operation will require. Likewise, the decision to buy a given piece of equipment in preference to another can be made in the same manner. But there are many areas where computations are not applicable. In these areas the executive often is asked to make a judgment, and the reference point for determining the soundness of the decision is a personal value held by the decision maker. The necessity for compromise is essential to success and may be accomplished by modifying the goal or the means of obtaining the goal. The question is one of determining when a given compromise becomes too much compromise. In a sense, a personal value is being compromised. Also, it is a judgment based on personal values that guides the executive in determining how much of the truth in any given situation should be revealed, whether a decision should be made even though all the necessary facts are not available, and in determining the upper limits of the number of mistakes on the part of a subordinate that may be tolerated. In addition, a manager must retain a degree of individuality in personal life, and must strive to broaden and deepen personal intellectual horizons even though the office image calls for a person of action. The above-mentioned situations are not susceptible to quantification and mathematical analysis but must be viewed as questions of personal values that determine one's relations with others.[9]

<hr>

[9]The above discussion is based upon Louis W. Norris, "Moral Hazards of an Executive," *Harvard Business Review*, Vol. 38, No. 5 (September–October, 1960), pp. 72–79.

Conflict of Interest Problems. Much has been said about conflict of interest as it applies to high-ranking government officials. It is now customary for the President of the United States and other high officials to divest themselves of the shares they hold in public corporations, or to establish a trust fund so that they are not aware of the specific shares held and have no control over the purchase or sale of their equities. Such action has been considered necessary in order to minimize or eliminate situations that might lead to a conflict of interest. It is only normal that a potential conflict of interests exists when an individual is simultaneously a member of one or more groups. Potential conflict is present because a person as a member of a group is expected to perform those actions necessary for the support of that group. Thus, it seems reasonable to assume that the possibility of conflicting interests may be controlled by limiting the number of groups in which an individual may participate at any given time.

The conflict of interest situation that arises most frequently originates when an official employed by one company has interests in a second company that either supplies or purchases from the employing firm. This possible conflict of interest is illustrated by the following questions: If an executive has a major financial interest in a supplying firm, will the executive, as an employee, be sufficiently forceful in demanding the best price and quality? Will the executive be more forceful in demanding the best if the executive has no personal interests in the profits of the supplying firm?

Interpersonal Relationships. Ethical problems recognized primarily as matters of interpersonal relationships arise as the result of actions intended to assist the company in meeting its objectives. They may be categorized in the same manner as are types of objectives — external and internal. The external interpersonal relationships are those relationships with customers, as illustrated in Case Problem 3-A, with other companies (both suppliers and competitors), and with governmental agencies.

There are three areas of interpersonal relationships with individuals and groups internal to the firm — those with nonmanagerial employees, those with shareholders, and superior-subordinate relationships. Although company objectives that call for equitable relationships with employees and stockholders may guide an executive in making critical judgments, such objectives do not offer much help when there is an honest difference of opinion as to what constitutes fairness in a specific situation. Examples are the periodic negotiations a company has with the union representing its employees in matters pertaining to wages and other conditions of employment. Likewise, an honest difference of opinion may arise when shareholders, as owners of the business, desire a greater return on their investment. Finally, management is asked to determine what part of earnings should be retained in the business in order that the company might maintain or improve its competitive position. The apportionment of company earnings is not an easy decision to make and requires an ethical judgment concerning the validity of the claims of each segment of the business: the employees, the shareholders, and the needs of the business itself to fulfill its stated objectives.

In addition, the manager's relationship with superiors often calls for ethical judgments. One phase of the subordinate-superior relationship, in which the subordinate is forced to rely upon personal ethical standards in determining proper conduct, is the subordinate's decision that defines proper action in obtaining promotions. Can the subordinate establish a reputation for honesty and integrity and at the same time be an opportunist who takes advantage of others for self-advancement? Another decision dependent upon a subordinate's ethical standards centers around judgment as to what constitutes an honest job in the completion of assigned duties. The other phase of this relationship — from superior to subordinate — has been touched upon in the discussion of those decisions that must be made that are dependent upon an ethical judgment as a criterion. In particular, it is mentioned that superiors are faced with the problem of determining the extent to which they can permit subordinates to make mistakes while the superiors accept responsibility for those mistakes. Superiors also face ethical problems in determining how much they should compromise with subordinates and the extent to which they can reveal all the facts of a situation to their subordinates.

Value Systems of Managers

The personal value system of the individual manager has a strong influence on that manager's perception of a situation and consequent behavior. The reference point in determining the soundness of a decision is often a personal value held by the decision maker. Compromises almost always represent to some extent the compromise of a personal value. Personal value systems also influence the way in which a person looks at other people and groups of people, thereby influencing interpersonal relationships. Also, the personal value system largely determines one's concept of what is or is not ethical behavior. A personal value system may be viewed as "a relatively permanent perceptual framework which shapes and influences the general nature of an individual's behavior."[10]

Though similar to attitudes, values are regarded as being broader in scope, unrelated to specific objects or events as are some attitudes,

---

[10]George W. England, "Personal Value Systems of American Managers," *Academy of Management Journal*, Vol. 10, No. 1 (March, 1967), pp. 53–68. England examines the personal value systems of 1,072 American managers. He also presents a theoretical model for studying the effect of values on behavior. A detailed analysis of data obtained is presented. The discussion that follows is based upon England's study.

and more stable in nature. A personal value system is a series of concepts with each concept having a degree of personal worth and meaning. Personal value systems determine for an individual what is right or wrong, good or bad, successful or unsuccessful, pleasant or unpleasant, or any other similar bipolar evaluation.

George England studied the personal value systems of American managers through a personal values questionnaire (PVQ). Professor England based his research upon an underlying theoretical model. Two sets of personal values are recognized. *Operative values* have the greatest influence on behavior and play a significant role in the development of alternative solutions to problems and in decision making. As a result, they serve to channel behavior. The second set of values, *intended and adopted values*, serve primarily as a means of screening incoming information, commonly referred to as perceptual screening, thus having an indirect effect upon behavior. As a result of behavioral channeling and perceptual screening, the range of behavior is limited in nature because of the value systems. Behavior is limited even further by the interaction of the value system of the individual manager and environmental influences and constraints. The result of the interaction of all these factors is a specific behavior for a given period of time and for a given situation.

The 66 concepts of the personal values questionaire (PVQ) — concepts about which most individuals have a personal value judgment — are reproduced in Figure 3-1 and are arranged into the following five groups: goals of business organizations, personal goals of individuals, groups of people, ideas associated with people, and ideas about general topics. The managers completing the PVQ were asked to make four value judgments for each of the concepts shown in Figure 3-1. The first evaluation is known as a *power mode*, an evaluation of the concept on an important-unimportant scale. Next, it was necessary to determine why individual managers rated a given item as important or unimportant; therefore, three secondary modes of evaluation were utilized. The three secondary modes selected were a *pragmatic* mode of evaluation using a successful-unsuccessful scale, an *ethical-moral* mode using a right-wrong scale, and an *affect*, or feeling mode of evaluation using a pleasant-unpleasant scale. Thus by using the secondary modes of evaluation one can determine why a given concept is rated as highly important, of average importance, or of low importance.

The Value Profile. Figure 3-2 shows the value profile of the managers and the concepts that are ranked as successful with high importance, average importance, and low importance; those that were ranked as right with high importance, average importance, and low importance; and those that were ranked as pleasant with high, average, and low importance.

	Goals of Business Organizations	Personal Goals of Individuals
	High Productivity	Leisure
	Industrial Leadership	Dignity
	Employee Welfare	Achievement
	Organizational Stability	Autonomy
	Profit Maximization	Money
	Organizational Efficiency	Individuality
	Social Welfare	Job Satisfaction
	Organizational Growth	Influence
		Security
		Power
		Creativity
		Success
		Prestige

Groups of People	Ideas Associated with People	Ideas About General Topics
Employees	Ambition	Authority
Customers	Ability	Caution
My Coworkers	Obedience	Change
Craftsmen	Trust	Competition
My Boss	Aggressiveness	Compromise
Managers	Loyalty	Conflict
Owners	Prejudice	Conservatism
My Subordinates	Compassion	Emotions
Laborers	Skill	Equality
My Company	Cooperation	Force
Blue-collar Workers	Tolerance	Liberalism
Government	Conformity	Property
Stockholders	Honor	Rationality
Technical Employees		Religion
Me		Risk
Labor Unions		
White-collar Employees		

Figure 3-1
CONCEPTS USED TO MEASURE MANAGERS' VALUES

England summarizes his interpretation of Figure 3-2 as follows:

1. The 29 concepts which are rated as "high importance" and are viewed as "successful" represent the operative values for these managers. They are considered important and fit the primary orientation (pragmatic) pattern of the group and should influence the behavior of the managers more than the ideas and concepts in any other cell in the Value Profile. For example, the fact that managers value the characteristics Ambition, Ability, and Skill more than they value the characteristics Loyalty, Trust, and Honor would be reflected in their own behavior and in their expectations about others' behavior.

Figure 3-2

MANAGERIAL VALUE PROFILE

	High Importance	Average Importance	Low Importance
Successful	High Productivity, Industrial Leadership, Organizational Stability, Profit Maximization, Organizational Efficiency, Organizational Growth, Employees [Operative Values] — Customers, My Co-workers, Craftsmen, My Boss, Managers, Owners, My Subordinates, My Company, Stockholders, Technical Employees, Me — White-collar Employees, Ambition, Ability, Skill, Cooperation, Achievement, Job Satisfaction, Creativity, Success, Change, Competition	Labor Unions, Aggressiveness, Influence, Power, Compromise, Conflict, Risk — [Adopted Values—Situationally Induced]	Prejudice, Force
Right	Employee Welfare, Trust, Loyalty, Honor, Dignity, Individuality, Government, Property, Rationality, Religion — [Intended Values—Socio-culturally Induced]	Social Welfare, Laborers, Blue-collar Workers, Obedience, Compassion, Tolerance, Authority, Caution, Conservatism, Equality, Liberalism	
Pleasant		Leisure, Autonomy, Money, Security, Prestige, Emotions — [Values with Low Behavioral Relevance]	Conformity

2. The 9 concepts found in the cells labeled "Adopted Values — Situationally Induced" are those that have been observed as being successful in the manager's organizational experience but which he finds difficult to internalize and view as being of high importance. Managers seem to be saying, for example, that Labor Unions are successful (they do have a large impact on what goes on in organizations) but that they should not be considered as important as other groups such as Customers or Managers or Owners. The values represented by these 9 concepts would not be expected to influence the behavior of managers to the extent that operative values would, since managers are not as wholly committed to adopted values as they are to operative values.

3. The 10 concepts found in the cells labeled "Intended Values — Socioculturally Induced" are those that have been considered as highly important by the manager throughout most of his life [but] do not fit his organizational experience. Here the interpretation would be that managers, for example, have viewed "rationality" as an important criterion for behavior but that their organizational environment has not always rewarded "rationality." It is as if they were saying that we have always considered it important to be rational but don't see it as being highly useful in our organizational life. The complexities of organizational requirements do not square with individual notions of what is and what is not rational. These intended values where there is conflict between what one has learned to believe and what one sees in his accepted environment have been termed professed or talking values by a number of authors. Employee Welfare, for example, is viewed as highly important as an organizational goal by managers but it may not affect their behavior greatly because it doesn't fit their primary pragmatic orientation. It is a professed value but not one that is operative or directly influential of behavior to any large extent.

4. Finally, the 18 concepts found in the cells labeled "Values with Low Behavioral Relevance" are those that would not be expected to influence a manager's behavior to any large extent since they are not considered important and do not fit the pragmatic orientation of managers.[11]

Significance of Personal Value System. The results of this study show that values, even though complex, may be measured. Clearly, a general value system emerges and is best described as pragmatic; that is, a value system measured in terms of whether or not a concept is successful or unsuccessful — does it work or does it not work in operation. At the same time there are individual differences in managers with respect to the number of operant values held and the specific nature of these values. Personal values are significant not only as determinants of one's own decisions, but also as determinants of corporate objectives and strategy. Differences in personal values may account for much of the conflict in organizations. It is suggested that

---

[11]*Ibid.*, pp. 60–62.

accommodation may occur more readily between individuals who have compatible value systems. Finally, personal value systems, both the operative system and the intended and adoptive values, determine one's perception of the ethical content of a situation and the subsequent evaluation of a specific action as being ethical or unethical.[12]

How Ethical Are Executives?

In an earlier study by Raymond C. Baumhart 1,700 representative executives were questioned to determine their attitudes toward ethical problems.[13] The survey establishes four problem areas: the extent to which business executives are aware of their social and ethical responsibilities, current practices in industry that are accepted yet recognized as unethical, a description of specific areas requiring ethical judgments, and an analysis of the determinants of ethical standards and practices in industry.

Awareness of Social and Ethical Responsibilities. Awareness of ethics as related to business is illustrated by the overwhelming number of executives, 99 out of every 100, who indicate complete agreement with the following statement: "Sound ethics is good business in the long run." In addition, there is considerable evidence that executives recognize the multiple nature of business objectives. Five out of six believe that it would be unethical to act in the interest of shareholders only and exclude the interests of employees and consumers. However, one out of six, or approximately 16 percent, does not agree that sound ethics is good business.

When the statement, "Sound ethics is good business in the long run," is paraphrased so that it becomes "Whatever is good business is good ethics," 15 percent of those queried indicate agreement with the paraphrased statement. In conclusion, it appears that the vast majority of executives are acutely aware of the social and ethical implications of their actions, but there is also evidence that approximately 15 percent of those included in the survey have a different value system.

---

[12]A replication of the 1966 England study was completed in 1972, using the 1971 edition of Standard and Poor's Directory of Corporations, Executives and Directors. The results of the 1972 study show a remarkable similarity to the 1966 study performed by England, thereby demonstrating a high degree of stability in the personal value systems of American managers. Edward J. Lusk and Bruce L. Oliver, "American Managers' Personal Value Systems — Revisited," *Academy of Management Journal*, Vol. 17, No. 3 (September, 1974), pp. 549–554.

[13]R. C. Baumhart, "How Ethical Are Businessmen?" *Harvard Business Review*, Vol. 39 (July–August, 1961), pp. 6–12, 175. The discussion following is based upon the questionnaire and findings reported by the Reverend Raymond C. Baumhart, S.J., Doctoral Candidate, Harvard Business School. The study reports a wealth of detailed material that is of unique value in that it is a statement of how business executives define ethical problems and how they react to problems involving ethical concepts.

Current Practices: Accepted, Yet Unethical. Within many industries there are practices that are tolerated and sometimes even accepted though they fall far short of ideal standards of ethical behavior. In order to obtain direct information on accepted, yet unethical practices, the following question was asked: "In every industry there are some generally accepted business practices. In your industry are there any such practices which you regard as unethical?"

Actions intended to buy loyalty for the company and its products are mentioned most frequently as the one practice that should be eliminated. Among the methods used to secure preferential treatment for the company and its products are gifts, gratuities, lavish entertainment, and outright bribes. Twenty-three percent of those queried indicate that these practices ranked first among those that should be eliminated. Unfair practices in pricing, such as price discrimination, are listed as the next most undesirable practice, with 18 percent indicating that these practices should be eliminated. Dishonest advertising ranks first on the list of practices to be eliminated by 14 percent of those queried. Miscellaneous unfair competitive practices; cheating customers, unfair credit practices, overselling; price collusion by competitors; dishonesty in making or keeping a contract; and unfairness and prejudice in hiring are mentioned, but in no case did more than 10 percent rank any one of these practices as the one practice that should be eliminated.

The preceding information is important for several reasons. First, it illustrates the extent of unethical practices and details some of those practices. Second, the practices of an industry influence the executive's behavior by forming the ethical climate in which an executive must operate. And lastly, the existence of unethical but accepted practices sets the stage for a certain degree of conflict within the executive. Common industry practice may require the executive to act in a manner unethical according to personal standards.

Problem Areas Requiring Ethical Judgments. The giving of gifts, gratuities, and lavish entertainment, which is intended to obtain loyalty for a company or its products, is ranked as the number one unethical practice that should be eliminated. Thus, it would seem that the problem situation most frequently giving rise to conflict would be in connection with these activities. However, such is not the case. Instead, problems of interpersonal relationships ranked first as the business situation causing the deepest source of concern. Interpersonal problems create a conflict within the individual between what is expected of a profit-conscious executive and what is expected of an ethical person. Yet it must be noted that only 75 percent of the executives participating in the study indicate that there are any ethical problems. Apparently the 25 percent who do not perceive any problems do not regard the following interpersonal problems as having an ethical content. This 25 percent has a personal value system that differs from the majority and may be best described as one that has "hard" operative values. The problem areas considered as causing the deepest concern for the majority surveyed are firings and layoffs; honest communications; collusion and sharp practices in pricing; gifts, entertainment, and kickbacks; and pressure from superiors.

Determinants of Ethical Standards and Practices. The degree of awareness of social and ethical responsibilities has been reviewed; current practices — accepted, yet unethical — have been examined; and the five problem areas causing concern because the decisions required involve ethical judgments have been mentioned. Though this information is significant, the major contribution of Reverend Baumhart's study is that it points the way toward the development of a principle of ethics. Before the principle can be developed, it is necessary to know the factors determining the degree of ethical behavior in the business community. The executives included in the survey were asked to rank the influences which, in their opinion, contribute most to ethical behavior and the influences contributing most to unethical behavior. The results of the ranking are shown in Figure 3-3.[14]

When answering the question calling for influences that create ethical behavior, the factor given first rank is the individual's personal code of conduct. Tied for second place in importance as determinants

FACTORS DETERMINING ETHICAL DECISIONS

Factor	Average Rank
An Executive's Personal Code of Behavior	1.5
The Behavior of Superiors in the Company	2.8
Formal Company Policy	2.8
Ethical Climate of the Industry	3.8
The Behavior of Equals in the Company	4.0

FACTORS DETERMINING UNETHICAL DECISIONS

Factor	Average Rank
The Behavior of Superiors in the Company	1.9
Ethical Climate of the Industry	2.6
The Behavior of Equals in the Company	3.1
Lack of Company Policy	3.3
Personal Financial Needs	4.1

Figure 3-3 DETERMINANTS OF ETHICAL BEHAVIOR

[14]*Ibid.*, p. 156.

of ethical behavior are two factors in the executive's immediate business environment: (1) the behavior of the executive's superiors in the company, and (2) a formal statement of company policy. Though the ethical climate of the industry and the behavior of the executive's equals in the company are important, they are not as significant in determining ethical behavior as the first three factors.

What are the influences leading to unethical decisions? Moving to first rank in importance in determining unethical behavior is the behavior of an executive's superiors. The climate of the industry, in reality a composite of the behavior of all the executives of that industry, is second in importance as a determinant of unethical actions. The remaining three factors — behavior of an executive's equals, lack of company policy, and personal financial needs are of significance, but in each case the ranked value is greater than three.

Thus, it seems that regardless of the manner in which the question is worded; i.e., whether the emphasis is placed upon ethical or unethical behavior, two factors stand out as major determinants of ethical behavior. They are: (1) the individual executive's personal code of conduct and (2) the behavior of the executive's superiors. In the last analysis, the superior's behavior is governed, in turn, by a personal code of conduct.

The above conclusion, which indicates the ultimate dependence upon a personal code of conduct and ethics, has a familiar ring. In Chapter 2, in the discussion of Fayol's principle of authority, it is mentioned that the solution to questions concerning the abuse of authority lies in the integrity of the person holding that authority. Fayol's full statement concerning this point is as follows: "The best safeguard against abuse of authority and against weakness on the part of a higher manager is personal integrity and particularly high moral character of such a manager, and this integrity, it is well known, is conferred neither by election nor ownership."[15]

A Concluding Concept

Fundamental to the development of a clear concept is the recognition that the business community is composed of many industries which, in turn, are made up of many companies. Each company has its own management, and each and every member of that management is at the same time an individual, a subordinate, and a superior. An individual's own personal code of conduct exerts the greatest influence in determining the degree to which that person's behavior is judged as ethical. A subordinate's code is reinforced and supported by the actions of superiors. A superior exerts a great positive influence in encouraging ethical behavior on the part of subordinates and potentially

---

[15]Henri Fayol in Harwood F. Merrill (ed.), *Classics in Management* (New York: American Management Association, 1960), p. 220.

has an even greater influence in contributing to a subordinate's unethical behavior. The conclusion is clear: *The ethical standards of any industry are determined by the ethical standards of individual executives of each member company in that industry.*

Code of Ethics

Though the ethical standards of a group are dependent upon the standards of each individual member of the group, the establishment of a code of ethics may serve a useful purpose. The chief value obtained from the establishment of a code is that it offers a framework within which individual members of the group may work. Guides are provided to aid in reaching decisions on those problems having a high ethical content. Ethical codes tend to be an expression of the ideal and, as such, they have the effect of raising the level of conduct of the group governed by the code. There have been many criticisms of codes of ethics. Chief among these criticisms is that, for the most part, such codes are established voluntarily and are difficult to enforce. Usually the penalty for violating a code is expulsion from a group, which has the effect of leaving the violator free from further criticism. Codes are also criticized as being at best an expression of good intentions and not an accurate statement of conditions as they are.

Nonetheless, several industries and groups associated with industry have developed codes of ethics. In 1957 the AFL-CIO formulated a statement called the AFL-CIO Ethical Practices Code. This code lists six ethical practices to be followed by members of the AFL-CIO. Included are regulations governing the issuance of charters for local unions, the honest administration of trust funds, and the conduct of honest elections for union officials. Also mentioned are conditions limiting eligibility to hold office in the AFL-CIO or any affiliated union, limitations on outside financial interests of union officials, and provisions designed to insure maintenance of accurate and honest records of all union transactions. In 1958, the National Association of Manufacturers (NAM) issued a two-part statement setting forth the beliefs of management in regard to moral and ethical standards. The first part of the statement outlines the beliefs of the NAM in regard to the type of political economy that industry should support and suggests the proper relationships between industry and government, suppliers, customers, and stockholders. The second part of the statement outlines the beliefs of the NAM with respect to relationships between employers and employees.[16]

In the opinion of many, the two codes of conduct have fallen short of their goals. Neither all unions, nor all managements, conduct themselves according to the standards set forth by their respective groups.

---

[16]*Moral and Ethical Standards in Labor and Management* (New York: National Association of Manufacturers, 1958), pp. 1–7.

The following three industrial situations all describe an employee-employer relationship. In each instance the employer used a form of surveillance, either closed-circuit television or wiretapping, to secure information that it might not otherwise have.

Case Problem 3-B
ELECTRONIC SURVEILLANCE

Since formal organizations are made up of individuals who are members of management or of the work force, it is not surprising that there are occasionally charges from the members of the work force that management is not acting in an ethical manner. When the employees of a company are members of a union, the process of arbitration provides a means of settling such disputes between management and its employees through the selection of a third party, an arbitrator. The decision of the arbitrator is usually final and binding. The following incidents concerning the use of electronic surveillance have been ruled on by arbitrators. You are asked to decide for each incident whether or not the management of the company was justified in using electronic surveillance.[17]

Incident No. 1

The company installed a closed-circuit television network in one of its plants. The employees contend that the use of closed-circuit TV is a violation of their privacy, that it amounts to employer spying, and that it violates a provision of the agreement between the employees and management which provides that present conditions of employment beneficial to employees shall not be changed unilaterally by the management of the company. There was no evidence presented during the arbitration hearing by the company indicating any need for the closed-circuit TV as

a means of improving production either in respect to quantity or quality.

Incident No. 2

Again closed-circuit television was installed by management, and again the employees filed a grievance contending that it violated their right to privacy. However, there are some differences between this incident and incident 1. In this case management had reason to suspect that there was pilferage in the receiving room. One of the monitors from the television camera was located in an office where a salaried employee controlled the flow of materials through the plant by radio contact with forklift truck drivers. Thus, the device aided the company in maintaining a more even flow of materials to the production departments. The union contends that the dignity of the workers was being violated by the use of this device. The company, on the other hand, contends that the use of television in the receiving room is in effect another supervisor and affords another "pair of eyes," allowing observations which would normally be made had another supervisor been employed.

Incident No. 3

In this instance a large drug company had reason to believe that one of its employees was "writing numbers" on a large scale. The management of the company also believed that this activity was disruptive in addition to being illegal, and decided to obtain evidence against the employee. The evidence was obtained by tapping a telephone located in the warehouse. Conversations between the employee who was writing numbers and the person for whom he was writing numbers were recorded on a tape recorder. Based upon the information obtained, the company

[17]The Bureau of National Affairs, Washington, D.C., publishes a complete Labor Reporting Service. Among the reports published are current labor arbitration cases selected by BNA for publication in its Labor Arbitration series. The following are the references for each of the incidents:

Incident No. 1 — 44 LA 563
Incident No. 2 — 46 LA 335
Incident No. 3 — 31 LA 191

discharged the employee. The union protested the discharge claiming, among other things, that it was an invasion of privacy and that such evidence should not be admitted that was obtained by means of wiretapping.

PROBLEMS

1. How would you rule as an arbitrator in each of the above cases?

2. Are the three incidents described properly considered as problems of ethical relationships between employer and employee?

3. The last two incidents described are concerned with illegal activities on the part of employees; incident No. 2 is concerned with possible theft, and incident No. 3 is concerned with illegal gambling. If the company is denied the right to use electronic surveillance, how can it stop such practices?

CHAPTER QUESTIONS FOR STUDY AND DISCUSSION

1. One of the characteristics of an objective is that it should be well within the reach of an organization, yet difficult to obtain. With this in mind, comment on the following statement: The difficult we do today; the impossible we do tomorrow.

2. Why is the creation of profit a good example of an objective that simultaneously gives direction and motivates?

3. Why is it necessary for a firm to have an objective that states its desired overall position in relation to its competitors?

4. Why is it necessary to state several objectives for a firm rather than one general objective?

5. Evaluate the strengths and weaknesses of MBO.

6. Is it significant that the classification of interpersonal relationships follows the same general pattern as the classification of objectives; i.e., internal and external interpersonal relationships which correspond to those objectives that are internal to the firm and those objectives that are external to the firm?

7. Define in your own terms personal value system. Give an example showing how one's personal value system can influence perception of the ethical content of a situation.

8. England's study shows quite clearly that the primary personal value system for most American managers is best described as pragmatic. What is meant by the term, pragmatic, and is this an appropriate value for managers? Discuss.

9. Comment on the following statements: "Sound ethics is good business in the long run," and "Whatever is good business is good ethics."

10. The conclusion regarding ethics is worded with reference to an industrial situation; that is, to the ethical standards of an industry and the standards of the companies that make up that industry. Does this principle apply equally to professional groups such as teachers, physicians, and lawyers?

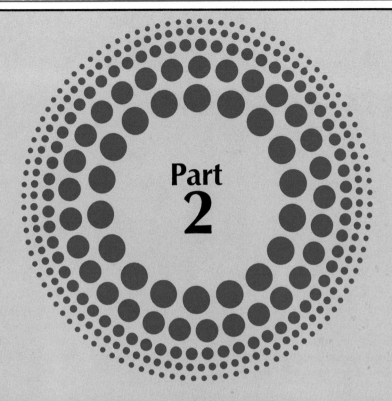

Part 2

The Planning Function

The planning function is accorded the position of primacy among the four functions of the management process since logically it is the function that occurs first. Planning is also regarded as pervasive as it shapes the other three functions of organizing, leading, and controlling. A taxonomy of plans is presented which results in plans being classified with respect to duration, function, or scope. Further, scope, or breadth, is divided into three subgroups — policies, procedures, and methods. Chapter 4 closes with a discussion of the criteria that may be used to evaluate plans.

Chapter 5 discusses the development of policy statements for each of the major business functions. First, the range of policy statements for finance is outlined. Next, the scope of policy statements for the marketing function is developed. The third area discussed is policy statements for the production function. Finally, policy statements for the personnel function are presented. The interrelationships between policy statements for each of the four functional areas are summarized in tabular form and are also integrated within the context of a servo system.

Effective planning requires timely and complete information; consequently, it is necessary to study the functions of a management information system. The development of electronic data processing is traced and the steps necessary for the design and installation of a completely integrated data processing information system are set forth. The case problems of Chapter 6 are of particular interest. Case Problem 6-A, the Parable of the Spindle, shows clearly that an information system breakdown can create behavioral reactions on the part of employees that are normally considered to arise as the result of poor practices in human relations. Case Problem 6-B provides insight into the problems of establishing computer security.

As part of the planning process it is usually necessary to select one plan from several alternatives; in short, a decision must be made. Since many business problems can be expressed as mathematical equations, some of the frequently used quantitative aids for decision making are described. The behavioral aspects of decision making are considered. First, the characteristics of a given individual and their result upon the decision-making process are discussed. Second, the advantages and disadvantages of group decision making are presented, and tested methods for encouraging group participation in the solution of business problems are summarized.

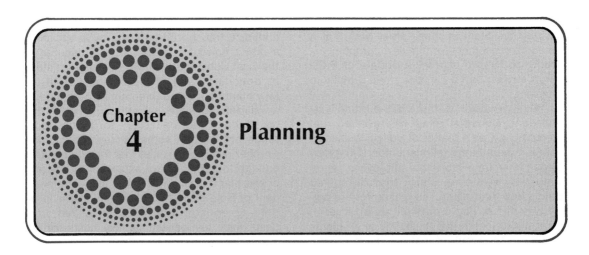

Chapter 4

Planning

Case Problem 4-A
SELECTING A PLANT SITE

The Bojo Corporation is an established manufacturer, located in a small town in southwestern New York State. The company was founded about 90 years ago and initially served both the railroad industry and the oil fields of northern Pennsylvania. At the present time, a large part of its business is still associated with the oil industry. In recent years, however, it has branched into other fields and has been able to develop applications of products originally used in the oil fields to other areas. The Bojo Corporation is a subsidiary company of a large national firm with headquarters in St. Louis. The national headquarters controls all capital expenditures, reviews operating budgets developed by the subsidiary corporations, follows up to insure the meeting of budgetary goals, and also exerts strong influence in the labor relations area. All labor contracts and labor policies are determined by the headquarters staff.

In recent years, the Bojo Corporation developed a new type of pipe coupling that is used to join two pieces of pipe without having to thread the ends of the pipes being joined or cutting them to an exact length. The coupling saves time and money and has experienced a remarkable sales volume from municipalities since it is used primarily to replace existing water and gas lines. There is every reason to believe that the market will expand and that the Bojo Corporation will receive a large share of the increase. Since the coupling is particularly useful in the replacement market with the oldest water and gas systems on the eastern seaboard, the greatest potential market for the immediate future is in this area.

Present manufacturing facilities, a department in the main plant, are now running at capacity; and in order to meet the anticipated increase in demand, new facilities are needed. Since the present plant location does not permit expansion, it has been decided that a new plant should be built to house the present coupling department and to provide for future increases in volume. A member of the St. Louis controller's staff, Ms. Minelli, has been assigned the task of conducting a plant location survey and submitting subsequent recommendations to the president of the Bojo Corporation and the officials of the parent company.

In preparing for her assignment, Ms. Minelli contacted several executives, among them the executive vice-president responsible for the Bojo Corporation and other subsidiaries in Pennsylvania, New York, and Massachusetts. It was the executive vice-president's wish that the plant be located on a direct route between Pittsburgh, Pennsylvania, and the present location, or between Buffalo, New York, and the present location. His reason for desiring the plant in these areas was that it would be convenient for him as a company executive to fly into either the Buffalo or Pittsburgh airport, rent a car, and drive directly to the plant.

A conversation with the home office vice-president, industrial relations, revealed that the company, as a matter of policy, wished to have a different international union in the new plant rather than have the employees represented by the same union that organized Bojo's New York plant. The reason for the policy was that having a different union in each plant would lessen the possibility of all plants closing as the result of a strike, since no one international union would represent more than one plant. The vice-president indicated that it would be necessary to locate at least 100 miles from the present plant in order to be assured of a different union. He also recommended analyzing the labor rates of any community proposed as a location for the new plant so that maximum savings might be realized from low initial labor costs. He stated further that by starting operations with labor rates as low as possible, the company would be in a better position to increase rates in the future.

When Ms. Minelli contacted the president of the Bojo Corporation and reviewed the wishes of the two central office executives, she found the president had a few ideas of his own to add to the picture. The president indicated that it was mandatory that the new location have complete rail facilities, since raw materials were received most economically by rail and many of the finished product shipments could be made by rail. He wanted the plant located east of the present facility to minimize transportation costs by establishing a direct flow of materials from Pittsburgh to the East Coast markets. He was also insistent, as operating head of the company, that the new plant be located in an area where there is a well-defined, stable tax structure. He felt that tax stability was necessary to predict long-range profits with some degree of accuracy. Another requirement was that the site be large enough to permit future expansion of the proposed plant to twice its initial size. The president of Bojo placed no exact limitations in regard to construction costs provided such costs were in line with typical costs for the area selected.

PROBLEMS

1. Assume that you are Ms. Minelli. Prepare an initial determination of the relative significance of the factors considered to be important by:

   a. The executive vice-president of the home office.

   b. The vice-president, industrial relations, home office.

   c. The president of the subsidiary Bojo Corporation.

2. Indicate in detail the steps that you would follow in conducting a study to evaluate alternate sites for the new plant.

3. Prior to Ms. Minelli's receiving her assignment, certain decisions had been made by the Bojo management. What were these decisions? What additional decisions must be made after a satisfactory location for the new plant has been found?

Planning is generally considered the first function performed in the management sequence of planning, organizing, leading, and controlling. The need for planning is not limited to the development of plans for the attainment of organizational objectives. Planning is needed to determine the kind of organization that is necessary to achieve stated objectives. Planning is also necessary to determine the methods and types of controls as well as the kind of direction best suited to the organization. Yet, the success or failure of an enterprise or the success or failure of specific plans is dependent upon the way in which the other three functions of the management process are performed, as well as upon the quality of the planning function.

In our study of the planning function we shall examine some of the fundamental concepts of planning and develop a definition of planning. The different types of plans are reviewed and classified, and in the last part of the chapter, criteria are developed for the evaluation of plans.

FUNDAMENTAL CONCEPTS OF PLANNING

In order to understand the nature of planning, the meanings of three terms — planning, the plan, and decision making — must be clarified. We also need to know the purpose of planning and why planning is important to the management process.

Planning

Planning is an activity performed by all levels of management. Differences in the complexity of the planning process and the resultant plans are, to a large measure, determined by the organizational level of the person who initiates the planning process. In Case Problem 4-A, Ms. Minelli has been asked to develop and analyze alternatives available to the Bojo Corporation in the selection of a new plant site. There are many factors that she must consider, among which are availability of land, cost of land, cost of building, availability of transportation, and location with respect to raw materials and markets for the finished product. She is required not only to list these factors but also to evaluate them with respect to their relative importance, which in turn means that value criteria must be developed. These are the kinds of managerial activities normally associated with planning.

The outstanding concern of planning is the future, and as a process it probes the future, literally attempting to foretell the effects of coming events, thereby enabling a firm to meet the future with some degree of success. Less apparent is planning's concern with the past. To develop a sound plan, it is necessary to review the past and evaluate information relevant to the present and the future. Analysis of forces of the present — internal and external to the organization — must also be considered. Thus, the planning function is defined as *the analysis of relevant information from the present and the past and an assessment of probable future developments so that a course of action (plan) may be determined that enables the organization to meet its stated objectives.*

The Plan

Planning, the process of evaluating all relevant information and the assessment of probable future developments, results in the statement of a recommended course of action — a *plan*. Plans should be regarded as blueprints for action. The kinds of plans commonly used in business operations are discussed in the next major topic of this chapter, "Types of Plans." The characteristics of plans and the effect that these characteristics have upon the probable success of plans are discussed in the section, "Criteria for Evaluating Plans."

Decision Making

Decision making is an activity that permeates the entire planning process. *Making a decision is making a choice between two or more alternatives.* The alternative selected is the decision. Planning requires the continuous collection, evaluation, and selection of data. Some data is rejected as not being pertinent to the problem at hand; other data is retained and used to formulate a recommended course of action. Selecting some information and rejecting other information constitutes a choice, or a decision. Ultimately one proposed course of action is recommended as being superior to an alternate course as a means of attaining desired objectives. Again, a decision has been made. These are the decisions of a planner as a plan develops.

Decision making is also used to describe an activity that is characteristic of executive positions. The responsible executive either accepts or rejects the plan. If the plan is accepted, the next step is its implementation. Plan implementation requires commitment of company resources, an action that initiates a chain of events which are sometimes irreversible. The difference between an executive's decision and a planner's decision is one of degree — not kind — since both are making choices. The executive's decisions are overt in nature and are recognized because they commit company resources, but the planner's decisions are covert and can be retracted and reevaluated at will.

Purpose of Planning

The purpose of planning is to provide information concerning a proposed course of action so that the relative probabilities of success or failure can be estimated. Planning does not eliminate the element of risk, but planning does provide a more accurate basis for estimating relative success or failure in more precise terms. As knowledge of the factors that influence the success or failure of a proposed plan is acquired, the greater is the probability that the final decision — either the acceptance or rejection of the plan — will be the correct one.

Importance of Planning

Planning is of importance for two reasons: its *primacy* from the standpoint of position in the sequence of management functions, and its *pervasiveness* as an activity that affects the entire organization.

Primacy of Planning. Planning has a position of primacy among the management functions. The reason for designating planning as the first of the management processes is that in some instances planning may be the only managerial function performed.[1] Planning may result in a decision that further action is not required or possible. When this happens, there is no need for the subsequent process of organizing, leading, and controlling. Had the Bojo Corporation, as a result of early planning, determined that they could manufacture couplings economically and in sufficient quantity by rearranging their present facilities, the present plant location study would not have been initiated, nor would the need arise to organize, lead, and control a new plant.

Pervasiveness. When need for further action is indicated, the pervasiveness of the planning function is revealed. Implementing plans affects the organizing, leading, and controlling functions. In addition, planning is required in order to perform the functions of organizing, leading, and controlling. The effect of planning on the other managerial functions is discussed below.

Organizing. Plans, the result of planning, have their effects upon the structure and functioning of an organization. Assume that there is a plan designed to raise a company's sales volume to $500 million. Further, the desired volume requires the acquisition of other companies producing related products as well as increasing the sales volume of products now being produced. Acquiring other companies may necessitate establishing a special staff group to study and evaluate potential acquisitions. Also, permanent organizational units must be created to administer and coordinate the companies purchased as a part of the plan to increase sales volume. To increase the volume of sales produced by the present organization, a realignment of the duties of key executives may be required to establish broad geographic divisions, with each division having the capabilities of attaining its own specified share of the expected increase.

Planning is required to define structure, authority relationships, and proper scope for each of the newly created or modified organizational units arising from the implementation of an accepted plan.

Leading. The results of planning have their effects upon the leadership of an organization. As we shall find in Chapter 14, "Leadership Patterns," the methods of leading subordinates range from those methods considered as highly participative to techniques of leadership regarded as authoritarian in nature. The degree of direction varies from extremely close supervision to direction that exemplifies a "hands off" policy. Several factors determine the leadership pattern best suited to meet organizational objectives. Some of these factors are the size of

---

[1]L. F. Urwick, "Management and Human Relations," in R. Tannenbaum, I. R. Weschler, and F. Massarik, *Leadership and Organization*, A Behavioral Science Approach (New York: McGraw-Hill Book Co., 1961), pp. 416–428. On page 423 Colonel Urwick states that planning must be considered a separate function, one which precedes an organization, because one of the possible conclusions of planning is that there is no need for subsequent organization.

the organization, the capabilities and needs of the members of the organization, the goals of the organization in relation to the goals of its members, the need for an interchange of information between members of the organization, and the extent to which the organization is meeting its stated objectives.

Controlling. Planning is closely related to the control process in that plans often serve as the basis for control. A fully developed plan incorporates a timetable that shows, in proper sequence, the activities necessary to reach a stated objective and includes an estimate of the time required to complete each step. Also, a well-presented plan includes a statement of organizational responsibility. Thus, with checkpoints defined and responsibility clearly designated, there is a framework for the control process. The checkpoints provide a basis for comparing present performance, and the designation of organizational responsibility facilitates and makes more effective the corrective action of control. The proper exercise of the control function frequently requires the formulation of new plans or the modification of existing ones — and again, the new or changed plans serve as the basis for continuing control. The continuing relationship between planning and control is frequently described as the planning-control-planning cycle.

TYPES OF PLANS

We have seen that the primary purpose of planning is to reduce the degree of risk in business operations and that planning is important because of its position of primacy and its pervasiveness in influencing the other management functions. The emphasis has been placed on planning as a function. Let us now examine the result of planning — the plan — in respect to its characteristics and application.

The following outline classifies plans with respect to characteristics and use or application:

1. Classification by time or duration
   a. Long-range plans
   b. Short-range plans
2. Classification by business function or use
   a. Plans concerning the marketing function
   b. Plans concerning the production function
   c. Plans concerning the personnel function
   d. Plans concerning the finance function
   e. Plans concerning any other major function
3. Classification with respect to breadth or scope
   a. Policies
   b. Procedures
   c. Methods

The above outline provides a useful basis for discussing the various types of plans. However, it must be remembered that any given plan includes more than one of the characteristics or uses shown in the outline. For example, a policy statement in the area of finance is considered a policy because of its breadth; it may also be a long-range plan if it pertains to long-term financial resources; and it is a plan concerned with a specific business function, finance. Similarly, a short-range plan may be applicable to any given business function and also be classified by its breadth or scope; e.g., a procedure to guide the preparation of a physical inventory.

Classification by Time

When plans are classified by their duration, they are recognized as either long-range plans or short-range plans.[2] Examples of long-range planning are numerous and almost always include financial plans. It is not unusual for companies to issue bonds with a 25-year maturity date as part of a long-range plan to develop desired financial strength. Research and development programs are planned for many years, and the long-range plans for research frequently emphasize the research of "pure science" as well as the development of new products. Research not directed specifically toward new products must be continued on a long-range basis since it has been demonstrated many times that the "pure" research of today leads to the development of products for tomorrow. Corporate public relations programs are also planned on a continuing basis since one of their express purposes is to create a stable public image.

The value of long-range planning is shown in a study conducted by Thune and House in which 17 of the 92 companies contacted indicated that they had formal long-range planning while 19 companies considered their long-range planning as informal. Five economic indexes were used to measure performance: sales, stock prices, earnings per common share, return on common equity, and return on total capital invested. In each of these respects those companies having formal planning outperformed those with informal planning. In addition, the study shows that some of the companies currently classified as formal planners — but formerly engaged in informal planning only — showed

---

[2] Long-range plans may be further subdivided in a manner that has proven to be useful in many instances. They may be regarded as being either *strategic* or *operational* in nature. Strategic plans are those plans that are concerned with the long-term well-being of the corporation; for example, financial plans. Operational plans are those plans primarily concerned with the allocation of company resources; for example, finances, plant facilities, or labor. Generally these operational plans extend for a period of three to five years and are consequently regarded as long-range in nature. For a further discussion of some of the characteristics of long-range planning and the characteristics of organization for long-range planning, the following are recommended:

Robert J. Litschert, "Some Characteristics of Organization for Long-Range Planning," *Academy of Management Journal*, Vol. 10, No. 3 (September, 1967), pp. 247–256.

Robert J. Litschert, "Some Characteristics of Long-Range Planning: An Industry Study," *Academy of Management Journal*, Vol. 11, No. 3 (September, 1968), pp. 315–328.

significant gains in sales, earnings per share, and stock price after the introduction of formal long-range planning. This study has been replicated by Herold with similar results.[3]

As might be expected, plans that encompass a relatively short period of time are referred to as short-range plans. There is, unfortunately, no precise cut-off point in time which enables one to designate categorically all plans extending beyond a given duration as long range and all plans up to that duration as short range. Short-range plans are best understood in their relation to long-range plans. Examples are found in the daily and even annual operations of a company. Typical short-range plans are production schedules for a period of a day, a week, or perhaps a month. Actually, production schedules may be considered short-range plans even though they extend over a period of a year, provided expanded facilities are planned for the foreseeable future. Thus, the designation of a plan as either short range or long range depends, to some measure, upon whether the plan considered as short range is part of a larger plan. Generally, if a plan is part of a large plan, it may be considered as a short-range plan.

The time span or duration of a plan is significant, not only as a basis for classifying plans, but also as an index of difficulty in evaluating its success. As a rule, it is more difficult to evaluate long-range plans than short-range plans because their duration is sometimes longer than the life span of their originator, or the life span of any one observer. Many times a treasurer retires or dies before that treasurer's mistakes are discovered. Since the duration of long-range plans makes a determination of their ultimate success difficult if not impossible, extreme care must be taken to insure highest standards in performing the planning function.

Classification by Function

Another basis for classifying plans involves their function or use. Classification by business function considers planning as applied to the marketing function, to the production and procurement functions, and to financial and personnel areas. Grouping plans by function is particularly useful when analyzing the operations of specific areas in an organization. Consequently, many companies find it convenient to develop policy statements for four major functional areas — finance, marketing, production, and personnel. Functional grouping of plans enables one to determine more clearly the interaction and interdependence that exist between major areas of operations and emphasizes the

---

[3]Stanley S. Thune and Robert J. House, "Long-Range Planning Pays Off," *Business Horizons*, Vol. 13, No. 4 (August, 1970), pp. 83–87.

David M. Herold, "Long-Range Planning and Organizational Performance: A Cross-Valuation Study," *Academy of Management Journal*, Vol. 15, No. 1 (March, 1972), pp. 91–102. Herold's study was designed to validate and extend the study by Thune and House. The data supports strongly the findings of Thune and House.

need for determining these interrelationships before plans are approved and put into effect. Specifically, a marketing department considering the installation of a sales order procedure should be aware that any such procedure will probably have a marked effect upon production and accounting procedures.

Classification by Scope

Classification with respect to breadth is the third way of grouping plans. Three distinct groups of plans are recognized when scope or breadth is the basis for classification. They are policies, procedures, and methods. Interestingly enough, this classification not only permits an immediate determination of the breadth of the plan but also reveals the organizational level that initiated the plan and the extent to which the plan is utilized in the organization.

Policies. Company policies are broad in their application, and, as a result, they often appear to be vague and nonspecific in their wording. They are intended to serve as guideposts that define the scope of activities necessary and permissible by the board of directors or by the executive committee of a company. It is rare for a department head to develop policy. A department head may recommend policy statements for approval by the executive committee or the board, but policies emanate from the highest levels of a company. Another characteristic of policies is their stability in that they do not change rapidly. They are not immutable, but their change is slow. Examples of change can be found in company policies relating to credit and methods of distribution. The J. C. Penney Company ultimately changed its credit policy from one of strictly cash to one that permits and even encourages customer charge accounts.[4]

Procedures. There is considerably more variation among procedures with respect to both origin and scope than there is among policies. For the most part, procedures are interdepartmental or intradepartmental in their breadth. They do not affect the entire organization to the same extent that policy statements do, even though they may be observed on a company-wide basis. The phrase "standard operating procedure" typifies the fact that procedures are more closely related to the daily operations of a company than policies. Examples of procedures are found in every major department of a company, with their

---

[4]The following two sources offer a comprehensive review of corporate policies. *Management Policies I* presents the development, formulation, and administration of corporate policies, and *Management Policies II* offers a source book of policy statements drawn from major United States corporations.

M. Valliant Higginson, *Management Policies I: Their Development as Corporate Guides* (New York: American Management Association, 1966).

M. Valliant Higginson, *Management Policies II: Sourcebook of Statement* (New York: American Management Association, 1966).

origin and application confined to one department, such as production, sales, or personnel. Procedures are, by definition, of sufficient breadth to have an impact upon the operations of related departments. Production control procedure, which has as its goal an organized flow of materials through a plant, modifies and is modified by the procedures of the sales department governing the receiving and entering of orders, and by procedures of the accounting department utilized to determine production costs.

Methods. Another group of plans, more specific in scope than procedures, are methods. Methods are applied within a given operating department and are regarded as plans that detail the manner and sequence of performing those individual tasks necessary to complete given assignments. A method is designed to influence the behavior of an individual; for example, there is a prescribed method for the completion of employment application forms. Likewise, there is an approved method for the assembly of a given product or the grinding and finishing of a machined part.

In conclusion, the classification of plans by breadth ranges from policies, which are the broadest of all plans and originate at the highest levels of an organization, through procedures, which are concerned with the operations of major functional departments and are interdepartmental in their effect, to methods, which are specific and stated as a guide to direct the performance of individuals.

CRITERIA FOR EVALUATING PLANS

Two approaches are available in developing criteria for the evaluation of plans. One approach, designated as *Approach A*, is a review and analysis of the procedures followed and the resultant characteristics that differentiate successful plans from unsuccessful plans. These criteria are descriptive in nature and serve as a checklist against which the plan under consideration may be judged. Approach A is a procedural analysis of the plan that is being evaluated.

A second approach to the development of criteria for judging plans, designated as *Approach B*, is the determination of the degree to which the plan under consideration is economic. The word "economic" is used here in its broadest sense; i.e., the effective utilization of resources. In order to determine the economic worth of a plan, it is necessary to use a technique that permits describing any plan in economic terms and to utilize this technique to the extent that it becomes a "way of thinking" about plans. Approach B is referred to as an economic evaluation of plans. We consider first those criteria developed from a procedural analysis and, second, the evaluation of plans in terms of economic effectiveness.

Approach A — Procedural Analysis

There have been many statements concerning the procedural characteristics to be used as criteria for judging plans.[5] The characteristics that may be considered as criteria for evaluating the probable success of plans are objectivity, degree of structuralization, and flexibility. To apply these characteristics as criteria, it is necessary to discuss more fully the meaning of each term and to present specific examples showing the application of the characteristic to the planning process and to the resultant plan.

Objectivity. Objective findings or conclusions, such as plans, are subject to verification by another observer. The greater the degree of objectivity, the greater is the likelihood that another observer will reach the same conclusion. The antithesis of objective findings is known as subjective and is based upon one's own feelings and beliefs. Conclusions based upon personal experiences and beliefs are not subject to verification by outside observers.

Objectivity results from the precise observation, recording, analysis, and interpretation of pertinent data, which is a form of analysis and reasoning known as the *scientific method*. The managerial process of planning can be accomplished by either subjective or objective means. The extent to which the scientific method is followed in the planning process determines the degree of objectivity of that process and the consequent objectivity of the resultant plans. The scientific method, as applied to planning, consists of the following six steps:

1. Statement of objective
2. Statement of problem
3. Designation of planning authority
4. Collection and interpretation of data
5. Formulation and testing of tentative plan
6. Statement of final plan

The application of each of these steps to the process of planning is discussed separately.

---

[5] Preston P. Le Breton and D. A. Henning, *Planning Theory* (Englewood Cliffs: Prentice-Hall, 1961), p. 23. This comprehensive work treats planning as it is performed at all levels in the industrial firm. The following 13 dimensions or factors of plans are presented: complexity, significance, comprehensiveness, time, specificity, completeness, flexibility, frequency, confidential nature, formality, authorization, ease of implementation, and ease of control.

Ralph C. Davis, *The Fundamentals of Top Management* (New York: Harper & Brothers, 1951), p. 46. Davis lists the following eight characteristics of a plan: objectivity, logical soundness, security, flexibility, stability, comprehensiveness, clarity, and simplicity.

In a more recent work Professor George A. Steiner presents five dimensions of planning and plans: subject, elements, time, characteristics, and organization. George A. Steiner, *Top Management Planning* (New York: Macmillan Co., 1969), p. 12. Steiner discusses the nature and concept of business planning, the process of developing plans, the tools for more rational planning, and planning in selected major functional areas.

Statement of Objective. A planner must always have a clear concept of the broad objectives of the firm and the specific objectives of any given plan. A plan should contribute to meeting these objectives. Having stated objectives for the planner minimizes the possibility of developing inappropriate plans.

Statement of Problem. When planning is required, there is the implication that the organization is not completely meeting its objectives, for, if it were, there would be no need for additional or new plans. The discrepancy between present performance and desired performance constitutes the problem area. The problem to be resolved by the planning process must be clearly stated. Stating the problem clearly and setting forth the limiting factors and conditions that must be met define the extent of the planning process and the scope of the resultant plan. In Case Problem 4-A, the problem is clearly defined. There is a need for a plant to manufacture a known product. Further, limiting conditions, such as shipping costs of raw materials and finished products, the cost and availability of labor, land requirements, and transportation facilities, are clearly stated. In contrast, a poorly defined problem fails to direct the planning process toward a specific goal and frequently results in inappropriate and ill-conceived plans.

Designation of Planning Authority. As part of the planning process, there must be a designated planning authority. After a company has stated the problem and is convinced that a plan or course of action should be developed as a solution to the problem, it is necessary that an individual or group be given the authority necessary to carry out an effective planning process and develop alternate plans. The planner's authority should be granted by that level of the organization that normally has the responsibility for performing those functions included in the approved plan. For example, a plan requiring a large capital outlay, such as the construction of a plant, is normally approved by the president or the executive committee. Determining the appropriateness of the source of the planner's authority provides an estimate of the extent to which the recommended plan will be approved and put into use.[6]

Collection and Interpretation of Data. The next step in the planning process is the collection and interpretation of available data. As stated in the definition of planning, consideration must be given to pertinent information from the present and the past, and an assessment must be made of probable future events.

---

[6]The matter of designating a planning authority specifically for long-range planning is discussed in R. L. Mason, "Developing a Planning Organization," *Business Horizons*, Vol. 12, No. 4 (August, 1969), pp. 61–69.

Daniel D. Roman, "Technological Forecasting in the Decision Process," *Academy of Management Journal*, Vol. 13, No. 2 (June, 1970), pp. 127–138. Professor Roman has advised that technological forecasting, the assessment of future technology transfer, be assigned a specific function separate from other planning functions.

Generally, the data used in planning falls into two broad categories — external data and internal data. Information pertaining to the national economy and the industry in which the company is operating is typical of *external data*. The financial resources of the firm, the past performance of the firm in the attainment of similar objectives, and the ability of personnel charged with executing the plan are representative of *internal data*. Available information from both sources along with estimates of probable future developments must be utilized and interpreted to insure a successful plan.

Formulation and Testing of Tentative Plan. Whenever possible, a tentative plan should be formulated and initiated on a trial basis. Although this step is not always feasible, it is desirable since a trial run reveals strengths and weaknesses and offers a basis for predicting the probable success of a plan. Training programs are sometimes adopted on a trial basis before being applied on a company-wide basis. New products may be introduced to a single geographic region to test the acceptability of the product and the effectiveness of the proposed marketing techniques before making a final decision concerning national distribution.

If plans can be presented as a mathematical formula, changes that would result from altering the value of any one factor or condition can be determined with precision. Analyzing the effect of change by using a model is called *simulation*. The effect of changes in proposed production schedules may be simulated, and the effect of changes in price and volume upon profit may also be predicted accurately. When plans are expressed in quantitative terms, the effects of changing conditions may be simulated as a way of testing a plan's potential success without having to commit company resources.

Statement of Final Plan. The last step in the planning process is the statement of the final plan. If a plan is to be considered objective, it must be derived from the data developed and analyzed. In this sense, a plan is a conclusion. The extent to which the analysis and reasoning of the scientific method have been followed in developing the final form of a plan indicates the degree of objectivity of the stated plan.

Degree of Structuralization. The determination of the degree of objectivity of a plan is essentially an analysis and evaluation of the planning process used in the development of the plan. The *degree of structuralization* is a criterion for evaluating the format of the plan and the extent to which the plan structures the actions of the organization. Well-structured plans are capable of precise execution. Factors considered in determining the degree of structuralization are: comprehensiveness, time span, assignment of duties, and control features.

Comprehensiveness. When evaluating the structure of a plan, one consideration is the degree of comprehensiveness. The complexity and the breadth of a plan are not necessarily measures of comprehensiveness. Simple plans that are well stated may be comprehensive. A production plan for a departmental supervisor may be for a period of one day and affect the work of only two people, yet answer a particular need. Similarly, a plan requiring 100 people for its execution and a time span of one year may not be comprehensive. Therefore, the comprehensiveness of a plan is the extent to which it provides solutions to the original problem.

Time Span. A well-structured plan has a definite statement of the length of time required for its completion. The statement of dates for the start and the completion of a plan should be specific; in addition, complex plans specify intermediate time goals. For example, a building construction plan should state the date for the first activity on the building site (usually commencing with surveying), the time that grading begins, the date that foundation work starts, and beginning and completion dates for all other events including an expected occupancy date. It is recognized that there are factors which may delay the completion of any intermediate goal; however, the sequence and the relationship of these intermediate points should be clearly stated in the original plan. When a delay occurs, full information concerning the sequence and relationship of all phases of the project facilitates the task of revising the plan.[7]

Assignment of Duties. The characteristics of comprehensiveness and time span refer to the structure of the plan itself. One of the expected results of a plan is that it structures the behavior of the organization responsible for carrying out the plan. In order to implement a plan effectively, it is necessary to assign specific duties to designated personnel in the organization. The mere listing of activities to be performed is not sufficient. Activities must be expressed as job duties and assigned as responsibilities to individual members of the organization.

Control Features. Another factor indicating the degree of structuralization is the extent to which a plan includes features which facilitate control. One method of controlling the execution of plans is the utilization of logical time-oriented control points. Budgets, a type of financial plan, generally provide for quarterly reviews as an integral part of the plan. Another aspect of control is the designation of personnel to review progress and recommend necessary control action. Also, it is desirable to indicate the amount of variance from the original plan that can be tolerated. Provisions should be made for reporting these exceptions to the responsible manager.

---

[7]See Case Problem 19-B, page 489, for an example of a plan stating specific dates throughout its duration.

Flexibility. Paradoxical as it may seem, the characteristic that contributes most to the stability and probable success of the plan is its flexibility. Rigid plans may appear to offer stability and firmness; however, rigidity also leads to an inability to meet the requirements of changing conditions.

Flexibility does not imply vagueness or instability. Flexibility results from the development of alternate courses of action. Developing plans that include alternatives has several advantages. First, flexibility permits management to meet changing external conditions rapidly and effectively. A plan without an alternate can result either in a blind-alley venture or reaching a point of no return, thereby dooming the plan to failure. Second, if a series of alternate actions is included in the plan, alternates are available immediately and avoid the delay that would result from having to develop a new plan. Lastly, it is much easier to gain approval for a plan in its initial stages when alternate courses are indicated. The presence of several choices implies that a fairly complete analysis of the problem has been made, and that one path has not been chosen and followed blindly.

When a plan is being submitted to a group having varied interests and goals, the inclusion of alternate choices increases the possibility of compromise; but when only one course of action is presented, the result may be a rejection of the entire plan. For example, if a plan is presented proposing that a quality control program be established and the only recommendation concerning its administration is that it be placed under manufacturing, and if a strong personal conflict exists between the vice-presidents of manufacturing and engineering, an impasse may develop resulting in the cancellation of the entire program. However, the inclusion of an alternate form of organization — the creation of a separate department reporting directly to the president — provides a ready compromise and the achievement of the goal of the original plan.

The preceding discussion — an analysis of the characteristics of plans — presents three criteria for judging the probable success of a plan. These criteria — objectivity, degree of structuralization, and flexibility — not only serve as a measure of the probable success of a given plan but also reflect the effectiveness of the planning process. The relationship between planning and plans is summarized as follows: *Effective planning results in plans that are objective, structured, and flexible, and the extent to which resultant plans possess these characteristics is a measure of their probable success.*

Approach B — Economic Effectiveness

Over a period of years it has been observed that good plans have the aforementioned characteristics. However, it is quite possible that a plan carried through to its successful completion may not have been the most appropriate plan for that specific situation. The concept of *economic effectiveness*, widely used in economics, may be applied to determine whether or not a plan makes the maximum contribution to company objectives.[8] The application of this concept as a management tool rests upon two basic assumptions:

1. Management of a business enterprise is primarily an economic activity, and the principles and techniques of economics should be applicable and transferrable as principles and techniques of management. The word *economics* means the effective utilization of all resources.
2. The primary objective of any organization is to maximize the return (units of output) in relation to the effort (units of input) expended. This premise is stated in broad terms because the concept of maximization of return applies not only to capital invested, sales, or production, but also to the management of a charitable foundation seeking the best (most economic) distribution of its funds; to a religious organization seeking converts; or to a labor union demanding increased benefits for its members.

The Law of Diminishing Returns. The second assumption implies that the units of return are compatible with organizational objectives. If so, the problem is one of determining the amount contributed by the last unit of input in relation to the amount contributed by the next to last unit of input. The method of making this determination can be accomplished in several ways, but all methods have one common characteristic — they represent a certain way of looking at input-output relationships. An example frequently presented in economics to illustrate input-output relationships assumes a unit of land (usually an acre), a worker, and corn, the product. The one worker farms the one acre and is able to produce 100 bushels of corn with certain given tools. It is reasonable to expect that, with the same tools, by increasing the number of workers there will be an increase in the yield of corn *up to a point*. Eventually, however, there are enough workers so that adding workers does not result in additional product. This phenomenon has been stated variously as the *law of diminishing returns* or the *law of variable returns*.

Now translate the classic economic example into a problem in production. Columns A, B, and C of Figure 4-1 indicate the three elements of our first example. Assume that the tools (that is, the plant and the facilities), the product, and the methods remain the same. One unit of

[8]Charles J. Hitch and R. N. McKean, *The Economics of Defense in the Nuclear Age* (Cambridge: Harvard University Press, 1960). This book represents combined staff efforts of the Rand Corporation and presents an economic analysis of the problems of defense. It ranges from an analysis of resources available, through concepts of efficiency, and a detailed presentation of specific problems and applications to military research, logistics, and the development of policies for the choice of military deterrents. The underlying economics are applicable to the management of business firms.

	A Units of Input	B Total Produced	C Average Produced	D Marginal Product
	1	10	10	—
Figure 4-1	2	24	12	14
RELATIONSHIP	3	39	13	15
BETWEEN UNITS	4	48	12	9
OF INPUT, TOTAL	5	55	11	7
PRODUCED,	6	60	10	5
AVERAGE	7	63	9	3
PRODUCED, AND	8	64	8	1
MARGINAL	9	63	7	−1
PRODUCT				

input is the work of one person for an eight-hour day. This one unit of input produces 10 units of output, the total produced. In this instance the average produced is also 10. Average production is obtained by dividing total units produced by the units of input. When another worker is added, the economic effectiveness of each worker increases and the total produced reaches 24; the average goes up to 12. The addition of the third worker results in total production of 39, with an average of 13. So far everything is increasing. When the fourth worker is added, total production continues to rise; but the average drops to 12. With the addition of a fifth worker, the production goes up and the average slips to 11; and with the addition of the sixth worker, the average is down to 10 again; however, the total number of units produced is 60, or six times as much as that produced by one worker. After the seventh, eighth, and ninth workers, the average production per worker is reduced to seven; and, by adding the ninth worker, the phenomenon of diminishing returns appears and the total production declines from 64 to 63.

This relatively simple example poses a problem that recurs as the central theme of many managerial decisions. Managers, in making their decisions, are asked to answer the following question: What combination of resources results in the greatest economic return consistent with the objectives of the organization? If it can be said of a plan that it represents the best (most economic) combination of resources resulting in the achievement of desired objectives, the plan can then be considered appropriate. Obviously, both aspects of the test must be met. If the plan does not result in the achievement of desired objectives, it is not appropriate; nor is it appropriate if in achieving the desired objectives there is anything less than the most economic use of resources.

The Concept of Marginal Product. How can it be determined when there is the most efficient use of available resources? The data in the first three columns of Figure 4-1 does not provide sufficient information, but it does indicate some difficulty as reflected in the average units produced per worker. Note that the average starts falling when the fourth worker is added. A second indication that all is not well is revealed by the amount of total production. This measure drops when the ninth worker is added. Since our concern is with input-output relationships, does it not seem logical to study these relationships more carefully and find out what happens each time an additional person is added? It is necessary to determine exactly how much *additional* output results from each *additional* unit of input. Economists refer to this incremental relationship between additional units of input and resultant additional units of output as *marginal product*. The terms marginal productivity, marginal revenue, or marginal profit, may be interpreted as *additional* productivity, *additional* revenue, or *additional* profit in relation to an *additional* unit of input.

In Figure 4-1, Column D shows the marginal (additional) product resulting from each additional unit of input. The first person working for eight hours (one unit of input) forms the base of the problem. The marginal productivity of this worker cannot be computed because there was no previous production. With the addition of the second worker, 24 units were produced, a gain of 14 units over that produced by the first worker alone (24−10). The marginal production for each additional worker is shown in Column D. The addition of the third worker results in the production of 39 units, 15 units more than the amount produced by the previous two-worker team. The addition of the fourth worker yields only nine additional units, compared to the 14 added by the second worker and the 15 added by the third worker. The average production also drops by one unit from 13 to 12. The incremental increase in production resulting from additional units of input continues to drop and at a more rapid rate than the decline in average production. With the addition of the ninth worker, the results are negative, a marginal (additional) increase of −1; and the total number of units produced also declines by one. An inspection of Column D shows that there are increasing amounts of additional production until the fourth worker is added; thus, it seems that the maximum utilization of available resources occurs when the third worker is added. Prior to this point, the operation is not at maximum efficiency since the cost of additional units of input is more than offset by the value of additional units of output. Beyond this point the operation loses efficiency as each additional unit of input results in the production of a smaller and smaller amount of additional product. The phenomenon of decreasing efficiency in the use of resources is revealed by the marginal product rather than by measures of average or total production. The average production is 12 when the second worker is added, and it is also 12 when the fourth worker is added; but in the first instance the marginal productivity is increasing while in the second case, i.e., with the addition of the fourth worker, it is decreasing.[9]

The concept of marginal output, or incremental changes in the rate of production in relation to each additional unit of input, is a means of determining how efficiently available resources are employed. Efficiency increases as long as the additional units of output increase at a faster rate than the rate of additional units of input. When the point is reached where an additional unit of input results in a smaller rate of increase in output than that resulting from the addition of the previous unit of input, the maximum, or most efficient, utilization of resources no longer exists.

The management of any organization must continuously ask if its action, or its proposed plan, maximizes the efficient utilization of resources in meeting its goals. When a choice must be made between two or more plans, each of which possesses to the same degree the characteristics of objectivity, structuralization, and flexibility, it is apparent that another measure is needed in order to reach a decision. *Economic effectiveness* is the fourth criterion for use in judging the worth of plans and provides a basis for selecting the appropriate plan. The importance of economic effectiveness as a criterion for evaluating plans is stated in the *concept of economic effectiveness: Economic effectiveness in planning results in plans that maximize achievement of company objectives through the most efficient utilization of the available resources.*

Cost-Benefit Analysis

The above discussion of economic effectiveness provides a conceptual framework for evaluating the economic worth of a plan, and as stated on page 84, its application as a management tool rests upon two basic assumptions. The first assumption is that we are dealing with

---

[9]The student who has had calculus will understand that the curve for marginal productivity is the derivative of the equation for the total product curve. The problem can be expressed as $MC = MR$, or marginal costs equal marginal revenue. In addition to standard calculus texts, the following references are suggested for the student interested in a better understanding of the mathematical expression of the concept of marginal product:

Charles J. Hitch and R. N. McKean, *The Economics of Defense in the Nuclear Age* (Cambridge: Harvard University Press, 1960), pp. 362–405. The appendix headed "The Simple Mathematics of Maximization" presents fundamental concepts of calculus as used in maximizing returns in relation to inputs.

Herbert G. Heneman, Jr. and Dale Yoder, *Labor Economics* (2d ed.; Cincinnati: South-Western Publishing Co., 1965), pp. 793–809. Heneman and Yoder discuss marginal wage theory. The discussion is directed to problems of marginal productivity as they affect wages; however, the concepts are applicable to any situation involving input-output relationships.

Milton H. Spencer, K. K. Seo, and Mark G. Simkin, *Managerial Economics*, Text, Problems, and Short Cases (4th ed.; Homewood: Richard D. Irwin, 1975), Chapter 7. This discusses the relationships that exist between simple production functions.

the management of a business enterprise that is primarily economic in nature with the result that the principles and techniques of economics should be applicable and transferable as principles and techniques of management. Implied in this assumption is the quantification of inputs and outputs so that marginal product may be determined. The second assumption is that the primary objective of any organization is to maximize the return (units of output) in relation to the effort (units of input) expended. However, there are many instances where these two assumptions are not appropriate, with the result that the concept of economic effectiveness is not applicable to the evaluation of specific plans. These instances may occur in business firms and, in addition, there are nonprofit organizations — governmental units, educational institutions, and religious and charitable organizations — unable to evaluate plans with respect to their economic effectiveness. For these situations cost-benefit analysis (also referred to as benefit-cost analysis) offers an analytical framework similar to that provided by the concept of economic effectiveness.[10]

Quantification Problems. Cost-benefit analysis is utilized when it is difficult to measure either the value of or the distribution of benefits and when it is also difficult to determine those costs that should be included, as well as determining those that should be excluded, in establishing the cost of a given plan. Difficulties in measuring benefits and establishing costs are encountered often by the nonprofit organizations mentioned above and by business firms in evaluating specific programs. Cost-benefit concepts have long been used by the United States government in the development of river and harbor projects (The River and Harbor Act of 1902) and extensively in the allocation of water resources and the building of dams (Flood Control Act of 1936).[11] Cost-benefit analysis may also be used in evaluating urban renewal projects; in determining a state's allocation of financial resources among a university, four-year colleges, and community colleges; and

---

[10]An easy to understand introduction to the concept of cost-benefit analysis is the discussion by Harley H. Hinrichs entitled, "Government Decision Making and the Theory of Benefit-Cost Analysis: A Primer," which appears in Harley H. Hinrichs and Graeme M. Taylor, *Program Budgeting and Benefit-Cost Analysis*, Cases, Text, and Readings (Pacific Palisades, Calif.: Goodyear Publishing Co., 1969), pp. 9–20. Hinrichs' work is used extensively as the basis for this discussion of cost-benefit analysis.

For a discussion of a related concept, cost-effectiveness analysis, the following book is recommended: Washington Operations Research Council, *Cost-Effectiveness Analysis*, New Approaches in Decision Making, edited by Thomas A. Goldman (New York: Frederick A. Praeger, 1967), pp. 17–32.

The following article includes a 90-item bibliography for those who wish to explore the subject of cost-benefit analysis in depth: A. R. Prest and R. Turvey, "Cost-Benefit Analysis: A Survey," *Economic Journal*, Vol. 75 (December, 1965), pp. 638–735. This paper is reprinted in American Economic Association, *Surveys of Economic Theory*, Vol. III: Resource Allocation (New York: St. Martin's Press, 1966).

[11]Hinrichs and Taylor *op. cit.*, p. v.

in determining benefits to be derived from each of several types of executive compensation plans.[12]

All of these problems have two characteristics in common: First, the costs in these situations are difficult to determine and second, anticipated benefits are extremely resistant to quantification. In fact, the quantification of benefits often results in an unrealistic oversimplification. Thus a value judgment must be made concerning the worth of anticipated benefits in relation to what amounts to, at best, an educated estimate of costs. Projected benefits may be expressed as statements which are, in turn, evaluated with respect to their desirability and assigned relative weights, a process of making value judgments. The method employed by England, described in Chapter 3, may be used if desired.[13]

Maximization Dilemma. Even if it were possible to quantify all costs and all benefits, thereby removing the implicit constraint of the first assumption, that inputs and outputs be expressed in quantitative terms, there would still remain the problem of maximization. Since we do not live in a simplistic world, problems seldom can be stated as one of "maximizing the goodies and minimizing the baddies." Frequently, the objective is not to "maximize"; instead, to use a term of Herbert Simon, it is to "satisfice."

For example, if the objective of a governmental agency or a business firm is to maximize welfare (defining welfare as a subjective state of well-being or the achievement of one's desires), can either the government or the business realistically maximize the benefit, *welfare*, for either its citizens or its employees, as the case may be? Aside from the problems inherent in the quantification of costs and benefits (welfare) several difficult choices must be made to achieve this elusive maximization.[14] First, the government can ignore ethnic groups and the needs

---

[12]The following two references are reprinted in Fremont J. Lyden and Ernest G. Miller, (ed.) *Planning, Programming, Budgeting,* A Systems Approach to Management (Chicago: Markham Publishing Co., 1968), pp. 199–241. The paper by Professor McKean shows clearly the impact of personal value systems in the analysis of relative benefits and costs while the article by Professor Maass discusses the application of cost-benefit analysis in making public investment decisions.

Roland N. McKean, "Cost and Benefits from Different Viewpoints," in Howard G. Schaller (ed.), *Public Expenditure Decisions in the Urban Community* (Washington: Resources for the Future, 1963), pp. 147–163.

Arthur Maass, "Benefit-Cost Analysis: Its Relevance to Public Investment Decisions," *Quarterly Journal of Economics*, Vol. 80, No. 2 (May, 1966), pp. 208–226.

The following article discusses the application of cost-benefit analysis to problems of executive compensation: George W. Hettenhouse, "Cost/Benefit Analysis of Executive Compensation," *Harvard Business Review*, Vol. 48, No. 4 (July–August, 1970), pp. 114–124.

[13]The use of qualitative judgments is suggested as one of the means of determining the scope of standards to be used as a basis for control, pp. 442–446 and the use of appraisal as a means of setting standards, p. 447. The method used by England is described on pp. 54–60, Chapter 3.

[14]The following discussion is based upon Hinrichs, *op. cit.*, pp. 10–13.

of special social classes; disregard political entities such as states, cities and counties; and concentrate its efforts toward maximizing the welfare of each and every citizen. In the same manner, a corporation could ignore divisions, plants, departments, customers, and stockholders; thereby devoting its energies to maximizing the welfare of each of its employees. Should the maximization of benefits for each and every individual prove too difficult, for either the government or the corporation, a second choice is open: Forget maximization; instead, make it possible for everyone to gain something. The third alternative is to arrange events so that some group (either citizens or employees) gains in benefits, but nobody loses. Fourth, should either of the first three choices prove unsatisfactory or unworkable, there is the possibility of having the winners, those who gain in benefits or welfare, outnumber the losers. Admittedly, the concept, welfare, is next to impossible to either quantify or maximize. For that matter so are the normal business objectives of innovation, manager performance and development, worker performance and attitude, and public responsibility.[15]

Thus the problem of analyzing benefits within the context of cost-benefit analysis becomes a problem of re-examining objectives and making a comparative value judgment concerning the relative worth of stated objectives. A copper mining company may state as one of its major objectives the desire to fulfill its obligations with respect to public responsibility. Undoubtedly, there are also objectives with regard to profitability. What are the benefits to be derived from the installation of a several million dollar device to control the pollutants from its smelter — surely a public responsibility — in comparison to maintaining its dividend to its stockholders and its position as an attractive investment? Though quantification and economic analysis may be helpful, the solutions to this and similar questions are based upon personal value systems, the essence of cost-benefit analysis.

We have reviewed the methods of evaluating the potential effectiveness of plans. Approach A is one of describing and evaluating the observable characteristics of the planning process itself. Approach B is one of evaluating the plan in terms of its economic effectiveness. The concept of marginal costs in relation to marginal revenues expressed by the formula, $MC = MR$, is one method of determining the effectiveness of incremental units of input in relation to incremental units of output. Another method of evaluating economic effectiveness is that of cost-benefit analysis, a method used when it is extremely difficult to quantify either the costs or the benefits.

Case Problem 4-B offers an opportunity to utilize cost-benefit analysis techniques in the area of the social responsibilities of a business organization.

---

[15]See Chapter 3, pp. 45–52 and Chapter 18, pp. 442–457.

COST-BENEFIT ANALYSIS
OF SOCIAL RESPONSIBILITY

A company manufacturing fabricated metal products employs approximately 400 hourly rated employees, most of whom are highly skilled machinists. The annual sales of the company are approximately $12 million with an annual payroll of approximately $4 million. The company is located in a city of approximately 200,000 and is one of the larger manufacturers in the city. Within the city there are approximately 15,000 low income, socially disadvantaged people who have moved into the area during the past 25 years. About 25 of this category are employed in the plant in unskilled jobs.

The president of the company is extremely active in community affairs and believes that the company has a social responsibility to aid in alleviating unemployment and improving housing, schooling, and other problems confronting this disadvantaged social group. As a result of these beliefs the president of the company has requested that $100,000 be budgeted during the coming year to aid the company in meeting its social responsibilities to the community. Once the decision to budget the $100,000 was made, an ad hoc planning committee was established to recommend how the $100,000 should be spent to gain the greatest benefits in aiding the company to meet its social responsibilities. The following are the alternatives presented by the committee. Anticipated benefits are stated for each of the five options.

1. Establish a training program for unskilled workers in order that they may progress to the skilled positions in the organization. There have been sporadic efforts in this direction in the past, and the records thus far indicate that out of five workers placed in a formal apprenticeship program only one or two ever develop the skills necessary to become qualified as a machinist. The other three

or four, though they remain with the company, are below average in output and quality of product produced. In addition, some employees resent the special treatment offered the socially deprived group and frictions develop between present employees and newly hired and trained disadvantaged employees.

2. Invest all of the $100,000 allocated for social responsibility in another industry, located in the town, that utilizes primarily unskilled and semiskilled workers. It is estimated that such an investment would create approximately 200 such jobs. This option would possibly result in the other company receiving the credit for creating the additional job opportunities rather than the company making the investment. In addition, there is potential criticism that by creating 200 relatively low-paying unskilled jobs, one is simply perpertuating the plight of the disadvantaged social group and that the jobs would be labeled as "dead-end" jobs.

3. Invest the $100,000 in research and development with the intent of developing a product line that would result in the creation of at least 50 semiskilled machine operator jobs. Such a move would result in the establishment of a product line of perhaps a lower quality than the present high quality product and could conceivably result in the company's image within the industry as a quality manufacturer being severely damaged. Also, the number of jobs created is relatively insignificant in relation to the number of jobs needed in the community.

4. Since the company is located on a piece of property much larger than is needed in terms of future expansion, spend part of the $100,000 to improve the landscaping and general appearance of the plant and offices and spend the remainder in building a community recreation center. Such a center could be used by many community organizations throughout the entire city. This option would have an immediate and long-range impact, hopefully favorable, on residents throughout the community and especially on those living

---

Case Problem 4-B is based upon the following article: David Novick, "Cost-Benefit Analysis and Social Responsibility," *Business Horizons*, Vol. 16, No. 5 (October, 1973), pp. 63–72.

in the neighborhood of the plant. It is also believed that such a move would enhance the image of the company.

5. Establish a public relations campaign including a well-organized institutional advertising program to inform the community of the current activities in which the company is involved. Any donations to such artistic groups as civic opera, symphony, or other cultural activities would become a part of the institutional advertising program. Current donations to civic and charitable groups should be made public. Such a campaign might have positive effects upon middle- and higher-income groups, but there is serious question concerning whether it would have a favorable reception by the low-income or disadvantaged groups. Also, it would not directly benefit such groups since normally they do not participate in this type of community activity.

1. Prepare a cost-benefit analysis for each of the five options stated above. In one column present anticipated social benefits and in the other column the costs, or potential liabilities, involved with each option. Rank each cost and each benefit on a scale from 1 to 10 in terms of its potential liability (cost) or its potential benefit. Then rank each option in terms of its desirability.
2. State the reasons for your ranking of each of the options.
3. Discuss the basic value systems underlying the decision of a company to enter into the area of social responsibility as well as continuing its objective of making a profit.
4. Is there any basic conflict between maximizing profit and simultaneously establishing and fulfilling social objectives?

CHAPTER QUESTIONS FOR STUDY AND DISCUSSION

1. Determining the objectives of a business was discussed in Chapter 3. Some writers include the determination of objectives as a part of the planning process and discuss objectives as a part of planning. Develop several reasons for the inclusion of objectives as a part of planning and several reasons for considering the determination of objectives as a function that precedes planning.
2. Develop an example that shows how the planning function can be applied to the other managerial functions of organizing, leading, and controlling.
3. Comment on the following statement: "Good decision makers are good planners."
4. Give an example of a decision made by a planner. How does this decision differ from an executive decision? Why?
5. What is meant by the concepts of primacy and pervasiveness as applied to planning?
6. Give several examples of "pure" research that has developed into today's products. What are some of the products of tomorrow that may develop from today's research?
7. Develop a policy statement for a specific functional area. Next, describe the procedures and methods necessary to implement the stated policy.

8. What is meant by the concept of objectivity when used to describe plans or the planning function?
9. What is simulation? Give an example of simulation and describe the conditions that must be met before simulation is possible.
10. Define in your own terms the concept of marginal productivity. Give an example of marginal product.
11. What are some of the circumstances that might make it advisable to continue production even though marginal product is declining?
12. Discuss the relationship that exists between personal value systems and the determination of benefits within the context of cost-benefit analysis.
13. Discuss the relationships that exist between objectives and cost-benefit analysis.

Chapter 5

Planning for Functional Areas

Case Problem 5-A

KWICKIE KAR KLEAN

Tim Jones, owner-manager of Kwickie Kar Klean, sat in his office mulling over the results of his first year's operations. Before entering the automatic car wash business, Tim had investigated carefully the claims of several manufacturers of automatic car wash equipment and found considerable variation in what was considered the optimum amount of automatic equipment necessary for a successful business. One manufacturer suggested an installation costing over $60,000 exclusive of land and buildings, and pointed out that the savings in labor would soon pay for the equipment. At the other extreme, there was a unit for $15,000 but it required almost twice as much labor on high-volume days. Tim chose the latter course; however, the equipment was designed to permit adding fully automatic units later.

He considered himself fortunate in being able to rent a building for $600 a month on a busy through street in the center of a large residential area. Thus, his only capital outlay was for equipment capable of washing at least 600 cars a week. A summary statement of average monthly expenses for Kwickie Kar Klean during its first year's operations appears at the top of the next column.

Expense	Average per month
Heat, light, and power	$ 140
Water...	125
Supplies (towels, detergents, etc.).......	75
Depreciation and repairs.................	160
Building and land rent....................	600
Labor...	2,600
Total expenses	$3,700

Tim regarded most of these expenses as fixed since there was little he could do to control the first five items. Therefore, he decided to direct his attention to controlling the amount of money spent for labor and improving output per man-hour.

The conveyor that pulls the cars through the washing process is 80 feet long. At the front of this line there is a portable vacuum cleaner used in cleaning the interior of the car. Next, there is a steam cleaning unit used to steam the wheels, bumpers, and grill; and following this is the mitting area where one employee on each side washes the entire car with detergent as it is pulled through by the conveyor. The next three operations are automatic: a side and top brush unit (including automatic pre-rinse) washes the top and sides of the car; an automatic rinsing unit removes detergent and loosened dirt left by the washing unit; a drying unit completes the automatic process. The car is moved forward to the front of the building to be wiped and finished by hand.

Tim carefully studied the time required for each operation and concluded that the production bottleneck was at the end of the line where the cars are manually wiped. He discovered that two employees could wipe one car in three minutes and concluded that his total daily production should be 20 cars per hour, or a total of 200 cars per day since the auto laundry remained open 10 hours each day. However, such was not the case because customers did not appear on a regular schedule. He decided to record the total number of cars washed during a 10-hour day for varying crew sizes. Here is a summary of the production records for the car wash:

Number of employees	Total cars washed in 10 hours
3	90
4	120
5	155
6	180
8	230
10	270
12	350

When three employees worked, one at the front of the line operated the vacuum cleaner and the steam cleaner, while the other two washed the car in the mitting area, one on each side of the car. Then, as the car moved through the automatic units of the line — the side and top brush unit, the rinsing unit, and the drying station — the two mitters moved to the end of the line and served as wipers after

Tim drove the car from the conveyor to the front of the building. When the crew consisted of four, the additional person was placed on the end of the line to help the mitters in wiping the car. The addition of a fifth employee meant that there was still one at the front of the line, two mitters now remaining in the mitting area, and two functioning solely as wipers. Though this arrangement yielded the highest average per employee for a 10-hour day, it was found that there were times during the day, for example during the lunch period, when the effective crew actually consisted of four people. Also, if one of the five was absent, the result was a definite undermanning; and if it was a good day for business, Tim felt that he lost customers when they drove by and a saw a line of cars waiting to be washed. Consequently, he decided that for the weekdays, Monday through Friday, he would regularly employ six people, which almost always assured him of an effective crew of five, thus allowing him to handle peak periods on these days with ease. With a crew of six, one vacuumed, one operated the steam cleaner, two were in the mitting area, and two wiped.

During the first year, Kwickie Kar Klean washed an average of 500 cars a week, but the number washed was not distributed evenly throughout the six working days. Usually by Friday evening only 40 to 60 percent of the week's total had been completed, which meant that in order to reach the weekly average of 500, it was necessary sometimes to wash as many as 350 cars on Saturday. The addition of two more wipers, making eight, could handle 250 cars, but this was not enough for the busy days. And increasing the total crew to 10, with six of them wiping, enabled Tim to turn out only 20 more cars per employee in a 10-hour day. After analyzing the production of a crew of 10, Tim decided that the cars were not being prepared fast enough for the conveyor line, so he decided to put two people on the vacuum cleaning, two on the steam cleaning, and, of course, two in the mitting area. These six on the front of the line seemed to be able to keep the six wipers supplied with cars even during rush periods.

1. Evaluate Tim's original decision to staff with a crew of six during weekdays.
2. There were many weeks during the year when the total output, Monday through Friday, was 300 cars with the standard crew of six. It is possible for these six employees to wash approximately 200 cars on Saturday, thus bringing the weekly total to 500. Yet, Tim called in six additional employees on Saturday to raise the possible output to 350, or 650 for the week. How much is it costing Tim to be prepared for the additional 150 cars? Would you recommend that this practice be continued? Why?
3. Under what circumstances would you recommend that fully automatic equipment be purchased, assuming that the purchase of such equipment would eliminate four employees — the two in the mitting area and the two in the steam cleaning area?
4. What additional related items could be sold at a car cleaning operation?

In Chapter 4, on page 74, a classification of plans is presented. Plans are classified according to time or duration, according to major business function, and with respect to breadth or scope. It is the purpose of this chapter to examine more closely the planning function as applied to the major business functions of finance, marketing, production, and personnel. The emphasis is upon planning for policy statements in each of these four functional areas.

Figure 5-1 presents a summary of the scope of policies for each of the four major functional areas. A cursory examination shows that there is a high degree of interrelationship between each of the functional areas. The availability of capital and the manner in which capital is employed have their effect upon the production process. There is also a close relationship between the policies governing the production function and the marketing function. The quantity and quality of the product or service produced sets the upper limits of the level of achievement of the marketing function. Well formulated and properly executed personnel policies have their effect on all the other functional areas. A brief discussion of the nature of each function is presented, and the scope of policies for each of these functional areas is examined.

THE FINANCE FUNCTION

As shown in Figure 5-1, the finance function encompasses the acquisition of capital, the utilization of capital, and the distribution of profit. Since profit is necessary for the survival of a business organization, it is necessary to have an understanding of the various meanings associated with the term *profit*.[1]

---

[1] Carl A. Dauten and Merle Welshans, *Principles of Finance* (4th ed.; Cincinnati: South-Western Publishing Co., 1975).

J. Fred Weston and Eugene F. Brigham, *Managerial Finance* (4th ed.; Hindale: Dryden Press, 1972).

Figure 5-1 SUMMARY OF THE SCOPE OF POLICIES FOR EACH FUNCTIONAL AREA

FINANCE	MARKETING	PRODUCTION	PERSONNEL
Acquisition of Capital	*Product Selection*	*Product Policies*	*Staffing*
Long-term capital	Product diversification	Diversification	Selection
	Product obsolescence	New products	Promotion
Stock	Product style	Integration	Termination
Bonds	Product quality	Make or buy	
Mortgages	Product standardization		*Development*
Long-term notes		Quality	
	Pricing the Product	Standardization	Training
Short-term capital			Management development
	Product costs	Inventory	
Commercial credits	Competition		*Compensation*
Bank loans	Pricing new products	*Facility Policies*	
Commercial factors	Terms of sale		Amount of compensation
		Location	Method of payment
Utilization of Capital	*Channel of Distribution*	Capacity	Employee benefit plans
		Maintenance	
Fixed assets	*Promotion*		*Labor-Management Relations*
Working capital		*Selection of Vendors*	
Inventory	Direct selling		Organizational climate
Credit and collections	Advertising	Number of vendors	Relation with nonunion
	Special promotional	Reciprocity	employees
Distribution of Profit	devices		
Dividends			
Reinvestment			

The Meaning of Profit

Profit has been viewed as a form of compensation to the individual owner or to the stockholders of a publicly held corporation. It has also been defined within the framework of an economic process, a concept that states that profit is the result of a firm's operating in an economic environment that is not perfect. Differences in the desirability of location or holding a patent on a manufactured product are examples of these imperfections which are known as *frictions*. Profit can be considered the result of innovations, either with respect to the product or to the method in which the business is operated. Profit may be defined as the amount remaining after all expenses associated with conducting a business have been met. However, such definition leaves much to be desired since it is passive in nature and can lead one to believe that profit is something left over. Profit must be regarded as an integral portion of the sales dollar and a management goal that can be realized through proper planning. Profit creates new capital to provide for expansion. Consequently, the continuance and growth of any industrial enterprise depend upon its ability to produce profit.

Profit may be measured as total dollars earned or may be expressed as a ratio. The most commonly used method of expressing a company's profit is total dollars earned during a specified period of time. However, additional information is required in order to make this measure meaningful. Knowledge of past performance provides a basis for comparing a company's present performance with its past record. Profit for a given firm must be considered in light of the performance of its industry so that profitability in relation to other companies may be ascertained. The meaning of the statement that a company has increased its profits 10 percent over its profits for the preceding year changes significantly when it is known that the average profit for other companies in the same industry also increased 10 percent. Similarly, the meaning changes if the industry average decreased 10 percent or remained constant during the same period.

The two most frequently used ratios, or percentages, to express profitability are: (1) percentage return on capital invested, and (2) percentage return on sales. In the opinion of many analysts, return on invested capital is by far the most important measure because it indicates the effectiveness of management's stewardship and has a marked effect on the company's ability to attract new investment capital. Consequently, a company's rate of growth is directly influenced by its return on invested capital. Percentage return on sales is a measure closely associated with the operating statement of a company and is affected directly by changes in operating costs. When expressed as a percentage of sales, profit decreases by the same amount that sales volume decreases unless costs are reduced correspondingly. Conversely, when sales volume increases profits should show the same percentage increase, provided that operating costs remain constant.

Acquisition of Capital

The sources of capital for an individual starting a business are savings, borrowed capital, or both. The same sources used by the individual — savings, or prior earnings, and borrowed capital — are available to a corporation. Capital acquired from outside sources is usually classified according to the length of time for which the financing is desired. Financing required for periods greater than one year is referred to as *long-term capital*, and capital required for a period of less than one year is referred to as *short-term capital*.

Long-term Capital. The sources of long-term capital are: stock, bonds, mortgages, and long-term notes, each of which has distinct advantages and disadvantages.

The sale of *stock*, representing a share of ownership, is one of the most widely used means of raising capital for a corporation and may be designated as either *preferred stock* or *common stock*. When formulating policies concerning the issuance of preferred stock, a company must recognize that there may be occasions, especially when earnings are less than anticipated, that may result in the elimination of dividends on common stock in order to pay dividends on preferred stock. There is no such obligation with respect to common stock. Also, the concept of equity must be considered. Without a corresponding increase in fixed assets, the issuance of additional stock results in dilution of stockholder equity. Consideration must be given to determining whether the payment of a dividend on common stock is necessary to make the purchase of such equities an attractive investment.

When a company issues *bonds*, another means of long-term financing, it agrees that it will repay the face value of the bond on a specified date and that a fixed rate of interest will be paid until that date. One advantage of bonds is that management's control of the company is not jeopardized as it may be when additional stock with voting rights is issued. Second, the fixed rate that a company pays for a bond issue is an expense item and not taxed as income; however, dividends paid to stockholders come from profits after the payment of income taxes. A disadvantage resulting from the issuance of bonds is the obligation to pay interest, thus resulting in an additional fixed charge to the issuing company.

Another means of obtaining capital is through *mortgages* secured by part or all of the company's real property. Most modern mortgages enable a company to retain its present management and control as long as payments on principal and interest are met as agreed. *Long-term notes* are also used as a means of raising capital. Again, interest payments are considered an expense item. However, there may be distinct disadvantages if the lender places restrictions on the payment of dividends or the purchase of additional assets, or requires representation on the board of directors.

Short-term Capital. Short-term capital supplements the company's existing cash and may be used for such things as the purchase of additional inventory or taking advantage of cash or quantity discounts. The most frequently used source of short-term capital is bank loans; however, the degree to which banks are used as a source of credit depends upon the company's reputation and the relationship it has established with the banking community. *Commercial credits* are another source of short-term capital. Commercial credits, which are similar to an individual's charge account, are extended by vendors to customers with good credit ratings. Such credits imply a deferral of payments for 30, 60, or even 90 days, thus establishing a source of short-term capital. A third source is *commercial factors*. These firms specialize in short-term financing usually through the purchase of a company's accounts receivable. In some instances factors prepare the required invoices and perform all the paperwork necessary to collect the accounts. To firms without an adequate clerical staff, the use of commercial factors may offer an attractive means of acquiring short-term capital.

Utilization of Capital

Once capital has been acquired, financial policies must be developed for its proper utilization. Elements to be considered in determining the most effective utilization of capital are the amount of capital to be placed into fixed assets, the ratio between fixed assets and working capital, the amount of inventory, and policies concerning credit and collections. Each of these elements demands cash; and unless there are policies that specify the amount to be allocated for each use, a serious imbalance may result, thereby impairing the firm's position.

Fixed Assets. In its simplest form, the policy decision concerning the amount of capital to be allocated to fixed assets is a question of leasing or buying. The latter choice results in increasing fixed assets. The problems of obsolescence, maintenance, replacement, and the rate of return on specific assets arise. Tax liability must be considered since money paid for rentals or leases is usually considered an expense and tax deductible. Such tax advantages may be offset by a depreciation allowance on fixed assets. Fixed assets may also be converted into cash, should the need arise.

Working Capital. Closely related to the amount of capital to be placed in fixed assets is the capital to be retained and utilized for the operation of the business. Such capital is referred to as *working capital* and is used for the purchase of materials and services, for payment of payrolls, and for contingencies. Balance should be maintained between fixed assets, all of which require money to operate, and the working capital available for their operation. Policies define the proper ratio for a given company.

Inventory. Policy statements with regard to inventory should include a determination of the size of inventory of both in-process and finished goods, expressed as a unit portion of annual sales. A determination of the rate of inventory buildup and turnover is necessary in order to take advantage of price fluctuations of raw materials and to minimize the risk of obsolescence.

Credit and Collection. Virtually every business is forced to extend some credit to its customers. The extent to which credit is granted may be determined by general industry practices, or it may be the result of attempting to secure a better competitive position. In either event, clear-cut policies are needed to determine the amount of credit to be extended. Closely allied to credit policies are policies governing the collection of accounts receivable and the granting of discounts from list price for prompt payment. Accounts receivable, unless closely watched, may become abnormally large and reduce cash flow.

Distribution of Profit

The third area of financial policy determination concerns the distribution of profit. Policies must be developed to determine the amount to be retained for operating expenses and for expansion. Consideration must also be given to the allocation of funds for dividends.

Dividends. It is necessary to formulate policy statements concerning the payment of dividends in order to assure a fair return on investment to those who have invested in the firm and to make the continuing purchase of equities in the firm an attractive investment. Such policies may express the amount to be paid out in dividends as a percentage of profit earned. When profits increase so does the amount returned to investors; however, when profits decrease, dividends do also. The alternative is one of stating a fixed rate of return modified periodically based on long-term trends in earnings.

Reinvestment. The establishment of adequate cash reserves and the payment of dividends must also relate to policies concerning *reinvestment*. Questions to be answered are what portion of the profit is to be reinvested in the firm and how this money is to be reinvested. It may be placed in fixed assets, as a means of increasing sales volume. A method of increasing sales not ordinarily classified as reinvestment is to direct capital into an expanded advertising program or to establish sales territories not currently served by the company. Another major area for the utilization of capital is research and development.

THE MARKETING FUNCTION

The *marketing function* of a business organization encompasses those activities necessary to move goods and services from the producer to customers or consumers in a manner that satisfies both the needs of the organization and the needs of the customers or consumers. The business activities included in the above definition are the determination of (1) the product or service to be offered, (2) the price of the product or service, (3) the method of distribution so that the product or service is made available to consumer, and (4) the method of promotion to be used in order to enhance the volume of the product or service being offered. Each of these aspects of the marketing function is discussed in turn.[2]

Product Selection

The determination of policies concerning the product or service involves not only the marketing function but also the other functional areas. The contribution of the marketing department in forming product policies is its estimate of the potential market and its responsibility for the distribution of the product to the customer. There are four policy determinations that influence product selection. They are (1) product diversification, (2) product obsolescence, (3) product quality, and (4) product standardization.

Product Diversification. The phrase, *product diversification*, refers to the number of products produced and distributed and the extent to which they differ from each other in terms of physical characteristics, manufacturing processes, and selling methods. Product diversification implicitly refers to the acquisition of additional products. However, diversification policies should serve not only as guides for the acquisition of additional products but also should show the need for reducing the number of items in an existing product line. Factors to be considered in the acquisition of new products are available financing, the production facilities required, and the method of distribution. The qualifications of available personnel, particularly their ability to perform continuing research and development work, is a necessary consideration if a position of leadership is desired. Anticipated market size, the level of sales volume, and profitability serve as effective guides in determining whether an existing product should be retained or dropped from the product line.

Product Obsolescence. *Obsolescence* of durable goods occurs when a product is no longer usable for any one of several reasons. Durable goods, both consumer and capital, become obsolete when worn out, thereby having served their useful life. There is also the concept of *forced obsolescence* which is the direct result of a policy decision. Continued product improvement or change may be used to create consumer dissatisfaction with the product in its present form. Changes in

[2]Weldon J. Taylor and Roy T. Shaw, *Marketing*, An Integrated, Analytical Approach (3d ed.; Cincinnati: South-Western Publishing Co., 1975).

E. Jerome McCarthy, *Basic Marketing*, A Managerial Approach (5th ed.; Homewood: Richard D. Irwin, 1975).

style, for example in wearing apparel, are another means of inducing forced obsolescence. Policy statements concerning product obsolescence determine the extent and frequency of changes in design and style in order to create a desire for a product that is either new in appearance or better in performance.

Product Quality. *Quality* refers to those characteristics that are relevant in measuring the degree to which a product meets predetermined standards of performance. Quality is not an absolute value; yet there is an implied relationship between quality and excellence of design, workmanship, materials, and price. One policy question that must be resolved is the determination of how many levels of quality are to be produced or sold. Any given firm must determine whether or not it is going to carry multiple-quality product lines. Another policy consideration concerning quality is determining whether or not truly outstanding quality can be used as the primary basis for promotion.

Product Standardization. *Standardization* is closely related to the number of levels of quality in the product line. A reduction in the number of levels of quality or the number of models produced and distributed is a move toward product standardization, usually resulting in a lowering of production and distribution costs. Hence, policy statements setting forth the optimum degree of standardization of a given product line, with respect to either quality or the number of models, is a choice between potentially lower costs in production and distribution or the possibility of increased market share potential.

Pricing

It is recognized that the costs of production and distribution have a direct bearing upon price. However, cost is but one of several factors that must be considered in establishing pricing policies. The actions of competitors often influence price. When pricing a new product, it is necessary to consider the proposed price in relation to the price structure of the current product line and whether or not the product should be introduced at a relatively low price then raised when it has gained market acceptance. The alternative is to price the product relative to actual cost and hope that as the result of increased volume to ultimately lower the price due to reduced production and distribution costs. Finally, the terms of sale, including the availability of credit and discount privileges, modify the significance of the stated price.

Channel of Distribution

One of the underlying assumptions in selecting the channel of distribution is that certain functions are inherent in the process of distribution and must be performed. The decision to sell either directly to the consumer or through a series of intermediaries to the consumer is the selection of a channel of distribution. Orders are received, the product is drawn from stock, shipments are sent to the customer, a statement of the amount due is prepared, and provisions for collection are provided. Any of these functions may be combined or transferred to another position in the distribution cycle, but the function itself is not eliminated. A company selling directly to the consumer performs all of these functions. However, if one or more intermediaries, called variously jobbers, distributors, wholesalers, or retailers, are introduced into the cycle some of these functions may be transferred to the intermediary. Sometimes the selection of the channel of distribution is determined by industry practices. Even so, the selection of a market channel offers an opportunity for innovation. Avon Products, Inc., for example, sells directly to the consumer through its own field sales force, while competitors distribute similar products through wholesalers, to retail stores, and ultimately to the consumer. The factors to be considered in selecting one channel of distribution in preference to another, assuming that such choice is possible, are (1) the costs incurred as the result of performing the functions of the distribution cycle and (2) the advantages gained by controlling the selling effort with the company's own sales force and direct contact with the customer. There is also the possibility that more than one channel of distribution may be utilized.

Promotion Policies

The final policy question to be considered is determining an effective means of persuading the customer to buy the product — the selection of the methods of *promotion*. Personal selling, advertising, and sales promotion are the most frequently used forms of promotion.

The process of a salesperson persuading a customer to buy a product is referred to as *personal selling*. Two aspects of personal selling are particularly significant in formulating promotion policies. The first is establishing the importance of the role of sales personnel in persuading the customer to buy a given product. At one extreme are those people — such as those employed by variety chains and supermarkets — who function as sales clerks and whose only contribution to the selling process is to respond to requests of customers. At the other extreme of the selling process are the agents of life insurance companies who seek and locate a prospect, create a felt need for the product, and finally persuade the prospect to buy an intangible item that may never offer a tangible reward to the buyer personally.

The second aspect of personal selling is determining the optimum degree of control necessary to realize the greatest benefit from sales personnel. A close degree of control is usually possible when those who sell the product are employees of the company making the product. Many industrial products, such as machine tools, are sold in this manner; however, relatively few consumer products are sold by a sales force employed by the manufacturer. Instead, they are sold through the efforts of employees of the retailer. If the efforts of sales personnel are incidental to the selling process, such personnel are usually not employed by the producer of the product. As a result, emphasis is placed upon *advertising* or *sales promotional devices*, such as point-of-sale demonstrations used in department stores and other retail outlets. However, when sales personnel are the decisive factor in persuading the customer to buy, the producer of the product usually employs and exercises close control over the sales force. Consequently, advertising and other promotional devices are of lesser importance.

THE PRODUCTION FUNCTION

As a nation we are noted for both the effectiveness and efficiency of our production processes. By *effectiveness of production* we mean providing those goods and services desired by consumers. Effective production is the result of a close liaison between the demand side of business, sales, and the supply side of business, production. The efficiency of our industrial enterprise results from the production manager continually seeking answers to the following two questions: (1) What is the maximum attainable output with a given sets of inputs? (2) What are the minimum inputs required to achieve a stated level of output? These questions form the framework within which policy decisions are made with regard to the production function.[3]

The Nature of the Production Function

The production function is present in all formal organizations; however, it is easier to recognize that function in those organizations that manufacture a product. The factors of input in manufacturing are the physical facilities, the raw materials that are converted into a final form, and the human resources needed to produce the product. The output of the manufacturing firm is a tangible product. A service organization, such as a firm of certified public accountants, works with data supplied by its clients and offers as an end result an interpretation of that information based upon its members' professional training and judgment. An airline has as its production function the moving of passengers and freight from one city to another, an operation that requires the utilization of airport facilities, ground crews, aircraft, and flight crews — all factors of input. Finally, the wholesale distributing organization, typically considered a part of the marketing process, performs a function similar to that of the airlines in that the products to be distributed must arrive at a specified place at a given time.

---

[3]A. C. Laufer, *Operations Management* (Cincinnati: South-Western Publishing Co., 1975).

Elwood S. Buffa, *Modern Production Management* (4th ed.; New York: John Wiley & Sons, 1973).

Decisions concerning the product are responsibilities of the production function as well as of the marketing function since production is charged with producing the required product or service. Physical facilities are another phase of production policy, and the selection of sources of supply, or vendors, is the third area of production policy.

Product Policies

Marketing policies concerning the product encompass product diversification, obsolescence and style, quality, and standardization. Production policies also cover these aspects of the product, with the possible exception of policy statements on obsolescence and style — an area that is usually reserved primarily for the marketing function because of its close contact with customer needs. In addition, the production function is charged with the establishment of policies governing inventory levels. The close relationship and the degree of overlap between the role of the marketing function and that of the production function concerning the product are shown clearly in the second and third columns of Figure 5-1.

Diversification. Marketing policies concerning product diversification include both the acquisition of new products and the decision as to whether or not existing products should be retained in the product line. Production policies relating to product diversification are also concerned with these aspects of diversification. In addition, the production function is concerned with the problem of integration and the question of whether to make or to buy a component part of the end product.

New Products. Product policies relating to the acquisition of new products must be closely coordinated with the efforts of the marketing department so that there is a full utilization of the existing sales force and channels of distribution. In addition, questions peculiar to the production process itself must be considered. Will the new product utilize present production facilities or will it require new or additional facilities? Will the same raw materials be used and the same human skills be required in its production? Will the knowledge gained as the result of research and development on the new product benefit existing products? Almost every business has the opportunity to acquire new products or offer additional services that conform to existing sales and production capabilities. For instance, the automatic car wash service described in Case Problem 5-A can offer its customers additional services such as polishing and waxing. The answers to the above questions are generally referred to as a question of integration or the question of make or buy.

Integration. The combining of a sequence of distinct production processes that sometimes may exist in the form of separate companies is known as *vertical integration*. For example, some steel companies have integrated vertically in both directions. These companies have acquired raw material sources, iron ore mines, and have also directed the expansion of their operations so that they are able to convert their basic product, steel, into finished consumer goods such as steel pails and even prefabricated houses. The result is a vertically integrated production process that mines ore, produces steel, and fabricates the finished consumer product. Occasionally the term *backward integration* is used when companies acquire raw materials, and the term *forward integration* is used to describe those situations in which companies extend their product lines into a finished consumer product.

Make or Buy. The *make-or-buy* decision is a miniature of the integration decision and usually refers to whether a company should make or buy a specific component part used in its product. Ball bearings are an example of a part that may be purchased from an independent source of supply or manufactured by the user. The following questions are useful in formulating policies concerning whether or not a company should integrate other related production operations into its present structure and in resolving the make-or-buy decision:

1. Can present facilities be used, or are new facilities required?
2. What new technical skills and knowledge are required?
3. Is the present source of supply satisfactory with respect to quantity, quality, cost, and reliability of service?
4. Will making the new product result in an excess quantity that must be sold by the marketing department?

Quality. The production function (along with the marketing function) is concerned with the formulation of policies relative to the quality of the product. Production policies concerning quality emphasize the cost of quality rather than the sales potential associated with the level of quality. Figure 5-2 is a model showing the relationship of the three variables considered in formulating policies that define the desired level of quality control for a given product or service. The general term, "corrective action," is used since the model is a statement of the factors that must be considered when taking any managerial action designed to improve performance. The vertical axis is a measure of cost, and the horizontal axis indicates units of corrective action. Assume that the quality of a given product can be improved when additional inspectors are added to an assembly line. The cost of additional inspection is shown by line *A*, the rising diagonal line — the cost of corrective action inputs. Line *B*, a downward sloping curve, shows the decreasing costs resulting from the corrective action (in this case, the use of additional inspectors). Total costs, line *C*, form a U-shaped curve. When there is no inspection the cost is zero, but the cost resulting from poor quality due to excessive scrap, replacement of defective parts, and loss of sales is high; consequently, the total production cost

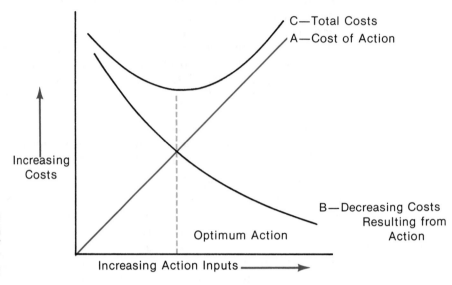

Figure 5-2
MODEL SHOWING
THE EFFECT OF
MANAGEMENT
ACTION

of the product is also high. As additional inspection is added, the cost of such inspection increases; but this rising cost is being offset by the decreasing costs attributable to poor quality, with the result that total costs decline until an optimum point is reached. Beyond that point, total costs again rise since the cost of inspection is greater than the decreasing costs resulting from improved quality. The cost of additional inspection has been used as an example; however, the same reasoning applies when establishing any control in any of the functional areas whether it be finance, marketing, production, or personnel.

Standardization. From the viewpoint of marketing, the addition of models that vary in size, color, function, or quality means that a greater share of the potential market may be gained. Yet each variation in the product increases the complexity of the production function with an attendant increase in production costs. Nonetheless, it is possible to achieve a relatively high degree of standardization in some instances without seriously compromising sales volume and maintain relatively low production costs. The standardization of parts and subassemblies that make up the finished product offers such an opportunity. For example, a manufacturer of refrigerators may standardize the insulating materials, compressors, hinges, door latches, and quality of steel plate used in its product in order to increase production efficiency and still continue to produce a variety of sizes and colors in order to maximize its share of the market.

Inventory. Inventory policies determine the practices that a company follows in carrying raw materials, parts in process, or finished goods. The model presented in Figure 5-2 may be applied to the general problem of determining an optimum inventory level. Since establishing a given inventory level is the result of management action, let the horizontal axis represent increasing amounts of inventory and the rising diagonal, line *A*, the increasing cost of carrying an inventory. The downward sloping curve, line *B*, shows the decreasing costs that might be expected as the result of fewer stock-outs. When stock-outs are frequent, total costs, line *C*, are also high since stock-outs may mean either a loss in sales volume as the result of not being able to fill customer orders, or increased production costs as the result of frantic efforts to fill a succession of small orders. As the amount of inventory increases, so does the cost of carrying that inventory increase, line *A*; but the cost of inventory is offset by the decreasing number of stock-outs which enables the company to fill customer orders promptly and to increase the efficiency of the production process through longer production runs. The optimum level of inventory, as measured by total cost, is reached when the actual cost curve, line *C*, reaches its lowest point. Beyond this point the cost of carrying additional inventory is greater than any advantage gained as the result of further reduction in the number of stock-outs, and total costs again begin to rise.

Facility Policies

The physical facilities of production include the land, buildings, and all equipment used in the production process. The natures of some processes — for example, paper making — offer relatively few degrees of freedom to the manager in selecting either equipment or location; and some production, such as steelmaking, is so technical that only those who are highly trained in the industry can appreciate the problems involved. For these reasons a discussion of the selection of specific facilities for a given industry is beyond the scope of this book. Nonetheless, there are three aspects of facility policies that are broad in scope and applicable to most business firms.

Location. First, there is the question of facility location. For many businesses the location decision has been made and usually little can be done about it; but for those that are contemplating expansion or establishing a new business, the decision may be crucial, particularly when choosing the location of a new retail or service establishment. Among the factors to be considered are availability of raw materials and ready access to the market, the cost of space, of construction, of services such as heat, light, and power, and the availability and cost of labor.

Capacity. Second, a decision must be made concerning the optimum capacity of either the proposed or existing facility. If facilities are too large, waste is inevitable; if the facilities are too small, loss in sales volume and inefficiencies in the production process may result. Policies relating to capacity for production should provide for maximum flexibility so that variations in output may be handled in the most efficient manner.

Maintenance. Third, there are decisions concerning the maintenance of facilities. Again, Figure 5-2 serves as a model for determining the optimum degree of maintenance of facilities. The reduction of losses due to breakdown is shown by the downward sloping curve of line *B*. As sound preventive maintenance increases, the cost of such maintenance also increases (shown by line *A*). But this cost is offset by the decreasing cost of production failures that are reduced by the maintenance program. Consequently, total costs are also declining as shown by the U-shaped curve of total costs, line *C*. When total costs are at the lowest point, the optimum degree of preventive maintenance is attained. When total costs rise excessively as the result of an extensive maintenance program that becomes necessary to keep worn equipment in operation, consideration should be given to replacing existing facilities with new equipment requiring less maintenance.

Selection of Vendors

Policies relating to the selection of vendors are developed to insure an uninterrupted flow of materials and supplies vital to the production process. Usually the factors of quality, service, and price are of prime importance in selecting a vendor; however, attention must be given to the number of vendors, and in some instances it is necessary to consider the question of reciprocity.

Number of Vendors. The number of vendors may be of significance since vendors are frequently pitted against each other by large purchasers as a means of improving quality and insuring prompt service. Multiple vendors are also used as a means of providing a continuing source of materials in the event that one supplier is unable to make delivery because of difficulties arising from strikes or mechanical failures. However, small companies frequently find it advantageous to patronize a single source of supply. They do this because their volume may be so small that if divided among several sources it would not warrant special attention and service; but when orders are placed with a single source, the firm may merit special attention. In formulating policies concerning the number of vendors, a company must view itself as a customer as well as analyze its own needs as a purchaser.

Reciprocity. Reciprocal agreements are possible when the purchaser of a given item produces a product or service that can, in turn, be used by the vendor. The existence of reciprocity between purchaser and vendor does not imply collusion or unethical conduct. There is no reason to develop a policy statement barring reciprocity provided such agreements are evaluated with respect to quality, service, price, and strategic position.

THE PERSONNEL FUNCTION

The functions of finance, marketing, and production are usually managed by an executive who is assigned sole responsibility for the performance of that particular function. If the organization is large enough, there is also an executive assigned responsibility for the performance of the personnel function; but, unlike other executives, the personnel manager shares the performance of the personnel function. The reason for the shared responsibility is inherent in the nature of the personnel function itself.[4]

The Nature of the Personnel Function

The personnel function includes all of the activities associated with the management of personnel. Since organizations are composed of people and the work of organization is accomplished by and through people, managers of operating units by necessity manage personnel. In addition, historically managers have performed, and still do in small organizations, all of the duties normally associated with the management of personnel — including selecting, training, compensating, and administering any additional benefits associated with employment. It has been only recently that personnel management has emerged as a separate function with a manager charged with the responsibility of administering the personnel function for the entire organization. Even so, many of the functions of personnel are still performed by other managers. For example, in most companies the responsible managers still retain the final decisions as to whom they will employ, make recommendations concerning promotions and level of pay, and are responsible for much of the training.

Several factors have contributed to the emergence of personnel as a separate function. First, as organizations grew in size and complexity it became increasingly difficult for the unit manager to continue successfully the performance of the personnel function. Second, knowledge developed from divergent sources has had a direct bearing upon the management of personnel. One source stressed the importance of measuring work, another the need for selection and training, and a third the need for determining the amount of compensation to be received for performing a job. Knowledge was also gained from the human relations approach to management, for it was this philosophy that emphasized that the worker was motivated by sociological and psychological factors as well as by economic interests. The development of labor unions and their bargaining for wages, hours, and other terms and conditions of employment forced companies to set up a

---

[4]Herbert J. Chruden and Arthur W. Sherman, Jr., *Personnel Management* (5th ed.; Cincinnati: South-Western Publishing Co., 1976).

George Strauss and Leonard R. Sayles, *Personnel*, The Human Problems of Management (3d ed.; Englewood Cliffs: Prentice-Hall, 1972).

counterpart to bargain with the unions. Indeed, the mere threat of unionization has forced many organizations to develop a competitive personnel program. Finally, the 1964 Civil Rights Act, as amended, has had a profound influence on personnel administration.

Perhaps the most obvious area of policy formulation is the process that creates employees — recruitment and selection. However, the problem is broader than recruitment of new employees. It also includes the placement of present employees in positions that are new for them. Therefore, the broader term, *staffing*, is used to designate the first area of personnel policies. After a person becomes an employee or is assigned to a new position, there is need for *training* or development, the second area of policy determination. Third, employees must be *compensated* for the work performed. For those organizations whose employees are represented by unions, it is necessary to develop policy statements concerning *labor-management relations*.

Staffing

Staffing policies affect an organization in two ways. First, effective staffing reflects itself by increasing the general level of competence of employees in the performance of their assigned duties. Secondly, staffing policies have a direct bearing upon the mobility of employees from one position to another within the organization, a factor that can contribute significantly to the motivation of employees. Three facets of the staffing process are significant in determining its effectiveness. Selection is a term that refers for the most part to the hiring of new employees who will best fit the needs of the organization. Also, since present employees are often selected to fill vacancies, policies concerning promotion become significant. Finally, provisions for the termination of employees must be considered.

Selection. An organization must know the training, education, and prior experience needed for the successful performance of its jobs. Without this information the selection process is little more than a game of chance. If those selected are underqualified, excessive turnover may result from terminations due to poor performance and dissatisfaction. Those who do remain are rarely capable of being promoted. Organizations that select candidates overqualified for the entry-level job may experience excessive turnover if these people become restless because they do not receive promotions. Also, it may be necessary to pay more than the entry-level job is actually worth in order to attract highly qualified people. The recruitment of college graduates is an example of hiring overqualified candidates for entering positions in order to have personnel with potential for growth.

Promotion. Strictly defined, *promotion* is vertical movement upward in the organizational hierarchy and usually is associated with an increase in pay. In practice the concept of promotion includes lateral transfers to other positions at the same organizational level since such transfers may be part of a long-range training plan. Also included in the concept of promotion are increased responsibilities in a current position with or without an increase in compensation. In any event, whether the new job is called a promotion, a transfer, or simply results in increased responsibilities, all movements represent a form of employee mobility. Consequently, all are potential motivators since they may satisfy the needs for growth, achievement, increased responsibility, and recognition. Policy statements encouraging promotion from within are effective only if there is a sufficient number of employees with the potential for promotion.

Termination. Policies governing the termination of employment have a marked effect upon the mobility of employees. When the phrase "termination of employment" is mentioned, one usually thinks of discharge for cause or resignation. Yet there are other and increasingly more frequent reasons for the termination of employment: to name one, retirement. Policies requiring retirement at a stated age provide opportunities for mobility since positions in the organization become available as incumbents reach the stated age limit. However, a mandatory retirement age may result in some employees, particularly executives, being forced to retire despite their potential contribution to the company. Ideally retirement policies should be flexible with provisions for extended service on a part-time or consulting basis and with provision for early retirement.

Development

Policies concerning the development of personnel are related to the policies established for promotion. For organizations committed to promotion from within, the development of personnel is viewed as a vital function since it provides the means for continued organizational development and performance. However, for those organizations that elect to fill vacancies with outside personnel, development may be regarded as a chore that should make minimal demands with respect to time and expense.

Either term, training or development, refers to the process of learning. However, the term *training* is used with greater frequency when the development of hourly employees is discussed, while the term *development* is used more often when referring to the development of managers. This distinction in terminology is observed in the discussion that follows.

Training. Training begins with first impressions. Orientation programs are designed to control first impressions. The extent of employee orientation may range from no formal program whatsoever, with the employees being directed to their work places and not even knowing their supervisors' names, to a carefully structured introduction to the organization. A well-planned orientation not only familarizes employees with all aspects of their immediate work situation, but also acquaints them with the nature of the organization, its objectives, and their roles in the attainment of those objectives. Orientation affords the organization an opportunity to create a favorable first impression.

The area of greatest concern in the training of hourly employees, both clerical and operative, is the development of job skills. The methods used in developing these skills vary considerably and include on-the-job training and a combination of on-the-job experience and formal classroom training. By far the most widely used method is on-the-job training which may be informal instruction by the supervisor or a carefully planned sequence of activities with a formal assessment of achievement. Reliance upon on-the-job training as a means of developing skills requires that supervisors be prepared as trainers if the method is to be most effective.

Management Development. Three terms are used, often interchangeably, to designate programs classified as development. These terms are: *executive development*, *management development*, and *organization development*. However, each term carries a slightly different connotation. "Executive development" emphasizes the development of the individual executive; "management development" indicates a plan for the development of all members of management, and "organization development" implies that the entire management structure is involved, not as individuals, but as members of the organization, so that the organization can function in a different or improved manner. Regardless of the program undertaken there is a twofold responsibility for its success: that of the organization and that of individuals.

Compensation

Compensation is defined as money paid for work performed. In establishing compensation policies, there are three major considerations. First is the selection of criteria to determine the level or amount of compensation, and second is a determination concerning the method of payment. In addition to payment received for work performed, referred to as a wage or salary, employees also receive other benefits — vacations, holidays, insurance, sick leave — that are economic in nature and may be considered a part of the total compensation plan. These are referred to as employee benefit plans.

Amount of Compensation. Determining the amount of compensation to be paid for a given job is not an easy task since there is no single criterion applicable to all companies or even to the same company over a period of time. At least three criteria are used by most companies in determining the level of compensation; however, the significance assigned each criterion varies considerably. The three criteria are: area rates, industry rates, and internal rate structure equity.

For many businesses the rates paid in a given geographic area are the controlling factor in determining wage levels. The geographic area encompasses the labor market that a company draws upon; thus, it may consist of a single, small community or a vast metropolitan complex. When rates higher than those paid in the area are established, it may be possible to secure better employees. When rates lower than those of the area are adopted, increased turnover, absenteeism, and poor performance may result. Area rates are the chief determinant in setting the level of payment of many clerical workers and employees of local retail establishments.

For larger industrial firms the prevailing rates of the specific industry may be the factor given the most weight. Industry patterns are prevalent in the manufacture of steel, autos, chemicals, and aircraft. To a large extent, industry rates are the result of collective bargaining agreements between the member firms of an industry and the unions representing that industry.

In addition to the determination of wage levels by either area or industry rates (external factors), internal criteria must also be satisfied. Within each organizational unit, such as a plant or headquarters office, there should be an equitable relationship between the amount paid for jobs requiring different levels of skill, responsibility, and training. Equitable pay structures are developed through the use of *job evaluation* procedures, a technique of weighting the various factors necessary for the performance of each job.

Method of Payment. Once the amount of compensation has been determined as the result of a judicious weighting of internal and external criteria, a method of payment must be selected. Fundamentally there are two methods of payment. One method is to pay for time spent on the job; the other is to pay for the amount of work produced. There is, of course, the possibility of a combined payment for both time and amount produced. However, such combinations are usually regarded as payment for work and are classed as incentive plans.

Payment for time is applicable to all levels of the organization even though the unit of time varies considerably. Production workers are paid for the actual number of hours worked, and the amount earned is usually computed and paid on a weekly basis. Time for nonexempt clerical employees, those who must be paid for overtime, is computed on a weekly basis and payment may be received weekly, semimonthly, or monthly. Although clerical workers are expected to work a predetermined number of hours each week, policy decisions determine whether or not pay is received for time not worked due to absence or tardiness. Those employees who are exempt from the provisions of the law requiring payment of overtime are called salaried employees, and their time is computed on a monthly basis with payment either monthly or semimonthly.

Payment for work performed, whether it be the piece rate of the garment industry with no hourly guarantee for time spent on the job or an hourly rate with additional pay for work produced in excess of a stated standard, rests upon two assumptions. First, it is assumed that the worker has control over the amount of work that can be produced; and second, that the worker will respond to the monetary incentive and earn more money by increasing output. The second assumption leads to the designation of compensation based on the work produced as incentive compensation plans, or more simply, *incentive plans*.[5]

Employee Benefit Plans. Unlike compensation which is directly related to the job performed, employee benefits are not directly related to the job itself; instead, they are peripheral to the job and are aptly called "fringe benefits." Included among the many fringe benefits are retirement plans, educational plans, tuition rebates, various forms of insurance, sick leave, recreation programs, supplemental unemployment compensation, and other items intended to improve the welfare of the employee. Employee benefits must be at competitive levels in order to attract and retain employees.[6]

Labor-Management Relations

The above discussion of staffing, development, and compensation is presented in a manner which implies that these are policies to be determined solely by the management of an organization. Such is not usually the case, particularly when employees are represented by a labor union, since unions are entitled to bargain for "wages, hours, and other terms and conditions of employment."[7] In addition, unions can and do use the strike as an economic weapon to obtain concessions from management. Though not participating formally in the development of personnel policies, labor unions have a marked impact upon policy statements. The impact is not limited to those organizations whose employees are union members but extends to nonunion employers competing in the same labor market or industry. The threat of unionization has forced many employers to meet or exceed union gains in wages and benefits in an effort to avoid unionization.

Organizational Climate. The major policy consideration is that of determining the organizational climate within which a given set of labor-management relations are to occur. Frequently the nature of these relationships is described as ranging from open hostility to one of cooperative effort between management and labor. Open hostility

---

[5]This subject is discussed in Chapter 16, pp. 383–388.
[6]See Chapter 16 for a discussion concerning the motivational values of employee benefit plans, pp. 391–393.
[7]Labor Management Relations Act of 1947 as amended, Sec. 8(d).

most likely occurs during union organization and the negotiation of the initial labor agreement. A more mature relationship between labor and management is often described as a business relationship and is similar in many respects to the relationship that exists between a company and its suppliers and customers. The open hostility disappears and each side recognizes the responsibilities and rights of the other. The ultimate in labor-management relations is evidenced by complete cooperation and understanding on the part of both the union and the company. It is recognized that a mature cooperative relationship between a company and a union depends on factors other than the establishment of a conducive organizational climate; for example, the goals and strength of the union and the economic condition of the company. However, organizational climate sets the upper limits of the extent to which cooperative efforts may be realized not only in the negotiation of successive labor agreements but also in the manner of their administration.

Nonunion Employees. There is also a decision to be made concerning the treatment of *nonunion employees*. It is seldom that all hourly employees, both clerical and production, belong to a union. Often the production workers are unionized while the hourly clerical employees are not, and in those instances in which clerical employees are unionized they rarely belong to the same bargaining unit as the production employees. When clerical employees are not unionized and hourly production workers are, it should be decided beforehand whether any improvement in wages or benefits extended to production workers should be granted to clerical employees. Or a company may decide to extend to its nonunion employees those increases in wages and benefits that it believes can honestly be made for all employees, union and nonunion alike. Further, the extent to which increases in hourly benefits should be extended to supervisory personnel must be decided. Decisions in these areas may modify or even determine the bargaining tactics of a company.

INTEGRATING POLICY STATEMENTS

The scope of policy statements for each of the four functional areas — finance, marketing, production, and personnel — are summarized in tabular form in Figure 5-1 and serve as the basis of this chapter. Another means of integrating the functional areas is examining them within the context of a servo system as shown in the schematic diagram of Figure 5-3. A *servo system* is a system capable of reacting to changes occurring in any of the subsystems or to changes in the external environment so that a state of balance, or equilibrium, is maintained. Financial inputs to the production process supply the raw materials and the physical facilities necessary to produce the product. Personnel inputs furnish the required skills, knowledge, and judgment.

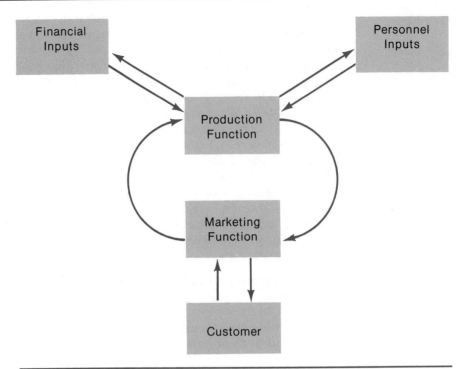

Figure 5-3
INTEGRATING
FUNCTIONAL
AREAS — A
SERVO SYSTEM

The marketing function is charged with the responsibility of selling the product to the customer. At this point, a feedback of information occurs which is interpreted and then relayed to production. If the customer buys the product in sufficient quantity the cycle continues, and production signals for a continuation of financial and personnel inputs. If the demand is greater than the quantity produced, production requests additional inputs. When customers do not buy, the signal from marketing calls for a reduction of inputs.

Note that there are both internal and external feedback loops. The loop between marketing and the customer provides information relating the efforts of the company to its external environment, specifically the customer. Information provided by this loop enables the firm to modify its product or service so that customer demand may continue. If these efforts are not successful, the level of production can be modified to prevent excessive inventory buildup. The other feedback loops are internal to the organization and relate financial and personnel inputs with the functions of production and marketing. Should either of these inputs be inadequate in any respect, the initial impact is felt in the production function, usually by a diminution of that function. The extent and nature of the needs for financial and personnel inputs are the result of information obtained from the combined production-marketing cycle.

Case Problem 5-B provides an opportunity to develop a set of consistent policies for a specific organization.

FORMULATING PERSONNEL POLICIES

Joe Beck, vice-president of industrial relations for Diversified Manufacturing, has just completed some notes that he had been preparing for his conference with Diana Santos, the personnel director who reports to him.

"Diana," he began, "we have been asked to prepare a draft of proposed personnel policies to be submitted to the board of directors when they have their annual meeting here in Chicago next month. It seems that we are being criticized because of what appears to be a lack of consistency in some of the decisions made concerning the personnel function."

"Is that criticism true?" Diana asked.

"I believe there is a good basis for it. Here are some of the incidents that have been brought to my attention." Joe handed Diana the notes he had been preparing. The following is a copy of Joe's notes:

1. In the western division's Los Angeles plant, there was a 45-day strike because the company insisted that an incentive plan be installed as a way to raise average earnings of employees. The union had proposed a general wage increase to bring the rates up to the average of the area. As the strike progressed, it became clear that the real issue was one of permitting union participation in setting time standards. The company stated that determining standards was a company prerogative and no concern of the union. Yet, in a New York plant a job evaluation plan had been installed with joint union-management participation.

2. The general manager of the eastern division responsible for both manufacturing and marketing had attended several management development seminars at the request of the president. These seminars emphasized the need for the establishment of a cooperative organizational climate as the backdrop for labor-management relations. Later other eastern division managers attended similar programs. Some of these managers were then transferred to the western division and have reported that they feel as though they were working for a different company. One even said that if he could not return to the eastern division he would resign.

3. The basis for determining wage levels is not clear. In the eastern division the company's position is that the area wage should be the basis for determining the wage level; yet, in the western division the company argues that the average of the industry, rather than the geographic area average, should determine the wage level. The union says the company is inconsistent.

4. Employee benefit programs are uniform throughout all plants in both divisions. As a result, there are locations where hospitalization benefits adequately cover the cost of hospitalization, and there are locations where the benefits received are inadequate. Uniform practices are also followed with respect to vacations, holidays, and leaves of absence; and, as in the case of the hospitalization benefits, there are instances where company practices are more liberal than those of other companies in the area and there are situations where company practices fall short of area standards.

5. The eastern division reimburses all employees for expenses for tuition and books after the completion of any course in an accredited school or college. This includes trade courses, secretarial courses, and degree courses. In addition, employees with five or more years' seniority are granted leaves of absence with one-half pay for

periods of one year in order to complete their college work. The manager of the eastern division contends that such programs contribute to the division's ability to promote from within. The western division has no subsidies for self-improvement.

6. In the eastern division the plant supervisors, along with other members of management, attend a regularly scheduled monthly dinner meeting to discuss production schedules and methods for the coming month and to review performance of the past month. No supervisory meetings are held in the western division.

After reading these six incidents, Diana returned the list to Joe and said, "It almost seems as though we are talking about two different companies."

"It certainly does, and our job is to develop some policies that will bring these two divisions together. Try and get a draft of such policies for me within the next couple of days."

PROBLEMS

1. What key determination must be made before any policies can be developed for this company?
2. Is it necessary, or even desirable, for a company to have consistent personnel policies within separate operating divisions? Give reasons to support each point of view.
3. Develop a proposed set of personnel policies for this company.

CHAPTER QUESTIONS FOR STUDY AND DISCUSSION

1. What measures are commonly used to measure profit? What are the advantages and limitations of each of the methods?
2. For what purposes does a company generally seek to secure long-term capital? Short-term capital? What factors should be considered when choosing among the various means of obtaining long-term capital; i.e., stock, bonds, mortgages, or long-term notes?
3. What policy decisions must be made regarding the utilization of capital? Discuss the effects of various types of imbalances in the allocation of capital.
4. Cite examples of the marketing policy questions that must be resolved when considering product diversification, obsolescence, quality, and standardization.
5. Compare the meanings of the phrase "product diversification" when used in reference to marketing policies and when used in reference to production policies. Which meaning is broader?
6. On pages 108–109, inventory is discussed from the standpoint of either a retail or manufacturing organization. How would you apply the same concepts to a service organization such as a firm of public accountants?
7. Show the application of Figure 5-2 to areas other than quality control (for example, the cost of advertising or the optimum number of sales representatives for a company).
8. Discuss the significance of each of the areas of personnel policy. Which is the most important in your opinion? Why?

9. Discuss the relationship between policies concerning promotion and policies established for the development and training of personnel. What effect do policies in the area of labor-management relations have on promotion and training?
10. Figure 5-3 shows a feedback loop between the marketing function and the external environment, the customer. What constitutes the external environment of the personnel function? Of the finance function?

Chapter 6

Management Information Systems

Case Problem 6-A

THE PARABLE OF THE SPINDLE

Once upon a time the president of a large chain of short-order restaurants attended a lecture on "Human Relations in Business and Industry." He attended the lecture in the hope he would learn something useful. His years of experience had led him to believe that if human relations problems ever plagued any business, then they certainly plagued the restaurant business.

The speaker discussed the many pressures which create human relations problems. He spoke of psychological pressures, sociological pressures, conflicts in values, conflicts in power structure, and so on. The president did not understand all that was said, but he did go home with one idea. If there were so many different sources of pressure, maybe it was expecting too much of his managers to

Reprinted from "The Parable of the Spindle" by Elias H. Porter, *Harvard Business Review*, May–June 1962. Copyright © 1962 by the President and Fellows of Harvard College; all rights reserved. The parable presented in this article, pages 58–61, is attributed to Professor William Foote Whyte of Cornell University. The remainder of the article discusses the spindle in the light of current systems theory. Mr. Porter is a member of the research staff of System Development Corporation, Santa Monica, California.

think they would see them all, let alone cope with them all. The thought occurred to him that maybe he should bring in a team of consultants from several different academic disciplines and have each contribute his part to the solution of the human relations problems.

And so it came to pass that the president of the restaurant chain and his top-management staff met one morning with a sociologist, a psychologist, and an anthropologist. The president outlined the problem to the scientists and spoke of his hope that they might come up with an interdisciplinary answer to the human relations problems. The personnel manager presented exit-interview findings which he interpreted as indicating that most people quit their restaurant jobs because of too much sense of pressure caused by the inefficiencies and ill tempers of co-workers.

This was the mission which the scientists were assigned: find out why the waitresses break down in tears; find out why the cooks walk off the job; find out why the managers get so upset that they summarily fire employees on the spot. Find out the cause of the problems, and find out what to do about them.

Later, in one of the plush conference rooms, the scientists sat down to plan their attack. It soon became clear that they might just as well be three blind men, and the problem might as well be the proverbial elephant. Their training and experience had taught them to look at events in different ways. They decided that inasmuch as they couldn't speak each other's languages, they might as well pursue their tasks separately. Each went to a different city and began his observations in his own way.

First to return was the sociologist. In his report to top management he said:

"I think I have discovered something that is pretty fundamental. In one sense it is so obvious that it has probably been completely overlooked before. It is during the rush hours that your human relations problems arise. That is when the waitresses break out in tears. That is when the cooks grow temperamental and walk off the job. That is when your managers lose their tempers and dismiss employees summarily."

After elaborating on this theme and showing several charts with sloping lines and bar graphs to back up his assertions, he came to his diagnosis of the situation. "In brief, gentlemen," he stated, "you have a sociological problem on your hands." He walked to the blackboard and began to write. As he wrote, he spoke:

"You have a stress pattern during the rush hours. There is stress between the customer and the waitress. . . .

"There is stress between the waitress and the cook. . . .

"And up here is the manager. There is stress between the waitress and the manager. . . .

"And between the manager and the cook. . . .

"And the manager is buffeted by complaints from the customer.

"We can see one thing which, sociologically speaking, doesn't seem right. The manager has the highest status in the restaurant. The cook has the next highest status. The waitresses, however, are always 'local hire' and have the lowest status. Of course, they have higher status than bus boys and dish washers but certainly lower status than the cook, and yet they give orders to the cook.

"It doesn't seem right for a lower status person to give orders to a higher status person. We've got to find a way to break up the face-to-face relationship between the waitresses and the cook. We've got to fix it so that they don't have to talk with one another. Now my idea is to put a 'spindle' on the order counter. The 'spindle,' as I choose to call it, is a wheel on a shaft. The wheel has clips on it so the girls can simply put their orders on the wheel rather than calling out orders to the cook."

When the sociologist left the meeting, the president and his staff talked of what had been said. It made some sense. However, they decided to wait to hear from the other scientists before taking any action.

Next to return from his studies was the psychologist. He reported to top management:

"I think I have discovered something that is pretty fundamental. In one sense it is so obvious that it has probably been completely overlooked before. It is during the rush hours that your human relations problems arise. That is when the waitresses break out in tears. That is when the cooks grow temperamental and walk off the job. That is when your managers lose their tempers and dismiss employees summarily."

Then the psychologist sketched on the blackboard the identical pattern of stress between customer, waitress, cook, and management. But his interpretation was somewhat different:

"Psychologically speaking," he said, "we can see that the manager is the father figure, the cook is the son, and the waitress is the daughter. Now we know that in our culture you can't have daughters giving orders to the sons. It louses up their ego structure.

"What we've got to do is to find a way to break up the face-to-face relationship between them. Now one idea I've thought up is to put what I call a 'spindle' on the order counter. It's kind of a wheel on a shaft with little clips on it so that the waitresses can put their orders on it rather than calling out orders to the cook."

What the psychologist said made sense, too, in a way. Some of the staff favored the status-conflict interpretation while others thought the sex-conflict interpretation to be the right one; the president kept his own counsel.

The next scientist to report was the anthropologist. He reported:

"I think I have discovered something that is pretty fundamental. In one sense it is so obvious that it has probably been completely overlooked before. It is during the rush hours that your human relations problems arise. That is when the waitresses break out in tears. That is when the cooks grow temperamental and walk off the job. That is when your managers lose their tempers and dismiss employees summarily."

After elaborating for a few moments he came to his diagnosis of the situation. "In brief, gentlemen," he stated, "you have an anthropological problem on your hands." He walked to the blackboard and began to sketch. Once again there appeared the stress pattern between customer, waitress, cook, and management.

"We anthropologists know that man behaves according to his value systems. Now, the manager holds as a central value the continued growth and development of the restaurant organization. The cooks tend to share this central value system, for as the organization prospers, so do they. But the waitresses are a different story. The only reason most of them are working is to help supplement the family income. They couldn't care less whether the organization thrives or not as long as it's a decent place to work. Now, you can't have a noncentral value system giving orders to a central value system.

"What we've got to do is to find some way of breaking up the face-to-face contact between the waitresses and the cook. One way that has occurred to me is to place on the order counter an adaptation of the old-fashioned spindle. By having a wheel at the top of the shaft and putting clips every few inches apart, the waitresses can put their orders on the wheel and not have to call out orders to the cook. Here is a model of what I mean."

When the anthropologist had left, there was much discussion of which scientist was right. The president finally spoke. "Gentlemen, it's clear that these men don't agree on the reason for conflict, but all have come up with the same basic idea about the spindle. Let's take a chance and try it out."

And it came to pass that the spindle was introduced throughout the chain of restaurants. It did more to reduce the human relations problems in the restaurant industry than any other innovation of which the restaurant people knew. Soon it was copied. Like wildfire the spindle spread from coast to coast and from border to border.

PROBLEMS

1. In your opinion, which of the three scientists offered the most plausible explanation of the restaurant's problems?
2. Are the personnel problems observed by the owner "problems" or are they "symptoms"? Defend your answer.
3. In recommending the spindle, the scientists are tacitly admitting that the restaurant is a form of system. Name the kind of system they are thinking of and show how the restaurant meets the requirements of a system.
4. Prepare a chart showing the flow of information in the restaurant and designate the major steps in this process.

Figure 5-3 of Chapter 5, "Planning for Functional Areas," depicts the business firm as a servo system. In the discussion of this figure it is stated that management receives and interprets information from internal and external sources and designates the corrective action necessary for the firm to continue operating successfully. Since management must receive, interpret, and transmit information in order to accomplish its stated objectives, the planning of an effective information system is an important management task. In order to design an information system it is first necessary to establish the meaning of the phrase, information system, and to determine the major functions of such a system. Second, it is necessary to understand fundamental electronic data processing techniques in order to design and evaluate an integrated data processing information system.

FUNCTIONS OF AN INFORMATION SYSTEM

The concept of a *system* implies a dynamic relationship between the components of a larger whole and at the same time permits the recognition of each part as a separate *subsystem* which makes its own unique contribution to the function of the whole. The human nervous system, a communications network, is composed of several subsystems. The autonomic nervous system monitors and controls the gastrointestinal and circulatory systems. The peripheral nervous system receives stimuli, such as heat or cold, from the external environment and warns of impending danger by transmitting a signal of pain. The central nervous system performs an integrative function by coordinating the many subsystems of the body.

In many respects an *information system* is analogous to the human nervous system. Patterns of information flowing from production and marketing may be likened to the impulses transmitted by the autonomic nervous system in controlling the vital functions of the body. Messages from the sales force, field engineers, and buyers are similar to the stimuli transmitted by the peripheral nervous system in that they represent contacts with an external environment. Management, like the central nervous system, must interpret the data received and transmit directions so that corrective action may be taken. Unlike the human organism, however, an organization is not created with a complete information (nervous) system. Therefore, management must design its own system so the organization may function properly. What are the components of such a system, and how does each part contribute to the operation of the complete system?

Components of an Information System

Information systems range in degree of complexity from the very simple as described in Case Problem 6-A, "The Parable of the Spindle," to the complex systems utilized by the major airlines. Regardless of the degree of complexity of the system, an effective information system has the following five parts: (1) *input device* — provides for placing information into the system, (2) *storage unit* — provides for the accumulation of information (performs a memory function), (3) *control unit* — selects the proper information from the storage unit and controls the operations of the processing unit, (4) *processing unit* — handles and interprets the data, and (5) *output device* — presents the original information in usable form after it has been processed.

Contribution of Each Part

Before discussing the contribution of each part of an information system to the functioning of the total system, it is well to recognize that all organizations have some form of information system. When the system functions imperfectly, as illustrated in Case Problem 6-A, the symptoms of such malfunction may become so acute that they appear to be the problem. Each of the three scientists consulted by the restaurant owner determined that the problem arose during rush hours; however, each presented a different interpretation of the causes. The sociologist described the situation in terms of stress patterns coupled with the concept of status; the psychologist saw ego involvement arising from a disregard of classic familial authority relationships; and the anthropologist explained the problem in terms of values. Fortunately, all agreed on one solution — an improved information system — though none of the three defined the basic problem as one resulting from the imperfect functioning of an inadequate information system. Let us determine the contribution of each part of the recommended system.

Input Device. The input device recommended as the first step of the new information system is a ticket on which the waitress writes a description of the desired order. Formerly the waitresses called their order to the cook, a method that invites error and confusion. In addition to decreasing the possibility of misunderstanding, a written record provides a means of checking the accuracy of the eventual output and serves as a basis for correcting errors should they occur. When written records are used, it is possible to designate the point of origin; in this instance the initials of the waitress serve that purpose. Further, an input record may serve more than one purpose. When the ticket is returned with the prepared order, it may be used as a bill to be presented to the customer and then retained by the manager as a permanent record of the day's activities. Thus, written inputs minimize the introduction of error, provide a basis for correcting errors when they do occur, indicate the origin of the input, and serve as a permanent record.

Storage Unit. The main contribution of the spindle to the flow of information is the effect it has upon the cook's work. With orders of the waitresses attached to the revolving spindle, it is no longer necessary for the cook to remember each order. The spindle is performing a function formerly performed by the cook's memory; consequently, a storage unit is frequently referred to as a *memory unit*.

Rarely does information enter a system at a uniform rate; instead, the flow of information during a normal business day forms a chart with many peaks and valleys. The introduction of a storage unit into an information system makes it possible to control the rate of flow to subsequent units. The spindle storage unit has another important feature in that data may be drawn from it without reference to the sequence followed in putting information into the system. Storage units that permit the withdrawal of information without regard to the sequence of input are called *random access* units. If the tickets had been placed in a box rather than on a spindle, the cook would be relieved of remembering each order and could control the rate of flow of information from the box by selecting one or two tickets at a time. However, the cook would see only the top ticket, and could not combine several orders so they might be filled more efficiently. The visual display of the spindle allows random access without regard to the sequence in which the orders are received. At a single glance, the cook has access to all written tickets and can determine the number of steak dinners on order, thus enabling him to prepare similar orders simultaneously. The spindle adequately performs the functions of a storage unit in that it stores, or remembers, the information; aids in regulating the flow of information to subsequent units in the system; and permits random access to the stored information.

Control Unit. In an information system the influence of the control unit is felt throughout the entire system. Though the unit cannot control the rate at which information enters the system, it can reject those items not suitable to the system or incapable of interpretation. The cook, who functions simultaneously as a control and a processing unit, may reject an order that is not on the menu (not suitable for the system) or ask that a ticket be rewritten because it is illegible. However, the cook cannot control the rate at which waitresses enter the orders.

In exercising control the cook may determine the sequence in which orders are selected from the random access memory unit. The control unit also determines the method to be used in processing the order and checks the final results to make sure that the original input request is fulfilled. In addition, the output of the processing unit is monitored in respect to quality, quantity, and rate of output. In complex systems employing electronic data processing equipment, the control unit and the processing unit are separate pieces of electronic equipment; yet the control function remains the same — checking the flow of information into the system, determining the sequence in which material will be drawn from the memory unit, setting up the methods to be used in processing, and controlling the quality, quantity, and rate of output.

Processing Unit. The chief task of the processing unit is one of interpreting information so that the output of the system conforms to requirements laid down by the control unit. Since the cook is performing the processing function as well as the control function, it is his task to interpret the symbols on the tickets and translate these symbols into action that produces the specified output — orders of food. Simple arithmetic computations are necessary to determine the number of orders on each ticket, and on occasion the cook may compute the total number of identical orders capable of being prepared at the same time, thereby increasing efficiency of output. In more sophisticated systems, computers form the processing unit. However, the function remains the same — the interpretation and manipulation of symbolic data to produce the desired output.

Output Device. The output of an information system is the final step in the sequence. Frequently the output of the processing unit is additional information, usually directions requiring action on the part of subsequent elements in the system. The cook could, for example, interpret the information stored on the spindle and give directions to his assistants, indicating the work that each is to perform. Or immediately after interpretation, the information may be converted into action that fulfills the objectives of the system, in this instance, the preparation of food. If the end result of the system is information, it should be capable of being checked against the original input so that the reliability of the entire process is insured. In our present example the original ticket may be placed with the prepared food, which enables both the cook and the waitress who placed the original information (order) into the system to check the accuracy of the final result.

In addition to providing a basis for discussing the major parts of an information system, "The Parable of the Spindle" points up the value of viewing business problems as occurring within a system rather than as isolated problems to be analyzed and solved as separate entities. Suppose that none of the scientists had recommended the installation of a spindle, but that one had recommended a more tolerant cook; another, a more stable manager; and the third, the selection of waitresses with a higher degree of emotional stability. Such recommendations represent an approach that emphasizes the strength of each element rather than the design of the system itself. The solution that was adopted, the installation of a spindle, illustrates the systems approach to the management process. Seymour Tilles has suggested that the manager's job is essentially one of managing systems and that a manager should define the company as a system, establish objectives for the system, create formal subsystems, and then integrate all such systems.[1] The chief advantage to be derived from regarding the

---

[1]Seymour Tilles, "The Manager's Job — A Systems Approach," *Harvard Business Review*, Vol. 41 (January-February, 1963), pp. 73–81; Richard A. Johnson, Fremont E. Kast, and James E. Roszenweig, *The Theory and Management of Systems* (3d ed.; New York: McGraw-Hill Book Co., 1973). These works emphasize the business organization as a complex of systems and the manager as a manager of systems. *The Theory and Management of Systems* relates the systems concept to the management functions.

manager's job as one of managing systems is the recognition of the interdependence and contribution of each part to the whole system and the realization that failure to meet objectives may be due to an improper design of the system itself rather than the result of shortcomings attributable to the individual components of the system.

ELECTRONIC DATA PROCESSING

"The Parable of the Spindle" provides a means of illustrating the components of an information system and the importance of recognizing the management of systems as an important element of the manager's job. Obviously, the number of business situations in which a spindle may be used as a storage unit is limited; also, most business situations are so complex that an information system that relies solely upon human capabilities for the functions of control, interpretation, and output of data would have extremely limited effectiveness. Fortunately, there are techniques available for the design of effective communication systems for those situations too complex for the spindle and the powers of human memory and reasoning. Modern communication, or information, systems rely upon the use of electronic data processing (EDP) equipment which may be combined into an integrated data processing (IDP) system. In discussing electronic data processing, we will touch upon its development, the steps in the design of an electronic data processing system, and an evaluation of electronic data processing.

Before discussing the development of electronic data processing, it is necessary to define some commonly used terms. *Data processing* refers to the act of handling information or data, either manually or automatically. Typical of the manual methods of handling data is the work of clerical employees such as bookkeepers, accountants, billing clerks, and payroll clerks. *Automated data processing* (*ADP*) is the handling of information by machines rather than by human beings. The punched card equipment discussed below is an example of automated data processing. The phrase, *electronic data processing* (*EDP*), means that the data is processed at high speed by electronic equipment. When the word electronic was first used to describe data processing equipment, it designated equipment that utilized the vacuum tube rather than the earlier electromechanical devices. The term electronic is still used to describe data processing units that are completely transistorized and no longer use vacuum tubes. Since the computer is the best known example of an electronic data processing unit, the phrase EDP also implies that a computer is part of the electronic data processing system. *Integrated data processing* (*IDP*), sometimes called *management information systems* (*MIS*), refers to the integrated collection, transmission, handling, and use of all data needed for the operation of a business. It must be recognized that there are varying degrees of integration and that technically IDP is not dependent upon any form of automatic equipment. For example, "The Parable of the Spindle" describes an integrated flow of information that is manually operated. However, as the term IDP is now used, it almost always means that EDP is being utilized, but the emphasis is upon the integrative aspects of management information rather than upon the means of processing the data.

Development of EDP

The origin of automated data processing may be traced to Charles Babbage, who in 1823 conceived the idea of a "Difference Engine" to compute and print mathematical tables.[2] Though he worked on this project for 10 years, it was never completed due to difficulties encountered primarily in its manufacture. The next major step in automated data processing occurred in 1890 when Dr. Herman Hollerith developed the now familiar punched card as an aid in tabulating the results of the 1890 census. Information was coded by means of holes punched in the cards; and an electrical contact completed through the holes activated mechanical counters. The first computer, started in 1937 by Professor Howard Aiken of Harvard University in conjunction with the International Business Machines Corporation, was placed in operation in 1944 and is still in use. The computer, the Automatic Sequence Controlled Calculator — Mark I, operated on electromechanical principles with the counters controlled by electrical relays. The first electronic computer, completed at the University of Pennsylvania's Moore School of Engineering in 1946, was called the Electronic Numerical Integrator and Calculator (ENIAC). This computer replaced the relays and counters of Mark I with 18,000 vacuum tubes. By 1950 there were approximately 20 different types of computers in use and in 1960 this number had reached at least 300.[3]

Five Generations of Computers

Estimates of the number of computers in use today vary from 60,000 to 120,000, depending upon whether one considers installations or individual computers within a given organization. In the 25-year period starting with 1950, two things happened. First, an entirely new industry — the computer industry — had grown to maturity; and second, the use of computers in formal organizations had become a way of life. One writer, Frederic G. Withington, identified four generations of computers already in use and foresaw the development of a fifth

---

[2]See Chapter 2, page 21.

[3]It is beyond the scope of this chapter to present a detailed analysis of the construction of electronic data processing equipment. The student is referred to the following reference as a broad source of information concerning the principles of electronic data processing equipment and its application to the behavioral sciences: Harold Borko (ed)., *Computer Applications in the Behavioral Sciences* (Englewood Cliffs: Prentice-Hall, 1962).

generation in the near future.[4] It is well to examine the names and approximate time periods of each of the generations, the hardware and software utilized by each, the major functions performed, and the location of and the effect each generation has had upon the organization. It must be remembered that there is considerable overlap between each of these generations and that many organizations still retain their first computer.

"Gee Whiz" — 1953–1958. The first generation of computers was acquired by large businesses between the years 1953 and 1958. Withington has designated this period as "Gee Whiz," because there was little sound cost justification for the purchase of these machines and one of the underlying motives for their purchase was the belief that in order to be progressive one must own a computer. The hardware, the computer and storage facilities, operated by vacuum tubes with magnetic records as the storage device. There was relatively little software, i.e., standard programs for the processing and compiling of data. The first applications were in formalized accounting systems of organizations, such as payroll and billing. As a result the computer was generally assigned to either the controller's or treasurer's office, and in many organizations it remains in that location today.

Though the actual effects of these computers on organization structure and function were relatively small, certain problems did arise. In some organizations there was considerable apprehension concerning possible unemployment. Instead, new jobs were created, such as computer operators and programmers. These positions had to be fitted into existing organizations, and, due to the scarcity of qualified personnel, salary problems arose relative to the rest of the organization.

The Paper Pushers — 1958–1966. The second generation of computers came as the result of technological advances — the development of the transistor and the use of magnetic cores to store information. The second generation was marked by advances in software including systems analysis and input-output controls. Most significant is that the second generation firmly established the use of computers in large-scale operations. Logic systems were improved, and, as a result of the use of transistors in place of vacuum tubes, the computers were able to handle vast amounts of information in an incredibly short period of time. Hence the designation "paper pushers."

During this period *on line* operations became possible; that is, from a remote terminal one could gain access immediately to the information stored in the computer. Classic examples are airline and

[4]Frederic G. Withington, "Five Generations of Computers," *Harvard Business Review*, Vol. 52, No. 4 (July-August, 1974), pp. 99–108. The following discussion of the five generations of computers is based upon Withington's analysis.

hotel reservation systems and stock market quotation systems. Further, these computers made possible the development of the universal credit card industry, the electronic sorting of checks by banks, and many other large-scale applications.

Because of their flexibility and the large amount of information that could be stored and retrieved, second generation computers appeared at all levels of the organization. These computers are used not only in the controller's or treasurer's office but also in marketing departments, to maintain inventory controls, and for the control of production, especially in the process industries such as petroleum. They are placed in divisional and field offices, thereby giving field managers and operating personnel immediate access to information that is useful and necessary in their operations.

The effects on the organization were marked. There was a significant impact on clerical personnel; however, technological unemployment did not materialize. There are two reasons: first, the length of time required to install EDP equipment is rather long (approximately two years); and as a result normal attrition, rather than layoffs, is the rule. Second, installation of EDP results in a change in the nature of clerical jobs rather than in a reduction in the number of clerical jobs in most installations. For example, check sorting by hand became a thing of the past, but new jobs such as keypunch operators were created. There is little evidence that the introduction of computers has meant a reduction in clerical personnel.

Groups of EDP specialists at the higher levels of the organization were developing the systems to be used in the second generation of computers. In some instances there was alienation of supervisors who felt that their jobs were being taken over by machines, and there was also criticism of the rigidities imposed by predetermined programs. On the other hand, some field operating personnel recognized that they were now able to have information needed to do their jobs properly.

The Communicators — 1966–1974. The third generation is called "the communicators" primarily because personnel using remote terminals can communicate with the computer, which is usually located in a central headquarters. The third generation is the result of another technological advance. Just as the transistor replaced the vacuum tube, the development of integrated circuitry replaced the transistorized computer and made possible the development of large-scale computers. Since most of the large-scale computers of this generation have remote terminals, computer operating controls became more significant. Consequently, the development of software became highly critical. Programs to control communications with the computer, to determine the sequence of processing information, and to control the type of processing for each kind of information by the computer itself became necessary. The functions that can be performed by the third generation seem almost limitless. Sales orders can be handled rapidly, thus improving customer service. Other business operations such as manufacturing can be improved, and in general there is a reduction in processing time.

The organizational changes resulting from the installation of the third generation of computers were significant. Most of these large-scale computers were placed in central locations because of their size and capacity with the result that most divisional and field managers had to give up their second generation computers and become dependent upon the central system. Also, these computers required the development of a highly centralized management information system group. Division managers who are assigned responsibility and held accountable to their superiors for the performance of their organizational unit are understandably apprehensive when they are no longer in control of the information necessary to operate their unit. Also, these computers require highly specialized professionals to develop both operating and informations systems. The problem is acute, because the supply of such personnel is limited.

The organizational impact of the third generation of computers is well illustrated by a store manager who is responsible for the operations of the store but who does not know the result of the operations for a given week until the information is sent from a central office. Often the statement is sent by mail and is received during the middle of the following week. However, the manager's superior has the information on Monday morning immediately following the close of the previous week. The store manager may receive a telephone call early Monday, but at that time may have no knowledge of prior operations and consequently is unable to answer questions intelligently or to explain the operations. Thus the manager becomes somewhat defensive and may believe that the superior is being unfair. These problems can be and are being resolved by most organizations, yet during the early installation of large-scale centralized information handling, the relationships between the organization's headquarters and unit managers often become somewhat strained.

The Information Custodians — 1974–c. 1982. We are now into the fourth generation of computers, called "information custodians," since they are capable of storing extremely large amounts of information. In addition, they can be tied to satellite computers dispersed geographically throughout the organization. The fourth generation is an evolutionary step and has not yet been fully exploited. These computers are capable of forming what is termed a *data base*, a large mass of information from which independent applications may be drawn. As indicated, the fourth generation of both hardware and software are still in their early stages of development, but it is expected that by the end of the 1970s fully developed hardware and software will be available.

Those organizations using the fourth generation anticipate substantial changes in management structure. Many of the large-scale functions such as personnel, procurement, and cash management, will be centralized simply because it is more economical to centralize these functions. At the same time, it is expected that information needed to make decisions for the operation of branches will be made available to branch managers through the use of satellite computers drawing from the centralized data bases.[5]

The potential impact of the fourth generation of computers upon organizational structure and function is illustrated by a bank or other financial institution that formerly required loans above a stated amount to be approved by the parent organization. With a satellite computer and access to centralized data including the credit ratings of potential borrowers, branch managers are now able to approve the same loans that formerly required approval from headquarters. After all, they have the same information available to them that formerly was available only to the central bank.

Action Aids — c. 1982–? Though fifth generation computers are not in use at the present time, research and development work is going forward and it appears that the fifth generation will be oriented primarily toward assisting managers in making decisions. Therefore, fifth generation computers may be appropriately termed "action aids." The functions performed by the "paper pushers" and the "information custodians" will still exist, but the new computers will aid primarily in decision making. The technology is uncertain, but the fifth generation will possibly be capable of reading handwriting and using laser equipment. New software, particularly simulation programs and new computer languages, will be developed. There will undoubtedly be intraorganizational and interorganizational linkage between computers. Thus it will be possible for a plant manager to determine immediately the status of a production schedule or inventory level. The plant manager would also be notified automatically when inventory falls below a predetermined level. Computers will link vendor and supplier, possibly carrying out predetermined communication of information. The automatic transfer of funds from one financial institution to another is in the near future.

Because the fifth generation is still in the developmental stage, its potential effect upon organizations is not known. There will undoubtedly be centralized data processing units. Large companies may have their own such organizational units, and smaller organizations may

---

[5]For a complete discussion of the concept of data bases; that is, large amounts of related data in a central location, the following are recommended: George Schussel, "Business EDP Moves to Data Bases," *Business Horizons*, Vol. 15, No. 6 (December, 1972), pp. 73–84; Richard L. Nolan, "Computer Data Bases: The Future is Now," *Harvard Business Review*, Vol. 51, No. 5 (September–October, 1973), pp. 98–114.

utilize service bureaus; that is, firms specializing in providing computer services to other organizations. As new programs are developed, remote terminal users should be able to gain access to and retrieve information from the centralized information system so that the decision-making processes will be improved.

The feasibility of the fifth generation of computers for most organizations is seriously questionable. One reason is that it is almost impossible to anticipate all of the information needs of a large organization at one time. Second, few organizations could afford the cost of the fifth generation which, according to Withington, is estimated to be between $10 million and $50 million. Few organizations can afford this amount of money in a lump sum, thus an annual capital budget must be prepared for the development of an organization-wide information system.[6]

Designing an EDP System

Electronic data processing is a powerful tool capable of handling large quantities of information in very short periods of time. Ideally the various applications of EDP should result in an integrated flow of information among all levels of the organization so that management has relevant and timely information for decision making. The following discussion outlines the major steps in designing an EDP system, reviews some of the problems encountered in each step, and offers suggested ways of overcoming these problems.[7]

Designate Authority. Before determining objectives and analyzing the present information system, it is necessary to designate authority for planning the system and its later administration. Usually it is best to choose one person to be responsible for both planning and administration since the knowledge gained of the organization and its information needs during the planning phase of the program is invaluable in administering the program. The person chosen should have a thorough knowledge of the company and a reputation that merits the confidence of the company's top officials. In small and medium-size firms the controller is usually designated, since the controller generally has a broad knowledge of the company and usually administers a large part of the present information system. In large companies — with several plants, a diverse product line, and several sales offices — it is best to create an information function independent of the controller's office. Frequently the manager of EDP carries the title of vice-president, administrative services. Regardless of title, the person in charge

---

[6]There is serious question as to whether a large organization can develop a single (integrated) management information system. For example, see John Dearden, "MIS is a Mirage," *Harvard Business Review*, Vol. 50, No. 1 (January–February, 1972), pp. 90–99.

[7]Joel E. Ross, "Computers: Their Use and Misuse," *Business Horizons*, Vol. 15, No. 2 (April, 1972), pp. 55–60.

of planning and administering EDP should report to the chief operating head of the company.

State Objectives. Company-wide objectives are normally expressed in terms of accomplishments in specific functional areas and do not specify the information needed to achieve these goals. Objectives should be reexamined and expressed as information needed for their achievement. A way of gathering the information required to meet objectives is to ask each department manager to develop the information needs required to improve the performance of that department. This approach, in addition to aiding in restating objectives, serves to acquaint the organization with the benefits to be derived from EDP and helps to allay fears associated with the introduction of automatic, high-speed processes. Figure 6-1 shows the information needed for the management processes of planning and control as well as the information needed for the major functional areas.

Analyze Present Systems. There are two divergent theories concerning the extent to which present information systems should be examined in order to develop a new EDP system.[8] One of these theories holds that there should be a detailed analysis of present systems even though the information gained is not completely relevant. Most companies have established procedures to describe a series of related tasks, such as payroll procedures, employment procedures, or accounting procedures. Procedures are usually implemented by methods, a descriptive statement of the precise way to perform a given job. Procedures and methods are examples of the flow of information; however, it is information flowing primarily in one direction since the major emphasis in developing procedures and methods is that of describing the manner in which a given task or job is to be accomplished. Since the purpose of procedures and methods is to accomplish work, rather than develop information for an integrated system, a detailed analysis of an existing system is of questionable value. Detailed analysis of present systems may build mountains of data that obscure real information needs.

The second theory holds that only information pertinent to the meeting of company information objectives should be analyzed and recorded. Selecting only pertinent data not only reduces the amount of work but also avoids one of the dangers inherent in the first theory — unconsciously trying to fit powerful electronic data processing techniques to existing procedures and methods that were originally designed to direct manual operations. In practice, a middle ground is

[8]James D. Gallagher, *Management Information Systems and the Computer* (New York: American Management Association, 1961), Research Study No. 51, p. 127. Mr. Gallagher's research study surveys the problems generally associated with information systems and contains two case studies of information systems of special interest: the American Airlines Sabre System and the system used by Sylvania Electric Products, Inc.

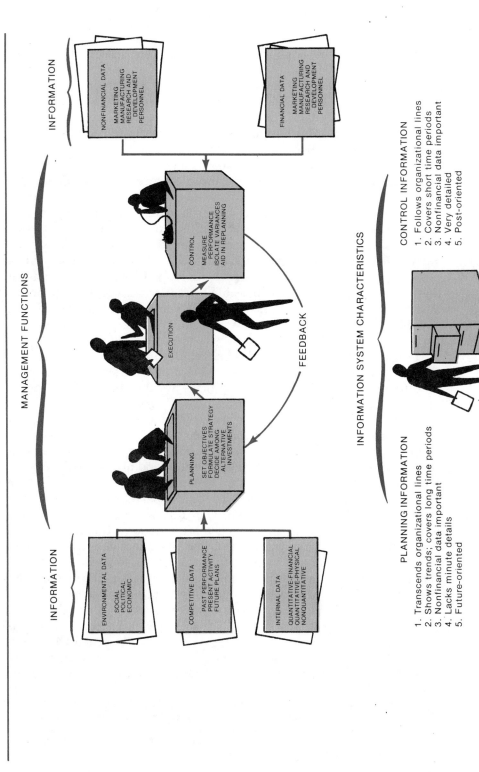

Figure 6-1
ANATOMY OF MANAGEMENT INFORMATION

INFORMATION

MANAGEMENT FUNCTIONS

INFORMATION

NONFINANCIAL DATA

MARKETING
MANUFACTURING
RESEARCH AND
DEVELOPMENT
PERSONNEL

FINANCIAL DATA

MARKETING
MANUFACTURING
RESEARCH AND
DEVELOPMENT
PERSONNEL

CONTROL

MEASURE
PERFORMANCE
ISOLATE VARIANCES
AID IN REPLANNING

EXECUTION

PLANNING

SET OBJECTIVES
FORMULATE STRATEGY
DECIDE AMONG
ALTERNATIVE
INVESTMENTS

FEEDBACK

ENVIRONMENTAL DATA

SOCIAL
POLITICAL
ECONOMIC

COMPETITIVE DATA

PAST PERFORMANCE
PRESENT ACTIVITY
FUTURE PLANS

INTERNAL DATA

QUANTITATIVE-FINANCIAL
QUANTITATIVE-PHYSICAL
NONQUANTITATIVE

INFORMATION SYSTEM CHARACTERISTICS

PLANNING INFORMATION

1. Transcends organizational lines
2. Shows trends; covers long time periods
3. Nonfinancial data important
4. Lacks minute details
5. Future-oriented

CONTROL INFORMATION

1. Follows organizational lines
2. Covers short time periods
3. Nonfinancial data important
4. Very detailed
5. Post-oriented

Source: D. Ronald Daniel, "Management Information Crisis," **Harvard Business Review**, Vol. 39 (September-October, 1961), p. 114. Copyright© 1961 by the President and Fellows of Harvard College; all rights reserved.

usually chosen. Thorough knowledge of present information is required, but the collection of voluminous data is avoided since the purpose and techniques of EDP differ from those of the existing system.

Install Short-Range Improvements. Some experts say that a complete management information system must be developed before making any changes in present procedures. On the other hand, there is much to be gained by installing short-range improvements provided such steps meet with the goals of a more comprehensive EDP system. Critics of short-range improvements state that until the entire systems analysis is complete, there is no way of knowing ultimate equipment requirements; however, modern EDP equipment is of modular design, and units acquired at a later date are usually compatible with existing units. Further, earlier experience with EDP influences the design of subsequent systems and demonstrates early the benefits resulting from EDP. In some instances it is possible to realize immediate reductions in cost, for example, in applications to inventory control procedures, payroll procedures, or the processing of sales orders.

Prepare for Organizational Change. Despite the many technical problems encountered in the installation of an EDP system, the greatest difficulties experienced by many firms are the effects of EDP upon the organizational structure of the company.[9] One factor is the obvious fear and resistance on the part of employees who might be displaced by electronic data processing equipment. Yet, in many respects, the major problems with people come from middle and top management. Organizational structures usually conform to and are derived from the work patterns of the organization. People doing similar work are grouped into units that may develop into departments. For example, those engaged in scheduling the product through production form the production control department, and those who keep financial records make up the accounting department. Supervisors of departments tend to develop a proprietary interest in the work performed in their departments and the people performing this work. An EDP system, by automating manual operations, frequently eliminates the need for entire departments and their respective supervisors. Consider the plight and attitude of the employees and the supervisor of a payroll department when it is learned that a new system will record the hours worked for each production worker, accumulate the total number of hours for each worker during the pay period, and at the close of the

[9] G. W. Dickson and John K. Simmons, "The Behavioral Side of MIS," *Business Horizons*, Vol. 13, No. 4 (August, 1970), pp. 59–71. Professors Dickson and Simmons discuss fully the behavioral aspects of the installation of a management information system. A similar discussion is found in Fred R. Bahr, "The Man-Machine Confrontation," *Business Horizons*, Vol. 15, No. 5 (October, 1972), pp. 81–86.

period compute all necessary extensions and deductions and print individual checks for the net amount due.[10]

Evaluation of EDP

Few companies have completely integrated data processing systems. However, most EDP installations are hopefully a first step toward an integrated management information system. A question that normally arises whenever the design and installation of EDP is being considered is the matter of cost. It is extremely difficult to develop meaningful figures because each company has unique information needs. Also, rental charges for equipment, depending upon the kind selected and the number of units required, range from a low of $1,000 per month to over $200,000 per month. Should the user decide to purchase equipment, the cost of a fifth generation computer ranges between $10 million and $50 million.[11]

There have been isolated instances where the installation of EDP resulted in marked reductions in the number of clerical personnel, as illustrated by the Treasury Department's installation of a computer programmed to reconcile the government payroll and print checks. This system resulted in a reduction of clerical workers from 755 to 270. In addition, Federal Reserve banks were able to eliminate some 400 employees as the result of this move.[12] However, the personnel reductions experienced by the government are not typical of industry's experience since personnel reductions of this magnitude occur only when an extremely large volume of repetitive clerical work is mechanized. For most companies the number of clerical workers remains the same and many firms have been forced to increase their clerical staff. The reasons for this paradox are not due to the inefficiencies of EDP but are attributable to normal expansion of and the accumulation and use of data not readily available when manual information systems are used.

Although for some companies there are potential savings resulting from a well-planned EDP information system, the major value to be

[10]The following two references are recommended for their discussion concerning the impact of computer technology and EDP upon management organizations: William E. Reif, *Computer Technology and Organization* (Iowa City: Bureau of Business and Economic Research, The University of Iowa, 1968); Floyd E. Moan, "Does Management Practice Lag Behind Theory in the Computer Environment?" *Academy of Management Journal*, Vol. 16, No. 1 (March, 1973), pp. 7–23.

[11]An interesting method of determining the value of a management information system is discussed in Charles A. Gallagher, "Perceptions of the Value of a Management Information System," *Academy of Management Journal*, Vol. 17, No. 1 (March, 1974), pp. 46–55.

[12]*Use of Electronic Data Processing Equipment*, Hearing before the Subcommittee on Post Office and Civil Service, House of Representatives, 80th Congress, 1st Session (Washington: U.S. Government Printing Office, 1959) Appendix A, pp. 34–40.

derived from such an installation is the improved effectiveness of the business organization as an information-decision system. Peter Drucker expresses the value of an improved information-decision system as follows:[13]

> The new organization, whether an army or a business, is above all an information and decision system. Information, ideas, questions, flow from the outside environment as well as from people within. They not only have to be perceived and transmitted; the relevant has to be separated from the merely interesting. Then somebody has to make a decision which in turn has to flow back to the places where it can become effective action. Information and decision systems are around us everywhere; every living being is one, and so is every machine. But the organization is probably the most complex.

One of the major problems of organizations utilizing sophisticated computers is that of security. Case Problem 6-B, Computer Security, outlines some of the difficulties encountered in making the computer secure from fraudulent use and the protection of vital information that should not be released to other than authorized personnel. As yet, there is no method that offers complete security. The purpose of the case is to designate the areas in which computers are most vulnerable to fraudulent use and to show the complexity and difficulty of the overall problem of keeping information secured that is stored in a computer.

Case Problem 6-B
COMPUTER SECURITY

Instances in which computers have been misused for fraudulent purposes are numerous and have been recounted so many times that they are now almost legendary. For example, one enterprising non-employee managed to steal almost $1 million of inventory from a West Coast utility over a two-year period. There is also the Eastern railroad that lost 200 boxcars, and the teller of a New York bank who placed $30,000 a day in bets on the horses for an extended period of time with his favorite bookie. In 1971, there were 12 cases of computerized bank embezzlement with an average loss to the bank in each instance of slightly in excess of a million dollars. One of the most distressing aspects of computer theft is that almost all such thefts have been uncovered accidentally rather than through the normal audit procedure of following "the paper trail." There is no paper trail in many computer operations, thus rendering largely ineffective traditional internal and external audit procedures.

Part of the reason for the difficulty in controlling computer security lies in the very nature of the computer itself. First, the computer was designed to perform rapid calculations and its first applications were of a scientific or mathematical nature. Thus, little thought was given to the problem of security. Second, with the development of remote access terminals it became possible for users either to enter the

[13]Peter Drucker, *Landmarks of Tomorrow* (New York: Harper & Brothers, 1959), p. 92.

main computer of their own organization or to enter the computer of a service bureau on a time-sharing basis with other organizations. Though there are access controls in the form of passwords and codes to screen incoming requests, such codes and passwords cannot be too complicated. The computer is a service tool and a legitimate user does not want to become engaged in an argument with a computer about access for a service for which the user is paying. As a result, these controls are by and large ineffective. Another significant factor is that remote access terminals utilize telephone lines leading to the central computer. Such lines can be tapped by individuals who want to learn the passwords and codes for entry. With a little ingenuity and a minicomputer of their own, they can secure both the operating and processing programs. Also, the very nature of the software, the programs controlling the operation of the computer itself and the application or manipulation of data, is such that it must be susceptible to modification and change by the legitimate user. These same characteristics make software susceptible to modification and change by the illegitimate user.

One authority, Robert Courtney of I.B.M., lists the following six factors, in descending order of importance, as the basis for computer losses:

The largest category, accounting for around half of all losses, is simply errors and omissions by clerical and data-processing employees. Next in order is employee dishonesty. Then come losses of data and equipment in fires; sabotage by disgruntled employees; water damage (i.e., floods and sprinkler system malfunctions); and finally, an 'other' category that includes remote manipulation of the system by outsiders.[14]

Courtney has also found that employee dishonesty since 1972 has risen from fourth place to second place as a cause of computer losses.

In an article entitled "Embezzler's Guide to the Computer," Professor Brandt Allen of the University of Virginia describes six areas in which computer fraud has been committed and the difficulty inherent in establishing adequate controls and security.[15] First, there is disbursement fraud. Usually a dummy company is set up and the computer is instructed to disburse funds to the dummy company for services or products that have not been performed or received. The second major area is in the manipulation of inventory records. In the case of the railroad that lost the 200 boxcars, inventory records showed that the cars were either wrecked or scrapped. In fact, they were sent to a yard where they were repainted, rebuilt, and sold. The manipulation of sales is also an area difficult to control because shipping documents can be changed. Improper bills can be prepared, or excess credits can be arranged and paid to a dummy company. One Canadian department store sent large appliances coded "Special Pricing" to a nonexistent customer at a cost that was a fraction of their real value. Fourth, there is the opportunity for payroll fraud; i.e., keeping employees on the payroll that have long since been terminated. Closely related is the continuation of pension benefits and annuities to employees who are deceased. Finally, accounts receivable can be manipulated.

Though means to make dishonest access to the computer more difficult are in development, several questions raise doubts concerning the value of such means as preventive measures. First, it is estimated that there is approximately $17 billion of current remote

[14]Tom Alexander, "Waiting for the Great Computer Rip-off," Fortune, Vol. 90, No. 1 (July, 1974), pp. 143–150. As indicated by the title of this article, many are apprehensive that large thefts by computer will occur in the future. Courtney's statement appears on p. 144.

[15]Brandt Allen, "Embezzler's Guide to the Computer," Harvard Business Review, Vol. 53, No. 4 (July–August, 1975), pp. 79–89. The six areas discussed are presented in detail by Professor Allen who shows the extreme difficulty of detecting such losses through normal audit procedures. He also emphasizes that manufacturing concerns are as vulnerable to theft and loss as are banks.

access hardware in use. What is to become of this investment if it should be made obsolete? Second, it is estimated that there are over a million people in the country who have some knowledge of programming. If only one percent of these programmers decide to use that knowledge for fraudulent purposes, there are 10,000 programmers available for misappropriation of funds. Finally, there is no reliable estimate of the number of frauds committed. It has been estimated that only one out of a hundred computer frauds are detected and made public. Many companies that detect frauds prefer not to make the matter public.

An unknown number of frauds are not detected. Therefore, there is no accurate estimate of the extent of computer fraud.

PROBLEMS

1. In light of the above outline of the misuses of the computer, would you recommend to a company that they keep vital information (for example, information on patents and product development) stored on computer tapes? Discuss.
2. Do you believe it feasible to design a completely secure computer system? Discuss.

CHAPTER QUESTIONS FOR STUDY AND DISCUSSION

1. Is it possible for an information system to function with one or more of the five components missing? If so, which components could be omitted? If not, why not?
2. Does EDP eliminate the possibility of human error? If not, where is human error most likely to occur?
3. What is meant by "random access" and why is it a desirable feature of a management information system?
4. What is meant by the statement that failure to meet objectives is more often due to an improper design of the system rather than to the shortcomings of the separate components of the system?
5. State what is meant by and give an example of each of the following abbreviations: ADP, EDP, and IDP.
6. When are the meanings of EDP and IDP synonymous?
7. Do you believe that it is possible for a large organization to have a single integrated data processing system or a single management information system? Explain.
8. Which in your opinion is more important — the technological advances that made the successive generations of computers possible or their acceptance and usefulness by large organizations?
9. How does EDP aid the manager in making decisions? Does this necessarily mean that the manager's decisions are easier to make?
10. What is meant by the statement that the major problems of installing an information system are people oriented rather than machine oriented?
11. Comment on the statement: Most companies experience a sharp reduction in the number of clerical personnel as the result of an EDP installation.

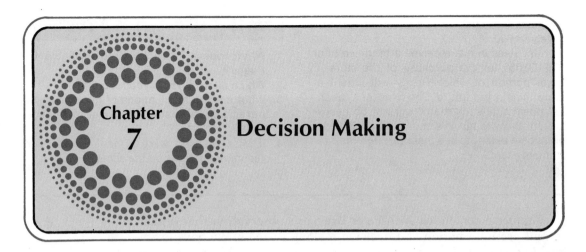

Chapter 7 — Decision Making

Case Problem 7-A

PERSONAL VALUES AND DECISION MAKING

Peggy Gleeson has been employed for the past 11 years as a pharmacist in a large chain of drugstores in a growing metropolitan area. She presently earns $14,000 a year. The organization for which she works is expanding at the rate of three to five new stores each year. This expansion is creating additional managerial positions in the organization, some of which pay as much as $27,000 a year including the company's rather generous profit-sharing plan. Pharmacists are sometimes promoted to the position of store manager and, while such managerial positions have not been open to women in the past, Miss Gleeson believes that such opportunities will become available in the near future.

Recently Peggy's father, who owns his own pharmacy, was forced to retire because of poor health. Mr. Gleeson hired a recent graduate pharmacist on a temporary basis to operate the pharmacy, and Peggy's mother continues to manage the other departments of the drugstore. Peggy's father would like for her to return home to manage the store which she will ultimately inherit. The small town in which the store is located is experiencing a growth in population because of the completion of a large lake resort development near

the city. As a result, the possibility for growth and expansion of the drugstore is better than it has been for a number of years.

In discussions with her parents, Peggy has found that the present volume of sales of the drugstore is about $100,000 a year and the gross margin on sales is roughly $39,000. Before Mr. Gleeson's retirement, he and Mrs. Gleeson were drawing salaries of $22,000, and had additional operating expenses of about $16,000 annually, which left a net profit before taxes of $1,000 a year. Since Mr. Gleeson's retirement, the level of profit from the drugstore has remained basically the same. Mr. Gleeson is presently paying the pharmacist he hired a salary of $12,000, and Mrs. Gleeson receives a salary of $10,000 a year. Mr. Gleeson no longer draws a salary from the business.

Should Peggy decide to assume the management of the drugstore, Mr. Gleeson has proposed that she draw a salary of $14,000, her present earnings. He further proposed that Peggy's share of the profits from the store's operation be 25 percent initially, increasing to 50 percent after two years. Since Mrs. Gleeson will no longer work in the store, it will be necessary to hire a part-time clerk to assist Peggy in the operation of the store, and Mr. Gleeson estimates that such expense will be approximately $4,600.

Mr. Gleeson has received a tentative offer of $150,000 for the purchase of the store, a major portion of which Peggy will inherit at some time in the future. The Gleesons' financial position is such that it will not be necessary for them to tap this source of capital to a significant extent to see them through their retirement years.

PROBLEMS

1. What courses of action are available to Peggy?
2. Which alternative do you recommend?
3. What are the implications of her system of personal values on the decision she makes?
4. If Miss Gleeson were a man, would your recommendations be the same?

Chapter 6 concluded with Peter Drucker's observation that organizations are information and decision making systems. We have examined in some detail the nature of information systems. Now it is necessary to study the decision-making phase of the information and decision-making cycle. In this chapter we analyze the decision-making process, examine some of the quantitative aids to decision making, and consider some of the behavioral aspects of the decision-making process.

THE DECISION-MAKING PROCESS

Decision making is frequently defined as the selection of one course of action from two or more alternate courses of action. This definition has the advantage of brevity, is easy to remember, and focuses attention upon the essential element of decision making — making a choice. Though brief, the definition is satisfactory provided we understand that making a decision is part of a process which includes the following four steps: definition of the problem, analysis, development of alternate solutions, and selection of a decision. A fifth step must be included if management decisions are to be effective in meeting company objectives. The fifth step is execution.[1]

Definition of the Problem

The intellectual process that culminates in making a decision is referred to as *problem solving* or *reasoning*. It is an activity undertaken

---

[1]Peter F. Drucker, *The Practice of Management* (New York: Harper & Brothers, 1954). For a later discussion by Peter Drucker on the decision-making process, see "The Effective Decision," *Harvard Business Review*, Vol. 45, No. 1 (January–February, 1967), pp. 92–98. For an advanced discussion of human problem solving, the following is recommended: Allen Newell and Herbert A. Simon, "Human Problem Solving: The State of the Theory in 1970," *American Psychologist*, Vol. 26, No. 2 (February, 1971), pp. 145–159. The article appears in Allen Newell and Herbert A. Simon, *Human Problem Solving* (Englewood Cliffs: Prentice-Hall, 1972).

by an individual to resolve tensions created by a situation that thwarts a normal course of activity. Problems are personal in that they thwart the activity of an individual. Herein lies an explanation of the difficulty frequently encountered by managers in securing employee participation in solving company problems — there is no problem for the employee unless the situation creates tensions which may be resolved through problem-solving activity. Employee suggestion systems are an attempt to elicit problem-solving activity through the creation of a problem — how can I get the money? — and offering a suggested means of attaining the goal — suggesting an improvement in company operations. Suggestion plans are successful only to the extent that they create within employees tensions that are capable of resolution as the result of problem-solving activity.

No amount of care and effort in the subsequent steps of analysis and development will yield a decision capable of reaching desired objectives unless the problem is properly defined. It is a common error in the diagnosis of problem situations to confuse obvious symptoms, usually those characteristics that attract attention, with the problem itself. Poor decisions are many times correct solutions to the wrong problem and are considered poor because they do not contribute to stated goals. We have seen in "the Parable of the Spindle," Case Problem 6-A, how an inadequate information system may result in poor human relations. Likewise, unsatisfactory sales volume may be the result of factors such as an incompetent sales force, an excessively high sales price, an improper channel of distribution, or poor quality of product. It is not easy to differentiate between symptoms and problems. A good way of getting behind the symptom and to the problem itself is to ask *why*: Why are the people upset? Why is sales volume too low? This approach usually involves listing all the possible causes and consumes considerable time and effort; nonetheless, it is better than solving the wrong problem.

Also, it is helpful to ask the following question: Would the solution to the problem as diagnosed provide an effective means to the desired end or goal? This question is stated diagrammatically below.

Problem $\longrightarrow$ Solution = Means $\longrightarrow$ End

When enlisting the help of others in solving a problem, it may be necessary to restate the problem in terms understandable to those asked to participate. A sales manager would be well advised to restate the problem of attaining a desired percentage of the market in terms that present a challenge to each salesperson. This may be done by having all salespeople define the problem in their territories and develop plans that will result in increased sales volume from existing customers and the acquisition of new customers.

Analysis

When the problem has been satisfactorily defined and there is reasonable assurance that its satisfactory solution provides a means to a desired end, the next step is the analysis of available information. At first glance, it may seem that this step implies the gathering and analysis of facts not presently at hand, an assumption which is correct in most instances; however, there are at least two classes of problems that require no additional information for their correct solution. First, there are those problems that clearly fall within the scope of existing policies. One of the major purposes of a policy statement is to provide a predetermined course of action, in effect, a solution to a multitude of similar problems. A personnel director, when asked to decide whether or not an employee's request for early retirement should be granted, has a ready answer after the question is properly defined and it is determined that it falls within the province of the company's retirement policy. The second class of problems not requiring the acquisition of additional information consists of those problems that fall within the decision maker's range of experience. The decision maker may possess, as the result of prior experience and training, the factual information and conceptualizations necessary to resolve the question and make a decision. The ability to synthesize past experiences so that they form a cohesive network of information that can be used in solving current problems is one of the primary reasons for the emphasis placed upon past experience as a factor in the selection of managers.

For those situations that do not fall within the range of existing policies or within the decision maker's experience background, it is necessary to acquire additional information, a process of "getting the facts." One step that may be taken to assure proper information for analysis is the building of information systems and data bases as described in Chapter 6. When information systems provide a timely flow of relevant information to management, they become information-decision-making systems. Such systems are of particular value in providing the information necessary for decisions concerning production schedules or optimum inventory levels, for they provide up-to-date and accurate information. Even so, there is need for judgment. Too much information may be gathered, with resultant masses of data, not relevant facts. Judgment is also required in determining when it is advisable to make a decision even though all necessary facts have not been acquired or analyzed.

Development of Alternate Solutions

Having defined the problem and analyzed the available information, the decision maker is now ready for the third step, the development of alternate courses of action. Logicians refer to this step as the formulation of hypotheses — tentative explanations or conclusions. Alternate solutions come as the result of weighing the concepts derived from the analysis of data in the preceding step. Concepts are weighed and interpreted in the light of past experience; and continuing effort should be made to rearrange the information of the second step, analysis, so that new concepts emerge and, in turn, may be examined and evaluated. Both inductive and deductive reasoning processes are used, and the validity of the tentative conclusions may be tested against the rules of logic. The development of alternatives is usually regarded as the central step of the decision-making process, for it is during this step that creative, or original, solutions to problems come into being. Suggestions for the encouragement of creative solutions to problems are discussed later in this chapter. Operations research techniques and other applications of the computer have been developed as special aids in the development of alternate courses of action. These, too, are discussed later in the chapter.

Selection of the Decision

The selection of a decision is the process of making a choice between two or more alternatives. The number and quality of choices available are dependent upon the degree of productiveness and originality employed in the third, or developmental, stage. It is unusual for a manager to have only two alternatives from which to make a selection; rather the problem is that of selecting one from many. In addition to the choices that represent new courses of action, there is always one other alternative — to do nothing. Volkswagen's decision not to change body styles is in every sense of the word as much a decision as Detroit's annual selection of one body style, from among many, to be adopted for the coming year.

Making the correct choice is not easy. Seldom is there only one correct choice with all others classed as incorrect. Instead, business decisions are neither black nor white; for the most part they are grey. Part of the difficulty in making the final or correct decision stems from the element of risk. It is difficult to assess the probable success or failure of a projected plan since the environment in which business operates is continually changing. In addition to the element of change, incomplete and unavailable data often limits the number and quality of concepts developed during the third stage of the decision-making process. Because of the difficulties encountered in selecting the best decision, the development of criteria for determining the worth of decisions is very important. The following three questions form a basis for judging decisions:

Does the decision contribute toward the attainment of stated objectives? Implied in this question is recognition that a course of action is but a means to an end, and if a proposed solution to the problem does not further the stated objectives, it should not be adopted.

Does the decision represent the maximum degree of economic effectiveness? The decision selected should represent the maximum utilization of all available resources; anything less than this would not contribute toward maximum economic effectiveness.

Is the decision capable of execution? Here we are asking whether or not it is possible to develop a plan to make the decision effective.

The use of the above questions to judge the worth of a decision is another application of the concept of the objective, the concept of economic effectiveness, and the concept of planning. These concepts are also used as criteria in the formulation of policies, and they are useful in evaluating any projected course of action. The act of deciding does not stand for long by itself as a single act; it rapidly merges into a series of actions designed to implement the decision.

Execution

The fifth and final step of the decision-making process, execution, converts the selected decision into action. The manager must follow through to make the choice effective. When measured in terms of contribution to company objectives, there is no difference between no decision at all and an ineffective decision that is not feasible. A decision has been made possible as the result of utilizing the flow of information from both inside and outside the firm; now the information-decision-making cycle must be completed with information flowing to those people in the organization who will translate the decision into action. It must be recognized that the current decision is but one of a series and, when translated into action, additional problems will arise that will demand solutions and subsequent decisions. The decision to build a new plant in Chicago provides an answer to two questions, whether or not a plant should be built and where it should be located; but it also opens the door to a flood of new questions related to the construction of the plant.

When communicating a decision, every effort must be made to use clear, concise terms understandable by those who will translate the decision into action. Perhaps it will be necessary to point out the logic of the decision and state the reasons for making it. The extent to which such persuasion, or selling, is necessary serves as a measure of the probable success of the decision, since it reveals the degree of participation on the part of those directly affected by the decision. Group participation in both decision making and creative thinking is discussed in the last section of this chapter.

QUANTITATIVE AIDS IN DECISION MAKING

In our discussion of the second step in the decision-making process, analysis, we mentioned that policies may serve as an aid to decision making provided the problem under consideration falls within the scope of the existing policy. For this reason, policies have sometimes been called *standing plans*, and as such provide the means for making these decisions effective. However, policies and other standing plans are of assistance only in the solution of recurring problems. During World War II, certain mathematical techniques were developed to aid in the resolution of complex military problems and in recent years have been applied to aid managers in their decision making. A general term used to describe these rather sophisticated mathematical techniques is "operations research."[2] The following discussion defines operations research, reviews some of its major techniques and applications, and suggests limitations.

Definition of Operations Research

Operations research (OR) is a term that apparently means different things to different people. It is, above all else, an application of the scientific method to problem situations; however, the scientific method is not the distinguishing characteristic of OR. Nor is the decision maker who faithfully follows the five steps of the decision-making process, an application of the scientific method, using operations research techniques. In OR the scientific method is applied to the analysis of the operations of a system rather than to the solution of a specific problem.

The phrase, operations of a system, implies that the problems undertaken by OR are much broader than those susceptible to solution by other decision-making techniques. Examples of operating systems that have been analyzed by operations research are weapons systems, man-machine systems such as aircraft, and business organizations. Further, the research on the system being studied is directed toward an understanding of the functioning of the entire system and ultimate improvement of the degree of control over the operation of the system. The specific techniques of OR demand that the system be represented as a mathematical model; that the solution to the problem be obtained by solving the mathematical equations representing the system (i.e., the model); and in addition, that the obtained solution be tested and recommendations made for its application.

---

[2]The phrase management science is often used as a synonym for operations research. See Harvey M. Wagner, *Principles of Operations Research with Applications to Managerial Decisions* (2d ed.; Englewood Cliffs: Prentice-Hall, 1975), Chapter 1.

Operations research may be defined as: *(1) an application of the scientific method to (2) problems arising in the operations of a system which may be represented by means of a mathematical model and (3) the solving of these problems by resolving the equations representing the system.*[3]

OR — Techniques and Applications

The following introduction to operations research techniques and applications indicates a few major applications of OR and touches briefly upon some of the underlying mathematical techniques.

Linear Programming — Allocation Problems. *Linear programming* techniques are most useful in those situations requiring an optimum allocation of resources. As the name implies, linear programming is concerned primarily with analyzing those relationships capable of being expressed mathematically as linear functions. In most instances there are several such linear functions operating simultaneously.

One of the classic applications of linear programming is of assistance in determining the location of an additional plant within an existing complex of plants and warehouses. Assume that a company has existing plants in Milwaukee and Philadelphia and that the single product of these plants is being distributed to warehouses in Chicago, St. Louis, New York, and Atlanta. Further, preliminary studies have narrowed the choice of a possible new plant site to Memphis or Indianapolis. If optimum allocation of resources is defined as least cost, including both manufacturing cost and the cost of transporting the finished product from plant to warehouse, a partial statement of the problem is determining which location offers the lower cost. However, the introduction of a new plant into the existing system of plants and warehouses necessitates revision of the allocation of the output of present plants to warehouses; therefore, the problem stated in its entirety is determining which of the two proposed systems offers the lower cost.

In addition to providing solutions to location problems, linear programming also aids in determining the most profitable product mix, whether to make or buy, and economic inventory levels. *Quadratic programming*, like linear programming, is an algebraic technique developed for analyzing those systems whose functions are nonlinear in nature.

Queuing Theory — Intermittent Servicing Problems. *Queuing theory*, sometimes called *waiting-line theory*, is of value in determining the correct balance of factors necessary for the most efficient handling of intermittent service. There are costs involved in having a waiting

---

[3]C. West Churchman, Russell L. Ackoff, and E. Leonard Arnoff, *Introduction to Operations Research* (New York: John Wiley & Sons, 1957), p. 18.

line, whether it be customers waiting for service in a restaurant or machines waiting to be repaired and returned to production. Time lost in waiting, particularly the downtime of machines needing repair, is also a factor of cost; and if the line is one of impatient customers, sales volume is reduced. In order to eliminate the line or decrease its length, thereby reducing waiting-line costs, it is necessary to increase servicing capacity. In turn, there is an increase in the cost of physical facilities and labor necessary to perform the desired service. The restaurant has to enlarge its seating capacity and hire more employees to reduce its line of waiting customers; the industrial plant needs more maintenance workers and a larger stock of repair parts to minimize production losses resulting from idle machines waiting for repair.

Another important factor in determining the optimum size of servicing facilities is time of arrival. Occasionally, actual observations may be made and a tally kept of the exact number of units requiring service during each hour of the workday. In many instances, such observations cannot be carried on for a long enough period of time to produce a stable pattern of work load. The *Monte Carlo* technique is used to produce a sample of random arrivals for those situations where actual observation is impracticable or impossible. Essentially, the Monte Carlo technique provides a large sample of random numbers that may be generated by a computer. From the large Monte Carlo sample, rather precise determinations may be made in regard to the expected servicing load for each hour of the day. Queuing theory is of value in reaching decisions concerning the optimum balance between the cost of service and the cost of having a waiting line; and when combined with the Monte Carlo technique, projections may be made for those situations where the work load varies in a random fashion.

Game Theory — Simulation of System Operation. "War games" have been used for many years as a means of training personnel and testing plans and equipment under field conditions. The process of obtaining the essential qualities of reality without the reality itself is known as *simulation*. "Management games" have been developed to provide training in decision making by providing laboratory situations that simulate as nearly as possible real-life operations. The development of a management game is incredibly complex, particularly if it is a game involving a situation in which there is a competitor aware of changing conditions — an increase in price or volume of goods produced — who responds with counter moves. At the moment, the application of game theory to business problems has been used primarily for training purposes rather than for solving competitive problems because of the complexities in analyzing and programming the many variables as they exist in real life.

Another example of simulation is the analysis of an actual system through the use of a simulated system programmed into a computer.

United Airlines has simulated the operations of aircraft at New York's LaGuardia Airport by running a program of a "station model" on an IBM 704 computer. The elements included in this program are time of day, week, and year; weather conditions; maintenance required; type and length of repair job; availability of spare aircraft; delays in landing or take-off; absenteeism of personnel; and number of maintenance personnel. By varying any one or a combination of factors, the functioning of the system may be observed under changed operating conditions, and subsequent analysis reveals operating efficiencies and cost.[4] Game theory and simulation techniques offer a means of training managers and analyzing system operations under changing conditions.[5]

Probability Theory — Determining Degree of Risk. Statistical techniques in their simplest form provide a descriptive statement of the characteristics of a group. For example, a wage survey may show that the average wage for tool and die makers in an area is $5.00 an hour. Further analysis, an application of *probability theory*, results in a measure of the reliability or accuracy of the obtained average. A probable error of ±5 cents an hour is interpreted to mean that the chances are 50–50 that the true average wage of all tool and die makers in the area falls between $4.95 and $5.05 an hour. A probable error of ±3 cents an hour indicates that the chances are 50–50 that the true average wage lies between $4.97 and $5.03. Thus, the smaller the probable error, the greater the degree of confidence that can be placed in the average. Measures of probable error are significant when dealing with a sample, or a part, of an entire population by not only showing the reliability of the obtained data but also by revealing whether or not additional time and money should be spent in securing more information.

Predictions concerning the probable outcome of future events are inferences based upon careful statistical analysis of existing data. Life expectancy tables used by insurance companies in setting their rates are statements of the probable death rate expected for each age group of the entire population during the present year. Statistical quality control is another application of the theory of probability. The volume of goods produced in high-speed manufacturing is so great that the cost of inspecting each item produced would be prohibitive. But a detailed inspection of a small sample, say one of every thousand, and periodic checking of the production equipment make it possible for a

---

[4]Elizabeth Marting (ed.), *Top Management Decision Simulation* (New York: American Management Association, 1957), pp. 50–51. In addition to United Airlines' "station model," a simulated distribution and inventory control model used by Imperial Oil Limited of Canada is presented. There is also a description of the development of the AMA game.

[5]Professor Whybark of Purdue University reports the results of an experiment which offers a means of determining whether or not the cost of the development of a mathematical model is worthwhile. D. Clay Whybark, "Comparing an Adaptive Decision Model and Human Decisions," *Academy of Management Journal*, Vol. 16, No. 4 (December, 1973), pp. 700–703.

quality control supervisor to predict with high accuracy the number of defective products that may be expected in every thousand produced.

Limitations of OR

Operations research is a direct aid to the decision-making process through its contribution to the steps of analysis and development, and, indirectly, OR forces a clearer statement of the problem. It does not, however, make the final choice nor translate the decision into action. The effectiveness of OR is limited to the analysis and comparison of relationships that may be expressed quantitatively and transformed into a mathematical model. Even so, there are times when the subjective judgment of the decision maker must override the recommendations of OR. Operations research may set the economic level of raw material inventory for an auto manufacturer, but in the face of an impending steel strike, the judgment of the individual executive should control. As yet, OR techniques are not adaptable to the prediction of customer reactions to a given style or color, nor do they clarify alternatives in human relations problems.

Finally, there seems to be a wide gulf separating the management scientists and the real world of management. In recounting his experiences as chairman of the Price Commission during the Nixon administration, C. Jackson Grayson offers the five following reasons why he, one who was well trained in the field of management science, did not use the model building or mathematical techniques described above. First, there was a shortage of time; second, an inaccessibility of data. Much of the data needed was not available and much that was available was not in the proper form. Third, he recognized that there would be resistance to change among his staff, and he simply did not have the time to overcome such resistance. Fourth, there is a long response time. Managers must make decisions within the constraints of relatively short periods of time; however, management scientists prefer to work at a more leisurely pace. The fifth reason given by Mr. Grayson is that management science tends to oversimplify the real situation.[6]

BEHAVIORAL ASPECTS OF DECISION MAKING

The preceding discussion of the sequence of the decision-making process and the brief review of quantitative aids describe the decision-making process as an exercise in logic — purely cognitive, or intellectual, in nature. However, there are other behavioral factors significant to the decision-making process. One group of factors is the personal characteristics of the decision maker. Also, most business decisions are rarely made by a single individual; instead, they are the result of the interaction between individuals who function as members of one or more groups. Consequently, the behavioral aspects of decision making

---

[6]C. Jackson Grayson, Jr., "Management Science and Business Practice," *Harvard Business Review*, Vol. 51, No. 4 (July–August, 1973), pp. 41–48.

may be conveniently classed as those factors attributable to the characteristics of the individual decision maker and those that are the result of group behavior.

Individual Factors

One of the fundamental observations of psychology is that individual differences exist in virtually every measurable human characteristic. Decision making is no exception. These differences are manifested in the way in which different people define the problem, the extent and breadth of the search for and the analysis of relevant data, and the number and kinds of alternative solutions developed. Also, differences between individuals determine the characteristics of the solution ultimately chosen and influence the degree of vigor and decisiveness shown in its execution. Though there are many behavioral characteristics influencing the decision-making process, the following three seem most significant. First, there is the way in which the person perceives the problem; second, there is the matter of ability and willingness to process information in the search for and the analysis of data, a prerequisite for the development of alternate solutions; and third, there is the personal value system of the decision maker, a factor of great significance in determining the final choice or decision.

Perception of Problem. *Perception* is a psychological process utilizing both incoming data from the sense organs and information learned from past experience so that meaning is attached to incoming data. Perception may be visualized as being midway on a continuum with direct sensory awareness (hot, cold, pain) at one extreme and thinking (not requiring external stimulation) at the other extreme.

The process of "making sense" out of what we see, hear, feel, taste, or smell obviously depends to a great degree on the nature of the external stimuli; however, of equal importance, if not more so for our purposes, is the past experience of the person receiving the stimulation. When the same objective data is given to people of differing backgrounds, there is always the likelihood that each will perceive a different problem. For example, Case Problem 6-A (pp.122–124) tells of a restaurant owner who observes that his waitresses break down in tears, that the cooks walk off the job, and that his managers become so upset that they summarily dismiss employees. His statement of the symptoms of the problem was verified by each of three consultants — a sociologist, a psychologist, and an anthropologist. Each observed and reported the objective data describing the behavior of the waitresses, cooks, and managers as reported by the restaurant owner. Yet each perceived a different problem; for one it was a sociological problem, for another it was psychological in nature, and for the third the problem was anthropological in nature..Given the same data each consultant perceived the problem in the light of his own background.

In addition to influencing how one perceives the problem, the first step of the decision-making process — the perceiver's experience — operates in a similar manner in subsequent steps of the decision-making process. Of significance is the manner in which alternative solutions are perceived. The same background factors that influence the perception of one aspect of a problem as being more significant than another may also influence the perception of one solution as being more desirable than another. If perception of one solution as being more desirable than another occurs early in the development of alternatives, there is the likelihood that other alternatives will not be fully developed; therefore the quality of the final solution to the problem will be strongly influenced.

Ability to Process Information. In addition to differences in how problems are perceived, there are also wide individual differences in the ability to process and store information. The effect of these differences is most evident in the second and third steps of the decision-making process — the search for and analysis of data and the development of alternative solutions. Some decision makers make decisions with relatively little data and the development of few alternatives because they are incapable of handling large quantities of data and wish to avoid the discomfort and confusion occasioned when confronted with new and unfamiliar information. The inability to handle information may result in an extreme stance either to the right or to the left of broad social issues as indicated in this quotation from Boulding:

> There is also a considerable relationship between the capacity of a decision maker to handle large quantities of information and his ability to widen his agenda. People who have narrow agendas, the bigots, the Birchers, the Marxists, the Nationalists, and the schizophrenics, are by and large people whose information processing capacities are highly limited. They retreat into narrow agendas because they cannot bear the information overload which would seem to result from the wide ones.[7]

The breadth of a person's agenda is frequently characterized as either open-mindedness or closed-mindedness. If one is open-minded there is a flexibility in approach and a willingness to consider a wide range of data and alternative solutions, but the closed-minded person tends to consider only that data and those solutions supporting a preconceived position. Thus the process of search is undertaken only to verify an *a priori* position. There are many characteristics of open-mindedness; however, the three suggested by Rokeach seem most useful in understanding managerial decision making.[8] First is the ability

---

[7]Kenneth E. Boulding, "The Ethics of Rational Decision," *Management Review*, Vol. 55, No. 2 (February, 1966), p. 167.

[8]Milton Rokeach, *The Open and Closed Mind* (New York: Basic Books, 1960), pp. 392–393.

to remember information, including new data, relevant to the solution of the problem. Second, there is a willingness to consider and explore various alternate solutions; and third, the breadth of one's past experience is an index of willingness to accept new ideas. The broader one's range of past experience the greater is the likelihood that new ideas can and will be accepted since breadth of experience is a measure of past encounters with new ideas.

In addition to the ability to process and store information and the willingness to accept new ideas (open-mindedness) there are also differences in the characteristic way in which information is handled. For some their *forte* is the gathering and analysis of data, while others excel in the synthesis and interpretation of information. These differences may have a marked effect upon the quality and type of decision eventually developed. The ability to synthesize tends to improve the quality of the final decision and enhances the probability of creative decisions. Thus the ability to handle information, the willingness to accept new information, and the proclivity to either analyze or synthesize are all behavioral characteristics of the individual decision maker that profoundly influence the outcome of the decision-making process.

Personal Value System. Since a personal value system is a series of concepts with each concept having a degree of personal worth and meaning, the individual values of the decision maker influence the decision-making process.[9] Values are significant determinants, not only in the selection of the final choice from among several alternates, but also as determinants of the statement of the problem. The ultimate decision for Peggy Gleeson (Case Problem 7-A, problem 3) is based on her value system.

In Chapter 4 (pp. 87–90) cost-benefit analysis, a technique used in those situations where anticipated benefits or costs are either difficult or impossible to quantify, is discussed. Frequently cited business objectives such as innovation, manager performance and development, worker performance and attitudes, and public responsibility are examples of hoped-for benefits not readily amenable to quantification. When alternate solutions are developed with each intended to increase benefits in any one of the above mentioned areas, the final choice is often based upon the personal values of the decision maker. If, for example, alternatives are proposed for a manager development program, the decision maker's personal values concerning the relative merits of each of several types of educational activities may form the basis for decision.

Personal values are important in initiating the course of the decision-making process. Problems frequently can arise as a result of the general question, "What must be done to achieve a stated objective?"

---

[9]Chapter 3, pp. 55–60, discusses the value system of American managers.

Objectives are often the organizational counterparts of personal objectives. Personal objectives, by their very nature, are a reflection of what is important to a person. The individual's desire for achievement, growth, excellence, or originality indicates that these attributes are significant to the person holding such values. A manager has the opportunity of fulfilling personal objectives through the instrumentality of the organization. Thus the organizational problems that emerge and the subsequent decisions to be made are shadows cast by the personal values and objectives of the manager.

Group Factors

In formal organizations it is rare for an individual to complete the entire decision-making process without functioning as a member of a group. Even in those instances in which an individual is designated as being responsible for solving a specific problem, the execution of the decision requires the participation of others. The observation that more than one person is required for the execution of a decision is significant because it implies that there is a need for commitment on the part of others. The participation of groups in the earlier steps in the decision-making process introduces factors that may either enhance or inhibit the decision-making process. The following are observations concerning the major advantages and disadvantages inherent in group participation in decision making.[10]

Advantages of Groups. One of the greatest advantages of group decision making is that potentially the group has a wider range of knowledge than any single member of the group since each individual brings to the group a different experience background. The extended range of knowledge should be of benefit in the definition of the problem and in the development of alternatives, and should result in a more critical analysis of the alternatives developed. Further, participation in decision making usually results in a better understanding of the decision reached. When commitment on the part of the group is needed in the execution of the decision, having been a participant increases the probability of commitment by each member of the group.

Disadvantages of Groups. The major limiting factor in determining the effectiveness of group participation in decision making arises as a result of social pressures.[11] In formal organizations the relationship

---

[10]Norman R. F. Maier, *Problem Solving and Creativity in Individuals and Groups* (Belmont, Calif.: Brooks/Cole Publishing Co., 1970), pp. 431–444. Study Number 37 was originally published in the *Psychological Review*, 1967, Vol. 74, pp. 239–249. This volume brings together the results of 15 years of study on individual and group problem solving conducted in Professor Maier's laboratory. Most of the studies have been published in other sources. The summary presented above is based upon Study 37.

[11]Chris Argyris, "Interpersonal Barriers to Decision Making," *Harvard Business Review*, Vol. 44, No. 2 (March-April, 1966), pp. 84–97. This study reports the findings of an analysis of the decision-making process in six companies. It analyzes the behavior of 165 top executives in these companies during the decision-making process.

between superior and subordinate may result in no real participation on the part of subordinates; instead, there may be mere acquiescence. Or the subordinates, in order to enhance their positions with the superior, may elect not to participate in developing the decision but rather to go along with the wishes of the superior. Even though hierarchical pressures are not normally present in informal groups, there are nonetheless definite social pressures. Sometimes the desire for acceptance by the group prevents a significant contribution to the decision-making process, thus having the same effect as hierarchical pressures. Questions are also raised concerning the quality of group decisions. Often a proposed solution is accepted without thorough evaluation of its quality simply because there is a concensus favoring that solution. In addition, there is the potential of individual domination of a group with a resultant diminution of group activity. Further, on occasion members of groups become engrossed with winning the argument rather than seeking the highest quality decision. Also, groups generally require more time, measured in total worker-hours, to reach a decision than that required by an individual.

Group Participation in Creative Thinking. People are recognized as being social in nature and one of the characteristics of such gregariousness is the influence exerted by a group on an individual and the effect that the individual, in turn, has upon the other members of the group. The capacity to be stimulated by a group and at the same time contribute to shaping the group's behavior is called *social facilitation*. Because of the phenomenon of social facilitation, groups are occasionally established for the primary purpose of engaging in creative thinking; that is, coming up with a new idea or a new application.[12]

Several techniques have been developed as group aids to creativity and their success is dependent upon the following two basic psychological phenomena:

1. Free association of ideas is a process of producing ideas in rapid succession with a minimum of inhibiting or restraining action. The original stimulus word is presented by the group leader and immediately the free associations thus produced function as additional stimuli for the group.
2. Social facilitation, as defined above, increases the productivity of each individual. Increased individual productivity further stimulates other members of the group.

A summary of the rules and suggestions for conducting two types of group sessions in creativity is presented in Figure 7-1.[13] Each of

---

[12]Robert J. Zajonc, "Social Facilitation," *Science*, Vol. 149, No. 3680 (July, 1965), pp. 269–274. In this paper Zajonc reviews the conditions under which social facilitation occurs.
[13]Charles S. Whiting, "Operational Techniques of Creative Thinking," *Advanced Management* (October, 1955), pp. 24–30. In addition to the Osborn and Gordon techniques, Whiting discusses several forced-relationship methods.

OSBORN BRAINSTORMING

Rules:

1. Judicial thinking or evaluation is ruled out.
2. Freewheeling is welcomed.
3. Quantity is wanted.
4. Combinations and improvements are sought.

Suggestions for the Osborn technique:

1. Length: 40 minutes to 1 hour, sessions of 10 to 15 minutes can be effective if time is short.
2. Do not reveal the problem before the session. An information sheet or suggested reference material on a selected subject should be used if prior knowledge of a general field is needed.
3. Problem should be clearly stated and not too broad.
4. Use a small conference table which allows people to communicate with each other easily.
5. If a product is being discussed, samples may be useful as a point of reference.

GORDON TECHNIQUE

Rules:

1. Only the group leader knows the problem.
2. Free association is used.
3. Subject for discussion must be carefully chosen.

Suggestions for the Gordon technique:

1. Length of session: 2 to 3 hours are necessary.
2. Group leader must be exceptionally gifted and thoroughly trained in the use of the technique.

GENERAL SUGGESTIONS THAT APPLY TO BOTH TECHNIQUES

1. Selection of personnel: a group from diverse backgrounds helps. Try to get a balance of highly active and quiet members.
2. Mixed groups of men and women are often more effective, especially for consumer problems.
3. Although physical atmosphere is not too important, a relaxed pleasant atmosphere is desirable.
4. Group size: groups of from four to twelve can be effective. We recommend six to nine.
5. Newcomers may be introduced without disturbing the group, but they must be properly briefed in the theory of creative thinking and the use of the particular technique.
6. A secretary or recording machine should be used to record the ideas produced. Otherwise they may not be remembered later. Gordon always uses a blackboard so that ideas can be visualized.
7. Hold sessions in the morning if people are going to continue to work on the same problem after the session has ended; otherwise hold them late in the afternoon. (The excitement of a session continues for several hours after it is completed, and can affect an employee's routine tasks.)
8. Usually it is advisable not to have people from widely differing ranks within the organization in the same session.

Figure 7-1
SUMMARY OF
RULES AND
SUGGESTIONS
FOR GROUP
SESSIONS

Reprinted by permission of the publisher from Charles S. Whiting, "Operational Techniques of Creative Thinking", *S.A.M. Advanced Management Journal*, October, 1955, p. 28.

these types, Osborn's brainstorming and the Gordon technique, is discussed below.

Brainstorming. Brainstorming was developed by Alex F. Osborn as an aid in producing ideas for an advertising agency; however, since that time the technique has been applied in many other situations where there is a need for the production of a large number of new solutions in answer to a specific problem. In order to develop the desired quantity of ideas, an atmosphere conducive to the free flow of ideas is created. The group leader informs the participating members of the desired objective and the quantity of new ideas, and cautions them against being critical of their ideas. He encourages "freewheeling," and usually all criticism of ideas is barred. Occasionally checklists and suggestions for developing new ideas are distributed to the group. One such list, developed by Osborn, is as follows:[14]

1. Put to other uses
2. Adapt
3. Modify
4. Magnify
5. Minify
6. Substitute
7. Rearrange
8. Reverse
9. Combine

One of the major criticisms of brainstorming is that, by its very nature, it tends to produce rather superficial ideas since the problem is worded in specific terms and thus limits the development of broad free association. Also, the technique may be very time-consuming; for in addition to the hours spent in the session itself, time is required to evaluate the ideas produced. Nonetheless, it is a valuable group aid to encourage creative thinking, particularly in those situations in which a specific answer is desired such as a name for a new product or an advertising slogan. Above all else, it tends to create an atmosphere within the organization that encourages individual creative thinking long after the session had ended.

Gordon Technique. William J. J. Gordon developed a technique to meet the needs of Arthur D. Little, Inc., a consulting group specializing in industrial research and other technical problems. The participants of a Gordon session, unlike those of a brainstorming group, are not aware of the specific problem under consideration. For example, if the desired result is an improved method of dehydrating food, the key word selected might be preservation, a stimulus which would elicit suggestion for the preservation of many items other than food. Also, it must be remembered that the Gordon technique was developed for the highly trained staff of the Arthur D. Little organization. Proponents of

---

[14]Alex F. Osborn, *Applied Imagination* (New York: Charles Scribner's Sons, 1953), p. 284.

Gordon's approach to conducting group sessions in creativity claim that the technique results in a higher quality of ideas since the generic key word does not tend to limit ideas, nor is there the likelihood of a member developing pride of authorship because he has no information concerning the application of his idea. In addition, many of the ideas produced may be of value in later projects even if they are not applicable to current problems. If the leader is highly skilled and the participants have both depth and breadth of knowledge in the field in question, the Gordon method is an excellent means of generating new ideas.

Evaluation of Group Decision Making

There are two aspects of group decision making that may be considered advantageous under certain circumstances; yet those same characteristics may be liabilities under other conditions. First, there is a tendency for those holding extreme positions to move toward the norm of the groups when that norm represents a middle ground. Second, there is a tendency for a group to select a decision representing a higher degree of risk, defining greater risk as increased uncertainty with respect to the probability of achieving expected outcomes. The tendency for extremes to approach the mean is desirable if an extreme position interferes with the execution of the decision or does not contribute significantly to any step of the decision-making process; however, if the extreme position represents the highest quality decision, such movement toward the center automatically impares the quality of the final decision. Likewise, the degree of riskiness of the decision varies in its desirability. When there is an increased payoff associated with increased risk, the greater risk may be desirable; but if the payoff appears to be no greater, the increased risk may not be desirable.

Although the potential benefits of group participation in decision making is great, such potential is seldom achieved in actual practice.[15] Membership in a group does not insure participation; hence, the knowledge that each might contribute to the decision-making process is not always tapped. In addition, the social pressures that develop, even in informal groups, seriously impair the quality of the decision-making process. The answer to the effectiveness of group decision making is dependent upon the quality of leadership. The leader of the group most be skilled in creating an environment that encourages each member to make a full contribution. The leader must help individuals in recognizing, and in placing in proper perspective, conflicting individual and group goals, and must guide the discussion so that the highest quality decision, consistent with the stated objectives, is

---

[15]Argyris, *op. cit.*

reached. In effect, the leader must function as the central nervous system so that each member of the group makes the maximum contribution to the group effort.[16]

On pages 144–148, the steps of the decision-making process — definition of the problem, analysis, development of alternate solutions, selection of the decision, and execution — are discussed. In Case Problem 7-B you are asked to make a series of decisions, a decision task known as the NASA Moon Survival Problem.[17] First, the project provides a measure of your ability to make decisions as an individual; second, since the subject matter is relatively new, a measure of creativity in decision making is required.

Case Problem 7-B

THE NASA MOON SURVIVAL PROBLEM

Directions: You are a member of a space crew originally scheduled to rendezvous with a mother ship on the lighted surface of the moon. Because of mechanical difficulties, however, your ship was forced to land at a spot some 200 miles from the rendezvous point. During reentry and landing, much of the equipment aboard was damaged and, since survival depends on reaching the mother ship, the most critical items available must be chosen for the 200-mile trip. Below are listed the 15 items left intact and undamaged after landing. Your task is to rank order them in terms of their importance for your crew in allowing them to reach the rendezvous point. Place the number 1 by the most important item, the number 2 by the second most important and so on through number 15, the least important.

_____ Box of matches

_____ Food concentrate

_____ 50 feet of nylon rope

_____ Parachute silk

_____ Portable heating unit

_____ Two .45-calibre pistols

_____ One case dehydrated Pet milk

_____ Two 100-lb. tanks of oxygen

_____ Stellar map (of the moon's constellation)

---

[16]For a similar evaluation of group participation in decision making the following are recommended:

Charles R. Holloman and Hal W. Hendrick, "Adequacy of Group Decisions as a Function of the Decision-Making Process," *Academy of Management Journal*, Vol. 15, No. 2 (June, 1972), pp. 175–184.

L. L. Cummings, George P. Huber, and Eugene Arendt, "Effects of Size and Spatial Arrangements on Group Decision Making," *Academy of Management Journal*, Vol. 17, No. 3 (September, 1974), pp. 460–475.

[17]Jay Hall and W. H. Watson, "The Effects of a Normative Intervention on Group Decision-Making Performance," *Human Relations*, Vol. 23, No. 4 (Plenum Publishing Corporation, August, 1970), pp. 299–317. The directions and the items to be ranked in importance are presented in the Appendix of the article, pp. 316–317. The NASA Moon Survival Problem was developed by Jay Hall in 1963.

_____ Life raft   _____ Signal flares

_____ Magnetic compass   _____ First aid kit containing injection
                                          needles

_____ 5 gallons of water   _____ Solar-powered FM receiver-transmitter

---

CHAPTER QUESTIONS FOR
STUDY AND DISCUSSION

1. Why is the fifth step, execution, included as part of the decision-making process even though it may be argued that execution is not a part of decision making?
2. In defining a problem, how does one distinguish between the symptoms resulting from the problem and the problem itself?
3. Give an example of a correct decision to an improperly defined problem.
4. Give several examples of the need for restating problems in terms that are understandable to those who are asked to help in solving the problem.
5. What is the relationship between established policies and decision making? Give an example of a recurrent business decision that could be eliminated by establishing a policy.
6. Why is experience valuable in making decisions? What are some of the dangers in relying too heavily on experience?
7. What is meant by the term operations research? What is the relationship between OR and the scientific method?
8. Discuss the following statement: Most modern applications of OR would be impossible without the aid of the computer.
9. Which of the three personal characteristics of the decision maker — perceptual characteristics, ability to process information, personal value systems — do you consider to be most important? Why? Which of these three characteristics is most closely related to intelligence?
10. In Figure 7-1 a summary of the rules and suggestions for the Osborn and Gordon group sessions is presented. Note that Osborn calls for sessions of 40 minutes to 1 hour in length while the Gordon technique requires a session length of 2 to 3 hours. Also, Osborn requires a clear statement of the problem, but Gordon requires that only the group leader know the problem. Are these differences contradictory in nature, or do they merely serve to limit the usefulness of each technique to a certain class of problem? Under what circumstances would you recommend Osborn's brainstorming? When would you recommend the technique suggested by Gordon?

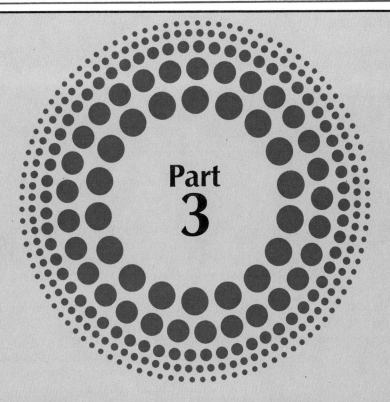

Part
3

The Organizing Function

Underlying organization theory are assumptions, often implicit, concerning the structure and functions of organizations. One set of assumptions concerning work and the people performing that work is known as the work-centered, or classical, theory of organization. Another approach, with different assumptions concerning work and people, is people centered and sometimes called neoclassical theory. The third approach to understanding organizations is within the context of a system and is termed a contingency approach. The concepts of the work-centered and people-centered approaches to organization theory and resultant organizational characteristics are compared. Chapter 8 concludes with a contingency approach to organization theory, and specific parameters, all appearing with significant frequency in the literature, are stated.

Although the contingency approach to organization theory is recognized as current in the study of organizations, there is much to be learned from the past. For this reason the classical concepts of organization structure, organization relationships, and organization processes are examined carefully. Departmentation, the prime determinant of organization structure, and recommendations for the subsequent arrangement of departments into effective spans of management are discussed in Chapter 9. Since committees are found in most organizations, they are considered within the framework of organization structure. There are two widely divergent views concerning the source of authority. One holds that authority is derived from an institutional, or societal, source; the other states that authority is derived from acceptance by subordinates. Both views concerning the source of authority and the authority relationships between line and staff personnel are discussed. The analysis of the processes of transferring authority within organizations, delegation and decentralization, also considers the behavioral aspects of delegation and offers guides to determine the optimum degree of decentralization.

Since social organizations are not static, it is necessary to prepare for the inevitable change that is certain to occur. One form of change may be rather sudden in nature and stems from an organization analysis setting forth specific recommendations for change; the other form of change is evolutionary in nature and is the result of planned organization development. The tools for organization analysis and the steps necessary to establish an effective organization development program appear in Chapter 12.

Case Problem 8-A

AN EXPERIMENT IN PARTICIPATIVE MANAGEMENT
PART I The Experiment

Non-Linear Systems, Inc. (NLS) was founded in 1952 in Del Mar, California, by Andrew F. Kay, the sole owner. The company manufactures a line of digital electrical measuring instruments that range in price from $500 to over $20,000 per unit. By 1960 the company was a leader in its field. For many years it was one of seven companies that held 95 percent of the available market with approximately 50 other companies sharing the remaining 5 percent. The number of employees grew from 5 to a high of 340 in the 1960s.

The experiment began in 1960 as the result of Mr. Kay's belief that the human relations approach would work in an organization. Prior to the beginning of the experiment there was much consultation with experts in human relations. Also, there was continuing discussion and consultation with the employees of

the company. When the experiment was put into effect, all personnel were thoroughly familiar with the goals of the experiment. It was begun as the result of a decision made solely by Andrew Kay.

In brief, the human relations approach to organization theory is as follows:

(1) Work is a natural phenomenon and if satisfying it will be performed voluntarily.

(2) If the employee is committed to the objectives of the organization, there is little need for external control.

(3) The degree of commitment to objectives is primarily a function of the rewards associated with these objectives.

(4) Many people are not only willing to accept responsibility, they actually seek such responsibility.

(5) Powers of imagination, creativity, and ingenuity are widely distributed throughout the general population and the organization and not limited to a few people at the top of the organization.

(6) Modern industrial organizations only partially utilize a person's intellectual abilities. (For a complete discussion of these assumptions, see pp. 174–179).

Erwin L. Malone, "The Non-Linear Systems Experiment in Participative Management," *The Journal of Business of the University of Chicago*, Vol. 48, No. 1 (January, 1975), pp. 52–64. Case Problem 8-A and its sequel, Case Problem 8-B, are based upon the authoritative report of the Non-Linear Systems experiment as reported by Erwin L. Malone. Dr. Malone spent two weeks at Non-Linear Systems shortly after the termination of the experiment. He interviewed all levels of management and hourly employees and had free access to all records.

The experiment translated these assumptions concerning people into action by changing the organizational characteristics of NLS. The following changes in the organization were made.

Wages At the time the experiment began, hourly workers were receiving $1.90 an hour ($76 a week). They received a 60¢ an hour increase and were classified as salaried workers receiving $100 a week. No records were kept of tardiness or absenteeism. Coffee and fatigue breaks were taken at the employee's convenience. Shortly after the experiment began, at the request of some of the senior employees new employees were started at $85 a week rather than at $100. They were then advanced to the $100 a week salary at the end of a variable probationary period.

Organization The classic organization structure is discussed on p. 172 and is essentially pyramidal in nature as shown in Figure 8-1. At NLS a quite different approach was taken. Three zones of management were established. Zone I was the level of trustee management and consisted of the board of directors of the company including Andrew F. Kay, chairman of the board. Zone I had the responsibility of determining the basic policies and direction of the organization. Zone II was one of general management. It was an eight-member executive council consisting of seven members in addition to Mr. Kay. Essentially, Zone II consisted of the vice-presidential level covering the functions of innovation (product development), productivity, physical and financial resources, profitability, manager performance and development, marketing, legal counsel and public responsibility. It should be noted that the office of president was eliminated; however, Kay did function as a member of the trustee management, Zone I, and general management, Zone II. Zone III corresponded to departmental managers. There were 30 department units, also referred to as project teams. Each unit consisted of 3 to 12 employees including the departmental manager. Departmental managers were responsible for the day-to-day operations of their respective units. The functions of the 30 departments included

product development, the assembling of instruments, shipping and receiving, personnel services, and sales functions including both sales promotion and distribution within specified geographic regions.

Production Set-up Prior to the experiment the product was assembled by two assembly lines, each of which produced one of the two basic models of digital voltmeters. Minor changes in either of the basic models resulted in adaptations for the special needs of customers. These assembly lines were discontinued at the beginning of the experiment and replaced by departmental units each headed by a manager with 3 to 12 other people and each unit was responsible for building the complete instrument. Each group worked at its own rate of speed and determined whether one person would make a complete instrument or whether it would be done by three to twelve people.

Indoctrination Programs A thorough indoctrination program at all levels of the organization preceded the experiment. When new employees were hired subsequent to the beginning of the experiment they were thoroughly indoctrinated in the basic aims and goals of the company and the reasons for its operations.

Training Procedures The indoctrination for new employees was followed by considerable on-the-job training. Training facilities both inside and outside the company were used widely. Employees who received training outside the company were reimbursed by the company upon the completion of each course.

Time Clocks Since punching a time clock is viewed by many as degrading and implies mistrust, all time clocks were removed.

Record Keeping Records are a form of external control; therefore, they were literally abolished. NLS became a company that maintained very little in the form of formal records of productivity or product costs.

Accounting The accounting department as a formal unit was dismantled. The personnel of that department worked in each of the

Zone III departments. Individual records were kept for each of these departments, with summary statements being sent periodically to the treasurer.

Inspection The formal inspection department was eliminated. Each of the production units performed its own inspection. Thus there was no external control in this area.

1. Does the organization described above more closely parallel a Theory X organization or a Theory Y organization? Explain.
2. Based upon your own experience and the materials presented in the chapter, what is your prediction concerning the outcome of the experiment?

It is a truism that organizations are a major force in determining the course of our lives; yet few of us recognize the extent to which organizations shape our behavior. We are born in hospitals and immediately the process of adapting to formal organizations begins; for the hospital, an organization, imposes a schedule of eating, sleeping, and bathing. There is a brief respite from formal organizations during the next five years; then at the age of six, when school begins, we become members of a succession of formal organizations — grade and high school, college, and the places where we work. Retirement from active employment does not mean retirement from all organizations, for usually memberships in social clubs, civic organizations, and churches continue.

The word, organization, has two distinct meanings, one of which refers to an organization as an *entity* in itself, and the other one which refers to organization as a *process*. Some of the more common organizations, as entities, are mentioned above — schools, places of employment (including industrial organizations, governmental agencies, or private institutions), social clubs, civic service organizations, and churches. There are three characteristics common to each of the organizations above: first, each is composed of people; second, each has a distinct purpose or goal to achieve, thus offering a reason for its existence; and third, each has a degree of formality in the structure of the organization that results in a definition and limitation of the behavior of its members. *Thus, as an entity, an organization is a group of people bound together in a formal relationship to achieve organizational goals.*

The second meaning of organization is that it is a *process of structuring, or arranging, the parts of the organization;* a meaning exemplified by the phrase, "what this place needs is more organization." The question arises, what is being organized? There are three possible answers to this question; first, *work* is being organized; second, *people* are being organized; and third, *systems* are being organized. The answer you choose as being most descriptive of the process of organization is dependent upon certain fundamental assumptions with regard to the nature of work and the behavior of human beings in a work situation. These assumptions, known as theories of organization, are important for they determine the structure of an organization and the methods used in administering the organization. The theoretical framework leading to the conclusion that organization is a process of organizing *work* is known as *Theory X*; those assumptions concluding in the belief that *people* are the central theme of organization form *Theory Y*; and an approach that emphasizes the organization of *systems* is designated as a *contingency approach* to organization.

THEORY X — A WORK-CENTERED APPROACH

Underlying every management action is a set of implicit assumptions concerning the nature of work and the nature of human beings. Theory X is a group of assumptions that results in what is referred to as the traditional, or classical, approach to organization.[1] In discussing Theory X, let us first examine the basic assumptions concerning work and the nature of human beings in a work situation.

Assumptions of Theory X

Theory X rests upon four implicit assumptions. The first of these assumptions is concerned with the nature of work, and the remaining three describe the behavior of human beings in a work situation.

1. Work, if not downright distasteful, is an onerous chore to be performed in order to survive.
2. The average human being has an inherent dislike of work and will avoid it if he can.
3. Because of this human characteristic of dislike of work, most people must be coerced, controlled, directed, threatened with punishment, to get them to put forth adequate effort toward the achievement of organizational objectives.
4. The average human being prefers to be directed, wishes to avoid responsibility, has relatively little ambition, wants security above all.[2]

Briefly, Theory X states that there is no intrinsic satisfaction in work, that humans avoid it as much as possible, that positive direction is needed to achieve organizational goals, and that workers possess little ambition or originality. Let us assume that Theory X is an accurate statement of conditions as they exist today. How do these assumptions affect the structure and processes of an organization?

---

[1]Douglas McGregor, *The Human Side of Enterprise* (New York: McGraw-Hill Book Co., 1960). Professor McGregor summarizes the assumptions of traditional management under the heading of Theory X, and presents those assumptions which result in a human relations approach to management under the heading of Theory Y. The theoretical assumptions of both theories are presented in Part I of the book; Part II is a discussion of Theory Y in practice; and Part III is a discussion of the development of management talent.

[2]*Ibid.*, pp. 33–34. Assumptions 2, 3, and 4 are quoted directly from McGregor. Assumption 1 has been added as an explicit statement of the nature of the work to which humans are reacting. For a good treatment of work theory, see Dale Yoder, *Personnel Management and Industrial Relations* (6th ed; Englewood Cliffs: Prentice-Hall, 1970), Chapter 4.

Effect on Organization

Adherence to Theory X results in a *work-centered* organization. As noted earlier, one of the characteristics of an organization is that it has a goal — a raison d'étre. It is normal to be concerned about the work of an organization, and when work is distasteful, something to be avoided like the plague, firm steps must be taken to assure its accomplishment. An external force is needed to accomplish organizational objectives under the conditions prescribed in Theory X. This force is dependent upon the traditional concept of authority; indeed, it is so dependent upon authority that organizations which subscribe to Theory X are frequently referred to as *authoritarian* organizations. Once the foundation of an organization has been laid upon the cornerstone of authority, the location of the decision-making process is determined, the organizational structure acquires certain characteristics, and the roles of the supervisor and the individual member of the organization are sharply defined.

Authority. Authority has been succinctly defined as *the right to command and the power to exact obedience*, a definition that raises two questions: (1) the source of the right and (2) the method of power. One source of authority, used by the early European monarchies, is expressed by the phrase, the divine right of kings. A corresponding point of view applied to the management of industrial enterprises regards authority as emanating from the right to own property and the attendant obligation to manage that property. The power of the monarch in enforcing obedience is absolute, because the monarch can exact the supreme penalty, death, if it is deemed necessary. In the industrial situation the supreme penalty for disobedience is discharge, a penalty that prohibits an employee from fulfilling economic needs. It is interesting to note that many arbitrators, when writing decisions concerning the discharge of an employee, equate the death penalty to discharge by an employer. We will see when we discuss Theory Y that there is another concept of authority. But Theory X rests upon an assumption of complete authority as the motivating force directing the course of the organization.

Location of Decision Making. The analogy of a political monarchy and a highly authoritarian industrial organization continues as an effective means of describing the location of the decision-making process. In the monarchy, decision making is highly centralized and located at the apex of the organization, the king, since it is the king who has the divine right to command. For the authoritarian industrial organization, the nominal head of the organization is the locus of the decision-making process; again this is a logical location when the right to manage is derived from ownership. Centralized decision making requires a certain form of organizational structure if the decisions are to be carried out effectively.

Organization Structure. When authority to make decisions is centralized at the top of the organization and its primary purpose is the accomplishment of work, a structure must be designed that permits the ready exercise of authority at all levels of the organization, and maximum effectiveness in the accomplishment of work.

Figure 8-1 is a model showing the structure of the traditional work-centered, or authoritarian, organization. Note that authority to manage flows from the owners through the board of directors to the president who is appointed by the board. Reporting to the president are several vice-presidents, each of whom is in charge of a specific phase of the work of the organization. Figure 8-1 is an exploded diagram of the organization reporting to the vice-president of manufacturing; similar pyramidal structures could be developed for each of the other vice-presidents. Reporting to the manufacturing vice-president is the manager in charge of a specific manufacturing unit, a plant. The major operations of the plant — receiving, machining, assembly, and shipping — are assigned to four general foremen who report to the plant manager. The general foremen direct the efforts of foremen who are in charge of the operating departments within each of the four major functions. Four assistant foremen, each of whom directs the work of a specific area, report to each foreman; and, finally, production employees report to their respective assistant foreman.

Figure 8-1 refers to production workers as rank and file employees, a phrase borrowed from the military expression used to describe the rows and columns of the infantry platoon. Another military phrase, *chain of command*, is used to describe the means of transmitting the president's authority so that ultimately production employees produce the desired work. Authority is transmitted through a chain of command, the successive levels of management, between the president and the production worker. When Figure 8-1 is read from top to bottom, the chain of command, which permits the ready exercise of authority at all levels in the organization, is easily followed; and when viewed from left to right, the division of the organization into units of work is apparent.

Role of Supervisor. The pyramidal structure of the organization determines the role, or function, assumed by supervisors. First, supervisors are an integral part of the chain of command, and as such it is their function to transmit authority to the succeeding lower levels of the organization. Decision making is a minor, if not nonexistent, function, for the authority to make decisions is vested in the head of the organization. Thus, supervisors are agents of a higher authority. Second, as agents of higher authority, they have the function of optimizing the goals of the organization; therefore, they may be expected to emphasize production. If, in addition, a particular supervisor is an agent of an organization built on the premise that work is distasteful

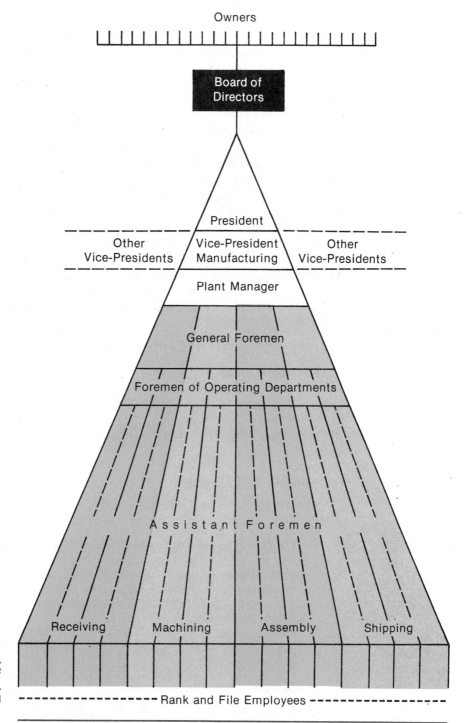

Owners

Board of Directors

President

Other Vice-Presidents

Vice-President Manufacturing

Other Vice-Presidents

Plant Manager

General Foremen

Foremen of Operating Departments

Assistant Foremen

Receiving   Machining   Assembly   Shipping

------------------- Rank and File Employees -------------------

Figure 8-1 PYRAMIDAL STRUCTURE OF TRADITIONAL ORGANIZATION

and that people tend to avoid work, is it any wonder that all the supervisor's efforts are oriented toward production?

Role of Individual. The role of the individual worker is that of a cog in a machine. Workers are to be directed, coerced if need be, and controlled so that they will put forth the effort necessary for the achievement of organizational objectives. Their function is to perform their present jobs; there is little encouragement for self-development or advancement. The phrase, rank and file, is used to describe production workers in Figure 8-1; perhaps an even more descriptive appellation is "hired hands," a term that implies that only hands, not complete people, are being hired. However described, production workers in a Theory X organization are regarded as individual units reporting only to their direct supervisor. They are not considered members of a group, or for that matter members of several groups; instead, each stands isolated reporting to and influenced only by the supervisor.

The discussion above outlines the organizational effects implicit in the assumptions of Theory X and may seem exaggerated. However, there are many organizations that actually parallel the Theory X organization. The propositions of Theory X and the effectiveness of the authoritarian, work-centered organizations are evaluated following the presentation of Theory Y.

THEORY Y — A PEOPLE-CENTERED APPROACH

The assumptions of Theory Y concern the nature of human behavior based upon an interpretation of modern behavioral sciences. The same format used in the presentation of Theory X is used in presenting Theory Y; first, the assumptions of the theory are stated and, second, the consequent effects of these assumptions upon the organization are reviewed.

Assumptions of Theory Y

The assumptions of Theory Y are the antitheses of those of Theory X. The six assumptions of Theory Y are as follows:

1. *The expenditure of physical and mental effort in work is as normal as play or rest.* The average human being does not inherently dislike work. Depending upon controllable conditions, work may be a source of satisfaction (and will be voluntarily performed) or a source of punishment (and will be avoided if possible).
2. *External control and the threat of punishment are not the only means for bringing about effort toward organizational objectives. People will exercise self-direction and self-control in the service of objectives to which they are committed.*
3. *Commitment to objectives is a function of the rewards associated with their achievement.* The most significant of such rewards, e.g., the satisfaction of ego and self-actualization needs, can be direct products of effort directed toward organizational objectives.

4. *The average human learns, under proper conditions, not only to accept but to seek responsibility*. Avoidance of responsibility, lack of ambition, and emphasis on security are general consequences of experience, not inherent human characteristics.

5. *The capacity to exercise a relatively high degree of imagination, ingenuity, and creativity in the solution of organizational problems is widely, not narrowly, distributed in the population.*

6. *Under the conditions of modern industrial life, the intellectual potentialities of the average human being are only partially utilized.*[3]

Effect on Organization

Adherence to Theory X results in work-centered, authoritative organizations. Theory Y is an approach to organizational problems that emphasizes human relations and results in an organization characterized as *participative*. The two forms of organization, authoritative and participative, are the extreme points of a continuum. Between these poles are many gradations of organizational behavior. One writer distinguishes the following steps: (1) exploitive authoritative, (2) benevolent authoritative, (3) consultative, and (4) participative group.[4] Thus, when discussing the effect of the propositions of Theory Y on organizational structure and processes, it is well to remember that we are dealing with the other end of the continuum in order to present in clear, sharp lines the differences existing between the two approaches.

Authority. Authority, as presented in Theory X, is the right to command and the power to enforce obedience. However, there is more to authority than right and power as illustrated by the following brief story:

> An agent for the Textile Workers Union of America likes to tell the story of the occasion when a new manager appeared in the mill where he was working. The manager came into the weave room the day he arrived. He walked directly over to the agent and said, "Are you Belloc?" The agent acknowledged that he was. The manager said, "I am the new manager here. When I manage a mill, I run it. Do you understand?" The agent nodded, and then waved his hand. The workers, intently watching this encounter, shut down every loom in the room immediately. The agent turned to the manager and said, "All right, go ahead and run it."[5]

Unquestionably the manager has the right to run a plant, and it is possible, under certain circumstances, for the manager to exercise power and discharge all workers for engaging in an unauthorized work

---

[3]Douglas McGregor, *The Human Side of Enterprise* (New York: McGraw-Hill Book Co., 1960), pp. 47–48. Another work by McGregor, published posthumously, *The Professional Manager*, edited by Warren G. Bennis and Caroline McGregor (New York: McGraw-Hill Book Co., 1967), discusses how a Theory Y organization may be developed.

[4]Rensis Likert, *New Patterns of Management* (New York: McGraw-Hill Book Co., 1961), Chap. 14, "A Comparative View of Organizations," pp. 222–236. This book is recommended as a summary of research in organizational behavior and leadership.

[5]McGregor, *The Human Side of Enterprise*, p. 23.

stoppage. Then the manager can start anew with a different group of workers, but this seems the hard way to manage a plant. Theory Y presents people as rational beings who are willing to work; in fact, they must work in order to satisfy deep-seated psychological needs (propositions 1 and 3). Also, they have intelligence and are capable of making their own decisions. Among the decisions that an individual makes is that of deciding *which* leadership to accept. The above incident does not portray a situation in which there is no authority; on the contrary, there was a great deal of authority — in the hands of the agent for the union. The workers in the mill had decided to accept one source of authority and reject another source. Thus, *acceptance* of authority, rather than right of authority, is one of the major differences between Theory Y and Theory X.

If authority based upon the concept of the right to command is displaced by authority which must be accepted to be effective, what happens to power? Power, too, is displaced. Look at proposition 2 of Theory Y, which states that "people will exercise self-direction and self-control in the service of objectives to which they are committed." One tool available to management to replace power in gaining an employee's commitment to organizational objectives is *persuasion*; another means is to afford an opportunity for *participation* in setting objectives.

Location of Decision Making. Setting objectives is one form of decision making and, according to Theory X, is retained by the nominal head of the organization. Proposition 5 of Theory Y states that "the capacity to exercise a relatively high degree of imagination, ingenuity, and creativity in the solution of organizational problems is widely, not narrowly, distributed in the population." Under these circumstances it is no longer necessary to retain decision making in the hands of a few. As a result, decision making in the Theory Y organization is widespread and diffuse, and it may occur at any level of the organization. Herein lies the meaning of participation; it is participation in decision making, including the determination of objectives.

Organization Structure. Figure 8-1 shows the pyramidal structure of the typical traditional organization with successive layers of supervision and the development of work functions for each supervisor. The relationships between superior and subordinate at any level of the organization appear in the usual organization chart as shown in Figure 8-2.

Figure 8-2 emphasizes the work-centered aspects of the organization. Each subordinate is in charge of a specific function. It is an organization constructed primarily for the downward flow of authority in order to accomplish work. Communications between superior and subordinates are illustrated in Figure 8-3.

Figure 8-3 implies that interpersonal face-to-face relationships occur only between a superior and each subordinate in succession. The

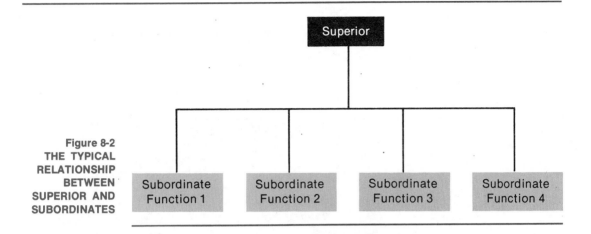

Figure 8-2
THE TYPICAL
RELATIONSHIP
BETWEEN
SUPERIOR AND
SUBORDINATES

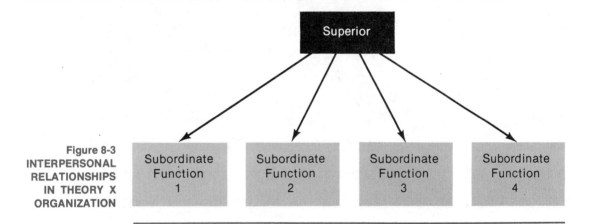

Figure 8-3
INTERPERSONAL
RELATIONSHIPS
IN THEORY X
ORGANIZATION

individual is the basic unit of the organization, and at best there can be no more than two-way communication between superior and subordinate. Earlier in this chapter an organization was defined as a *group* of people bound together in a formal relationship to achieve organizational goals. Theory Y emphasizes that organization has to do with groups and that the individual who accepts organizational goals does so as a member of a group. Thus, the group, not the individual, becomes the basic unit of organization. The reasons for recognizing the group as the basic unit are found in proposition 3 of Theory Y. Since the degree of commitment to organizational objectives is a function of the rewards derived from satisfying ego and self-actualization needs, which include participation in and recognition by a group, it is logical that superior and subordinates be considered a functional group. The large triangle of Figure 8-4 enclosing superior and subordinates represents the group as the primary organizational unit. Figure 8-4 also illustrates free communication of ideas between every group member.

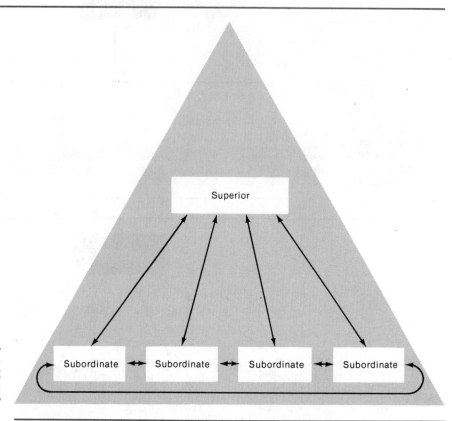

**Figure 8-4
SUPERIOR-
SUBORDINATE
FUNCTIONING
AS A GROUP**

Role of Supervisor. Under the conditions of Theory X, the supervisor, a vital link in the chain of command, is an agent of higher authority. The supervisor's role is to optimize the goals of the organization by directing the efforts of individuals. But Theory Y replaces authority with the concept of acceptance and replaces power with persuasion and participation. Also, the supervisor is no longer dealing with individuals but is now working with a group which includes the supervisor. Thus, he has an *intragroup* function of leading his own group. At the same time he is a member of a supervisory group which means that he has an *intergroup* function to perform — coordinating the efforts of the two groups to which he belongs. Likert refers to this coordinative function as the "linking pin" function.[6] Note the arrows in Figure 8-5; these are the linking pins which denote that the supervisor has an intergroup and an intragroup coordinative function.

---

[6]Likert, *op. cit.*, pp. 113–115.

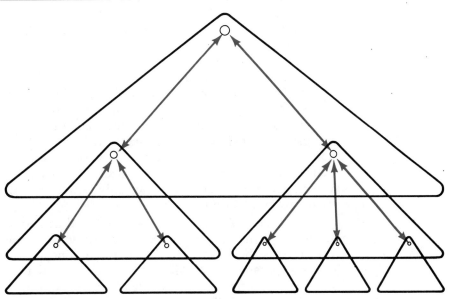

Figure 8-5
THE "LINKING
PIN" FUNCTION

Source: Adapted from Rensis Likert, **New Patterns of Management** (New York: McGraw-Hill Book Co., 1961), p. 113.

Role of Individual. Theory X regards the individual as an isolated worker whose function is that of a cog in a machine. Personal responsibility is limited to quality and quantity of production, control of work is ever present and from external sources, and there is little opportunity or need for individual growth and development. The assumptions of Theory Y portray an intelligent, willing person functioning as an integral member of a group and contributing to the success of that group; thus, the need arises for maximizing the contribution of each member of the group by encouraging individual growth and development. External control and coercion are replaced by self-control and motivation derived from satisfying ego and self-actualization needs. The individual is creative and should participate in determining the objectives of the group, for it is through the act of participation that the goals of the organization and the goals of the individual become congruent. It must be remembered that although Theory Y encourages individual growth and development, the employee is not an isolated individual but a participating member of a group. The group is the smallest functioning unit of the organization.

Evaluation of Theories X and Y

Before presenting a contingency approach to organization theory, a summary statement of the positions of Theory X and Theory Y and an evaluation of the two theories are in order. One such summary asserts that Theory X describes "organizations without people," while Theory Y describes "people without organizations."[7]

Describing a Theory X organization as an organization without people is admittedly an overstatement. Organizations using the Theory X approach also have been termed work-centered, traditional, classical, and authoritative. Such characterizations place these organizations at one extreme of a continuum of theoretical approaches to organization theory. A Theory X organization often appears to ignore the psychological needs of its members. External controls and the accompanying overt resistance to these controls are very much in evidence. Further, the imposition of additional controls merely aggravates original problems which usually center around the quantity and quality of production.

The Theory Y organization — described as people without organizations — is the other extreme of the continuum and has been termed variously as the neoclassical, human relations, participative, or democratic approach to organization. Seemingly, all that is needed is the freedom and opportunity for members of the organization to express their latent capabilities. Such an opportunity for self-expression would result in the achievement of organizational goals and at the same time fulfill the psychological needs of the individual member. Despite the limitations inherent in the extreme stance of each theory, acquaintance with the implicit assumptions of Theory X and Theory Y is of value for it defines the limits of the approaches to organization theory.

Both theories suffer from too much generalization in that sweeping statements are made concerning work and human behavior. A study of the findings of both sociology and psychology tells us that such generalizations are not a correct statement of conditions as they actually exist. There are marked variations in the demands placed upon persons as the result of work, and what is considered as pleasant work by one individual is boredom and drudgery for another. Likewise, the behavioral characteristics suggested by each theory represent the extremes of the distribution of personality traits in the general population. Few people consistently demonstrate the characteristics postulated by either theory.

A second criticism that applies equally to each theory is that neither Theory X nor Theory Y is consistently in accord with research findings. The "organization without people" description of a Theory X organization is all too familiar to students of management, but not all Theory X organizations have such problems. Yet for those that do, the prescriptions of Theory Y — creation of jobs with intrinsic satisfaction,

---

[7]W. G. Bennis, "Leadership Theory and Administrative Behavior," *Administrative Science Quarterly*, Vol. 4 (December, 1959), pp. 259–301.

a democratic form of supervision, and participation in the decision-making process — do not consistently cure the problems of the Theory X organization.

A CONTINGENCY APPROACH

Fortunately there is an approach to organization theory holding promise that eventually the effects of organizational changes and the most effective form of organization for a given situation can be predicted. It is an approach that views the problems of organization as one of organizing a system. The systems concept is first introduced in Chapter 1 as an approach to the study of the management process, and in Chapter 5 (pp. 117–118, Figure 5-3) the major business functions are discussed as a servo system. The concept is presented again in Chapter 6 in connection with information systems and expanded in Chapter 7 into information-decision-making systems. We know that a cybernetic system is a recirculating type of process and is capable of a degree of corrective action, either as the result of internal changes within the system or in response to external environmental changes. A system is usually made up of subsystems, and the capabilities of the entire system depend on the capabilities of each subsystem; in turn, any change in the function or capacity of the larger system requires corresponding changes in the subsystems. Inputs into the total system may originate from outside the system or from the internal subsystems; the same is true of outputs — they may be placed outside the system or fed back into any one of the subsystems.

The above discussion of systems theory is rather abstract and has therefore not proven to be of significant value in the design and operation of organizations. What is needed is an approach that is more concrete and applicable to organizations as we know them. Such an approach is known as a contingency approach or contingency view of organizations. It does not abandon the systems concept; rather, it translates that concept into a less abstract language recognizing that the structure and functioning of an organization is contingent upon many situational factors, both internal and external to the organization. It is not a simplistic view of the organization which states that there is only one form of a successful organization under all situations or circumstances, nor is it the abstract view presented in general systems theory. It is a mid-range view adaptable to organizations.[8]

---

[8]Fremont E. Kast and James E. Rosenzweig, "General Systems Theory: Applications for Organization and Management," *Academy of Management Journal*, Vol. 15, No. 4 (December, 1972), pp. 447–465.

Jay W. Lorsch and Paul R. Lawrence (ed.), *Studies in Organization Design*, (Homewood: Richard D. Irwin, 1970).

Fremont E. Kast and James E. Rosenzweig, *Organization and Management: A Systems Approach* (2d ed.; New York: McGraw-Hill Book Co., 1974).

Parameters of a Contingency Approach

One of the main problems in developing a contingency approach to organization theory is determining the parameters of the organization. What are the factors of organizational design, structure, and function to be considered in such an approach? March and Simon in their book, *Organizations*, consider 206 variables as parameters of organization.[9] Many of the variables are new and as yet have not been tested by research; in addition, it is almost impossible to comprehend 206 variables and all the possible interrelationships that might arise. March and Simon's work stresses the belief that organizational effectiveness depends on recognizing and adapting to many variable and interdependent situational factors, and that what is considered effective organization for one situation may be woefully inadequate for another.

At the other end of the spectrum, Theory X and Theory Y utilize only two factors — work and the nature of people — as the parameters of organizations. A middle ground suggests the following six interacting, situational variables as factors that determine the appropriateness of any given organizational structure or process: (1) size of organization, (2) degree of interaction, (3) personality of members, (4) congruence of goals, (5) level of decision making, and (6) state of system.[10]

---

[9]James G. March and Herbert A. Simon, *Organizations* (New York: John Wiley & Sons, 1958). *Organizations* is primarily a systems approach to the study of organizations. The list of 206 variables is contained in the appendix, pp. 249–253. The book is recommended to the advanced student interested in organization theory.

[10]Raymond A. Katzell, "Contrasting Systems of Work Organization," *American Psychologist*, Vol. 17 (February, 1962), pp. 102–108. In this paper, Professor Katzell's presidential address to the Division of Industrial Psychology of the American Psychological Association, five situational parameters are presented. They are: size, degree of interaction and interdependence of organization members, personality of organization members, the degree of congruence or disparity between the goals of the organization and that of its employees, and who in the organization has the necessary ability and motivation to take action that will further its objectives. Professor Katzell has suggested the name, Theory Alpha and Omega, for the theoretical approach based upon these variable constructs. Perhaps the best method of developing the parameters of organization theory would be to use multivariate analysis as a technique for determining the dimensions of organizations. The following studies are suggestive of this approach:

William B. Eddy, Byron R. Boyles, and Carl F. Front, "A Multivariate Description of Organization Process," *Academy of Management Journal*, Vol. 11, No. 1 (March, 1968), pp. 49–61. This study is a multiple factor analysis of 24 performance measures obtained from a firm's records. One group of variables is drawn from monthly financial statements; another group is taken from information concerning the firm's labor force; some reflect the utilization of labor and its costs; and the last group contains ratios pertaining to productivity.

Stanley E. Seashore and Ephraim Yuchtman, "Factorial Analysis of Organizational Performance," *Administrative Science Quarterly*, Vol. 12, No. 3 (December, 1967), pp. 377–395. In this paper the annual performance data of 75 insurance sales agencies over an 11-year period are subjected to multiple factor analysis methods.

J. H. K. Inkson, D. S. Pugh, and D. J. Hickson, "Organization Context and Structure: An Abbreviated Replication," *Administrative Science Quarterly*, Vol. 15, No. 3 (September, 1970), pp. 318–329.

A. J. Grimes and S. M. Klein, "The Technological Imperative: The Relative Impact of Task Unit, Modal Technology, and Hierarchy on Structure," *Academy of Management Journal*, Vol. 16, No. 4 (December, 1973), pp. 583–597.

Size of Organization. As size (defined as number of people) increases, organization structure becomes more formal and complex, with the result that the appropriate processes of motivating employees toward the achievement of organizational goals become more formal and directive, rather than informal and participative.[11]

Degree of Interaction. As the need for interaction between members of an organization increases in order to accomplish the prescribed work, the organization structure should permit a free flow of information and exchange of ideas, and the accompanying processes of motivation should become more participative and informal.[12]

Personality of Members. Effective organizational structure and processes conform to the personality and expectations of members of the organization. Members who do not expect participation and who are dependent upon others for motivation react best to formal patterns of structure and motivation, while those who expect participation and are motivated largely from within react best to participative processes and informal organizational structure.[13]

Congruence of Goals. When the goals of the organization and those of its members are congruent, participative processes and a less formal structure are appropriate; but when organizational goals and members' goals are divergent, greater reliance must be placed upon external controls and formal structure to assure adequate control.[14]

---

[11]The following studies indicate the significance of size as a dimension of organization theory:

Geoffrey K. Ingham, *Size of Industrial Organization and Worker Behaviour* (Cambridge: Cambridge University Press, 1970), p. 170.

D. S. Pugh, *et al.*, "Dimensions of Organization Structure," *Administrative Science Quarterly*, Vol. 12, No. 3 (June, 1968), pp. 65–105.

Henry Tosi and Henry Patt, "Administrative Ratios and Organizational Size," *Academy of Management Journal*, Vol. 10, No. 2 (June, 1967), pp. 161–168.

William A. Rushing, "The Effects of Industry Size and Division of Labor on Administration," *Administrative Science Quarterly*, Vol. 12, No. 2 (September, 1967), pp. 273–295.

[12]The following studies indicate the importance of interaction between members of an organization:

John J. Morse and Jay W. Lorsch, "Beyond Theory Y," *Harvard Business Review*, Vol. 48, No. 3 (May-June, 1970), pp. 61–68.

Paul R. Lawrence and Jay W. Lorsch, "Differentiation and Integration in Complex Organizations," *Administrative Science Quarterly*, Vol. 12, No. 1 (June, 1967), pp. 1–47.

[13]Victor H. Vroom, *Some Personality Determinants of the Effects of Participation* (Englewood Cliffs: Prentice-Hall, 1960), p. 91.

William W. McKelvey, "Expectational Noncomplementarity and Style of Interaction Between Professional and Organization," *Administrative Science Quarterly*, Vol. 14, No. 1 (March, 1969), pp. 21–32.

Chris Argyris, "Personality and Organization Theory Revisited," *Administrative Science Quarterly*, Vol. 18, No. 2 (June, 1973), pp. 141–167.

Carl M. Lichtman and Raymond G. Hunt, "Personality and Organization Theory: A Review of Some Conceptual Literature," *Psychological Bulletin*, Vol. 76, No. 4 (October, 1971), pp. 271–294.

[14]W. Keith Warner and A. Eugene Havens, "Goal Displacement and the Intangibility of Organizational Goals," *Administrative Science Quarterly*, Vol. 12, No. 4 (March, 1968), pp. 539–555.

Level of Decision Making. The hierarchical level of decision making is primarily a function of the technology of the organization. When technology permits and decision-making functions are retained within the primary work group of an organization, participative processes and informal structure are effective. As the decision-making processes move upward in the organizational hierarchy and away from the work group affected by those decisions, formal structure and directive processes are more appropriate.[15]

State of the System. When the performance of an organization is relatively poor with respect to the achievement of organizational goals (thereby creating a state of system imbalance), directive processes of motivation and formalized structure become necessary to initiate corrective action; however, as the organization achieves stated goals, participative processes and informal patterns of organization become more effective and are expected by the members of the organization.[16]

The Contingency Approach Summarized

The parameters stated above form the framework of a contingency approach to the study of organizations. These dimensions are not broad generalizations concerning the nature of work and the characteristics of human beings, nor do they prescribe "the one best way." Instead, the parameters of a contingency approach offer a means of analyzing each organizational situation as it arises so that the most

Lawrence and Lorsch, *op. cit.*

Seashore and Yuchtman, *op. cit.*

George W. England, "Organizational Goals and Expected Behavior of American Managers," *Academy of Management Journal*, Vol. 10, No. 2 (June, 1967), pp. 107–117.

[15]The following discussion illustrates the effect of electronic data processing and management information systems (information technology) upon the locus of decision making:

William E. Reif, *Computer Technology and Organization* (Iowa City: Bureau of Business and Economic Research, University of Iowa, 1968). See discussion beginning on page 109.

To the extent that organizational structure is a function of technology, the following references are pertinent:

L. Vaughn Blankenship and Raymond E. Miles, "Organizational Structure and Managerial Decision Behavior," *Administrative Science Quarterly*, Vol. 13, No. 1 (June, 1968), pp 106–117.

Joan Woodward, *Industrial Organization*, Theory and Practice (London: Oxford University Press, 1965).

David J. Hickson, D. S. Pugh, and Diana G. Pheysey, "Operations Technology and Organization Structure: An Empirical Reappraisal," *Administrative Science Quarterly*, Vol. 14, No. 3 (September, 1969), pp. 378–396.

Jerald Hage and Michael Aiken, "Routine Technology, Social Structure, and Organization Goals," *Administrative Science Quarterly*, Vol. 14, No. 3 (September, 1969), pp. 366–376.

D. S. Pugh *et al.*, "Dimensions of Organization Structure," *Administrative Science Quarterly*, Vol. 12, No. 3 (June, 1968), pp. 65–105.

[16]Gwen Andrew, "An Analytic System Model for Organization Theory," *Academy of Management Journal*, Vol. 8, No. 3 (September, 1965), pp. 190–198.

appropriate organizational structure and process may be designed to fit the needs of that particular situation. One might well preface each statement with the phrase, "other things being equal," for the parameters expressed above function as a system and a change in the value of one factor modifies the significance and function of the remaining five variables. In the chapters that follow concerning the organizing function, the contingency approach to the study of organizations is utilized.

Case Problem 8-B sets forth what happened after five years of the experiment in participative management described in Case Problem 8-A.

Case Problem 8-B

AN EXPERIMENT IN PARTICIPATIVE MANAGEMENT
PART II The End of the Experiment

Between 1960 and 1965 there were many visitors to NLS. Most reported high praise for the experimental organization and few were aware that there were any defects. Yet in 1965 there were a series of changes in the organization of NLS that clearly marked the end of the experiment in participative management. The following changes occurred:

1. "Line" organization procedures were reestablished at the top levels.
2. Direct supervision was provided.
3. Specific duties and responsibilities were assigned.
4. Standards of performance and quality were reestablished.
5. Authority was delegated commensurate with responsibility.
6. Records were reinstituted and maintained.
7. Remuneration was related to effort.
8. Factory department units were accorded a large measure of autonomy to schedule work within their units in the fashion they wished. In this respect the department units functioned reasonably closely to the manner in which

they operated during the years of the experiment.[17]

It is difficult to evaluate why the experiment failed. Some of the reasons for ending the experiment were that sales volume was not at the level expected, and both administrative and sales costs were high in relation to sales volume. In addition, there was restlessness and dissatisfaction at the managerial levels of the organization. There were layoffs in 1963, 1964, and 1965. Competition in the industry had increased. Significantly, the sales force resisted all efforts to decrease sales cost, and finally the company was becoming progressively less profitable. Sales volume did increase during the time of the experiment; however, it was at a much lower rate with significant declines late in 1963 and 1965. The company was slow in carrying out its layoffs because it believed that such layoffs would be in conflict with the stated objectives of job

_____

[17]Erwin L. Malone, "The Non-Linear Systems Experiment in Participative Management," *The Journal of Business of the University of Chicago*, Vol. 48, No. 1 (January, 1975), p. 57.

and personal security. Thus the company tended to keep more people than needed.

There was dissatisfaction at the upper levels of the organization. At the council level the vice-presidents had formerly been very active in their respective areas, but as part of the experiment they functioned only as "sideline consultants." Their duties were not well defined and they were unable to function without clearly defined duties and the authority commensurate to fulfill these duties. At the Zone III level the departmental managers were also dissatisfied. They sought advice from the Executive Council as a whole rather than from individual members of the council who were formerly vice-presidents. The members of the council contacted at any given time may or may not have had the expertise in the area in which advice was sought. Some of the departmental managers, particularly those with minimal experience, needed the advice, counsel, and direction of someone with expertise in a specified functional area.

As mentioned in Part I, remuneration was increased from a wage of $76 a week to a salary of $100 a week, a 32 percent increase in direct labor costs. There is no evidence that there was a corresponding increase in productivity. The increased labor costs increased the sales costs of the product approximately 5 percent. It is difficult to evaluate productivity fully because of the absence of records, but it is known that in 1963 the production output was approximately 30 percent more than in 1960. However, the increase was not what it appeared to be on the surface. The total number of employees had risen from 240 to 340, an increase of 42 percent, over the same period of time. Thus there was an actual decrease in productivity. There is no evidence that production efficiency increased at any time during the experiment.

One of the most significant findings was related to the attitude and behavior of the sales force. At the beginning of the experiment NLS recognized the increasing competition by expanding its research and development efforts and enlarging its sales force to cover the entire country. Prior to the experiment the product had been distributed through sales representatives, but with the beginning of the experiment, salaried salespeople were employed and district sales offices were established with a stated annual sum to cover all sales expenses. Each office had its own bank account, paid its own bills, and sent receipts to the home office. Many salespeople considered servicing customers somewhat beneath their dignity, and there were no sales reports or expense books required of the sales force. In 1965 salaried salespeople were replaced by sales agents paid on a commission basis.

There appears to have been no significant difference in product quality with and without inspection.

The degree of job satisfaction was entirely a function of where one happened to be in the organization. The production workers, in general, reported that they were more satisfied with the experimental conditions than with the normal operations. There was no change in absenteeism or turnover rates between 1960 and 1965 as measured within NLS itself, nor was it significantly different from the Del Mar area in which the plant was located.

At the higher levels of the organization, job satisfaction was at a very low ebb. The following summary of what happened at Zone II, the vice-presidential level, indicates the severity of the problem:

> Initially, three of the seven had favored the plan, two had cooperated even though unconvinced of its merit, and three had cooperated while privately believing that it could not succeed. During the 5 years of the experiment, one new member was added, and one was dismissed and then later rehired. After the end of the experiment in 1965 three were given long advance notice of employment termination, a fourth left of his own volition after refusing a salary reduction, and death overtook two.[18]

There is no evidence whatsoever that there was any increase in creativity or innovation on the part of employees.

---

[18]Ibid., p. 62.

Profits had increased yearly from 1953 to 1960. Though an increase in profitability was not one of the goals of the experiment, one would not have expected that profits would decline continually from 1961 until the losses incurred compelled the abandonment of the experiment in 1965.

PROBLEMS

1. Does the organization established at the close of the experiment more closely resemble the Theory X organization or the Theory Y organization? Explain.

2. State in your own words why you believe the experiment was a failure, or if you do not believe it a failure, why you do not believe that it failed.

3. Would a contingency approach to organization have been of help in this situation rather than the full application of Theory Y — the human relations approach? Discuss your answer.

CHAPTER QUESTIONS FOR STUDY AND DISCUSSION

1. Give examples from your experience that illustrate the two meanings of the term, organization. Are these meanings mutually exclusive or is there a degree of overlap between the two meanings? Discuss your answer.

2. After reviewing the assumptions of Theory X, describe a work situation that reflects these assumptions as nearly as possible.

3. Describe a work situation that reflects the assumptions of Theory Y.

4. In your opinion, in our industrial society do most work situations conform more closely to the assumptions of Theory X or of Theory Y?

5. Compare a Theory X organization and a Theory Y organization with respect to the type of authority, the location of the decision-making process, the characteristics of the organizational structure, and the roles of the supervisor and the individual members of the organization.

6. Is it possible to have an organization that conforms to Theory X in some respects and to Theory Y in other respects? Give an example.

7. Describe in your own terms what is meant by a systems approach to organization theory.

8. The contingency approach presents six parameters for the characteristics of organizations. If you were to reduce the number to three, which three would you present? If the parameters for a contingency approach to organization theory were to be increased, which ones would you add?

Chapter 9

Organization Structure

Case Problem 9-A

SPAN OF MANAGEMENT

Excelsior Products, originally a sales organization owned and operated by a manufacturer's representative, is now a wholly owned subsidiary of Triumph Chemical Company, a relatively large concern in its industry and engaged in the development, manufacture, and distribution of industrial maintenance chemicals. Excelsior, like the parent company, sells direct to the industrial consumer and counts among its best selling items degreasers, waxes, detergents, insecticides, weed killers, special paints, and liquid fertilizers. All told, there are 85 products currently in the line; new products are added at a rate of about ten a year and usually the five poorest selling items are dropped from the line.

The sales force is composed of commission sales representatives who are among the highest paid of any industry. Although the commission rate varies from a low of 20 percent on some items to a high of 35 percent on a very few items, the average rate paid — based on current sales analysis — is 25 percent of total sales volume. Representatives earn an average gross income of $14,000 a year, and out of this amount they pay their own expenses. However, many representatives who have been with the company for more than a year earn at least $25,000.

The sales expense of Excelsior Products includes the 25 percent direct selling cost

paid to sales representatives as commissions and 8 percent allocated to advertising in trade journals, printed specification sheets carried by all representatives and distributed to customers, semiannual national sales meetings, and other miscellaneous sales expenses. Thus, from the $56,000 sales volume generated by each sales representative, the total sales expense is $18,480, or 33 percent.

During the first complete year of operations following the acquisition by Triumph, all five of the sales representatives employed by the former owner of Excelsior remained; true to expectation, they produced a total sales volume of $280,000. During this year no effort was made to expand the sales force by Thomas Jackson, a former district sales manager for Triumph and the new general manager of Excelsior. In the second year Jackson hired and trained ten new sales representatives, but by the year's end only five of the new representatives remained; however, sales for that year totaled $375,000. At the beginning of the third year, Jackson had ten good representatives, each capable of producing a sales volume of $56,000. The plans for the third year called for hiring and training two new representatives each month. Actually this goal was not realized, but he did hire 20 representatives, 12 of whom were still with the company at the end of the third year. Fortunately, none of the ten representatives working at the beginning of the year quit, and as a group they produced $570,000. This amount, combined with the volume of the new representatives — none of whom sold for a full year — totaled $810,000. Jackson is convinced that the 22 representatives presently employed are capable of producing a sales volume of $1 million in a full calendar year. These 22 representatives are located in the following areas: Los Angeles, 2; San Francisco, 2; St. Louis, the home office, 5; Dallas, 2; Houston, 2; Florida, 1; New York City, 3; Chicago, 3; Detroit, 1; and Colorado, 1.

Now Jackson is planning for the coming year and realizes that the growth of Excelsior Products is dependent primarily upon the number of sales representatives hired. Most of the representatives live in relatively large cities and sell not only to customers in that city but also to customers in the small towns in that section of the state. He recognizes that he has only one sales representative in the southeastern part of the United States and none in the Northwest or New England.

Jackson spends most of his time in recruiting and training new sales representatives. Some of the new representatives are referred to the company by present sales representatives, but most are recruited through newspaper advertising. Usually a new representative is sent out on the road for a period of one week with an experienced representative; then Jackson spends a week with the new representative in the territory assigned to him. Jackson realizes that the training received under these circumstances is probably inadequate, but it is all that time allows. In addition to recruiting and training new sales representatives. Jackson conducts two national sales meetings a year in order to introduce new products, and these meetings afford an opportunity to brush up on sales techniques. Although the laboratories of the parent company develop new products, it is the general manager's responsibility to choose the product name, approve the package design, and prepare the layout and copy of the specification sheets that describe the product and are carried by all sales representatives. In the home office there are three clerical employees who process sales orders as they are received from the field. The billing of customers, the computation of commissions, and the payment of sales representatives are performed by personnel of the parent company. Jackson realizes that if Excelsior Products is to continue to grow, he needs more managerial help, but he feels obligated to stay within the 33 percent selling cost imposed by the parent corporation.

PROBLEMS

1. Develop an organization structure for Excelsior Products that will permit the company to attain a sales volume of $5 million annually. Will this structure be effective when sales reach $15 million?
2. Of what significance are the findings of Graicunas in understanding Jackson's problems?
3. Is it possible to change the organization structure of Excelsior Products and still remain within the 33 percent overall selling cost? State the reasons for your answer. How does the answer to this question affect the recommendations made concerning organization structure in your answer to Problem No. 1?

Three approaches to organization are presented in Chapter 8, each of which emphasizes a different aspect of organizing. Theory X presents organization as centered around the work to be performed; Theory Y stresses the people of the organization. The contingency approach to organization recognizes the situational factors that determine organizational structure and function and integrates the requirements of the work to be performed and the desires and capabilities of the people who make up the organization. The alert student has probably observed that the three theories talk more of people than organizations, an observation which has considerable merit, for it is through people that the work of an organization is accomplished. Nonetheless, the structure of the organization — the arrangement of the component parts, people and work — is a major determinant in shaping the behavior of people, and, in turn, determines the extent to which organization goals are realized. One writer makes the following statement about the relationship between organization and people:

> People have about the same relationship to the organization as the driver and passengers in an automobile have to the automobile itself. If we want to improve the effectiveness of the automobile in reaching its objectives, that is, improve it as a means of rapid, safe, and comfortable transportation, we can do a number of things. We can improve the design of the automobile to better adapt it to the people who will probably use it. We can modify it to better conform to the characteristics of the roads it will travel. We can alter the furnishings of the automobile or adjust certain of its mechanical features to human needs. Such flexibility is inherent in good design. The design of the automobile must always be predicated upon the characteristics of the people who will use it and the environment in which it is to be used. The automobile is neither the people nor the environment, but it is inextricably linked with both.[1]

We all know something about the design of an automobile in relation to its purpose and the people who use it. If the automobile is to carry 50 people, it becomes a bus; if it is to enter the Indianapolis 500, there is room only for the driver; and Ford learned as the result of a survey, which surprises no one who has given the matter much thought, that engaged couples do not like bucket seats. We all know something about the structure and design of organizations, even though an organization is not a tangible entity like an automobile. When organizing a business or professional group for a social outing, one of the first items to be considered is the part that each person is to play in preparing for and conducting the event. Five members may be chosen to arrange transportation, three more to assume responsibility for providing food and beverages, and a third group to select and make advance arrangements for the site. Each group has a leader who works closely with the person in charge of special social events so that the efforts of all groups will be coordinated.

The example of a group preparing for an outing illustrates three characteristics of organization structure. First, the work to be accomplished is divided and then arranged into manageable portions. The

---

[1]From *Management and Organization* by Louis A. Allen. Copyright © 1958 by Louis A. Allen. Used with permission of McGraw-Hill Book Company. This book is a presentation of organization which emphasizes an orientation toward the work to be accomplished.

The following work, the result of a major research study, also emphasizes the point of view that organizations are not people: Peter M. Blau and Richard A. Schoenherr, *The Structure of Organizations* (New York: Basic Books, 1971).

word used to describe the process of analyzing, dividing, and arranging work into manageable portions is *departmentation*. Second, the leader of each group works closely with the permanent social chairperson so that the efforts of each group may be coordinated. The number of work groups reporting to the chairperson is a structural characteristic resulting from the manner in which the work is organized. To the chairperson, these are the number of groups that must be coordinated, or managed; hence, the expression, *span of management*. Third, each of the groups coordinated by the chairperson functions as a committee. In many organizations committees are a permanent part of the organization structure. This chapter discusses departmentation, span of management, and committees.

DEPARTMENTATION

A reservation concerning the use of the term, organization, must be made. For the most part, organization is actually *reorganization*. Seldom is an entire organization projected from scratch; instead, it is a process of changing and refining present structure and personnel. Problem 1 of Case Problem 9-A requests that you develop an organization structure for Excelsior Products and reflects a common use of the word, organization, in management literature. A more precise, though cumbersome, wording would request a reorganization. We will continue to use the expression, organization, as it appears in most management writings, but it is well to remember that in practically all instances we are discussing reorganization.

The need for departmentation, defined as the grouping of work or individuals into manageable units, is easily understood. Usually the process of creating manageable units is the first step in building an organization structure. It is conceivable that one person can perform all the work of an enterprise provided the individual has the necessary skills, knowledge, and time. A hamburger stand is illustrative of a business whose *functions* are managed by one person. As the business prospers, the owner finds that there is not enough time to perform the work of preparing food and serving customers. Thus as a first step in organization, the work is divided into units that can be completed by one person. Perhaps a cook who performs all functions associated with the preparation of food is hired, and the owner retains those functions connected with serving customers and managing the business. If the hamburger stand continues to grow and becomes a restaurant capable of seating 100 customers, the work of the cook is further subdivided. A chef is now in charge of the preparation of food and is responsible for all work performed in the kitchen. The chef supervises the work of several assistants, each of whom is skilled in the preparation of a certain type food. A supervisor of the dining room directs the waiters and waitresses who serve the customers. The owner is performing the managerial function of coordinating the efforts of all personnel. Should a chain of restaurants develop, each restaurant may be regarded as a manageable unit. Thus, departmentation, the grouping of work and people, occurs at all levels of an organization. What are the bases most commonly used in determining departmental structure?

Bases of Departmentation

Certain well-recognized and accepted bases for departmentation have developed over a period of years. These bases, which are common to all types of organizations, appear with such frequency and consistency that they may be regarded as common denominators of organization. The units created through the process of departmentation combine to form the total structure of the organization, and are work-centered in their origin and application since the primary goal is an effective division of work. The most frequently used bases of departmentation are: (1) function, (2) product, (3) customer, (4) geography, (5) process, and (6) sequence. Each basis for dividing work is discussed below.

Function. *Function* denotes related activity. It is a relationship that is apparent because of the similarity of the skills required to perform a given kind of work, or a relationship that binds together a group of tasks in the accomplishment of a common goal. The fundamental appeal of function as a basis for dividing work is its logical simplicity. What is more natural than grouping together all work requiring the skills necessary to operate machine tools and placing employees with those skills under the direction of one supervisor? By the same token, all employees having the required skills to assemble the product form the assembly department. These and other seemingly unrelated skills may be grouped together on a functional basis because the application of each skill results in the accomplishment of a specific task; and when these tasks are combined, a logical relationship may be perceived, for machining and assembling are activities (functions) necessary to accomplish a common goal — the production of the product.

The functions usually identified in the top echelon of business organizations are production, finance, and marketing, or sales. These functions have been described as primary, vital, or organic; the implication is that the absence of any one of the three functions would result in the death of the organization. The terminology used to describe these functions and the significance of these and other functions varies from one type of enterprise to another. Manufacturing firms use the terms production (or manufacturing), finance, and marketing. Wholesalers recognize the functions of finance and sales, but production takes the form of buying, warehousing, and distribution. Airlines use the word, operations, to describe their production function — the movement of passengers. For some organizations one or more of the functions may be vestigial in nature; for example, hospitals and banks have no marketing function per se; rather, these organizations refer to the function of public relations. On the other hand, it is difficult to imagine a function more vital to pharmaceutical firms than research, because over half of their current sales volume results from products which were unknown ten years ago.

In addition to the primary functions, there are auxiliary functions such as personnel that must be performed. Traditionally, auxiliary functions — frequently called staff functions — are considered supportive in nature and supplement the primary functions of the organization. Delicate interpersonal relationships between those performing primary functions and those carrying out auxiliary functions often arise and are discussed in considerable detail in the next chapter.

Product. Companies with diversified product lines frequently create managerial units based upon the product. Three forms of product departmentation are shown in Figure 9-1. Chart 1 shows the division of both the sales and the manufacturing functions into product departments, while Chart 2 shows product departmentation applied to the sales function only. In Chart 3 the manufacturing function is departmentalized according to product, and sales remains as a single unit. Figure 9-1 also illustrates that the process of creating departments quite properly employs more than one basis. In this instance, the bases of function and product are used.

Customer. Retail stores may organize their sales forces to meet the needs of a specific class of customer by forming special departments to cater to teenagers, collegians, or brides. An industrial firm manufacturing valves might divide its sales force so that one part of it sells to original equipment manufacturers and the other part sells to the replacement market.

Geography. At one time, poor communications was the reason given to justify departmentation based on territorial or geographic units. While this reason may still have some validity for those companies with foreign operations, the quality of communications is usually no longer a valid reason for geographic departmentation within the United States. When the number of people to be supervised is large and dispersed over a wide area, territorial units afford a logical means of developing manageable units. The creation of regional units offers a possible solution to the organization problem confronting Excelsior Products in Case Problem 9-A.

Process. The process or equipment used in producing a product may be the basis for determining departmental lines at the plant level. The grouping of all milling machines into one department and the placing of lathes in another department is illustrative of departmentation by equipment. In other industries the process serves as the basis for determining effective departmentation. Thus, in a chemical plant a process such as distillation becomes the operating unit.

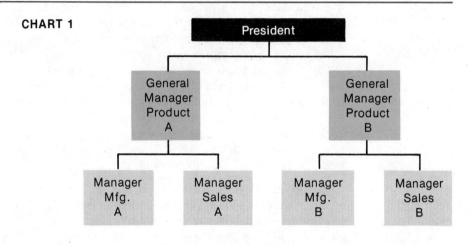

CHART 1

President

General Manager Product A — General Manager Product B

Manager Mfg. A — Manager Sales A — Manager Mfg. B — Manager Sales B

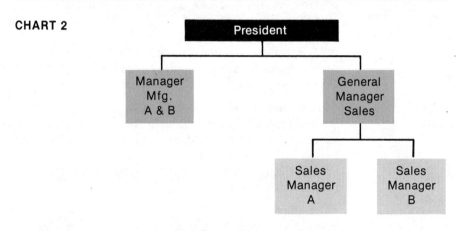

CHART 2

President

Manager Mfg. A & B — General Manager Sales

Sales Manager A — Sales Manager B

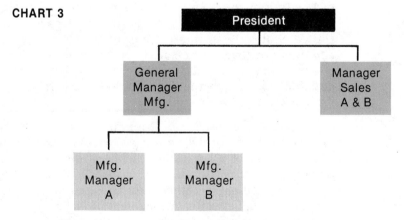

CHART 3

President

General Manager Mfg. — Manager Sales A & B

Mfg. Manager A — Mfg. Manager B

Figure 9-1
THREE POSSIBLE ARRANGEMENTS OF DEPARTMENTATION BASED UPON PRODUCT

Sequence. Departments sometimes conform to alphanumeric or time sequences. For those organizations not yet computerized the bookkeeping section may be subdivided into two units, one of which posts accounts for customers whose last names begin with the letters A through M; the other unit posts for those customers whose names begin with the letters N through Z. Numerical sequence is often the basis for dividing undifferentiated labor gangs into controllable units; i.e., every 30 employees are placed under the direction of a straw boss. Plants operating 16 or 24 hours a day establish separate shifts, and each shift is a distinct administrative unit.

Creating Manageable Departments

The above bases of dividing work are an extension of the definition of departmentation and a description of the building blocks that make up the organization structure. Creating manageable departments is not an end in itself; instead, it is a means of facilitating the achievement of organizational objectives. There is no set of rules that prescribes the one best pattern of organization structure; however, there are guides, discussed in Chapter 11, which are useful in selecting the most appropriate structure.

SPAN OF MANAGEMENT

Once the bases of departmentation are determined — whether by function, product, customer, geography, process, sequence, or any combination of these criteria — another problem in organization structure immediately arises: How many departments are to be placed under the direction of one individual? This problem is frequently referred to as *span of control*; however, the phrase *span of management* describes the question more accurately because an executive performs the functions of planning, organizing, and leading, as well as the function of control. The span of management has a direct bearing upon the number of levels in an organization; the number of levels, in turn, is a measure of the length of that organization's *lines of communications*.

For example, Thomas Jackson of Excelsior Products in Case Problem 9-A, has 22 sales representatives and three clerks in the home office reporting to him, a span of management of 25 employees. Let us assume that he names a chief clerk and appoints four regional sales supervisors; his span of management is reduced from 25 to 5, but there is now one level of supervision through which communications between him and the sales representatives and clerks must pass. Suppose that he appoints an eastern division sales manager and a western division sales manager, each of whom supervises three regional sales managers. Jackson's span of management is reduced to three people. He must now communicate to his sales representatives through two levels of supervision, the divisional and the regional managers.

From the discussion above, it is apparent that if the span of management is decreased, the lines of communications are lengthened; and, conversely, if the lines of communication are shortened, the manager's span is increased. Yet, there are writers in the literature of management who advise the chief executive to simultaneously reduce span of management and shorten the organization's communication lines. Let us review the reasons frequently advanced in support of a limited span of management and then examine the experience of several companies that have deliberately increased the manager's span.[2]

Reasons for a Limited Span

One of the earliest recommendations in support of a limited span of management is found in Jethro's advice to Moses that he establish "rulers of thousands, and rulers of hundreds, and rulers of fifties, and rulers of tens."[3] In modern literature the development of the concept that supports a limited span of management is attributed to the work of three men. First, there is the statement of Sir General Ian Hamilton; second, the work of V. A. Graicunas; and third, the formal statement of a principle by Lyndall F. Urwick.

Hamilton's Recommendations. General Hamilton's conclusions are drawn from his experiences as a military officer. He begins his line of reasoning with the statement that the average human brain finds its optimum work level when handling three to six other brains. His observation that a noncommissioned officer is not fully occupied when directing only three soldiers and that a lieutenant general finds it difficult to direct the activities of six divisional generals is recognition that the number of persons under the direction of one supervisor should be greater at the lower levels of the organization than the number supervised at the top of the organization. General Hamilton recommended that "the nearer we approach the supreme head of the whole organization, the more we ought to work toward groups of six."[4]

The Theory of Graicunas. An important consideration in establishing an appropriate span of management is the number of potential interactions that might occur between the manager and subordinates. V. A. Graicunas, a Lithuanian management consultant, developed a

---

[2]For a discussion of the factors that determine the span of management and number of levels in an organization, the following is recommended: D. S. Pugh, "The Measurement of Organization Structures," *Organizational Dynamics*, Vol. 1, No. 4 (Spring, 1973), pp. 19–34.

[3]See page 20, for a more complete analysis of Jethro's recommendations which are contained in Exodus 18: 13–26.

[4]Sir Ian Hamilton, *The Soul and Body of an Army* (London: Edward Arnold Publishers, 1921), p. 221.

formula for determining some, but not all, of the relationships inherent in a given span.[5]

If, for example, one supervisor, *S*, has two subordinates, *A* and *B*, a *direct relationship* may occur between the supervisor *S* and *A*, and between the supervisor *S* and *B*. But there are times when *S* talks to *A* with *B* present or to *B* with *A* present; thus, two *group relationships* are possible. Further, *cross relationships* may exist between *A* and *B* and between *B* and *A*. As shown in Figure 9-2, these three sets of relationships — direct, group, and cross — combine to form six possible interactions between one supervisor and two subordinates. When a third subordinate, *C*, reports to *S*, one additional direct relationship is

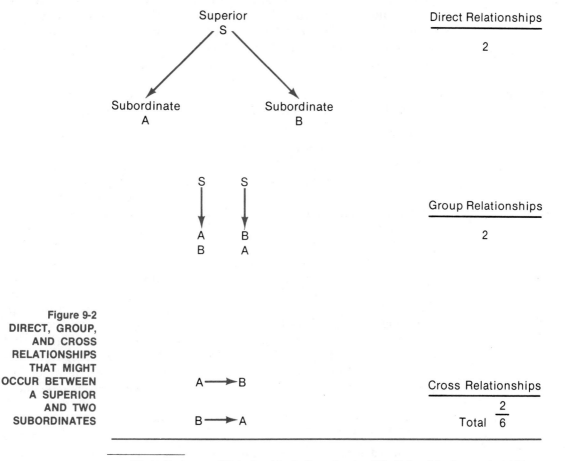

Figure 9-2
DIRECT, GROUP, AND CROSS RELATIONSHIPS THAT MIGHT OCCUR BETWEEN A SUPERIOR AND TWO SUBORDINATES

[5]V. A. Graicunas, "Relationship in Organization," *Bulletin of the International Management Institute*, Vol. 7 (March, 1933), pp. 39–42, reprinted in *Papers on the Science of Administration*, edited by Luther H. Gulick and Lyndall F. Urwick (New York: Institute of Public Administration, Columbia University, 1937), pp. 183–187.

established between S and C; but seven additional group relationships (AC, CA, BC, CB, ABC, CBA, and BAC) are possible. Also, four more cross relationships ($A{\blacklozenge}C$, $B{\blacklozenge}C$, $C{\blacklozenge}A$, and $C{\blacklozenge}B$) are added, thus bringing the potential number of interactions to 18. A fourth subordinate raises the theoretical interactions to 44, the fifth results in an even 100 relationships, and the executive with eight subordinates is the center of a web of 1,080 potential relationships.[6]

Graicunas's mathematical analysis of the potential relationships in a given span of management is significant for two reasons. First, his theory emphasizes the complex social processes that occur between a superior and subordinates and between the subordinates themselves. Second, the application of his formula stresses the alarming rate at which the complexity of these social processes increases with each additional subordinate. The addition of the fifth subordinate raises potential interactions from 44 to 100, the eighth subordinate moves the potential from 490 to 1,080, and the fourteenth subordinate finds the total relationships soaring to 114,872 from 53,404 with 13 subordinates. Fortunately, the relationships envisioned by Graicunas do not occur on a daily basis, or for that matter may not occur at all; but the warning is clear — somewhere there is one additional subordinate who is the straw that breaks the managerial camel's back.

Urwick's Principle. Lyndall F. Urwick, a noted management consultant who credits Sir General Ian Hamilton as the first to call attention to the concept of a limited span of management, encouraged Graicunas in developing his mathematical analysis of relationships. Urwick offers as a reason to support a limited span the observed psychological phenomenon that a person has a limited "span of attention" — a limit to the number of items that may be attended to simultaneously. Other limitations in human spans, such as the amount of energy available to a supervisor to perform the job, may be advanced. Further, time may be a limiting factor. Admittedly, not all the relationships recognized by Graicunas develop during the course of a single day, but if only a small fraction of the 1,080 potential relationships that might arise with eight subordinates occurs with any degree of regularity, an executive's span is limited by the amount of time that may be allocated to each personal contact. Graicunas recognizes that the number of cross relationships between subordinates, a major factor in determining the complexity of a supervisor's job, is dependent

---

[6]The number of relationships, r, may be determined by the following formula, in which n represents the number of subordinates:
$$r = n\,(2^{n-1} + n - 1)$$
As mentioned in the text, Graicunas does not take into account all possible relationships. Any one of the subordinates could conceivably initiate action, which in effect doubles the number of potential direct relationships; in addition, the supervisor could participate as a member of each group, with successive members of that group assuming the dominant role.

upon the nature of the work being performed. Colonel Urwick recognizes the variable complexity of a supervisor's job as a function of the work being performed in the following statement of principle:

"No supervisor can supervise directly the work of more than five or, at the most, six subordinates whose work interlocks."[7]

Span of Management in Practice

Lyndall Urwick's recommended limitations on the span of management — "five or, at the most, six subordinates" — is rather specific; but it must be noted that the suggested limitations are modified by the qualifying phrase, "whose work interlocks." How valid is this precept? One way of determining the validity of the concept of a limited span of management is to examine industrial practice in this respect. If there are differences between practice and recommendation, why do the differences exist? Two studies, one reported in 1952 and the other in 1967, present a good picture of practices and trends with respect to existing spans of management.

The American Management Association study (1952) presented the results of a survey of the then current practices regarding the span of management of the presidents of 141 companies that were "all known to have good organizational practices."[8] In the 1967 study, Ernest Dale conducted a questionnaire survey for the American Management Association.[9] The results of both studies were presented separately for large companies (over 5,000 employees) and for medium-size companies (500 to 5,000 employees). The 1967 study involved 93 companies with a single chief executive and seven companies having a form of group

---

[7]Lyndall F. Urwick, "The Manager's Span of Control," *Harvard Business Review*, Vol. 35 (May-June, 1956), pp. 39–47. Colonel Urwick's article is an excellent discussion in support of a limited span of management. The principle stated above first appeared in Lyndall F. Urwick, *Scientific Principles and Organization* (New York: American Management Association, 1938), Institute of Management Series No. 19, p. 8.

For a more recent discussion of the work of Graicunas and Urwick's comments about his own principle, the following is recommended: Lt. Col. L. F. Urwick, "V. A. Graicunas and the Span of Control," *Academy of Management Journal*, Vol. 17, No. 2 (June, 1974), pp. 349–354.

[8]Ernest Dale conducted two studies on organization, both published by the American Management Association. The first study was published in 1952 and the second study was published in 1967.

Ernest Dale, *Planning and Developing the Company Organization Structure* (New York: American Management Association, 1952), Research Report No. 20, p. 56. This research report is divided into two parts. Part I discusses the dynamics of organization with respect to determining objectives, delegating authority, span of control, the staff assistant, the staff specialist, group decision making, and decentralization. Part II presents established procedures in the mechanics of organization, including the development of charts and manuals. Many people consider this work a "handbook" of organization.

[9]Ernest Dale, *Organization* (New York: American Management Association, 1967), pp. 94–96. This study on organization is not a revision of the 1952 study; rather, it is based upon a new survey of practices in large and medium-sized companies. Further, it includes some of the recent behavioral work on organizations.

management at the top with lines of authority leading from this group rather than from a single executive. The median number of executives reporting to the president in 1952 and 1967 in large companies was between eight and nine, a number considerably above the limits recommended by Colonel Urwick. In the medium-sized companies, the results were essentially the same. The median number was between six and seven for both surveys. However, in 1952 the range in the number reporting to the chief executive was 1 to 17, and in 1967 the upper limits of this range increased to 22.

It was evident that more than half of the companies in each group did not adhere to the recommendation that "five, or at the most, six" subordinates report to each superior. Nor did it seem possible that the deviation from the recommended five or six was due to work of subordinates that did *not* interlock. Again, there was marked similarity between the two groups of companies with respect to the functions performed by the subordinates reporting to the president. Among those functions most frequently mentioned by both groups that were supervised by the president were production, sales, industrial relations, legal counsel, controller, treasurer, finance, purchasing, research, plant management, and engineering. The nature of these functions is such that there is usually a high degree of interrelationship between them.

COMMITTEES

Committees are a major part of organizational structure, and most students of management sooner or later serve as a member or chairperson of a committee. A study of committees is necessary for a full understanding of the process of organizing and the potential assignment as a committee member. First, let us examine some of the underlying assumptions implied when a managerial task is assigned to a committee rather than to an individual, then evaluate committees to determine those situations that lend themselves best to committee action. Second, the committee is analyzed as it functions in business organizations; and third, the concept of the plural executive is discussed.

Evaluation of Committees

Before discussing the advantages and disadvantages of the use of committees, it is helpful to examine the underlying assumptions whenever a committee is created as part of an organizational structure. At least one of the following two assumptions is implicit in the creation of any committee. The first of these assumptions is that somehow, as a result of interaction between the members of a committee functioning as a group, the results produced by the committee should be better than the results achieved by an individual. The benefits of interaction between the members of a group may take one of several forms. If ideas are sought from the group, interaction will hopefully increase either the quantity or quality of ideas produced; and if action is desired as a result of committee deliberation, the fact that all members of the committee have participated in determining the course of action is likely to improve the quality and forcefulness of such action. The assumption that the interaction of the members of a group is beneficial is best described as a *participative belief* — a belief in the efficacy of participation per se.[10]

The second assumption implicit in the creation of a committee is that as an organization increases in complexity, primarily as the result of the increased number of delegated functions and the complexity of the individual functions, it becomes necessary for the managers of these various functions to meet periodically to exchange information. The need for an exchange of information between the managers of the major functions of an organization is illustrated in Case Problem 9-B. Committees formed as the result of a need to exchange information perform not only a message-center function, thereby improving the quality of communications, but they also perform a coordinative function as the result of channeling information.

Advantages of Committees. Advantages resulting from the use of committees are discussed under the following four headings: (1) group judgment, (2) improved motivation, (3) as a check on authority, and (4) improved coordination. The first three of these advantages are attributable to the interaction of the members of a committee functioning as a group, while the fourth advantage is attributable to the committee performing a coordinative function made possible by the exchange of information.

Group Judgment. The idea that the judgment of a group is superior to that of an individual is expressed in the phrase, "two heads are better than one." We all know that two heads are not necessarily better than one; however, there are certain situations in which the judgment of a group tends to be better than that of a single individual. A problem requiring diverse knowledge and varied experience for optimum solution is ideally suited for group consideration, since it is more likely that a group is able to contribute knowledge and experience broader than the knowledge and experience of an individual. The final determination of whether a given product should be placed in a company's product line is a good example of a situation requiring diverse information from production, finance, and marketing. A word of caution is in order, however. Even with problems requiring information drawn from each of the major functions of the company, it is not always necessary that the managers of these functions act as a group

---

[10]Although mentioned only in passing in this chapter, the concept of participative beliefs is reviewed in detail in Chapter 14. An example of participative beliefs in action is presented in Case Problem 8-A, An Experiment in Participative Management.

to obtain the values derived from such diverse backgrounds. The president of the company can talk with the head of each department separately and acquire from each manager the breadth of information required for a sound decision. Staff specialists who conduct a survey by interviewing many department heads are gaining the values associated with broad experiences without the necessity of meeting as a group.

In addition to values attributable to breadth of knowledge and experience, group judgments are sometimes improved by the internal self-criticism developed within the group as the result of interaction between its members. Self-criticism may result in a compromise solution containing the best aspects of several solutions proposed by individuals. Impulsive decisions and actions are minimized by the self-criticism generated by the group. A further benefit possible from interaction when meetings are conducted as brainstorming sessions, as described in Chapter 7, is an increase in the quantity of ideas produced by the group.

Another valuable characteristic of group judgment occurs when the membership of the group is carefully selected so that all interested parties are represented, thereby increasing the likelihood that the final decision takes into consideration the needs and interests of each member of the group. The daily production meeting of a manufacturing plant usually includes representatives from each production department, shipping, production control, and quality control, so that any action taken considers the needs of all participating departments.

Improved Motivation. Although the values received from the pooled knowledge and experience of committee members are often cited as the major contribution of a committee, there is much to indicate that one of the underlying reasons for committees, if not the dominant reason, is to assure cooperation in the execution of any plan developed by the committee. Cooperation, or improved motivation, in the execution of the plan may result from having participated in the work of the committee, for one of the benefits directly traceable to participation is increased knowledge, and, consequently, greater understanding of concepts that were formerly unknown or rejected. Another advantage resulting directly from participation is best described as pride of authorship. It is difficult not to support the execution of a plan developed, at least in part, by one's own efforts. An example of a committee owing its success to the positive values derived from participation is a salary or compensation committee that describes and evaluates all jobs and then develops and administers a plan of compensation.

An additional characteristic of committee participation that contributes toward better motivation is obtained by using membership on a committee as a means of "selling" or persuading a lukewarm member to go along with the majority. Such persuasion may range from the benefits gained by a better understanding acquired through participation to the implied pressure created by the stamp of approval that comes as the result of being a member of the committee.

A Check on Authority. One of the functions of a committee that may be considered an advantage is its operation as a check on authority. The use of committees in business organizations to limit authority is not frequent, yet committees are used for this purpose in other forms of organizations — governmental, religious, social, and educational — to such an extent that a brief discussion of the subject is warranted. The Supreme Court of the United States is, in effect, a nine-member committee that serves to check the authority of all agencies of the government; and the two houses of Congress serve, not only as a check on the powers of the chief executive, but also as a check and balance upon the powers of each other. Most religious and social organizations such as fraternal groups are governed by boards that effectively restrain the powers of designated officials. In universities we find good examples of restraint through the action of committees. The president of a university is usually restrained not only by the committee that appoints him or her, often called a board of regents, but also by committees of the faculty that may have authority ranging in scope from determining the curriculum to administering faculty pay increases and determining tenure policy.

The use of a committee as a restraining agent is not as clear cut in business organizations. Perhaps it is because many businesses have their origin as a result of the efforts of a single individual, or it may be the recognition that there are inefficiencies inherent in committee organization. Even so, the board of directors, a committee elected by the stockholders, serves as an effective check on the powers and actions of the president.

Improved Coordination. The three advantages of committees described above — group judgment, improved motivation, and a check on authority — are advantages that are believed to be derived from the participation of a group. Improved coordination resulting from committee action is not so much the result of participation per se; instead, it is the result of receiving, interpreting, and channeling information. A committee whose purpose is to transmit information and coordinate the activities of the various functions of the organization is formed at the upper level of an organization and may be called an executive committee or an operating or management committee. Usually this group is composed of the managers of functional areas such as marketing, manufacturing, engineering, and finance. The person-to-person contact afforded by regularly scheduled meetings permits all interested parties to receive and exchange information with considerable savings in time and an improved degree of understanding.

A further strength of committees whose purpose is one of coordination is that such committees may be granted an authority greater than that possessed by any of the individual members. For example, a new products committee, composed of the heads of marketing, manufacturing, engineering, and finance, may be granted the authority to accept or reject a given product, thereby exercising an authority greater than that of any of its members. By granting superior authority to the committee, rather than to an individual, the coordinative purpose of the committee is emphasized.

In Case Problem 9-B, the Electric Manufacturing Corporation can achieve improved coordination by creating an executive or management committee whose function is primarily the exchange of information. Such a group, meeting on a regularly scheduled basis, would serve to channel information to Ray Talbert so that he could better coordinate the various management functions. Also, if Talbert's health problems persist, the committee could be delegated sufficient authority to coordinate and administer the affairs of the company.

Disadvantages of Committees. The disadvantages and criticisms leveled at committees often result from the misuse of committees as well as from weaknesses inherent in the committee system itself. The criticism most frequently leveled at the committee system is that the cost is greater than the value received. Committees are also charged with not being able to produce good decisions since their very nature tends to develop a compromise decision rather than the one solution that is best for the situation; and lastly, the composition of a committee with its several members and semblance of democratic action makes it difficult to establish accountability. Each of these criticisms is discussed below.

Cost. The costliness of committees comes not only from the direct cost of each man-hour spent in committee service but also from the losses incurred when timeliness is a factor in determining the worth of the decision. Committees are very time consuming, since one of the premises upon which they operate is that the committee serves as a forum in which all members have a right to express a point of view no matter how trivial or inconsequential. If there is an important item under discussion, it is highly unlikely that any action will be taken without a review of the written minutes of the meeting by each individual member, an action that results in further delay and expense.

Though it is difficult to determine the cost of committees, particularly when measured against value received, the following approach is suggested. First, determine the number of man-hours spent per year in meetings by multiplying the total number of meetings, times the average length of each meeting, times the average number of executives in attendance. Add to this figure the cost of the secretary of the committee and other clerical and staff work; then assign an average dollar cost to the total time spent (remember that the cost of a $25,000 a year executive is about $15 an hour). Review the work of the committee for the past year and place a monetary value on its accomplishments. Balance this value of work accomplished against total cost; then determine whether the work of the committee could be carried on as effectively if the committee were dissolved.

Compromise Decisions. Although the value of group judgment derived from varied backgrounds and experiences of the members of a committee is listed as one of its chief values, it is a value realized only under relatively limited conditions. Far too often the decision of a committee may result in a compromise at what appears to be the level of the lowest common denominator. The reasons for poor quality in committee decisions are not hard to find. Committees often develop a belief that they should reflect a unanimity of opinion, and unless a unanimous decision can be achieved, there is a tendency to delay any decision. The desire for unanimity, even though it means compromise, is understandable when there is a decision requiring execution because a recalcitrant member can sabotage the entire action of the committee by refusing to aid in carrying out the plan. Another reason for compromise is that committees within a company are made up of people who must work together in many different capacities, with the result that there is opportunity for a degree of political trading and a reluctance to force unpleasant situations — conditions that encourage compromise.

Still another factor affecting the quality of committee decisions is the control of a committee by a minority, a control particularly effective when there is a tradition of unanimous action. Such control may be exercised by the power of veto, or as illustrated in national politics by the power of the filibuster. Although the filibuster is not operative as a formal institution in business, there are times when a subject is avoided rather than invite what everyone knows is going to be a protracted discussion of an issue.

If decisions are not compromised, either in an attempt to secure unanimity or as the result of minority control, the other extreme may occur, a single dominant person hiding behind the screen of a committee composed of a group of "Yes men." If such is the case, the following question should be raised: Why have a committee in the first place?

Lack of Accountability. In discussing the process of delegation in Chapter 11, the three steps of the process are set forth: (1) the assignment of duties or responsibilities, (2) the delegation of authority, and (3) the creation of an accountability on the part of the subordinate to the superior. Committees, like individuals, may be assigned responsibilities and may be granted delegated authority. However, the establishment of accountability to the one who appoints the committee is very difficult. Theoretically, all members of a committee may be held accountable for the action of the committee, yet this is not a practical point of view when the final position of the committee is a compromise reached as the result of many hours of discussion. One might wish to hold the chairperson accountable, but the chairperson may have no effective control over the individual members of the committee. The inability to establish accountability clearly and to take any necessary subsequent corrective action makes committees particularly ineffective as an organizational structure when the responsibility assigned is one of action or execution.

Committees in Use

The use of the committee as a part of the organization structure of top management is relatively recent, the first notable example being the top management committee established in 1921 by E. I. du Pont de Nemours & Company.[11] Since 1921 the use of committees has grown extensively; however, before discussing the extent to which committees are used, it is helpful to develop a means of classification because committees vary widely in the functions assigned and the degree of authority granted to them.

Classification of Committees. When classified by function, committees may be grouped as either *general management* committees or *restricted* committees. The major function of a general management committee is policy making and the effect of its work is usually company-wide in scope. Those committees not engaged in general management activities are classified as restricted committees and their scope is limited to one function or, at the most, to a group of related functions. Typically, restricted committees are concerned with such functions as marketing, production, or personnel. Both of these broad categories, general management committees and restricted committees, may be further subdivided in the degree of delegated authority possessed by the committee. If the committee has the power to make decisions and has an effective means of carrying out these decisions, it is regarded as an *authoritative* committee. If the committee is not capable of carrying out its recommendations, or if it is organized solely for the purpose of studying and advising, the committee is classified as *nonauthoritative*.[12]

Functions of Committees. There are two studies of the extent to which committees are used and the functions assigned to them. M. R.

[11]M. R. Lohman, *Top Management Committees* (New York: American Management Association, 1961), AMA Research Study 48, p. 5. Research Study 48 of the American Management Association presents information gathered from 93 firms that have a total of 319 management committees of all types and discusses the status of committees in American industry.

[12]*Ibid.*, pp. 13–21.

Lohman's survey of 319 top management committees in 93 companies reveals that 78 of the 93 companies have general management committees. Of these general management committees, two thirds of them receive their authority from the president of the company and the other one third is appointed by and receives its authority directly from the board of directors. Twenty-five percent of these general management committees are classified as authoritative and 25 percent are classified as nonauthoritative. The remaining 50 percent have some degree of authority in specific areas of operations, but the authority is not of sufficient breadth to warrant their classification as authoritative. It is interesting to note that of those general management committees appointed by the board of directors — one third of the total — 83 percent are classed as authoritative, while only 20 percent of the committees reporting to and drawing their authority from the president of the company are regarded as authoritative. Seemingly, the degree of authority granted top management committees is related to the source of authority. Only 12 of the 78 firms reporting the presence of a general management committee are limited to that one committee; 66 of the 78 firms have at least one restricted committee in addition to the general management committee. All the firms surveyed reported some form of top management committee.[13]

The other study, conducted by Rollie Tillman, Jr., is a survey of 1,200 executives regarding the functioning and extent of committees in their companies. The presence of a regular, or a "standing" committee, is to some extent related to the total number of employees of the company. Of those firms with fewer than 250 employees, only 63.5 percent have one or more regular standing committees, while 93.8 percent of those firms with more than 10,000 employees report one or more standing committees. The average for all firms represented by the 1,200 executives who participated in the study shows that 81.5 percent have one or more standing committees.[14] One aspect of Tillman's study is that it presents in concise form the major functions assigned to each of the various types of standing committees. The distinction between standing or regular committees and those that are temporary in nature is that the temporary committee is usually organized for a specific purpose and dissolved when that purpose is satisfied. Temporary committees are generally called ad hoc committees.

The committees listed by Tillman conform to the classification developed by Lohman. Sixty-seven percent of the executives serving on general management committees report the primary function of the committee as one of setting policy, and the functions of planning and making operating decisions are second and third in importance. The remaining types of committees — finance and control, marketing,

---

[13]*Ibid.*, pp. 10–11.

[14]Rollie Tillman, Jr., "Committees on Trial," *Harvard Business Review*, Vol. 38 (May–June, 1960), pp. 6–8, 11, 12, 162–164, 166, 168, 171–173.

production, labor and personnel, research and development and new products, public relations, and other — correspond to Lohman's classification of restricted committees.

It is interesting to note the variation in the major function assigned to each of the restricted committees. The committees of finance and control, production, and research and development are engaged primarily in the function of planning, while marketing mainly performs a review function. Very few of those serving on marketing committees report a policy function for this committee; apparently the policies of marketing are determined by general management committees. The function most frequently performed by the labor and personnel committee is that of making operating decisions and is probably due to the necessity for these committees to interpret labor agreements as they affect company operations. The committees on public relations most frequently serve in an advisory capacity. Although Tillman's study shows definite trends in the functions assigned to various management committees, it is unwise to generalize concerning the purpose of a given committee since there is substantial variation in the functions assigned to general management committees and to each of the restricted committees. Nonetheless, the study is of value in that it shows succinctly the wide range of activities that may be delegated to various committees.

The Plural Executive

When committees assume the responsibilities of an executive, they are referred to as a *plural executive*; and, as the phrase implies, the group functions as a single executive. In Dale's 1967 survey (p. 199), of the 100 large companies, seven of them did not have a single chief executive. Instead, these seven companies operate with a small group that is often referred to as *office of the president*. The office of the president is an example of a plural executive and functions as a single executive. Another example of a committee that almost invariably functions as a plural executive is the board of directors. It must be remembered that not all committees are regarded as a plural executive. Among those not considered as a plural executive are committees whose function is advisory in nature or whose function is research and study.

Case Problem 9-B describes a company whose problems may be solved by the formation of a committee. Whether the committee be advisory in nature or functions as a plural executive is one of the choices that must be made.

A PROBLEM IN COORDINATION

Ray Talbert, the president and founder of Electric Manufacturing Corporation (Emcorp), is wondering how he can follow the advice of his doctor, who told him to take it easy after last year's coronary attack. Emcorp manufactures a full line of fractional horsepower electric motors sold to both original equipment manufacturers and distributors throughout the country. At the present time, the company employs approximately 1,000 people.

Talbert, an engineer, has maintained tight control over all major functions throughout the years; and though each of the heads of the engineering, manufacturing, sales, finance, and personnel departments has the title of vice-president, they come to Talbert for approval before making any changes in procedure. Usually, each of these executives sees Talbert several times a day. The personnel director once suggested a weekly meeting, but Talbert vetoed the idea as too time consuming. Now, worried about his health as well as the problems of the company, Talbert is beginning to feel the need for some relief from the constant pressure.

The manufacturing department shows a picture of rising costs, consistent failure to meet delivery schedules, and an increasing number of quality complaints. John Stroud, vice-president of manufacturing, admits to poor performance, but says that the cost figures from accounting are pure history and of no use since they do not reach manufacturing until the 15th of the month following the month in which the work is completed. He states that his failure to meet delivery schedules is due almost entirely to the fact that the sales department makes unrealistic promises and does not bother to check manufacturing schedules. Stroud attributes most of the quality problems to the incessant flow of engineering changes that come without warning and with no time to work out the production problems present in all new products. Talbert admits to himself that he forgot to tell Stroud that he had approved the last set of engineering changes and that he had asked Frank Smyth, vice-president of engineering, to put all of the approved changes into production immediately.

The vice-president and general manager of sales, Rita Linder, recognizes that she has no knowledge of the manufacturing schedules and realizes that she, too, is being criticized by Talbert for the many broken promises in regard to delivery dates. However, Linder's chief complaint at the present time is the result of having sold a large order of standard motors to a distributor having a supply of replacement parts in stock and then discovering that engineering had changed specifications — a change that made all replacement parts in the field obsolete. Another irritant for Linder is the tightened credit requirements instituted by the finance department without prior consultation with the sales department. Again Talbert admits privately that it is the same engineering change which caused so much trouble in manufacturing that is causing trouble for the sales department and obsoleting the existing stock of replacement parts. He also realizes that at his request, due to an unusually short cash position, the finance department tightened up on credit requirements.

PROBLEMS

1. Define the major problem facing Emcorp's management.
2. Would the formation of a committee be of any value in this situation? If a committee is needed, assign a title to the committee and indicate who should be members of the committee. Is there a need for an outside member on the committee?
3. Would an ad hoc committee be of any value?
4. In the event that Talbert decides to retire, would the presence of a committee make it easier or more difficult for Talbert's successor? Discuss.

CHAPTER QUESTIONS FOR
STUDY AND DISCUSSION

1. The quotation from Louis A. Allen on page 190 presents an analogy that compares the design of an organization to the design of an automobile. What is the lesson to be learned from this analogy? What similar analogies can you develop?

2. What is meant by the statement that most of what is called organization is actually reorganization?

3. What is meant by the term departmentation? Give an example of each of the six bases of departmentation.

4. Comment on each of the following statements: (a) The characteristics of people should be given prime consideration in the creation of departments. (b) The characteristics of the work performed should be given prime consideration in the creation of departments.

5. Why is the phrase span of management used in the text rather than the phrase span of control? Which phrase do you prefer? Why?

6. Comment on the advisability of shortening the lines of communication and at the same time decreasing an executive's span of management.

7. Evaluate the reasons presented by Hamilton, Graicunas, and Urwick for a limited span of management.

8. What phrase in Urwick's principle makes possible the justification of increased spans of management? Does this seem a valid reason for increasing the span of management?

9. What assumptions are implied whenever a committee is formed? Which assumption is more applicable to the formation of a general management committee? Which is more applicable to the formation of an ad hoc or restricted committee?

10. Under what conditions is the judgment of a group likely to be superior to that of an individual? Is the information presented in Chapter 7 concerning brainstorming applicable to the improvement of the judgment of a group? How?

11. Why are committees not used as a check on authority more frequently in business organizations?

12. What problems concerning accountability arise when a committee is granted the authority to make decisions? How can the chairperson of a committee be held accountable for the action of the group?

Case Problem 10-A

A STRIKE VOTE

The Muskegon Machine Works is a Delaware corporation that operates two plants. One is located in Muskegon, Michigan, and employs 700 people; the other is located in Nashville, Tennessee, and employs 300 people. The Machine Works, as it is known locally, is proud of its relations with its stockholders and their active participation in annual meetings. At the last meeting the present board of directors was reelected and, in turn, the board reappointed the present officers of the company. A meeting of the board of directors of the Machine Works is now in progress.

"Gentlemen," John Johansen, president of the company and a member of the board, began. "I have asked for a meeting so that we might review our current labor negotiations. We have been negotiating with the local union for the past 60 days in an effort to reach an agreement satisfactory to both parties. Two months ago we met in this same room and authorized our negotiating team to hold the line with a 7 cent an hour increase, some slight improvement in the pension plan, and a modification of our group insurance to bring the benefits in line with the daily room charges of the local hospitals. Mr. Lasker, chairman of our negotiating committee, tells me that the union is adamant in its demands: a 12 cent an hour wage increase, one additional holiday which brings the total to 9, and 4 weeks' vacation for all employees with 10 years' service.

The 7 cents an hour represents an increase in labor costs of $145,000 a year for the company since we give the same increase to the Nashville plant that we settle for here. The 12 cents that the union is demanding would add another $100,000 to the $145,000. You are well aware that our average hourly rate in Muskegon is 20 cents an hour above the average for the industry and 30 cents more than our average in the Nashville plant. Also, I am told that the union is meeting tonight to take a strike vote on our final offer presented to them this morning and in line with the instructions we gave our committee at the start of these negotiations. We have a meeting scheduled with the union tomorrow, the expiration date of our current labor agreement; if we don't reach an agreement then, the union is free to strike. Shall we stand firm in the face of what promises to be a long and costly strike?"

All issues are discussed thoroughly and the board votes unanimously in support of the company's final offer and instructs the negotiating team not to change its present position.

* * * *

In another part of town a special meeting of the local union is in progress. Norvell Slater, a 39-year old electrician with 20 years' seniority, is speaking to the membership. He has been an active member of the union since its certification as the bargaining agent of the employees of the Muskegon Machine Works by the National Labor Relations Board more than 15 years ago.

"I am reporting to you as president of the local and chairman of your bargaining committee. For the past two months we have been meeting with company representatives in an effort to reach agreement on a new contract. So far, not much has been accomplished. We have gained some slight improvement in our pension plan, and the daily room allowance of the hospitalization insurance has been increased so that it now covers the full cost of a hospital room. The real problem seems to be wages. When we started negotiations, we decided that we wouldn't take less than 12 cents an hour. The company says that they won't give more than 7 cents. They say that we are getting 20 cents an hour more than the rest of the industry and 30 cents more than Nashville. I don't know about that. All I know is that we are getting 10 cents an hour less than other workers here in Muskegon for the same kind of work and we live here, not in Nashville." At this point there is a roar of approval from the floor.

"The other things we can't get together on are holidays and vacations. Pat Toms, our international representative, tells us it would be a feather in our cap if we could lead the parade for once and get something first in this town. Getting that ninth holiday would put us out in front for a change. And about the four weeks' vacation for those of you with 10 years' service; you should get that now and not have to wait 20 years for it like I did. Anyway, that fourth week doesn't seem like much to me when you compare it to the three-month vacations that some companies are giving. Any questions?"

Again all issues are discussed thoroughly and the vote to strike is unanimous unless the company meets the union's demands for wages, vacations, and holidays.

At nine o'clock the next morning the negotiating teams meet in a downtown hotel. The meeting ends at 6 p.m. with no agreement. As the meeting closes, Norvell Slater makes this comment: "You know our contract expires at midnight. We have a strike vote backing us up, and since we can't get together we have no choice but to strike. Pickets will be placed around the plant in the morning."

The next morning pickets are at every gate and none of the hourly employees, all members of the union, make any effort to cross the picket line.

PROBLEMS

1. What is the source of authority granted to the board of directors of the Muskegon Machine Works? Did the board exceed that authority in authorizing the company negotiating committee to stand fast in the face of a certain strike?
2. What is the source of authority that permits the local union to enforce its contract demands by striking? Has the union exceeded its authority in the above case?
3. Does the action taken by the union, i.e., an economic strike, negate or cancel in any way the authority of the management to operate the plant? If so, how?
4. What are the obligations of the employees of the Machine Works to (a) the company and (b) the union?

In the discussion of theories X and Y in Chapter 8, brief statements were made concerning the *source* of authority. It was mentioned that Theory X assumes that the source of authority is related to the right to own property and the attendant obligation to manage property, while Theory Y states that in order for authority to exist, it must first be accepted by those who are being subjected to that authority. These two positions concerning the source of authority are diametrically opposed; one regards authority as being granted by a source external to the organization and the other views authority as being granted internally by the members of the organization through their acceptance of the exercise of authority. The first purpose of this chapter is to discuss the nature of authority and to reconcile these opposing points of view concerning the source of authority. In addition to understanding the sources of authority, it is necessary to appreciate the relationships between two types of authority that are exercised in most formal organizations. These different types of authority are usually called *line* authority and *staff* authority. The second part of the chapter discusses the important organizational relationship of line-and-staff authority.

AUTHORITY

One way of developing an understanding of the differences concerning the source of authority is to present statements representative of each point of view. However, before presenting and analyzing these statements, let us examine various familiar meanings of the word authority.

Meanings of Authority

There are many different meanings to authority. A board or a commission empowered to act in a specific area may be termed an authority; for example, the port authority. We recognize government as an authority in the phrase, the authority of the state. An individual may be recognized as competent in a given field of learning or possessing technical qualifications that enable that person to speak with authority. Technical writers and expert witnesses are examples of this kind of authority. When we refer to the authority of the president, we associate authority with an office or a position.

Authority is an abstract concept and, as shown by the above examples, it is a concept applicable to many situations. When used in management literature, the term authority has yet another meaning. Managerial authority may be defined as *the right to act or to direct the action of others in the attainment of organizational goals*. This definition states explicitly two characteristics of authority: (1) authority is a *right* and (2) as a result of possessing this right, one is entitled to *act*, either directly or indirectly through the actions of others. Implied, but not stated explicitly, is a third characteristic of authority — (3) the *power* to employ penalties or rewards so that the desired action is completed. Power remains implicit, for there is a great deal of variation in the amount of power associated with managerial authority; in fact, there is one form of authority, staff authority, that may be purely advisory in nature with no power whatsoever. There are also situations in which two or more conflicting or overlapping authorities are entitled to act and the power assigned to one authority may outweigh the power of the others; yet, the authority of those with lesser power remains.

Sources of Authority

Theory X, the work-centered approach, relates the source of authority to the right to own property. The right to own property and the association of authority with that right are dependent upon the organization of the society in which we live. Relating the source of authority to the right to own property and the subsequent management of that property may be termed an *institutional* source of authority since it is dependent upon the institution of organized society. Theory Y, the people-centered approach, regards authority as a situational phenomenon. Authority exists only when the subordinates of a situation accept another individual as having the authority to direct them. Therefore, this source of authority may be designated as *subordinate acceptance*.

Institutional Source. To state that authority is derived from the right to own private property is a narrow view of the source of authority and not entirely correct since there are instances of managerial authority not dependent upon the ownership of property. To discover the source of authority one must first determine why it is possible to own private property. Our constitutional form of government in the United States rests upon the concept that government represents the will of the people, a will expressed through the action of elected representatives in Congress and enforced by a judicial system. One aspect of our legal system is that it permits the ownership of private property and the management of that property in accordance with established law. Thus, the real source of managerial authority lies not in the right to own property, but rather in the laws that permit the ownership of property. Case Problem 10-A states that the Muskegon Machine Works is a Delaware Corporation, a statement which indicates that the company is created by law and, as such, possesses the authority necessary for its operation. Further evidence emphasizing that authority is derived from law and not the ownership of property is illustrated by the Tennessee Valley Authority. The managerial authority exercised by the managers of TVA, a publicly owned and operated utility, is derived from an action of Congress, which created the Tennessee Valley Authority. The authority of the management of TVA can come from no other source than law since the ownership of private property is not involved.[1]

Subordinate-Acceptance Source. Do you remember the following story that appears in Chapter 8?

---

[1]Cyril J. O'Donnell, "The Source of Managerial Authority," *Political Science Quarterly*, Vol. 47 (December, 1952), pp. 573–588. Professor O'Donnell's article is a skillful presentation of authority derived from institutional sources.

An agent for the Textile Workers Union of America likes to tell the story of the occasion when a new manager appeared in the mill where he was working. The manager came into a weave room the day he arrived. He walked directly over to the agent and said, "Are you Belloc?" The agent acknowledged that he was. The manager said, "I am the new manager here. When I manage a mill, I run it. Do you understand?" The agent nodded and then waved his hand. The workers, intently watching this maneuver, shut down every loom in the room immediately. The agent turned to the manager and said, "All right, go ahead and run it."[2]

The story illustrates, according to the subordinate-acceptance approach, that the manager has no authority because the subordinates, the workers in the mill room, refuse to accept his authority.

Among the first to dissent from the institutional concept of authority was Chester I. Barnard, a successful business executive, who, in the words of Morton J. Mandeville, "writes with authority about authority."[3] The following quotations from Barnard present his definition of authority and the related concept that the source of authority is its acceptance by a subordinate.

Authority is the character of a communication (order) in a formal organization by virtue of which it is accepted by a contributor to or "member" of the organization as governing the action he contributes, that is, as governing or determining what he does or is not to do so far as the organization is concerned.[4]

Barnard's statement concerning the source of authority follows:

If a directive communication is accepted by one to whom it is addressed, its authority for him is confirmed or established. It is admitted as the basis of action. Disobedience of such a communication is a denial of its authority for him. Therefore, under this definition the decision as to whether an order has authority or not lies with the person to whom it is

---

[2]Douglas McGregor, *The Human Side of Enterprise* (New York: McGraw-Hill Book Company, 1960), p. 23.

[3]Morton J. Mandeville, "Organizational Authority," *Academy of Management Journal*, Vol. 3 (August, 1960), pp. 107–118. An adaptation of Professor Mandeville's article appears in Paul M. Dauten (ed.), *Current Issues and Emerging Concepts in Management* (Boston: Houghton Mifflin Company, 1962), pp. 199–207. Mandeville presents the entire range of opinion concerning the definition of authority. Immediately following Mandeville's "Organizational Authority," in *Current Issues and Emerging Concepts in Management*, is a reply by C. Edward Weber entitled "The Nature of Authority: Comment" and Mandeville's reply to Weber's comment, pp. 208–212. The original citation for Professor Weber's article is as follows:

C. Edward Weber, "The Nature of Authority: Comment," *Academy of Management Journal*, Vol. 4 (April, 1961), pp. 62–66.

Robert Albanese, "Substitutional and Essential Authority," *Academy of Management Journal*, Vol. 9, No. 2 (June, 1966), pp. 136–144.

The student who reads these articles will gain insight into a management issue that is far from settled.

[4]Chester Barnard, *The Function of the Executive* (Cambridge: Harvard University Press, 1938), p. 163.

addressed, and does not reside in "persons of authority" or those who issue these orders.[5]

Before us are two conflicting views of authority. One, the institutional approach, says that authority is derived from the laws of the society in which we live. The other view of authority, the subordinate-acceptance approach, says that there is no authority unless the person who is the object of that authority accepts the order or directive as authoritative. One approach to reconciling these different views concerning the source of authority is to examine the factors contributing to the effectiveness of authority.

Effectiveness of Authority

Effective management requires a manager to have a clear understanding of the nature of authority. Managerial authority is not absolute; however, a manager cannot afford to be reduced to a state of indecision resulting from self-questioning concerning the right to manage. On the other hand, the manager cannot blithely assume that every action or directive will result in the fulfillment of organizational goals. There are three factors that limit the effectiveness of managerial authority: (1) superior authority, (2) overlapping authority, and (3) subordinate acceptance of authority. Note that subordinate acceptance does not negate or cancel managerial authority; *it merely limits the effectiveness of that authority*. Let us examine each of the three limitations on authority.

Superior Authority. The actions of the officers of a corporation are subject to review and limitations imposed by the board of directors. In Case Problem 10-A, the president of the company calls for a meeting of the board to review current labor negotiations. In so doing he is recognizing the higher authority of the board and seeking a course of action that meets with their approval. The board, in turn, is subject to the legal authority of the owners, the state, and the federal government. Companies impose limitations on the authority of managers by establishing policies and procedures; for example, a plant manager may be authorized to make capital expenditures up to $1,000 without prior approval, but required to submit for approval expenditures in excess of $1,000. These instances illustrate that authority is not absolute; rather, it is always subject to limitation by higher authority.

Overlapping Authority. Problem 3 of Case Problem 10-A asks whether or not the action of the union, i.e., the calling of a strike, negates or cancels the authority of management. If the source of authority lies in the acceptance of that authority by subordinates, then the

---

[5]*Ibid.*

answer to Problem 3 is affirmative. Now, analyze the situation carefully. The company, a corporation created by law, is exercising proper authority in determining what it believes to be best for its economic welfare. The union, too, is created by law and is certified by the National Labor Relations Board as the official bargaining agent for the employees of the Muskegon Machine Works. Also, the union is exercising properly the authority granted by law in enforcing its economic demands by striking. Thus, here is a situation in which both parties are exercising legally constituted authority to determine the wage rates of the employees of the company. Clearly, there is overlapping and dual authority, with each authority having the same source, law, and each authority being properly exercised. The rejection of the company's offer by the union and the subsequent strike do not negate the authority of management; it simply means that at this time the power of the union is sufficient to prevent the management from exercising its authority to operate the plant. Later, as the strike progresses, the company may accede partially or fully to the union's demands, or the union may agree to the original offer made by the company. Authority is not cancelled by power conflicts, which arise frequently when authority overlaps; it is only held in abeyance until the forces of power are resolved.

Subordinate Acceptance. Some proponents of the subordinate-acceptance concept of authority leave the impression that disobedience and the rejection of authority are the normal behavior for members of an organization. Nothing could be further from the truth. The institutions of society, including authority, serve a purpose desired by the majority of that society; however, occasions do arise when subordinates refuse to accept authority. Most authority carries with it rewards and penalties that may be used to encourage compliance. Those who recognize authority as derived from the acceptance of subordinates also recognize that the weighing of rewards and penalties by subordinates is an important factor in their determining whether or not to accept authority. The weighing of rewards and penalties is in effect a recognition of authority. Disobedience does not cancel authority, but it does render it ineffective for that particular situation unless the reward or punishment is sufficient to exact compliance.

LINE AND STAFF RELATIONSHIPS

The preceding discussion emphasizes superior-subordinate relationships — the relationships between the managers and the workers of an organization. There is another authority relationship that is equally important — the relationship between two different types of authority exercised by the managers of an organization. These two forms of authority are called *line authority* and *staff authority*, designations of authority that result in the corresponding expressions of *line organization* and *staff organization*, phrases which classify the entire organization according to the predominant type of authority exercised. In discussing line-and-staff authority relationships, we seek answers to the following four questions:

1. What is line authority and what are its functions?
2. What is staff authority and what are its functions?
3. What are the problems inherent in line-and-staff relationships?
4. Is the line-and-staff concept of authority obsolete?

Line Authority

The concept of line-and-staff authority recognizes that within an organization there are two types of managerial authority. There are also two aspects to the definition of line authority. First, line authority may be defined as a relatively simple authority relationship that exists between a superior and a subordinate. Second, line authority may be defined in terms of the organizational function supervised by a manager. When line authority is defined with respect to organizational function, the critical characteristic of the function that determines whether it is line or staff is the degree to which the function in question contributes to the direct achievement of organizational objectives. Let us examine each aspect of line authority.

An Authority Relationship. When defined as an authority relationship, *line authority entitles a superior to direct the work of a subordinate — in essence a command relationship*. It is a command relationship extending from the top of the organization to the lowest echelon and is aptly described as the *chain of command*. As a link in the chain of command, a manager has the authority to direct the work of subordinates, and, in turn, is subject to the direction of a superior. Each manager reports "in line" to a superior and is a part of the line organization. Figure 10-1 shows the relationships that form the chain of command in an organization.

Contribution to Organizational Objectives. The second definition of line authority does not contradict the above view which holds that line authority is a command relationship between superior and subordinate. It does, however, shift the emphasis of the definition from one of relationship between superior and subordinate to organizational function. The shift in emphasis results in the following definition: The line functions of an organization are those functions that contribute directly to the creation and distribution of the goods or services of the organization.

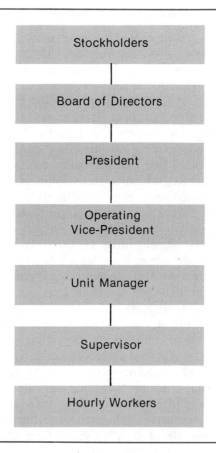

Figure 10-1
LINE AUTHORITY
RELATIONSHIP
AS A CHAIN OF
COMMAND

The key to distinguishing between line and staff is not the function itself; rather it is the degree to which the function contributes directly to the achievement of organizational objectives. In an army, the infantry, the artillery, and armored units are known as "line" since they contribute directly to organizational objectives — engaging the enemy in battle; the supporting services — ordnance, medical, engineering, and supply — are regarded as auxiliary in nature and referred to as "staff." In manufacturing organizations, production and sales are regarded as line functions, while purchasing (supplies) is usually classified as staff. Yet in a department store, the purchasing function, called buying, and sales make up the line organization. Most firms regard finance as a staff function, but for a loan company the acquisition and management of capital is part of the line organization. In each of these examples, the basis for designating a function as line is the contribution of that function to the direct achievement of organizational objectives.

Staff Authority

Staff authority is advisory or service in nature. *A member of management possessing staff authority advises or provides a service for line managers.* An organization may function quite effectively without any designated staff managers, and in small organizations such is the case.

In Case Problem 9-A, Thomas Jackson, the general manager of Excelsior Products, is effectively managing an organization of 22 sales representatives and 3 clerks. Assume that, as a first step in developing an organization structure capable of extended growth, Jackson appoints five regional sales managers, each of whom is responsible for the sales in one geographic area. These managers are line managers since they report directly to Jackson. They have the authority to direct the work of the sales representatives and are fully responsible for and contribute directly to the achievement of the organization's primary goal of selling its product. The first step in the development of staff might occur when Jackson employs Tom Richards as a *personal* assistant. At first, the duties of Tom Richards are not specified, but in a letter to the sales managers, Jackson states that Richards is to function as his personal assistant. Perhaps Richards' first assignment is to make all arrangements for the next sales meeting. Then he completes a statistical analysis of the dollar volume of sales for each of the many products that Excelsior sells. Eventually, Jackson may assign Richards to the specific job of training new sales representatives and discover that training demands the full time of a specialist. As a next step, he may hire someone whose sole function is the training of new sales representatives. Thus, the undifferentiated work of the personal assistant may develop into a specialized staff role.

This example illustrates that the need for staff services arises partially as the result of increasing size in an organization with an attendant increase in the work load of the chief executive.[6] Consequently, one of the functions of staff is to ease the load of top management. The personal assistant is frequently engaged as a means of easing the work load. As size increases, operations usually become more complex and the need for specialized services arises and results in the creation of a specialized staff. These two forms of staff, which are termed *personal staff* and *specialized staff*, are discussed briefly.

Personal Staff. There is need to define clearly the difference between an *assistant-to* a manager and an *assistant* manager. The assistant-to is a personal assistant to the manager. Duties vary widely from one organization to another and they also vary considerably from time

---

[6]For a discussion of the relationship between size and complexity in the staff function the following is recommended: S. R. Klatzky, "Relationship of Organizational Size to Complexity and Coordination," *Administrative Science Quarterly*, Vol. 15, No. 4 (December, 1970), pp. 428–438.

to time within the same company. The assistant-to receives the necessary authority to perform duties from the manager and usually the authority is granted on a limited basis; that is, it is extended for a specific job and for a relatively short period of time. The duties of an assistant-to may range from the routine task of opening the chief executive's mail to negotiating a purchase agreement for a new plant site as a personal representative of the chief. Note that the assistant-to usually has no specific function to perform; duties vary with the assignment at hand. Second, there is no authority associated specifically with the position; it is authority granted only for each individual assignment. Third, the assistant-to acts only as a personal representative of the superior.

The assistant manager is not regarded as staff, but rather as part of the line. As shown in Figure 10-2 (A), the operating executive reports through the assistant general manager to the general manager. In the absence of the general manager, the assistant manager acts in his stead. The assistant-to, Figure 10-2 (B), usually does not have the authority to act as general manager when the latter is absent. The general manager may assign certain specific functions to the assistant manager. For example, all activities related to manufacturing may be reported to the assistant manager, while the general manager supervises those activities associated with sales. Another possible arrangement is for the general manager to oversee the line functions of the organization, while all staff services report to the assistant manager. In each of these possibilities we note that (1) subordinates report directly to the assistant manager, (2) the assistant manager is assigned

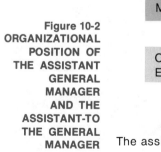

Figure 10-2
ORGANIZATIONAL
POSITION OF
THE ASSISTANT
GENERAL
MANAGER
AND THE
ASSISTANT-TO
THE GENERAL
MANAGER

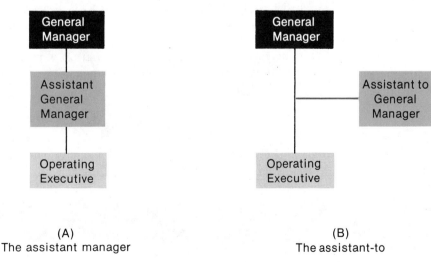

(A)
The assistant manager

(B)
The assistant-to

fairly constant, well-defined responsibilities, and (3) in the absence of the general manager, the assistant manager assumes the full authority of the general manager's position.

Specialized Staff. As an organization grows in size and complexity, the undifferentiated role of the personal assistant develops into specialized staff assignments. There is no unanimity concerning the functions that may be performed by specialized staff personnel, nor is there complete agreement concerning the type of authority that may be exercised by staff managers. Nonetheless, the following three types of specialized staff authority appear in formal organizations with great frequency:

1. A staff specialist may have the authority to provide a specific *service* for the line organization and thus exercise *service authority*.
2. Not all staff positions are created for the purpose of providing service; some have as their sole function the offering of advice concerning a special group of problems. Staff personnel in these positions exercise *advisory authority*.
3. Another type of specialized staff authority is *functional authority*, an authority that provides the staff specialist with considerable latitude and freedom to make decisions in a given functional area.

It must be understood that these three forms of staff authority are not clear cut; there is considerable overlap, and many positions utilize all three forms of staff authority.

Figure 10-3 shows a typical staff organization at the plant level of a manufacturing firm. The production planning and control supervisor is responsible for planning and controlling the flow of production; the purchasing supervisor serves by making necessary purchases; and the plant engineer is responsible for maintaining physical facilities. The supervision of each of these functions exercises *service authority* in providing a service for the line organization. The authority of the personnel supervisor may be either service authority or advisory authority. When performing the employment function of recruiting and screening applicants, the personnel supervisor is clearly rendering a service for

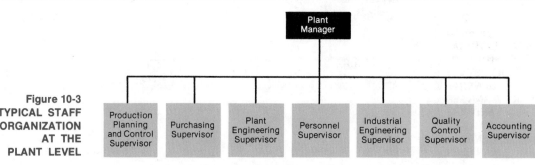

**Figure 10-3
TYPICAL STAFF
ORGANIZATION
AT THE
PLANT LEVEL**

the line. Other duties may include the administration and analysis of morale surveys with the purpose of advising the line regarding actions necessary to improve employee morale. The staff supervisor, when offering advice to the line, is drawing upon advisory authority. The industrial engineer, the quality control supervisor, and the head of the accounting department have as their primary function the offering of advice in specialized areas; and though there is a strong element of service in the work that each performs, it is best to regard their authority as *advisory* in nature.

Functional authority broadens the concept of service and advisory authority so that a staff manager may exercise effective direction and control of a functional specialty. There are two ways of exercising functional authority. First, staff managers may be granted functional authority over their counterparts who are in lower levels of the organization; and second, the particular functional specialty in question may be separated from the line manager's job and assigned to the appropriate staff specialist.[7] Figure 10-4 shows both forms of functional authority. Note that the plant supervisor of each staff function reports functionally (usually indicated by a dotted line) to the staff counterpart at the next higher level. In large organizations this next higher level may be a geographic division, and the managers at the divisional level report to their counterparts on the corporate staff. In addition, the plant staff supervisor performs that portion of the production foreman's job which falls within a specialty. Thus, there are cost clerks in the production department who report to the supervisor of cost accounting and prepare all production costs. The plant industrial engineer supervises time studies and institutes changes in methods, and the quality control supervisor directs the work of inspectors who accept or reject the finished product. Although functional staff authority is limited to a specific function, it may sometimes be quite absolute within that particular function, with the result that the authority of the line manager may be severely restricted.[8]

Problems in Line-Staff (L/S) Relationships

The duality of the line-staff (L/S) concept inherently creates problems of interpersonal relationships. Two authorities exist within an

---

[7] Frederick W. Taylor referred to the assignment of the specialized portions of the production foreman's job to the appropriate staff specialist as "functional foremanship." Further, he recommended that all of the "brain work" be eliminated from the foreman's job and that the worker come in contact with many members of management for directions rather than just one member — the foreman.

Frederick W. Taylor, *Scientific Management* (New York: Harper & Brothers, 1947), pp. 98–99.

[8] For a discussion of the functional authority of a specific staff specialist, the controller, the following is recommended: Dale A. Henning and Robert L. Moseley, "Authority Role of a Functional Manager: The Controller," *Administrative Science Quarterly*, Vol. 15, No. 4 (December, 1970), pp. 482–489.

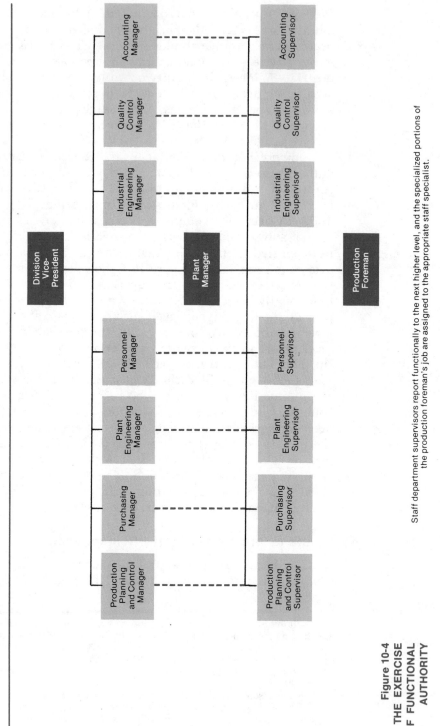

Figure 10-4
THE EXERCISE
OF FUNCTIONAL
AUTHORITY

Staff department supervisors report functionally to the next higher level, and the specialized portions of the production foreman's job are assigned to the appropriate staff specialist.

organization — line authority with its right to command, and staff authority with its right to advise. There is a duality of function — the line function is associated with the achievement of primary company objectives and the staff function supports the line. It is a duality that results in referring to an organization as though it were two separate units — the line organization and the staff organization. The concepts of dual authorities, functions, and organizations set the stage for some rather serious misunderstandings between those who are designated as line and those designated as staff. The reasons for L/S misunderstandings and friction may be traced to the way in which the individuals involved define their respective roles within an organization with respect to responsibility and importance of function.[9]

Responsibility. It is generally agreed that the line manager is responsible for achieving the primary objectives of the organization. When the organization is small and there is no staff, there are no restraints other than superior line authority on the line manager's freedom to make decisions and initiate action necessary to achieve the stated goals. When staff is introduced, restraints appear, for it is implied that the line manager should consult with staff. Frequently, line managers view consultation with staff as an infringement upon their authority to manage, and the resulting resentment toward staff is expressed through such statements as "staff is impractical," "staff does not appreciate the technical problems," and "consultation means delay." Line may accuse staff of trying to take all the credit when things go well and at the same time be unwilling to accept any responsibility for failure.

However, it is the presence of functional staff with its authority to administer its own particular function that presents the severest test of interpersonal L/S relationships. For example, the president of a company that is one of several subsidiaries of a large corporation is responsible for the profits of that subsidiary; and as a means of emphasizing this responsibility, a part of the president's incentive pay is based upon the profitability of the company. At the same time the corporate industrial relations staff, empowered by functional authority, is expected to negotiate the labor agreements for all subsidiary companies to prevent the various unions from playing one company against another. Thus, the president is responsible for profits, but one of the major cost factors — wages and work rules — is determined to a large

---

[9]For a discussion of line-staff relationships within the context of a systems framework, see Charles Coleman and Joseph Rich, "Line, Staff, and the Systems Perspective," *Human Resource Management*, Vol. 12, No. 3 (Fall, 1973), pp. 20–27.

For a study of how individuals perceive themselves as either line or staff, the following is of value: Philip J. Browne and Robert T. Golembiewski, "The Line-Staff Concept Revisited: An Empirical Study of Organizational Images," *Academy of Management Journal*, Vol. 17, No. 3 (September, 1974), pp. 406–417.

extent by staff personnel who do not report to the responsible executive. Is it any wonder that resentment toward staff arises? It is only normal that friction builds up in a situation in which one feels that a significant part of the decision making and control necessary to operate effectively is lost, and the resulting tensions are expressed as a specific resentment toward staff. The same situation holds for the line managers in lower levels of the organization. The production foreman may be responsible for the costs of a department, yet the requirements of staff may force the hiring of additional clerks. To summarize, one of the main sources of friction between line and staff is the manner in which the line manager defines responsibilities. When the line manager defines responsibility, or when it is defined for the manager, as *total* responsibility, it is only normal to resent any intrusion of authority that tends to weaken the manager's control of the situation.

Importance of Function. Staff's infringement upon the line manager's authority to manage is the major cause of L/S conflict from the point of view of line, but the idea that staff functions are supportive, with the attendant implication that they are secondary and somehow less important, is the main source of L/S conflict as viewed by staff managers. To understand staff's position, it is necessary to state briefly the personal characteristics of staff personnel. As a rule, staff personnel are highly ambitious and eager to advance, and they are somewhat younger and have a higher level of formal education than their line counterparts. Staff managers are also aware that the reason for their employment is their specialized knowledge, and since they are ambitious and desire to advance, it is only natural that they advance by the avenue which seems most logical to them — advancing their ideas. When their ideas are restricted by line, they are told that it is the function of line to decide and that their role is supportive in nature. To the staff employee the statement that line makes the decision is a distortion of what happens in practice, if not pure fiction. The following example supports staff's contention that it is staff, not line, who makes critical decisions or, at the very least, makes it possible for the line manager to decide.

In a typical manufacturing organization, the manager of manufacturing is responsible for producing the product and the sales manager is responsible for distribution of the product. Both are line managers whose activities are coordinated by a higher line authority, a president or a general manager. Who determines how much of each product is to be manufactured and the sequence in which these items are to be produced and sold? As a result of analyzing market trends and customer needs, the staff manager of the market research department recommends the optimum product mix. The manager of production planning and inventory control, another staff department, interprets and translates the findings of market research into production schedules that specify quantity and sequence for manufacture of each product.

Though the sales manager approves the recommendations of market research and the production manager approves schedules developed by production planning and inventory control, it is understandable why staff managers of market research and production planning consider that they in effect make the decisions. It is difficult to relegate either staff function to a supportive role when the very nature of these functions influences so greatly the success of the company in fulfilling its primary objectives — the manufacture and the distribution of a product.

Is Line-Staff Obsolete?

Conflict between line and staff has long been recognized as a major deterrent to organizational effectiveness, with the result that many students of management have offered suggestions to minimize such conflict. Such recommendations state that line has the final responsibility for the successful operation of the company and consequently should have the authority to make operating decisions. Staff functions are carefully defined as providing either service or advice to the line; an advice or service that should be presented when requested by line and also when, in the opinion of staff, it is considered necessary. It is suggested that whether or not staff's advice or service is accepted depends entirely on the judgment of line, and line is urged to seriously consider staff recommendations. The last recommendation suggests that both line and staff have the right of appeal to higher authority.

The recommendations presented above are helpful in some cases; however, such recommendations are of limited value primarily because they rest upon assumptions that are of questionable validity. These assumptions are: (1) line managers will accept the advice and recommendations of staff and (2) staff is able and willing to accept a supportive role in the organization and continue to put forth its best effort when in fact its recommendations may be ignored. Also, recommendations for improving line-staff relationships implicitly assume that the line-staff concept is necessary for organizational effectiveness. There are two alternatives to the line-staff concept that deserve careful consideration.

Functional-Teamwork. Functional-teamwork is an organizational concept presented by Gerald Fisch, a management consultant, as an alternate to the line-staff concept.[10] It is suggested that three functional areas be defined and each area represent a function significant to the well-being of the organization. In addition to defining functional

---

[10]Gerald G. Fisch, "Line-Staff Is Obsolete," *Harvard Business Review*, Vol. 39 (September-October, 1961), pp. 67–79. This section is based upon Fisch's article which states the author's belief that the line-staff concept is obsolete. In place of the line-staff (L/S) concept, Fisch suggests *functional-teamwork* (F/T). The first part of the article presents a careful analysis of the line-staff concept and the second part presents in detail the functional-teamwork concept.

areas that are grouped under *time, resources,* and *human interrelations,* the task of top management is carefully defined. Let us see how the many activities of a business organization that are classed as either line or staff are treated under the functional-teamwork concept.

Process Functions. All functions within the business that must be controlled with *time* as a major element are classed as *process functions.* Included as process functions are product design, purchasing, manufacturing, advertising, physical distribution (sales), and billing. Note that in this arrangement the usual line functions of sales and manufacturing are grouped with functions normally regarded as staff to form a functional unit concerned with the movement of the product from its inception in product design, through manufacturing, the distribution system, and the final billing — all related activities accomplished under the pressure of time; hence, they are process functions.

Resources Function. All resources — physical, monetary, and human — are considered as part of the resources of a company, and it is the function of the resources manager to acquire, maintain, and utilize these resources in the most efficient manner possible. Physical facilities, capital invested in the business, the skills of employees, and patents on products or processes are all considered as resources that should be carefully controlled and utilized.

Relations Function. The relations function can be summed up in one word, communications, and it includes both internal and external communications. Business in our society has an acute communications problem; and, in most companies, little is being done to present a consistent, coherent picture of the company and its problems to employee groups, shareholders, the community, various government agencies, and customers. These are the relations that would be supervised by the director of the relations function.

General Management. Though not a function in the same sense as the above three functions, general management deserves particular attention under the functional-teamwork concept. With the day-to-day work allocated to the three functional managers, the top management of the organization is free to establish corporate goals and objectives, to offer leadership when needed, to coordinate and realign the functions when necessary, and to control the entire operation.

There are several characteristics of the functional-teamwork concept that differentiate it from the line-staff concept of organization. First, there is only one authority, managerial authority, that is exercised by each of the managers of the process, resources, or relations function within each functional area. Second, once the goals of the organization are established and the resources determined to be adequate for the project at hand, the decisions concerning the production of the company's product or services fall within a logical framework.

Third, a structure encouraging teamwork is stressed so when the actions of one function touch upon those of another function, the problem is one of resolving the question on a teamwork basis rather than determining which party has the superior authority. Also, top management is free to encourage a teamwork solution to problems as they arise.

Task Force Organization. The functional-teamwork concept implies a fundamental redesign of the organization structure. An approach similar to functional-teamwork, though generally much more limited in its scope, is often called *task force organization* or *task force management*. Like functional-teamwork, a task force is essentially a team effort. There are several distinctive characteristics of a task force. First, it is a tightly organized unit under the direction of a manager who usually has broad powers of authority. Second, a task force is organized to accomplish a specific task or goal such as the introduction of a new product or building and placing into operation a new physical facility. A task force is working against a time deadline since its objectives must be accomplished by a certain date. Third, the personnel who make up the task force possess a diverse range of skills and abilities, thus making it possible for each member of the group to make a unique contribution to the solution of the problem.[11]

A good example of the application of the task force concept of organization to the solution of a specific problem is Minneapolis-Honeywell's Polaris Missile task force headed by a manager of the team with a production manager, an account manager, a subcontract manager, and a procurement manager reporting to the manager. The task force organization is also successfully used in such diverse activities as construction, advertising, military fighting units, and motion picture film production. Whenever there is a need for *concerted* team effort to accomplish a specific goal within a relatively short period of time, the creation of a task force may offer a means of creating an organization capable of accomplishing the desired goals.[12]

There is no universal answer to the question raised at the beginning of this section — is line-staff obsolete? The line-staff concept

---

[11]The following two papers discuss some of the problems that might arise in either functional-teamwork or task force organization: Hans J. Thamhain and Gary R. Gemmill, "Influence Styles of Project Managers: Some Project Performance Correlates," *Academy of Management Journal*, Vol. 17, No. 2 (June, 1974), pp. 216–224; David L. Wilemon and John P. Cicero, "The Project Manager — Anomalies and Ambiguities," *Academy of Management Journal*, Vol. 13, No. 3 (September, 1970), pp. 269–282.

For a discussion of the concept of the application of task force organization to new product development see James D. Hlavacek and Victor A. Thompson, "Bureaucracy and New Product Innovation," *Academy of Management Journal*, Vol. 16, No. 3 (September, 1973), pp. 361–372.

[12]A. K. Wicksberg and T. C. Cronin, "Management by Task Force," *Harvard Business Review*, Vol. 40 (November–December, 1962), pp. 111–118. In this article the authors stress team effort in task force management and offer practical suggestions for the reassignment of personnel after the completion of a specific project.

serves many companies very well, particularly those companies operating in an environment of minimal change. However, when stress situations appear with the accompanying need for prompt action in order to survive, many companies turn to the functional-teamwork concept of organization by creating a task force to solve the immediate problem. Since the application of the concept of functional-teamwork is effective in a crisis situation, it is only logical to consider the possibility of applying the functional-teamwork approach to organization as a continuing form of organizational structure to insure the maximum utilization of resources in meeting the daily challenges of competition. In addition to stress situations with their accompanying need for prompt action, the introduction of integrated information-decision-making systems also calls for a reexamination of the line-staff concept. Such systems cut across traditional departmental lines and functions with a resultant change in the locus of the decision-making function. Modern information systems also result in the creation of large functional units composed of several traditional line-staff departments. Further, when the need for interaction between the members of an organization is high, the functional-teamwork concept offers a structure that makes possible highly effective communications.

Case Problem 10-B offers you an opportunity, as a chief executive, to resolve a typical conflict taking place between a line manager and a staff specialist.

Case Problem 10-B
LINE-STAFF RELATIONSHIPS

The Glass Container Company, with headquarters in Chicago, is a large manufacturer of glass containers that operates 18 plants located throughout the United States. The company has three geographic divisions — Eastern, Central, and Pacific — each of which is headed by a vice-president and general manager who is responsible for the sales and manufacturing functions within that division. The Central Division's general manager is a young, aggressive executive who seems destined to become the president of the company. Under his direction the profits and sales volume of the division have grown each day, a growth due in large part to the successful operations of the Minneapolis plant. The manager of the Minneapolis plant, a graduate engineer, was brought into the company as a plant manager

as part of a planned program to strengthen the management of the company. Plans are now being made to transfer the Minneapolis manager to the corporate headquarters in Chicago, thus making it necessary to select a new manager for Minneapolis.

In Chicago, there is a director of organizational planning who is a member of the corporate staff and reports directly to the president of the company. At the suggestion of the director of organizational planning, the Minneapolis plant manager was recruited from outside the company since a survey of key personnel indicated a need for technically trained managers. Normally the director of organizational planning works directly with the division vice-presidents in an advisory capacity; and when she and the vice-president agree upon a proposed move of key personnel, the move is made without consulting the president of the company. However, when there is disagreement, the matter is usually referred to the president who makes the final decision.

There is still a need for graduate engineers capable of filling top managerial positions that are presently available and those expected to develop within the next five years as the result of expansion and the retirement of present personnel. It is believed by all concerned that sound preparation for top management should include two or three years of experience as a plant manager as a means of learning the technical aspects of the glass container industry.

In regard to the Minneapolis position, there are three possible choices. First, another manager can be recruited from outside the company and be assigned to the Minneapolis plant as manager, thus providing a period of training with subsequent assignment to a more responsible position in the corporation. Second, there are several young assistant plant managers who would profit from experience as manager of a large plant; and although it would probably take longer for any of them to develop, they too could be promoted to more responsible positions. The third possibility is to promote the present assistant plant manager, a man who is 50 years old with 25 years' service with the company. The assistant plant manager is responsible to a large extent for the success of the plant since he directly supervises the operating departments and is thoroughly familiar with the technical aspects of glass making. However, he has indicated an unwillingness to move from the Minneapolis area and has expressed a desire to retire upon the completion of 30 years' service at age 55, which is permissible under the terms of the company's pension plan.

In discussing these three possibilities with the vice-president of the Central Division, the director of organizational planning recommended either of the first two choices and pointed out that if the third choice were adopted, it would mean the blocking of a valuable training position for at least a five-year period. She also stated that should the assistant plant manager elect to work until normal retirement at age 65, it would mean an even longer period of time before the plant could be used as a training position. However, the division vice-president insists upon promoting the present assistant plant manager. He readily admits that the promotion of the assistant plant manager will effectively block the use of that position as a training position; but he does not want to see any of the younger assistant plant managers in the Minneapolis position, nor will he approve the recruitment of a manager from outside the company. To him, either of the first two choices means putting an unknown quantity into an important operating position that markedly affects the profitability of his division. In summing up his position, he tells the director of organizational planning:

"I'm charged with the responsibility of maintaining profitable operations in the plants under my direction, and the extent to which I meet this responsibility determines to a large extent my future in this company. For me to accept either a new manager from outside or a younger manager from within the company whom I don't know personally is to run the risk of being responsible for a less profitable plant. I realize that you are responsible for planning for corporate organizational needs, but I'm responsible for the operating success of this division."

Since the matter could not be resolved with the vice-president of the division, the director of organizational planning decided to refer the question to the company president.

PROBLEMS

1. As president of the company, how would you decide the matter?
2. Should the director of organizational planning be given the authority to overrule the division vice-president in the functional area of organizational planning?
3. Is the concept of functional-teamwork applicable in this situation? If so, how?

CHAPTER QUESTIONS FOR
STUDY AND DISCUSSION

1. What concept of authority is reflected in the following statement: Authority emanates from the office or the position that a person holds and not from the person? Cite examples of such authority.

2. Do you believe that the use of power — that is, the use of rewards or punishment to enforce direction — is prevalent in most industrial organizations? What alternative is available to executives in accomplishing the work for which they are responsible?

3. What is meant by the statement that managerial authority has its source in law rather than as the result of a right to own property?

4. Has the plant manager in the story quoted on page 215 lost the authority to manage the plant since it is no longer in operation? Why or why not?

5. What conditions limit the effectiveness of managerial authority? Can you give examples of such conditions other than those cited in the text?

6. The designation of a function as either line or staff depends upon the directness of the contribution of the function to a particular organization. Under such circumstances does a differentiation between line and staff authority have any usefulness? Explain.

7. Under what conditions can one find a chain of command within a staff department?

8. What is the nature of staff authority? Under what conditions may the line responsibilities of a given manager become staff functions?

9. What advantages result from utilizing the L/S concept in industrial groups?

10. Can the functional-teamwork or the task force type of organization be utilized in all organizations? Discuss.

11. Under what conditions is the traditional L/S organization most effective? What circumstances or conditions within the organization call for a reorganization along the lines of the functional-teamwork or task force type of organization?

Chapter 11

Organizational Processes — Delegation and Decentralization of Authority

Case Problem 11-A

A NEED FOR DELEGATION

Thomas Dayton, now 41 years old, is one of several candidates who are being considered for the position of general manager of manufacturing for Engineering Products, a firm with seven manufacturing plants. A review of Tom's personnel file indicates that he joined the firm as a design engineer immediately after receiving his degree in mechanical engineering from the state university. His first assignment was on the board as a draftsman, and a notation by the supervisor of the drafting department indicates that Tom did this job willingly and well. The notation reads in part:

"Mr. Dayton is now in his sixth month as a member of the design department. There have been several occasions when he has come in voluntarily on weekends to rework drawings so that they meet the most exacting specifications. It is unheard of for Mr. Dayton to turn in work that is smudged or messy in any way."

At the end of 18 months Tom was promoted to section chief and placed in charge of ten draftsmen. As might be expected, the work from his section was almost perfect. One reason for the high level of accuracy was that Tom actually performed the work of the section checker and personally reviewed all drawings thoroughly and carefully before passing them on to the head of the department. On more than one occasion Tom reworked the drawings of his subordinates in order to meet specified deadlines.

Following these early years in the design section, Tom's rise was steady and sure. During the time that he served as assistant manager of the research laboratory, there were several important product modifications, primarily the result of his own work and effort. After several years in research, he was transferred to one of the larger plants as assistant manager in charge of all production departments so that he could supervise the introduction to manufacturing of one of the products which he had developed. He remained in this position for over five years and during most of this time the production costs for the manufacturing departments under Tom's supervision were the lowest in the company. Upon the retirement of the plant manager, Tom was moved up to manager with the honest congratulations of all concerned. There were no reservations concerning his ability to work long and hard in order to get the job done; nor was his loyalty to the company ever questioned.

It did not take long to realize the success predicted for Tom as plant manager, that is, success measured by the operating statement. Operating efficiency increased slightly, and when combined with the substantial reduction in administrative expenses, the result was a marked increase in the profitability of the plant. However, all was not well with Tom's administration. The chief industrial engineer

233

of the plant resigned and told Tom his reason for resigning was that he had been offered a similar position in another company at considerably more money. Yet in a conversation with the corporate general manager of industrial engineering, the following remarks were made:

"We no longer have any weekly staff meetings at the plant. These were stopped about a month after Tom became plant manager. He told us then that they were a waste of time and that if we had any special ideas about improving operations we should see him personally. Also, he now approves all changes in pay. As a department manager, I used to be able to approve pay changes for the engineers in my department as long as they were within the provisions of the corporate salary plan; but not now, because he approves all changes in pay, regardless of the amount or whether they are within the terms of the salary plan. As for overtime, he approves all overtime in advance, not only in the general administrative departments but also within the production departments, a responsibility that normally lies within the control of the assistant plant manager. And the cost control program results in his actually running all departments. We are supposed to run our departments within the limitations set by the annual budgets, but not any more. Tom wants all expense accounts sent directly to him; as department managers, we no longer see them. The switchboard operator sends him a daily tally of all long-distance telephone calls with the name of the party called, the name of the person making the call, and the amount of the call. But what really irritates me is that he plans the work of my department and calls my people into his office to check on the accuracy of their work. If he wants to run the industrial engineering department, he is welcome to do so, but he doesn't need a department manager for the job — he needs a chief clerk."

Mr. Thompson, the present general manager of manufacturing, is slated to move to the presidency of the corporation. He is a staunch supporter of Tom Dayton and points to Tom's outstanding record of success in the company. The general manager of manufacturing coordinates the production of all seven plants and is accountable to the president of the company for the performance of the plants. Traditionally there is a substantial degree of delegation of authority to the individual plant managers for day-to-day operations. Such a policy of delegation results, on occasion, in some rather expensive mistakes on the part of plant managers and the attendant temptation to step in and correct things immediately; but the net result is the development of strong plant managers and a highly efficient manufacturing organization. Mr. Thompson realizes that Tom Dayton is not a good delegator, but he believes that as president of the company, he can develop Tom into a good manufacturing manager and teach him how to delegate.

PROBLEMS

1. What are the underlying causes of Tom's failure to delegate?
2. Do you agree with Mr. Thompson that Tom can be taught how to delegate?
3. Why should a manager be criticized for his failure to delegate?

Chapter 10 examines the sources of authority and the interpersonal relationships that exist between those people performing line functions and those who are engaged in staff work. Fundamental to the exercise of managerial authority, either as line authority or staff authority, is an organizational process that permits the transmission of authority from superior to subordinate — a process called the *delegation of authority*. It is the process of delegating authority from superior to subordinate that makes it possible for organizations to grow. The extent to which organizations consistently delegate authority downward to lower-level organizational units is called the process of *decentralization of authority*. In this chapter we discuss the nature of the process of delegation of authority and the behavioral aspects of delegation. Decentralization of authority is discussed with emphasis on the relative nature of decentralization. The last part of the chapter applies the contingency approach to organization theory, presented in Chapter 8, to problems of organization structure, line/staff relationships, and the processes of delegation and decentralization.

DELEGATION OF AUTHORITY

Delegation of authority is an organizational process that permits the transfer of authority from superior to subordinate. There is general agreement that the process of delegation consists of three distinct steps; however, there is considerable variation in the terminology used to describe each of the three steps. The following quotation from Louis Allen, a management consultant, illustrates the variation in terminology used to describe each of the three steps of the process of delegation:

> We have now described the three essential aspects of delegation: the entrustment of *work*, or *responsibility*, to another for performance; the entrustment of *powers and rights*, or *authority*, to be exercised; and the creation of an *obligation*, or *accountability*, on the part of the person accepting the delegation to perform in terms of the standards established.[1]

The Process of Delegation

This text uses the following terms to describe the three aspects of the process of delegation:

1. The assignment of responsibility.
2. The delegation of authority.
3. The creation of accountability.

Assignment of Responsibility. The term, *responsibility*, is used to refer to the work assigned. There are several reasons for limiting the meaning of responsibility to duties, or work, to be performed in fulfilling an assignment. In our everyday speech we frequently equate responsibility and duties by referring to the responsibilities of a parent or the responsibilities of a student. Also, many companies in their descriptions of managerial positions state the responsibilities of a given position as duties to be performed. Another reason for limiting the meaning of the word responsibility to assigned duties is that there is a

---

[1]From *Management and Organization* by Louis A. Allen. Copyright © 1958 by Louis A. Allen. Used with permission of McGraw-Hill Book Company. On pages 116–117, footnote 3, there is a brief discussion of the various terms used to describe the process of delegation.

specific term, *accountability*, which is used to describe the obligation created by the assignment of responsibilities.

Thus, responsibility is defined as *all of the duties that must be performed in order to complete a given task.*

Delegation of Authority. Delegation has a precise meaning. One who delegates to another person *empowers that person to act for the delegator*. Two facets of this definition deserve careful attention. First, the delegator *empowers* the delegatee. In Chapter 10, authority is defined as the right to act or to direct others to act. Since responsibilities — or duties — are assigned as the first step in the process of delegation, it is necessary that the person to whom responsibility is assigned either act or direct others to act in the performance of those duties. Authority empowers such action; hence the expression, the delegation of authority, with the result that the delegatee is empowered to act or to direct others to act.

The second facet of the definition deserving careful attention is the phrase, *for the delegator*. A person possessing delegated authority is acting for, or representing, the person who delegated the authority. The implications of acting for another are significant as an organizational process because it means that even though authority is delegated to subordinates so that they may successfully fulfill their assigned duties, the delegator still retains full control over the delegated authority and may recall that authority as the occasion demands. Delegation in no way implies abdication. When a king abdicates, he divests himself of all responsibility and authority; however, an executive who delegates remains responsible for the accomplishment of assigned duties and retains full control over delegated authority.

Creation of Accountability. The moment one accepts a loan from a bank, an obligation is incurred to repay the money borrowed. Likewise, when a subordinate accepts responsibility and the authority necessary to carry out those responsibilities, an obligation is incurred — a duty to perform the assigned work and to properly utilize the delegated authority. The creation of such an obligation on the part of a subordinate, when viewed as an organizational process, is defined as the creation of *accountability*. Subordinates are *accountable* to their superiors for the proper exercise of authority and performance of assigned responsibilities. An easy way to differentiate between the concepts of responsibility and accountability is to remember that a subordinate is *responsible for* the completion of assigned work and is *accountable to* a superior for the satisfactory performance of that work.

Conditions for Effective Delegation

The preceding analysis of delegation presents a process that is relatively easy to understand and seemingly simple in nature; however, in actual practice a great deal of difficulty is experienced in achieving effective delegation. There is general agreement among students of management and management practitioners that three conditions must be met for the process of delegation to be most effective. These conditions are:

1. Parity of authority and responsibility.
2. Absoluteness of accountability.
3. Unity of command.

Each condition is discussed briefly below.

Parity of Authority and Responsibility. *For effective delegation, the authority granted to a subordinate must equal the assigned responsibility.*

The concept of parity of authority and responsibility recognizes the need for delegated authority and emphasizes that delegated authority should be of sufficient scope so that the assigned responsibility may be accomplished. Too little authority usually manifests itself by managers having to consult their respective superiors before making relatively routine decisions. A manager of manufacturing, charged with the responsibility of producing the company's product within specified cost and quality limits, should be able to make decisions pertaining to purchasing raw materials, maintenance of equipment, selection and training of personnel, and the determination of the most efficient methods of manufacturing. In short, the authority granted should be of sufficient scope so that all related activities may be accomplished.

Although the granting of too little authority is a frequent reason for ineffective delegation, failure to fully understand and recognize the limitations normally inherent to managerial authority causes most of the difficulty in the application and interpretation of the principle of parity of authority and responsibility. One limitation, not always understood or appreciated, is that managerial authority seldom carries with it the power necessary for the literal achievement of the assigned responsibilities.

For example, a sales manager cannot force customers to buy, nor can a personnel director force a union to cooperate with management; yet, it is not uncommon to say that the sales manager is "responsible" for the sales in one territory and that the personnel director is "responsible" for establishing cooperative relations with the union. Another limitation on managerial authority results from restrictions imposed by the organization itself. Authority is not absolute; instead it is circumscribed by statements of company policy and procedure that have the effect of defining the limits of authority for each level of the organization. A regional sales manager may have a substantial advertising budget and the authority to select the media appropriate for a given geographic area, yet the total spent may not exceed the budgeted amount without prior approval from superior authority. Restrictions set by higher authority exist for every position within a company.

We have described three conditions that may result in an imbalance between authority and responsibility. First, there may be too little authority granted for the task at hand; second, there are situations in which a manager has little or no power to direct the actions of others; and third, organizational policies and procedures often limit the extent of a manager's authority. With such restrictions on authority, one might reasonably ask whether or not a concept of parity of authority and responsibility is practical. The answer is yes, because knowledge of the difficulties encountered in creating coextensive authority and responsibility should help in developing effective techniques of delegation and in realistically assessing the extent to which an executive should be held responsible for the accomplishment of assigned duties.

Absoluteness of Accountability. *Although responsibility may be assigned to and authority may be delegated to subordinates, accountability to one's superior can neither be assigned nor delegated.*

When the process of delegation is defined as the assignment of responsibilities, the delegation of authority, and the creation of accountability, it is evident that both responsibility and authority may be transferred. Indeed, the continuing redelegation of authority and reassignment of responsibility make organizations possible. Departmentation, the dividing of work into manageable units, is an example of the assignment of responsibility. When major departments are created, the chief executive is dividing responsibility — the work load — so that others may more effectively accomplish the tasks necessary for the achievement of organizational goals. At the same time that responsibilities are assigned, commensurate authority is also delegated so that managers of the newly created work units may effectively act or direct others to act. In turn, the major departmental units are further subdivided, with the managers of the subunits receiving assigned responsibilities and delegated authority. But accountability, the obligation to report to one's superior, cannot be delegated nor assigned. The president of a company, although assigning to a marketing vice-president the responsibility and delegating to that person the authority necessary to carry out the marketing function, remains accountable to superior authority, the board of directors, for the successful discharge of the marketing objectives. In turn, the marketing vice-president, though redelegating authority and reassigning responsibility to division marketing managers, remains accountable to superior authority, the president, for the successful discharge of the marketing function. In theory, the concept of accountability is absolute and cannot be transferred. However, in practice it is recognized that assigned responsibilities are performed by subordinates whose work may fall short of expected standards of performance. For example, the marketing vice-president considers the number of new and inexperienced sales representatives when evaluating the performance of a division marketing manager; and the president considers these facts when appraising the work of the vice-president.

Unity of Command. *Each subordinate should be accountable to one, and only one, superior.*[2]

The unity of command concept states something we all know — no person can serve two masters well. The expression, unity of command, stresses that the sources of command should be so unified that a subordinate receives assigned duties and delegated authority from one superior and is accountable only to that superior. The following four examples represent situations that result in a subordinate's having more than one master and serving none well.

Undifferentiated Organizations. Occasionally in small organizations there are work groups that are undifferentiated with respect to rank or job assignments. Frequently the head of such a group characterizes the work force as "one big happy family." An employee who is a member of an undifferentiated work group is not certain what is expected or sure of the relative powers of the several persons who offer direction. As a result, the subordinate is forced to select from several job assignments those believed to be most effective in placating the several supervisors. Even though an employee may succeed in keeping a job by "greasing the wheel which squeaks the loudest," it is doubtful that organizational objectives are being met effectively. Objectives may be attained much more efficiently when an organization structure is established so that each supervisor knows clearly the subordinates accountable to him or her and each subordinate knows to which supervisor to report.

Intentional Disregard of Unity of Command. Frequently organizations that have progressed beyond the undifferentiated work-group stage and have established well-defined superior-subordinate relationships intentionally assign one subordinate to two or more supervisors. Such assignments are justified on the grounds that the work load is light and that it is necessary for an employee to work in several departments in order to keep fully occupied. However, it must be recognized that disputes may arise when one supervisor demands more than the allotted share of time. These difficulties can be avoided or minimized by designating in advance a higher authority to determine which department has precedence.

---

[2]There is little empirical evidence to support the three classical principles relating to effective delegation. However, the following study supports the view that at least in a bureaucratic organization, a governmental agency, violation of the concept of unity of command results in dysfunctional consequences as evidenced by a change in attitudes of managers: Martin J. Gannon and Frank T. Paine, "Unity of Command and Job Attitudes of Managers in a Bureaucratic Organization," *Journal of Applied Psychology*, Vol. 59, No. 3 (June, 1974), pp. 392–394.

Bypassing Intermediate Supervision. A third violation of the unity of command concept arises as the result of leapfrogging or bypassing one or more levels of intermediate supervision. For example, a plant manager who ignores the superintendent and directs a foreman to change a production schedule is bypassing an intermediate level of supervision. Such action is unfair to the foreman who is put into the position of serving two masters and carrying out two sets of conflicting directions. It is also unfair to the superintendent who remains accountable to the plant manager for the performance of subordinates even though effective control over their actions has been lost. The remedy for the difficulties and misunderstandings which appear as the result of bypassing is not found in recommending that each supervisor have contact only with one immediate superior and with immediate subordinates; rather, it is found in clearly defining the nature of these personal contacts. It is desirable and necessary for an executive to be aware, as the result of personal observation and contact, of the activities of all levels of the organization; however, the actual direction of subordinates should remain the specific responsibility of each subordinate's designated supervisor.

Staff Relationships. Figure 10-4 on page 224 illustrates the concept of functional staff authority and shows the relationship that may exist between two or more levels of staff personnel and between line-and-staff personnel at the plant level. The exercise of strong functional authority may result in circumstances that violate the unity of command concept.

Dual command arises when the supervisor of quality control at the plant level receives instructions establishing acceptable levels of quality from the division manager of quality control that conflict with those standards established by the plant manager, the direct-line superior. In the same manner, a production foreman may be placed in the position of receiving orders from more than one source of authority when the plant quality control supervisor sets quality standards in conflict with those previously stated by the plant manager. The potential difficulties resulting from the dual authority sources of line and staff are minimized when the functional authority of staff is clearly defined and it is emphasized that even though staff properly has authority within a given functional area, any direct orders are to be issued only by the immediate-line superior.

Practical Suggestions for Successful Delegation

The conditions for effective delegation discussed above provide a basis for understanding more fully the process of delegation and recognizing the conditions that may result in ineffective delegation. Admittedly, a delegation of sorts can occur even though all three conditions are violated simultaneously, yet few deny that observance of the conditions of delegation results in more effective delegation. The following practical suggestions for successful delegation are offered as a means of putting into practice the conditions for effective delegation.[3]

1. Determine Objectives. Remember the principle of the objective: *Before initiating any course of action, the objectives in view must be clearly determined, understood, and stated.* The process of delegation affords an excellent opportunity for the application of the principle of the objective. As a first step, it is necessary to determine the goals expected as the result of a specific work assignment. A statement of goals is important to the process of delegation for two reasons: First, the duties and responsibilities of a job are derived from and directed toward the achievement of stated objectives. Second, persons who are assigned work are accountable to their respective superiors for the successful completion of those duties; consequently, unless work performed is pertinent to achieving stated goals, the concept of accountability becomes exceedingly vague.

2. Assign Duties and Delegate Commensurate Authority. Determine all the duties that must be performed to complete the task at hand; then assign the whole job — not just parts of it. There are too many instances where supervisors assign only the minor or routine details of a job and retain the key decision-making aspects of the job for themselves. Such assignments are not delegation in the true sense of the word since there is little need for the delegation of authority. Defining the whole job at the very start of a project brings into proper perspective the amount of authority needed to insure parity of responsibility and authority. Also, subordinates are more likely to be better motivated by assignments that encompass the whole job.

3. Select Subordinate. Select the candidate for the job in light of what is expected. Assigned responsibilities are in effect the duties of a job; and duties, if they are to be completed successfully, require certain skills and knowledge. In addition to possessing the necessary skills and knowledge, the best candidate for the job is the person who is willing to accept full responsibility for achieving stated objectives. Among the many reasons for a subordinate's unwillingness to accept responsibility are lack of understanding of what is expected, fear of failure or criticism, and insufficient motivation. Whatever the reason, if a choice must be made between two subordinates with one possessing the necessary skills and experience but unwilling to assume responsibility, and the other short on experience but willing to assume responsibility, it is probably better to choose the latter.

[3]Louis A. Allen, *Management and Organization* (New York: McGraw-Hill Book Co., 1958), Chapter 7, "Better Methods of Delegation," pp. 134–155. Chapter 7 presents an extensive discussion of specific methods that may be used for more effective delegation.

4. Establish Necessary Controls. The discussion of the second step of the process of delegation, the delegation of authority, states explicitly that delegation is not synonymous with abdication. Instead, the delegator retains the right to recall delegated authority and remains accountable for the responsibilities assigned to others. Thus it is necessary for the delegator to establish and exercise control over the actions of subordinates so that the delegator's obligations may be fulfilled. Essential to proper control is the maintenance of clear channels of communication between superior and subordinate so that a complete interchange of information is possible. Controls also imply that corrective action may be taken if needed to insure the fullfillment of stated objectives. Resentment of controls on the part of subordinates is minimal when the subordinate participates in establishing the controls to be used.

BEHAVIORAL ASPECTS OF DELEGATION

Thus far, our discussion of delegation includes an analysis of the three steps in the process of delegation, a statement of three conditions that should be observed for most effective delegation, and specific practical suggestions for successful delegation. Yet if this were all of delegation, or even a major portion of the process of delegation, there would be little reason for discussing delegation so extensively in management literature. The real problems of delegation lie not in the observance of the conditions of delegation nor in following the practical suggestions for successful delegation. Instead they are found in the personality of the person doing the delegating.

The behavior of the superior who finds it difficult to delegate is characterized by an excessive attention to details, coupled with a marked distrust and questioning of the ability of subordinates. There are many reasons for these two characteristics, which for purposes of discussion may be grouped into four broad categories. First, there are those who seemingly have always been interested in activities and studies that require precision and exactness. These people often follow vocations requiring and emphasizing precise action. Second, there are those who immerse themselves in details as a means of avoiding the central problems of a situation. Third, there are those who refuse to relinquish any part of their job to others because of a deep-seated fear of failure. The fourth group who refuse to delegate and must retain all of a job for themselves are those who have a paranoid (fear of persecution) distrust of others. Let us examine each of these groups separately, realizing that there is considerable overlapping between each group and that most failures to delegate can be traced to one or more of the four categories.

Vocational Choice

Any discussion of personality factors and vocational choice may evolve into the proverbial question of which comes first, the chicken or the egg. In other words, does one enter a given vocation because of certain underlying personality traits or does the specific vocational training received mold the personality? Admittedly, both processes operate simultaneously. There is much in our culture that emphasizes the importance of doing a job well and following it through to completion. Some people have been brought up with the admonition, "If you want a job done well, do it yourself." Whatever the sources of desire for personal accomplishment, we are taught to respect those capable of hard and effective work.

There are specific forms of vocational training that tend to reinforce the normal inclinations of attending to detail. Accounting and engineering are good examples of such vocational training in that both courses of study require a meticulous attention to detail, a liking for exactness expressed in the form of numbers to the third decimal place, and considerable hard work and drudgery to complete the course. Upon graduation, the engineer may be doing exacting work on a drafting board and the accountant may be performing the work necessary for a detailed audit. It is the ability to do this first assignment — close attention to detail — and to do it well that results in promotion. Is it any wonder that a person with a normal liking for detail, reinforced by four years of college training in precise work and subsequently reinforced en route to success and promotions, should find it difficult to let go of the detail part of a job and turn it over to others?

Some of these highly trained people, and Thomas Dayton of Case Problem 11-A is one of them, are frequently very competent in their field of work, a competency often expressed by the phrase, "I can do it better myself." Although they may not be able to do it better, they usually can perform the work as well. Another characteristic is the 12- to 16-hour day, which with few exceptions is the result of an inability to delegate rather than due to the press of important affairs. It is difficult to change people such as Thomas Dayton and make them successful delegators. Basic to the difficulty is their liking for work and their ability to do it well. Admonitions concerning health may fail to encourage them to delegate. Even after the occurrence of physical breakdown, some are still unable to slow down and delegate their work to others.

Avoidance of Major Issues

Attention to detail sometimes offers a security and comfort not possible when one's attention is directed toward the major problems at hand. In extreme cases the ability to attend to detail rather than to the central issue is important for life itself. On occasion facing the real problem may be so overwhelming that one would be unable to carry on. An example of the extreme is illustrated in the following brief quotation describing the plight of a refugee:

> The refugee was a peasant woman from down San Carlos way. She was complaining of the haste with which she and her family had had to flee. The burden of her complaint was that her husband's new suit and his Sunday gloves had had to be left behind. I had heard exactly the same kind of protest years ago in China; I was to hear it later in Austria and Czechoslovakia. The mind of the refugee, dazed and uprooted, concentrates upon the small, specific losses that it can cling to with understanding. To be homeless and without food or shelter as a result of the "policy" of foreign dictators and prime ministers — that is a state so terrible that it cannot be taken in all at once. The new suit, the Sunday gloves, these are the losses one can still comprehend.[4]

Although managers may not be faced with problems of such personal magnitude as those confronting the war refugee, there are instances where some managers simply cannot cope with the central issues of their environment and as a result direct their attention to peripheral details that are related to, but are not the real problem. The marketing manager who personally reviews each sales representative's expense account and then tallies the amount spent on telephone calls may be avoiding the real problem of increasing the number of new customers. The president of a company who reviews every change in salary may hold down payroll costs and then complain that there is not enough time for the major task of coordinating the development of new products.

Fear of Failure

Feelings of personal insecurity with the attendant fear of failure may be the cause of inability to delegate. These are not the feelings of insecurity and unsureness associated with lack of knowledge and experience that are normal when one undertakes a new job; rather, it is the unsureness derived from a feeling of personal inadequacy. For some, fear of failure may be very real and imminent, for they may be on the brink of failure and realize that one more mistake can cost them their job or, at the very least, an opportunity for promotion. For others, failure may not be near, but there is the constant fear of what might happen if failure does occur. In either case, whether failure is imminent or imagined, the underlying thought processes are somewhat as follows: This is a very difficult job to be done. It is full of problems and pitfalls; it requires a great deal of attention, hard work, and skill. It is going to

---

[4]Vincent Sheehan, *Not Peace but a Sword* (New York: Doubleday Doran, and Company, 1939), p. 86. Reprinted by permission of Doubleday & Company, Inc.

tax my abilities to the limit. Since it is such a hard job for me to do, how can anyone else possibly do this job?

Whatever the cause of personal inadequacy, the result tends to be the same — a refusal to delegate, with the firm belief that the job is so taxing that it is inconceivable that anyone else can possibly handle it. As expected, it is extremely difficult to persuade these individuals to let go, because the motivating force is a fear of personal failure. It is a fear that immobilizes action since there is a complete inability to take a risk.

Distrust of Others

A fourth reason for not assigning duties and delegating authority to subordinates may be the result of a paranoid distrust of the motives of others. The word paranoid is used to describe a person who has delusions or false beliefs of persecution. The phrase, paranoid distrust, as used here refers to a distrust of others based upon the false belief that a subordinate's drive for success is founded upon a desire to displace or discredit the boss. The supervisor who distrusts and fears subordinates may refuse to delegate authority to them as a means of countering their threat. Such refusal weakens organizational processes. There is also a long-range effect on the organization, for when a supervisor tormented by fears of distrust has the opportunity to select subordinates, there is understandably a strong tendency to select only those persons who are so submissive that they are incapable of threatening any superior's position.

To summarize, whatever the reasons for failure to delegate, whether it be a liking for detail work, a defense against having to face the central issues of a problem, the fear of failure, or the desire to maintain one's own security through weakening competition, the results are essentially the same. First, the refusal to delegate and let subordinates carry projects through to their normal completion results in the elimination of valuable training experiences. If the reason for reluctance to delegate lies in a well-founded belief that subordinates are not trained or capable, the sad fact remains that by not delegating, subordinates never become trained or capable since the opportunity to learn through experience is denied. Second, refusal to delegate has the effect of stifling initiative, with the result that suggestions and new ideas may cease entirely. The subordinate is wondering, "Why should I say anything? I'm not allowed to do anything around here anyway." The third effect of refusing to delegate is that the better people, defining better people as those who need to develop and accept more responsibility, leave the company at the earliest opportunity. The industrial engineer of Case Problem 11-A is a case in point. The net result is not a pretty picture — a frustrated superior incapable of delegating and surrounded ultimately by subordinates incapable of accepting responsibility, even if it were offered.

DECENTRALIZATION OF AUTHORITY

Delegation of authority is described in the first part of this chapter as a process that transfers authority from superior to subordinate in an organization. The extent to which authority is delegated to organizational units is a measure of the degree of decentralization of authority within that organization. The concept of decentralization of authority is relative; an organization is never completely centralized nor is it completely decentralized. Complete centralization of authority would require one person with no subordinates — hardly an organization — while complete decentralization implies that there is no longer a central authority, again a situation resulting in no organization.

In discussing decentralization of authority, it is necessary to define decentralization and to establish guides for determining the extent to which a company is decentralized. Next, the probable effects of the application of integrated information-decision-making systems upon the extent of decentralization within an organization are examined.

Definition of Decentralization

Before defining decentralization, it is well to differentiate between decentralization and two other processes often confused with it. These two processes are departmentation and geographic dispersion. In Chapter 9, *departmentation* is defined as the grouping of work and people into manageable units, and the bases most frequently used in the creation of departments are discussed. These bases are departmentation by function, product, customer, geography, process, and sequence. However, the mere creation of separate departmental units does not constitute decentralization. For example, the vice-president of marketing who appoints five marketing managers, each in charge of a different product, is further departmentalizing the marketing function along product lines but is not necessarily decentralizing the marketing function. The division of one large manufacturing plant into six widely separated smaller plants certainly results in *geographic dispersion*, but not necessarily in decentralization. The key to whether the appointment of product marketing managers or the building of geographically separate plants is decentralization or merely further departmentation is revealed by analyzing the effect of such changes upon the decision-making process within the organization.

Decentralization is the delegation of authority to make decisions to the managers of lower echelon organizational units. The decentralization of the decision-making function is relative, and the degree of decentralization depends upon the following three characteristics of the decisions made at lower levels of the organization: (1) frequency of the decisions, (2) breadth of the decisions, and (3) the extent of the controls exercised over lower level decisions. Let us examine briefly each characteristic.

Frequency of Decisions. The greater the frequency or number of decisions made at lower levels of an organization, the greater is the degree of decentralization in that organization.

Breadth of Decisions. The broader the scope of decisions made at lower levels of an organization, the greater is the degree of decentralization. The breadth of decision making is determined by the number of functions affected by the decisions. A plant whose manager is limited to making only those decisions directly affecting production is less decentralized than the plant whose manager's scope of decision making includes, in addition, the negotiation of labor agreements with a union.

Extent of Controls over Decisions. The extent of controls exercised over the decisions made at lower levels of an organization is an important measure of the degree of decentralization. Decisions are frequently classified in terms of the number of dollars involved, with dollar limitations placed upon decisions that may be made without prior approval. Thus, an organization that permits a sales manager to approve customer credit up to $5,000 is more decentralized, other things being equal, than the organization that permits approval by the sales manager of only $1,000 credit. Timeliness of approval is also a factor. There is less decentralization when approval is required before the decision is made than when a superior is notified after the decision is made or when higher authority is not even informed. The number of approvals required prior to making a decision is also an index of the degree of decentralization. Generally, the fewer the persons who must be contacted for approval, the greater is the degree of decentralization.

Electronic Data Processing and Decentralization

The proper degree of decentralization is determined by carefully considering all factors in relation to the objectives of the organization. One factor that causes a great deal of interesting speculation is the effect of the introduction of high-speed electronic data processing equipment upon decentralization. For example, there are information systems capable of receiving an order for an electric motor from a customer, selecting the warehouse nearest the customer, and preparing in printed form the customer's name, address, and pertinent credit information. If the order reduces the inventory level below a predetermined point, the manufacturing plant is notified and that type motor is scheduled for production. It is also possible for large customers to place their orders directly from remote terminals in their own offices, thereby bypassing the local sales office.

When one considers that customers can order directly through an information processing system, it is easy to point to the sales office and conclude that the decision-making role of middle management is weakened with the introduction of electronic data processing. With the undermining of middle management's decision making and the centralization of information handling, one can develop the argument that modern information systems are more conducive to a centralized rather than decentralized form of organization. Whether or not this argument is valid depends on the definition of middle management decision making and the company's basic philosophy regarding decentralization. If middle management's decisions are defined as the processing of orders, the checking of inventories, and the performance of other routine functions, then in all probability these functions are better handled by electronic equipment. Also, if the basic philosophy of the company is one of centralization — the desire to place as many decisions as possible in the hands of a few top executives — modern information-decision-making systems tend to strengthen that philosophy. But if the underlying philosophy of the company is one of decentralization, it is possible to direct the flow of information to subordinate managers so that they may make better decisions, thereby increasing their contribution to the organization and making their positions more secure. Companies which are centralized because needed information is complex and must be laboriously handled in a central location may find that modern data processing eases the burden of handling such information, thereby making it possible to decentralize. Thus, whether electronic data processing strengthens or weakens the trend toward decentralization depends upon the definition of decision making on the part of middle managers and the company's basic philosophy regarding decentralization.[5]

A CONTINGENCY APPROACH TO ORGANIZING

Chapter 8 presents a contingency approach to organization theory (pp. 181–185). The six situational factors of a contingency approach to organization are expressed in broad terms of organization structure and processes. In Chapter 9, the structural aspects of organization — departmentation, span of management, and committees — are discussed. Chapter 10 discusses the authority relationships between line and staff personnel. In this chapter we have analyzed the organizational processes of delegation and decentralization of authority. Now we reexamine each of the situational factors of a contingency approach —

---

[5]William E. Reif, *Computer Technology and Management Organization* (Iowa City, Iowa: Bureau of Business and Economic Research, The University of Iowa, 1968). In this empirical study, Mr. Reif analyzes the effects of the installation of electronic data processing systems upon a bank, a utility, and a manufacturing organization. The effect of computers on the degree of centralization is discussed in full in Chapter 7, pp. 91–108.

size of organization, degree of interaction, personality of members, congruence of goals, level of decision making, and state of the system — and show how each influences the organizing function. In the discussion that follows, the application of each of the parameters to departmentation, span of management, committees, line and staff relationships, delegation, and decentralization is summarized briefly.

Size of Organization

Perhaps the greatest effect of size of organization, defining size as number of people, is on the degree of formalization of both structure and processes. As size increases, the need for departmentation becomes evident. Whatever the basis selected for the creation of departments, whether it be function, geography, product, or any other unifying characteristic, an increase in the number of departments also results in an attendant increase in the span of management of the chief executive. Committees are also characteristic of large organizations primarily because increased size requires a greater degree of coordination. Committees in large organizations, such as an executive committee, may also be charged with responsibility for decision making.

In large organizations there is a clearer delineation between line and staff functions than in small organizations. Specialized staff appears and is assigned responsibility for a given functional area throughout the entire organization. Delegation of authority with attendant responsibility for the completion of assigned duties becomes imperative in large organizations. The decentralization of authority to make decisions to the managers of lower level organizational units is another characteristic. In summary, the greatest effect of size of organization is the increased degree of formalization of both organizational structure and processes.

Degree of Interaction

An important guide in determining effective departmentation is the need for interaction between the members of an organization in order to achieve organizational goals. Need for interaction arises when several persons find it necessary to communicate with each other in order to solve a common problem or when they are developing and using the same information. Occasionally the formation of committees satisfies the need for interaction.

The degree of interaction between persons supervised by one superior is often a factor in determining the upper limits of an effective span of management. The geometrically progressive increase in the number of relationships described by Graicunas is primarily a function of the cross relationships between those being supervised. It is a function recognized by Urwick in the qualifying phrase, "whose work interlocks."

There is need for interaction between line and staff personnel. Although the line organization is responsible for the achievement of organizational goals, it is necessary that there be free interaction between line and staff personnel in order that the services of staff may be utilized most effectively.

The need for interaction between superior and subordinate is obvious if there is to be an effective process of delegation. Similarly, the need for interaction often serves as a guide in determining whether the decentralization of decision-making authority to lower level echelons improves organizational effectiveness. The decentralization of authority that appears in many marketing departments is recognition of the need for close interaction between the customer, the salesperson, and the local marketing manager in reaching satisfactory solutions to common problems. However, when decisions require close interaction between the members of several organizational units, it may be necessary to centralize the decision-making process at a higher organizational level rather than to move toward a greater degree of decentralization.

Personality of Members

The personality of the members of an organization (defining personality as the sum total of skills, abilities, expectations, interests, and personal characteristics) is an important consideration in determining departmental lines. Work is often departmentalized according to the skills utilized, an arrangement which encourages specialization and the maximum development of individual skills and abilities. Specialized knowledge concerning a specific product or function may well serve as the basis for defining a department. However, it is essential to maintain a balance between specialization, which often facilitates training and results in a high level of skill, and the enrichment of jobs so that there is a resultant maximum utilization of the capabilities of all personnel.

Personality is an important consideration in determining the upper limits of an effective span of management. First, consider the personality of the manager. It is axiomatic that there are variations in the capabilities of managers in respect to range of interests, breadth and depth of knowledge, and the amount of energy expended on the job. In addition to these readily recognized characteristics, there is that rare quality — the ability to inspire others. Managers who have the ability to inspire subordinates to "play over their heads" should have larger spans of management so that their dynamic qualities of leadership may influence as many subordinates as possible. The personality of subordinates is also a determinant of an effective span of management. If subordinates are well trained, interested in their jobs, and desirous of making their own decisions, less supervisory effort is required, thereby increasing the effective span of management. On the other hand, subordinates requiring close supervision decrease the effective span of management. Personality of members is also significant in the formation of committees. When problem solving is the goal it is often best to assign committee members who have a diversity of background, knowledge, and interests.

One of the basic problems existing between line and staff personnel arises from the manner in which the respective roles are perceived. Because of education staff managers have difficulty in accepting a secondary or supportive role. At the same time it is difficult for line managers to relinquish any authority believed necessary to accomplish line objectives. Policy statements setting forth well-defined relationships between line and staff personnel may reduce tensions between the two groups.

The personality of the chief executive is highly significant as a predictor of the extent and effectiveness of delegation and decentralization within an organization. If the chief executive is unable to delegate because of personality, the concept of decentralization of authority to lower level echelons is neither encouraged nor understood. However, if the chief executive is capable of delegating authority, the first step toward effective decentralization of authority is assured.

Congruence of Goals

When the immediate goals of several diverse activities are the same, such congruence may serve as a basis for establishing departments. Plant maintenance departments include personnel possessing the diverse skills of millwrights, electricians, plumbers, steamfitters, and machinists — a variety which seems to have little in common. Yet all are concerned with the immediate objective of keeping plant facilities in good repair. The placement of sales and service personnel under the direction of a sales manager is another example of combining personnel having a congruent goal — customer satisfaction. In the same fashion a committee composed of members having diverse backgrounds yet a common goal often increases the probability of developing creative solutions to a given problem.

When applied as a guide in determining an effective span of management, congruence of goals refers not only to the similarity of goals of each of the various work groups, but also includes the degree of congruence between the immediate goals of the individual and those of the organization. An argument often presented in support of incentive plans, relating pay to productivity, is that such plans are a means of making the goals of the individual congruent with those of the organization. In general, as the immediate goals of subordinates become congruent with the goals of the organization, the span of management may be increased.

When line and staff managers recognize that their respective goals contribute to the goals of the organization, misunderstandings and conflicts between line and staff personnel may be reduced. Also, when goals are congruent the delegation of authority from superior to subordinate is more likely to be successful. One method of increasing the probability of success of the process of delegation and increasing the effectiveness of decentralization of authority to lower level organizational units is to implement a management-by-objectives program.

Level of Decision Making

In some organizations the power to make important decisions is retained by the chief executive and senior vice presidents. In others, decision making occurs at all levels of the organizational hierarchy. The hierarchical location of decision making is primarily a function of the technology of the organization. Some technologies result in an information flow where only the top level of the organization possesses sufficient information for sound decisions. Committees or departments may be created for the specific purpose of placing decision making at the level where it is most effective. The creation of decentralized divisions with decision-making powers is an example of the downward movement of decision making. The reasons most frequently advanced for such decentralization are the need for timeliness, better coordination, and the ability to meet and take full advantage of local factors such as the actions of competitors and the needs of customers.

The level of decision making in an organization has a direct bearing upon the breadth of an executive's span of management. The executive who retains the responsibility for making decisions usually has a reduced span of management. If subordinates are permitted to make decisions, the span of management may be increased.

The relationship between line and staff personnel is also influenced by the level of decision making. In those organizations with highly centralized decision-making processes, it is not uncommon for staff personnel to exercise considerable authority in their functional speciality. If the organization is diversified and has many product lines, it may be better to place the decision-making function of both line and staff personnel at lower levels of the organization. When decision making is located at the top of the hierarchy, there may be a reluctance to delegate decision-making authority to lower level subordinates. Yet it is quite possible that a greater degree of delegation and decentralization might be more effective if the practical suggestions for effective delegation discussed on pages 240–242 were followed.

State of the System

The extent to which the organization is achieving its stated goals, the state of the system, is an important consideration in determining departmental units. Cost reduction, a continuing goal for most organizations, is frequently achieved by combining departmental units, thereby avoiding duplication of effort. At the same time, the needs of the organization may be such that it becomes necessary to emphasize a particular function by creating a separate department or committee reporting directly to the chief executive; for example, research and development. The desire to reduce costs or to emphasize a particular function are examples illustrating the elimination or creation of departments as the result of viewing the organization as a system and evaluating the extent to which that organization is meeting its stated goals.

The extent to which the goals of the organization are stabilized and the degree to which an organization is achieving these goals serve as guides in determining an effective span of management. When the organization is failing to meet its goals, the chief executive may decide to decrease the span of management as a means of structuring the organization so that it may be better controlled. One result is a more rapid adaptation to changing internal and external forces. However, if the organization is relatively stable and successfully fulfilling its goals, such conditions contribute to the effectiveness of an extended span of management.

The relationship between line and staff personnel is influenced by the extent to which an organization is meeting its goals. When line personnel fail to meet expected standards of performance it is likely that staff personnel will exercise more positive staff authority in order that such standards may be met. Similarly, when line personnel meet established standards and the organizational system is in a state of equilibrium, staff's role becomes less apparent and directive in nature.

The narrowing of the span of management in order to exercise a high degree of control during a crisis usually results in relatively limited delegation of authority. As the crisis is resolved it is probable that more subordinates will be assigned broader responsibilities and will be delegated the commensurate authority to fulfill those responsibilities. The state of the system is an important consideration in determining the optimum degree of decentralization. In addition to considering the extent to which organizational goals are being achieved during a crisis, consideration must also be given to the stage of organizational growth, the nature of the organization's purpose, and the availability of controls. As an organization succeeds in achieving stated objectives, it is possible to exercise a more permissive form of leadership and decision making. More permissive leadership and participation in decision making tend to further the process of decentralization.

The decentralization of authority to make decisions is not an *either-or* proposition as implied by the expression, centralization vs. decentralization. Instead, the extent of decentralization is a point on a continuum with a high degree of centralization and a high degree of decentralization marking the limits of the continuum. Case Problem 11-B illustrates that the definition of the degree of decentralization depends upon one's position in the organization. The chairman of Dynamic Industries honestly believes that the corporation is highly decentralized, but the president of a subsidiary company questions that view. The case also shows how a few well-chosen corporate controls — capital expenditures, budgets, and centralized industrial relations — effectively limit the degree of decentralization.

Case Problem 11-B

DECENTRALIZATION — FACT OR FICTION

Dynamic Industries, a diversified manufacturer of automotive replacement parts, is a company that is growing rapidly as the result of an aggressive policy of acquisition. Board chairman John Rafferty believes that the growth of his company is sound and that the main reason for the extremely rapid growth is due to the operation of the company on a highly decentralized basis. Since growth is the result of acquiring companies that are going concerns, Rafferty encourages the managements of the subsidiary companies to carry on as they had prior to joining Dynamic Industries. At present, discussions regarding merger are being held with Central Electronics, a company that manufactures a broad line of electronic components, many of which have applications in the defense and space industries. Central Electronics is interested in Dynamic Industries because Dynamic could supply the much-needed capital to complete the final stages of the development of a high-performance transformer and the building of a plant in which to manufacture the new product. However, Rosa Vasquez, the founder and president of Central, realizes the potential dangers of merging with another company in that she might lose control of her own firm and be placed in the position of being an employee for a larger corporation.

But Rafferty continually assures Vasquez that Dynamic Industries operates on a highly decentralized basis and describes their concept of decentralization as follows:

"We expect you, as the president of a subsidiary company, to manage as you have in the past. You are successful with your own company and there is no reason why you shouldn't continue to be a success operating as a part of Dynamic. The major functions of sales, manufacturing, engineering, and product development are all yours to do with as you see fit. In a sense, we are sort of the banker; that is, we supply the money that you need for capital improvements and expansion. Even though the profits of each subsidiary company go into the corporate till, it is still like having your own company because your pay for the year is a combination of a guaranteed salary and a percentage of the net profits of your company."

Thus assured, Vasquez decided to merge with Dynamic Industries. During the first six months all went well, and Vasquez saw very little of anyone from corporate headquarters. At the beginning of the seventh month, the corporate controller paid Vasquez a visit and explained to her in detail the company's requirements for profit planning and requested that Vasquez develop a profit plan, a detailed forecast of Central's revenues and operating expenses, for the coming year. Though very pleasant, the controller made it quite plain that should the performance of the company deviate significantly from the forecast, a team of cost analysts and industrial engineers would arrive from headquarters to determine the cause of the deviation and to recommend necessary changes.

Shortly after this experience with the controller, the industrial relations vice-president of Dynamic Industries called on Vasquez and informed her that a member of the corporate industrial relations staff would be on hand to conduct the coming negotiations with the union representing Central's employees. Vasquez protested, saying that she had been negotiating her own labor contracts for years; however, it was explained to her that because of company-wide employee benefit plans, such as pensions and insurance, and to prevent the unions from pitting one subsidiary company against another in the area of wages, centralized control over negotiations was very necessary. At the time of this visit, the provisions of the company's salary plan were outlined to Vasquez and arrangements were made for the installation of the corporate clerical and supervisory salary plans by a member of the headquarters industrial relations staff.

The following month Vasquez called Rafferty and asked what steps should be taken to secure capital for the new building intended for the manufacture of the high-performance transformer. Rafferty answered by saying, "I'll have someone from the treasurer's office call on you and show you how to fill out the forms used in requesting funds for capital expansion. It's quite a process, but remember you are only one of 15 subsidiaries and they all seem to want money at the same time. Whether or not you get it this year depends not only upon your needs but also upon the needs of the other 14 companies."

PROBLEMS

1. Has Dynamic Industries decentralized its operations as much as possible?
2. As Rosa Vasquez, president of Central Electronics, would you regard the management policies of the parent corporation as primarily centralized or primarily decentralized?
3. Is Dynamic Industries exerting too much control over Central Electronics? Why or why not?
4. Recommend the optimum degree of decentralization for the situation described in this case.

CHAPTER QUESTIONS FOR STUDY AND DISCUSSION

1. Why is it necessary to define the term *to delegate* precisely? How does such a definition contribute to an understanding of the control exercised by a person who does the delegating?
2. Why is it necessary to have three principles or conditions that must be met for the process of delegation to be most effective? Explain what would happen if accountability were not considered absolute.
3. Should the president of a company be held accountable for the following actions of subordinates?
   (a) Price fixing that is in violation of federal laws and stated company policies.
   (b) Failure to meet stated company sales objectives.
   (c) Loss of competitive position in development of new products.
4. If one or more of the conditions of delegation is violated, is it possible for the process of delegation to work? Discuss.
5. How valid is the concept that an executive should be held accountable for the performance of a function even though there is no

power to control the actions of others (for example, the sales manager who cannot force customers to buy)?

6. Give an example of each of the four situations that result in a violation of the condition of unity of command.

7. If delegation includes the granting of authority and empowers a subordinate to act, why is it necessary to establish controls to see that the subordinate performs as expected?

8. What is meant by the idea that the real problems of delegation are found in the personality of the person doing the delegating?

9. Differentiate between decentralization and geographic dispersion. Can geographic dispersion be transformed into decentralization of authority? Discuss.

10. Discuss the following statement: The development of electronic data processing systems tends to centralize authority and limit the decision-making powers of the middle manager.

11. Discuss each of the criteria which are used to determine the extent of decentralization.

12. How is the concept of decentralization of authority related to the concept of delegation? In what respects do these two concepts differ? In what respects are they the same?

Organizational Change — Analysis and Development

Case Problem 12-A

CHARTING AN ORGANIZATION

Twenty-five years ago Stanley Johnson founded the Johnson Valve Company, which has grown and prospered over the years. Mr. Johnson, now 62 years old, realizes that he cannot continue as president indefinitely, but there are no well-formulated plans for management succession. The stock in the company is closely held by Mr. Johnson and members of his immediate family, with only ten percent held by an outsider, the attorney who serves as the only outside member of the board and as general counsel for the corporation. The attorney has suggested that the position of executive vice-president be created and a person brought in from another company to be moved up to the presidency upon satisfactory performance and Mr. Johnson's expected retirement at age 65. Currently the organization is as follows.

Reporting directly to Mr. Johnson as an "assistant-to" is a man in his early thirties who has a master's degree in marketing. Although his title is "assistant-to," his primary function is to conduct market research studies in the valve industry and to prepare detailed analyses of current sales. Johnson often refers to his assistant as "my forward planning unit." Also reporting to the president are the treasurer, the vice-president of sales, the purchasing director, the production vice-president, the

chief engineer, and the plant manager. The plant manager, now nearing retirement, has been ill most of the past year, so in effect the plant superintendent reports directly to the president.

The treasurer, who for several years was the firm's only accountant, has been with the company since its founding. Reporting directly to the treasurer is the office manager who not only manages the office but also performs the personnel function for all salaried and clerical personnel. The controller, responsible for the cost accounting section, and the supervisor of general ledgers also report to the treasurer. The vice-president in charge of sales has been an officer of the company for the past five years; however, for many years she was in charge of the field sales force and the entire sales function with the title of sales manager. Although there is now a sales manager reporting to her, the vice-president actually directs the sales force and the sales manager spends most of his time in the office handling the paper work generated by the sales representatives. The supervisor of the sales order department also reports to the sales manager.

The purchasing director, with a staff of two buyers and a clerk, reports directly to the president as a result of Mr. Johnson's desire to control the cost of raw materials. Formerly, the director of purchases reported to the production manager, who is a vice-president and Mr. Johnson's sister-in-law, but the only person now reporting to the production manager is the head of the production scheduling department. The chief engineer, also an officer of the company, knows the product well and supervises the section chief of the drafting department, the chief metallurgist, and the director of the research laboratories.

Most of Johnson Valve Company's current problems center in the production area. The plant manager's staff consists of the maintenance foreman, the plant personnel and employment manager, and the foreman of the tool room; but for the past year, as the result of the plant manager's illness and absence, the plant staff has been reporting directly to the plant superintendent, who also reports on paper to the plant manager. Normally reporting to the plant superintendent are the shipping and receiving foreman, the machining foreman, the quality control manager, the factory stores supervisor, the assembly foreman, and the supervisor of the experimental shop, which is engaged primarily in carrying out projects assigned by the chief engineer.

PROBLEMS

1. Prepare an organization chart showing the present structure of Johnson Valve Company.
2. Prepare a plan for reorganization. Include a new organization chart and your justification for the changes suggested.

Organizations are not static structures; instead, organizations are made up of dynamic interrelationships existing between people performing those functions necessary for the achievement of organizational goals. As either goals or people change, the need for modification of organization structure and function arises. Symptoms calling for organizational change, such as those described below, reflect inadequacies or inefficiencies in any part of the organization.

1. *Faulty decision making.* Decision making may be too slow to gain full advantage of the situation, or erroneous decisions are being made. Perhaps the difficulty in decision making may be traced to the placement of the responsibility for decisions at a level of the organization not having access to necessary information.
2. *Poor Communications.* The Parable of the Spindle, Case Problem 6-A, is illustrative of the complete breakdown of an information system with its resultant personnel problems.
3. *Failure in Functional Areas.* There may be failure or inefficiency in any one of the major functional areas. Production may not meet schedules or it may show excessive costs and quality defects. Sales may show a steady loss of customers and failure to achieve expected market penetration, while finance may reveal an inability to provide for long-range corporate demands. In the area of personnel, the need for organizational change may arise as the result of personnel not meeting the requirements of changing positions, with poor performance as a result; or the need for change may be highlighted by excessive personality clashes between employees (again, the Parable of the Spindle).
4. *Lack of Innovation.* There may be a dearth of new ideas, either in the form of new products or new and better ways of performing present functions. When innovation ceases, growth ceases also.

The presence of any of the above symptoms indicates the need for organizational change. Such change may occur within a relatively short period of time as a result of organizational analysis and an evaluation of organizational effectiveness — an approach that emphasizes change in structure. Or organizational change may occur as a result of implementing a long range plan of organizational development that stresses the development of individual managers — an approach that emphasizes change in behavior. Each approach, structural or behavioral, has its place.[1] Discussed first is organizational analysis, including the procedures and techniques usually used in such studies, and a method of evaluating organizational effectiveness. Planned organizational development programs emphasizing the development of executives or managers are discussed in the second part of the chapter.

ORGANIZATIONAL ANALYSIS

When conducting organizational analysis, one is planning for the future of the organization; therefore, it is helpful to follow a procedure based on an objective method. As a result the procedures used in organizational planning follow very closely the procedures discussed in Chapter 4.

Procedures for Organizational Analysis

The procedures for sound organizational analysis are an application of the scientific method. They are: (1) assign responsibility, (2) collect data, (3) prepare alternate plans of organization, and (4) install the best plan and follow up.

Assign Responsibility. There are three questions to be answered in the assignment of responsibility for organizational analysis. The first of these questions is, who is to initiate the study; the second, who is to collect the necessary data and develop recommended changes; and third, who is to approve the recommended changes and place them into effect? An early study by K. K. White of 118 companies sheds some light on what is actually done by industrial firms in one phase of organizational analysis, preparing the organization chart.[2] White's study shows that the company president initiates the charting of the

---

[1]William F. Glueck, "Organization Change in Business and Government," *Academy of Management Journal*, Vol. 12, No. 4 (December, 1969), pp. 439–449. Professor Glueck discusses the approaches to organizational change, both structural and behavioral, and outlines the dimensions of organizational change. The following book expresses a similar point of view: Newton Margulies and John Wallace, *Organizational Change*, Techniques and Applications (Glenview: Scott, Foresman & Co., 1973).

[2]K. K. White, *Understanding the Company Organization Chart* (New York: American Management Association, 1963), Research Study Number 56, pp. 16–17. A more recent study setting forth the role of the management consultant in organization analysis and change is Neil G. Davey, *The External Consultant's Role in Organizational Change* (East Lansing: Graduate School of Business Administration, Michigan State University, 1971).

organization in 42 percent of the companies surveyed; a company vice-president in 22 percent of the companies; and the personnel executive in 12 percent of the companies. In most instances, 25 percent of the companies surveyed, the personnel executive compiles the necessary data and prepares the chart. The president of the company does the charting in 17 percent of the cases, a company vice-president in 14 percent, or an outside consultant in 13 percent of the companies. Final approval for any organizational change must come from top management itself. It goes without saying that the chief executive, usually the president, must approve any changes and, to insure maximum cooperation, approval of other members of top management is much desired.

Collect Data. Once the responsibility for analysis and preparation of proposed changes is established, it is necessary to collect all pertinent information so that any proposed change is founded on fact, not upon supposition. The availability and type of information sought varies from one situation to another. Certain historical records are of interest, particularly those that show the growth of the company with respect to the number of people, their titles, their duties, and their personal backgrounds and qualifications.[3] The pattern of growth of the company as reflected by gross sales is of value, especially when these figures can be correlated with the need for personnel. In this manner, definite trends may be established, and personnel needs for expected future levels of sales may be projected. The analysis of current reports and forms, for example the monthly distribution of manufacturing costs, shows the flow of information within the company. Activity charts showing the distribution of an employee's time for each day or week may be prepared for key jobs or for all the jobs within a department. When interpreted in the light of information gained from an analysis of existing reports, the activity chart indicates whether the information is needed. Information gained from the organization questionnaire (discussed below) is of value in defining authority relationships, the nature of assigned responsibilities, and the extent of authority delegated to carry out these responsibilities. The gathering of data for an organizational analysis is often a long and tediuous task, but it is an important step for it establishes the factual basis for any proposed change.

Prepare Alternate Plans. Ultimately, any proposed change in organization must be sold to key personnel and alternate plans should be prepared as a form of insurance. Among these plans, there should be

---

[3]The following is recommended as a discussion of computer-based models in manpower planning: James W. Walker, "Models in Manpower Planning," *Business Horizons*, Vol. 14, No. 2 (April, 1971), pp. 87–95.

an "ideal" structure that is theoretically desirable, but not necessarily attainable. Using the ideal as a starting point, modifications in the plan that consider the economic and competitive position of the company may be developed. If only a single plan is presented, it may be rejected by one displeased executive; an alternate plan is necessary since organizational change is a situation in which "half a loaf is better than none" and the adoption of the alternate plan is at least a step in the right direction.

Install the Best Plan and Follow Up. When the plan is approved, it should be installed and there should be provisions for continuing study and analysis so that any necessary modifications can be made. This task is usually assigned to the group that proposes the initial change. Proper follow-up and modifications of the plan, when needed, emphasize the continuing nature of organizational change.

Tools of Organizational Analysis

There are many tools available for use in organizational analysis. Among those most commonly used are the organization questionnaire, the position description, the organization chart, and the organization manual. Each of these techniques used in studying organizations is discussed briefly.

The Organization Questionnaire. One of the first steps in describing the present organization is to determine the functions and positions of present personnel. Organization questionnaires have been found useful in securing information from executives, supervisors, and department heads concerning their positions in the organization. The first portion of most questionnaires contains identification material such as the name of the employee, the department, the major division, title of position held, and the location of the position. Also, the name and position title of the employee's immediate supervisor is requested. The employee is also asked to give the names and titles of subordinates along with the activities of subordinates and an indication of whether actions taken by subordinates are reported prior to action, reported after action has been taken, or not reported at all. The employee may also be asked to describe the responsibilities of the position held and close relationships with other personnel in the organization. The nature of authority is generally defined in terms of whether or not the employee may establish policy, incur expenses, make personnel changes, or establish procedures and methods. Membership on committees is also included and, if chairing the committee, the employee is asked to state the goals and accomplishments of the committee. The basic records that must be kept and regular or occasional reports that are required are also listed. Finally, the employee may be asked to make suggestions concerning changes which would improve the functioning of the organization.[4]

There are two methods of securing the information called for by the questionnaire. One method is to have the employee in the position fill out the questionnaire and return it to the person conducting the study; the other method is to secure the information through interview. While the latter method is more costly and time consuming, it is generally agreed that the interview yields much more information and understanding of the organization as a result of aside remarks and nuances of meaning implied in the way in which answers are given. Once the questionnaires have been completed, they are usually reviewed with the next higher level of authority. It is at this stage that significant discrepancies in the opinions of superior and subordinate with respect to the nature of assigned duties, the nature and extent of delegated authority, and the lines of accountability may emerge.

The Position Description. The data obtained from the questionnaire is the primary source of information for preparing the *position description*, a written statement that describes a specific position in the organization. Whether a written position description merely sketches the major duties of the job or whether it goes into minute detail depends on its intended use. If the purpose is to define the major positions in the organization and show their relationships to each other, the description may be relatively brief; if however, the primary purpose of the description is for training, the job duties may be detailed so that they approach the completeness of a procedural manual.

Most position descriptions usually include the following information. There is a section that *identifies* the job and may range from a statement of the title only to the inclusion of statements indicating the title of the immediate superior, the date of preparation of the description with dates of revision, and the number and types of employees supervised. Generally, the name of the position holder is not included since a change in personnel would necessitate a revision of the description. Next, there is a statement of the major responsibility or *primary functions* of the job, a capsule description of the purpose of the position. A statement of *responsibilities* presents the major tasks that must be performed in order to fulfill the functions of the job. It is this portion of the description, when developed in great detail, that may serve as a useful training device; but for the most part, executive and supervisory descriptions are limited to a statement of between six and ten major responsibilities. The *authority* delegated to the position in order to perform the required functions may appear as a separate section of

---

[4]Harry Levinson, Janice Molinari, and Andrew G. Spohn, *Organizational Diagnosis* (Cambridge: Harvard University Press, 1972). This work presents an in-depth study of the many techniques used in organizational diagnosis including the questionnaire. The use of the questionnaire and interviews are discussed thoroughly.

the position description or it may be combined with the statement of primary responsibilities. The last section of most descriptions is a statement of *relationships*. The reason for stating relationships is two-fold. First, it shows the position in its proper relationship to other positions within the company and relationships to people outside the company such as vendors, auditors, or public relations contacts. Second, a statement of relationships tends to answer the criticism often made of position descriptions that these descriptions force an employee into a narrow role, oblivious to other events and employees in the company.

As a general rule, position descriptions do not include a statement of the specifications and qualifications required of the position holder. If such specifications are prepared, they are on a separate sheet and include requirements regarding education, experience, and other personal characteristics. Specifications are of value as an aid in evaluating and selecting potential replacements.

The Organization Chart. An organization chart presents in graphic form the major functions and the lines of authority of an organization as of a given moment in time. Charts range in complexity from the simple chart shown in Figure 12-1 to complex charts that use color and the photographs of the holders of key positions. However, for purposes of organizational analysis and reference, it is best to keep charts as simple as possible.

The mechanics of constructing an organization chart are not difficult. Figure 12-2 presents ten suggestions for preparing organization charts. These are not hard-and-fast rules and they should be modified when the occasion demands. By far the most common form of organizational charting is the *vertical* chart (Figure 12-1), which shows the organizational hierarchy ranked from top to bottom. A variation of the vertical chart is the *horizontal* chart, which is read from left to right rather than from top to bottom. A more complex form of charting is the *circular* organization chart, which places the chief executive in the center of the circle with the horizontal lines of the vertical chart forming a series of concentric circles around the chief executive. Proponents of the horizontal form of charting contend that we normally read from left to right and that a horizontal chart follows this natural tendency. Those who favor the circular chart claim that dynamic relationships are better portrayed through a series of concentric circles. However, precedent and ease of construction and interpretation favor the continued use of the vertical chart.

The Organization Manual. An *organization manual* is a compilation of descriptive statements usually bound in manual form concerning the organization of a specific company. The content of organization manuals varies widely; however, two of the tools of organizational analysis are included in almost all manuals — position descriptions

ORGANIZATION CHART — XYZ CORPORATION

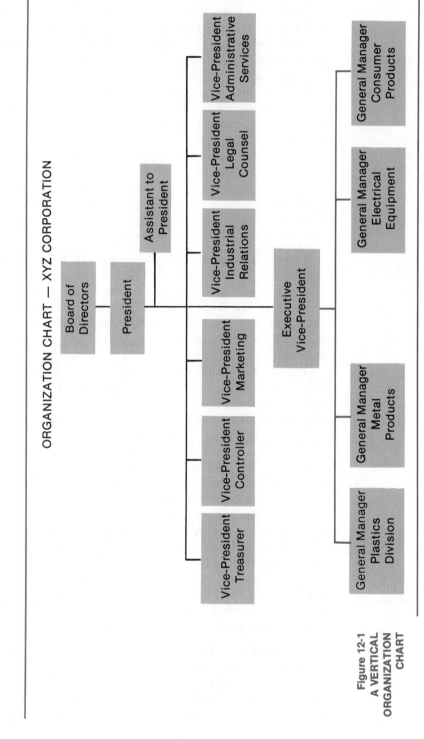

Board of Directors

President

Assistant to President

Vice-President Treasurer

Vice-President Controller

Vice-President Marketing

Vice-President Industrial Relations

Vice-President Legal Counsel

Vice-President Administrative Services

Executive Vice-President

General Manager Plastics Division

General Manager Metal Products

General Manager Electrical Equipment

General Manager Consumer Products

Figure 12-1
A VERTICAL
ORGANIZATION
CHART

Figure 12-2
SUGGESTIONS
FOR PREPARING
AN
ORGANIZATION
CHART

1. Identify the chart fully by showing the name of the company, date of preparation, and title of person or name of department responsible for preparation. If the chart is for one division of the company only, include such information as part of the title.

2. Use rectangular boxes to show either an organizational unit or a person. Plural executives and other committees occupy one box.

3. The vertical placement of the boxes shows relative positions in the organizational hierarchy; however, due to space limitations, line units are frequently shown one level below staff units. (See Figure 12-1.)

4. Any given horizontal row of boxes should be of the same size and should include only those positions having the same organizational rank.

5. Use vertical and horizontal solid lines to show the flow of line authority.

6. If necessary, use dotted or broken lines to show the flow of functional authority. (See Figure 10-4.)

7. Lines of authority enter at the top center of a box and leave at the bottom center; they do not run through the box. Exception: the line of authority to a staff assistant or an "assistant-to" may enter the side of the box. (See Figure 12-1.)

8. The title of each position should be placed in the box. The title should be descriptive and show function. For example, vice-president is not sufficient as it does not show function. The functional area, e.g., manufacturing, should be included even though it is not a part of the official title. Titles should be consistent; if necessary, revise titles so they are both consistent and descriptive.

9. Include the name of the person currently holding the position unless personnel turnover is so great that revision of the chart is burdensome.

10. Keep the chart as simple as possible; include a legend if necessary to explain any special notations. When preparing a separate chart for an organizational unit, include the superior to whom the unit reports.

and organization charts.[5] The combination of these two instruments shows the lines of authority and accountability, the major functions of each position, the responsibilities and authority for each position, and the primary interrelationships between key positions. In addition, organization manuals may include statements of company objectives and company policy. In large companies, it is not uncommon to find organization manuals consisting of several volumes, one for each of the major functional areas of the company. In such cases, each volume includes a statement of company objectives, policies, and the organization charts and position descriptions for that specific functional area.

[5]For a discussion of the use of organization charts as a means of planning for an organization's future the following is recommended: William L. Brockhaus, "Planning for Change With Organization Charts," *Business Horizons*, Vol. 17, No. 2 (April, 1974), pp. 47–51.

Evaluation of Formal Organizational Analysis

Not all companies believe in using the formal tools of organizational analysis. The extent to which formal tools of analysis are used is related to the size of the company. The absence of charts, position descriptions, and organization manuals in small companies may be due to a belief that they are not needed, a lack of personnel to prepare such materials, or any of a number of similar reasons. However, large companies without charts have not prepared them because it is felt that the disadvantages of charting the organization outweigh the advantages. Let us examine the advantages and disadvantages usually attributed to the use of formal tools of organizational analysis.

Advantages of Formal Organizational Analysis. The advantage most frequently cited in support of preparing a formal analysis of an organization is that the process of analysis itself forces the key executives of the company into critical thinking directed toward organizational problems. The process of analysis leads to a reexamination of present structure and functions and makes possible the correction of organizational defects. Second, charts and manuals are of use in training replacements for present personnel. True, the person holding the position at present may not benefit greatly, but new people coming into the organization or a person moving into a new position find charts and manuals helpful during their period of orientation. The third reason advanced for formalizing the organization structure is that charts and position descriptions offer an authoritative source which describes the major functions and responsibilities for each position and thus become a means of settling disputes that may arise concerning lines of authority and accountability.

Disadvantages of Formal Organizational Analysis. Those who prefer not to use formal analysis claim that the formalization of organization structure by charts and position descriptions leads to rigidity and inflexibility in organization structure and function. They point out that a new person coming into a position complete with chart and position description is bound by precedent and does not have the full opportunity for self-expression and for showing an ability to contribute to the organization. In a sense, these critics of charting are saying "Put a person into a square and you have one." In addition to organizational inflexibility and the stultifying effects that charting may have on individuals, opponents of formal analysis state that formal charting ignores completely the informal organization — the many interpersonal relationships, lines of communications, and influence — which exists among people who work together every day and is often quite different from the formal relationships shown on the chart.

There is a need for balance. Charting is not intended to stultify or limit the achievement of individuals. It is intended to show in broad strokes major functions and relationships. Nor is charting intended to promote organizational inflexibility; on the other hand, an organization with relationships that change from day to day or with every crisis cannot properly be called an organization.

Evaluating Organizational Effectiveness

The application of the tools of organizational analysis — the organization questionnaire, the position description, and the charting of the present organization — is the second step in the process of organizational analysis. In order to complete the third step of analysis, to prepare alternate plans of organization, and move on to the fourth step of selecting the best plan for a given situation, it is necessary to establish a basis for evaluating present organizational effectiveness. Due to the dynamic nature of organizations resulting from patterns of leadership, the structure of the organization, the types of organizational authority, the efficiency of organizational processes such as delegation, and the utilization of groups to perform organizational functions, any concept of measuring effectiveness must recognize these variables and interpret them in terms of the needs of each specific organization. Figure 12-3, Checklist of Organizational Effectiveness, is a systematic means of checking each major factor contributing to organizational effectiveness. Let us examine Figure 12-3, remembering that the characteristics of organization are not absolutes — either black or white.

Overall Planning. The extent of overall planning lends direction and purpose to an organization and is basic to the effectiveness of any enterprise. In the collection of data for organizational analysis, the examination of company records may determine the extent of overall planning. Two questions are asked in this regard: is there a written statement of company objectives, and is there a written statement of company policy? Objectives define the goals of the organization, while policy statements indicate the broad framework within which each of the functional areas of the firm should operate in achieving the objectives. As an absolute minimum, there should be policy guides for each of the major functional areas of finance, production, marketing, and personnel. Unless objectives and policies are clearly stated, there is very little hope for establishing effective organizational structure and processes.

Patterns of Leadership. Chapter 8, discusses Theory X, a work-centered approach to organizational leadership, and Theory Y, a people-centered or human relations approach to leadership. The contingency approach to organization theory holds that the most effective leadership pattern, whether it be predominantly authoritative or participative, is dependent upon the characteristics of the organization and its

Figure 12-3
CHECKLIST OF
ORGANIZATIONAL
EFFECTIVENESS

1. OVERALL PLANNING
Written Statements of Company Objectives _____
Company Policies _____
  Marketing _____
  Finance _____
  Production _____
  Personnel _____
  Other _____

2. PATTERNS OF LEADERSHIP
Primarily
  Authoritative _____
  Participative _____
  Appropriate _____

3. ORGANIZATIONAL STRUCTURE
Departmentation
  Function _____
  Product _____
  Customer _____
  Geography _____
  Process _____
  Sequence _____
Span of Management
  One over One _____
  Two or Three _____
  Three to Seven _____
  Eight or More _____
Overall Impression
  Proper Balance _____
  Proper Emphasis _____

4. AUTHORITY RELATIONSHIPS
Factors Limiting Effectiveness of Authority
  Overlapping Authority _____
  Superior Authority _____
  Provisions for Subordinate Acceptance _____
Line and Staff Relationships
  Use of "Assistant-to:" _____

Limits of Line Authority _____
Limits of Staff Authority _____
Task Force Organization _____

5. DELEGATION
Parity of Authority and Responsibility _____
Absoluteness of Accountability _____
Availability of Controls _____
Unity of Command _____
Personality Factors _____

6. DECENTRALIZATION
Definition of Decentralized Unit _____
Scope, Type, and Frequency of Decisions _____
Availability of Controls _____
Statement of Goals for Unit _____
Degree of Decentralization _____
  Optimum _____
  Too Little _____
  Too Much _____

7. USE OF COMMITTEES
Committees
  Ad Hoc _____
  Advisory _____
  Management _____
  Composition _____
  Benefits _____
Board of Directors
  Outside Members _____
  Inside Members _____
  Contribution _____

8. PROVISIONS FOR CONTROL
Definitions of Standards _____
Units of Measurement _____
Reporting of Exceptions _____
Timeliness of Controls _____
Strategic Placement of Controls _____
Control Information for Line Managers _____

members. As the organization grows in size, defining size as number of people, there is a tendency for leadership patterns to become more authoritative. The same tendency exists when there is little need for interaction between members, when members of the organization are submissive and dependent, when the goals of individuals and the organization are divergent, when decision making occurs at a high level of the organization, and when the organization is under pressure to survive and meet stated objectives. The converse of the above situation — a small organization or unit, need for interaction, independent members, congruent goals, decision making at all levels in an organization achieving its objectives — calls for a participative form of leadership. Although a judgment concerning the effectiveness of leadership is highly subjective in nature and its worth dependent upon the skill of the person performing the organizational analysis, such a judgment should be made in evaluating an organization.[6]

Organization Structure. When evaluating the structure of an organization, three structural characteristics are considered: departmentation, span of management, and an overall impression of balance and emphasis. The most frequently used bases for departmentation are function, product, customer, geography, process, sequence, and any combination of these. The basis chosen for forming a department varies from one level of the organization to another and there may be variation in the bases for departmentation among units of the same level. The test of proper departmentation is whether or not the result is a grouping of activities that is capable of functioning effectively.

Span of management is the number of departments or functions under the direction of one manager. The checklist in Figure 12-3 provides a basis for grouping the span of management into four broad categories. When a one-over-one arrangement is found, it deserves careful examination. A situation in which a one-over-one arrangement is probably effective and necessary is that of an executive vice-president as the sole person reporting to the president. In this instance, the president's other duties, such as relations with the board of directors and with groups outside the company, may make it mandatory that only one person report to the president. However, one-over-one relationships at lower levels of the organization should be regarded with suspicion. The designation of an assistant manager, a line relationship showing only one subordinate, may be justified if there is a clear understanding of those functions to be performed by the manager and those functions to be performed by the assistant manager.

---

[6]For a discussion of the influence of the chief executive officer's behavior upon organizational development, the following is significant: Chris Argyris, "The CEO's Behavior: Key to Organizational Development," *Harvard Business Review*, Vol. 51, No. 2 (March–April, 1973), pp. 55–64.

An overall impression of the effectiveness of an organizational structure includes evaluating the structure; i.e., departmentation and span of management, with respect to the *balance* and *emphasis* accorded those functions and activities most closely related to the objectives of the organization. It is helpful to view the structure as components of a system, and the parameters of the contingency approach, as discussed in Chapter 8, are helpful as a basis for determining whether the departmentation, span of management, and the degree of balance and emphasis represent the optimum for organizational effectiveness.

Authority Relationships. In reviewing authority relationships, our concern is directed toward those factors that limit authority, the clarity of established line-and-staff relationships, and ultimately a consideration of the feasibility of a task force form of organization. When determining the effectiveness of lines of authority, it is necessary to determine the extent to which there is overlapping authority between managerial functions. The source of this information is the questionnaire and the position description. Occasionally authority may be ineffective because provisions for subordinate acceptance of authority are inadequate and may result in ineffective performance, lack of cooperation, and, on occasion, refusal to follow directions. The pattern of leadership is an important item to consider when assessing provisions for subordinate acceptance.

When checking line-and-staff relationships, review any position entitled "assistant-to" and question the practicality of designating a specific staff title more descriptive of the functions performed. In small organizations or in the case of new positions, descriptive titles may not be practical. When determining the authority relationships of established line-and-staff positions, attention is directed toward the degree to which authority relationships are defined — the stating of definite limits of authority for each, and the extent to which each authority understands the role of the other. In some organizations, characterized by changing projects, with well-defined objectives and limiting time tables, it is well to consider the possibility of using a task force organization designed for the specific task at hand. It is necessary that responsibility for the entire project be stated and that provisions be made for the reassignment of personnel upon the completion of the project.[7]

Delegation. Violation of any of the three conditions for effective delegation may result in ineffective delegation. Admittedly, these conditions are ignored on many occasions; but when ignored and when the resultant delegation seems effective, it is effective in spite of the fact that the conditions have been disregarded. Also, poor delegation

---

[7]For an evaluation of functional structure and matrix organizational design for the completion of projects, the following is recommended: Jay R. Gilbraith, "Matrix Organization Designs," *Business Horizons*, Vol. 14, No. 1 (February, 1971), pp. 29–40.

may be due to personality characteristics of either the superior or the subordinate which make the process of delegation ineffective.

Decentralization. The measure of the effectiveness of decentralization of authority is whether it meets the needs of the organization. The parameters of the contingency approach form a useful set of guides concerning the appropriateness of the degree of decentralization. Additional questions may be raised concerning the definition of the decentralized unit, the scope and type of decisions made within the unit, provisions for adequate control, and the statement of goals for the unit. An overall determination of effective decentralization expresses the degree of decentralization as optimum, too little, or too much.

Use of Committees. When properly used, committees may perform quite effectively the managerial functions assigned to them. In rating the effectiveness of committees, it is necessary to determine the extent to which the duties assigned to the committee are in keeping with the functions normally assigned to a given type of committee. Ad hoc committees are temporary in nature and are formed to consider a specific question. They are disbanded upon the completion of their assignment. Ad hoc groups may appear at any level of the organization and the functions assigned may range from making recommendations to making decisions and taking action necessary for the completion of the assignment. Advisory committees are, as the name indicates, assigned advisory functions with the right to take action reserved for another, usually the person to whom the committee reports. The management committee, whose members are from the top level of the company, offers a means of coordinating the work of individual functional areas and may operate as a plural executive. Benefits derived from the proper use of committees are the value of pooled judgments coming from the diverse knowledge of the individual members, the creation of a favorable training situation, and improved cooperation on the part of individual members as the result of having participated in the work of the group.

In determining the contribution of a board of directors, review the backgrounds of individual members, not only regarding their status as employees of the corporation which determines whether they are inside or outside members, but also with respect to the amount of time each member is able to devote to the company. The contributions of a board depend on the manner in which they perform their directive functions of setting corporate objectives, selecting management, and subsequently reviewing and guiding management's efforts.

Provisions for Control. Though the control process is not discussed fully until Part Five of this textbook, items concerning the control function are included in the checklist for organizational effectiveness for the sake of completeness. In evaluating control provisions, it is necessary to determine the extent to which standards of performance are clearly defined — particularly for the production and marketing functions. The units of measurement employed to measure performance against standard should be appropriate and as objective as possible. Consideration is also given to the degree to which controls report the exceptional deviation from standard, to their timeliness, and to their strategic placement. Since the last step of the control process may require corrective action, controls should provide necessary information for the responsible manager so that appropriate corrective action may be taken.

ORGANIZATION DEVELOPMENT

As noted in Chapter 5 in the discussion of personnel policy statements concerning management development (page 114), three terms are used, often interchangeably, to describe the long range process of organizational change that emphasizes the development of executives or managers. These terms, all emphasizing a change in behavior as opposed to structural change, are: *executive development, management development,* and *organization development.* However, each descriptive term carries with it a slightly different connotation. *Executive development* emphasizes the development of the individual executive; *management development* indicates a plan for the development of all members of management; *organization development* implies that the entire management structure is involved, not as individuals but as members of an organization, so that the organization functions in a different or improved manner.[8]

In discussing organization development the following topics are considered. First, there is a review of several points of view now existing in organization development; second, a review of the elements of a formal organization development program; and third, a discussion of one of the major problems in evaluating an organization development program, the measurement of performance.

Approaches to Management Development

Douglas McGregor describes two extremes in the approaches to management development. The earliest approach to management development regards development as an automatic process requiring little attention on the part of management. This approach assumes that competent managers, like cream, will rise to the top and can be skimmed off when needed. There is much to be said for this view, provided conditions are such that the cream can rise to the top. For most

[8]The following article summarizes the various approaches that have been used in organizational development and differentiates between management development and organization development: George Strauss, "Organizational Development: Credits and Debits," *Organizational Dynamics*, Vol. 1, No. 3 (Winter, 1973), pp. 2–19.

companies the "hands-off" approach did not produce enough qualified managers, with the result that during the last 20 years another way of developing managers emerged. The second method may be called the "manufacturing" approach, in which the development of managers is looked upon as a production problem. When development programs are considered to be a problem of producing managers, people are "assigned the *engineering* task of *designing* a program and *building* the necessary *machinery*, toward the end of *producing* the needed *supply* of managerial talent."[9] The major criticism of the manufacturing approach to executive development is that all too frequently companies become so engrossed in the mechanics of the program that they lose sight of the original objectives of management development — the development of managers for the organization. Let us review briefly the current thinking in regard to management development that lies between the two extremes outlined by McGregor. First, the development of executives is recognized as a process of change; second, the role of the individual being developed or changed is considered; and third, the contributions of the organization are evaluated.

A Process of Change. When a company expresses a need for organizational development, it is in effect saying that change is desired so that the organization may become more effective. Change may be accomplished in several ways. Occasionally it may be necessary to transfer an executive to another post or terminate an executive's services with the company. The duties of the position may be modified so that the present holder's abilities are sufficient for the changed job requirements, or it may be necessary to undertake an extensive reorganization to align job requirements and personnel capabilities. The recruitment of executive talent from outside the company is frequently used as a means of introducing organizational change. However, our concern is the development of management personnel — itself a process of change — as a means of changing organizations.

A question arises concerning the objectives of management development programs — what is it about the executive that needs changing? It could be the acquisition of professional knowledge and skills such as those possessed by engineers or accountants. However, most managers have such skills at the time they are employed; and in those instances where additional knowledge or skill is required, either company or university training programs seem to meet this need satisfactorily. *Development programs are aimed toward producing a set of attitudes that differentiate the competent, professional manager from the*

---

[9]Douglas McGregor, *The Human Side of Enterprise* (New York: McGraw-Hill Book Co., 1960), p. 191. Italics are McGregor's. Chapter 14, "Management Development Programs" and Chapter 15, "Acquiring Managerial Skills in the Classroom," pp. 190–226, provide a good general discussion of management development.

incompetent or immature manager.[10] Part of the difficulty in achieving desired results in management development is due to an unsureness and inability to define the attitudes required, and part is due to our failure to apply consistently what is known about the process of changing an individual member of a social organization — a form of *influence*. Edgar H. Schein, a psychologist at Massachusetts Institute of Technology, offers a model for change capable of being used in evaluating the potential effectiveness of management programs.[11] The model consists of the following three steps: (1) unfreezing, (2) changing, and (3) refreezing.

Unfreezing. All learning, whether it be the acquisition of skills, knowledge, or changed attitudes, assumes that the learner is ready to learn. The learner is *set* for the experience and motivated. When attitudes are being changed, it is necessary to "unfreeze" present attitudes so they may be dropped and new ones acquired. Coercion may be used as an aid in unfreezing, as in the case of the brainwashing of the Chinese Communists; however, management development assumes that the manager is ready to learn. There is some evidence that such is not the case. An early study shows that even top-level executives have ill-defined goals and merely wish "to get ahead" and that many middle- and lower-level managers fail to see the purpose of management development in terms of either company needs or their own needs.[12] Other factors that aid in the unfreezing of old attitudes to make room for the new include a completely new environment, thus removing the individual from the sources of old attitudes, a certain amount of punishment and humiliation for holding on to old attitudes, and a carefully planned series of rewards and punishments to emphasize the value of change. The hazing of fraternity pledges offers a good example of removal from an old environment, humiliation, and selected rewards and punishment.

---

[10]For a similar point of view regarding organizational development programs the following is recommended: John B. Miner, "The OD-Management Development Conflict," *Business Horizons*, Vol. 16, No. 6 (December, 1973), pp. 31–36. The limitations of management education programs are set forth in J. Sterling Livingston, "Myth of the Well-Educated Manager," *Harvard Business Review*, Vol. 49, No. 1 (January–February, 1971), pp. 79–89.

[11]Edgar H. Schein, "Management Development As a Process of Influence," *Industrial Management Review*, Vol. 3 (May, 1961), pp. 59–76. Dr. Schein's article is a well-reasoned statement of the application of current knowledge concerning social influence as a factor in changing attitudes. He applies the model he develops to the brainwashing of the Communists, the training of a nun, and the development of managers. For a critical evaluation of another model, operant conditioning, the following article is recommended: Craig Eric Schneier, "Behavior Modification in Management: A Review and Critique," *Academy of Management Journal*, Vol. 17, No. 3 (September, 1974), pp. 528–548.

[12]Reed M. Powell, "Growth Plans for Executives," *Business Horizons*, Vol. 4 (Summer, 1961), pp. 41–50. This report is part of a study on the impact of university-sponsored development programs upon executives. For a more detailed treatment of the study, see the following article: Kenneth R. Andrews, "Reaction to University Development Programs," *Harvard Business Review*, Vol. 39, No. 3 (May–June, 1961), pp. 116–134.

In order to have successful management development programs, companies must communicate their organizational needs to prospective participants to insure an understanding of the aims of the program. The participants themselves must have clearly defined goals congruent with those of the organization and must perceive the need for change on their part. The use of environmental factors that aid in the unfreezing process poses a real problem in developing a planned company program of attitude change. The difficulty is not one of physically removing the executive from the old environment since there are many university training programs that meet this requirement; rather, it is the nature of the change process, the second step of the change model.

Changing. According to Schein's model, a change in attitudes is accomplished either as the result of *identification* or *internalization*. The opportunity to identify one's self with a person having the desired attitudes facilitates the acquisition of those attitudes. The executive who describes his or her early years with the company by referring to a superior with the words, "He treated me like a father," or "She treated me as though I were her son," is expressing identification with a former boss. Herein lies the problem of removing the trainee from the organizational environment — the trainee is prevented from identifying with someone in the company. The same difficulty is present when executive development programs are conducted by staff members. Regardless of how competent staff personnel are, it is rare that a line executive will identify with a staff employee.

Internalization is the process of trying, adopting, and using the new attitudes as a way of solving problems and learning how to live with them. Training programs away from home grounds usually offer an excellent opportunity for internalization since the environment is relatively controlled and other trainees are going through the same process of experimenting with new attitudes. Further, rewards in the form of approval by the leader and other members of the group tend to encourage the adoption of the desired changes. It is difficult, if not impossible, to internalize attitudes if training is sandwiched in between the regular course of a day's work. Attitudes must be lived, studied, and experimented with in order that they may finally be accepted and integrated into one's personality.

Refreezing. Refreezing is the final acceptance and integration of the desired attitudes so they become integrated as a permanent part of one's personality. Time and organizational support are needed for this phase of the process of change. In Chapter 17 the importance of organizational climate is discussed as a factor in the training of supervisors, and it is stated that unless the climate is favorable, training programs may be a complete waste of time and money. An organizational climate that encourages executives to exercise their newly formed attitudes and rewards them for using the attitudes is essential to the process of refreezing.

The Individual and Change. The above discussion presents attitudinal change as a relationship between an individual undergoing the process of change and an organization inducing that change. Let us examine more closely the role of the individual, particularly with respect to those changes which are desired through the process of management development.

First, there is evidence that members of middle and lower management are not ready for change, as evidenced by their lack of understanding of the organization's goals for management development and their failure to perceive within themselves the need for change. Without proper motivation and readiness to learn, the desired change in attitude cannot be reasonably expected.

Identification with another person seems to be an essential ingredient of attitudinal change. As part of psychological growth children attempt an identification with one or both parents, symbols of authority. If identification is not completed with either or both parents, it may occur with a coach, a teacher, or some other adult figure. If the father or mother is rejected as an object of identification, or if identification is discouraged by either parent, psychological growth is stunted and at the same time symbols of authority are rejected. One of the characteristics of organizations is that they are authoritarian to some degree. The son or daughter who has failed to form identification with authority figures and who has become a manager in an organization has attitudes towards authority that are incompatible with the concept of authority as it operates in formal organizations. Usually there is difficulty in accepting authority, understanding it, submitting to authority, or using delegated authority wisely. The ability to identify and the related attitudes toward authority are well established before one finishes college, yet management development programs are challenged to change these attitudes five or ten years after a manager has completed professional training. The difficulty of the task is evident. There is also mounting evidence that success or failure as a manager is dependent to a considerable extent upon personality factors. Again we are dealing with behavioral patterns established early in life, and to change long-established patterns of personality is a tedious and difficult task.[13]

---

[13]Thomas W. Harrell, *Managers' Performance and Personality* (Cincinnati: South-Western Publishing Co., 1961). This book presents a summary of the literature concerning personality and its relation to performance in the upper levels of business management. The following quotation from page 172 supports the concept that authority relationships are dependent upon identification with an adult figure early in life.

(Continued on page 277)

These three items — the readiness to learn new attitudes, the ability to identify with a person having the desired attitudes (along with the implications of former identifications), and the significance of personality as a determinant of managerial success — are characteristics of the individual manager who is the object of the desired change. It must be recognized that for one reason or another every manager is not subject to change; and for those who are capable of change, the direction and the degree of change vary with each individual.

The Organization and Change. The role of the organization in the process of change is of utmost importance in the unfreezing of the unwanted or old attitudes and the *refreezing* of the new or desired attitudes. In his analysis of management development as a process of influence, Dr. Schein describes the institution's total control over the environment in the shaping of attitudes. He cites the environmental control exerted by the Chinese Communists in their brainwashing technique and the rigid structure imposed by the convent in the training of nuns. Other less rigorous examples of institutional control over the individual that result in the fixing of attitudes acceptable to that institution would include the internship and residency of a physician, and the various military and naval academies. To a lesser degree the college fraternity system accomplishes the same end. An important element in institutional control of environment is that the administrators of such institutions have been through the same process of influence and change — a condition that goes a long way toward explaining the rigidity of institutions. At the same time these administrators become acceptable objects for identification and thereby facilitate the acquisition of the new attitudes. Their presence, their behavior, and their attitudes serve to reinforce the new attitude during the process of *refreezing*.

Industrial organizations cannot and do not exert the same degree of control over the environment of their managers. Most companies have top managements with no common institutional background with the result that there is no clear attitudinal pattern to transmit to

---

"Relations to one's parents appear to offer the best explanation for the development of a personality similar to that of successful general managers. Who the parents are, especially what is the father's occupation, has already been discussed. Relations with parents regardless of their socio-economic status are also crucial. Many young presidents have been reported to be comparing with their fathers whom they respected but wanted to match or outdo. The mobile elite, who by definition did not have highly successful fathers, occupationally were still trying to prove themselves worthy of the acceptance they had not had from their fathers, and often had developed an identification with some other father figure who inspired them to great effort."

A recent study supporting the position of Harrell is found in the following: Albert N. B. Nedd, "The Simultaneous Effect of Several Variables on Attitudes Toward Change," *Administrative Science Quarterly*, Vol. 16, No. 3 (September, 1971), pp. 258–269.

managers, nor is there a uniform image of managerial success as an object of identification.

The practice of *coaching*; i.e., individual counsel and guidance, is used frequently in management development, but its contribution to the development of managers is questionable. Lack of time is usually cited as the reason why coaching is not conducted on a systematic basis; however, the real reasons are a lack of understanding of the dependency needs of subordinates and the need for identification, an environment that tolerates precious few mistakes, and the fact that very few companies include development of subordinates as a major function of an executive's job.

The above outline of the knowledge we have available concerning the optimum conditions required for a change of attitudes shows the difference between industrial organizations and those organizations better suited for instilling a prescribed set of attitudes. Yet the development of managers and organizational planning are necessities for the industrial firm. The following section describes the major steps in the administration of an organization development program.

An Organization Development Program

The steps necessary to establish an organization development program are outlined in Figure 12-4. Step one of the outlined program, the analysis of the present organization, is developed in the first part of this chapter. The determination of the objectives of the program and the establishment of opportunities for development are the result of personnel policy statements in regard to staffing (pp. 261–265) and define the direction and scope of any organization development program. However, the fourth major step of an organization development program, the evaluation of the program itself, relies heavily on performance appraisals and for that reason it is well to discuss in considerable detail the nature of performance appraisals.

Performance Appraisals

The main purpose in evaluating an organization development program is to provide feedback so that the effectiveness of the program with respect to its contribution to the development of the entire organization may be determined. Evaluation of results is also necessary to revise personnel requirements and to bring up-to-date the information contained in the personnel inventory. Opinion and attitude surveys of those who have participated in the program are of value; however, there is evidence that the information elicited from such surveys may express at best only a general satisfaction with the "broadening effects" of management development rather than provide the specific

I. Analyze Present Organization
A. Preparation of Organization Charts (Figure 12-1)
B. Preparation of Organization Manuals
C. Completion of Organizational Checklist (Figure 12-3)

II. Determine Objectives of the Program
A. Management Personnel Requirements
1. Replacement Needs
2. Growth Needs
a. Historic Growth
b. Planned Expansion
3. Improved Performance Needs
B. Management Personnel Inventory
1. Inventory of Current Capabilities
2. Appraisal of Current Performance
3. Estimate of Potential Growth

III. Establish Opportunities for Development
A. Internal Sources
1. Training Programs
2. Job Rotation
3. Committee Assignments
4. Coaching
5. Planned Promotional Sequence
B. External Sources
1. University Programs
2. Professional Meetings
3. Industrial Conferences

IV. Evaluate Program
A. Continue Performance Appraisals
B. Opinion and Attitude Surveys
C. Feedback to I and II above

**Figure 12-4
AN
ORGANIZATION
DEVELOPMENT
PROGRAM**

data necessary for the improvement of such programs.[14] The most common device used to evaluate the development of managers is the *performance appraisal*. Since the performance appraisal is used not only as a means of evaluating a management development program

---

[14]Reed M. Powell and Charles S. Davis, "Do University Executive Development Programs Pay Off?" *Business Horizons*, Vol. 16, No. 4 (August, 1973), pp. 81–87. Powell and Davis conclude that university development programs have little influence on the participants in those programs.

For a critical analysis of the Powell and Davis study, the following is recommended: H. R. Smith, "Executive Development Programs," *Business Horizons*, Vol. 17, No. 2 (April, 1974), pp. 39–46.

but also as a means of supplying information for the management personnel inventory, there is considerable criticism concerning performance appraisals. Although a subordinate's performance is always appraised in some fashion by the superior, the introduction of formal performance appraisals into an organization is invariably met with resistance. Such resistance is usually evidenced by the inability to complete the required appraisals within the allotted time limits. Resistance is due in part to the lack of a clear statement of the purpose of appraisals, a definition of expected standards of performance, and an understanding of the objectives of the appraisal interview.

Purpose of Appraisals. There are two questions to be resolved in determining the purpose of performance appraisals. First, is the appraisal intended to measure current performance, or is it intended to measure the subordinate's potential for promotion? Second, is the appraisal to be used to determine advances in salary, or is it to be used as a basis for self-improvement?

It is difficult enough for a manager to appraise current performance without, as Douglas McGregor phrases it, "playing God" by being required to estimate a subordinate's potential capabilities in the organization.[15] Admittedly, a manager makes such estimates and an estimate of potential is reflected each time a subordinate is selected for promotion, but having to state potential capabilities in writing and perhaps having to reveal and defend the estimate to the subordinate during the interview is one of the major causes of resistance to formal appraisal systems. An appraisal is not only a statement of a subordinate's performance but also a mirror of the superior's personality and concept of adequate performance. If the superior lacks self-confidence and perhaps has lost hope of being promoted, these attitudes may be reflected in the appraisal of subordinates. Further, few managers have a sound basis for determining the ability required for any position other than their own. Indeed, the question of capabilities and manager performance has only begun to be answered. Thus, it seems wise to limit appraisals to an evaluation of current performance.

Having determined that the appraisal should be limited to an evaluation of current performance, the second question — whether the results of the appraisal should be used to determine salary or used as a basis for self-improvement — remains to be answered. When appraisals are used to determine whether a subordinate should receive an increase in salary, there is a tendency to distort the appraisal of current performance so that the decision in regard to salary may be justified.

[15]Douglas McGregor, "An Uneasy Look at Performance Appraisals," *Harvard Business Review*, Vol. 35, No. 3 (May–June, 1957), pp. 89–94.

L. L. Cummings and Donald P. Schwab, *Performance in Organizations*, Determinants and Appraisal (Glenview: Scott-Foresman & Co., 1973). *Performance in Organizations* is one of the more recent comprehensive books on performance appraisal. Of significance is an annotated bibliography which makes up the final chapter.

Performance is only one of several factors determining whether or not an increase in pay should be granted. Availability of funds, length of time on the job, salary ranges, and the subordinate's position within the range are a few of the other factors that must be considered. Since the goal of a management development program is the development of individual managers, appraisals of performance should serve as a basis for improving that performance in the future. Objective discussions of current performance are possible only when salary considerations are set aside and attention is directed toward the improvement of performance and the development of the individual. Decisions concerning salary should be made at a separate time and should include all aspects of the company's salary policy.

Standards of Performance. Another problem encountered in the use of performance appraisals is that of developing criteria for measuring performance on the job. In many appraisal systems the manager is asked to rate subordinates on a five-point scale using a list of personality traits such as loyalty, promptness, and willingness to work. All too frequently this approach may again become a reflection of the rater's personality. Occasionally a superior is asked to rate the performance of each subordinate against that of each of the other subordinates. The shortcomings of this method are obvious, particularly when subordinates have different jobs requiring different abilities and levels of achievement. A third type of criteria is defined in terms of the goals of the job itself. However, for job goals to be effective standards of performance, they must be clearly stated, measurable, and within the control of the subordinate.

The Appraisal Interview. Most formal appraisal systems require an interview between subordinate and superior. The interview is supposed to offer an opportunity for the subordinate to discover where he or she stands, at which time the superior should outline steps to be taken for the improvement of job performance and self-development. An extensive study of the typical appraisal interview conducted at General Electric shows that praise has little effect, either positively or negatively, that criticism has a negative effect on future achievement, and that defensiveness results from criticism with no improvement of performance.[16] The same study indicates that discussions concerning salary should be held at a separate time and not as a part of a performance review. It is questionable whether the typical line manager has the necessary training or inclination to conduct a broad evaluative interview. As McGregor has noted, there is a reluctance to "play God,"

---

[16]Herbert H. Meyer, Emanuel Kay, and John R. P. French, Jr., "Split Roles in Performance Appraisal," *Harvard Business Review*, Vol. 43, No. 1 (January–February, 1965), pp. 123–124. The following article discusses performance appraisals in several other major United States corporations: Herbert E. Meyer, "The Science of Telling Executives How They're Doing," *Fortune*, Vol. 89, No. 1 (January, 1974), pp. 102–112.

with the result that the typical interview is resisted by both superior and subordinate and usually becomes a mere formality, with little of the developmental benefits that should result from it.

Improving Performance Appraisals. The weaknesses of the typical performance appraisal are attributable to failure to define the purpose of the appraisal, the need for a well-defined set of criteria, and the inadequacy of the appraisal interview. Appraisals may be conducted to determine the potential of a member of management, to evaluate performance in his present job, or to develop a plan for self-improvement. Criteria may consist of a list of illusive personality traits, the performance of a subordinate's peers, or a statement of job goals. The inadequacy of the interview may result from the superior's having to evaluate performance and justify salary action at the same time, or from being required to assess personality and potential development — tasks the superior is not trained to do. The following five-step program eliminates the conflicting points of view in regard to purpose and criteria, and as a result places the appraisal interview on much safer ground.

1. The individual discusses his job description with his superior and they agree on the content of his job and the relative importance of his major duties — the things he is paid to do and is accountable for.
2. The individual establishes performance targets for each of his responsibilities for the forthcoming period.
3. He meets with his superior to discuss his target program.
4. Checkpoints are established for the evaluation of his progress; ways of measuring progress are selected.
5. The superior and subordinate meet at the end of the period to discuss the results of the subordinate's efforts to meet the targets he had previously established.[17]

The five-step program suggested by Kindall and Gatza corrects the major weakness of the usual performance appraisal since the purpose of the appraisal is clearly defined as the appraisal of current performance, the goals of the job are determined and agreed upon by both superior and subordinate, and the interview is confined to a discussion of performance with superior and subordinate equally interested in improving that performance. General Electric uses an appraisal system, called the Work Planning and Review program, that incorporates these five steps, and finds the program to be far more effective than the traditional approach to appraisals in improving job performance.[18]

---

[17]Alva B. Kindall and James Gatza, "Positive Program for Performance Appraisal," *Harvard Business Review*, Vol. 41, No. 6 (November–December, 1963), p. 157. Copyright © 1963 by the President and Fellows of Harvard College; all rights reserved. This article presents a brief statement of the shortcomings of the typical appraisal program and then develops a plan for the installation of the five steps.

[18]Meyer, Kay, and French, *op. cit.*, pp. 127–129.

Case Problem 12-B poses a series of questions encountered sooner or later by most companies and offers an opportunity to plan an organization development program. There is an obvious need for the development of a planned approach to the replacement of key executives of a company who are due to retire within the next few years under the provisions of the company's mandatory retirement plan. Contemplated expansion increases the need for a planned program of organization development since the requirements of an expanded organization must be met as well as the needs arising as the result of attrition in the present organization.

Case Problem 12-B
ORGANIZATION PLANNING

Wanda Evans, president of Toolco, Inc., looked up as Robert Kessler, the director of industrial relations, entered her office. She asked, "What kind of progress are you making on the report I asked for last week?"

"Here are some notes I have prepared covering key executives in the company," Kessler answered as he handed Evans a copy of Exhibit 1 (pages 284 and 285). "It appears that the compulsory retirement plan that went into effect the first of this year is going to create a real need for replacements within the next five years."

"We not only have a replacement problem," Evans rejoined, "we also have some problems coming up as the result of our decision to move into the industrial products area and create a new industrial products division. As you know, our existing product line is purchased by individuals through department and hardware stores; however, the new division means not only manufacturing new products, it also means a new method of distribution."

"There is another factor other than replacement and expansion to be considered," Kessler stated.

"What is that?"

"The information I just handed you pertains only to replacements due to reaching the mandatory retirement age; thus far we have no information about the needs that might arise if we were to evaluate some of these people in terms of the quality of their performance. We both know that some of our managers are not doing the job that we would like to see done."

"Are you suggesting that we get into the area of performance appraisals?" Evans asked.

"We're going to have to get into it sooner or later; otherwise, how are we going to know who is promotable to these key positions when they open up due to retirement?"

"Bob, as you know, we have an executive committee meeting at the end of next week. I wonder if you could show our needs in some graphic form that would impress everyone at the meeting. There are still some doubting Thomases who believe that the cream will rise to the top — personally I don't think it will, and even if it does I doubt that we have that much time. When we have this meeting, will you also recommend some definite name to designate this program we're going into? You and I have at various times called it executive development, management development, or organization development, and even organization planning. We ought to settle on a title that has meaning to everyone." Evans returned the notes Kessler had given her and closed with, "See me again a day or two before the committee meeting so that I can review the recommendations that you intend to present at the meeting."

Exhibit I

President — Age 62, founder of company and the driving force behind the institution of the company's compulsory retirement plan a year ago.

Reporting to the President:

Director of Marketing — Age 40, has been in position only a little over one year, former director of economic research for an advertising agency. Performs economic research; has staff of two: a statistical typist and a statistician — both in early 30's. It was his recommendation that company enter industrial products field.

Legal Counsel — Age 45, functions primarily as liaison between engineering and outside firm of attorneys in patent matters. Occasionally handles real estate transactions; has one legal secretary.

Vice-President and Treasurer — Age 50, a CPA who has been with the company 20 years; formerly head of the cost accounting section. Has heads of cost and general accounting sections reporting to her; responsible for all financial affairs of the company. As the company grew, it was her idea that the position of controller be established as a separate function reporting to the president.

Controller — Age 45, has been with the company only three years; has a small clerical staff; is in the process of establishing and refining budgets in the manufacturing plants. Though the chief of the cost section reports to the treasurer, the controller maintains a close working relationship with him.

Director of Industrial Relations — Age 40, has been with the company five years; chief negotiator for the company; his staff consists of a secretary, a clerk, and a research assistant. Each plant has its own personnel director. Administers company-wide salary plan and employee benefits, including insurance and the new retirement plan. It will be his responsibility to administer any executive development program agreed upon.

Director of Purchasing — Age 60, formerly a purchasing agent in one of the plants. Serves in an advisory capacity to plant purchasing agents for the most part, although occasionally does purchase those items that can be used by all plants.

Executive Vice-President — Age 62, formerly vice-president in charge of manufacturing; over 20 years' service with the company; started as a plant manager in its number 2 plant.

Reporting to the Executive Vice-President:

Vice-President, Manufacturing — Age 55, has been with the company five years; came to company as vice-president, manufacturing, when the post of executive vice-president was created. At that time it was believed that the plant manager of the number 2 plant, then 55 years old, was capable of filling the vice-president position, but there was no suitable replacement for him in his plant. Since the number 2 plant is the largest plant in dollar volume and profit, he was kept in that position. Reporting to the vice-president, manufacturing, in staff positions are the director of industrial engineering and the director of quality control. These positions were created shortly after his taking the job. Both are in their early 40's and well trained for their positions. Both have worked previously with the vice-president, manufacturing, in another company.

The managers of the five manufacturing plants report to the manufacturing vice-president. Each plant manager has managers of personnel, quality control, industrial engineering, purchasing, accounting, product engineering, and an assistant plant manager. Each staff department head has at least three exempt employees and several clerical employees. The assistant plant manager supervises directly the plant engineer (building maintenance), the master mechanic who is responsible for the tool room and the machine shop, and the general foremen in charge of the production departments. The following summary shows the ages of the plant managers, the number of hourly employees, and the number of general foremen and foremen for each plant.

Plant No.	Age of Plant Manager	Total Hourly Employees	General Foremen	Foremen
1 (outboard motors)	50	250	3	20
2 (engine plant)	60	700	4	32
3 (power hand tools)	45	400	3	18
4 (lawn mowers and edgers)	50	300	3	15
5 (power tools)	56	500	4	24

Exhibit I (continued)

Vice-President, Engineering — Age 48, has been with the company 22 years. She has been in her present position five years. There are five supervising design engineers who report to her, one for each of the product lines. There is also a chief metallurgist who directs the metallurgical laboratory.

Vice-President, Sales — Age 61, has the advertising manager (age 50), the head of the sales order department (age 60), and the assistant general sales manager (age 58) reporting to him. Most of his efforts are devoted to the various advertising programs and promotional campaigns. The head of the sales order department acts as liaison between plants 1 and 4 since these plants purchase 50 percent of the output of the engine plant. The assistant general sales manager directs four regional sales managers. Each regional manager has a clerical staff of two and approximately 15 sales representatives reporting to him. The manager of the Eastern region is 62 years old, the manager of the Central region is 58, the Southern regional manager is 50, and the manager of the Pacific region is 55.

PROBLEMS

1. Prepare an organization chart that shows clearly the replacement needs of Toolco for the next five years.
2. What title would you choose to designate the program being considered by Toolco? Why would you choose this title?
3. How many people would you include initially as a part of any proposed development program?
4. Prepare a set of recommendations to be submitted to Evans prior to the committee meeting. Outline and justify each step in the proposed program.

CHAPTER QUESTIONS FOR STUDY AND DISCUSSION

1. What basic similarity exists between organizational analysis and planning for production and sales?
2. Discuss briefly the tools commonly employed in organizational analysis.
3. Rearrange Figure 12-1 so that it appears as a horizontal chart and as a circular chart. What are the advantages attributed to each form of charting — vertical, horizontal, and circular?
4. Discuss the strengths and weaknesses of formal organizational analysis. When would the disadvantages of formal analysis outweigh the advantages?
5. Why is it important to evaluate organizational effectiveness? Should this be done before introducing any organizational change or after the change has been introduced?
6. What is meant by the statement that most organizational studies are actually reorganizational studies?
7. Two extreme approaches to the development of managers are described by McGregor. Evaluate each of these extremes and then describe a middle-of-the-road approach.

8. Most of us can agree on some of the basic attitudes necessary for the practice of medicine. Develop a similar set of attitudes for the successful practice of management.
9. Describe in your own terms the change process. What condition must exist prior to the beginning of this process for the change to be most effective? If this condition does not exist, how does the first step of the change process serve to induce a readiness to change?
10. Based upon the discussion concerning the problems of identification with authority, do you believe that men or women are more likely to succeed as managers? Discuss.
11. Would it be desirable for industrial organizations to exert the same degree of control over the environment and actions of new managers as that exercised by a convent over noviates or a military academy over cadets? Discuss.
12. Discuss performance appraisals with respect to the following factors: purpose, strengths, weaknesses, and methods of improving performance appraisals.

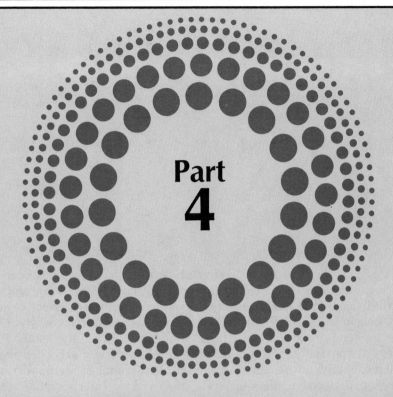

Part 4

The Leadership Function

The quality of leadership determines the degree of effectiveness in the performance of the functions of planning, organizing, and controlling. The experimental method and its conceptualization of independent, intervening, and dependent variables offer a convenient way of discussing organizational behavior. Organizational climate, and leadership is a part of that climate, influences the behavior of organizational members; but the effect that climate has upon behavior is determined by the individual's perception of the organization. Organizational behavior takes many forms; however, the discussion in Chapter 13 is limited to organizational role, sources of conflict, and the resultant stress that may occur in organizations.

A review of the theories of leadership reveals that there has been interest in the personality of the leader, in the situation, and in the interaction of the situation and the leader as the major determinant of effective leadership. A contingency model of leadership which considers the style of the leader, the structure of the task, the relationship between the leader and the members of that leader's group, and the degree of power accorded the position of leadership is presented. Chapter 14 also makes an important differentiation between leadership style, the type of interpersonal relationships between leader and subordinate, and leadership behavior which includes all of the things a leader does as a manager.

Communication is one of the tools of effective leadership. Much of the communication that occurs in organizations is informal in nature; for example, the grapevine and communications between superior and subordinate. The psychological factors in communication are considered and guides for effective communication and listening are presented.

The last two chapters are concerned with problems related to the behavior of employees in organizations. In Chapter 16 the problem of motivation is discussed in terms of basic psychological needs. These concepts are applied to problems of motivation in industry; the role of job satisfaction as a factor in performance is examined; and a model is developed that relates job performance, the type of rewards received, and the interpretation of those rewards in relation to goal attainment and consequent job satisfaction. Chapter 17 discusses the role of the supervisor as the one member of management who links the management of an organization to nonmanagerial operating employees, and in this role the supervisor is a determining factor in productivity.

Case Problem 13-A

MEASURING ORGANIZATIONAL CLIMATE

In the chapter that follows, organizational climate is considered to be those relatively permanent characteristics of an organization that influence the behavior of its members. Also, the characteristics of organizational climate serve to differentiate one organization from other organizations. Since most of the users of this text are members of an organization — a college or university — we limit the problem of measuring organizational climate to determining the climate of the school that *you* are attending.

Several approaches may be used in assessing the organizational climate of a college.[1] The demographic characteristics of the institution may be tabulated and classified with respect to size, source of revenue (private or public), location (rural or urban), student/faculty ratio, number of courses and majors, and other similar objective data. Another way of determining climate is to study the students. What are their socioeconomic backgrounds, levels of intelligence, values, high school grade point averages, and vocational and social aspirations? Third, direct measures of organizational behavior may be

obtained by observation or by asking students to report their behavior. Such questions would include the number of blind dates, hours of study per week, hours of work per week, number of classes cut, and other direct accounts of behavior. A fourth, and perhaps the most fruitful approach, is to determine how a member of an organization perceives that organization. The student is asked to report on many facets of the environment as he or she sees, or perceives, it to be. In so doing, the student draws a personal psychological map of the organization.

It is the last approach, your perception of the organization, that is used in this case. You are asked to describe the climate, or environment, of the school that you are attending.

---

[1] C. Robert Pace, *College & University Environment Scales: Technical Manual* (2d ed.; Princeton: Educational Testing Service, 1969), p. 7. The four approaches discussed in this case problem are outlined in greater detail by Professor Pace.

PROBLEMS

1. Complete the college and university environment scales (CUES II) presented in Appendix A, pp. 535–541.
2. What characteristics of the environment do you believe are measured by CUES II? Which of these factors have the greatest influence on your behavior?
3. How would you expect your professor or dean to describe the organizational climate of your school? Discuss.

A summarization by Warren Bennis, presented in Chapter 8, "Organization Theory," states that Theory X describes "organizations without people" and Theory Y describes "people without organizations."[2] To many readers it may appear that the chapters subsequent to Chapter 8 concerning the concepts of organization structure, authority processes, committees, and methods of analysis and change, like Theory X, are devoid of people. If such is the impression, it should be corrected in this chapter for here we study the behavior of people in organizations.

As a first step in the study of organizational behavior it is necessary to examine briefly the research methods of the behavioral sciences. There are two reasons for the study of methodology. First, knowledge of the methods employed in a given study enables one to infer and assign a degree of confidence to the results obtained. Second, the experimental method, used in the study of organizational behavior, provides the conceptual framework of independent, intervening, and dependent variables — a useful way of thinking about problems of organizational behavior. Following the discussion of methodology the independent, intervening, and dependent variables of organizational behavior are examined in greater detail.

BEHAVIORAL SCIENCE RESEARCH METHODS

The behavioral sciences — primarily psychology, sociology, and anthropology — are all concerned with the study of human behavior, yet each discipline emphasizes differing aspects of behavior.[3] As a result it is difficult to develop a classification system of research methods for the behavioral sciences that applies equally well to each discipline; consequently many schemes have been developed. Research may be classified in terms of its purpose, e.g., descriptive, exploratory, or hypothesis-testing studies. The method used in collecting data may be the basis for classification; for example, observation, interview, questionnaire, or the examination of written documents. The locus of the study — in the field or in a laboratory — may be used as a basis for distinguishing between types of research. The degree of scientific rigor, ranging from the observations of a competent observer, very difficult to replicate, to the laboratory experiment which may be replicated, is another method of classification. Any system of classification is largely arbitrary and contains many overlapping categories. For our purposes, the classification of research methods into two broad categories —

---

[2]W. G. Bennis, "Leadership Theory and Administrative Behavior," *Administrative Science Quarterly*, Vol. 4 (December, 1959), pp. 259–301.

[3]Review Case Problem 6-A, The Parable of the Spindle (pp. 122–124), as an example of differing explanations offered for the same phenomena by a psychologist, a sociologist, and an anthropologist.

field studies and experiments — is a useful way of studying organizational behavior.[4]

Field Studies

As the term implies, *field studies* are conducted within the environment of an existing organization. The data used in field studies may be the observed behavior of the members of an organization, recorded by a neutral observer; also, members of the organization may be asked to provide information during an interview or by completing a questionnaire or other similar instruments. Written documents, such as contractual agreements between labor and management and company policy and procedure statements, along with objective measures of production and quality, are part of field study data.

The purpose and design of field studies vary widely. Some studies are intended to survey current practices within an organization or an industry; some may be designed as case studies to provide comparative data between cultures, industries, companies, or individual members of organizations. Studies that show development and change in organizational behavior over a period of time are referred to as longitudinal studies. A brief discussion of each design reveals the breadth and scope of field studies.[5]

Survey Study. Survey studies are designed to present a broad spectrum of events. Usually, such studies are cross-sectional in nature and represent a sample of organizational behavior drawn from many different individuals who may be representative of many companies and industries. A survey study describing the behavior of a large number of American managers is reported in Chapter 3.[6] In the study by England, 1,072 managers responded to a value system questionnaire.

Survey studies are of value in that they may establish statistical indexes of behavior and, when verified by subsequent research, trends may be observed. To draw reliable conclusions, the representativeness

---

[4]A relatively brief discussion of methodology may be found in Peter M. Blau and W. Richard Scott, *Formal Organizations*, A Comparative Approach (San Francisco: Chandler Publishing Co., 1962), pp. 15–26.

The following is recommended for a more complete discussion of research methods. Leon Festinger and Daniel Katz (eds.), *Research Methods in Behavioral Sciences* (New York: Dryden Press, 1953), pp. 13–172.

[5]The following survey indicates the extent to which the services of psychologists and other behavioral scientists are used in industry: Spencer Hayden, "Psychology on the Business Scene," *Organizational Dynamics*, Vol. 1, No. 1 (Summer, 1972), pp. 43–55.

[6]George W. England, "Personal Value Systems of American Managers," *Academy of Management Journal*, Vol. 10, No. 1 (March, 1967), pp. 53–68. See Chapter 3, pp. 55–60.

For an analysis of reactions to feedback concerning attitude surveys the following is suggested: Stuart M. Klein, Allen I. Kraut, and Alan Wolfson, "Employee Reactions to Attitude Survey Feedback: A Study of the Impact of Structure and Process," *Administrative Science Quarterly*, Vol. 16, No. 4 (December, 1971), pp. 497–514.

of the study sample must be established and the statistical methods used must be appropriate.

Case Study. The purpose of a case study is to provide an in-depth analysis of an industry, a company, or an organizational unit within a company. A case study may, and often does, use many sources of data, including the researcher's observation of the organization, information supplied by the members of the organization during interviews and in questionnaires, and objective indexes of organizational performance such as cost, profits, and the quantity and quality of production. Normally, one thinks of a case, in contrast to the longitudinal study, as a still camera shot in that it portrays an organization during a short time period.

Longitudinal Study. The case study method is well adapted for tracing the development of a particular organization or the behavior of members of an organization over an extended period of time. Such studies are called longitudinal studies and provide insight into the dynamics of organizational behavior and change.[7]

Comparative Study. There are two distinct approaches to the design of comparative studies. First, the researcher may seek two or more organizations that differ in characteristics believed to have an effect on the behavior of their members, and determine whether or not these differences do have such an effect; or the researcher may start with observed differences in the behavior of the members of two or more organizations, then describe and measure the organizational characteristics to determine whether or not there is a relationship to the observed differences in behavior. Among the organizational variables that have been considered as having potential influence on members' behavior are size, style of leadership (autocratic vs. democratic), organization structure, and the interdependence of employees in various work groups. Behavioral differences that have been used as the starting point for organizational studies include quantity and quality of production, absenteeism, turnover rate, accident frequency and severity, and perceived job satisfaction.[8]

---

[7]An example of a longitudinal study is the account of the acquisition of Weldon Manufacturing Company by the Harwood Manufacturing Company. The first part of the book is an in-depth case study of the Weldon Manufacturing Company, the second part of the study outlines the change strategies, and the concluding portion of the study describes Weldon after the changes were introduced. The study encompasses a two-year period. Alfred J. Marrow, David G. Bowers, and Stanley E. Seashore, *Management by Participation* (New York: Harper & Row, Publishers, 1967).

[8]The following study is a summary of comparative studies of the cultural effects of given societies upon organizational behavior: Karlene H. Roberts, "On Looking at an Elephant: An Evaluation of Cross-Cultural Research Related to Organizations," *Psychological Bulletin*, Vol. 74, No. 5 (November, 1970), pp. 327–350.

Another study analyzing the factors that have emerged as significant in the comparative analysis of organizations is Karl O. Magnusen, "A Comparative Analysis of Organizations: A Critical Review," *Organizational Dynamics*, Vol. 2, No. 1 (Summer, 1973), pp. 16–31.

Experimental Studies

Field studies provide much information concerning organizational behavior; yet, their very complexity and the absence of controlled conditions make it extremely difficult to say with assurance that a given form of behavior is the direct result of a specific organizational characteristic. Fortunately, the experimental method overcomes many of the shortcomings inherent in the methodology of field studies.

In theory, the concept of the experiment is quite simple. By isolating and manipulating a single variable, and at the same time holding all other variables constant, the experimenter is able to measure the effect that the manipulated (independent) variable has upon the behavior (dependent variable) of the subject of the experiment. In practice, the design and execution of experiments in the behavioral sciences is quite difficult. Formal organizations are complex with many characteristics potentially capable of influencing the behavior of members. While it may be possible to isolate and vary one of the independent variables, e.g., style of leadership or physical working conditions, seldom is it possible to control and hold constant all of the remaining organizational variables that might influence behavior. Also, it is difficult to obtain precise measures of behavior, the dependent variable. The quantity of work performed, absenteeism, resignations, accidents, and job satisfaction are but a few of the dependent variables. Further, experimental studies with living subjects are confounded, or contaminated, by a group of variables known as *intervening* or *moderating* variables. Included as intervening variables are such factors as the degree of motivation, the ability to learn, and the individual's perception and reaction to the changing independent variable.

Despite the difficulties encountered in applying the experimental method to the study of organizational behavior, it is regarded as the most rigorous method of the behavioral sciences. However, all experimental studies do not possess the same degree of rigor since there are variations in the degree of control exercised over independent and intervening variables and in the definition and measurement of dependent variables. The natural experiment, the field experiment, and the laboratory experiment, presented in ascending degrees of rigor, are discussed below.[9]

The Natural Experiment. The natural experiment is the result of a series of fortuitous circumstances. It may be argued that the natural experiment is not an experiment since the experimenter does not exercise control, directly or indirectly, over any of the independent variables in the situation.[10] Nonetheless, there are instances in which the

---

[9]For a complete discussion of laboratory experiments see "Laboratory Experiments" by Leon Festinger, Festinger and Katz, *op. cit.*, pp. 136–172.

[10]The following reference recognizes a natural experiment as distinct from the field experiment and the laboratory experiment: Dorwin Cartwright and Alvin Zander (eds.), *Group Dynamics*, Research and Theory (3d ed.; New York: Harper & Row, Publishers, 1968), pp. 32–33.

natural experiment approximates the field or laboratory experiment since only one major independent variable is changed and there are objective and varied measures of organizational performance and behavior available. The following illustrates the natural experiment.

Walter R. Nord and Robert Costigan report the results of a study made to determine the effects of a change from a workweek of five 8-hour days to four 9½ hour days. The study is one of the first attempts to assess the effects of change in attitudes toward the four-day week over a period of time. Questionnaires were administered to some 100 workers employed in a nonunion pharmaceutical company in St. Louis six weeks, twelve weeks, and approximately one year after the new work schedule was introduced. Data was collected by age, sex, marital status, and children living at home. Though Nord and Costigan suggest that the results of the study should be interpreted with caution, several findings did emerge. Most important was the observed tendency for significant patterns of response to occur over the one-year period rather than soon after the work schedule change. Though there was a consistently positive attitude toward the four-day week, its effects on the workers' home life were perceived as less favorable after one year. Further, such attitudes appear to be a function of a number of factors. The more plans workers had for leisure time activities, the better satisfied they were with the four-day week. Workers whose plans were task-oriented rather than recreation-oriented also perceived the four-day week as more favorable. Female workers, perhaps because the added day of "leisure" permitted them to attend to household chores with greater ease, reported more satisfaction with the new work schedule. However, people with one or more children living at home looked less favorably upon the effects of the four-day week on their home lives.[11]

The Field Experiment. The manipulation of the independent variable in the natural experiment is an event not controlled by the researcher, and seldom are control groups available. In the field experiment the researcher controls the timing and extent of the change in the independent variable; in addition, control groups may be established as further assurance that any change in the dependent variable, organizational performance or behavior, that occurs after the independent variable has been manipulated is the result of that specific change and not the result of extraneous, uncontrolled factors.

A classic field experiment by Morse and Reimer describes the effect of changing a major organizational variable — the hierarchical location of decision making. Four similar divisions, all engaged in clerical work, of a large industrial firm participated in the experiment. The independent variable was the location of the decision-making process

---

[11]Walter R. Nord and Robert Costigan, "Worker Adjustment to the Four-Day Week: A Longitudinal Study," *Journal of Applied Psychology*, Vol. 58 (1973), pp. 60–66.

in the organization structure. In two of the divisions (the autonomy program) formal changes in organization structure and decision-making processes were introduced so that rank and file participation in decision making was increased. In the other two groups changes were made so that supervision and upper-level management had an increased role in the decision-making process (hierarchical control). Pre- and post-experimental measurements of productivity, perception of changes by clerical and supervisory personnel, and job satisfaction measures were obtained.[12]

The Laboratory Experiment. The laboratory experiment, more rigorous than either the natural or field experiment, affords the greatest degree of control over independent, intervening, and dependent variables. A *laboratory* is defined as any setting where the variables of the experiment are subject to the control of the experimenter. Ideally, the laboratory experiment isolates and varies only one independent variable at a time. Intervening variables are held constant, or any change is also subject to control, and the effect of the change in the independent variable upon the subject's behavior is measured with precision.

The most frequent criticisms of laboratory experiments are that they are unrealistic and an oversimplification of organizational behavior. Realism may suffer when subjects are given the task of assembling washers and nuts on a bolt in contrast to the assembly of an automobile, and the study of the behavior of small groups in the laboratory is admittedly an oversimplification of the behavior of large groups of people in a formal organization. Yet it is precisely the capability of taking a complex situation and "cutting it down to size" that is the greatest strength of the laboratory experiment. It enables one to test a specific hypothesis or theoretical construct, to control and analyze the interaction of all variables, and to state with precision the effect of the manipulated variable upon the dependent variable.[13]

A laboratory experiment by Mackworth illustrates the effect of independent and intervening variables upon behavior in a laboratory situation. The environmental working conditions of heat and humidity usually are assumed to have an adverse effect upon the performance of a physical task. It is also assumed by many that a high degree of motivation tends to offset the effect of hot and humid climatic conditions.

---

[12]Although both groups showed an increase in efficiency as measured by reduced costs, the autonomy program produced a higher degree of job satisfaction than did the hierarchical control program. Nancy C. Morse and Everett Reimer, "The Experimental Change of a Major Organizational Variable," *Journal of Abnormal and Social Psychology*, Vol. 52 (January, 1956), pp. 120–129.

See Chapter 2, pp. 32–33, for an account of the Hawthorne Studies, a classic field experiment.

[13]A complete discussion of the application of the laboratory experiment to the study of organizations is found in Karl E. Weick, "Laboratory Experimentation With Organizations," published in J. G. March (ed.), *Handbook of Organizations* (Chicago: Rand McNally & Co., 1965), Chapter 5, pp. 194–260.

In Mackworth's study, the velocity of the air was controlled at 100 cubic feet per minute and humidity and temperature were varied so as to produce effective temperatures ranging from 61° to 92° Farenheit. The intervening variable, motivation, was recognized and varied by establishing two groups, one working under high incentive conditions provided by goal setting, immediate feedback of results, and encouragement from the experimenter. The other group operated under ordinary incentive conditions with no goal setting, knowledge of results, or comments from the experimenter. The task consisted of raising and lowering a 15-pound weight 2 feet every 2 seconds. As might be expected, the group performing under high incentive conditions outperformed the group working under normal incentive conditions, regardless of temperature, thus illustrating the significance of motivation as an intervening variable. However, when the room temperature reached an effective temperature of 79°, both the high and the ordinary incentive groups showed a marked decrement in performance. Thus Mackworth shows that there is a critical level of heat and humidity that results in a drop in physical output regardless of the degree of motivation.[14]

A Concluding Concept

The experimental method with its conceptualization of independent, intervening, and dependent variables provides a useful way of thinking about organizations and behavior. It offers a means of identifying those characteristics of organizations (independent variables) that influence the behavior of its members (dependent variables). The perceptions, capabilities, and expectations of the members of an organization are recognized as intervening or moderating variables. Thus behavior in organizations, as is true of all behavior, is best described as a function of the interaction between a person and the environment. With this concept in mind, let us examine the major independent, intervening, and dependent variables of organizational behavior.

INDEPENDENT VARIABLES — ORGANIZATIONAL CLIMATE

Case Problem 13-A requests that you describe the organizational climate of your college or university; not a simple task since educational institutions are complex. In addition, the phrase, organizational climate, has many meanings. However, a definition has been offered that is gaining wide acceptance. *Organizational climate* may be defined as "the set of characteristics that describe an organization and that (a)

---

[14]N. H. Mackworth, "High Incentives vs. Hot and Humid Atmosphere in a Physical Effort Task," *British Journal of Psychology*, Vol. 38 (1947), pp. 90–102.

distinguish the organization from other organizations, (b) are relatively enduring over time, (c) influence the behavior of people in the organization."[15] The limitation in the definition that the characteristics of climate enable one to differentiate one organization from another implies that these characteristics must be measurable; the limitation that the characteristics must be fairly enduring over a period of time eliminates those features of an organization that influence behavior for a relatively short period of time such as cost cutting during economic retrenchment. Finally, the limitation that organizational climate applies only to those characteristics that influence behavior is perhaps the most difficult aspect of the definition to clarify since the list of potential stimuli is varied and lengthy.[16]

Many classifications of the characteristics of organizational climate have been proposed, yet it seems that the grouping of characteristics into three broad areas serves our purposes best. First, and perhaps most obvious, are those formal actions of the executives of a company that are intended to motivate employees. Included are formal systems of rewards and punishments, various employee benefit programs, incentive pay plans, communication programs, and the quality of leadership offered by the top echelon of the organization and the resulting supervision exercised in the middle and lower levels of the managerial hierarchy. Each of these approaches to influencing the behavior of an organization's members are discussed in the remaining chapters of this part.[17] Also, the structural characteristics of the organization influence behavior. Since the first group of organizational characteristics is discussed elsewhere in the text, the following discussion is limited to structural characteristics and their influence on behavior. Structural properties are considered as independent variables and the resulting attitudes and job-related behavior are regarded as dependent variables.

In an extensive review of the literature, Porter and Lawler classify the structural properties of organizations into two broad groups: (1) characteristics of the *total-organization* (defining the total-organization as a company with a president and capable of selling its own stock independently of other companies), and (2) characteristics of *suborganizational units* (which range from subsidiary companies and decentralized divisions in large corporations, through plants in multiplant

---

[15]Garlie A. Forehand and B. von Haller Gilmer, "Environmental Variation in Studies of Organizational Behavior," *Psychological Bulletin*, Vol. 62, No. 6 (December, 1964), pp. 361–382.

[16]The following is a summary of research studies on organizational climate. Included in the article is an excellent table setting forth the major studies. Don Hellriegel and John W. Slocum, Jr., "Organizational Climate: Measures, Research and Contingencies," *Academy of Management Journal*, Vol. 17, No. 2 (June, 1974), pp. 255–280.

[17]See Chapter 14, "Leadership Patterns"; Chapter 15, "Communications"; Chapter 16, "Motivating Employees"; Chapter 17, "The Role of the Supervisor."

companies, down to and including departments and primary work groups within departments).[18] First, we examine the properties of suborganization, considered as independent variables in the literature; then we examine total-organization characteristics assumed to influence behavior.

Suborganization Properties

The structural characteristics of suborganization units are drawn from the relationships shown in the formal organization chart. The characteristics mentioned most frequently are *number of organizational levels*, *line and staff functions*, *span of management*, and *size* of the subunit, defining size as number of people. Though discussed separately, these characteristics should not be considered mutually exclusive. As shown in Chapter 9, there is a relationship between size and span of management which, in turn, has a marked influence on the number of levels within the organization. The effects of organization structure upon its members are measured in two areas — attitude and overt behavior. The term, *attitude*, includes opinions about one's job, company policy, supervision, and perceived satisfaction from the job. Overt behavior includes such measures as absenteeism, turnover rates, accident frequency, productivity, labor disputes, and progression or mobility within the organization.

Organization Levels. Early studies of organizational behavior, for example the Hawthorne Studies, were concerned with the attitudes and behavior of hourly production employees. Next, studies focusing on comparisons between managerial and nonmanagerial employees emerged, and most recently there have been many studies concentrating on differences between hierarchical levels within management. Almost without exception, these studies show a strong positive relationship between organizational level and the degree of perceived job and need satisfaction. Managerial employees of all levels report greater satisfaction with their work than that reported by hourly employees. Further, within the management structure there is a positive relationship between organizational level and satisfaction, with higher levels of management showing greater satisfaction than lower managerial levels.[19]

---

[18]Lyman W. Porter and Edward E. Lawler III, "Properties of Organization Structure in Relation to Job Attitudes and Job Behavior," *Psychological Bulletin*, Vol. 64, No. 1 (1965), pp. 23–51. Much of the material in the text has been drawn from the Porter and Lawler study. Also, their classification and sequence of structural factors are used.

[19]The following extensive study based upon data from 387 respondents working at all hierarchical levels in 14 different organizations shows a significant variation in the perceptions of organizational climate by hierarchical level held in the organization: Roy L. Payne and Roger Mansfield, "Relationships of Perceptions of Organizational Climate to Organizational Structure, Context, and Hierarchical Position," *Administrative Science Quarterly*, Vol. 18, No. 4 (December, 1973), pp. 515–526.

However, there is no such relationship between the perceived needs of organizational members and their level in the organization. Several studies utilizing hierarchically arranged needs — social, achievement, recognition, and fulfillment — show that needs are surprisingly the same for all levels of the organization. Differences are minor with lower levels of the organization being more concerned with aspects of their immediate work environment while the higher levels are more concerned with the entire organization. Consequently it seems that the relative importance of various kinds of needs are constant throughout the organization and not related to organizational level.

The frequently used indexes of overt organizational behavior — turnover, absenteeism, accident frequency, etc. — have been used as measures of hourly employee behavior and have not been used widely with managerial groups. Thus, there is relatively little data that compares managerial and nonmanagerial employees in these respects. Yet within the managerial hierarchy there are indications that face-to-face intra-organizational, interpersonal contacts decrease at the higher levels of management; but interpersonal contacts with individuals outside the organization increase. Decisions at the higher levels of management take longer to make, and a longer period of time for feedback concerning their correctness is evident. However, data is scanty at this time; therefore, any conclusions must be considered as tentative.

Line-Staff Structure. The distinction between line and staff functions and the problems inherent in line-staff relationships are discussed elsewhere.[20] Therefore the following is limited to observing differences in attitudes and behavior between the two groups. The evidence shows that the line manager consistently reports a higher degree of job satisfaction than does the staff manager. Also, line managers report a higher degree of need satisfaction, especially those needs related to esteem and self-actualization. For the most part, line and staff personnel express the same needs when stated in terms of desirable working conditions; however, there is a tendency for staff to desire greater autonomy and to perceive themselves as being more oriented toward getting along with others and more directed by others than are line managers.

There has been only a limited number of studies pertaining to the behavior of line and staff managers. Staff's mobility within the organization, the result of the nature of their jobs, makes them more informed than line managers on conditions within the organization. Also, the turnover rate of the staff manager is two to four times that of line personnel — in all probability the combined result of two factors. First, as noted, staff reports a lower degree of job satisfaction. Second,

---

[20] See Chapter 10, pp. 217–230.

staff skills are acquired largely as the result of education, as opposed to experience, and are more readily transferred to other organizations than are the technical skills of the line manager which usually are acquired in a single company or a specific industry.

Span of Management. Span of management is an easily recognized structural characteristic of organizations. As noted elsewhere, there are several interacting factors that determine the optimum span of management.[21] More than twenty-five years ago, based upon research conducted in Sears, Roebuck & Company, James Worthy stated that flat organization structures with the resultant increased span of management are positively related to morale.[22] Unfortunately, Worthy does not present any empirical data to support his statement. Nor has the study been replicated. Thus, there is no objective data relating span of management to either attitudes or overt behavior.

Size of Subunit. A subunit of the total organization is defined by boundaries that exclude the remainder of the organization. Subunits may consist of a primary work group, a department, a single plant in a multiplant company, a decentralized division of a corporation, or a subsidiary of a conglomerate. With such range in the size and type of subunits, the difficulties encountered in evaluating empirical studies concerning the effect of size are apparent. Nonetheless, some relatively firm conclusions concerning the effect of subunit size upon attitudes and behavior may be drawn.

Generally, small departments and work groups have more positive attitudes toward their work than do large departments and large work groups. But no sweeping generalizations can be made concerning all employees, since the studies reported measure the attitudes of hourly workers in relation to group size and virtually no studies report managerial job-related attitudes and group size. The size of the group has its effect upon attitudes other than job satisfaction. Perhaps because of the increased opportunity for interaction, smaller groups show a higher degree of intimacy and less control than larger groups. Group cohesiveness is also more pronounced in smaller groups than in larger groups. However, the larger the group the greater is the willingness to accept leader-directed activities and plans.

Most studies show a strong positive relationship between the absentee rates of hourly employees and subunit size; however, the few studies concerned with absenteeism among managerial employees show no consistent relationship between size and absenteeism. Again, there is a strong positive relationship between size and the appearance of labor disputes; but in all probability no causal relationship. Historically the strong militant unions have represented employees in industries where subunit size is large — automobile manufacturing, steel,

[21]Chapter 9, pp. 195–200.
[22]James C. Worthy, "Organization Structure and Employee Morale," *American Sociological Review*, Vol. 15 (1950), pp. 169–179.

and mining. The data is inconclusive in regard to turnover rates and productivity. The turnover rate data is equivocal with a slight tendency for turnover rates to be positively related to unit size. In the case of productivity, the data is inconsistent and shows no predictable relationship with subunit size — a finding that is not surprising when one considers the many factors that determine level of productivity.

Total-Organization Characteristics

There are difficulties in interpreting the literature concerning total-organization units because most studies do not state clearly whether the subject is a subunit of an organization or the total-organization itself. For example, many researchers loosely refer to the study of an organization when in reality the unit is but one plant of a multiplant company. An admittedly arbitrary definition is that a total-organization unit has a chief executive with the title of president or its equivalent and can sell its stock independent of other companies, even though it may be part of a larger corporation. Recognizing the lack of a consistent definition, let us continue the discussion of size.

Size of Total Organization. One study that *seems* to relate the size of the total organization to job satisfaction shows a correlation of $-.67$ between the satisfaction of hourly employees and size.[23] Although the study does include some total-organization units, the difficulty in interpreting the significance of the findings is one of determining whether the dissatisfaction stems from the size of the subunit (known to have a negative relationship with job satisfaction) or whether the dissatisfaction stems from the size of the total-organization unit.

There is a series of studies that sheds some light on the relationship between total-organization size and managerial attitudes. Questionnaire respondents were grouped into three categories based upon the size of the company in which they were employed. Companies with a total employment of less than 500 were regarded as small; the medium-size companies ranged in total employment from 500 to 4,999; and those companies with more than 5,000 employees were considered large. Managerial personnel of the small companies showed a greater degree of need satisfaction than those of the larger companies at the lower levels of the organization, but at the upper levels of management the greater need satisfaction appeared in the larger companies. These studies by Porter show clearly the mediating effect of organization level upon size.[24]

It must be noted that we know very little concerning the effect of total-organization size upon the behavior of either managers or

---

[23]S. Tallachi, "Organization Size, Individual Attitudes and Behavior: An Empirical Study," *Administrative Science Quarterly*, Vol. 5 (1960), pp. 398–420.

[24]Lyman W. Porter, "Job Attitudes in Management: IV. Perceived Deficiencies in Need Fulfillment As a Function of Size of Company," *Journal of Applied Psychology*, Vol. 47 (1963), pp. 386–397.

workers. For example, we do not know how the total company absentee, turnover, or accident rates of General Motors, Standard Oil of New Jersey, and Ford Motor Company compare to smaller companies with similar technologies and operating in the same geographical areas.

Shape of Organization. Organizations are sometimes characterized as being either tall or flat. Tall organizations have a greater number of managerial levels in relation to total size than do flat organizations. The key to whether a company is tall or flat is span of management. Given the same number of employees, reduced spans of management at each level produce a tall organization while increased spans of management create a flat organization.

Much of the interest concerning the shape of organizations stems from Worthy's statement that "Flatter, less complex structures, with a maximum of administrative decentralization tend to create a potential for improved attitudes, more effective supervision, and greater individual responsibility and initiative among employees."[25] Yet, as noted earlier, Worthy does not present any quantitative data to support his conclusion.

There are very few empirical studies that test Worthy's statement by reporting the effect of the shape of an organization on either attitudes or behavior. In one study, Porter and Lawler show that managerial employees in companies with fewer than 5,000 employees show a higher degree of need satisfaction in flat organizations than in tall ones.[26] However, the reverse is true in companies employing more than 5,000 since the managers in these companies with tall organizations perceive a greater need satisfaction. However, the apparent advantage of the tall organization is limited to those needs relating to social and security needs while the flat organizations are superior with respect to the needs concerning self-actualization. Thus no clear-cut superiority exists for either the tall or the flat organization.

Degree of Decentralization. Another facet of organizational structure is the degree of decentralization, defining decentralization as extending authority to make decisions to lower-level organizational units. Data relevant to the effect of centralization and decentralization upon either attitudes or behavior is sketchy at best. One study of a staff function, industrial relations, shows that those working in decentralized departments prefer it that way while those in centralized departments prefer centralization.[27] In one of the few other studies in

---

[25]Worthy, *op. cit.*, p. 179.

[26]Lyman W. Porter and Edward E. Lawler III, "The Effects of Tall vs. Flat Organization Structures on Managerial Job Satisfaction," *Personnel Psychology*, Vol. 17 (1964), pp. 135–148.

[27]Helen Baker and R. R. France, *Centralization and Decentralization in Industrial Relations* (Princeton: Princeton University Department of Economics and Sociology, Industrial Relations Section, 1954).

this area Weiss found no significant statistical relationships between the degree of decentralization and grievances, turnover rates, absenteeism, accident frequency and severity rates, number of white collar workers, and the age of managers. Though the differences were not statistically significant, there was a slight trend for each factor in favor of decentralization.[28] In a more recent study of 787 senior British managers working in 78 different organizations, Child reports that a structuring of activities and a high degree of centralization result in a relatively low level of conflict and a high degree of conforming behavior.[29]

In summary, the degree of centralization or decentralization and span of management show only modest effects upon either attitudes or behavior. However, the other five structural characteristics of organizations — organizational level, line-staff organizations, size of subunit, size of total-organization, and shape of organization — show significant relationships to either job-related attitudes or behavior, or both. Further, it is shown that these characteristics are interrelated and that one is capable of moderating the effects of another; for example, organizational level has much to do with one's job-related attitudes and perceived need satisfaction regardless of the size of the subunit or the total-organization.

INTERVENING VARIABLES — THE INDIVIDUAL

Throughout the above discussion of the effects of organization structure, an independent variable, the individual's *perceived* attitudes toward the job and degree of need satisfaction, is used as a measure of behavior, the dependent variable. Aspects of the organization that stimulate behavior are received and interpreted by the individual; hence, the individual's perceptions of what is "out there" acts as a *moderating* or *intervening* variable between organizational stimuli and resultant behavior.[30] Accordingly, knowledge of perception, especially how one person perceives another, leads to a greater understanding of organizational behavior. As a first step in learning more about perception we discuss briefly the nature of perception.

The Nature of Perception

In the early history of psychology much time was devoted to the study of perception. For the most part research concentrated on the perception of sensory stimuli such as sound, color, light, form, odor,

---

[28]E. C. Weiss, "Relation of Personnel Statistics to Organization Structure," *Personnel Psychology*, Vol. 10 (1957), pp. 27–42.

[29]John Child, "Strategies of Control and Organizational Behavior," *Administrative Science Quarterly*, Vol. 18, No. 1 (March, 1973), pp. 1–17.

[30]A similar point of view is taken by Schneider and Hall in their study of Roman Catholic diocesan priests: Benjamin Schneider and Douglas T. Hall, "Toward Specifying the Concept of Work Climate: A Study of Roman Catholic Diocesan Priests," *Journal of Applied Psychology*, Vol. 56, No. 6 (December, 1972), pp. 447–455.

and the various means of stimulating the senses of the skin. Soon it became apparent that there were marked differences between individuals in the way in which they perceived sensory stimuli; further, it was noted that the same individual sometimes perceived stimuli having constant physical properties differently from one day to the next. Also, it was found that peripheral or extraneous factors were significant as determinants of the meaning attached to external stimuli. In 1945, D. M. Johnson summarized research on object perception and the influence of so-called extraneous factors.

1. He may be influenced by considerations that he may not be able to identify, responding to clues that are below the threshold of his awareness. For example, a judgment as to the size of an object may be influenced by its color even though the perceiver may not be attending to color.
2. When required to form difficult perceptual judgments, he may respond to irrelevant cues to arrive at a judgment. For example, in trying to assess honesty, it has been shown that the other person's smiling or not smiling is used as a cue to judge his honesty.
3. In making abstract or intellectual judgments, he may be influenced by emotional factors — what is liked is perceived as correct.
4. He will weigh perceptual evidence coming from respected (or favored) sources more heavily than that coming from other sources.
5. He may not be able to identify all factors on which his judgments are based. Even if he is aware of these factors he is not likely to realize how much weight he gives to them.[31]

The above summary should not be interpreted as meaning that we respond only to the peripheral factors of a situation; however, it does indicate that peripheral factors can and do influence perceptual judgments.

In 1958, Jerome Bruner summarized the results of a series of experiments concerning the influence of social behavior upon perceptual processes that "came, rather waggishly, to be called the 'New Look' in perception."[32] These studies emphasize the behavioral aspects of perception such as social values, needs, attitudes, and cultural background, rather than the effect of the "out there" that marked the earlier studies. It is now recognized, as a result of the work of Bruner and others, that there is the phenomenon of perceptual readiness, or *set*, arising from the behavioral aspects of perception that largely determines the way in which we perceive social situations. The following study illustrates the effect of set.

---

[31]D. M. Johnson, "A Systematic Treatment of Judgment," *Psychological Bulletin*, Vol. 41 (1945), p. 206.

[32]Jerome S. Bruner, "Social Psychology and Perception," published in E. Maccoby, T. Newcomb, and E. Hartley, *Readings in Social Psychology* (3d ed.; New York: Holt, Rinehart & Winston, 1958), pp. 85–94.

In an experiment designed to determine the influence of predisposition, or set, Kelley investigated the effect of labeling a person as having a "warm" or "cold" personality.[33] Students were told that a guest lecturer would conduct the class, and a biographical sketch of the guest was distributed to the class. Two sketches were distributed and were identical except for one statement. One half of the class received a data sheet with a statement that described the guest as being a "very warm" person, and the other half of the class received data sheets that described him as being "rather cold." The guest led the students in a 20-minute discussion and following the discussion was rated by the class on a 15-item rating scale. Those who had received the sketch describing the guest as "very warm" rated him as being more popular, humane, humorous, sociable, and considerate of others than did those who had received the descriptive statement that the guest was "rather cold." Obviously, it pays to have a good press agent.

Factors Influencing Perception

The study by Kelley shows the effect of perceptual readiness and how quickly and easily it may be induced. There are other types of errors in perception, some of which are due primarily to the perceiver and some are the result of the characteristics of the perceived.

The Perceiver. In addition to perceptual readiness, there are other predispositions on the part of the perceiver that influence social perceptions. *Stereotyping* is the most frequently encountered source of perceptual bias. Although the term stereotype originally referred to a three-dimensional, relief type face made by a casting process, Walter Lippmann used the term in 1922 to describe "pictures in peoples' heads."[34] Stereotyping, as a perceptual process, is categorizing a group into a rather simplistic mold with the simplified characteristics ascribed to the group often having no basis in fact. Generally, the stereotyped ideas of a group are widely held within a given culture and are extremely resistant to modification. Stereotypes are frequently associated with ethnic groups, and there are also stereotypes for various professions as well as for other classes of people.

Stereotypes exist within organized labor with regard to management personnel and vice versa. In an experimental study concerning the stereotypes that management and labor hold toward each other, Haire asked a group of labor officials and a group of management personnel to judge the personality of two individuals based upon a short biographical sketch and a photograph. One half of each group, labor and management, received photographs indicating that Person A was

---

[33]H. H. Kelley, "The Warm-Cold Variable in First Impressions of Persons," *Journal of Personality*, Vol. 18 (1950), pp. 431–439.

[34]Walter Lippmann, *Public Opinion* (New York: MacMillan Co., 1922).

a secretary-treasurer of the union and that Person B was a branch manager of a manufacturing company. For both groups the biographical data accompanying each photograph were the same. The other half of the management group and the other half of the labor group received the same biographical data, the same photographs, but the designation of role as being a member of labor or management was reversed. None of the four groups responded to the photographs or the biographical data; instead, they responded to the designation of role as being either a union official or a branch manager. The union officials perceived the secretary-treasurer of the local much more favorably than the branch manager, while management personnel perceived the branch manager as having the more desirable characteristics.[35]

The *halo effect* is a perceptual phenomenon that has received a great deal of attention because of its effect on the rating of subordinates. When rating a subordinate there is a tendency to focus attention on a single trait, either favorable or unfavorable, thereby forming a "halo" that surrounds the rating of other traits. If the dominant trait is favorable, other traits are likely to be classified as favorable; however, an unfavorable dominant trait usually results in unfavorable ratings on all other traits. The halo effect also operates in determining employees' perceptions of their companies. The clerical employees of a Chicago firm that had been in receivership for a period of six months were surveyed with respect to ten aspects of job satisfaction. As might be expected, they rated their company low in regard to job security; however, the halo spread and the employees perceived working conditions, such as office space and furnishings, pay, and other items not related to job security, as being low. Yet, these characteristics were, by objective standards, superior to those of other offices in the area.[36] Similarly, if hourly workers perceive inequities with respect to pay, supervision, job security, advancement opportunities, working conditions, intrinsic aspects of the job, or social aspects of the job, such perceptions may lead to increased turnover.[37]

Projection, a defense mechanism, is a means of transferring, or projecting, the blame for one's shortcomings to an object or to another person. The saying, "A poor workman blames his tools," is a good example. Projection also operates as a perceptual bias in the perception of others and can result in unduly favorable or unfavorable impressions. An insecure supervisor with a borderline record of performance

---

[35]Mason Haire, "Role-Perceptions in Labor Management Relations: An Experimental Approach," *Industrial and Labor Relations*, Vol. 8 (1955), pp. 204–216.

A similar study supports Haire's original findings: Warren H. Chaney, "A Study of Facilitating and Inhibiting Personality Dimensions in Occupational Identification" (Doctoral dissertation, North Texas State University, 1974).

[36]B. A. Grove and W. A. Kerr, "Specific Evidence on Origin of Halo Effect in Measurement of Morale," *Journal of Social Psychology*, Vol. 34 (1951), pp. 165–170.

[37]Charles S. Telly, Wendell L. French, and William G. Scott, "The Relationship of Inequity to Turnover among Hourly Workers," *Administrative Science Quarterly*, Vol. 16, No. 2 (June, 1971), pp. 164–172.

has a strong tendency to perceive subordinates as having these same traits. Thus it is very difficult for such a supervisor to recognize a subordinate as being ready for promotion. In the same manner, managers who have difficulty in delegating to subordinates for reasons of personality usually perceive their own supervisors as also having difficulty in delegating and for the same reasons.[38]

The Perceived. Perceptual biases resulting from stereotyping, the halo effect, and projection are attributable to the perceiver; however, there are errors that are induced by the person being perceived. The organizational position of the person being perceived is significant. Characteristics are attributed to the person being perceived because of *status*, i.e., the person's position within the organization. For example, it has been shown that persons with high status are perceived as willing to cooperate, while persons with lower organizational status are viewed as having to cooperate.[39] Closely related to status is *role*, behavior that is expected and prescribed by the organizational position that one holds. Status and role are significant because they provide important cues to the observer who may then place the observed into a predetermined stereotype. The *visibility* of certain traits of the perceived forces one to attend to those traits and possibly ignore more significant characteristics because they cannot be readily visualized and determined. Aggressiveness and level of energy draw one's attention simply because they are visible, but the characteristics of integrity or honesty are not readily visible and often ignored. The high visibility of certain ethnic groups serves as a constant reinforcement of bias and prejudice.

Improving Perception

From the preceding discussion, one is almost tempted to conclude that there is no "real" world; the world is only as it is perceived. For the effective management of organizations, administrators should learn to recognize the differences between their perceptions and the perceptions of others. First, it is suggested that the perceiver be constantly aware of the sources of perceptual errors. Recognition that such errors do exist and knowledge of the common causes of these errors is helpful. Second, there is mounting evidence that the degree of personal adjustment on the part of the perceiver determines what will be seen in others. Those who are well adjusted and secure perceive positive traits in others, while those who are insecure and unable to recognize and accept their shortcomings tend to perceive others as having the same characteristics. In other words, the recommendation

---

[38]See Chapter 11.
[39]J. W. Thibaut and H. W. Riecken, "Some Determinants and Consequences of the Perception of Social Causality," *Journal of Personality*, Vol. 24 (1955), pp. 113–133.

is more than "know thyself"; it also includes "accept thyself." At the same time one must learn to know and accept others.[40]

DEPENDENT VARIABLES — ORGANIZATIONAL BEHAVIOR

There are many dimensions of the dependent variable, organizational behavior. Job-related attitudes are mentioned in the discussion of the effects of organization structure and are examined more closely in Chapter 16, "Motivating Employees." Productivity, another significant form of organizational behavior, is discussed in Chapter 17, "The Role of the Supervisor." Our concern in this chapter is the examination of organizational behavior in broad terms in order to develop a general model for understanding behavior. First, every individual who enters a formal organization assumes a role, a form of behavior that is expected and prescribed by the position. Second, conflict is a normal part of organizational life; to believe otherwise is to engage in wishful thinking. Third, stress, a subjective state perceived in varying degrees by each person, is present in all organizational behavior. These three forms of organizational behavior — role, conflict, and stress — are discussed in turn.

Role

The neat squares and the straight lines of the organization chart may lead one to believe that the organization is a spatial arrangement of physical entities much like the stones of an arch with the president occupying the keystone position. But the squares of the chart do not possess the physical properties of stone; instead, they are symbolic of events and the actions of people. The title, President, in the square of the chart is indicative of the events and actions associated with that position and differentiates that office from the events and actions implied by the title, Controller. When one person leaves a position, another steps in and assumes the mantle of the office, thereby giving constancy and durability to the otherwise ephemeral actions of people. Thus role, expected behavior associated with an office, is central to the concept of enduring social organizations.

It has been suggested that the organization may be likened to a large fishnet with each knot representing an office and the strings of the net showing the functional relationship between the positions.[41] When one picks up the net by a single knot it is possible to visualize

---

[40]For a discussion of counseling techniques and their value the following is recommended: "Conversation with Fritz Roethlisberger," *Organizational Dynamics*, Vol. 1, No. 2 (Autumn, 1972), pp. 31–45 (an interview with Fritz Roethlisberger by William F. Dowling, Editor, *Organizational Dynamics*).

[41]Daniel Katz and Robert L. Kahn, *The Social Psychology of Organizations* (New York: John Wiley & Sons, 1966), p. 174. This work is recognized as an outstanding theoretical contribution to the study of organizations and social institutions. Most of the discussion concerning the role episode and conflict are drawn from this work.

immediately adjacent and related positions. Positions closely associated within a given office are those of the immediate superior, subordinates (if any), and peers. Since role is an expected form of behavior derived from the office, it is well to understand how such expectations are established. The cycle of the role episode helps to provide such understanding.[42]

Role Expectations. One aspect of role expectations, the first step in the role episode cycle, is the position description. Such descriptions usually specify the main functions, responsibility and authority, and the primary interpersonal relationships necessary to accomplish the job. Although descriptions are important and form a part of the basis upon which performance is judged, there are other expectations in the minds of persons closely associated with a given office or position. Influence, in varying degrees, is associated with each organizational office. Also, there are expectations regarding the kind of authority, the type of leadership pattern, the exercise of power, and general behavioral characteristics of the employee.[43]

Role Sending. The second step of the role cycle episode is role sending, the exercise of influence that affects the role behavior of another person in the organization. It may range from a grumpy "good morning" or a wave of the hand to an explicit written memorandum requesting the performance of certain job duties by a subordinate. Roles may also be sent to peers and superiors. Role sending is a process of influence and communication, and, as such, it indicates the degree of freedom the receiver, or *focal* person, has in carrying out the assigned (sent) role behavior. Sent roles also vary in the strength of their attempt to influence behavior. Implied in role sending, especially to subordinates, is the use of power, rewards if role expectations are fulfilled and penalties if they are not.

The Received Role. The role received by the focal person is, in effect, a *perceived* role. The receiver's perception of the role sent has varying degrees of congruence with the sent role as defined by the sender. Yet it is the received role, the person's own psychological map of the organization, rather than any objective description of the organization that directly determines role behavior. It must be recognized that for any one person in an organization there is more than one received role since roles may be received from more than one superior, from subordinates (if any), and from peers. In addition to complications arising from the reception of multiple roles there is the person's own expectations concerning the roles received. Thus role behavior is

---

[42]*Ibid.*, pp. 174–184.

[43]The following study shows the relationship between position, power, status, and influence upon interpersonal relationships in formal organizations. The formal organization studied is a school of nursing. Linda E. Rice and Terence R. Mitchell, "Structural Determinants of Individual Behavior in Organizations," *Administrative Science Quarterly*, Vol. 18, No. 1 (March, 1973), pp. 56–70.

a result of forces created by multiple sent roles, multiple received roles (including perceptual errors), and the person's own preconceived expectations for each of these roles.[44]

Role Behavior. Role behavior in an organization ranges from the relatively simple to the very complex. At the simple end of the continuum, there is the assembly line worker who performs a repetitive task determined largely by the work situation and reinforced by verbal communication (role sending) when necessary. The repetition of a single task is the expected role behavior for the office of assembly line worker. Further, the office is occupied by one person. There is a unitary arrangement of one task, one role, one office, and one person. Moving away from the simple end of the continuum, there is a possibility of multiple tasks, typing and filing for example, that combine into a single role, an office held by one person. Multiple roles with implied multiple tasks often combine into a single office. Supervisors carry out the role of subordinates to their superiors, superiors to their subordinates, and that of peers in relation to other supervisors. These multiple roles combine into a single office held by one person, a supervisor. Finally, there are those situations that combine multiple tasks, multiple roles, and multiple offices all held by one person. The president of a company, in addition to holding the office of president, may hold the office of chairman of the board and also occupy the position of chairman of the United Fund, the presiding office of a completely separate organization. As one moves from the simple to the complex in role behavior it is apparent that conflict may arise in the performance of multiple tasks, the performance of multiple roles, or the holding of multiple offices since in each instance the execution of the required roles is by a single person.

Conflict

The description of behavior within the context of the role episode — role expectations, role sending, the received role, and role behavior — provides a framework for understanding behavior in organizations, particularly the phenomena known as conflict and the

---

[44]The following studies discuss the effects of sent roles, received roles, and preconceived expectations concerning roles upon organizational behavior.

John M. Ivancevich and James H. Donnelly, Jr., "A Study of Role Clarity and Need for Clarity for Three Occupational Groups," *Academy of Management Journal*, Vol. 17, No. 1 (March, 1974), pp. 28–36.

Charles N. Greene and Dennis W. Organ, "An Evaluation of Causal Models Linking the Received Role with Job Satisfaction," *Administrative Science Quarterly*, Vol. 18, No. 1 (March, 1973), pp. 95–103.

Dennis W. Organ and Charles N. Greene, "The Perceived Purposefulness of Job Behavior: Antecedents and Consequences," *Academy of Management Journal*, Vol. 17, No. 1 (March, 1974), pp. 69–78.

Henry O. Pruden and Richard M. Reese, "Interorganization Role-Set Relations and the Performance and Satisfaction of Industrial Salesmen," *Administrative Science Quarterly*, Vol. 17, No. 4 (December, 1972), pp. 601–609.

attendant subjective state, stress. Conflict, like change, is one of the constants of organizational life. The problem is not the elimination of conflict; rather, it is understanding the sources and types of conflict and learning how to cope with conflict in a way that minimizes the resulting stress upon the organization and its members. Katz and Kahn suggest the following four types of conflict associated with organizational roles: intra-sender, inter-sender, inter-role, and person-role.[45] In addition, inter-person conflict is considered.[46]

Intra- and Inter-Sender Conflict. These sources of conflict are considered together because they pertain to the messages sent to the receiver. Intra-sender conflicts have their origin in the sender and arise when the role sender requests conflicting behavioral responses on the part of the receiver. The degree of conflict may range from a situation that requests responses that are incompatible and consequently difficult to perform in conjunction with each other to those instances where the behavioral patterns required are mutually exclusive. The plant manager who requests higher unit production, and at the same time issues directives restricting the amount of overtime, may be requiring responses that are difficult to execute and in some cases the responses may be mutually exclusive.[47]

Inter-sender conflict arises when a person receives messages from one or more sources calling for behavioral responses that again may range from those that are merely incompatible to those that are mutually exclusive. The unity of command concept is the prescriptive statement designed to minimize inter-sender conflict; yet it should be noted that inter-sender conflict arises in situations other than those resulting from attempting to serve two masters. The production worker urged by management to respond to an incentive system may also receive pressure from the peer group to restrict output. Similarly, a supervisor is often the "man in the middle" trying to respond to conflicting requests from superiors and from subordinates.

Inter-Role Conflict. All organizational members experience inter-role conflict in some degree because every person is simultaneously a member of more than one group. The demand for overtime hours, an organizational role expectation, may conflict with the time demands required by one's role as a member of a family. Simultaneous multiple roles within the same organization are also a source of conflict; for example, the multiple roles of committee leader and department head

---

[45]Katz and Kahn, *op. cit.*, pp. 184–185.

[46]A general discussion of the concept of conflict is presented by Schmidt and Kochan in the following: Stuart M. Schmidt and Thomas A. Kochan, "Conflict: Toward Conceptual Clarity," *Administrative Science Quarterly*, Vol. 17, No. 3 (September, 1972), pp. 359–370.

[47]Henry Tosi, "Organization Stress as a Moderator of the Relationship Between Influence and Role Response," *Academy of Management Journal*, Vol. 14, No. 1 (March, 1971), pp. 7–20. The article by Tosi examines role conflict and its relationship to job satisfaction and stress.

often result in conflict. Thus, inter-role conflict may arise from multiple roles within a single organization or as the result of being a member of two separate organizations.

Person-Role Conflict. Inter-sender, intra-sender, and inter-role conflicts describe situations in which the sent role is external in nature and there are situations when conflict arises as a result of conflicting internal and external roles. Internally perceived roles and their expectations are the result of a person's perceptions of self, code of ethics, and values. Externally imposed roles that require a violation of one's self perception create person-role conflict. Being required to offer a kickback in order to obtain a sale or the assumption of a subservient position by one who perceives himself as a professional, are illustrative of person-role conflict.

Inter-Person Conflict. Inter-person conflicts are most frequent between persons whose roles place them at an organizational *interface*, a position that requires interaction with other segments of the same organization or with other organizations. The production manager, typical of a role at the interface, is in frequent contact, and often conflict, with counterparts in the operating departments. For the most part such conflict is not personal in nature; rather, it is the result of conflicting roles, with each employee an honest protagonist for a segment of the organization. The purchasing agent's role often conflicts with that of the person representing the vendor, and the industrial relations manager's role is often in conflict with that of the representative of the international union. Though many inter-person conflicts arise solely from the nature of the roles involved, there are situations complicated by personal animosity and dislike.

Stress

The above conflict situations, derived from the role episode, provide an objective analysis of conflict. Conflict situations often result in the subjective state known as *stress*. Stress is defined as a state of tension, strain, or pressure and is a normal reaction resulting from the interaction between an individual and the environment.[48] Those forces that induce stress are known as *stressors*, thus conflict often acts as a stressor. The individual's perceptions of the environment are also significant in determining the degree of the resulting stress; yet, there is evidence that an individual may experience stress without being aware of it. Within the context of organizational behavior the stressors most frequently noted are *role ambiguity* and *role overload*.

Role ambiguities have their origin in the conflicting role situations described above and create doubt, uncertainty, and even frustration on

---

[48]Hans Selye, *The Stress of Life* (New York: McGraw-Hill Book Co., 1956).
Hans Selye, *Stress Without Distress* (Philadelphia: J. B. Lippincott Co., 1974).

the part of the person receiving the role. The messages sent may be ambiguous; thereby making it impossible to determine with clarity the meaning of the sent role, or the source of the ambiguity may lie in determining the expected and desired role performance. Inability to accept an expected role, not consonant with one's self-image, is another form of ambiguity. Whatever the source, ambiguity functions as a stressor and creates the subjective state of stress for the person experiencing the ambiguity with resulting feelings of doubt, uncertainty, or frustration.

Role overload is another stressor associated with organizational role. Unlike role ambiguity, characterized by uncertainty, role overload occurs when the person receiving the sent roles cannot perform the expected activities within prescribed time limits. More often than not, there is no question concerning the legitimacy of the request, no lack of understanding concerning what is wanted, and no incompatibility between the expected responses. Instead, the problem is one of completing as many expectations as possible within a limited time period. Often quality is sacrificed for quantity, and difficult decisions must be made to determine which responses are most significant and to be performed first with the realization that others must be excluded. More than any other single factor, role overload characterizes the pressures of large formal organizations.

Regardless of the nature of the stressor, role ambiguity or role overload, the individual as an adaptive organism usually attempts to resolve the resulting stress. Much of the problem behavior exhibited in organizations is either exploratory or adaptive and reflects the individual's attempt to resolve the stress created by the conflict situation. Although much has been written concerning the psychology of adjustment, there is little agreement concerning the classification of adjustive processes. However, two broad groupings do emerge: those reactions to stress that are characterized by physiological changes and those that are primarily a modification of overt behavioral patterns.[49]

Physiological Reactions. Historically there has been a dichotomy between "mind" and "body." As a result of this dualistic concept, behavior is regarded as a function of the "mind," and changes in physiological functions, especially disease processes, are regarded as a function of the "body." However, in recent years there has been recognition that many of the so-called physical disorders and illnesses, if

---

[49]The following describe some of the physiological reactions occurring as the result of stress and offer a means of reducing stress for some persons. Herbert Benson, *The Relaxation Response* (New York: William Morrow & Co., 1975).

The following is an article drawn from this book by Dr. Benson: Herbert Benson, "Your Innate Asset for Combating Stress," *Harvard Business Review*, Vol. 52, No. 4 (July–August, 1974), pp. 49–60.

For another popular account about stress the following is suggested: Walter McQuade, "Doing Something About Stress," *Fortune*, Vol. 87, No. 5 (May, 1973), pp. 250–261.

not having their origin as the result of psychological processes, are profoundly influenced by the psychological make-up and attitude of the person. These illnesses are often called *psychosomatic* disorders, a rather unfortunate choice of terms since it tends to perpetuate the separation of mind (psyche) and body (soma). The term *somatization reactions*, used in the Army psychiatric classification system, is much preferred since it avoids the mind and body dualism. Somatization reactions are differentiated from other reactions by two distinguishing characteristics: (1) they are the result of the interaction between a person, the environment, and organic factors, and (2) demonstrable pathological changes in either the structure or functioning of bodily organs are evident.

Although there is relatively little specific data on the effects of stress resulting from role ambiguity, there is mounting evidence that cardiovascular disorders, particularly susceptibility to heart attacks, is closely associated with role overload.[50] For many years Jenkins and his co-workers have been studying the relationship between the incidence of coronary heart disease and basic personality type. They recognize two broad personality types, designated as Type A and Type B as defined as follows:[51]

> Type A is characterized primarily by excessive drive, aggressiveness, ambition, involvement in competitive activities, frequent vocational deadlines, pressure for vocational productivity, and an enhanced sense of time urgency. . . . The converse pattern, Type B, is characterized by the relative absence of this interplay of psychological traits and situational pressures. The Type B subject is more relaxed and more easy going, seldom becoming impatient and takes more time to enjoy avocational pursuits. He is not easily irritated and works steadily, but without a feeling of being driven by a lack of time. He is not preoccupied with social achievement and is less competitive in his occupational and avocational pursuits.

Many studies, reviewed and summarized by Sales, indicate that the Type A person is more prone to heart attacks than a Type B counterpart.[52] Further, there is evidence that each group is different with respect to biochemical characteristics. With dietary factors held constant, Type A persons show a higher serum cholesterol (closely associated with coronary disease) than a similar group of Type B persons.

Sales has shown that a relatively simple role overload situation results in a five-percent increase in serum cholesterol as compared to

---

[50]The following study is one of the few that addresses itself specifically to attitudes and behavior resulting from role ambiguity. John R. Rizzo, Robert J. House, and Sidney I. Lirtzman, "Role Conflict and Ambiguity in Complex Organizations," *Administrative Science Quarterly*, Vol. 15, No. 2 (June, 1970), pp. 150–163.

[51]Reprinted with permission from C. D. Jenkins *et al.*, "Development of an Objective Psychological Test for the Determination of the Coronary-Prone Behavior Pattern in Employees," *Journal of Chronic Diseases*, Vol. 20 (Pergamon Press Ltd. © 1967), p. 371.

[52]Stephen M. Sales, "Organizational Role as a Risk Factor in Coronary Disease," *Administrative Science Quarterly*, Vol. 14, No. 3 (September, 1969), pp. 325–336.

the statistically insignificant change in serum cholesterol during an underloaded period. The subjects of this experiment, male undergraduates, solved anagrams for a period of one hour. The overloaded group was provided with 35 percent more anagrams than they could decode in each five minute period, while the underloaded group was idle and waiting for additional work for approximately 30 percent of the one hour experimental period. These results are rather striking when one considers the short time period of the experiment, one hour, and the simplistic nature of the overload compared to the duration and type of overload existing in real organizations. For the objectively overloaded group, those perceiving a high degree of overload show a greater rise in serum cholesterol than those that perceived a low overload. Those working under objectively underloaded conditions, yet perceiving a state of overload, show a decrease in serum cholesterol, while those in the objectively underloaded group who perceived a low degree of overload show only a slight increase in cholesterol.

In addition, Sales notes that quite independent of the degree of overload, measured either subjectively or objectively, those reporting satisfaction with the task show less increase in cholesterol than those reporting low satisfaction with the task. Consequently there is experimental support for Wolf's clinical observation that people who work "without joy" are more prone to coronary disease than those who work "with joy."[53] Perhaps the industrial psychologist's interest in job satisfaction may gain wide support as a contribution to employee health.[54]

Behavioral Reactions. Stressors and the attendant state of stress do not always result in somatization reactions. In all probability, behavioral evidences of stress are more frequent than somatization reactions. A discussion of behavioral reactions to stressors within the space of a few pages is a virtual impossibility. One survey of eight textbooks of mental hygiene and related fields that discuss behavioral adjustment processes shows that no less than 32 adjustment mechanisms are listed and of these 32 there are only 2 that appear in all eight books.[55] Obviously, the selection of any kind of classification system is essentially arbitrary.

A summary prepared by Costello and Zalkind, Table 13-1, lists 13 adjustive reactions, defines each reaction, and illustrates the reaction

[53]S. Wolf, "Disease as a Way of Life," *Perspectives in Biology & Medicine*, Vol. 4 (1961), pp. 288–305.

[54]Coronary disease is discussed as a physiological reaction primarily because of its significance as a health factor and its lethal nature. The same general observations may be made about gastro-intestinal disorders. An early experimental investigation in this area is S. Wolf and H. G. Wolff, *Human Gastric Function*, An Experimental Study of a Man and His Stomach (2d ed.; New York: Oxford University Press, Inc., 1947).

[55]Laurance F. Shaffer and Edward J. Shoben, Jr., *The Psychology of Adjustment* (2d ed.; Boston: Houghton Mifflin Co., 1956), p. 158. Part Two is recommended as a highly readable discussion of adjustive reactions, pp. 157–306.

ADJUSTIVE REACTIONS	PSYCHOLOGICAL PROCESS	ILLUSTRATION
Compensation	Individual devotes himself to a pursuit with increased vigor to make up for some feeling of real or imagined inadequacy.	Zealous, hard-working president of the Twenty-five Year Club who has never advanced very far in the company hierarchy.
Conversion	Emotional conflicts are expressed in muscular, sensory, or bodily symptoms of disability, malfunctioning, or pain.	A disabling headache keeping a staff member off the job, the day after a cherished project has been rejected.
Displacement	Re-directing pent-up emotions toward persons, ideas, or objects other than the primary source of the emotion.	Roughly rejecting a simple request from a subordinate after receiving a rebuff from the boss.
Fantasy	Day-dreaming or other forms of imaginative activity provides an escape from reality and imagined satisfactions.	An employee's day-dream of the day in the staff meeting when he corrects the boss' mistakes and is publicly acknowledged as the real leader of the industry.
Identification	Individual enhances his self-esteem by patterning his own behavior after another's, frequently also internalizing the values and beliefs of the other; also vicariously sharing the glories or suffering in the reversals of other individuals or groups.	The "assistant-to" who takes on the vocabulary, mannerisms, or even pomposity of his vice-presidential boss.
Negativism	Active or passive resistance, operating unconsciously.	The manager who, having been unsuccessful in getting out of a committee assignment, picks apart every suggestion that anyone makes in the meetings.
Projection	Individual protects himself from awareness of his own undesirable traits or unacceptable feelings by attributing them to others.	Unsuccessful person who, deep down, would like to block the rise of others in the organization and who continually feels that others are out to "get him."

Table 13-1 ADJUSTIVE REACTIONS TO FRUSTRATION, CONFLICT, AND ANXIETY

Reaction	Definition	Example
Rationalization	Justifying inconsistent or undesirable behavior, beliefs, statements motivations by providing acceptable explanations for them.	Padding the expense account because "everybody does it."
Reaction-Formation	Urges not acceptable to consciousness are repressed and in their stead opposite attitudes or modes of behavior are expressed with considerable force.	Employee who has not been promoted who overdoes the defense of his boss, vigorously upholding the company's policies.
Repression	Completely excluding from consciousness impulses, experiences, and feelings which are psychologically disturbing because they arouse a sense of guilt or anxiety.	A subordinate "forgetting" to tell his boss the circumstances of an embarrassing situation.
Fixation	Maintaining a persistent nonadjustive reaction even though all the cues indicate the behavior will not cope with the problems.	Persisting in carrying out an operational procedure long since declared by management to be uneconomical as a protest because the employee's opinion wasn't asked.
Resignation, Apathy, and Boredom	Breaking psychological contact with the environment, withholding any sense of emotional or personal involvement.	Employee who, receiving no reward, praise, or encouragement, no longer cares whether or not he does a good job.
Flight or Withdrawal	Leaving the field in which frustration, anxiety, or conflict is experienced, either physically or psychologically.	The salesman's big order falls through and he takes the rest of the day off; constant rebuff or rejection by superiors and colleagues pushes an older worker toward being a loner and ignoring what friendly gestures are made.

Source: Timothy W. Costello and Sheldon S. Zalkind, *Psychology in Administration: A Research Orientation* (Englewood Cliffs: Prentice-Hall, 1963), pp. 148–149.

by citing recognizable forms of organizational behavior.[56] Careful study of the table and close observation of fellow workers or students provides insight into the causes of many seemingly inexplicable forms of behavior.

In conclusion, it is evident that there is much we do not know about stress. For example, we do not know why some persons react to stressors with the development of cardiovascular diseases while others develop gastric disorders. Nor do we know why some individuals develop behavioral modifications rather than physiological reactions, or why a given behavioral reaction develops instead of another. Stress is one of the normal aspects of life. It cannot be avoided; however, there is evidence that much can be done to reduce the effects of stress. But there is no simple prescriptive statement that, if followed, would guarantee minimization of stress. The statement by Somerset Maugham in *The Summing Up*, his autobiography, provides a rare insight into one man's perception of his own limitations in relation to his work and may be of value to others.[57]

> I discovered my limitations and it seemed to me that the only sensible thing was to aim at what excellence I could within them. I knew that I had no lyrical quality. I had a small vocabulary and no efforts that I could make to enlarge it much availed me. I had little gift of metaphor; the original and striking simile seldom occurred to me. Poetic flights and the great imaginative sweep were beyond my powers . . . I was tired of trying to do what did not come easily to me. On the other hand, I had an acute power of observation and it seemed to me that I could see a great many things that other people missed. I could put down in clear terms what I saw. I had a logical sense, and if no great feelings for the richness and strangeness of words, at all events a lively appreciation of their sound. I knew that I should never write as well as I could wish, but I thought with pains I could arrive at writing as well as my natural defects allowed.

Case Problem 13-B, What Killed Bob Lyons?, is a descriptive statement of the interaction of one man and his environment. Although the dynamics underlying Bob Lyons' decision to suicide are not discussed in the text, they are readily available elsewhere.[58] For some persons

---

[56]Timothy W. Costello and Sheldon S. Zalkind, *Psychology in Administration*, A Research Orientation (Englewood Cliffs: Prentice-Hall, 1963), pp. 148–149.

[57]W. Somerset Maugham, *The Summing Up* (New York: Doubleday, Doran & Company, Inc., 1938), pp. 29–30. © 1938 by W. Somerset Maugham. Reprinted by permission of Doubleday & Company, Inc.

[58]Harry Levinson, "What Killed Bob Lyons?" *Harvard Business Review*, Vol. 41, No. 1 (January–February, 1963), pp. 127–128. © 1963 by the President and Fellows of Harvard College; all rights reserved. The introductory material of this article appears as Case Problem 13-B. Dr. Levinson's statement of the reasons why Bob Lyons' reaction to his environment resulted in suicide and some practical conclusions to be drawn from this study are presented in the *Student Enrichment Activities*.

there would be little stress in the situation described; for others, assuming that there is stress, the reaction might have been a somatization reaction or one of the many behavioral adjustive reactions described in Table 13-1.

Case Problem 13-B

WHAT KILLED BOB LYONS?

Those who knew Bob Lyons thought extremely well of him. He was a highly successful executive who had an important position in a large company. As his superiors saw him, he was aggressive, with a knack for getting things done through other people. He worked hard and set a vigorous pace. He drove himself relentlessly. In less than ten years with his company, he had moved through several positions of responsibility.

Lyons had always been a good athlete. He was proud of his skill in swimming, hunting, golf, and tennis. In his college days he had lettered in football and baseball. On weekends he preferred to undertake rebuilding and repairing projects around the house, or to hunt, interspersing other sports for a change of pace. He was usually engaged, it seemed, in hard physical work.

His life was not all work, however. He was active in his church and in the Boy Scouts. His wife delighted in entertaining and in being with other people, so their social life was a round of many parties and social activities. They shared much of their life with their three children.

Early in the spring of his ninth year with the company, Bob Lyons spoke with the vice president to whom he reported. "Things are a little quiet around here," he said. "Most of the big projects are over. The new building is finished, and we have a lot of things on the ball which four years ago were all fouled up. I don't like the idea of just riding a desk and looking out the window. I like action."

About a month later, Lyons was assigned additional responsibilities. He rushed into them with his usual vigor. Once again he seemed to be buoyant and cheerful. After six months on the assignment, Lyons had the project rolling smoothly. Again he spoke to his vice president, reporting that he was out of projects. The vice president, pleased with Lyons' performance, told him that he had earned the right to do a little dreaming and planning; and, furthermore, dreaming and planning were a necessary part of the position he now held, toward which he had aspired for so long. Bob Lyons listened as his boss spoke, but it was plain to the vice president that the answer did not satisfy him.

About three months after this meeting, the vice president began to notice that replies to his memos and inquiries were not coming back from Lyons with their usual rapidity. He noticed also that Lyons was developing a tendency to put things off, a most unusual behavior pattern for him. He observed that Lyons became easily angered and disturbed over minor difficulties which previously had not irritated him at all.

Bob Lyons then became involved in a conflict with two other executives over a policy issue. Such conflicts were not unusual in the organization since, inevitably, there were varying points of view on many issues. The conflict was not a personal one, but it did require intervention from higher management before a solution could be reached. In the process of resolving the conflict, Lyons' point of view prevailed on some questions, but not on others.

A few weeks after this conflict had been resolved, Lyons went to the vice president's office. He wanted to have a long private talk, he said. His first words were, "I'm losing my grip. The old steam is gone. I've had diarrhea for four weeks and several times in the past three weeks I've lost my breakfast. I'm worried and yet I don't know what about. I feel that some people have lost confidence in me."

He talked with his boss for an hour and a half. The vice president recounted his achievements in the company to reassure him. He then asked if Lyons thought he should see a doctor. Lyons agreed that he should and, in the presence of the vice president, called his family doctor for an appointment. By this time the vice president was very much concerned. He called Mrs. Lyons and arranged to meet her for lunch the next day. She reported that, in addition to his other symptoms, her husband had difficulty sleeping. She was relieved that the vice president had called her because she was beginning to become worried and had herself planned to call the vice president. Both were now alarmed. They decided that they should get Lyons into a hospital rather than wait for the doctor's appointment which was still a week off.

The next day Lyons was taken to the hospital. Meanwhile, with Mrs. Lyons' permission, the vice president reported to the family doctor Lyons' recent job behavior and the nature of their conversations. When the vice president had finished, the doctor concluded, "All he needs is a good rest. We don't want to tell him that it may be mental or nervous." The vice president replied that he didn't know what the cause was, but he knew Bob Lyons needed help quickly.

During five days in the hospital, Lyons was subjected to extensive laboratory tests. The vice president visited him daily. He seemed to welcome the rest and the sedation at night. He said he was eating and sleeping much better. He talked about company problems, though he did not speak spontaneously without encouragement. While Lyons was out of the room, another executive who shared his hospital room confided to the vice president that he was worried about Lyons. "He seems to be so morose and depressed that I'm afraid he's losing his mind," the executive said.

By this time the president of the company, who had been kept informed, was also becoming concerned. He had talked to a psychiatrist and planned to talk to Lyons about psychiatric treatment if his doctor did not suggest it. Meanwhile, Lyons was discharged from the hospital as being without physical illness, and his doctor recommended a vacation. Lyons then remained at home for several days where he was again visited by the vice president. He and his wife took a trip to visit friends. He was then ready to come back to work, but the president suggested that he take another week off. The president also suggested that they visit together when Lyons returned.

A few days later, the president telephoned Lyons' home. Mrs. Lyons could not find him to answer the telephone. After 15 minutes she still had not found him and called the vice president about her concern. By the time the vice president arrived at the Lyons home, the police were already there. Bob Lyons had committed suicide.

PROBLEMS

1. Describe in your own words the reasons for Bob Lyons' suicide.
2. Was Lyons' reaction attributable primarily to his work situation, to his personality, or to an interaction between his personality and his work environment? Explain.
3. How much of Lyons' problem is attributable to this particular work situation? Describe a situation that would minimize stress for him.
4. Is it possible that somatization or adjustive behavioral reactions might appear in a stress situation of this type? Under what conditions?

CHAPTER QUESTIONS FOR STUDY AND DISCUSSION

1. What is the meaning of the phrase, scientific rigor?
2. In general, which of the two broad types of studies, field studies or experimental studies, is considered the more rigorous? Under what conditions would the type of study that you designate less rigorous become more rigorous than the other type of study?

3. Differentiate between and give an example of each of the following: natural experiment, field experiment, and laboratory experiment. What are the major factors that determine the experimental method to be used in a given study?
4. Define in your own terms the phrase, organizational climate. Drawing from your experience as a member of a formal organization, either a college or an industrial organization, give examples of characteristics of the organization that seem to meet the criteria set forth in the definition.
5. Summarize in your own words the effects of organizational structure upon behavior of its members. What major factors mediate, or moderate, the effect of organization structure upon behavior?
6. What is meant by the term *perception*? How does readiness or set influence perception?
7. In addition to readiness or set, there are other perceptual biases, some traceable directly to the perceiver and some to the perceived, that influence interpersonal perceptions. Give an example of each of these sources of perceptual error.
8. How does one's degree of personal adjustment influence the accuracy and quality of interpersonal perceptions?
9. What is meant by *role*? Why is the concept of role significant to the study of formal organizations?
10. How does the concept of role relate to the concept of conflict? Is it possible for an organization to exist without conflict? Discuss.
11. What is the relationship between role and stress? Is stress always perceived?

Chapter
14

Leadership Patterns

Case Problem 14-A

MEASURING LEADERSHIP STYLE

Among the many factors that contribute to the effectiveness of leadership are the behavior of the leader, the nature of the task, the composition of the group being led, and the leader's position within the group. In this problem we examine one aspect of the leader's behavior, leadership style. In the chapter that follows criteria are developed for determining the structure of the task, and in Case Problem 14-B measures are presented for the evaluation of the group and the position of the leader.

The phrase, leadership behavior, is broad in meaning and includes the managerial functions of planning, organizing, and controlling as well as the function of leading or directing. Leadership style is a narrower concept. It refers to the characteristic way in which a given leader relates to subordinates and the task assigned to the group. Leadership style is considered to be primarily a function of the leader's personality. Although many terms have been used to describe leadership style, most classifications result in two broad groups: those who are essentially interested in maintaining good interpersonal relationships and those who are essentially interested in the accomplishment of the task.

There are many ways of measuring style. One method is to ask direct questions about

the leader's action in a given situation. Another method used to determine leadership style is by inference — asking a person to describe his or her least preferred co-worker. Your description of the person with whom you would least like to work — either someone you now know or have known in the past — is used to measure your leadership style.

PROBLEMS

1. Before describing your least preferred co-worker and computing your average LPC score, do you consider yourself to be a leader who is primarily motivated to maintain good interpersonal relationships with your co-workers or do you consider yourself to be one who is primarily motivated to complete the assigned task, even at the expense of good interpersonal relationships?
2. Exhibit I on pages 323 and 324 provides a way of determining your leadership style. Read the directions, and complete the LPC scale presented in the exhibit. Directions for scoring and the rationale of the scale are described on page 340.
3. Does your average LPC score support your own evaluation of your leadership style? Discuss.

People differ in the ways they think about those with whom they work. This may be important in working with others. Please give your immediate, first reaction to the items on the following two pages.

Below are pairs of words which are opposite in meaning, such as "Very neat" and "Not neat." You are asked to describe someone with whom you have worked by placing an "X" in one of the eight spaces on the line between the two words. Each space represents how well the adjective fits the person you are describing, as if it were written:

Very neat :_____:_____:_____:_____|_____:_____:_____:_____: Not neat

8	7	6	5	4	3	2	1
Very neat	Quite neat	Some-what neat	Slightly neat	Slightly untidy	Some-what untidy	Quite untidy	Very untidy

FOR EXAMPLE: If you were to describe the person with whom you are able to work least well, and you ordinarily think of that person as being *quite neat*, you would put an "X" in the second space from the words Very Neat, like this:

Very neat :_____: X _:_____:_____|_____:_____:_____:_____: Not neat

8	7	6	5	4	3	2	1
Very neat	Quite neat	Some-what neat	Slightly neat	Slightly untidy	Some-what untidy	Quite untidy	Very untidy

If you ordinarily think of the person with whom you can work least well as being only *slightly neat*, you would put your "X" as follows:

Very neat :_____:_____:_____: X |_____:_____:_____:_____: Not neat

8	7	6	5	4	3	2	1
Very neat	Quite neat	Some-what neat	Slightly neat	Slightly untidy	Some-what untidy	Quite untidy	Very untidy

If you would think of that person as being *very untidy*, you would use the space nearest the words Not Neat.

Exhibit I
A MEASURE OF
LEADERSHIP
STYLE

Very neat :_____:_____:_____:_____|_____:_____:_____: X _: Not neat

8	7	6	5	4	3	2	1
Very neat	Quite neat	Some-what neat	Slightly neat	Slightly untidy	Some-what untidy	Quite untidy	Very untidy

Look at the words at both ends of the line before you put in your "X." Please remember that there are *no right or wrong answers*. Work rapidly; your first answer is likely to be the best. Please do not omit any items, and mark each item only once.

LPC

Think of the person *with whom you can work least well*. The person may be someone you work with now or may be someone you knew in the past. The individual does not have to be the person you like least well, but should be the person with whom you had the most difficulty in getting a job done. Describe this person as he or she appears to you.

Pleasant	:___:___:___:___|___:___:___:___:	Unpleasant	8 7 6 5 | 4 3 2 1
Friendly	:___:___:___:___|___:___:___:___:	Unfriendly	8 7 6 5 | 4 3 2 1
Rejecting	:___:___:___:___|___:___:___:___:	Accepting	1 2 3 4 | 5 6 7 8
Helpful	:___:___:___:___|___:___:___:___:	Frustrating	8 7 6 5 | 4 3 2 1
Unenthusiastic	:___:___:___:___|___:___:___:___:	Enthusiastic	1 2 3 4 | 5 6 7 8
Tense	:___:___:___:___|___:___:___:___:	Relaxed	1 2 3 4 | 5 6 7 8
Distant	:___:___:___:___|___:___:___:___:	Close	1 2 3 4 | 5 6 7 8
Cold	:___:___:___:___|___:___:___:___:	Warm	1 2 3 4 | 5 6 7 8
Cooperative	:___:___:___:___|___:___:___:___:	Uncooperative	8 7 6 5 | 4 3 2 1
Supportive	:___:___:___:___|___:___:___:___:	Hostile	8 7 6 5 | 4 3 2 1
Boring	:___:___:___:___|___:___:___:___:	Interesting	1 2 3 4 | 5 6 7 8
Quarrelsome	:___:___:___:___|___:___:___:___:	Harmonious	1 2 3 4 | 5 6 7 8
Self-assured	:___:___:___:___|___:___:___:___:	Hesitant	8 7 6 5 | 4 3 2 1
Efficient	:___:___:___:___|___:___:___:___:	Inefficient	8 7 6 5 | 4 3 2 1
Gloomy	:___:___:___:___|___:___:___:___:	Cheerful	1 2 3 4 | 5 6 7 8
Open	:___:___:___:___|___:___:___:___:	Guarded	8 7 6 5 | 4 3 2 1

Exhibit I (continued)

Source: Fred E. Fiedler, *A Theory of Leadership Effectiveness* (New York: McGraw-Hill Book Co., 1967), Table 3-1, pp. 40–41.

Within the framework of independent, intervening, and dependent variables presented in the preceding chapter, leadership is regarded as an independent variable — an input into the organization intended to influence the behavior of the members of the organization. As an independent variable, the function of leadership in formal organizations is the attainment of organizational objectives by means of interpersonal relationships with other members of the group. It is a function that is present at all levels of an organization. The president, by stimulating, directing, and coordinating the functions assigned to the line and staff officers, starts the process of organizational accomplishment. In turn, each key executive serves in the dual role of subordinate and leader. As the result of personal interaction with subordinates, each contributes a share to the attainment of stated goals. At the lowest level of the management hierarchy, a production foreman or a supervisor in the accounting department meets departmental goals by interaction with and the coordination of the efforts of workers who have no supervisory responsibilities.

Despite the general agreement that exists regarding the interpersonal nature of the leadership function and its presence in all organizations — admittedly in varying degrees of effectiveness — there is no concensus concerning the primary role, or function, of leadership. The various roles ascribed to the leadership function have been termed by some writers as theories of leadership and are discussed first. As might be expected there have been many approaches to the study of leadership. A review of the literature reveals that most of the early studies were directed toward the measurement and description of the characteristics of the leader as a person. The next period shows an emphasis on the nature of the situation in which leadership occurs. Most recently, studies of leadership stress the interaction between the leader, the situation, subordinates, and the task to be accomplished and is known as a contingency, or interactionistic, approach to leadership. Each of these various approaches to the study of leadership is presented. Finally, the studies of leadership show that the behavior of the leader, termed leadership style, is significant in its own right. The last part of the chapter presents a convenient means of classifying leadership behavior according to its style and a basis for selecting the most effective form of leadership for a given situation.

THEORIES OF LEADERSHIP

Defining leadership as a process of interpersonal relationships between the leader and members of the group does not indicate the nature of these relationships nor does it reveal the role, or function, of leadership. In part, the nature of these interrelationships depends on underlying organization theory. If one accepts the work-centered approach to organization theory, the role of the leadership function and subsequent interpersonal relationships are different from the role and relationships implied by a people-centered approach to organization theory. In the discussion of organization theory, Chapter 8, a third approach is presented — a contingency approach. Similarly, there is a third approach to understanding the role of leadership; however, it is termed a revisionist approach. The three approaches to the role of leadership — work-centered, people-centered, and revisionist — and the consequent function of leadership that results from each role definition are discussed in turn.[1]

Scientific Management — A Work-Centered Approach

Scientific management is discussed in Chapter 2, "The Development of Management Concepts," and some of its implied assumptions concerning the nature of human behavior are presented as Theory X in Chapter 8, "Organization Theory." The role of the leader is determined as a result of these assumptions concerning human behavior. Since people are assumed to be slothful and prone to make errors, such behavior must be corrected so that the organization may survive. Scientific management offers a means of correction by strengthening the organization. This may be accomplished in two ways — by improving the structure and definition of the organization, and by improving the methodology of the organization. Improvements in structure and definition are directed toward management itself. Policies, procedures, and standard practices are established to minimize the chance for error resulting from human frailty. The manager is taught to respect and revere the organization at all times. Thus, the bureaucrat, the "organization man," emerges. The reward for subservience to the organization is economic security in the form of continued employment, advancement through a well-defined path of promotions, and the acquisition of status symbols which serve to denote rank to others in the organization.

Improvements in methodology are directed toward controlling the behavior of lower echelons. If problems of quality control appear, the answer lies in engineering the product so that errors in production are reduced to an absolute minimum, not in training the worker to perform with greater skill. Quantity of production is controlled by measurement, not motivation. Under these conditions many of the problems of leadership disappear. All questions are resolved in favor of the

---

[1]Warren G. Bennis, "Revisionist Theory of Leadership," *Harvard Business Review*, Vol. 39, No. 1, (January-February, 1961), pp. 26–36, 146–150. The discussion of theories of leadership is based largely upon the excellent review of the revisionists' work in organization theory written by Bennis.

For another discussion of theories of leadership the following is recommended: Ralph M. Stogdill, *Handbook of Leadership: A Survey of Theory and Research* (New York: The Free Press, 1974). Professor Stogdill's *Handbook* is a complete survey of theory and research on leadership. Theories of leadership are discussed in Chapter 3, pp. 17–23. In Chapter 3, Professor Stogdill discusses the revisionist approach presented by Warren Bennis.

organization. What is best for the organization is, by definition, best for the individual, a member of the organization and dependent upon its welfare for survival.

Human Relations — A People-Centered Approach

The human-relations approach to leadership emphasizes the potential strength and contribution of each member of the organization rather than the organization's structure and methodology. Instead of tinkering with the organization, management motivates the members of the organization to reach their full potential. Employees are viewed as individuals with basic psychological needs that must be satisfied; further, it is believed that these needs can be satisfied within the framework of the modern industrial organization. Employees need recognition, the feeling of belonging to a group, and the opportunity to develop their capacities so that they may realize their full potential. The role of the manager-leader changes with these assumptions of human behavior. The manager must recognize that there is both a formal and an informal organization and deal with both, but the prime task is one of developing and guiding the members of the organization in order that they may reach their full potential. The leader's function is that of a catalyst. Questions are resolved in favor of the individual, since individual needs must be satisfied in order that leadership may reach its full potential and maximum contribution.[2]

The Revisionists — Expressions of Doubt

Admittedly, the above descriptions of the work-centered approach and the people-centered approach to the role of leadership are overdrawn. There has probably never been a successful organization either entirely work centered or completely people centered, but the exaggerated statements representing the scientific-management and the human-relations views of leadership serve a useful purpose. They bring into sharp focus a problem confronting all managers — balancing the needs of the organization with the needs and desires of its individual members. Expressions of doubt have arisen concerning the validity of either point of view. An interesting expression of doubt comes from Douglas McGregor, one of the first exponents of the human-relations approach, after six years as a college president:

> I believed, for example, that a leader could operate successfully as a kind of adviser to his organization. I thought I could avoid being a "boss." Unconsciously, I suspect, I hoped to duck the unpleasant necessity of making difficult decisions, of taking the responsibility for one course of action among many uncertain alternatives, of making mistakes and taking the consequences. I thought that maybe I could operate so

---

[2]For a discussion of the human relations approach, the following is suggested: Fred J. Carvell, *Human Relations in Business* (London: Collier-MacMillan, 1970).

that everyone would like me — that good "human relations" would eliminate all discord and disagreement.

I couldn't have been more wrong. It took a couple of years, but I finally began to realize that a leader cannot avoid the exercise of authority any more than he can avoid responsibility for what happens to his organization.[3]

The revisionists, unlike the early proponents of either of the polar approaches described above, realize that there are distinct needs for the organization and for the individual. Three of the revisionists, Robert N. McMurry, Chris Argyris, and Douglas McGregor, deserve attention, for each recognizes organizational needs and the needs of individual members. Their differences lie in their assessment of human needs and capabilities.

A Benevolent Autocracy. Robert N. McMurry's position results in a call for the organization to become a "benevolent autocracy" and for its head to be a "great man." He has no quarrel with participative management and the development of individuals to their fullest capacities. He simply believes, based upon many years of experience as a consulting psychologist working in an industrial setting, that the capacity for most humans to participate and contribute significantly to the organization is rather limited. The basic human need postulated by McMurry is a need for security and direction, a need that is readily met by the well-structured organization. Members of middle management need well-defined positions of authority derived from structure, since they are, for the most part, incapable of personal leadership. At the top of the pyramid there is room for a mere handful of dynamic individuals to direct the workings of the organization. Though this view is strikingly similar to the scientific-management approach there is a major difference. McMurry's "benevolent autocracy" not only satisfies the needs of the organization, it also satisfies the dependency needs of the individual members of the organization.[4]

Yes, But. Another revisionist, Chris Argyris, expresses a more optimistic view in his book, *Personality and Organization*.[5] To a degree Argyris is answering McMurry by saying "yes, but." He agrees that at present most workers are dependent, but they do not need to remain in

---

[3]Douglas M. McGregor, "On Leadership," *Antioch Notes* (May, 1954), pp. 2–3.

For a similar change in position on the part of a former student and colleague of Douglas McGregor after administrative experience the following is of interest: "Conversation with Warren Bennis," *Organizational Dynamics*, Vol. 2, No. 3 (Winter, 1974), pp. 51–66 (an interview with Warren Bennis by William F. Dowling, Editor, *Organizational Dynamics*).

[4]Robert N. McMurry, "The Case for Benevolent Autocracy," *Harvard Business Review*, Vol. 36, No. 1 (January-February, 1958), pp. 82–90.

[5]Chris Argyris, *Personality and Organization*, The Conflict Between System and the Individual (New York: Harper & Row, Publishers, 1957). The appendix, "Some Basic Categories of a Theory of Organization," pp. 239–250, summarizes Argyris' position.

a continued state of dependency. He disagrees entirely with McMurry as to the effect of the formal organization upon the individual. McMurry sees the organization as a means of answering dependency needs; for Argyris, the goals of the typical organization are in basic conflict with the needs and goals of the individual. By fragmenting jobs into discrete activities such as the assembly line and emphasizing the formal relationship, the organization creates dependency and restrains the development of the individual to his fullest capacities. But Argyris sees hope for the future through the enlargement of jobs, employee-centered leadership, and a reality leadership that recognizes the needs of the organization and the individual.[6]

A Middle Ground. The position of the third revisionist, Douglas McGregor, is not so glum as that expressed by McMurry, nor is it so optimistic as the expression of Argyris. In his book, *The Human Side of Enterprise*, McGregor outlines four steps as a possible solution to the problems confronting the leaders of organizations.[7] He suggests, first, that goals be determined jointly, a step that facilitates the second phase of his recommendations, which is collaboration between superior and subordinate. The third step, the development of self-control, is based upon the belief that people are capable of learning and exercising self-control. The last step is the integration of the goals of the individual and the organization, a bit of give and take on both sides, toward the solution of a mutual problem. McGregor does not claim that his approach will work; he only says that it *may* work.

COMPONENTS OF LEADERSHIP

The preceding discussion of the varying concepts concerning the function of leadership indicates a range from the belief that the primary purpose of leadership is to support the organization and its goals to the belief that the major function of leadership is that of supporting the needs of individual members. The middle ground offers hope that both the needs of the organization and the needs of individual members can be met simultaneously. A similar triad emerges when one examines the literature directed toward an understanding of the components, or factors, contributing towards effective leadership. The first studies were directed toward an understanding of the leader as the critical element in the leadership process, an emphasis usually designated as the trait approach to leadership. Next, the emphasis shifts to situational characteristics as being the more significant factors in

---

[6]For a discussion of the problems inherent in adapting behavioral theory to organizations the following is recommended: James A. Lee, "Behavioral Theory vs. Reality," *Harvard Business Review*, Vol. 49, No. 2 (March-April, 1971), pp. 20–28 and 157–159.

[7]Douglas McGregor, *The Human Side of Enterprise* (New York: McGraw-Hill Book Co., 1960).

determining effective leadership. Finally, there is the current approach to the components of leadership known as the contingency, or interactionistic, approach. Each of these approaches is discussed in turn.[8]

The Trait Approach to Leadership

There are many studies dealing with the traits required for successful leadership. Generally, the traits listed include such attributes as objectivity, judgment, initiative, dependability, drive, a liking for and understanding of people, and decisiveness. Also mentioned frequently are emotional stability and maturity, a strong desire to achieve, the ability to cooperate with others, and a high degree of personal integrity. After surveying the literature, Stogdill concludes that leadership is associated with the following personal factors: (1) intelligence, including judgment and verbal facility, (2) a record of past achievement in scholarship and athletics, (3) emotional maturity and stability, expressed in dependability, persistence, and a drive for continuing achievement, (4) the ability to participate socially and to adapt to various groups, and (5) a desire for status and socio-economic position.[9]

Another summary lists the following characteristics of a successful executive:

> (1) the ability to meet people from all walks of life and talk with pleasure on a wide range of subjects, (2) the ability at all times to work at "a mad pace" and sometimes with the "reflectiveness and slow tempo of a Buddhist priest," (3) an interest in world affairs and events in the personal lives of those around him, (4) pleasure in talking and the confidence required for isolation and pondering, (5) the ability to drive people hard when necessary, yet be subtle and tactful at other times, (6) the ability to take a witty or serious approach, as circumstances may require, (7) the capacity to deal with both concrete and abstract problems, (8) the capacity for originality and willingness to follow precedent, (9) the willingness to be conservative but at other times to take risks no gambler would dare to take (that is, the executive must know when to take risks and when to seek security), (10) assurance in decision making and humility in advice seeking.[10]

---

[8]For a complete review of the literature concerning the components of leadership, Part II, Leader Personality and Behavior, pp. 35–169, of the *Handbook of Leadership* is recommended: Ralph M. Stogdill, *op. cit.*

[9]R. M. Stogdill, "Personal Factors Associated with Leadership: A Survey of the Literature," *Journal of Psychology*, Vol. 25 (January, 1948), pp. 35–64. Another summary of the literature yielding similar results was prepared in 1959. R. D. Mann, "A Review of the Relationship Between Personality and Performance in Small Groups," *Psychological Bulletin*, Vol. 56, No. 4 (July, 1959), pp. 241–270.

[10]Zygmunt A. Piotrowski and Milton R. Rock, *The Perceptanalytic Executive Scale*, A Tool for the Selection of Top Managers (New York: Grune and Stratton, 1963), p. 4.

There are several shortcomings in the trait approach as a means of analyzing and understanding leadership: (1) Trait studies, as a general rule, do not assign weightings to each of the traits so that the relative importance of each trait as it contributes to leadership can be determined. (2) There is considerable overlap between the various traits mentioned. Seldom are they mutually exclusive. Also, there are many instances of conflicting or incompatible traits, such as the ten traits listed above. (3) An analysis of personality traits makes no differentiation between those traits of value in acquiring leadership positions and those traits necessary to hold or maintain leadership. (4) Trait analysis is based upon the rather shaky assumption that personality is a composite of discrete traits, rather than viewing personality as an integrated functioning whole with a continually shifting pattern of characteristics with respect to both their significance and their strength. (5) The trait approach to leadership ignores situational factors in the environment that influence the effectiveness of leadership. Let us discuss briefly how situational factors influence leadership.

Situational Factors in Leadership

Experienced executive recruiters are frequently confronted with the problem of determining whether an applicant is available for a new position because personality factors created an inability to function as an effective leader in his former position, or whether environmental factors beyond the applicant's control limited the expression of his leadership abilities. The following classic experiment conducted by Alex Bavelas shows the importance of situational factors as determinants of leadership.[11]

Each experimental group consisting of five subjects was arranged in the positional patterns shown in Figure 14-1. Each member of a group had a card on which there were printed five symbols from a total set of six; however, there was only one symbol that appeared on all five cards. The problem was completed when, as the result of passing information back and forth to each other, the group correctly determined the full set of six symbols. At the end of 15 trials each group was asked whether or not it had a recognized leader. The number of votes received by each member of each group is shown in the circles representing the individual members of each group. Note that in Group A every member receives at least one vote, yet no one member emerges clearly as the leader of the group; however, in Groups B, C, and D, there is definite recognition of one member of the group as the leader.

---

[11]Alex Bavelas, "Communications Patterns in Task-Oriented Groups," in D. Lerner and H. D. Lasswell (eds.), *The Policy Sciences* (Stanford: Stanford University Press, 1951), pp. 193–202.

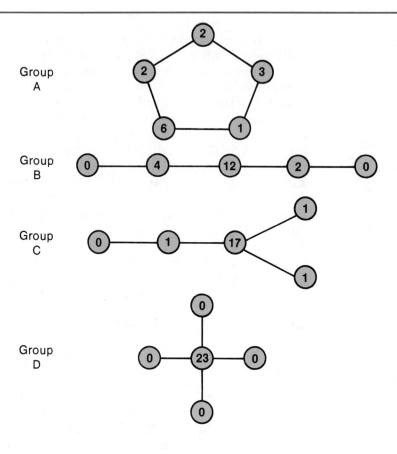

Figure 14-1
**Figure 14-1
THE EFFECT OF
POSITION AS A
DETERMINANT
OF LEADERSHIP**

The number within each circle is the number of votes each person received as recognized leader of the group. (From Bavelas, "Communications Patterns in Task-Oriented Groups," op. cit.)

In order to solve the stated problem it is necessary for the members of each group to pass information; in other words, to function as a part of an information system. The positions of the members determine the pattern of the informational network, and, as the pattern changes, the strategic value of each position also changes. In Group A, arranged in the form of a circle, every member receives at least one vote, but there is no one person emerging without question as the leader. In Group B, arranged as a straight line, neither of the individuals on each end of the line receives a single vote. Each of the persons on either side of the middle member of the group receives several votes, while the central figure receives 12 votes as the recognized leader. In Group C the person at the juncture of the Y receives the greatest number of votes, and in Group D, the person at the hub of the wheel is the only member receiving any votes as the recognized leader.

In Group B each of the members at the end of the straight line can communicate directly with only one other member of the group. The ones next to the end position can communicate directly with two members, but the one in the center communicates with two members directly and has only one intermediary when he desires to communicate with those on the end positions. Likewise, the person at the juncture of the Y communicates directly with three members of the group and is only one removed from the person at the end of the stem of the Y. The person at the hub of the wheel can communicate directly with each of the other members and there is no need to pass information through an intermediary. Thus, the one in the center receives all the votes. The positioning of each member of the group was determined by chance, with no consideration given to personality factors; therefore, the conclusion of this study is inescapable: recognition as a leader is dependent upon the strategic value of one's position in a communication network — a situational factor — and not upon personality characteristics.

Other Situational Factors

In a study of employees of 88 companies, Professor J. C. Wofford, using multiple factor analysis technique, established five independent situational factors that influence the effectiveness of leadership behavior.[12] The first of these factors, centralization and work evaluation, refers to the degree of centralization of the decision-making functions in the organization and the extent to which work is closely controlled by supervision. Second is the factor of organizational complexity and the corresponding degree of technical knowledge required of organization members. Usually a high degree of group cohesiveness and high levels of technical skill are associated with high organizational complexity. The third factor is the size of the total organization which is associated with highly structured work tasks. The fourth situational factor refers to the structure of the work group itself. A high rating in this respect implies a small work group with the members preferring group meetings and participation in the decision-making process. The last factor, organizational layering and communications, refers to the number of levels in the organization and communication between peers in the organization.

---

[12]J. C. Wofford, "Managerial Behavior, Situational Factors, and Productivity and Morale," *Administrative Science Quarterly*, Vol. 16 (March, 1971), pp. 10–17. This study clearly shows the effect of situational factors, as extracted by multiple factor analysis, upon the effectiveness of leadership styles with the criteria being productivity and morale. Professor Wofford indicates that the probable reason for having more than two leadership styles is that he included in his rating forms the managerial processes of planning, organizing, and controlling as well as the function of leading.

The entire March, 1971, issue of *Administrative Science Quarterly* is noteworthy as it is devoted entirely to organizational leadership.

Using the same multiple factor analysis techniques Wofford also develops five dimensions of managerial behavior. Group achievement is the first dimension and describes the manager who uses group processes in decision making and who organizes and plans the work carefully. The second dimension, personal enhancement, describes the manager whose primary means of influencing subordinates is the use of authority. Third is personal interaction, the dimension that describes the warm, friendly manager. Dynamic achievement is the fourth dimension and characterizes the manager who sets goals with his subordinates, then measures performance in relation to these goals. The fifth dimension, security and maintenance, describes the manager who is aloof and conscientious in that he continually checks with higher authority. By remaining apart, the manager provides some freedom in subordinates' activities; however, standards of performance are not clearly defined.

The results of this study show that the manager whose behavior is best described by dimension five is most effective in large complex organizations, where apparently the people are skilled and competent, with little need for guidance. The manager whose forte is personal interaction is most effective in operations that are relatively simple and highly structured. If the manager's behavior emphasizes group achievement and order, he does best where he can work with small groups having relatively unstructured tasks and the need for group meetings. Dynamic achievement is also associated with small groups; however, there is evidence of manager job security. Personal enhancement, the direct reliance upon authority, is associated with relatively simple situations that can be controlled effectively by direct supervision.

Wofford's study is significant for several reasons. First, it shows clearly the effect of situational factors upon the effectiveness of certain styles of leadership behavior. Second, it clearly illustrates the interaction between situational factors and the personality and behavioral characteristics of the leader. Effectiveness, measured either in terms of productivity or morale, is the result of these two forces rather than the result of one or the other.[13]

A CONTINGENCY MODEL OF LEADERSHIP EFFECTIVENESS

Before any definite statement can be made specifying the nature of the interaction between situational variables and the behavior of the leader, it is necessary to develop a model and test the elements of that

---

[13]Wofford's findings are supported by another study that examines leadership and success in tall and flat organizations: Edwin E. Ghiselli and Jacob P. Siegel, "Leadership and Managerial Success in Tall and Flat Organizations," *Personnel Psychology*, Vol. 25, No. 4 (Winter, 1972), pp. 617–624.

model by subjecting each element to objective scrutiny and verification. Such a model, capable of verification by objective research methods, has been developed by Professor Fred Fiedler and is known as *a contingency model of leadership effectiveness*.[14]

Assumptions and Definitions

In order to understand the contingency model it is necessary to define and examine the factors that contribute to effective leadership. First, the group in which leadership occurs is defined and a classification system is developed. Then the other factors — position power, the task structure, and leader-member relationship — are discussed in turn. Finally, a group-task classification system is presented in model form.

The Group. Fiedler defines the small group within which most leadership occurs as "a set of individuals in face-to-face interaction who perceive each other as interrelated, or as reciprocally affecting each other, and who pursue a shared goal."[15] Groups vary considerably with respect to the degree and nature of the interaction between members, with the result that three types of groups emerge — *interacting*, *coacting*, and *counteracting*.[16]

Interacting groups are characterized by a high degree of interdependence between members of the group. In interacting groups each member must complete a task in order that the other members may successfully perform their assigned tasks. Athletic teams, musical groups, airline crews, and restaurant employees are examples of interacting groups. The degree to which the goals of the group are shared by its members is high, and the leader must develop within such a group the coordination necessary to reach group goals.

The members of coacting groups may perform their respective individual tasks independently from those of other members of the group. The faculty of a university is a good example of a coacting group since each instructor can, and often does, conduct teaching, research, or writing activities with little dependence upon other

---

[14]The most complete statement of Fiedler's Contingency Model is found in Fred E. Fiedler, *A Theory of Leadership Effectiveness* (New York: McGraw-Hill Book Co., 1967). This book is the primary source of the contingency model discussion. For a briefer statement see Fred E. Fiedler, "Engineer the Job to Fit the Manager," *Harvard Business Review*, Vol. 43, No. 5 (September-October, 1965), pp. 115–122.

A more recent discussion of the effectiveness of a contingency model of leadership is the following book: Fred E. Fiedler and Martin M. Chemers, *Leadership and Effective Management* (Glenview: Scott, Foresman & Co., 1974).

[15]Fiedler, *A Theory of Leadership Effectiveness*, p. 18.

[16]Support is given to Fiedler's conceptualization of leadership occurring within a group in the following study: Steven A. Richards and James U. Cuffee, "Behavioral Correlates of Leadership Effectiveness in Interacting and Counteracting Groups," *Journal of Applied Psychology*, Vol. 56, No. 5 (October, 1972), pp. 377–381.

members of the faculty. Law firms and medical clinics are also typical coacting groups. Coacting groups need coordination only in the achievement of group goals and in those instances where the goals of an individual member may be in conflict with those of another member.[17]

A counteracting group, such as the labor-management bargaining team or a purchaser-vendor negotiating group, may not appear to be a group in that each side is pursuing separate goals. Yet, for ultimate success each is dependent upon the other in the solution of the problem at hand. Leadership in counteracting groups is very difficult, because in most instances there are two leaders — one for each side. Further, hostility and competition may be very marked. Leadership in these groups is primarily one of conflict resolution.

To date, most of the work done in the development and validation of the contingency model is based upon interacting groups.

Position Power. Even a cursory examination indicates that one of the factors determining the effectiveness of the leader is the power associated with the position of leadership. Case Problem 14-B presents one of many scales that have been used to measure the position power of the leader. Indicators of high position power are the right to hire and fire, to reward or withhold promotions or changes in pay; the appointment to the position and designation of title endorsed by the organizational hierarchy; and the accompanying external signs that clearly indicate the position of the office within the organization. A leader with low position power might be designated as temporary or acting, be elected by and subject to removal by peers or subordinates, have no power to select or retain subordinates, and no designation of rank or authority. An elected committee chairman or a group leader are examples of leaders with low position power.

Though position power is usually recognized as one of the factors determining the effectiveness of leadership, its precise effect is not clear since the results of empirical studies are ambiguous. A leader with high position power has at least an initial advantage in that this leader has the support of the organization and consequently should feel more free to interact openly with the members of the subordinate group. On the other hand, leaders with low position power do not have such freedom initially, and must first convince the members of their groups to accept their leadership and direction. The situation is particularly critical for leaders with low position power if they may safely be ignored or even deposed by their subordinates.

---

[17]In a review of the literature published subsequent to *A Theory of Leadership Effectiveness* (1967) Fiedler suggests that coacting groups be further subdivided. He recommends that task-oriented groups such as those mentioned in the text be differentiated from coacting groups that exist primarily for the benefit of the individual, such as groups of trainees: Fred E. Fiedler, "Validation and Extension of the Contingency Model of Leadership Effectiveness: A Review of Empirical Findings," *Psychological Bulletin*, Vol. 76, No. 2 (August, 1971), pp. 128–148.

The Task Structure. Another factor determining the effectiveness of leadership is the task itself. Some tasks by their very nature are relatively easy to define, to accomplish, and to measure. Such tasks are regarded as having a high degree of structure. There are also tasks that have a low degree of structure with the result that it is more difficult to define and to measure progress toward their accomplishment.

Fiedler uses four criteria in determining the degree of task structure. First is the extent to which the decision or solution may be verified. Those solutions that can be verified by comparison with a model or by subjecting them to an objective evaluation are regarded as structured. The work of an assembler may be verified by such means, but the conclusions of a research worker in the social sciences may not be as readily verified. The clarity of the goal and the extent to which it can be communicated to and understood by the members of the group is the second dimension of task structure. Third, multiplicity of available alternate pathways or solutions is significant. Usually there is only one way to correctly assemble a mechanical product, but there are many alternates, perhaps each being equally effective, available to the members of a research and development team in the development of a new product. Finally, there is the specificity of the solution. Most arithmetic problems have only one solution; others, such as a square root have two, a plus and a minus. At the other extreme, problems dealing with human relations, value judgments, and matters of opinion may have as many solutions as there are participants in the group. Consequently the structure of the task itself is a significant factor in determining the effectiveness of leadership.

There is also evidence that the size of the group and the task interact as determinants of leadership effectiveness. There is a positive relationship between both productivity and leader-member relations in those situations consisting of highly structured tasks. A supervisor of a highly structured task is likely to have a better performing group and more cooperation when size makes it unlikely that the supervisor can give close attention to each member of the group. However, when the task is relatively less structured there is no significant difference in size with respect to both productivity and leader-member relations, thus suggesting that the contribution of the supervisor to the members of the group is not particularly significant.[18]

Leader-Member Relationship. There is the personal relationship that exists between the leader and the members of the group that is significant in determining leadership effectiveness. The personality characteristics of a leader are important, but of equal importance are the composition and history of the group. In most formal organizations a group exists prior to the advent of the designated leader. With

---

[18]Robert C. Cummins and Donald C. King, "The Interaction of Group Size and Task Structure in an Industrial Organization," *Personnel Psychology*, Vol. 26, No. 1 (Spring, 1973), pp. 87–94.

legitimacy of position and the position power conferred by the organization, most designated leaders are able to demonstrate some degree of effectiveness. If the leader succeeds in building a strong interpersonal relationship by demonstrating competence and achieving goals and at the same time by supporting the needs and desires of the group, the position is further enhanced, thus making subsequent leadership tasks easier to achieve. At the other extreme of the continuum of leader-member relationships is the mutinous rejection of the leader by the group. Under such conditions the leader has little or no influence upon the actions of the group.

There are several ways of measuring the nature of these leader-member relations. One way is to obtain the leader's rating of the group atmosphere. It is a rating based upon a scale quite similar to the one presented in Case Problem 14-A for the measurement of the characteristics of the least preferred co-worker. A group atmosphere scale appears in Case Problem 14-B. When measuring leader-member relations the leader is asked to describe the group atmosphere rather than the characteristics of the least preferred co-worker. Admittedly, there is the possibility of a difference between the leader's perception of the group and the group's perception of their leader; yet this potential discrepancy does not seem to damage the effectiveness of the measure.

Group-Task Classification

These three characteristics — position power, task structure, leader-member relationships — are shown in Figure 14-2. Note that octants 1, 2, 3, and 4 represent those situations where the leader-member relationships may be termed as good while octants 5, 6, 7, and 8 describe those situations in which leader-member relationships are described as moderately poor. Table 14-1 summarizes the complete classification of group task situations on the basis of the three factors — leader-member relations, task structure, and position power.

Leadership Style

In addition to the task group situations which may be described by any one of the eight octants of Figure 14-2, the leadership style of the leader is also significant as a determinant of leadership effectiveness. Fiedler makes a clear distinction between leadership behavior and leadership style. Leadership behavior includes all the things that a leader might do in a work situation. It would include his efforts in the areas of planning, organizing, structuring the task, and controlling as well as his interpersonal relationships with his subordinates.[19] Leadership style refers to "the underlying need structure of the individual

---

[19]Wofford, *loc. cit.* It will be remembered that Wofford used such a definition in his measurement of the factors contributing to managerial behavior.

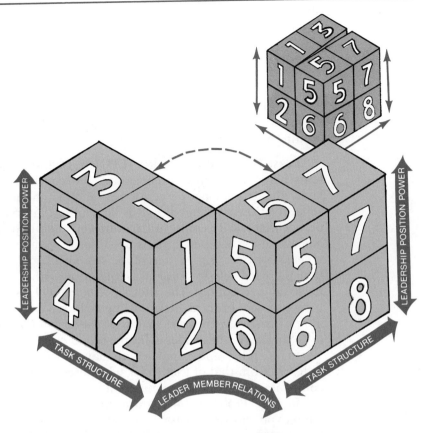

**Figure 14-2
A MODEL FOR
CLASSIFYING
GROUP-TASK
SITUATIONS**

Octant	Leader-Member Relations	Task Structure	Position Power
I	Good	High	Strong
II	Good	High	Weak
III	Good	Weak	Strong
IV	Good	Weak	Weak
V	Moderately poor	High	Strong
VI	Moderately poor	High	Weak
VII	Moderately poor	Weak	Strong
VIII	Moderately poor	Weak	Weak

**Table 14-1
CLASSIFICATION
OF GROUP TASK
SITUATIONS ON
THE BASIS OF
THREE FACTORS**

which motivates his behavior in various leadership situations. Leadership style thus refers to the consistency of goals or needs over different situations."[20]

It is difficult to summarize the terminology that has been used as descriptive of leadership style since the literature concerning leadership is so vast. Yet it seems the style of leadership is described most frequently as being either democratic, participative, supportive, or people oriented on the one hand, or autocratic, directive, or task oriented on the other. Fiedler's measure of leadership style follows a similar bipolar dichotomy.

Least Preferred Co-worker (LPC). In Chapter 13, some of the problems associated with interpersonal perceptions are discussed. We know that a person's perception of another influences their interpersonal relationships. Further, it is known that interpersonal perceptions do not necessarily conform to an objective statement of the situation. Nonetheless, such perceptions are relatively enduring and stable over a period of time; e.g., a stereotype. We also know the kind of behavior that is most likely to occur in conjunction with a certain type of interpersonal perception. The mother who perceives her noisy, ill-mannered, spoiled brats as little darlings will have a smoother interpersonal relationship with them than the mother who perceives them as they are. Similarly, the leader who perceives subordinates as cooperative, warm, friendly, and capable will have an interpersonal relationship different from that of the leader who perceives subordinates as hostile, cold, antagonistic, and incompetent.

In Case Problem 14-A you are asked to describe the person with whom you can work least well, either someone you work with at present or someone that you know from the past. In order to obtain your average LPC score add each of the scaled values that you indicated for each of the 16 traits; then divide by 16 to obtain the average score. A high average LPC score ranges from 4.1 to 5.7 and a low LPC score ranges from 1.2 to 2.2.[21]

Leadership Style and LPC. Persons with a high LPC — those who rate their least preferred co-worker in favorable terms — are people-oriented and are interested in establishing good interpersonal relationships. They are usually more considerate and supportive in their relationships with their subordinates. Those with a low LPC — those who rate their least preferred co-worker in unfavorable terms — are more task-oriented than they are relationship-oriented. They are more punitive toward the inefficient worker, more goal-oriented, and more efficient. Fiedler summarizes the significance of high- and low-LPC scores as follows:

---

[20]Fiedler, *op. cit.*, p. 36.
[21]*Ibid.*, pp. 43–44.

Thus, high-LPC leaders are concerned with having good interpersonal relations and with gaining permanence and self-esteem through these interpersonal relations. Low-LPC leaders are concerned with achieving success on assigned tasks, even at the risk of having poor interpersonal relations with workers. The behaviors of high- and low-LPC leaders will thus be quite different if the situation is such that the satisfaction of their respective needs is threatened. Under these conditions, the high-LPC leader will increase his interpersonal interaction in order to cement his relations with other group members while the low-LPC leaders will interact in order to complete the task successfully. The high-LPC person is concerned with gaining self-esteem through recognition by others, the low-LPC person is concerned with gaining self-esteem through successful performance of the task. Both types of leaders may thus be concerned with the task and both will use interpersonal relationships, although the high-LPC leader will concern himself with a task in order to have successful interpersonal relations, while the low-LPC leader will concern himself with the interpersonal relations in order to achieve task success.[22]

Leadership Style and Effectiveness

In view of the complexity of the task-group situation portrayed in Figure 14-2, it seems highly unlikely that one leadership style would be equally effective in all task situations and with all groups.[23] Figure 14-3 shows how the style of effective leadership varies with the situation. In all cases the groups studied are performing well, and as the task-group situation varies so does the effective style of the leader. Note that for situations described by octants 1, 2, 3, and 8 a controlling, active, structuring form of leadership (low-LPC) is most effective while in situations represented by octants 4, 5, 6, and 7 the relations-oriented (high-LPC) style of leadership appears most effective.

Fiedler's contingency model of leadership effectiveness is presented in considerable detail since it offers a way of showing the interaction between situational factors and the characteristics and needs of the leader, termed leadership style. The model is so constructed and presented that the tentative conclusions shown in Figure 14-3 are subject to verification or modification by subsequent research.[24] To date,

---

[22]*Ibid.*, pp. 45–46.

[23]It is because of the complexity of the task group situation that mixed results concerning the effectiveness of leadership training have been obtained. Fiedler summarizes the effects of leadership training and experience within the context of a contingency model in the following article: Fred E. Fiedler, "The Effect of Leadership Training and Experience: A Contingency Model Interpretation," *Administrative Science Quarterly*, Vol. 17, No. 4 (December, 1972), pp. 453–470.

[24]The following review is highly critical of the contingency model of leadership effectiveness. George Graen, Kenneth Alveris, James B. Orris, and Joseph A. Martella, "Contingency Model of Leadership Effectiveness: Antecedent and Evidential Results," *Psychological Bulletin*, Vol. 74, No. 4 (October, 1970), pp. 285–296.

A more recent criticism of the contingency model appears in the following: J. Timothy McMahon, "The Contingency Theory: Logic and Method Revisited," *Personnel Psychology*, Vol. 25, No. 4 (Winter, 1972), pp. 697–710.

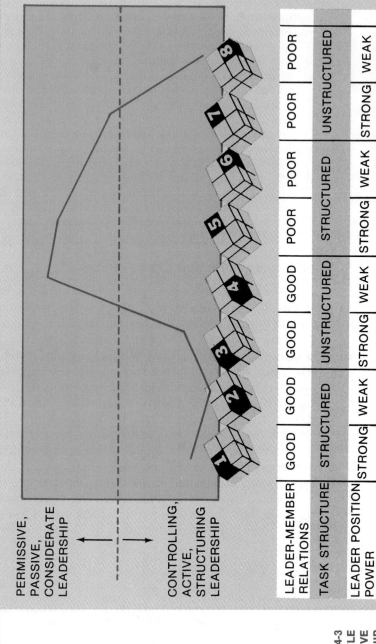

Figure 14-3
**HOW THE STYLE
OF EFFECTIVE
LEADERSHIP
VARIES WITH THE
SITUATION**

PERMISSIVE,
PASSIVE,
CONSIDERATE
LEADERSHIP

←——→

CONTROLLING,
ACTIVE,
STRUCTURING
LEADERSHIP

LEADER-MEMBER RELATIONS	GOOD	GOOD	GOOD	GOOD	POOR	POOR	POOR	POOR
TASK STRUCTURE	STRUCTURED		UNSTRUCTURED		STRUCTURED		UNSTRUCTURED	
LEADER POSITION POWER	STRONG	WEAK	STRONG	WEAK	STRONG	WEAK	STRONG	WEAK

Source: Fred E. Fiedler, "Engineer the Job to Fit the Manager," **Harvard Business Review**, Vol. 43, No. 5 (September–October, 1965), p. 118.

the studies that have been reported are based on interacting groups; little is known of the leadership requirements for co-acting or counteracting groups. Further, the effectiveness of leadership style is based only upon studies that include those with a high-LPC or a low-LPC score. What is the effectiveness of those leaders who have an intermediate LPC score?[25] In spite of these shortcomings, the contingency model of leadership effectiveness provides a useful way of thinking about and analyzing leadership situations.

HOW TO SELECT A LEADERSHIP PATTERN

As indicated, one of the shortcomings of the contingency model of leadership effectiveness in its present state of development is that it reports effectiveness only for those leaders with either a high- or low-LPC score. To this extent it perpetuates the extreme positions discussed in the first part of this chapter, "Theories of Leadership." One of the weaknesses of dichotomizing leadership style into two distinct categories is that we build stereotypes of each style — the inflexible "autocrat" making decisions without regard for human values and the permissive "democrat" working with fully satisfied subordinates. The discussion that follows emphasizes that the leadership style is better described as points along a continuum instead of viewing the style of the leader as falling into one of two dichotomous classifications.

Leadership, a Continuum

Managerial leadership involves much more than the kind of interpersonal relationship between superior and subordinate. The situation must be appraised by the manager with respect to available resources and the possible actions of external forces, such as the action of competitors, labor unions, or governmental agencies. There is also need to assess the capabilities of the personnel of the organization. The nature of the decision or the problem to be solved has to be evaluated, and lastly, the capabilities and personality of the manager influence the type of leadership. With so many factors determining successful executive action, it seems highly unlikely that the interpersonal relationships between superior and subordinate can be neatly classified into one of two categories — autocratic or democratic. Instead, the relationships between the manager and the person or groups being led follow a continuum described by Professors Tannenbaum and Schmidt

---

[25]Fiedler, *op. cit.*, pp. 261–265. In the concluding chapters, Professor Fiedler presents a concise statement of conclusions that may be drawn to date and problems that remain unanswered by a contingency model in its present state of development.

in an article that has now become a classic, "How to Choose a Leadership Pattern."[26] Let us discuss briefly each of the seven gradations of leadership behavior or style as described by Tannenbaum and Schmidt and shown in Figure 14-4.

Manager Able to Make Decision Which Nonmanagers Accept. This form of leadership behavior represents the most autocratic form; i.e., there is little opportunity for the nonmanager to express opinions either in the formulation or the solution of the problem. The manager formulates the problem, solves it, and announces the decision. Coercion, to assure the acceptance and execution of the decision, is not necessarily implied since nonmanagers may be willing to follow such directions. In order for this form of leadership to be either effective or possible, the manager must have a large degree of freedom and the degree of freedom for nonmanagers must be relatively small. In addition, nonmanagers do not have significant power or influence relative to that of the manager.

Manager Must "Sell" Decision Before Gaining Acceptance. At this stage, the manager recognizes the needs of nonmanagers and the possibility that there might be resistance to the initial decision. Consequently, the manager attempts to persuade nonmanagers to recognize the merits of the decision. However, the manager is still in control of all phases of the decision-making process.

Manager Presents Decision But Must Respond to Questions from Nonmanagers. The third form of managerial behavior marks the beginning of a degree of participation on the part of nonmanagers — at least they are being asked to express their ideas. It may result from nonmanagers having increased power and influence, or the degree of freedom for nonmanagers, compared to the manager, has increased. However, the manager has made the decision. Nonetheless, the presentation of a proposal to nonmanagers with the opportunity of their expressing themselves opens up the possibility that the decision may be modified.

Manager Presents Tentative Decision Subject to Change after Nonmanager Inputs. Here, at the midpoint of the range of leadership styles, there is definite participation by nonmanagers in shaping a

---

[26]Robert Tannenbaum and Warren H. Schmidt, "How to Choose a Leadership Pattern," *Harvard Business Review*, Vol. 34 (March-April, 1958), pp. 95–101. Copyright © 1958 by the President and Fellows of Harvard College; all rights reserved.

"How to Choose a Leadership Pattern" was again published as a *Harvard Business Review* Classic in the following issue: *Harvard Business Review*, Vol 51, No. 3 (May-June, 1973), pp. 162–180. Also included is a retrospective commentary prepared by Professors Tannenbaum and Schmidt fifteen years after the publication of their original article. In the 1958 article manager-subordinate relationships were discussed. The 1973 commentary uses the terms "managers" and "nonmanagers," thereby including nonmanagerial personnel in other organizations such as competitors, labor unions, and governmental agencies.

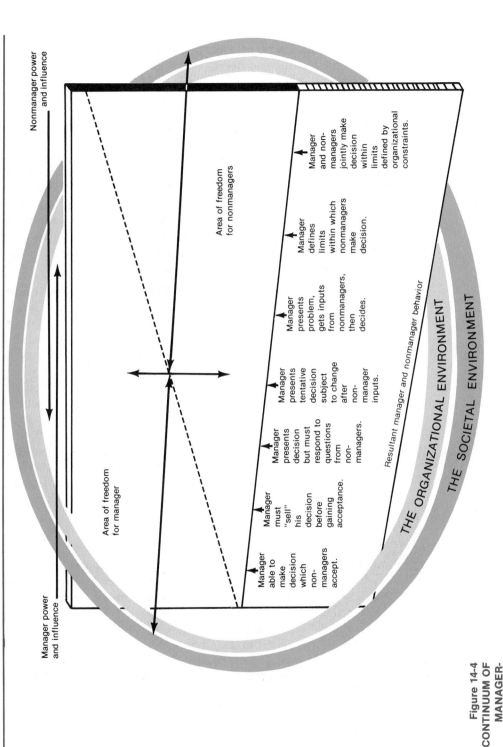

Figure 14-4
CONTINUUM OF MANAGER-NONMANAGER BEHAVIOR

Nonmanager power and influence

Manager power and influence

Area of freedom for nonmanagers

Area of freedom for manager

Manager and nonmanagers jointly make decision within limits defined by organizational constraints.

Manager defines limits within which nonmanagers make decision.

Manager presents problem, gets inputs from nonmanagers, then decides.

Manager presents tentative decision subject to change after nonmanager inputs.

Manager presents decision but must respond to questions from nonmanagers.

Manager must "sell" his decision before gaining acceptance.

Manager able to make decision which nonmanagers accept.

Resultant manager and nonmanager behavior

THE ORGANIZATIONAL ENVIRONMENT

THE SOCIETAL ENVIRONMENT

Source: Robert Tannebaum and Warren H. Schmidt, "How to Choose a Leadership Pattern," **Harvard Business Review**, Vol. 51, No. 3 (May–June, 1973), p. 167. Copyright© 1973 by the President and Fellows of Harvard College; all rights reserved.

final decision. Although the manager's decision is tentative, the manager still defines the problem and works out the initial solution.

Manager Presents Problem, Gets Input from Nonmanagers, Then Decides. Up to this point the decision is made by the manager with varying degrees of participation and input on the part of nonmanagers in influencing the final decision. Although the manager still defines the problem in general terms, consultation with nonmanagers prior to making a tentative decision increases the number of possible solutions.

Manager Defines Limits Within Which Nonmanagers Make Decision. Gradation Six is the first instance in which nonmanagers make the decision. It may be the result of increased degrees of freedom or increased power and influence for nonmanagers; or it may be the result of less power and influence and a smaller degree of freedom on the part of the manager. However, the manager still states the problem and the limits within which the decision must be made. Usually these limits are expressed in terms of cost, time, or feasibility.

Manager and Nonmanagers Jointly Make Decision Within Limits Defined by Organizational Constraints. The last stage of the relationship between managers and nonmanagers represents the maximum degree of nonmanagerial participation within formal organizations. The manager is limited in the extent to which participation may be permitted by both intra-organizational and inter-organizational factors. The same constraints are placed upon nonmanagers especially when they are members of other organizations. They, too, have organizational constraints within which they must operate. Typical of the situations in which decisions are jointly made are those between managers and nonmanagers (who are managers in their own organizations) representing labor unions or governmental agencies. When the manager and nonmanagers are members of the same organization the decisions are usually made within limits consistent with organizational policy and objectives.[27]

Determinants of Effective Leadership

Tannenbaum and Schmidt, as outlined above, suggest that there are forces in the manager, in nonmanagers, and in the situation, including society external to the organization, that must be weighed in order to select the most effective form of leadership style. In addition, it is well established that it is wise to differentiate between managerial leadership, defining leadership as an interpersonal relationship, and managerial behavior which includes the functions of planning, organizing, and controlling in addition to the function of leading. Thus, the

---

[27]For a similar taxonomy of leadership behavior see Victor H. Vroom, Chapter 34, "Leadership," pp. 1527–1551. This article appears in Marvin D. Dunnette (ed.), *Handbook of Industrial and Organizational Psychology* (Chicago: Rand McNally College Publishing Co., 1976).

most effective form of leadership in a given situation is a combination of the proper interpersonal behavior (leadership style) between manager and subordinates or other nonmanagers and managerial behavior in executing the processes of planning, organizing, and controlling.

Case Problem 14-B offers an opportunity to test the contingency model of leadership effectiveness. For those of you who now hold a position of leadership, the model may provide insights that will enable you to improve your leadership effectiveness. For those not presently in a position of leadership, the contingency model may provide you with a better understanding of those situations in which you served as a subordinate.

Case Problem 14-B
PREDICTING LEADERSHIP EFFECTIVENESS

In Case Problem 14-A you completed a rating form descriptive of your least preferred co-worker. It is also a measure from which certain inferences may be drawn concerning your style of leadership. Criteria for evaluating the structure of a task are discussed on page 337. Using Fiedler's Contingency Model of Leadership Effectiveness as a guide, there are two further measures necessary for the prediction of leader effectiveness in a given situation. One of these is leader-member relations, a relationship that can be inferred by the leader's rating of group atmosphere. The other measure, the leader's position power, is found by completing a checklist of items descriptive of the power of the position. These instruments are included as Exhibits II and III for you to complete.

Describe the atmosphere of your group by checking the following items.

8   7   6   5   4   3   2   1

1. Friendly   :___:___:___:___:___:___:___: Unfriendly

2. Accepting   :___:___:___:___:___:___:___: Rejecting

3. Satisfying   :___:___:___:___:___:___:___: Frustrating

4. Enthusiastic :___:___:___:___:___:___:___: Unenthusiastic

5. Productive   :___:___:___:___:___:___:___: Nonproductive

6. Warm   :___:___:___:___:___:___:___: Cold

7. Cooperative :___:___:___:___:___:___:___: Uncooperative

8. Supportive   :___:___:___:___:___:___:___: Hostile

9. Interesting   :___:___:___:___:___:___:___: Boring

10. Successful   :___:___:___:___:___:___:___: Unsuccessful

Exhibit II
GROUP
ATMOSPHERE
SCALE

Source: Fred E. Fiedler, *A Theory Of Leadership Effectiveness* (New York: McGraw-Hill Book Co., 1967), p. 269.

1. Compliments from the leader are appreciated more than compliments from other group members.

2. Compliments are highly valued, criticisms are considered damaging.

3. Leader can recommend punishments and rewards.

4. Leader can punish or reward members of his own accord.

5. Leader can effect (or can recommend) promotion or demotion.

6. Leader chairs or coordinates group but may or may not have other advantages, i.e., is appointed or acknowledged chairman or leader.

7. Leader's opinion is accorded considerable respect and attention.

8. Leader's special knowledge or information (and members' lack of it) permits leader to decide how task is to be done or how group is to proceed.

9. Leader cues member or instructs them on what to do.

10. Leader tells or directs members what to do or what to say.

11. Leader is expected to motivate group.

12. Leader is expected to suggest and evaluate the members' work.

13. Leader has superior or special knowledge about the job, or has special instructions but requires members to do job.

14. Leader can supervise each member's job and evaluate it or correct it.

15. Leader knows his own as well as members' job and could finish the work himself if necessary, e.g., writing a report for which all information is available.

16. Leader enjoys special or official rank and status in real life which sets him apart from or above group members, e.g., military rank or elected office in a company or organization. (+5 points)

17. Leader is given special or official rank by experimenter to simulate for role-playing purposes, e.g., "You are a general" or "the manager." This simulated rank must be clearly superior to members' rank and must not be just that of "chairman" or "group leader" of the group during its work period. (+3 points)

18. Leader's position is dependent on members; members can replace or depose leader. (−5 points)

Exhibit III
MEASURE OF
POSITION POWER

Note: The dimension of leader position power is defined by the above checklist in which all "true" items are given 1 point, except for items 16, 17, and 18, which are weighted +5, +3, and −5 points respectively.
Source: Fred E. Fiedler, *A Theory of Leadership Effectiveness* (New York: McGraw-Hill Book Co., 1967), p. 24.

1. Recall some recent task-oriented situation in which you had a position of leadership. Rate this situation regarding group atmosphere and the power accorded the position. Now, rate the task in accordance with the criteria presented in the text in Figure 14-3. How well does the model predict the effectiveness of your leadership? Discuss.

2. If you are unable to recall a situation in which you had a position of leadership, describe the task, the position power, and the group atmosphere from your position as a subordinate. It will be necessary for you to assume the style of the leader. Again, prepare a model containing all of the information presented in Figure 14-3. Does the model predict the effectiveness of leadership as it actually occurred? Discuss.

CHAPTER QUESTIONS FOR STUDY AND DISCUSSION

1. Do you believe that there has ever been a successful organization that was entirely work centered or entirely people centered? Why?
2. Much of the literature of management equates management with leadership. Do you believe that managing is necessarily leading? Discuss.
3. From your own experience describe a manager (or a teacher) whom you would characterize as typifying the scientific management approach to leadership. Describe one who typifies the human relations approach. Which one was more effective? Why?
4. How would you describe the revisionists' approaches to leadership?
5. What are some of the characteristics of leadership as revealed by the trait approach to the study of leadership? What are the shortcomings of this approach?
6. Describe a business situation that supports the situational aspects of leadership.
7. Certain positions in an organization, such as the presidency, carry with them a traditional prestige. Could this be considered similar to a situational factor? How?
8. What is meant by a *contingency* model? Evaluate fully Fiedler's Contingency Model of Leadership Effectiveness. Does it successfully integrate the trait and situational approaches to leadership?
9. Why is there a need for flexibility in leadership patterns?
10. Give an example illustrating how a manager of a given organization interacts with a nonmanager of the same organization at Stage 7, Manager and Nonmanagers Jointly Make Decision Within Limits Defined by Organizational Constraints.
11. Compare the same stage (Stage 7) using a manager of Organization A interacting with a nonmanager of Organization A who is at the same time a manager of Organization B. Discuss the possible effects resulting from the power and influence possessed by each manager in their respective organizations.

Chapter 15

Communications

Case Problem 15-A

A MESSAGE FOR MANAGEMENT

Regina Osterman, president of Federated Manufacturing Company, recognizes the importance of keeping employees informed about the economic problems of the company. She realizes that her company is entering a difficult competitive period resulting from a steady decline in prices. Osterman knows that she must lower prices in order to retain her share of the market.

She believes that her monthly letter, entitled *From The President's Desk*, which is sent to all employees, is adequate as a means of transmitting information. However, when a major crisis arises, she summons all department heads to the austere oak-paneled board room, an action which, in her opinion, assures them that they are a part of management and participating in major decisions. The established protocol for these meetings requires that all attending personnel be seated prior to the scheduled time and that they arise when Mrs. Osterman enters the room and remain standing until asked to be seated again. Regina Osterman has made her entrance and has indicated by a curt nod of her head that all may be seated.

"I have called you together to explain our dire economic situation. We are face to face with competitive wolves who are snapping at our heels. They are making us sell at prices which are too low and delivery schedules that are utterly impossible to meet. If this great company of ours — one of the bulwarks of free enterprise — is to survive, we must all pitch in and pull together. Let me tell you what I mean."

Following her opening remarks, Regina Osterman glared at everyone in the room as though she were daring them to speak. No one spoke, since all knew that any expression of opinion would be classified as negative thinking by Mrs. Osterman.

"First, what we need here is imagineering. We need positive thinkers and everyone has to play on the same team. We have to optimize production and nothing can be left out of account when we are considering cost reduction. To implement this crash program of cost reduction, I have gone outside the company and hired a top-drawer production manager.

"The second thing we have to do is maximize quality. Quality means everything in this business. Every machine has to be inspected on a regular schedule by the supervisor of the department and when that machine starts up in production, it means that the supervisor has given it the stamp of approval. Nothing is too small to overlook when we are thinking of quality.

"Third on my list of items deserving serious consideration is beefing up our sales force. Customers are the lifeblood of this business, and even though they are not always right, they still must be handled with kid gloves. Our sales representatives have to learn how to put themselves across and make every call count. Our method of compensating sales representatives is eminently fair, but even so, we're going to try to sweeten the pot by upping the commission rates on slow-moving items. We would do it across the board, but we have to hold the line on costs.

"The last thing on my list is teamwork. This we need more than anything else. Unless we all pull together, we can't make it. Leadership is teamwork, and teamwork is striving and straining for the same goal. You are the representatives of management, you are the leaders, and you know what our goals are. Now let's all put our shoulders to the wheel and wrap up the whole ball of wax immediately. Remember, we're one big happy family."

As Regina Osterman concluded, all arose and stood by their chairs while she gathered her papers and left the board room through the connecting door to her office.

PROBLEMS

1. What was the purpose of this meeting?
2. What is Regina Osterman trying to say? Rewrite her remarks in simple, direct language. Do you think that her analysis was correct?
3. What factors besides language cause a communication barrier in this case problem?
4. How would you arrange the above meeting to assure two-way communication?

The word, communication, as it is used in management literature has two distinct, yet compatible, meanings. One of these meanings emphasizes the dissemination of information and is commonly referred to as formal communication. The other meaning of the term refers to interpersonal communications between two or more people. Interpersonal communications transmit much more than information since psychological needs, motives, and feelings are often revealed that may be in conflict with the expressed verbal message.

Since formal communication is based on the science of semantics, we examine some of the fundamental concepts of semantics. Next, formal communications are considered, then problems inherent in interpersonal communications are examined, and lastly, the means of improving both formal and interpersonal communications are discussed.

THE MEANING OF MEANING

Communication is defined in its broadest sense as *the transmission of meaning to others*. However, the definition as it now stands does not mean or signify much, since two words used in the definition — *transmission* and *meaning* — need further elaboration. The word *transmission* as used in the definition is broad and does not limit the methods of communication to the use of language in either spoken or written form. The word *meaning* is also broad. It includes information consisting not only of facts and descriptive statements of objects and other people but also attitudes and feelings that may be conveyed to others. For purposeful communications, such as those in a formal organization, it is necessary to restrict our definition further by stating that communication is the transmission of *intended* meaning to others. The above restriction implies that the sender of the communication has a clear concept of the meaning to be conveyed; and in order for the communication to be purposeful, the receiver must interpret the message in such a manner that the intended meaning is received.

The scientific study of meaning is known as *semantics*, a word derived from the Greek term, *semantikos*, which means significant. Semantics is concerned with the relationship between (1) objects and/or events, (2) the thought processes involved in interpreting these objects and/or events, and (3) the signs and/or symbols used to express a given thought or to describe a specific object or event. First, let us discuss these three aspects of semantics and then apply the lessons learned in analyzing Case Problem 15-A.

The Triangle of Meaning

The relationship between objects and events, their interpretation, and the development of signs and symbols are shown in Figure 15-1, The Triangle of Meaning.[1] Objects and events are known as the *referent*; thoughts, interpretations, and emotions are called the *reference*; and devices used to express the reference are called *signs* or *symbols*.

The following example shows the relationship between a referent, a reference, and the way in which meaning is attached to a sign or a symbol. The object in question is taken from the ocean; it is elliptical in shape, three inches long, an inch and one half in width, an inch thick. The surface is a rough, brown, shell-like substance. Three persons are observing (thinking about) this object. One of them, a scientist, recognizes the object immediately and labels it a bivalve mollusk of the genus *Ostrea*. The second observer "sees" a dozen such objects

---

[1]C. K. Ogden and I. A. Richards, *The Meaning of Meaning* (8th ed.; New York: Harcourt, Brace & Co., 1956). *The Meaning of Meaning*, first published in 1923, still stands as one of the basic works in the field of semantics. Figure 15-1 is adapted from a figure on page 11 entitled Thoughts, Words, and Things. *The Meaning of Meaning* is a good reference for the serious study of semantics.

The following references are also suggested:

Alfred Korzybski, *Science and Sanity*, An Introduction to Non-Aristotelian Systems and General Semantics (4th ed.; Lancaster: Science Press Printing Co., Distributors for the International Non-Aristotelian Library Publishing Co., 1958). Count Korzybski, a mathematician, applies general semantics to all fields of science as they existed in 1933. *Science and Sanity* is recommended only for the advanced student.

Samuel I. Hayakawa, *Language in Thought and Action* (2d ed.; New York: Harcourt, Brace & World, 1964).

William V. Haney, *Communication and Organizational Behavior* (3d ed.; Homewood: Richard D. Irwin, 1973).

Anatol Rapoport, "What is Semantics?" *The Use and Misuse of Language*, edited by S. I. Hayakawa (Greenwich: Fawcett Publications, 1974).

Bess Selzer Sondel, *The Humanity of Words* (Cleveland: World Publishing Co., 1958).

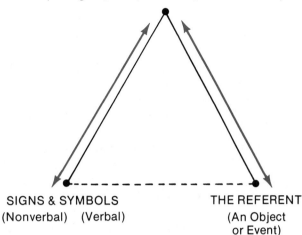

THE REFERENCE
(Thoughts, Interpretations, and Emotions)

SIGNS & SYMBOLS
(Nonverbal)   (Verbal)

THE REFERENT
(An Object
or Event)

**Figure 15-1
THE TRIANGLE
OF MEANING**

on the half shell ringing a platter full of ice; to him it is an object to be eaten, an oyster. The third person takes one look, grimaces, turns pale, and leaves the room. All have seen the same object, yet three distinct meanings are reflected in their labeling of the object. The scientist uses the symbol, bivalve mollusk of the genus *Ostrea*, to label the object; to that individual it is one more form of marine life to be classified in relation to other forms of life. To the person who calls it an oyster, the object is food and a source of delight. However, the third person does not use a symbol (word) to label the object. Instead, there is an eloquent expression of the interpretation of the meaning of the object by the signs of grimacing, becoming pale, and leaving the room — the object is a source of disgust.

Let us examine each element of the triangle in greater detail.

Signs and Symbols. Signs and symbols, the left-hand base of the triangle (Figure 15-1), are the labels used to initiate a particular thought, or reference, with regard to a specific referent. The two terms, signs (nonverbal) and symbols (verbal), are used to emphasize that communication is not dependent upon language. There is no intrinsic meaning in the color red, yet a red light as part of a traffic signal means that one must stop; but when used as a running light on a boat, red indicates the port side. Likewise, silence on the part of a supervisor may express disapproval as effectively as a dozen words. Status in an organization is conveyed almost entirely by signs; for example, a carpeted office, special parking privileges, punching a time clock, and the hour at which one reports for work all designate status.

Note that the base of the triangle is a dotted line and that the two sides of the triangle are solid. There is a direct relationship between the referent that calls up a certain thought and between the thought and the symbol used in its expression. Similarly, there is a direct relationship between symbol and thought and between thought and referent. There is, however, no such direct relationship between the label (symbol) and the object itself. The label, either a sign or a word, is *not* the object; it is used only to identify a specific object. Labels are arbitrary, and to be meaningful they must establish the same reference (thought) in both the sender and the receiver of a communication. Yet, one of the most common causes of misunderstanding results from filling in the base of the triangle and assuming that the label is the referent. Loyalty oaths are a good example of filling in the base of the triangle. The act of signing an oath does not make one loyal; yet, the assumption underlying such oaths is an identity between loyalty and the act of signing an oath.

Verbal symbols vary considerably with respect to their value as tools for communication. All words are abstractions; they are not the object or event itself. As words become more abstract; i.e., further removed from the specific object or event, their meanings become more difficult to transmit and their value as instruments for communication decreases. Words as names of things may be classified as follows:

1. *Names for objects* are a table, a chair, a milling machine, a lathe, an automobile, a truck, a machinist, and a clerk. When naming an object, we are at a relatively low level of abstraction, and there should not be too much misunderstanding since the referent may be seen and touched, and its characteristics may be detailed with a high degree of accuracy.

2. *Events* are more complex in their nature since action and time, in addition to an object, are implied. A table turning over, a milling machine cutting metal, a moving automobile, and a machinist reporting late for work are all statements of events — something happening to a specific object at a specified time.

3. Labels may be used to designate *clusters*, *groups*, or *collections of objects or events* which are composed of elements that have varying degrees of similarity. We refer to furniture, machine tools, motor vehicles, and employees.

4. At the highest level of abstraction, the referent may not be an object or event at all; instead, the referent is an *essence* or *value judgment* of an object or event. The furniture is described as beautiful, machine tools are valuable, motor vehicles are either necessities or luxuries, and the employee is lazy (the machinist reported late for work). Also in this category of high-order abstractions are such labels as democracy, free enterprise, truth, and honesty.

Reference and Referent. There are at least two persons involved in communication — a sender and a receiver. Symbols should create within the receiver a thought process (call it a mental image, if you wish) that leads the receiver down the right-hand side of the triangle to the desired referent. Conversation has been described as the art of saying something when there is nothing to be said. In contrast, communication is saying something when there is something to be said and saying it clearly. The purpose of communication is to influence the behavior of another person. Behavioral changes may consist of additional knowledge, a change in attitude, or action on the part of the receiver. Conversation takes place almost entirely on the left side of the triangle, from symbol to thought and back to another symbol again. There is no need for a common meaning between sender and receiver because the purpose of conversation is merely to occupy time. In communication, however, there is a purpose; and in order for the intended meaning to reach the receiver, both sender and receiver must travel the same route around the triangle from symbol, to reference, to referent.

A Semantic Analysis

A great deal can be told about how much meaning is transmitted through a given communication by answering these questions:

1. What is the purpose of the communication?
2. Do the symbols used by the sender have a precise meaning understandable to the receiver?

Let us ask these two questions in our semantic analysis of Case Problem 15-A, A Message for Management. At the same time we must keep in mind the triangle of meaning — symbol, reference, and referent.

What Is the Purpose of the Communication? Before there can be any communication, the sender must determine the purpose of the communication. Why has Regina Osterman called her department heads together? In the first paragraph of her talk, she states that she has called them together to explain "our dire economic situation." She closes her opening remarks with the statement that she is going to explain what she means. Apparently, Osterman is trying to state four things that the company needs in order to survive the dire economic situation. These needs are imagineering, which she does not define; instead, she talks about cost reduction. The second need is quality, the third is beefing up the sales force, and the last is teamwork. The conclusion is inescapable; Osterman is not sure of what she wants to say or why she wants to explain an economic condition to her department heads.

The purpose of the meeting is not to explain; instead, it is to influence or modify the behavior of the department heads — to change their actions so that the company may make a profit and at the same time lower the prices of its product to the level established by competition. Information concerning the actions of competitors and the development of attitudes resulting in teamwork and effective leadership are necessary if management is to do its job well. The purpose of the meeting is to change behavior.

Do the Symbols Have a Precise Meaning for the Receiver? Look at the first paragraph of Osterman's speech again. It is filled with abstractions having no precise meaning. She starts with a high-order abstraction, "dire economic situation," and does not bother to define what she means. Somehow she manages to drag into her remarks "The bulwarks of free enterprise," again without definition. Further, her use of metaphors indicates that she is not thinking clearly. How can she be "face to face with wolves snapping at her heels?" Prices are too low, but what does too low mean? If the delivery schedules are utterly impossible, how does the company manage to stay in business? The remainder of her talk is nothing but a collection of worn-out, meaningless words and phrases. What is "imagineering"? What is "positive thinking"? Are they going to play on the same team or are they working for the same company? What does she mean by "beefing up" the sales force? Does she want the sales representatives to gain weight? Is leadership teamwork? If so, leadership is striving and straining for the same goals. How does one simultaneously "put her shoulder to the wheel" and "wrap up a ball of wax"?

Regina Osterman is having a wonderful time running up and down the left-hand side of the triangle — from symbol to reference and back to symbol without once attempting to go down the right-hand side of the triangle to a common referent. To some of you, Osterman's *Message for Management* may seem overdrawn and exaggerated. It is not. It is hoped that you will not have to sit through many such meetings as a member of management and that you *never* conduct a meeting as Regina Osterman did. Remember this case as an example of how *not* to communicate.

The above analysis of A Message for Management answers two questions. When the questions are recast as statements, they form a guide for effective communication.

For effective communication the sender must determine the purpose of the communication and use symbols having the same meaning for sender and receiver.

The following guides are presented to aid in developing effective communication:

1. Determine and state the purpose of the communication.
2. Develop a plan of presentation. Consider the information to be transmitted and the interests and abilities of the receiver.
3. Eliminate unnecessary words.

4. Use words known to the receiver. Establish the meaning of abstractions by referring to objects and events within the experience range of the receiver.[2]

FORMAL COMMUNICATIONS

Although the transmission of intended meaning is the central problem in formal communications, there are areas other than the lack of agreement on intended meaning that contribute to communication problems. For example, in Chapter 6, Management Information Systems, the functions and characteristics of information systems are discussed. Case Problem 6-A, The Parable of the Spindle, describes an information system used in a restaurant and shows the positive relationships between system design and effective communication. Prior to the introduction of the spindle the system was inadequate with the result that there was a complete breakdown in communications. Also in Chapter 6, Figure 6-1, Anatomy of Management Information, necessary planning and control information is shown pictorially. In addition to formal management information systems, usually utilizing electronic data processing, there are other forms of formal communications available to the manager. One of the difficulties in formal communication is that all too often managers are not aware of the media available for communication; hence, a brief analysis of commonly used media is presented.[3]

Communication Media

Communication media within a company may be classified either with respect to the method used to transmit information or according

---

[2]It is beyond the scope of this book to develop a manual of style. The following references are presented for students who want additional help in improving their ability to express their thoughts clearly:

George Orwell, "Politics and English Language," *Shooting an Elephant and Other Essays* (New York: Harcourt, Brace and World, 1950). Reprinted in Norman R. F. Maier *et al.*, *Superior-Subordinate Communication in Management* (New York: American Management Association, 1961), AMA Research Study 52, pp. 78–88. Orwell's essay is one of six presented in the AMA research study. Orwell presents six rules for clarity of expression and although his essay is concerned primarily with the language of politics, it is applicable to all subject matter. The annotations of George H. Hass provide many examples of hackneyed expressions used in business communications.

William Strunk, Jr., and E. B. White, *The Elements of Style* (New York: MacMillan Co., 1959). *The Elements of Style* deals with English usage and style. Professor Strunk had the book privately printed and for many years used it in his English classes at Cornell University. The 1959 edition, revised by E. B. White, includes a chapter on how to write. *The Elements of Style*, dubbed "the little book" by Professor Strunk, reduces English rhetoric to 18 rules with examples of correct and incorrect usage to illustrate each rule.

[3]For a discussion of new approaches to the study of communication, both formal and interpersonal, the following is recommended: Richard V. Farace and Donald MacDonald, "New Directions in the Study of Organizational Communication," *Personnel Psychology*, Vol. 27, No. 1 (Spring, 1974), pp. 1–19.

to the directional flow of the communication. Using the means of transmission as a basis for classifying media, communications are either *written* or *oral*. When directional flow is the basis for classification — defining direction in terms of the organizational hierarchy — communications flow *downward*, *upward*, *horizontally*, and *diagonally*. Examples of written and oral communications are discussed briefly below.

Written Communications. Letters, memos, and reports are examples of written communications used to transmit information either downward, upward, or horizontally within an organization. Formal statements of policies, procedures, and methods are designed primarily for downward communications. Bulletin boards, house organs, annual reports, and handbooks are also directed downward. Written grievances, suggestion systems, and union publications serve as a means of upward communication. The information gained from attitude and morale surveys provides another means of directing information to higher levels of the organization. Letters and memos between department heads are examples of the horizontal or diagonal flow of communications. The distribution of carbon copies of written materials to all interested parties may be used as a means of directing information in several directions at one time.

Oral Communications. Even though a business may consume tons of paper during the course of a year in written communications, by far the greater percentage of information is transmitted by informal oral communications, either face to face or by telephone. Oral communications may involve as few as two people or as many as hundreds attending a training session or conference. All oral communication offers the potential of two-way information flow; and, depending on the relative organizational positions of the participants, the communication may be directed either vertically or horizontally. Most members of an organization prefer oral to written communications because they seem quicker and offer an immediate feedback in the form of questions and expressions of approval or disapproval. The advantages of speed and feedback may be more imagined than real, since oral messages are notoriously subject to misinterpretation and to the effects of barriers arising from interpersonal relationships.[4]

INTERPERSONAL COMMUNICATIONS

Thus far the discussion has been directed to one of the meanings of communication, the dissemination of information, with the emphasis upon the type of information needed. Interpersonal communications

---

[4]Keith Davis, "Success of Chain-of-Command Oral Communication in a Manufacturing Management Group," *Academy of Management Journal*, Vol. 11, No. 4 (December, 1968), pp. 379–387.

permit not only the transfer of information but also the expression of psychological needs and motives. Superior-subordinate communications are considered first with an assessment of the degree of understanding and the common barriers to effective communications that exist between superior and subordinate. Next, some of the problems encountered in horizontal communications are reviewed; and finally, the ubiquitous grapevine and its role are examined.

Superior-Subordinate Communication

It is generally assumed that superior-subordinate communication operates as a two-way information system permitting a free flow of information upward as well as downward. Yet, there are barriers in the superior-subordinate relationship that markedly interfere with free two-way flow of information. Before discussing these barriers, it is well to determine the effectiveness of superior-subordinate communication in a relatively objective and limited area — in relation to a subordinate's job.

Superior-Subordinate Understanding. In an early study the American Management Association conducted a statistical research project to determine the extent of agreement between superior and subordinate concerning the subordinate's specific job duties.[5] Fifty-eight superior-subordinate combinations from the upper management levels of five different companies were selected for this study, and the information from both members of each pair was obtained by patterned depth interviews. The following specific areas of the subordinate's job were discussed:

1. Job duties — a descriptive statement of what the subordinate does in the performance of his job.
2. Job requirements — a statement of the skills, background, experience, formal training, and personal characteristics needed for the job.
3. Future changes in job duties — anticipated changes in either job duties or requirements that might be anticipated in the next several years.
4. Obstacles in the performance of the job — problems that interfere with getting the job done, as seen by the subordinate and as viewed by the superior.

---

[5]Norman R. F. Maier *et al.*, *Superior-Subordinate Communication in Management* (New York: American Management Association, 1961), AMA Research Study 52. In addition to the presentation and interpretation of the statistical results of the study, there are six interpretative comments on the project and its findings in Part 2 of the report.
Another study designed specifically to complement the American Management Association study and one which yields the same basic results is the following: Bradford B. Boyd and J. Michael Jensen, "Perceptions of the First-Line Supervisor's Authority: A Study in Superior-Subordinate Communication," *Academy of Management Journal*, Vol. 15, No. 3 (September, 1972), pp. 331–342. Boyd and Jensen note that the American Management Association study is the only published work prior to their study dealing with communications within management itself.

The results of the study are presented in Table 15-1. An analysis of Table 15-1 shows that 85 percent of the pairs interviewed agree on one half or more of the subordinate's job duties (Columns 2, 3, 4), but the extent of the agreement with respect to subordinate qualifications drops to 63.7 percent. Only 53.3 percent of superiors and subordinates agree upon anticipated changes in the subordinate's job within the next few years. In interpreting the obstacles in the way of subordinate success, 68.2 percent showed either no agreement or agreement on less than half of the obstacles. The following is a narrative summary of the study by the authors:

> If a single answer can be drawn from this detailed research study into superior-subordinate communication on the managerial level in business, it is this: If one is speaking of the subordinate's specific job — his duties, the requirements he must fulfill in order to do his work well, his intelligent anticipation of future changes in his work, and the obstacles which prevent him from doing as good a job as is possible — the answer is that he and his boss do not agree, or differ more than they agree, in almost every area. Also, superior and subordinate very often disagree about priorities — they simply don't see eye to eye on which are the most important and the least important tasks for the subordinate.[6]

Barriers to Communication. The effect of communication barriers, whether they arise from semantic problems or from one of the specific superior-subordinate relationships discussed below, results in either a

	0 Almost No Agreement on Topics	1 Agreement on Less Than Half the Topics	2 Agreement on About Half the Topics	3 Agreement on More Than Half the Topics	4 Agreement on All or Almost All Topics
Job Duties..............	3.4%	11.6%	39.1%	37.8%	8.1%
Job Requirement (Subordinate's Qualifications)......	7.0%	29.3%	40.9%	20.5%	2.3%
Future Changes in Subordinate's Job	35.4%	14.3%	18.3%	16.3%	18.7%
Obstacles in the Way of Subordinate's Performance	38.4%	29.8%	23.6%	6.4%	1.7%

Table 15-1 COMPARATIVE AGREEMENT BETWEEN SUPERIOR-SUBORDINATE PAIRS ON BASIC AREAS OF THE SUBORDINATE'S JOB

Source: Norman R. F. Maier *et al., Superior-Subordinate Communication in Management* (New York: American Management Association, 1961), AMA Research Study 52, p. 10.

[6]Maier *et al, op. cit.*, p. 9.

distortion of meaning because of embellishment or a filtering of information by suppression or withholding. Semantic barriers usually result in a distortion of meaning. Distortion also occurs as the result of introducing errors into a message. Filtering information results in only a part of the message getting through. Filtering of communications by either the sender or the receiver of the message may be intentional or unintentional. The following barriers are frequently found in superior-subordinate communications; nonetheless, remember that these same barriers may occur in any two-way personal communication.

Semantic Problems. One barrier to communication, not limited to superior-subordinate relationships, is a semantic problem — determining a common referent and meaning for the symbols used in communication. In the research study described above, descriptions of the subordinate's job, of necessity, require the use of high-order abstractions. These are middle management jobs and, unlike operative jobs, they cannot be described as movements to be completed in a given sequence. Judgment, the interpretation of data, anticipation of future events, and skill in interpersonal relations are the important requisites for managerial jobs, and all of these characteristics are abstractions. Rudolf Flesch, in his comment on the study, believes that the problem of superior-subordinate communication as presented in Table 15-1 presents a somewhat exaggerated view of the inability of superior and subordinate to communicate effectively.[7] According to Flesch, who interpreted the same data, the lack of agreement is no greater than what might be expected when the subject is abstract and viewed from two entirely different positions; i.e., superior and subordinate. In brief, Flesch is saying that to some extent the results of the study are due to the methodology used in the study.

Status. Another barrier arises from the relative positions of the superior and subordinate in the organization. There is a strong tendency in formal organizations to express hierarchical rank through the use of signs known as status symbols. Status symbols within an organization, such as a better type of office furniture, may be deliberate as an attempt to reinforce the superior's position of authority. However, too much emphasis upon status may increase a subordinate's perception of organizational distance and consequently widen the communication gap between subordinate and superior.

Pressure of Time. In business organizations the pressure of time plays an important role as a communication barrier. The busy superior with many subordinates simply does not have the time to see all of them as frequently or to talk with them as fully as might be desired. Also, busy subordinates do not have the time nor the inclination to

---

[7]*Ibid.,* "Is the Problem Exaggerated?" pp. 60–67. Flesch discusses the results of the study as a semantic problem.

report every detail of every problem to their superiors. Supporting the subordinate's position is the concept of delegation. Responsibilities have been assigned, and the authority to fulfill these responsibilities has been delegated. In addition, accountability to one's superior has been established. It might be argued quite properly that as the effectiveness of the process of delegation increases, the need for detailed communication between superior and subordinate decreases. The pressure of time and the presence of an effective delegation process may decrease the amount and frequency of superior-subordinate communication; but even so, communication may be more than adequate because information necessary for the operation of the business is being transmitted.

Value Judgments. Making value judgments of a message prior to receiving the entire communication interferes with receiving the intended meaning of the message. A value judgment is the assignment of overall worth to a message and may be based upon its origin, its reliability, or its anticipated meaning. When value judgments are made too hastily, the receiver hears only that part of the message that he wishes to hear. Closely related to hearing only selected parts of a message is the lack of sensitivity to the emotional content of the communication, which is often reflected by the mannerisms and tone of voice of the sender. In many instances the real message is conveyed not by the words of the sender, but by the emotions and feelings accompanying the expression of the message.

Subordinate's Mobility. A specific characteristic of the superior-subordinate communications is the dependency relationship of subordinates upon their superiors for advancement within the organization — either more pay for the present position or attaining a higher position. Several studies support the hypothesis that the more a subordinate desires to advance in an organization, the greater the tendency to filter information sent upward to one's superior. If the subordinate desires to advance, only good news and the positive aspects of achievement are sent upward. Problem-oriented aspects of the subordinate's work are suppressed or filtered. It has also been reported that the amount and nature of the information transmitted upward, even by the subordinate strongly desiring advancement, is influenced greatly by the degree of trust subordinates have toward their superiors and the extent of perceived influence of superiors. As trust in the judgment and understanding of one's superior increases, and as the perceived influence of that superior on the subordinate becomes greater, the amount of problem-oriented information communicated upward increases.[8]

---

[8]The following two studies discuss the needs of subordinates in organizations and their effect upon superior-subordinate communication.

(Continued on page 363)

Horizontal Communication

Traditional organization theory with its concepts of line authority and the chain of command emphasizes vertical lines of communication between superior and subordinate. Figure 15-2 shows in schematic form the transmission of a message from D_1, supervisor of production department 1, to D_2, supervisor of production department 2, using the chain of command as a channel of communication. The advantage claimed for this formalized line of communication is that A, who is responsible for both production departments, is better able to coordinate the functioning of the two departments when fully informed of the activities of each department. The obvious disadvantages of following these formal lines of communication are the amount of time taken to transmit a message, the increased risk of error and distortion, and the loss of flexibility necessary to meet emergencies. The extent to which an organization insists that its lines of communication conform to the organizational lines of authority depend to a large extent on the technology of that organization. Failure to recognize communication needs arising from and depending on technology often results in poor communications.

There are several empirical studies that show the need for horizontal and diagonal communications between first-line supervisors as a function of the technology, or method, of production. In one of the earliest studies of an automobile assembly line, Blau found that the role of the foreman is one of problem solving and expediting material

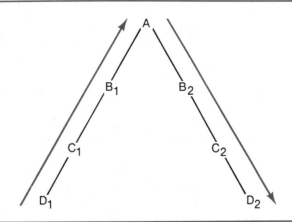

**Figure 15-2
TRADITIONAL
VERTICAL
COMMUNICATION**

John C. Athanassiades, "The Distortion of Upward Communication in Hierarchical Organizations," *Academy of Management Journal*, Vol. 16, No. 2 (June, 1973), pp. 207–226.

Karlene H. Roberts and Charles A. O'Reilly, III, "Failures in Upward Communication in Organizations: Three Possible Culprits," *Academy of Management Journal*, Vol. 17, No. 2 (June, 1974), pp. 205–215.

flow. The line itself determines the pace of production, and the jobs on the line are well defined. Under these circumstances there is relatively little need for the traditional vertical communications of giving orders to subordinates and there are not many orders received from one's superior. The result is that the bulk of the foreman's communications is with other foremen on the assembly line and with other departments such as material handling and maintenance.[9] All of these relationships are either horizontal or diagonal. However, Faunce in a study of a highly automated automobile factory finds, in an apparent contradiction, that there is a marked need for vertical communications through the traditional chain of command.[10] Simpson, in a study of the spinning department of a textile mill, obtains results similar to those of Blau; namely, a decrease in the need for vertical communications between superior and subordinate and an increase in the need for communications between supervisors on the same level.[11] In Simpson's study, the primary direct communication between the general foreman of the department and subordinate foremen consists of a written message stating the type and amount of material to be produced on each machine for each shift.

Simpson also resolves the apparent discrepancy between his findings, similar to those of Blau, and the findings of Faunce. He describes three broad types of technology used in production and suggests that the relative need for vertical or horizontal communication is determined by the technology. First, in unmechanized operations there is a relatively greater need for vertical communications than there is for horizontal communications. In this situation the various production departments are relatively independent, and the amount of work produced is determined by the effectiveness of the supervisor of the department. The manager responsible for coordinating the work of all departments needs detailed information from each supervisor. Second, when technology is characterized by mechanization, such as a textile mill or an automobile assembly line, separate departments are bound together by that technology. The success of the foreman of an assembly line depends on the right part arriving at a certain place in the line at a scheduled time and on the reliable functioning of the tools used in production. Providing the necessary parts for assembly is the function of the production control and material handling departments, and the proper operation of the tools for production is the function of the maintenance department. Rate of output is determined by the speed of the assembly line or other automatic equipment. Under these circumstances the need for horizontal communications among the foremen of

---

[9]Peter M. Blau, "Formal Organization: Dimension of Analysis," *American Journal of Sociology*, Vol. 62 (July, 1957), pp. 58–59.

[10]William A. Faunce, "Automation in the Automobile Industry," *American Sociological Review*, Vol. 23 (August, 1958), pp. 401–407.

[11]Richard L. Simpson, "Vertical and Horizontal Communication in Formal Organizations," *Administrative Science Quarterly*, Vol. 4 (December, 1959), pp. 188–196.

the various departments increases. Third, in highly automated plants where the breakdown of a single machine may result in the shutdown of all production facilities, the need for control becomes greater and the need for vertical communications also increases.

In summary, no mechanization or a low degree of mechanization emphasizes vertical communications; moderate mechanization (such as the assembly line) requires a great emphasis upon horizontal communications; and highly automated production facilities reestablish the need for vertical communications.

The Grapevine

Our discussion of the problems of communication has been directed toward formal channels and methods of communication. It is necessary for management to recognize that there are also informal methods of communication that may be far more effective in some respects than the formal means of transmitting information. An informal system of communication is generally referred to as the *grapevine*. As the name suggests, the grapevine is entwined throughout the entire organization with branches going in all directions, thereby short-circuiting formal vertical and horizontal channels.

Two characteristics of communications via the grapevine are noted by those who have studied it. First, the grapevine is often an exceedingly rapid form of communication; and second, the information transmitted is frequently subjected to a great deal of distortion. Formal channels of communication, particularly those following the vertical chain of command, usually pass information from one person to another — a time-consuming process. In contrast, the grapevine transmits information along a pathway described as a *cluster chain*.[12] Instead of passing information from one person to another, as in superior-subordinate communication, information is passed to a group of three or four persons, and from this initial link in the cluster chain, one or two individuals inform other groups. Thus, there is an ever-increasing rate in the flow of information. In part, this is due to the makeup of the grapevine; people who work near each other or whose work regularly brings them in contact with others are frequently on the same grapevine. The grapevine that includes the mail clerk, the switchboard operator, or any other person whose work requires contact with several groups transmits information much more quickly

---

[12]Keith Davis, "Communication Within Management," *Personnel* (New York: American Management Association, 1954). In this article Professor Davis discusses a method of communication analysis and applies the method to the communications of one company. He also discusses the grapevine in management communications.

The following article presents another method of analyzing informal communication known as the semantic differential: William E. Reif, Robert M. Monczka, and John W. Newstrom, "Perceptions of the Formal and the Informal Organizations: Objective Measurement Through the Semantic Differential Technique," *Academy of Management Journal*, Vol. 16, No. 3 (September, 1973), pp. 389–403.

than formal channels of communication. Another factor encouraging rapid communication is that the information carried by the grapevine reflects the interests and personal concerns of its members; for example, news of an impending layoff, an increase in pay, or news about other people.

The grapevine is notorious for distorting information, so much so that information received from this source is often referred to as rumor. In the discussion of superior-subordinate communications, the filtering of information — passing on only certain parts of a message — is mentioned as one of the causes of distortion. The grapevine information at its source is often fragmentary and incomplete, with the result that there is a strong tendency to fill in the missing parts. Since the grapevine is informal, there are no formal lines of accountability. Consequently, members of the grapevine do not have to answer to their superiors for any misstatement of facts. Further, the elaboration of a fragment of news into a full-blown story offers to some people an opportunity to express feelings of self-importance and to compensate for feelings of insecurity.

The characteristics of the grapevine are summarized by Davis as follows:

1. People talk most when the news is recent.
2. People talk about things that affect their work.
3. People talk about people they know.
4. People working near each other are likely to be on the same grapevine.
5. People who contact each other in the chain of procedure tend to be on the same grapevine.[13]

IMPROVING COMMUNICATIONS

Two approaches are available for the improvement of communications. The first of these approaches is from the point of view of the sender of the message. Recognize the purpose of the communication, the significance of the symbols used, the organizational lines through which the communication travels, and its possible effect on the receiver. These and other ways of improving one's ability to communicate clearly as a sender of messages are discussed below as ten general rules for improving communications. The last of these rules states that in order to achieve effective communication it is necessary to learn how to listen. It is a listening to the feelings and emotional content of messages expressed by others as well as being able to understand the factual information that is being presented. The process of learning how to detect the emotional content of communications is discussed under the heading, *empathetic listening*.

---

[13]Davis, *op. cit.*, p. 212.

Rules for Improving Communications

The American Management Association refers to the following rules as the Ten Commandments of Good Communication:

1. *Seek to clarify your ideas before communicating.* The more systematically we analyze the problem or idea to be communicated, the clearer it becomes that this is the first step toward effective communication. Many communications fail because of inadequate planning. Good planning must consider the goals and attitudes of those who will receive the communications and those who will be affected by it.

2. *Examine the true purpose of each communication.* Before you communicate, ask yourself what you really want to accomplish with your message — obtain information, initiate action, change another person's attitude? Identify your most important goal and then adapt your language, tone, and total approach to serve that specific objective. Don't try to accomplish too much with each communication. The sharper the focus of your message the greater its chances of success.

3. *Consider the total physical and human setting whenever you communicate.* Meaning and intent are conveyed by more than words alone. Many other factors influence the overall impact of a communication, and the manager must be sensitive to the total setting in which he communicates. Consider, for example, your sense of timing — i.e., the circumstances under which you make an announcement or render a decision; the physical setting — whether you communicate in private, for example, or otherwise; the social climate that pervades work relationships within the company or a department and sets the tone of its communications; custom and past practice — the degree to which your communication conforms to or departs from, the expectations of your audience. Be constantly aware of the total setting in which you communicate. Like all living things, communication must be capable of adapting to its environment.

4. *Consult with others, where appropriate, in planning communications.* Frequently it is desirable or necessary to seek the participation of others in planning a communication or developing the facts on which to base it. Such consultation often helps to lend additional insight and objectivity to your message. Moreover, those who have helped you plan your communication will give it their support.

5. *Be mindful, while you communicate, of the overtones as well as the basic content of your message.* Your tone of voice, your expression, your apparent receptiveness to the responses of others — all have tremendous impact on those you wish to reach. Frequently overlooked, these subtleties of communication often affect a listener's reaction to a message even more than its basic content. Similarly, your choice of language — particularly your awareness of the fine shades of meaning and emotion in the words you use — predetermines in large part the reactions of your listeners.

6. *Take the opportunity, when it arises, to convey something of help or value to the receiver.* Consideration of the other person's interests and needs — the habit of trying to look at things from his point of view —

will frequently point up opportunities to convey something of immediate benefit or long-range value to him. People on the job are most
responsive to the manager whose messages take their own interests
into account.

7. *Follow up your communication.* Our best efforts at communication
may be wasted, and we may never know whether we have succeeded
in expressing our true meaning and intent, if we do not follow up to
see how well we have put our message across. This you can do by
asking questions, by encouraging the receiver to express his reactions, by follow-up contacts, by subsequent review of performance.
Make certain that every important communication has a "feed-back"
so that complete understanding and appropriate action result.

8. *Communicate for tomorrow as well as today.* While communications
may be aimed primarily at meeting the demands of an immediate
situation, they must be planned with the past in mind if they are to
maintain consistency in the receiver's view; but, most important of
all, they must be consistent with long-range interests and goals. For
example, it is not easy to communicate frankly on such matters as
poor performance or the shortcomings of a loyal subordinate — but
postponing disagreeable communications makes them more difficult
in the long run and is actually unfair to your subordinates and your
company.

9. *Be sure your actions support your communications.* In the final analysis, the most persuasive kind of communication is not what you say
but what you do. When a man's actions or attitudes contradict his
words, we tend to discount what he has said. For every manager this
means that good supervisory practices — such as clear assignment of
responsibility and authority, fair rewards for effort, and sound policy
enforcement — serve to communicate more than all the gifts of ora-
tory.

10. *Last, but by no means least: Seek not only to be understood but to understand – be a good listener.* When we start talking we often cease to
listen — in that larger sense of being attuned to the other person's
unspoken reactions and attitudes. Even more serious is the fact that
we are all guilty, at times, of inattentiveness when others are attempting to communicate to us. Listening is one of the most important, most difficult — and most neglected — skills in communication. It demands that we concentrate not only on the explicit
meanings another person is expressing, but on the implicit meanings, unspoken words, and undertones that may be far more significant. Thus we must learn to listen with the inner ear if we are to
know the inner man.[14]

Empathetic Listening

The tenth rule admonishes us to listen to others — listen to the
explicit meaning and also the implicit meaning. Explicit meaning is

---

[14]"Ten Commandments of Good Communication," (New York: American Management Association, Copyright, 1955).

conveyed by the meaning of the words used by the sender; and in order to understand, it is necessary that we pay careful attention to what is being said. However, we must also listen with the "inner ear" if we are to hear the "inner person." Hearing the inner person, the implicit meanings of the message, calls for *empathy* — the ability to put oneself in the other person's place, to assume that person's role, viewpoint, and emotions. *Empathetic listening* is hearing and understanding the emotional content, the feelings, and the mood of the other person. Empathetic listening requires a special technique of listening.

Case Problem 15-B, A Case of Misunderstanding, should be read now, for it is the basis of our discussion of empathetic listening. As stated in the third paragraph of the case, we do not know exactly what Hart, the supervisor, said to Bing, the worker. We do know what each said to the personnel representative. With this information, let us reconstruct the conversation between Hart and Bing.

Hart: "Bing, I want to talk to you."

Bing: "Yeah?"

Hart: "Listen, why don't you try to get along here like other people do for a change?"

Bing: "How?"

Hart: "Well, for one thing, stop deliberately upsetting this department by going to lunch early and asking others to go with you."

Bing: "I haven't been to lunch early for a week."

Hart: "You have, too. And another thing, I want you to stop carrying three panels at one time over to your bench for inspection — you know the rules on that."

Bing: "That's what I want to talk to you about. I've got an idea . . ."

Hart: "Never mind your ideas, just follow the rules and you'll get along better."

Bing: "I want a transfer."

Hart: "We'll see about that. In the meantime, stop singing around here. What do you think this is, a nightclub, and you're Frank Sinatra?"

The above conversation and the comments made by Hart and Bing to the personnel representative show quite clearly that Hart is not listening to Bing. It appears that he is more interested in telling Bing off than he is in trying to determine the reasons for Bing's behavior. Hart is *not* using the techniques of empathetic listening. Without empathetic listening there cannot be two-way communication.

Listen with Understanding. Empathetic listening as a part of two-way personal communications is a concept borrowed from the methods of nondirective psychotherapy that have been highly developed by

Dr. Carl Rogers.[15] In this form of psychotherapy the role of the therapist is one of encouraging not only good communications between the therapist and the patient, but also good communications within the patient. The patient must learn how to express himself or herself and have the opportunity for that expression. Although a supervisor and other members of management are not therapists, if they are to have successful two-way communications with others, the others must have the opportunities to express themselves. In order to encourage such expression, nondirective techniques are employed. The one conducting the interview encourages the expression of the feelings, emotions, and desires behind the words of the other persons. In order to do this the interviewer listens instead of talking. In the conversation above, Hart does most of the talking, not Bing. If he were listening with understanding, his comments would have been designed to encourage Bing to talk and the following conversation might have occurred:

Hart: "Bing, I want to talk to you."
Bing: "Yeah?"
Hart: "I've noticed that you have been carrying three panels over to your bench for inspection. Do you have a new idea for a methods change?"
Bing: "Well, maybe."
Hart: "Um-hum."
Bing: "Well, maybe it won't work all the time, but with these smaller panels there is no reason why three of them can't be carried at once."

With this approach to communication, Hart is encouraging Bing to talk, not to defend himself. The problems caused by his leaving for lunch early and his singing may be explored in the same easy manner.

Guides for Listening. The following guides for empathetic listening have been found to be as effective in industrial settings as in their original clinical setting.

1. *Avoid Making Value Judgments.* Value judgments are global in nature and made from the point of view of the listener, not from the frame of reference of the person doing the talking. Such judgments place a single value — good or bad, desirable or undesirable, true or false — on a

---

[15]Carl R. Rogers and F. J. Roethlisberger, "Barrier and Gateways to Communications," *Harvard Business Review*, Vol. 30 (July-August, 1952), pp. 46–52. The first part of the article is written by Dr. Rogers, who suggests that the major barrier to communication is the tendency to evaluate and that the main gateway to communication is listening with understanding. In the second part of the article, Dr. Roethlisberger analyzes a communications situation and suggests positive steps that may be taken to improve communications.

For a full discussion of Dr. Roger's views on therapy, see: Carl R. Rogers, *Client-Centered Therapy* (Boston: Houghton Mifflin Co., 1953).

The following brief article, autobiographical in nature, summarizes Rogers' perception of his own work: Carl R. Rogers, "In Retrospect: Forty-Six Years," *American Psychologist*, Vol. 29, No. 2 (February, 1974), pp. 115–123.

series of complex statements, each of which varies considerably with respect to any given characteristic. In addition, the origin of value judgments is often derived from an earlier judgment of the source of the statement. How can Bing say anything worthwhile to Hart when he is prejudged by Hart as being mentally deficient and a sow's ear? Once the value judgment is made, the mind is closed and it becomes impossible to understand the other's point of view.

2. *Listen to the Full Story*. In the first interview, Bing started to say that he has an idea, but is stopped abruptly by Hart. In order to understand, listen to the whole story. Time is a critical factor in empathetic listening, and arrangements must be made for adequate time and a place where there will be no interruptions. Ask the other person to be seated; if he or she smokes, offer a cigarette. Do everything you can to put the other person at ease.

3. *Recognize Feelings and Emotions*. Remember, empathetic listening is putting yourself in the position of the other person. Try to pinpoint the meaning of the feelings and emotions behind the statements being made, rather than the meaning of the words being said. Look for signs of eagerness, hesitancy, hostility, anxiety, or depression. At the same time watch for evasions, the things left unsaid, or areas of discussion consistently avoided.

4. *Restate the Other's Position*. As a test of your understanding, restate the other person's statement from his or her point of view, not yours. For example, Hart might say, "You believe that I'm watching you like a hawk, treating you like a naughty kid, and as a result you feel like a marked man." Imagine the change in Hart's behavior if he can make the statement above with the same feeling that Bing would put into it.

5. *Question with Care*. The simplest way to keep the conversation going is to use the noncommittal "um-hum." If this is insufficient, phrases such as "and then what happened" or "what did you do" may start the story again. Occasionally restatements such as the one mentioned in (4) may be rephrased as questions. Avoid argumentative statements such as "that isn't true" or "I don't believe you." These statements not only cause you to lose your objectivity and become emotionally involved, but also put the other person on the defensive, thus making it impossible for the individual to express his or her true feelings.

The guides for empathetic listening are relatively easy to remember; however, their application requires a skill that may take years to develop. As a manager you will have to develop these skills to achieve two-way communication. Solving the problems for Case Problem 15-B is the first step in learning the techniques of empathetic listening and effective communicating.[16]

---

[16]F. J. Roethlisberger, "The Administrator's Skill: Communication," *Harvard Business Review*, Vol. 31 (November–December, 1953), pp. 55–57. Copyright © 1953 by the President and Fellows of Harvard College; all rights reserved. This case (names and places disguised) is adapted from a case in the files of the Harvard Graduate School of Business Administration.

Case Problem 15-B

A CASE OF MISUNDERSTANDING

In a department of a large industrial organization, there were seven workers (four men and three women) engaged in testing and inspecting panels of electronic equipment. In this department one of the workers, Bing, was having trouble with his immediate superior, Hart, who had formerly been a worker in the department.

Had we been observers in this department we would have seen Bing carrying two or three panels at a time from the racks where they were stored to the bench where he inspected them together. For this activity we would have seen him charging double or triple setup time. We would have heard him occasionally singing at work. Also, we would have seen him usually leaving his work position a few minutes early to go to lunch, and noticed that other employees sometimes accompanied him. And had we been present at one specific occasion, we would have heard Hart telling Bing that he disapproved of these activities and that he wanted Bing to stop doing them.

However, not being present to hear the actual verbal exchange that took place in this interaction, let us note what Bing and Hart said to a personnel representative.

WHAT BING SAID

In talking about his practice of charging double or triple setup time for panels which he inspected all at one time, Bing said:

"This is a perfectly legal thing to do. We've always been doing it. Mr. Hart, the supervisor, has other ideas about it, though; he claims it's cheating the company. He came over to the bench a day or two ago and let me know just how he felt about the matter. Boy, did we go at it! It wasn't so much the fact that he called me down on it, but more the way in which he did it. . . . I've never seen anyone like him. He's not content just to say in a manlike way what's on his mind, but he prefers to do it in a way that makes you want to crawl inside a crack on the floor. What a guy! I don't mind

being called down by a supervisor, but I like to be treated like a man, and not humiliated like a school teacher does a naughty kid. He's been pulling this stuff ever since he's been . . . promoted, he's lost his friendly way and seems to be having some difficulty in knowing how to manage us employees. He's a changed man over what he used to be like when he was a worker on the bench with us several years ago.

"When he pulled this kind of stuff on me the other day, I got so damn mad I called in the union representative. I know that the thing I was doing was permitted by the contract, but I was intent on making some trouble for Mr. Hart, just because he persists in this sarcastic way of handling me. I am about fed up with the whole damn situation. I'm trying every means I can to get myself transferred out of his group. . . . He's not going to pull this kind of kid stuff any longer on me. When the union representative questioned him on the case, he finally had to back down, because according to the contract an employee can use any time-saving method or device in order to speed up the process as long as the quality standards of the job are met.

"You see, he knows that I do professional singing on the outside. He hears me singing here on the job, and he hears the people talking about my career in music. I guess he figures I can be so cocky because I have another means of earning some money. Actually, the employees here enjoy having me sing while we work, but he thinks I'm disturbing them and causing them to 'goof off' from their work. Occasionally, I leave the job a few minutes early and go down to the washroom to wash up before lunch. Sometimes several others in the group will accompany me, and so Mr. Hart automatically thinks I'm the leader and usually bawls me out for the whole thing.

"So, you can see, I'm a marked man around here. He keeps watching me like a hawk. Naturally, this makes me very uncomfortable. That's why I'm sure a transfer would be the best thing. I've asked him for it, but he didn't give me any satisfaction at the time. While I remain here, I'm going to keep my nose clean, but whenever I get the chance, I'm going to slip it to him, but good."

WHAT HART SAID

Here, on the other hand, is what Hart told the personnel representative:

"Say, I think you should be in on this. My dear little friend, Bing, is heading himself into a showdown with me. Recently it was brought to my attention that Bing has been taking double and triple setup time for panels which he is actually inspecting at one time. In effect, that's cheating, and I've called him down on it several times before. A few days ago it was brought to my attention again, and so this time I really let him have it in no uncertain terms. He's been getting away with this for too long and I'm going to put an end to it once and for all. I know he didn't like my calling him on it because a few hours later he had the union representative breathing down my back. Well, anyway, I let them both know I'll not tolerate the practice any longer, and I let Bing know that if he continues to do this kind of thing, I'm going to take official action with my boss to have the guy fired or penalized somehow. This kind of thing has to be curbed. Actually, I'm inclined to think the guy's mentally deficient, because talking to him has actually no meaning to him whatsoever. I've tried just about every approach to jar some sense into that guy's head, and I've just about given it up as a bad deal.

"I don't know what it is about the guy, but I think he's harboring some deep feelings against me. For what, I don't know, because I've tried to handle that bird with kid gloves. But his whole attitude around here on the job is one of indifference, and he certainly isn't a good influence on the rest of my group. Frankly, I think he purposely tries to agitate them against me at times, too. It seems to me he may be suffering from illusions of grandeur, because all he does all day long is sit over there and croon his fool head off. Thinks he's a Frank Sinatra! No kidding! I understand he takes singing lessons and he's working with some of the local bands in the city. All of which is o.k. by me; but when his outside interests start interfering with his efficiency on the job, then I've got to start paying closer attention to the situation. For this reason I've been keeping my eye on that bird and if he steps out of line any more, he and I are going to part ways.

"You know there's an old saying, 'You can't make a purse out of a sow's ear.' The guy is simply unscrupulous. He feels no obligation to do a real day's work. Yet I know the guy can do a good job, because for a long time he did. But in recent months he's slipped, for some reason, and his whole attitude on the job has changed. Why, it's even getting to the point now where I think he's inducing other employees to 'goof off' a few minutes before the lunch whistle and go down to the washroom and clean up on company time. I've called him on it several times, but words just don't seem to make any lasting impression on him. Well, if he keeps it up much longer, he's going to find himself on the way out. He's asked me for a transfer, so I know he wants to go. But I didn't give him an answer when he asked me, because I was steaming mad at the time, and I may have told him to go somewhere else."

PROBLEMS

1. Based upon Hart's (and Bing's) report to the personnel supervisor, what are the factors that would make empathetic listening difficult for Hart to achieve?
2. Reconstruct in full the conversation as it probably occurred.
3. Reconstruct in full an interview between Bing and Hart utilizing the techniques of empathetic listening.
4. Discuss Bing's responsibility to listen empathetically to Hart.

1. Explain in your own words the triangle of meaning. Why is it important that the triangle have a dotted line for its base?
2. What are some of the things transmitted by an oral face-to-face message other than facts descriptive of a situation? Can these other things be transmitted as effectively in written form? Discuss.
3. Does highly effective and efficient communication between people eliminate conflict between them? If not, why not?
4. Why is conversation not necessarily communication?
5. Why are superior-subordinate communications more susceptible to certain types of communication problems than communication between two persons on the same organizational level?
6. Differentiate between embellishment and filtering. Are communications directed downward in an organization likely to be filtered or embellished? Explain.
7. Develop an argument that supports the thesis that sound processes of delegation minimize the need for face-to-face communication between superior and subordinate.
8. Develop several examples showing how the technology of the organization influences the need for and the type of formal communications.
9. How can the grapevine be used effectively as a communications device?
10. Since communication is primarily the sending of a message, why is it necessary to be able to listen empathetically?
11. What is meant by a value judgment? Why are value judgments often barriers to effective communication?

Chapter
16

Motivating Employees

Case Problem 16-A
PART I: AN EMPLOYEE BENEFIT PROGRAM

Acme Manufacturing Company, located in an eastern metropolitan area, produces a complete line of small household electrical appliances such as toasters, blenders, coffee percolators, and electric can openers. The products are of good quality and are distributed through department stores and mail-order houses under private labels. The small fractional horsepower motors and heating elements used in the products are purchased; however, the company does its own stamping, machining, plating, painting, and assembly. Two hundred hourly paid workers perform these operations.

The personnel policies of Acme Manufacturing are not stated in writing, nor is there an employee handbook. The company conducts an annual wage survey and maintains its wage level at the average of the area for similar jobs. There has not been the same effort to maintain fringe benefits at a competitive level. Surveys concerning employee benefits are not conducted on a regular basis, the last survey having been completed about five years ago. The company never conducted an attitude or morale survey.

John Rider, the general manager, is somewhat puzzled by one aspect of the monthly personnel department activity report. For the second successive month there are 10 production jobs to be filled. To the best of his knowledge there have been no changes in production schedules, nor has he authorized any additional factory personnel. Consequently, Rider wonders why the 10 openings exist. He has called the personnel manager to determine the reasons for the vacancies.

As the personnel manager, Margaret Marlow, entered his office, Mr. Rider said, "Margaret, I notice that for the second straight month we have 10 vacancies in our plant labor force. If this rate of turnover continues, we will be replacing over half of our labor force within a year. What is the reason for our hiring so many new employees?"

"Part of the reason is that we still have four vacancies to be filled from the preceding month, and the other six are vacancies that were created by employees with less than six months' service who quit last month," Marlow answered.

"About the four jobs remaining from last month, why haven't we filled them?"

"Well, these are all skilled jobs. Even so, we managed to hire two people, but they didn't report for work. Both called and said that they had taken better jobs somewhere else."

"Do you know where they went to work?" Rider asked.

"Yes, and neither company has a higher wage rate than we have." Anticipating the next question, Marlow continued, "The only reason for their going to these other companies is that they offer better employee benefits than we do; and in a tight labor market like the one we have now, that kind of difference is significant."

"I also notice from your report that our absentee rate is running about eight to ten percent a day — about twice what it was this time last year. Is that a part of the same pattern?"

"I believe it is," Marlow answered.

"In that case I suggest that we take a good look at our fringe benefits. After you have determined what is happening in the area, summarize the results and recommend the level that we should adopt for our company. I know that we have more or less paid the average in wages, but in view of our increasing quality problems and our productivity rate per man-hour, I'm willing to pay more for fringe benefits if they will help quality and production. Let me have the summary of the survey and your recommendations as soon as possible," Rider concluded.

Marlow returned to her office and took from her files a partial list of fringe benefits. The list is shown in Exhibit I.

PROBLEMS

1. Would you include all the items listed in Exhibit I in your survey of fringe benefits for Acme Manufacturing Company? If all items are not included in the survey, which should be included?
2. What is your recommendation regarding the level of fringe benefits that should be paid; i.e., below average, average, or in the upper quartile?
3. What can Acme expect as the result of a competitive employee benefit program with regard to turnover, absenteeism, productivity, and product quality?
4. How can a company measure the effectiveness of its employee benefit program?
5. Is there any justification for using the phrase, fringe benefits, to describe employee benefit programs?

One of the most difficult tasks of an organization is that of motivating its employees — managerial and nonmanagerial alike — to perform the work assigned to them in a manner that meets or surpasses expected standards of performance. Many methods are used to encourage employees to put forth their best effort. Among those commonly found in industrial firms are a variety of formulas intended to relate pay to performance, provisions for security on the job and during the later years of retirement, praise and reproof, and recognition in the form of special awards or promotion. The existence of so many different approaches to motivation suggests the complexity of the problem. Many factors are capable of motivating employees. Some of these factors are a normal part of the industrial situation and, as independent variables, can be controlled in some measure by the company; other factors have their origin in the individual employee, in his home, or in his community, and are beyond the company's control. Also, those forces that motivate a person today may be of little value as motivators next month or next year. Fundamental to the success of any plan for motivating employees is the extent to which the intended motivators meet the needs of the individual employees for whom they are designed.

I. For Added Leisure and Income

Call-back pay
Call-in pay
Clean-up time
Clothes-change time
Coffee breaks
Cost-of-living bonus
Downtime pay
Family allowances
Holidays
Hour limits
Jury duty pay
Leave, for illness
Leave, death of relative
Leave, for grievances
Leave, for negotiation
Leave, for voting
Lonely pay
Military bonus
Overtime pay
Portal-to-portal pay
Reporting pay
Rest pauses
Room and board allowances
Setup time
Shift differentials
Standby pay
Supper money
Travel pay
Vacations
Voting time

II. For Personal Identification and Participation

Anniversary awards
Athletic activities
Attendance bonus
Beauty parlor service
Cafeteria
Canteen
Car wash service
Charm school
Christmas bonus
Counseling
Credit union
Dietetic advice
Discounts
Educational aids
Financial advice
Food service
Home financing
Housing
Income tax aid
Information racks
Laundry service
Legal aid

Loan association
Moving aid
Music with work
Orchestra
Parking space
Quality bonus
Recreational programs
Savings bond aid
Safety clothes
Scholarships
Suggestion bonus
Thrift plans
Transportation aids
Year-end bonus

III. For Employment Security

Death benefits
Layoff pay
Leave for maternity
Retraining plans
Technological adjustment pay
Severance pay
Supplementary unemployment
    benefits
Unemployment insurance

IV. For Health Protection

Accident insurance
Dental care
Disability insurance
Health insurance
Hospitalization
Illness insurance
Life insurance
Medical care plan
Medical examinations
Optical services
Plant nursing service
Sickness insurance
Sick benefits
Sick leave
Surgical care plan
Temporary disability insurance
Visiting nurse service
Workmen's compensation

V. For Old Age and Retirement

Deferred income plans
Old age assistance
Old age counseling
OASDI
Private pension plans
Profit sharing plans
Rest homes
Retirement counseling
Stock ownership plans

Exhibit I
A PARTIAL LIST OF EMPLOYEE BENEFITS AND SERVICES

Source: Dale Yoder, *Personnel Management and Industrial Relations* (5th ed.; Englewood Cliffs: Prentice-Hall, 1962), p. 494.

In this chapter we discuss first the basis of motivation as a means of developing certain concepts that will enable us to better understand the worth of intended motivators. Next, specific problems of motivation in an industrial situation are presented. In the last part of the chapter the concept of morale is developed and the relationship between job satisfaction and productivity is reviewed.

THE BASIS OF MOTIVATION

The study of motivation attempts to answer the *why* of human behavior. Why do people behave as they do? Why does Mary Jones consistently complete her work on time while Pete Smith has to be urged to meet the minimum requirements of his job? When we speak of motivation or, in more precise terms, motivated behavior, we are referring to behavior having three distinguishing characteristics. First, motivated behavior is sustained; that is, it persists for relatively long periods of time. Second, motivated behavior is directed toward the achievement of a goal; and third, it is behavior resulting from a felt need. The third characteristic, behavior resulting from a felt need, introduces a concept requiring further explanation.

Various terms have been used to describe the motivating forces of human behavior. Some of the terms are need, aspiration, and desire. Although each term has a precise meaning in psychological theory, they may be grouped together for our purpose, since each is felt and recognized by the individual as a motivating force. As a result of perceiving a need, a tension or imbalance is created within the individual that leads to activities intended to reduce the tension thus created. The process may be diagrammed as follows:

A Perceived $\longrightarrow$ Tension $\longrightarrow$ Activity $\longrightarrow$ Reduction of Tension
   Need   (Motivating   (Achievement of Goal)
               Force)

The importance of the discussion above is this: If the efforts of organizations to motivate employees are to be successful, management must either create felt needs within the individual or offer a means of satisfying needs already in existence within the individual. Thus, in order to motivate employees, we must know something about fundamental human needs.

A Hierarchy of Needs

Numerous systems have been developed for the classification of human needs, ranging from those that attempt to explain all human motivation as the result of satisfying one basic need or drive to classifications that list 25 or more separate needs. Among those who have sought to explain behavior in terms of a single need is Freud, who stressed the libido — a broad concept of the sex drive — as the basic motivator of man. Two of his students, Adler and Jung, also postulated single motives; the former designated the desire for power as the primary motivator, while the latter believed that a desire for individuality served as the basic source of motivation. The economists also have had a hand in trying to describe human motivation as evidenced by Marx's description of economic determinism as a primary motivator. However, one of the most useful and widely quoted classifications of human needs is that developed by Maslow who recognizes five basic needs. These are:[1]

1. Physiological needs
2. Safety needs
3. Affection needs
4. Esteem needs
5. Self-actualization needs

Each of these needs is discussed briefly below.

Physiological Needs. Hunger and thirst are considered classic examples of physiological drives. Also included in this category are the tissue needs such as maintenance of the proper water content of the blood; maintenance of proper amounts of salt, sugar, protein, fat, calcium, oxygen, and acid-base balance; and the maintenance of the proper temperature for the tissues and the blood stream.[2] Satisfaction of the physiological needs is necessary for the preservation of life, and in most industrial economies these needs are satisfied relatively easily. Once satisfied, they cease to operate as the primary motivators of behavior and are replaced by motivational forces of a higher order.

Safety Needs. When considered as a goal of motivated behavior, the meaning of the term, safety, is broad because it includes the desire for psychological security as well as the need for physical security. Factors such as clothing, shelter, and protection from attack contribute to physical safety, thereby preserving and reinforcing the satisfaction of physiological drives. Much of the effort of organized society at the community level, such as police and fire departments, is directed toward the maintenance of security needs.

The desire for psychological security is of particular interest to management since the safety needs may become the predominant motivators when the physiological needs are fulfilled. Psychological safety

---

[1]A. H. Maslow, "A Theory of Human Motivation," *Psychological Review*, Vol. 50, (July, 1943), pp. 370–396. The theory of motivation, first presented in 1943 as a journal article, is treated in greater detail in *Motivation and Personality* (New York: Harper and Brothers, 1954).

[2]W. B. Cannon, *Wisdom of the Body* (New York: W. W. Norton and Co., 1932). Cannon describes the functioning of the human body as a homeostatic system.

takes the form of ordering the environment into a predictable pattern and attempts to cope with anticipated difficulties of the future. Demands for supplemental unemployment benefits, pension plans, termination pay, and other forms of economic insurance stress the need for predictability and security. The desire for the familiar and the predictable goes a long way toward explaining the resistance to change found in many organizations. It is not the direction or nature of the change being resisted; it is the fact that change implies something new and unfamiliar — a psychological threat.

Affection Needs. Some writers combine physiological needs and safety needs into one category and call them the primary needs. They then refer to the needs for affection, esteem, and self-actualization as secondary needs. Such a classification is misleading because in our society the needs for survival and safety may be satisfied to a large extent. Consequently, the predominant needs are those of affection, esteem, and self-actualization. Need for affection and love is best described as the need to belong, not only as a wanted member of a family unit but also as a member of other relatively small groups such as work groups. Loyalty to a small work group and the need to belong to that group often outweigh the financial incentives and the logical appeals of management.

Esteem Needs. The esteem needs, like the needs for affection and group belonging, are particularly significant as motivators in the industrial setting. Esteem needs may be summarized as the need for self-respect, for accomplishment, and for achievement. An important corollary to the need for esteem and achievement, perhaps as important as the need itself, is that the achievement must be recognized and appreciated by someone else. Few people are able to continue a pattern of achievement and success without the added encouragement and additional motivation provided by recognition of success by others. The desire for prestige and status (in reality, a form of recognition by others) is an important aspect of the drive for achievement. Attaining goals leads to feelings of self-respect, strength, and confidence. On the other hand, continued failure, frustration, and defeat can result in feelings of inadequacy and a withdrawal from competitive situations.

Self-Actualization Needs. Self-actualization, the capstone of the hierarchy of needs, is self-fulfillment. Maslow's original statement — "what a man can be, he must be" — may be paraphrased to state that *what one can do, one must do*. Self-actualization takes many forms. We usually think of the creative works of painters, musicians, composers, and authors as expressions of self-fulfillment; however, the realization of one's full potential is not limited to expression in the creative arts. The woman who desires to be the ideal mother, the professional athlete, and the dedicated teacher are all doing what each must do. Complete self-actualization is rare, perhaps because all the other needs —

physiological, safety, affection, and esteem — must reach a level of minimal satisfaction before the self-fulfillment needs become the dominant motivation in one's life.[3]

Variations in the Hierarchy

The discussion of Maslow's hierarchy of needs serves a useful purpose, provided we recognize that the concept of a hierarchy is used only as a model and is not intended to imply that the emergence and the strength of needs follow a rigid pattern. There are many reversals and substitutions of needs. For some persons the sole goal in life seems to center upon the esteem needs, the acquisition of prestige, wealth, and status, to the exclusion of the needs for love and affection. Closer examination often reveals a thwarting of the love needs early in life, with a permanent dampening and suppression of those needs; thus, the drive for self-esteem may serve as a substitute for the need for love. There is evidence that needs for esteem and self-actualization may be blocked to such an extent that seemingly they disappear and do not emerge. Those who have faced a life of unemployment, or at best marginal economic adjustment, are often motivated mainly by the desire for safety and security to protect basic physiological needs.

There is probably no universal motivator for all mankind, nor is there a single motivating force for any one individual. Needs are relative in their strength, and it is not necessary to satisfy a "lower" need fully before a "higher" need may emerge and operate as a motivator. Assume that 90 percent of a person's physiological needs are satisfied, that 80 percent of the safety needs are fulfilled, and that 55 percent of the needs for love and affection are being met. This does not mean that there are no needs for esteem or self-actualization. Needs are felt gradually and may become motivators along with the other needs, even though the earlier needs are not completely satisfied. The complexity of the problem of motivation can be fully grasped when it is realized that the hypothetical percentages stated above vary from one person to another, that the significance of each need also varies, and that within the same person the relative degree of satisfaction and the significance of each need vary. In addition, there are factors other than

---

[3]There have been several studies designed to test empirically in industrial organizations the need hierarchy described by Maslow. For the most part these studies do not validate Maslow's need hierarchy in an industrial setting. The results are not surprising since Maslow's original article was written within the context of a clinical setting. The following two studies are typical:

L. K. Waters and Darrell Roach, "A Factor Analysis of Need-Fulfillment Items Designed to Measure Maslow Need Categories," *Personnel Psychology*, Vol. 26, No. 2 (Summer, 1973), pp. 185–190.

Benjamin Schneider and Clayton P. Alderfer, "Three Studies of Measures of Need Satisfaction in Organizations," *Administrative Science Quarterly*, Vol. 18, No. 4 (December, 1973), pp. 489–505.

the variable characteristics of the basic needs that influence motivation. Among those factors are a person's self-evaluation and the interpretation of one's environment.

Concepts of Self and Environment

A person's self-concept and interpretation of the immediate environment provide a source of consistency to behavior throughout one's life and determine to a large extent those motives having the greatest influence. The image of self is formed relatively early in life and is reflected to the outer world by the manner of dress, speech, posture, and actions. The reflection remains fairly constant throughout life, thereby enabling others to predict with considerable accuracy one's behavior under a given set of circumstances. In this sense it is true that clothes do not make a person; indeed, clothes (along with actions, posture, and speech) are the person.

There are many dimensions to the self-image. Of particular concern with respect to the problems of motivation in industry is a person's perception of personal competence and the ability to achieve. Biographical studies show that patterns of achievement appear early in life. Initial successes lead to later successes and reinforce one's estimate of competence and ability to achieve. By the same token, failures, either imagined or real, deflate one's self-image of competence and achievement. Achievement, or the lack of it, shapes the environment in which one lives. Those who achieve develop a sense of *power* over their environment, for they are able to cope with that environment and seemingly control it to their advantage.[4] A person who exercises power and control over the environment learns to expect a high degree of *reward* from that environment, and when received, the reward tends to make people feel that they are masters of their own destiny. On the other hand, persistent lack of reward leads to an environmental image that is hostile and unrewarding. There are also the possible combinations of people who believe that they have a low degree of power to control their environment, yet have expectations of relatively high rewards, and those who feel that they can control their environment but expect little reward in return for their efforts.

The potential combinations of one's perceptions of the extent to which the environment can be controlled and one's expectations of reward are shown in Figure 16-1. It must be remembered that there are many possible shadings and combinations of these two factors and

---

[4]For a discussion of power as a factor in development the following is recommended: David B. McClelland, *Power, The Inner Experience* (New York: Irvington Publishers, 1975).

For a discussion of the desire for power as being the result of a fear of failure the following is suggested: Joseph Veroff and Joanne B. Veroff, "Reconsideration of a Measure of Power Motivation," *Psychological Bulletin*, Vol. 78, No. 4 (October, 1972), pp. 279–291.

Figure 16-1
RELATIONSHIPS
BETWEEN
PERCEIVED
CONTROL OVER
ENVIRONMENT
AND
EXPECTATIONS
OF REWARD

High

Reward Expectations		
Low Control Over Environment High Reward Expectations IV.	High Control Over Environment High Reward Expectations I.
Low Control Over Environment Low Reward Expectations III.	High Control Over Environment Low Reward Expectations II.

Low   Perceived Control Over Environment   High

Source: Saul W. Gellerman, **Motivation and Productivity** (New York: American Management Association, 1963), pp. 194-197.

that the four-cell table of Figure 16-1 represents only an outline of possible combinations.[5]

MOTIVATION IN INDUSTRY

The preceding discussion of needs and the way in which they are influenced by the concepts of self and the environment is presented in general terms with little specific reference to the application of these concepts to the day-to-day motivation of employees in an industrial situation. At the beginning of this chapter it is stated that in order to motivate employees management must either create felt needs within the individual or must offer a means of satisfying those needs already in existence within the individual. Undoubtedly the most widely used incentive to motivate employees is money, yet the evidence is overwhelming that more money does not necessarily mean greater productivity. The factors limiting the usefulness of money as a tool for motivating employees and the research findings concerning employee motivation are discussed below.[6]

Money and Motivation

Money has no intrinsic value, yet we recognize the economic worth of money in that it can be exchanged for goods and services. There is

---

[5]Saul W. Gellerman, *Motivation and Productivity* (New York: American Management Association, 1963), pp. 194–197. *Motivation and Productivity* presents in very readable form a summation of the outstanding research in the field of motivation and its applications to the industrial setting. A complete bibliography is included. The four-cell classification in Figure 16-1 is based on Dr. Gellerman's discussion.

[6]The following book contains 33 readings, all pertaining to managerial motivation and compensation: Henry L. Tosi, Robert J. House, and Marvin D. Dunnette (eds.), *Managerial Motivation and Compensation* (East Lansing: Graduate School of Business Administration, Michigan State University, 1972).

also a psychological emotionally toned worth attached to money. The economic worth of money enables it to serve as a means of satisfying the basic physiological and safety needs. Its psychological value is that for many persons money may symbolize achievement, success, prestige, or power — a way of fulfilling the higher social needs.

Control Over Environment. However, not all people are capable of regarding money as an incentive. Refer to the four combinations of expected rewards and perceived power over one's environment shown in Figure 16-1:

1. High perceived control over environment and high reward expectations.
2. High perceived control over environment and low reward expectations.
3. Low in both perceived control over environment and reward expectations.
4. Low perceived control over environment and high reward expectations.

Those persons who are best characterized by either the first or second category are the ones capable of responding to money as an incentive. These are the people who perceive themselves as having a high degree of power in shaping their environment; the magnitude of the expected reward is secondary in importance. Those belonging to the first group are highly trained in either technical or professional fields, a training that by its very nature represents a pattern of success. For these people money readily becomes a symbol of success and achievement and can be exchanged for desired goods and services. Those in the second category who expect little but believe that they can effectively control their environment are likely to respond to money, not for its own sake, but as additional evidence of ability to control and shape the environment. Entrepreneurs (including successful managers) often belong to the second group. People characterized by groups three and four generally do not respond to money as an incentive since they do not perceive themselves as effectively controlling their environment.[7]

Conflicting Needs. The belief that money is and should be a strong motivator is deeply rooted, and not without foundation, as evidenced by those who believe that they can control their environment. For the most part these people respond well to monetary incentive plans in sales and managerial jobs, but similar plans for hourly production workers experience questionable success at best. Whyte estimates that only 10 percent of the hourly production workers in the United States respond to a financial incentive plan by producing to capacity, thereby

---

[7]For a discussion of power, the ability to control the environment, the following is suggested: David C. McClelland and David H. Burnham, "Power is the Great Motivator," *Harvard Business Review*, Vol. 54, No. 2 (March–April, 1976), pp. 100–110.

increasing their earnings.[8] What about the other 90 percent? Why don't they produce more, particularly when greater productivity means more money? Zaleznik and his co-workers at Harvard University offer some sound answers to this question; albeit the answers are not encouraging for management.[9]

Before discussing Zaleznik's work we must take another look at groups one and two mentioned above. These are the people — the physician, the lawyer, the accountant, the salesperson or the entrepreneur — capable of responding to financial incentives, people who believe that they can shape their environment and control it to a large extent. To them the world is not a foreboding place in which to live since there are more successes than there are failures. Further, success is the result largely of individual effort. Although any one of these people may work as a member or a leader of a group, each is usually recognized as an individual having a unique contribution to make to the group. Admittedly, membership in a small work group is necessary and highly prized, but it is not the key to success. Instead, success is attributable largely to individual effort. Members of groups one and two usually satisfy to a considerable extent their need for belonging; but even more important, the esteem needs — prestige, achievement, power, and recognition — also have a measure of satisfaction. Many are realizing a degree of self-actualization in that they are doing and being what they must do and be.

The environment of the production worker, as described by Whyte and Zaleznik, is one of sharp contrast to the environment described above. First, let us consider the production worker as an individual, then a group of production workers, and finally the statistical exceptions — Whyte's 10 percent who respond as individuals to incentives.

The Production Worker. It is often said that all generalizations are false, including this one. Nonetheless, the following generalizations help to place in perspective some of the problems of motivation in an industrial society. For some reason, or perhaps a combination of reasons, the production worker (think of the assembly line) has not become highly skilled. Lack of progress may be due to a lack of ability, lack of physiological drive and stamina, poor environmental factors, inability to acquire training as a youth due to economic conditions, or any one of a host of other reasons. Whatever the cause, the environment has not surrendered much over the years, with the resultant feelings of frustration and the conviction that the world is hostile and

---

[8]William F. Whyte, *Money and Motivation* (New York: Harper & Row, Publishers, 1955).

[9]Abraham Zaleznik, C. R. Christensen, and F. Roethlisberger, *The Motivation, Productivity, and Satisfaction of Workers*, A Prediction Study (Boston: Harvard University Graduate School of Business Administration, 1958). Both the Harvard study and Whyte's work emphasize the limitations of money as a means of motivating production workers and stress the importance of the work group as a motivating force.

unyielding. Expectations of reward may have been high during youth, but early socio-economic forces may have permanently limited expectations to a minimal level. If expectations were high, the years of frustration and lack of anticipated rewards serve to emphasize the hopelessness of ever achieving original goals.

The basic physiological and safety needs of the worker described above are, in all probability, fairly well satisfied. But what about the higher needs? It is difficult for most of us to imagine self-actualization or self-fulfillment on an assembly line. Punching a clock, being identified by number, and performing a routine task are not conducive to feelings of status, prestige, or high esteem in the eyes of others. Since these esteem needs are not satisfied, the next step in descending order of the hierarchy of needs is the need for belonging — for belonging to a group.

The Group. Imagine our hypothetical worker accepting a new job and a new clock number with a different employer. The new job is not much different than several previous jobs, nor are the opportunities for advancement appreciably different, at least as the worker sees the situation. Since the job is the same, the possibilities for satisfying the esteem and self-actualization needs are effectively blocked, but the opportunity is present to become a member of a group. The informal group is composed of people with similar backgrounds and perceptions of self and control over the environment. At the beginning our new employee is not a "regular" member of the group (and may never become a member of the inner circle), but seeks the group as a means of satisfying a basic need — the need to belong. Zaleznik refers to these groups as "frozen groups"; Gellerman calls them "sick." Frozen or sick, these are the groups that set patterns of behavior and shape the attitudes of workers in the plant.[10]

Conformity with respect to both overt behavior and attitudes is the price of membership in the group. One of the most noticeable aspects of the group's behavior is the restriction of output, in reality a reflection of attitudes toward management. Management is viewed with suspicion, and any change is regarded as ultimately resulting in an increase in the amount of work required from each member of the group or a reduction in the size of the work force. The objective of the group is to maintain a *status quo* since expectations of high reward and the belief that the environment can be shaped no longer exist. At least, present conditions assure the satisfaction of the physiological and safety needs, and membership in the group satisfies the need for belonging. For the new worker, joining or not joining the group may be a difficult choice in terms of need satisfaction. Conformity to the

---

[10]For a similar description of the work group the following is recommended: Robert F. Allen and Saul Pilnick, "Confronting the Shadow Organization: How to Detect and Defeat Negative Norms," *Organizational Dynamics*, Vol. 1, No. 4 (Spring, 1973), pp. 3–18.

group's standards of behavior and attitudes usually means giving up satisfying the esteem and self-actualization needs while on the job; but prior experience shows that the satisfaction of these needs is difficult and in the distant future. To pursue the higher needs could mean rejection by the group, with the resulting frustration of the belonging needs. For many workers the dilemma exists only in theory; the choice is made early in life to belong to the group, thus satisfying the belonging needs and foregoing the higher esteem and self-actualization needs. Yet for some, the rate buster for example, needs other than belonging to the group are more important.

The Rate Buster. A small percentage, Whyte's estimate is 10 percent, rejects the group's demand for conformity and responds to money as an incentive. These people are known as *rate busters*. Conceivably they could be responding to management's plan to reduce costs and improve productivity, but it is seldom that such is the case. For the rate buster who sought membership in the group and was rejected by the group, behavior may be a form of revenge, a means of showing up the group by outproducing them. Others who excel in production do so as the result of their socio-economic background rather than as the result of responding to the merits of a specific incentive plan.

Socially, rate busters tend to be "loners" both inside and outside the industrial organization. Further, they generally come from homes that stress the virtues of individual achievement and economic independence. They still believe that as the result of their own efforts they can shape their environment and improve their lot in life. Either reason, revenge against the group or socio-economic background, points up the irony of incentive plans. The 10 percent who respond to incentives are not responding to the plan itself; instead, they are motivated by forces that are seldom recognized by and far beyond the control of management.[11]

When Money Works. The above discussion shows the shortcomings of monetary incentives as a means of motivating the vast majority of production workers. Nonetheless, many companies are satisfied with incentive plans and attribute a reduction in cost and an increase in productivity to these plans. Admittedly, many such plans work, but they are not working as the result of the effectiveness of money as an incentive. There are other reasons why incentive plans often attain management's desired results. First, the presence of a realistic standard tends to motivate employees since it defines a goal to be reached within a specified period of time. In this respect a standard is the same

---

[11]For a discussion of the effects of demographic factors on the meaning of money and its efficacy as a motivator, the following is of interest: Paul F. Wernimont and Susan Fitzpatrick, "The Meaning of Money," *Journal of Applied Psychology*, Vol. 56, No. 3 (June, 1972), pp. 218–226.

as par in golf or a 200 game in bowling. Second, without stated standards, supervisors do not know what is expected of them and often reflect their unrest through aggressive attitudes toward production workers. When standards are in effect, the production workers who meet these goals are assured of more pleasant working relationships with their supervisors. A third reason is that prior to the installation of production standards there is usually a period of intensive methods analysis which improves the mechanics of actually performing the job, with the result that more work can be done with less effort and fatigue. Fourth, the introduction of standards forces management to improve the production control function so that the flow of work is at a more even pace with fewer periods of idleness due to time spent waiting for materials.[12]

A Two-Factor Theory of Work Motivation

The discussion of money and motivation should not lead us to the conclusion that money is unimportant in the total process of motivating employees; it is important. However, according to the two-factor theory of motivation, money is a *hygienic factor*, not a *motivator*. The two-factor theory differentiates between hygienic factors and motivators and is the result of research conducted by Dr. Frederick Herzberg and his associates of the Psychological Service of Pittsburgh.[13]

Several hundred engineers and accountants were interviewed and asked to recall incidents related to their work and to indicate the effect of these incidents upon their productivity and attitudes toward their jobs. The subjects of the Pittsburgh studies were also asked to indicate the duration of the feelings aroused by each incident.

Herzberg found that experiences which create positive attitudes toward work arise from the job itself and function as *motivators*. These incidents are associated with feelings of self-improvement, achievement, and the desire for and the acceptance of greater responsibility. The feelings thus generated are of a relatively long duration and result in increased productivity. Since the subjects of the Pittsburgh studies

---

[12]The following observation was made by Morris S. Viteles many years ago. Morris S. Viteles, *Motivation and Morale in Industry* (New York: W.W. Norton & Co., 1953), pp. 29–30. "In practice, the installation of a wage incentive plan is generally accompanied by other changes in working conditions, personnel policies, and practices which are frequently major in character . . . as a result, management and industrial engineers have frequently been unable to present clear-cut and unequivocal evidence as to the specific effect of wage incentive."

For a review of the literature concerning the effect of money as a motivator the following is recommended. Robert L. Opsahl and Marvin D. Dunnette, "The Role of Financial Compensation in Industrial Motivation," *Psychological Bulletin*, Vol. 66, No. 2 (August, 1966), pp. 94–118.

[13]Frederick Herzberg, Bernard Mausner, and B. Snyderman, *The Motivation to Work* (2d ed.; New York: John Wiley & Sons, 1959).

For a more recent statement of Herzberg's position the following is recommended: Frederick Herzberg, *Work and the Nature of Man* (Cleveland: The World Publishing Co., 1966).

were engineers and accountants, the change in productivity was more qualitative than quantitative in nature. The second set of factors related to productivity on the job are conditions peripheral to the job itself. Pay, working conditions (such as heating, lighting, and ventilation), company policy, and the quality of supervision are all part of the environment but peripheral to the job itself. When these factors are believed to be inadequate they function as *dissatisfiers*; but when present, they do not motivate employees to greater productivity. Instead, they are *hygienic* in character in that their presence makes it possible for the motivators to function. Positive feelings aroused by these peripheral conditions of work, such as a word of encouragement from a supervisor or an increase in pay, are relatively brief in duration. Another finding of the Pittsburgh study is significant. When employees are highly motivated and find their jobs interesting and challenging, they are able to tolerate considerable dissatisfaction with peripheral factors; however, a full measure of all hygienic factors does not make the job interesting.

One obvious limitation of Herzberg's work is that his subjects were engineers and accountants, people who have had the motivation to acquire professional training, who believe that they can shape their environment, and who expect considerable reward from that environment. Does the same hold true for the nonprofessional worker?

Hygienic and Motivating Factors at Work. Dr. M. Scott Myers, formerly Manager of Personnel Research for Texas Instruments Incorporated, using essentially the same technique employed by Herzberg, raises and answers these questions concerning employee motivation.

1. *What motivates employees to work effectively?* A challenging job which allows a feeling of achievement, responsibility, growth, advancement, enjoyment of work itself, and earned recognition.
2. *What dissatisfies workers?* Mostly factors peripheral to the job — work rules, lighting, coffee breaks, titles, seniority rights, wages, fringe benefits, and the like.
3. *When do workers become dissatisfied?* When opportunities for meaningful achievement are eliminated and they become sensitized to their environment and begin to find fault.[14]

Myers' study is not limited to the analysis of the professionally trained, since it is a representative sample of 282 employees from five different job classifications, three of which are salaried and two are hourly classifications. The salaried classifications included are scientists, engineers, and manufacturing supervisors; the hourly classifications include technicians (male) and assemblers (female). Although the

---

[14]M. Scott Myers, "Who Are Your Motivated Workers?" *Harvard Business Review*, Vol. 42 (January-February, 1964), p. 73. Copyright © 1963 by the President and Fellows of Harvard College; all rights reserved. Dr. Myers' report, pp. 73–88, presents in detail the findings of his research conducted at Texas Instruments. The article contains many pictorial presentations well worth careful study.

answers to the above questions apply to all job classifications, the differences in the importance ascribed to various motivational factors other than achievement warrant a brief analysis of the responses of each group.

Scientists. For scientists, 50 percent of the favorable incidents reported are related to achievement on the job. The most intense feelings of satisfaction; i.e., those feelings that endure for at least two months, are related to "work itself." The most frequently mentioned source of dissatisfaction stems from company policy and administration, implying that rules and regulations sometimes interfere with the achievement of scientific goals. However, the most intense feelings of dissatisfaction come from a feeling that their work lacks full responsibility.[15]

Engineers. Engineers show a motivational pattern much like that shown by the scientists with respect to the importance of achievement and the satisfaction derived from work itself. Yet they differ from scientists in that advancement and pay are also predominant sources of feelings of intense satisfaction. In addition to reporting a lack of responsibility and poor company policy as causes of dissatisfaction, the engineers report that incompetence and unfriendliness of supervisors and inadequate pay (in their estimation) create dissatisfaction.[16]

Manufacturing Supervisors. Although achievement is mentioned most frequently as a source of satisfaction, manufacturing supervisors — a nonprofessionally trained group — show a pattern distinctly different from that of the scientists and engineers. Advancement, recognition, and the possibility of growth create the intense feelings of satisfaction, with advancement being by far the greatest single source of intense satisfaction. Lack of responsibility, inadequate pay, and failure to advance are causes of dissatisfaction among manufacturing supervisors. The designation of advancement as the major source of satisfaction is not surprising since supervisors are frequently promoted from hourly classifications and seek such promotions because of their strong desire to achieve through advancement within the organization.

Hourly Technicians. Hourly electronic technicians, like manufacturing supervisors, do not mention work itself as either a frequent or intense source of satisfaction; to them, work itself is the greatest dissatisfier. Increased responsibility is by far the strongest motivator of technicians and is followed by advancement. It is quite possible that

---

[15]The following study presents similar findings: Frank Harrison, "The Management of Scientists: Determinants of Perceived Role Performance," *Academy of Management Journal*, Vol. 17, No. 2 (June, 1974), pp. 234–241.

[16]Similar findings are reported in the following study: H. Roy Kaplan, Curt Tausky, and Bhopinder S. Bolaria, "The Human Relations View of Motivation: Fact or Fantasy?" *Organizational Dynamics*, Vol. 1, No. 2 (Autumn, 1972), pp. 67–80. This study also presents a bibliography of studies that lend support to Herzberg's theory and a list of studies that do not support the theory.

enlarged responsibilities and successfully achieving these responsibilities are considered a means of advancing.

Female Assemblers. The preceding groups — scientists, engineers, manufacturing supervisors, and hourly technicians — are all characterized by Myers as motivation seekers or, at the very least, potential motivation seekers. These people can be motivated by factors within the job itself, but the female assemblers are described as *maintenance seekers* in that factors peripheral to the work itself are dominant in creating either strong positive feelings of satisfaction or negative feelings of dissatisfaction. Although achievement is mentioned most frequently as a source of satisfaction, the competence and friendliness of supervision along with pay offer the most intense feelings of satisfaction. By the same token, lack of recognition by supervision and lack of security (the threat of layoff) are the chief causes of dissatisfaction. Increased responsibility and advancement are not motivators; instead, recognition and understanding by the immediate supervisor motivate the female assembler.

Management's Choice. The results of Dr. Myers' study are presented in pictorial form in Figure 16-2, Employee Needs. Note that the inner circle — motivational needs — contains those factors directly related to the job, while the outer circle is composed of maintenance needs. Employees seek satisfaction in the area of maintenance needs — those factors peripheral to the job itself — when the motivational needs of growth, achievement, responsibility, and recognition are not satisfied. The relative importance of maintenance needs diminishes when motivational needs are satisfied. Thus, management has two broad alternatives: (1) directing its efforts toward the satisfaction of motivational needs by designing jobs having the capability of fulfilling those needs, or (2) directing its efforts toward the satisfaction of those needs peripheral to the job itself. Acme Manufacturing Company, Case Problem 16-A, has apparently decided to choose the second alternative and satisfy the peripheral needs. Let us discuss this alternative and the results that might reasonably be expected from this approach to employee motivation.

Employee Benefit Programs. In all probability no company has a vice-president in charge of fun and games, yet most companies of any size have several highly paid administrators in their personnel departments in charge of various phases of employee welfare and benefit programs. These programs are concerned with those items shown in the outer circle of Figure 16-2. Such activities are costly, not only in terms of dollars spent but more importantly because of their inefficiency as motivators. The dollar cost of maintaining these extrinsic factors at competitive levels is rising in a never-ending spiral. Unions have traditionally directed their bargaining efforts toward improvement of the physical and economic factors shown in the outer circle. Managements

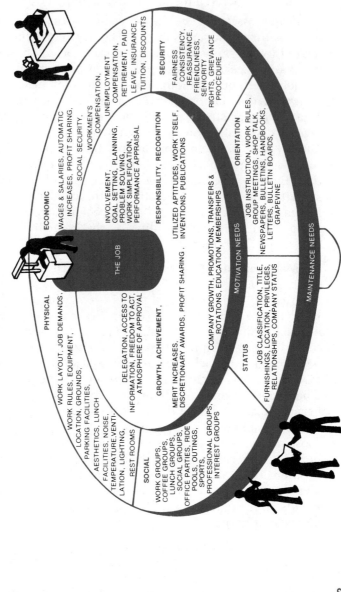

Figure 16-2
EMPLOYEE NEEDS —
MAINTENANCE AND
MOTIVATIONAL

Source: M. Scott Myers, "Who Are Your Motivated Workers?" **Harvard Business Review,** Vol. 42 (January–February, 1964), page 86. Copyright© 1964 by the President and Fellows of Harvard College; all rights reserved.

have, perhaps unwittingly, aided unions in their efforts to raise the level of employee benefits. Most companies take considerable pride in their benefit and welfare programs and in most instances are forced to keep them at competitive levels in order to attract needed personnel.

In addition to the ever-mounting total cost of these programs, a hidden cost lies in their inefficiency as motivators. When hygienic factors are absent, or not present in sufficient quantity, they function as dissatisfiers and can actually interfere with productivity. However, when present, they do not motivate personnel to greater productivity. They merely form a floor or base and represent the minimum acceptable conditions of employment. Employees who are best described as maintenance seekers are an insatiable group; maintenance needs are never fully satisfied. There is always a greener pasture offering more employee benefits. The designation of various employee benefits as fringe benefits is peculiarly apt, since they are on the fringe of the real benefits that should be derived from the job itself.

Job Design. If we are to tap the motivators of achievement, growth, responsibility, and recognition, we must examine closely the design of the job itself, for these factors are intrinsic. In some jobs, such as that of the scientist, the engineer, or the accountant, minor changes in company policy and administration might permit the potential motivators to operate effectively. However, there are many jobs in industry characterized by highly repetitive, monotonous activities offering few opportunities for growth, additional responsibility, or recognition. The obvious question arises: Can these jobs be designed in a manner that will offer greater motivation from factors inherently a part of the job? In answering this question, let us look first at current practices in job design and then at two alternatives for increasing job satisfaction.[17]

Current Job Design is based upon the concept of specialization, the nature of the production process, and the goal of lowest unit cost.[18] The concept of specialization is applied not only to the design of machinery used in the production process but also to the jobs performed by the workers. Jobs are composed of a sequence of individual tasks or

---

[17]David Jenkins, *Job Power*, Blue and White Collar Democracy (New York: Doubleday and Co., 1973). This book contains many case studies of job redesign both in the United States and in Europe.

Louis Davis and James Taylor, *The Design of Jobs* (Harmondsworth, England: Penguin Books Ltd., 1972). This work contains most of the important articles that have been written on the subject of job design.

Work in America (Cambridge: Massachusetts Institute of Technology Press, 1973). This work is the report of a special task force presented to the Secretary of Health, Education, and Welfare. Its primary goal is to show how to improve the quality of working life. An extensive bibliography is included.

[18]Louis E. Davis, "Job Design and Productivity: A New Approach," *Personnel*, Vol. 33 (March, 1957), pp. 418–430. Dr. Davis' article presents an excellent analysis of specialization and job design. It also contains a detailed review of the study conducted by Marks that is cited in footnote 21.

operations that are grouped and then assigned to a single individual. Usually a particular method for performing each of the separate tasks of a job is specified. In many instances the tasks performed by the worker are determined by the characteristics of the machine; for example, the bag catcher who removes and boxes bags made by a machine designed to produce a single product.

When there is a choice in determining which tasks should be combined into a single job, the criterion of lowest unit cost is applied. Since cost is to be minimized, it seems only logical to design tasks and combine them in such a fashion that the lowest level of skill is required. The application of this procedure usually results in a highly repetitive operation, composed of relatively simple movements requiring little skill, and capable of being learned by a large number of workers in a comparatively short period of time. Thus, training costs are at a minimum and an adequate potential of labor is assured. Assembly operations are typical of jobs composed of repetitive, unskilled tasks capable of being learned by most industrial workers.

How valid are these assumptions? Judging by this nation's level of productivity, consumption, and pay, the assumptions underlying the design of production processes and fitting jobs to these processes are quite effective. Yet it remains to be answered whether or not current practices of job design utilize the best available means of designing jobs since there are relatively few instances in which jobs have been designed to be more complex and challenging to the worker.

Job Enrichment, sometimes referred to as *job enlargement*, is the process of making industrial jobs more challenging and interesting by increasing personal responsibility for one's work and the opportunity for personal achievement and recognition, and by providing expanded opportunities for psychological growth and development.[19] The experience of Non-Linear Systems, Inc., described in Case Problems 8-A and 8-B, illustrates the experiences of one company with job enrichment.

One of the early studies leading to the belief that job enrichment might be a solution that would improve the attitudes and morale of industrial workers is the work conducted by Walker and Guest of the Institute of Human Relations at Yale University.[20] Their studies reveal

---

[19]The following book is recommended as a comprehensive statement of a job enrichment practices currently employed in industry. The cases presented cover a wide range of companies and also a wide range of industrial jobs that have been modified successfully through the process of job enrichment. John R. Maher (ed.), *New Perspectives in Job Enrichment* (New York: Van Nostrand-Reinhold Co., 1971).

For another summary of seven case studies from manufacturing and nonmanufacturing firms and a governmental agency of experiences with job enrichment the following report which contains a complete bibliography is recommended. The name of the author is Harold M. F. Rush, *Job Design for Motivation: Experiments in Job Enlargement and Job Enrichment* (New York: The Conference Board, 1971).

[20]C. R. Walker and R. H. Guest, *The Man on the Assembly Line* (Cambridge: Harvard University Press, 1952). C. R. Walker and R. H. Guest, "The Man on the Assembly Line," *Harvard Business Review*, Vol. 30 (May-June, 1952), pp. 71–83. *The Harvard Business Review* article presents a summary of feelings and attitudes of automobile assembly-plant workers as revealed by carefully conducted depth interviews.

a very low level of job satisfaction on the part of automobile assembly-line workers; in fact, the workers despise their jobs even though most of them indicate that pay, supervision, and working conditions are more than satisfactory. The reasons for the intense dislike of the work are reported to be due to the anonymity of the worker himself and the complete depersonalization of the job. Feelings of anonymity and depersonalization arise because the pace is determined mechanically by the speed of the line, the low level of skills required, the highly repetitive nature of the tasks performed, the lack of choice or control over methods and tools to be used, and the lack of social interaction resulting from an isolated and fixed position on the line.

Another early study, of value because it utilizes the experimental approach to enriching the job content of an assembly line operation, is described by A. R. N. Marks.[21] The total number of employees in the department was 35, of which 29 were female assemblers engaged in assembling a hospital appliance, and six performed supporting jobs of inspecting and supplying materials. Each assembler performed one of nine operations at a station on a conveyor-paced assembly line. Every two hours positions on the line were rotated to lessen fatigue and break the monotony. The speed of the conveyor determined the output for the group, and since positions on the line were rotated, there was no individual responsibility for quality. The experiment consisted of four stages:

1. Line Job Design — The normal method of assembling, performed on a conveyor-paced line with six workers supporting the 29 assemblers.
2. Group Job Design — The conveyor is eliminated but other conditions remain the same. In effect, the pace of the operation and consequently the output are determined by the worker.
3. Individual Job Design No. 1 — Each worker performs all nine operations at her own station and is responsible for procuring her own parts, inspection of the parts, and quality of the final assembly. This stage of the experiment was conducted in a room near the main production area to provide training in the new method. Each worker spent two days in this phase. The conveyor is eliminated.
4. Individual Job Design No. 2 — Following the two-day training period, each worker performs the assembly operation using the method of individual job design No. 1 in the main production area for six days. (In discussing the results of the experiment, individual job designs Nos. 1 and 2 are treated as a single method since design No. 1 served as a training period for design No. 2. The method is the same; the only variable is the location in which the work is performed.)

With the group job design method, which lasted only two days, productivity was considerably lower than the normal production of the line job design. Individual job design No. 1 resulted in a higher

---

[21]A. R. N. Marks, "An Investigation of Modifications of Job Design in an Industrial Situation and Their Effect on Some Measures of Economic Productivity" (Ph.D. dissertation, University of California, 1954).

level of productivity than that attained from the group job design, and the level of production of individual job design No. 2 continued to rise, with the average for the group being about 95 percent of the amount produced using the original line job design. These results are quite remarkable considering that the total number of days' experience in using the individual job design methods is only eight, while the average length of time on the line job design is over four years.

A detailed analysis of the production records of the individual job design method shows that production increased each consecutive day, and on the sixth day the average production for the group exceeded the average for the line design method. Further, as a result of each assembler operating independently of the others, individual differences in productivity were noted, with some of the women producing 30 to 40 percent more than the average for the line job design. In addition, the level of quality improved considerably — a 75 percent reduction in kinked (wiring) assemblies — and the six supporting workers who normally inspect final assemblies and procured parts were eliminated. Marks also found that those who participated in the experimental individual job design developed a more favorable attitude toward their jobs in that they desired more responsibility and were willing to put forth more effort, and when returned to the line job design method at the end of the experiment, they disliked the loss of personal responsibility that is inherent in a conveyor-paced assembly operation.

The experiment in job enrichment described above raises some provocative questions. The level of production on the sixth day of individual job design No. 2 exceeded the average of the line production method, thus challenging the assumption that the highly engineered assembly-line operation is the *optimum* arrangement for producing at the lowest unit cost. We do not know whether or not the individual job design method would result in productivity equal to that of the line job for a sustained period of time; in other words, did the high production of the assemblers on the sixth day result from the job design itself, or did it result from their awareness that they were participating in an experiment? How applicable are these results to other industries? Assume that individual job design does yield a higher degree of productivity; what is the capital investment required for individual job design as compared with line job design in assembling a complex product such as an automobile? Can the same procedures be applied to the routine, repetitive clerical jobs of a bank or an insurance company? And finally, how important are feelings of job satisfaction and productivity?[22]

---

[22]In a review of the literature concerning job enrichment Professors Hulin and Blood conclude that positive relationships between job size and job satisfaction cannot be assumed to be general; instead, the success of job enlargement programs is greatly dependent upon the backgrounds of the workers involved. Charles L. Hulin and Milton

The preceding discussion utilizes Herzberg's two factors with intrinsic job characteristics acting as motivators and peripheral job characteristics functioning as satisfiers or dissatisfiers but not as motivators. The two-factor theory is useful as a means of discussing the alternate courses available for motivating employees.[23] Implied in the above discussion, though not stated explicitly, is the assumption that job satisfaction is an independent variable with production the resultant dependent variable. However, such is not the case.

In order to place job satisfaction in its proper role as a dependent variable — the result of the total work situation — let us examine the concept of morale, and some of the studies of job satisfaction that utilize methods other than the interview. Then we review a part of the literature relating to job satisfaction and productivity and finally an instrumentality approach to the understanding of the causes of job satisfaction is presented.

Morale

Morale is a word with many meanings. Definitions include statements that morale is the absence of conflict, a feeling of happiness, good personal adjustment, those attitudes pertaining to work, and the extent of ego-involvement in one's job. Some definitions would limit the concept of morale to only those persons working in a group by defining morale as the extent of cohesiveness or "we feeling" of a group or the extent to which there is personal acceptance of the goals of the group. Dr. Robert Guion offers a definition of morale that includes most, if not all, of the attributes previously mentioned. *"Morale is the extent to which an individual's needs are satisfied and the extent to which the individual perceives that satisfaction as stemming from his total job situation."*[24] Guion's definition is of value since it stresses the

---

R. Blood, "Job Enlargement, Individual Differences, and Worker Responses," *Psychological Bulletin*, Vol. 69, No. 1 (January, 1968), pp. 41–55.

Professor Hulin has modified the above paper and presents it as a chapter in Maher (ed.), *op. cit.*, Chapter 9, "Individual Differences and Job Enrichment — The Case Against General Treatments," pp. 159–191. A complete bibliography is presented in both sources.

For another statement highly critical of job enrichment the following is suggested: Fred Luthans and William E. Reif, "Job Enrichment: Long on Theory, Short on Practice," *Organizational Dynamics*, Vol. 2, No. 3 (Winter, 1974), pp. 30–38.

[23]A criticism of the two-factor theory of job satisfaction and motivation is the following: Robert J. House and Lawrence A. Wigdor, "Herzberg's Dual-Factor Theory of Job Satisfaction and Motivation: A Review of the Evidence and a Criticism," *Personnel Psychology*, Vol. 20, No. 4 (Winter, 1967), pp. 369–389.

An alternate view, and one more in accord with current research findings, is presented in the last section of this chapter — "A Concluding View."

[24]Robert M. Guion, "Industrial Morale (A Symposium) 1. The Problem of Terminology," *Personnel Psychology*, Vol. 11 (Spring, 1958), p. 62. This symposium was presented at the 1957 meetings of the Midwestern Psychological Association in Chicago. Dr. Guion's article, pp. 59–61, summarizes varying concepts of morale.

importance of need satisfaction and applies equally to individuals as well as to those who are members of groups. It also emphasizes the complexity of the sources of morale by referring to the total job situation rather than to job satisfaction alone.

Other Studies of Job Satisfaction

There have been many studies showing that intrinsic job satisfaction is only one factor of the total job situation. An analysis of the job attitudes of 6,000 industrial workers in a midwestern tractor factory shows that there are four relatively independent factors contributing to satisfaction derived from the total job situation. They are: intrinsic job satisfaction, satisfaction with the company, satisfaction with supervision, and satisfaction with rewards and the opportunity for mobility.[25] Another study using the technique of multiple-factor analysis — a statistical tool for determining independent factors — investigated the needs to be satisfied by the total job situation. There is a general factor of morale resulting from overall satisfaction as a result of need fulfillment, the need for social recognition of status, and the need for self-respect.[26]

By far the most comprehensive study of job satisfaction, known as The Cornell Studies of Job Satisfaction, uses a carefully constructed checklist of items descriptive of the total job situation. The Cornell studies show that job satisfaction is composed of five relatively independent aspects of the work environment. They are the work itself, pay, supervision, opportunity for promotions, and the characteristics of co-workers. Further, it is shown that any one of these factors may serve as a source of satisfaction for a given group of employees and as a source of dissatisfaction for another group. Also, these factors shift in their significance to a given individual; that is, what is satisfying today may be dissatisfying tomorrow as the individual's needs and goals change.[27]

[25]Robert L. Kahn, "Productivity and Job Satisfaction," *Personnel Psychology*, Vol. 15 (Autumn, 1960), pp. 275–287. In addition to reporting the results of a multiple-factor analysis of employee attitudes, Kahn summarizes the major findings of the Survey Research Center of the University of Michigan in their studies of job satisfaction and productivity.

[26]Oakley J. Gordon, "A Factor Analysis of Human Needs and Industrial Morale," *Personnel Psychology*, Vol. 8 (Spring, 1955), pp. 1–18. This work complements the study of Kahn. Gordon's analysis is concerned with needs, while Kahn's is concerned with the job situation. Note that the definition of morale offered by Guion ties these two aspects of morale together.

[27]Patricia Cain Smith, Lorne M. Kendall, Charles L. Hulin, *The Measurement of Satisfaction in Work and Retirement*, A Strategy for the Study of Attitudes (Chicago: Rand McNally & Co., 1969). As indicated by the title, the Cornell studies measure satisfaction in retirement as well as satisfaction in work. The items measured in the Retirement Description Index (RDI) are activities and work, financial situation, health, and people you associate with. *The Measurement of Satisfaction in Work and Retirement* offers a detailed insight into carefully planned research strategy.

Productivity and Job Satisfaction

Psychologists have devoted a great deal of time and effort to studying the effects of reward and punishment upon human behavior. In general, it seems that situations that reward a person are satisfying and those situations that punish a person are dissatisfying. Further, people have a tendency to prolong or return to satisfying situations and to avoid those situations that are not satisfying. This line of reasoning is applied to the interpretation of morale as a factor in turnover and absenteeism. Thus, people with high morale (a high degree of perceived satisfaction of needs through the total job situation) can be expected to continue their job with a minimum amount of absenteeism, and those who quit or are chronically absent do so because the situation is not satisfying to them. Although this reasoning is plausible in explaining turnover and absenteeism, it does not follow that satisfaction with the job should or does result in a high level of productivity.

All individuals are simultaneously members of several social systems and the attainment of goals within each of these social systems serves to satisfy the needs of the individual. High productivity is seldom a goal, but high productivity may lead to the fulfillment of a goal, thereby creating a feeling of satisfaction. In this case, productivity is varying concomitantly with satisfaction (goal attainment); there is no causal relationship.

Katz and Kahn suggest that the industrial worker is a member of four social systems: (1) A system outside the plant and within the plant, (2) a system of relationships with other workers, (3) a system of the formal union structure, and (4) an organizational system of the company itself.[28] It might be argued that higher productivity is a means of achieving prestige, recognition, and higher status in the social system outside the plant. But evidence does not show that the majority of industrial workers are strongly motivated toward social achievement outside the plant.

Further, many industrial workers are in Gellerman's classifications of those who perceive little chance of control over their environment. In analyzing the relationships of industrial workers among themselves, we must remember Zaleznik's "frozen groups," groups that have pegged production at minimal levels, and the desire to belong to the group — an impossibility with high levels of production. Workers who have aspirations of achieving rank and position within the formal

---

[28]D. Katz and R. L. Kahn, "Some Recent Findings in Human Relations Research in Industry." From G. E. Swanson, T. M. Newcomb, and E. L. Hartley (eds.), *Readings in Social Psychology* (New York: Henry Holt & Co., 1952), pp. 650–665.

Arthur H. Brayfield and Walter H. Crockett, "Employee Attitudes and Employee Performance," *Psychological Bulletin*, Vol. 52 (September, 1955), pp. 415–422. Brayfield and Crockett present an excellent survey of the literature on employee attitudes in relation to productivity and use the four social systems suggested by Katz and Kahn as a format for their presentation.

structure of the union may do so without resorting to high production; in fact, high levels of productivity frequently serve as a detriment for advancement within the union. Seemingly the employee desirous of advancing within the company organization by receiving increased pay, a promotion, or a higher position in the hierarchy would be motivated to produce more. Yet, productivity is only one of several factors considered for advancement; quality, ability to get along with others, and dependability may outweigh productivity in determining advancement within the company.

In 1947 the Survey Research Center of the University of Michigan undertook a series of investigations to determine the relationships between supervisory practices, employee satisfaction, and productivity.[29] In the first study of the relationships of these three variables, the setting is the home office of a large insurance company. As might be expected, most of the employees are young women new to the labor force. Three indexes of satisfaction are used in this study. They are satisfaction with the company as a whole, satisfaction with pay and job status, and satisfaction with the job itself. The results show that there is no significant relationship between any of these indexes of satisfaction and the productivity of the work group. However, members of high-producing work groups recognize their groups as high producers; but this may not be satisfaction. Rather, it is a perception of the situation as it exists.

The design of the second study is the same as the first; however, the setting is as different as night from day. The work situation is the right-of-way maintenance jobs of approximately 300 railroad laborers and 72 foremen. The tasks performed are manual labor, not clerical functions; and the subjects are men, not young women. Yet, the results are the same. No consistent relationship is found between productivity and the three indexes of job satisfaction. Again, the members of high-producing work groups are able to perceive their groups as high producers, but this ability to perceive a situation as it exists is not necessarily job satisfaction.

The third study is different in several respects from the first two. Instead of using group measures of productivity, individual production records for 6,000 production workers of a midwestern tractor company were examined and compared against known time study standards for each job. Also, instead of assuming indexes of job satisfaction, a factor analysis of data obtained from a carefully constructed questionnaire was performed to determine the dimensions of job satisfaction. These dimensions — presented in the discussion of morale — are: intrinsic job satisfaction, satisfaction with the company, satisfaction with

---

[29]Robert L. Kahn, "Productivity and Job Satisfaction," *Personnel Psychology*, Vol. 15 (Autumn, 1960), pp. 275–287. Dr. Kahn also summarizes the results of the insurance study, the study of railroad workers, and the tractor study.

rewards and mobility. Again, none of these measures of satisfaction are related to productivity.

Current Theories of Work Motivation

There is no single theory concerning the motivation to work applicable to all individuals and to all work situations. Maslow's need hierarchy is a broad statement of human needs and provides a conceptual framework that offers a basis for understanding the forces that cause people to behave in certain ways in certain situations. Though Maslow's theory was developed primarily for application in the area of clinical psychology, it has been widely adapted and used in industrial situations. Gellerman's concept of how one learns to perceive the extent to which the environment can be controlled and how one learns to expect certain rewards from that environment is also useful. Gellerman's concept is of special significance because it emphasizes the effect of broad socio-economic factors. Herzberg offers a simplified two-factor theory of work motivation. To him, those factors that are intrinsic to the job itself are motivators and those factors extrinsic or peripheral to the job are hygienic in nature. The absence of the hygienic factors may cause certain forms of dissatisfaction with the work situation, but their presence even in above-average quantities does not lead to motivation — defining motivation as increased performance. The Cornell Studies resulting in the Job Description Index show that there are at least five factors, all related to the total work situation, that lead to job satisfaction. Further, the Cornell Studies show that the significance of each of these factors varies with different individuals and that even within the same individual the significance of each factor shifts over a period of time.

The Michigan Studies show that there is no clear-cut relationship between satisfaction and productivity. Also, an early review of the literature concludes that there is little evidence that there is either a simple or an appreciable relationship between employee attitudes toward their jobs and productivity.[30] Yet a later review of 23 studies shows that 20 of these studies result in a low but positive relationship; the average correlation being .14 between job satisfaction and productivity.[31] Remember, a coefficient of correlation is not a statement of causal relationship; it is merely a statement of covariance. Nonetheless, it is interesting to speculate why such a relationship exists.

VIE Theories. Perhaps the best basis for understanding the motivation to work is offered by several theories that have come to be

---

[30]Arthur H. Brayfield and Walter H. Crockett, "Employee Attitudes and Employee Performance," *Psychological Bulletin*, Vol. 52, No. 5 (September, 1955), pp. 415–422.

[31]Victor H. Vroom, *Work and Motivation* (New York: John Wiley & Sons, 1964). It should be noted that though these correlations are positive they are low in value and are not high enough to be useful as predictors.

known as valence, instrumentality, expectation (VIE) theories. These theories have several basic assumptions in common. First, there is the assumption that the individual worker's behavior is the result of a choice by the individual. That is, behavior cannot be reduced to a simple stimulus-response formula. Rather, work behavior is the result of a deliberate conscious choice in order to attain a predetermined outcome. Second, expectancy is defined as the belief that a certain form of behavior will lead to that particular outcome. Third, there must be a perceived instrumentality. Individuals must perceive that their behavior is instrumental in reaching that outcome. The concept of valence recognizes that all outcomes do not have equal force or attraction to the individual. Indeed, the valence of a given outcome may range from a -1.00 through $.00$ to a $+1.00$. Therefore, the valence of an outcome may cause an individual to either avoid or reject that outcome, to be neutral in attitudes and actions toward the outcome, or to be positively attracted by it. Fourth, VIE theories recognize rewards. Most statements of these theories differentiate between extrinsic and intrinsic rewards. However, such differentiation does not imply that either set of rewards — extrinsic or intrinsic — is more significant or desirable than the other.

In addition, there is the concept of equity of rewards. Equity is a social aspect of work. Equity of rewards is defined as a ratio between the effort put into a job and the reward obtained from that effort. If one perceives that the rewards being received are less than the perceived input and rewards of another person, then the rewards are being perceived as inequitable. Such a perception of inequity, dependent upon the individual, could result in a greater expenditure of effort in order to increase the reward. Or it could result in a withdrawal from the work situation because of the perceived inequity of rewards. Similarly, it is possible for a person to perceive that the rewards received are greater than the effort expended. An overreward could conceivably lead to a continuation of expending the same amount of effort in order to receive the overreward or it could lead to a diminution in the amount of effort expended. VIE theories of work motivation encompass many factors and though seemingly complex they offer at the present time the best understanding of motivation to work.

VIE Relationships. Figure 16-3 is a model showing the relationship between job performance, intrinsic and extrinsic rewards, perceived equity and instrumentality in goal attainment. All of these factors in combination determine perceived job satisfaction. Let us examine Figure 16-3 in detail. The first item to consider is goal attainment. Immediately several possible problems arise. The goals of the individual and the goals of the organization may differ. Not all organizational goals are accepted as personal goals by individuals. In certain instances the goals of the individual may be directly opposed to the goals of the

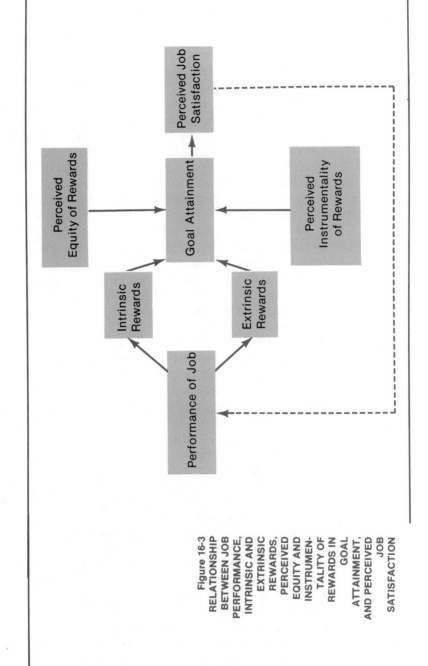

Figure 16-3
RELATIONSHIP BETWEEN JOB PERFORMANCE, INTRINSIC AND EXTRINSIC REWARDS, PERCEIVED EQUITY AND INSTRUMEN- TALITY OF REWARDS IN GOAL ATTAINMENT, AND PERCEIVED JOB SATISFACTION

organization. There is also the situation of the individual who has no goals. When such is the case there is little possibility of motivated behavior because one of the characteristics of motivated behavior is that it is goal-oriented.

The level of performance on the job — measured with respect to quantity, quality, and attitude — leads to certain rewards. These rewards may be intrinsic in that they arise from feelings of satisfaction from performing the job itself. It is not clear whether social contacts on the job should be regarded as intrinsic or extrinsic. The fact remains that they are derived from the work situation. Many programs of job enrichment have failed because the tradeoff in some instances has meant a change in the social structure of the job and some workers have not been willing to give up the socializing aspects of the job. There is no implication that either intrinsic or extrinsic rewards have a greater value. Their significance is dependent upon the value system and the goals of the individual. Extrinsic rewards, as we have seen from Gellerman's model (Figure 16-1, p. 383), may very well serve as motivators for some people. For other people and other jobs the intrinsic rewards may be more important.

The rewards received from performance on the job, whether they are intrinsic or extrinsic, must be perceived as being instrumental in the attainment of goals or outcomes if that performance is to continue. When one's behavior is not perceived or understood as contributing towards a certain outcome or goal, there is little reason for continuing that particular pattern of behavior. The perceived equity of the rewards, both intrinsic and extrinsic, is also of significance as a factor that leads to a continuation of a given level of job performance or a factor that inhibits job performance. In some cases a lack of either perceived instrumentality or perceived equity may lead the worker to leave that particular situation. The degree of attraction of the goals or outcomes of job performance may be either negative or positive. If the valence, degree of attraction, is negative there is no motivation to continue performance toward a goal that repels one. On the other hand, if the degree of attraction or valence is positive, one is motivated to continue that form of behavior.

When all of these factors are operating in the same direction, the result is likely to be one of perceived satisfaction with the work situation. The absence of any one of these factors or the operation of any one of these factors in a negative manner may diminish job satisfaction and ultimately result in dissatisfaction with the job and the work situation. In Figure 16-3 the dotted line from Perceived Job Satisfaction to Performance on the Job is in all probability the basis for the observation by Vroom that many studies on job satisfaction show a low positive correlation.[32] It is a form of feedback and though it is not

---

[32]*Ibid.*

sufficient to improve performance itself it does offer an explanation of the observed phenomena.[33]

In conclusion, the motivation of employees is not a simple matter. Jobs differ in their inherent attractiveness. People differ in the values placed on work and in their perceptions of the work place. There is also the possibility of inherent differences between the goals of organizations and the goals of people. Finally, perceptions regarding the significance of rewards, equity, and instrumentality are great. Work in an industrial setting is not the sum total of a person's life. There are many aspects to living other than working.

Case Problem 16-B describes the results experienced by Acme Manufacturing Company after having raised the level of its employee benefit program and poses another question to be resolved by the same management group: Should the company install a monetary incentive plan or should it embark upon a program of job enrichment?

Case Problem 16-B
PART II: INCENTIVES OR JOB DESIGN?

Approximately 18 months after the meeting described in Case Problem 16-A, Margaret Marlow, the personnel manager, and Al Conrad, the manager of industrial engineering, are in the general manager's office discussing ways of improving productivity and product quality. Following the survey of fringe benefits, Acme changed its practices with regard to holidays, vacations, life insurance, hospitalization insurance, and sick leave. After making these changes the company now ranks in the upper quartile of companies in the area with respect to these particular benefits. The company decided not to initiate employee services such as legal aid, counseling, a credit union, and a recreation program because these benefits are offered by very few companies in the area. There has been no

---

[33]The following three articles are summary statements of VIE theories. These articles have been cited since the number of specific studies is far beyond the scope of this book. Each of these reviews contains an extensive bibliography.

Terence R. Mitchell and Anthony Biglan, "Instrumentality Theories: Current Uses in Psychology," *Psychological Bulletin*, Vol. 76, No. 6 (December, 1971), pp. 432–454.

Herbert G. Heneman, III, and Donald P. Schwab, "Evaluation of Research on Expectancy Theory Predictions of Employee Performance," *Psychological Bulletin*, Vol. 78, No. 1 (July, 1972), pp. 1–9.

Orlando Behling and Frederick A. Starke, "The Postulates of Expectancy Theory," *Academy of Management Journal*, Vol. 16, No. 3 (September, 1973), pp. 373–388.

The following three studies are specific tests of VIE theories:

Robert D. Pritchard, Marvin D. Dunnette, and Dale O. Jorgenson, "Effects of Perceptions of Equity and Inequity on Worker Performance and Satisfaction," *Journal of Applied Psychology*, Vol. 56, No. 1 (February, 1972), pp. 75–94.

Robert D. Pritchard and Philip J. De Leo, "Experimental Test of the Valence-Instrumentality Relationship in Job Performance," *Journal of Applied Psychology*, Vol. 57, No. 3 (June, 1973), pp. 264–270.

H. Peter Dachler and William H. Mobley, "Construct Validation of and Instrumentality-Expectancy-Task-Goal Model of Work Motivation: Some Theoretical Boundary Conditions," *Journal of Applied Psychology*, Vol. 58, No. 3 (December, 1973), pp. 397–418.

change in the policy of setting wage levels equal to the average of the area.

Since increasing the level of its fringe benefits, the company has been able to hire replacements without undue delay; turnover, which had been most noticeable among employees with less than six months' service, has declined to its previous level; and the rate of absenteeism has been reduced. However, there has been no change in productivity per man-hour, nor has there been any improvement in product quality. An analysis by the quality control department shows that about 80 percent of the quality problems can be traced to errors in assembly.

Because of the persistent quality problem and the lack of improvement in productivity, Mr. Rider, the general manager, requested two feasibility studies. One of these, prepared by industrial engineering, discusses the feasibility of an incentive plan for hourly employees; the other is a report by the personnel department concerning job enlargement. After reading these reports, Rider asked for a conference with the heads of the industrial engineering and the personnel departments.

Rider turned to Conrad and said, "Apparently your department questions the value of incentives as a means of increasing productivity. Would you summarize your position for Margaret's benefit?"

"As you know," Conrad began, "we now have a measured day work plan; that is, we have time standards in most departments, but we do not have an incentive pay plan. The plant average is about 90 percent of standard for those departments that have standards. The press room, where we form the metal parts of our appliances, and the machining department average about 93 percent; the plating and painting departments run about 95 percent; the assembly department, about 85 percent; and in shipping and receiving the packers are the only ones on standards and they average about 85 percent also."

At this point Marlow commented, "It seems that assembly and the packers are the ones pulling the plant average down."

"That is right," Conrad continued. "Even so, a plant average near 90 percent is not too bad. Frankly, I question how much we would

gain with an incentive. In the press room and the assembly departments, the big factor in determining the output is the engineering design of the equipment and the manner in which it is maintained. Also, chrome plating requires a specified length of time for a given thickness of plate, and the capacity of the drying ovens is the limiting factor in our paint department. Improvement in production in these departments would be relatively small and the net gain in terms of earnings might be even smaller."

"Why is that?" Rider asked.

"To maintain standards for an incentive pay plan, I would have to double the size of my department. We would have to set additional standards for jobs that are run only infrequently. Complaints about standards would have to be answered promptly. All of this takes more people — I estimate at least an additional $50,000 a year in salaries alone. Sooner or later we would be forced into the position of paying the plant average to all workers — maintenance workers, janitors, shipping and receiving — because they will contend that they are having to do more work since more units are being produced; yet, actually their workload would change very little."

Looking at Margaret Marlow, Mr. Rider said, "It seems to me that it is questionable whether we would actually gain very much from an incentive pay plan in view of what Conrad has said. What about your recommendation of job enlargement?"

"Since most of our difficulty is in the assembly department, I would suggest that we start there by eliminating the assembly lines and having each person assemble the entire product and then pack it. There have been several instances where this approach has worked. If we had each person assemble the entire unit, inspect that unit, then insert an inspection slip into the box after packing the unit, we would have a much better control over quality."

"But assembly accounts for only one department," Conrad said. "What about the other departments?"

"In the press room and the machining departments we could have the operators learn how to make their own setups and make minor repairs instead of having the tool room make the setups and the maintenance department making all repairs, even the minor ones."

"You do that and we will have to pay all the machine operators a much higher rate since they will be classed as skilled rather than semiskilled," Conrad interrupted. "Also, we would be undertaking a tremendous training program, and at present we don't have that kind of staff."

Rider realized that he was no nearer a solution after talking to Conrad and Marlow than he had been before the conference. He decided to meet with them again in a week.

PROBLEMS

1. As the general manager of Acme, would you accept the recommendations of the personnel department? Why?
2. What additional information would you need to make a decision?
3. Is the industrial engineering department correct in not recommending an incentive plan? Discuss.

CHAPTER QUESTIONS FOR STUDY AND DISCUSSION

1. Why is it necessary for managers to know something about the fundamental needs of man in order to motivate employees successfully? From your own experience, describe an intended motivator that did not correspond to your own personal needs.

2. Of what significance are the physiological and safety needs in our economy today? Under what conditions would these needs become more significant?

3. What is meant by variations in the hierarchy of needs? Why is it necessary to recognize that such variations exist? In your opinion, which is the most important single variation in the hierarchy that can occur?

4. Evaluate the four categories of perception of one's self in relation to the environment as described by Gellerman. What is the probable outcome of using money as a means of motivation for each of Gellerman's four categories?

5. Give an example of conflicting needs in an industrial situation and show how this conflict affects employee motivation.

6. Why do monetary incentive plans achieve the desired goal of increased production in some companies if money is not a true motivator?

7. Differentiate between hygienic factors and motivators. Why is this distinction important?

8. What reasons can you advance to support the present practice of job design?

9. What is meant by job enrichment? What factors limit the opportunity for job enrichment?

10. Describe in your own words the meaning of the phrase "industrial morale."

11. Does it seem reasonable to you that whenever possible a company should strive to provide an industrial situation that will result in high morale on the part of its employees even though productivity is not increased? Discuss.

12. Evaluate your present job or current experiences in school in the light of Figure 16-3.

Chapter 17

The Role of the Supervisor

Case Problem 17-A

NO SMOKING

The managers of Apex Manufacturing, a company with approximately 750 employees, prided themselves in running what the company called a "tight ship." They are satisfied with the results of a recent attitude survey which shows that most employees believe that supervision is "strict, but fair." Like most of the other members of management, John Sweeney has come up through the ranks and is currently assigned to Department #40, the lacquer department, where he supervises 35 hourly employees. He has been with the company for 20 years, and for the last 10 years he has been a foreman. John tries to be fair to those working for him, and at the same time administer company policies in accordance with the wishes of the general superintendent who is very strict in the interpretation of company rules and regulations. John is waiting in his office for the arrival of Vera Huber, the union steward for Department #40.

"John, I'd like to talk to you about Jim Wilson, the worker you discharged yesterday afternoon."

"Not much to talk about, Vera," John replied. "You know he was smoking in restricted areas."

"That's just the point, John. The rules don't say that you have to discharge him. All they say is that anyone who violates any of the

Group One rules is *subject to* immediate discharge. That's a long way from saying that you *have* to discharge him."

"Look, Vera, I know that you have your job to do with the union and that you have a perfect right to question any action that I may take. But look at this case. Jim was with the company for over 12 years; certainly in that length of time he should know what the company rules mean. They are there for a reason. You know that this department could blow up the whole plant if there was a fire in here, what with this lacquer we have to work with. There are *No Smoking* signs all over the place and the workers in the spray booths even wear rubber soles so there is no chance for sparks. Sorry, nothing I can do about it; one mistake here would blow us all to hell and back."

"You say that Jim has been with us 12 years. That's true, but he's only been in your department for three months. He just forgot, maybe worried or something."

"I can't help that. Maybe it was some guy down the street last month who was just worried, or new, or something, and you know what happened. That fire took the lives of three employees in that plant and cost millions of dollars, and none of them are back to work yet. We don't want that happening here, and it won't if I have anything to do about it."

"John, you aren't leaving me much choice. I'm going to file a grievance, and I promise you this one will go all the way to arbitration. Twelve years of service without a single reprimand ought to mean something." With that remark, Vera Huber, the steward, left the foreman's office.

PROBLEMS

1. Do you agree with the action taken by John Sweeney, the foreman? Explain.

2. Has the steward presented her case well? Is she quibbling when she says that the words "subject to" do not mean that the foreman must discharge an employee?

3. The next step of the grievance procedure in Apex Manufacturing calls for a decision by the general superintendent. If he reverses Sweeney's stand, what effect will this have on Sweeney's relations with his workers?

4. Of what significance are the "fire down the street" and the "12 years of service without a reprimand"?

Many statements have been made concerning the importance of first-line supervisors because of their role in the attainment of the production goals of the organization and because their position in the managerial hierarchy results in their being the only members of management who direct the work of nonmanagerial employees. In the preceding chapter doubt is cast upon the value of monetary incentives per se or employee benefit programs as a means of motivating employees to higher levels of productivity. Further, the Michigan studies show that there is no consistent relationship between productivity and job satisfaction or morale. However, these studies do reveal a predictable relationship between supervisory practice and productivity; hence the importance of the supervisor in the achievement of the production goals of the organization.

This chapter is intended to provide an insight into the problems encountered by a supervisor. Many of the examples of supervisory practices refer to the manufacturing supervisor; however, it should be recognized that the supervisor of an accounting section or an order processing group has essentially the same problems. In order to provide insight into supervisory practices the following topics are discussed: (1) The Supervisor's Job, (2) Training of Supervisors, and (3) Improving Supervisory Performance.

THE SUPERVISOR'S JOB

The terms *supervisor* and *foreman* are frequently used interchangeably; however, in this chapter the term supervisor is used since it is somewhat broader in its application and also implies one of the major functions of supervision — to supervise. The term foreman is usually limited to supervisors in manufacturing organizations or to those supervising semiskilled or unskilled workers. The title supervisor is applicable to those who direct the work of others in laboratories, offices, retail establishments, and sales organizations as well as to those directing the work of hourly paid employees in manufacturing concerns. By definition, a supervisor is a part of management. The supervisor's position in management is unique — it is the only level of management charged with the responsibility of directing the work of nonmanagerial employees. Members of middle and top management perform various administrative tasks, and if they do direct the work of others it is the work of other managers.[1] The supervisor's position, between the upper levels of management and the hourly nonmanagerial employees has been described rather caustically, if not disparagingly, as the "man in the middle"[2] and the "marginal man of industry."[3] The supervisor has also been referred to as both "master and victim of double talk" as well as being "victim, not monarch, of all he surveys."[4] It is important to recognize that the supervisor is in the middle and because of that sometimes ambiguous position we have the key to the primary function of the job — "the linking-pin function."[5] Before developing the concept of the linking-pin function, let us review the legal definition of the supervisor's job.

Legal Definition

As defined by federal legislation, a supervisor is:

> . . . any individual having authority, in the interest of the employer, to hire, transfer, suspend, lay off, recall, promote, discharge, assign, reward, or discipline other employees, or responsibility to direct them, or to adjust their grievances, or effectively to recommend such action, if in connection with the foregoing the exercise of such authority is not of a merely routine or clerical nature, but requires the use of independent judgment.[6]

Another federal law, the Fair Labor Standards Act of 1938 (as amended), is often called the minimum wage law. One of its tests in determining whether or not a person is a supervisor is the amount of time spent performing work that is the same as that performed by the people under the supervisor's direction. Supervisors are expected to

---

[1] It is recognized that many members of middle and top management may have secretarial employees reporting to them, but the direction of these employees is incidental to the primary function which is usually administrative or the performance of a staff duty.

[2] B. B. Gardner and W. F. Whyte, "The Man in the Middle: Positions and Problems of the Foreman," *Applied Anthropology*, Vol. 4 (Winter, 1945), pp. 1–28.

[3] D. E. Wray, "Marginal Man of Industry: The Foreman," *American Journal of Sociology*, Vol. 54 (January, 1949), pp. 298–301.

[4] F. J. Roethlisberger, "The Foreman: Master and Victim of Double Talk," *Harvard Business Review*, Vol. 23 (September, 1945), pp. 283–298.

[5] Rensis Likert, *New Patterns of Management* (New York: McGraw-Hill Book Co., 1961), p. 113. Chapter 8, "An Integrating Principle and an Overview," pp. 97–118, presents a detailed discussion of the linking-pin function of supervision.

[6] National Labor-Management Relations Act (Taft-Hartley), 1947 (as amended), Section 101, Subsection 2 (11).

spend no more than 20 percent of their time doing the same kind of work that is performed by employees whom they are directing. In effect, the National Labor-Management Relations Act determines who is eligible to join an employees' union, and the Fair Labor Standards Act determines whether or not an employee is to be paid on an hourly basis (usually with overtime for hours in excess of a specified number) or whether the supervisor is to be paid a salary with no compensation required for overtime. Supervisors cannot join a union of production or clerical employees; however, they can form a union composed entirely of supervisors. Supervisors are paid a salary and are exempt from the provisions of the law requiring compensation for overtime. Hence, supervisors are commonly called "exempt" employees.

The net result of these two pieces of legislation is that supervisors are by definition a part of management, but supervisors do not always view themselves as the same as the other members of management.

The Self-Perception of Supervisors

We have mentioned that the supervisor's position is unique in that it requires interaction with nonmanagerial employees as well as with management. There is also a personal history characteristic that tends to set the supervisor apart from other members of management. Typically the first-line supervisor is promoted from the hourly ranks, and it is not at all unusual for the person to then supervise employees who have been known for years as friends and coworkers. Other levels of management usually start their careers as managers and are not in the position of having to change their attitudes as they advance in the organization. With this difference in background it is worthwhile to ask if the supervisor's self-perception is the same as other members of management.

Lyman W. Porter administered a self-description inventory consisting of 64 pairs of adjectives to 172 first-level supervisors, 291 upper-level management personnel, and 320 hourly production employees.[7] Each person was required to check one adjective of each pair that in his opinion offered the best self-description. The results of this study show that supervisors most frequently see themselves as planful, deliberate, calm, fair minded, steady, responsible, civilized, self-controlled, logical, judicial, and honest. Upper-level management personnel, a group including department heads, staff personnel, and vice-presidents, see themselves as resourceful, sharp witted, sincere, thoughtful, sociable, reliable, dignified, imaginative, adaptable, sympathetic, and generous. Hourly workers believe themselves to be ambitious, industrious, sharp witted, efficient, thoughtful, sociable, pleasant, reliable, and adaptable.

---

[7]Lyman W. Porter, "Self-Perception of First-Level Supervisors Compared with Upper-Management Personnel and with Operative Line Workers," *Journal of Applied Psychology*, Vol. 44 (June, 1959), pp. 183–186.

Note that there is a clear differentiation between each of the three groups. The supervisors see themselves as moderate, if not conservative, individuals who act as a stabilizing influence — an image not at all unsuited for "the man in the middle." The upper levels of management picture themselves as successful entrepreneurs who are imaginative, resourceful, and sharp witted; yet thoughtful, sympathetic, and dignified. The hourly worker is clearly on the way up. There does not seem to be any trend in self-image from the hourly ranks, through the supervisory group, to the upper levels of management. The supervisor's self-image does not retain the elements of the hourly image, nor has it acquired the outgoing self-confident characteristic of the higher levels of management.

Another study in a nonmanufacturing situation compared the attitudes of supervisors and managers toward their respective jobs. The sample consisted of 404 supervisors and 317 managers of the General Services Administration, a government administrative agency providing supply, maintenance, and protection services. Both supervisors and managers completed a 50-item questionnaire. Eight job attitudes were measured for each group. They are (1) equity of rewards, (2) adequacy of the work force, (3) goal quality, (4) commitment or initiative in the organization, (5) adequacy of performance appraisal, (6) adequacy of authority and freedom, or autonomy, (7) planning and coordination of work, and (8) skill utilization in the organization. Supervisors expressed more negative attitudes than managers with respect to the factors of equity of rewards, adequacy of the work force, and the degree to which their skills were utilized. The supervisors' attitudes toward the equity of rewards may be due to the fact that typically there is not too great a differential in pay between that of a supervisor and the hourly worker being supervised especially when one considers overtime earned by hourly workers. The second factor, adequacy of the work force, is the result of the supervisor's unique position. The supervisor is in direct contact with the work force while managers do not have such direct contact. The third factor in which supervisors differed, utilization of skill in the organization, shows that they perceive themselves as being capable of performing more responsible tasks.[8]

Dimensions of Supervisory Performance

The above discussion provides some insight concerning the way supervisors view themselves in comparison with other managers and in relation to hourly workers. It tells us little about the broad aspects of supervision or those factors that determine effective supervisory performance. Sandia Corporation, Albuquerque, New Mexico, wanted to know the independent dimensions or factors of administrative and general supervisory positions. Four hundred and fourteen supervisors

---

[8]Frank T. Paine and Martin J. Gannon, "Job Attitudes of Supervisors and Managers," *Personnel Psychology*, Vol. 26, No. 4 (Winter, 1973), pp. 521–529.

were asked to write an essay describing the performance of the best supervisor that they knew at Sandia Corporation. The descriptive statements were tabulated and a questionnaire containing 303 items describing supervisory performance was constructed. Three hundred and seventy-two supervisors then applied this questionnaire as a checklist to develop a descriptive rating of the best and the worst supervisor they knew. These ratings were analyzed by means of multiple-factor analysis, and six independent dimensions of supervisory performance were obtained:

1. Establishment of work climate.
2. Management ethics.
3. Self-development and subordinate development.
4. Personal maturity and sensitivity.
5. Knowledge and execution of corporate policies.
6. Technical job knowledge.[9]

Establishment of Work Climate. Descriptive statements characteristic of this factor are: expects a day's work, disciplines when necessary, and expects only the best. Supervisors rating high in this respect establish and maintain high performance standards. They are goal oriented and if necessary place the attainment of stated objectives above the likes and dislikes of subordinates.

Management Ethics. The essence of this dimension is ethical behavior on the part of a supervisor in interacting with other supervisors and members of top management. The same ethical behavior is also shown in those relationships with subordinates. Statements characterizing this trait are: gives credit where due, honest in discussing development of subordinates, no under-the-table deals, and doesn't promise anything that cannot be done.

Self-Development and Subordinate Development. Effective supervisors are interested in personnel development — the growth of subordinates as well as their own. They attempt to make assignments interesting and challenging and try to know their subordinates better so that they may direct their growth. They encourage outside study and pursue such activity themselves. They try to keep up with the professional aspects of management through reading and participation in outside groups.

Personal Maturity and Sensitivity. Two elements are closely related in this factor; one is personal maturity and emotional stability, and the other is empathy — a sensitivity to the feelings of others. Supervisors strong in this dimension maintain an "open door" policy, they

---

[9]Sherwood H. Peres, "Performance Dimensions of Supervisory Positions," *Personnel Psychology*, Vol. 15 (Winter, 1962), pp. 405–410. Seven factors were isolated; however, the seventh factor is a bias factor resulting from the halo effect present in rating scales. It is not a true factor of supervisory performance.

have a knack of saying the right thing at the right time, do not lose control under pressure, and seem to lighten serious situations with a sense of humor.

Knowledge and Execution of Corporate Policies. Note that knowledge of policy is not sufficient; there must also be execution of policy. Strong supervisors keep up with changes in policy and procedures and keep their subordinates informed of such changes. Those strong in this characteristic are orderly and tend to follow the "letter of the law." The result of this trait is that it gives a supervisor's behavior consistency and predictability.

Technical Job Knowledge. This dimension of supervision suggests not only technical knowledge but also the drive and willingness to get the job done. Supervisors usually have sufficient background and information to understand a new problem quickly. They are generally technically competent and do more than that expected of them.

The "Linking-Pin" Function

The legal definition of a supervisor cited at the beginning of this chapter details only the relationships between supervisor and subordinates. If questioned, many managers would also answer that a supervisor's job is to direct the work of subordinates. The above discussion of the dimensions of supervisory performance shows the narrowness and inadequacy of a definition that stresses the direction of subordinates. The analysis of supervisory positions at Sandia Corporation reveals that successful performance requires a person capable of much more than directing the efforts of others. Successful performance requires a structuring of the work situation; ethical behavior in personal relationships with superiors, peers, and subordinates; and effective execution of company policy.

The key to the primary function of supervision is the supervisor's singular position in the organization — the only member of management in direct contact with nonmanagerial personnel. As a result, the supervisor is the one member of management capable of linking management to operative personnel. For this reason the supervisor's major function is best described as a *linking-pin* function.[10]

Current Problems in Supervision

Though the Civil Rights Act of 1964, as amended, was passed more than a decade ago, its effect upon organizations in both the public and private sectors has been relatively recent. Section 703 (1) of the Act makes it unlawful to discriminate on the basis of "race, color, religion, sex, or national origin." Though much has been written about the Act

---

[10]Rensis Likert, *New Patterns of Management* (New York: McGraw-Hill Book Co., 1961), p. 113.

there have been relatively few research studies showing its effect upon the supervisory process. One such study conducted in the private sector shows the effect of a minority hiring program upon the first line supervisor. Another study compares the leadership behavior of male and female supervisors.

Supervisor Role Conflict. In an effort to combat the hard-core unemployment, a company employed 49 black males who met the following criteria.[11] They were between the ages of 21 and 50 years, residents of the inner city for a period of more than one year, and during the past two years had been employed for a period of less than six months. In addition, when last employed the employment had to be for a period of less than three consecutive months with the same employer. Prior to their actually going to work the supervisors to whom they would be assigned attended a special 12-hour training program divided into six equal sections of two hours each. During these training sessions anticipated problems and tentative solutions were discussed. Despite the preparation for the problems to be encountered, the employment of the hard-core unemployed created problems for the supervisors best expressed as role ambiguity — an inability to determine the proper supervisory role because of the conflicting messages being received.[12]

The supervisors complained that they did not have adequate information on the new hires. In part the complaint was true, because staff personnel had deliberately withheld some information concerning the background of individual workers since such information might bias the supervisor against the employees. The supervisors also complained that it was extremely difficult to communicate with the new employees. Perhaps the most serious complaint of all was that as supervisors they were forced to work with dual standards. For example, the management of the company indicated that the supervisors must accommodate the special group, but there was no change in expected production despite an excessively high absentee rate. Those employees who had been in the department prior to the special employment program complained that the new hires were being given preferential treatment, especially with regard to discipline and absenteeism.

There were many special problems to be solved by the supervisors. Much of the absenteeism was caused by inadequate transportation, so the supervisors had to advise these new employees concerning the bus routes and the establishment of car pools. There were also requests for

---

[11]This discussion is based upon a study which was conducted in a large midwestern city: R. A. Hudson Rosen, "Foreman Role Conflict: An Expression of Contradictions in Organizational Goals," *Industrial and Labor Relations Review*, Vol. 23, No. 4 (July, 1970), pp. 541–552.

[12]See Chapter 13, pp. 310–312 for a full discussion of role conflict.

advances in pay to tide them over until the first pay period. In addition, there were problems relating to poor health that resulted in taking an entire day off to go to a clinic rather than going to the company physician. All of these problems took additional time, yet there seemed to be a lack of recognition on the part of higher supervision that the work load had increased. The supervisors were unable to get support and direction from top management stating what was expected of them. Thus, with the complaints of subordinates who resented the dual standards and the pressures from superiors who demanded the same level of performance, yet failed to recognize changed conditions, the supervisor's role became intolerably ambiguous.

A Comparison of Male and Female Supervisors. In addition to providing equal employment opportunities for minorities, the Civil Rights Act has been interpreted as protecting the rights of women. Again, much has been said about the utilization of women in supervisory and managerial roles. Yet there are relatively few studies that compare the performance of male and female supervisors in similar positions. Traditionally private industry has not employed women as supervisors to any great degree. However, the federal government has made efforts to promote women to supervisory positions. The following study compares the leader behavior of male and female supervisors.[13]

Day and Stogdill report the leader behavior of 37 male supervisors and 36 female supervisors who were civilian employees of the United States Air Force Logistics Command in the continental United States. The leadership behavior of each group was analyzed with respect to leadership effectiveness, the relationship between leadership behavior and effectiveness, and the relationship between behavior, effectiveness, and biographical information for both male and female supervisors. In each instance, subordinates described the leader behavior and the effectiveness of their supervisors. The supervisory positions were comparable in nature.

The results of the study show that when rated by their immediate subordinates male and female supervisors occupying similar positions and performing similar functions show the same patterns of leadership behavior and effectiveness. Second, despite the description of leader behavior and effectiveness as being similar, such behavior and effectiveness is not related in the same manner for both groups with regard to advancement. For the male supervisors those rated as more effective advance more rapidly; whereas, the advancement of female supervisors is not related to effectiveness. Thus it seems that, though males and females as reported in this study exhibit the same behavior and

---

[13]David R. Day and Ralph M. Stogdill, "Leader Behavior of Male and Female Supervisors: A Comparative Study," *Personnel Psychology*, Vol. 25, No. 2 (Summer, 1972), pp. 353–360. This discussion is based upon the study by Day and Stogdill.

the same degree of effectiveness, there is a difference in the rate of advancement. Despite the fact that the study was performed in the public sector, the federal government, there is no reason to assume that the behavior and effectiveness of female supervisors in the private sector would be any different than in the public sector.

TRAINING OF SUPERVISORS

"You could dispose of almost all the leadership training courses for supervision in American industry today without anyone knowing the difference."[14]

The above statement, made by Robert H. Guest, is not intended as a criticism of the content or methods of leadership training programs for supervisors. Instead, it is intended to emphasize that the demands of the supervisor's job, such as those described in the hard-core employment program, are often such that it is difficult, if not impossible, to exercise the type of leadership expected. Despite the very real limitations on supervisory leadership imposed by the structure of the job, much effort and money are spent on supervisory training. In addition to training in leadership, programs are designed to improve other skills necessary for effective supervision.

The content of supervisory training programs is geared to the needs of the supervisor. Thus, there is considerable variation in content and method from one organization to another and within the same organization from one level of supervision to another. Figure 17-1 shows a useful classification proposed by Georgopoulos and Mann of the skills needed for supervision.[15] Note that the range of supervisory positions included in Figure 17-1 is from the first level of supervision, through department heads, and includes the highest level of administrators. With each step upward in the organizational hierarchy, the "mix" of supervisory skills changes. Technical skills are the skills and knowledge necessary for the performance of a given supervisory position in a specific industry. For the first-line supervisor, technical skills include the knowledge and skill required to perform jobs at the operational level. The technology of the industry must be known by the supervisors so that immediate subordinates can be trained. Administrative skills require a concept of the entire organizational system and the coordination of the component parts of the system. Planning, organizing, assigning work, and the establishment and exercise of necessary controls are administrative skills. For the first-line supervisor

---

[14]Robert H. Guest, "Of Time and the Foreman," *Personnel* (New York: American Management Association, 1956), p. 478.

[15]Basil S. Georgopoulos and Floyd C. Mann, *The Community General Hospital* (New York: Macmillan Co., 1962), Chapter 9. Reprinted in Robert A. Sutermeister (ed.), *People and Productivity* (New York: McGraw-Hill Book Co., 1963), pp. 381–385.

418   PART 4   THE LEADERSHIP FUNCTION

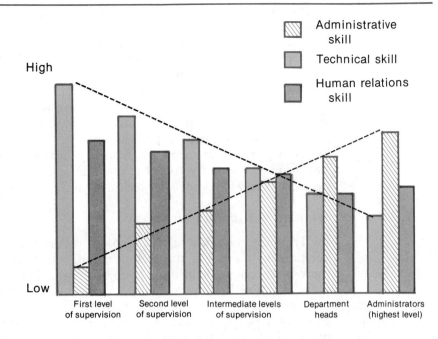

Source: Basil S. Georgopoulos and Floyd C. Mann, **The Community General Hospital** (New York: Macmillan Co., 1962), p. 431.

Figure 17-1 RELATIVE IMPORTANCE OF DIFFERENT SUPERVISORY SKILLS

these skills are relatively less important than the technical and human relations skills. Human relations skills require a knowledge of the principles of behavior and an ability to work with subordinates, peers, and superiors. Let us examine briefly some of the content and methods of technical and administrative training.

Technical and Administrative Skills

Technical training has as its goal the understanding of the technical aspects of a supervisory position. The supervisor in manufacturing must understand the design, operating principles, and maintenance of production equipment; the specifications of raw materials and component parts; and the quality standards of the finished product. The technical phases of a data processing supervisor's position include a working knowledge of the principles used in the design of electronic equipment, an understanding of the binary number system, and the ability to prepare computer programs. Training in the administrative area acquaints the supervisor with company policies and procedures as they apply to a specific department. The supervisor must know purchasing procedures, production scheduling methods, and the company's cost accounting system. Knowledge of the application and interpretation of company personnel policies is also required. If there is a labor union, one should be familiar with the provisions of the labor agreement.

The content of training programs in the technical and administrative areas is dependent upon the technology and administrative procedures of each individual company. As a result, most training programs are designed and conducted internally. The methods used are traditional in nature and rely heavily upon written materials such as technical manuals and statements of company policy and procedure. Formal classes are held at periodic intervals and may be supplemented by departmental meetings. In many large companies supervisors are furnished bound volumes of company policies and operating procedures to serve as a basis for technical and administrative decisions.

Training in Human Relations

Training in human relations poses problems not present in the development of skills in the technical and administrative fields. First, there is no concise definition of subject matter to be mastered. Second, there is typically a marked disparity between responses given in answer to written questions and the ability to transfer knowledge into effective supervisory patterns. Third, training in human relations requires the use of teaching methods quite different from those employed in the technical and administrative areas. Training programs in human relations stress: (1) communications, with particular emphasis placed on empathetic listening — the perception of the meaning and feeling of communications from subordinates; (2) the making of decisions involving people based upon the perceptions gained from empathetic listening; and (3) overcoming resistance to change, usually through the use of a participative leadership style.

In this section we present a brief overview of the methods used in human relations training and review experimental studies illustrative of specific problems in human relations encountered by all supervisors. The methods used in developing skills in human relations include the *case method*, the *incident process*, and *role playing*. Each of these methods is discussed briefly below.

Case Method. The case method of leadership training utilizes case problems much like those contained in this book. The case problem usually sets forth a sequence of events in such a manner that a question calling for a solution is posed. Or, as in Case Problem 17-A, No Smoking, the solution is provided as part of the case and the learner is asked to evaluate the given solution. In order to solve a case problem it is necessary to acquaint the participant with the principles or procedures to be applied, a task usually accomplished by lectures or assigned readings. Case problems should describe a situation that is part of the learner's background or a situation that is understandable to all learners. The case method arouses greater interest than that created by answering questions not related to a specific situation. Also, a case problem offers a chance to apply the principles and methods to be learned. Thus, the case problem offers an opportunity to increase interest, to participate in discussion, and to illustrate the application of principles, policies, or methods to simulated or real situations.

Incident Process Method. The incident process method, a variation of the case method, is used in small discussion groups. If Case Problem 17-A were rewritten as an incident, the incident described could be the fact that the supervisor discharged a worker for violating the no smoking regulations of the company. A bare statement of the fact — discharge for violation of a no smoking rule — cannot be evaluated without additional information. In the incident method, participants draw from the discussion leader all the information necessary to make a sound evaluation of the action taken and to recommend alternative courses that might have been available. Skill in questioning is developed by the incident method and experience is gained in gathering information needed in order to make sound decisions in the area of human relations.[16]

Role Playing. The role playing method offers the advantages of the case method and, in addition, provides training in the perception of the attitudes and feelings of other persons. As the name suggests, role playing is the assignment of a definite role to each member of a training group. There is usually a brief explanation and discussion of the supervisory problem under study prior to the assignment of roles.

Case Problem 17-A may be adapted for role playing in the following manner. The supervisors of the plant in which the smoking incident occurred might attend a company training session concerned with the enforcement of company rules. The rules may be explained, the need for their enforcement stated, and the duties of the union steward described. Following this general session for all supervisors, groups of three or four meet separately and each member of the small group is assigned a specific role. One is selected to be the supervisor, another the steward, and the remaining members assume the role of the employee in question who, in this instance, acts as an observer and evaluates the effectiveness of the steward in representing the case and the equity of the supervisor's decision. Each member is given a written statement describing the role to be assumed and is not aware of the details of the roles of the others in the group. The supervisor's statement may indicate that the employee *must* be discharged and cite as a reason the fire in a neighboring plant and the need to enforce company rules. The supervisor's role may or may not specify the employee's

---

[16]Paul Pigors and Faith Pigors, *Director's Manual: The Incident Process* (Washington: The Bureau of National Affairs, 1955). For a brief article describing the incident method see James L. Centner, "The Incident Process," *Advanced Management*, Vol. 21 (December, 1956), pp. 15–20.

long service record. The steward's role emphasizes that one who violates the rule is only "subject to" discharge, and the long, faithful record of the employee may be outlined for the steward. Remaining members of the small group — no more than one or two — are asked to evaluate the behavior of the supervisor and the steward from the standpoint of an employee with a long seniority who has admittedly violated a rule.[17] Roles may be rotated either within the same group or by forming new groups. Either way, each participant has the opportunity to assume the role of the supervisor and the steward and to evaluate the incident as the employee. Role playing is particularly effective in developing empathy — the understanding of the other person's feelings and attitudes.[18]

Specific Problems in Leadership Training

Let us study in detail two specific problems in the area of leadership training. The first is concerned with discipline; the second, with the effectiveness of training in group decision making.

Discipline. Maintaining discipline is one of the perennial problems of supervision. In general, there are two approaches to disciplinary problems: (1) a *judicial* approach — determining the rightness or wrongness of an act as defined by a specific rule and applying the penalty prescribed, and (2) a *human relations* approach — an emphasis on problem solving with an ultimate goal of improving the employee's behavior.[19] A judicial approach may be forced upon a supervisor by his superior as intimated in Case Problem 17-A. Some supervisors by reason of personality may be rigid, insecure, and incapable of flexibility. These persons find in the rule and its prescribed penalty a ready-made justification for their own rigidity. Still others would prefer the human relations approach but are fearful of where it may lead — they envision an ultimate state of complete anarchy. The studies described below show how supervisors tend to enforce company rules and point up the need for training in human relations.

The subjects of the study were approximately 500 supervisors from a variety of industries attending the Foremen's Conferences held at the

---

[17]The following article discusses the factors influencing decisions concerning disciplinary actions: Benton Rosen and Thomas H. Jerdee, "Factors Influencing Disciplinary Judgments," *Journal of Applied Psychology*, Vol. 59, No. 3 (June, 1974), pp. 327–331.

[18]Norman R. F. Maier and Lester F. Zerfoss, "MRP: A Technique for Training Large Groups of Supervisors and Its Potential Use in Social Research," *Human Relations*, Vol. 5 (May, 1952), pp. 177–182. This article is a relatively brief statement of the multiple role playing technique. For a more detailed treatment of role playing, see Norman R. F. Maier, Allen R. Solem, and Ayesha A. Maier, *Supervisory and Executive Development*, A Manual for Role Playing (New York: John Wiley & Sons, 1957).

[19]Norman R. F. Maier and Lee E. Danielson, "An Evaluation of Two Approaches to Discipline in Industry," *Journal of Applied Psychology*, Vol. 40 (October, 1956), pp. 319–323.

University of Michigan.[20] Following a lecture on attitudes and how to understand them, the supervisors were divided into workshop groups to study a "No Smoking" case using the role playing method. Each of the 172 role playing units consisted of three persons: the supervisor, the steward, and the employee. The case was much like Case Problem 17-A, with one important exception — the penalty for violating the rule was a three-day layoff rather than a discharge. The roles assigned made it clear that a violation of the rule had occurred, and that the worker knew the rule had been violated and knew the penalty involved. The worker acted as an observer in the role playing situation, with the interaction occurring between the supervisor and the steward who was instructed to press the worker's case. A 20-minute time limit was placed on the discussion between the supervisor and the steward.

Maier and Danielson found that slightly over half of the supervisors (52 percent) used the human relations approach and resolved the problem with an adjusted solution not calling for the three-day layoff penalty. Adjusted solutions ranged from no penalty, a warning or reprimand, or a one- or two-day layoff. Thirty-five percent of the supervisors followed the judicial approach and found the worker guilty, invoked the penalty, and refused to change their positions. The problem was not settled in the alloted time by 13 percent of the supervisors. The human relations approach resulted in greater satisfaction as judged by all three participants with a problem-solving type interview rather than argumentative, and the worker seemed more satisfied with the actions of the steward and less inclined to restrict future production. In another study the same authors found that only seven percent of the supervisors in a similar role playing situation laid off a worker who violated a safety rule.[21] In the safety case the situation was ambiguous: i.e., the supervisor was not sure that the employee, a lineman for a utility company, was wearing his safety belt and the penalty was much more severe — a three-week layoff. Despite the fact that 45 percent of the participants who played the role of the lineman admitted violating the safety rule, only seven percent were laid off in accordance with the prescribed penalty.

These two studies indicate that supervisors are inclined to use the human relations approach to discipline. Further, the formulation of strict rules with no latitude in their interpretation poses a dilemma for the supervisor. However, if the supervisor uses judgment and modifies the penalty, the wishes of the higher echelon are not being followed. Yet, by enforcing the letter of the law, the supervisor is demonstrating a lack of understanding and harshness toward subordinates.[22]

---

[20]*Ibid.*

[21]Lee E. Danielson and Norman R. F. Maier, "Supervisory Problems in Decision Making," *Journal of Applied Psychology*, Vol. 40 (October, 1956), pp. 319–323.

[22]For another statement of the human relations approach to discipline the following is recommended: John Huberman, "Discipline Without Punishment," *Harvard Business Review*, Vol. 42, No. 4 (July-August, 1964), pp. 62–68.

Training for Decision Making. In another study Maier investigated the effect of training in group decision making.[23] Forty-four role-playing groups of supervisors were given an eight-hour presentation of the methods of group decision making. These experimental groups also participated in four hours of discussion that permitted them to ask questions and to express their attitudes toward the role-playing problem which was introduced as part of the training. The 36 control groups were given no training in group decision methods, but were given one-half hour of instruction explaining the role-playing situation. The problem is a proposed change in method — a change sure to arouse resistance — for a group of three workers who normally rotate three production jobs among themselves at the end of each hour during an eight-hour day. There is a variation in the length of time it takes each worker to perform the duties of each position as shown in Table 17-1, Time Per Operation. A methods engineer has suggested that the work be assigned on a permanent basis as follows: Jack to the first position, Steve to the second position, and Walt to the third position. The reduction in time would amount to 2¼ minutes per cycle, a savings of 17 percent or 80 minutes per eight-hour day. In other words, compared to the "optimum" solution, the men are now loafing 80 minutes a day.

	Position 1	Position 2	Position 3	Total
Jack	3 min.	4 min.	4½ min.	11½ min.
Walt	3½ min.	3½ min.	3 min.	10 min.
Steve	5 min.	3½ min.	4½ min.	13 min.
				34½ min.

Table 17-1 TIME PER OPERATION

Source: Norman R. F. Maier, "An Experimental Test of the Effect of Training on Discussion Leadership," *Human Relations Journal*, Vol. 6 (May, 1953), p. 164. This table was originally published by John Wiley & Sons in Norman R. F. Maier's *Principles of Human Relations*, Applications to Management, 1952.

In the role playing situation, the supervisor desires to install the solution recommended by the methods engineer and is met with varying degrees of resistance on the part of each of the three workers. The result of the role-playing situations for trained and untrained supervisors, Table 17-2 — Percentage of Successes, Failures, and Compromises of Trained and Untrained Groups — shows clearly the effect of training. Only 4½ percent of the trained supervisors experience failure — with failure being defined as no solution, no change, or open rebellion against the supervisor's imposed solution. On the other hand,

---

[23]Norman R. F. Maier, "An Experimental Test of the Effect of Training on Discussion Leadership," *Human Relations Journal*, Vol. 6 (May, 1953), pp. 161–173.

50 percent of the untrained leaders experienced failure. However, the striking result is that the untrained leader did not produce a single compromise. It must be pointed out that many compromise solutions might in practice be the "optimum" or best solution, since the compromises contained varying plans for rotation of jobs to minimize the effects of monotony and boredom on production.[24]

	Failures	Compromises	Successes
Trained leader	4.5	36.4	59.1
Untrained leader	50.0	0	50.0

Table 17-2 PERCENTAGE OF SUCCESSES, FAILURES, AND COMPROMISES OF TRAINED AND UNTRAINED GROUPS

Source: Norman R. F. Maier, "An Experimental Test of the Effect of Training on Discussion Leadership," *Human Relations Journal*, Vol. 6 (May, 1953), p. 168. This table was originally published by John Wiley & Sons in Norman R. F. Maier's *Principles of Human Relations*, Applications to Management, 1952.

IMPROVING SUPERVISORY PERFORMANCE

In Chapter 16, "Motivating Employees," it is stated that no consistent relationship is found between measures of employee morale and productivity. Fortunately there is a distinct positive relationship between supervisory practices and productivity. There are many characteristics of effective supervisory action; however, four stand out above all others. The first factor determining effective supervision, *organizational climate*, is largely beyond the control of supervisors and determines how effectively they may exercise the other three characteristics of sound supervision. Good practices in *delegation*, the second factor, are necessary for effective supervision. The third requisite for effective supervision is an orientation toward the job, best described as a *situational* approach, with a balanced emphasis upon the task and the maintenance of good relations with subordinates.[25] The fourth requirement is an ability to use *employee participation* skillfully to introduce change.

Organizational Climate

The quotation from Guest's "Of Time and the Foreman," appearing at the beginning of the preceding section on training, dramatizes the limiting effects of organizational climate upon the efficacy of training. Fleishman also emphasizes the limitations of training unless the "leadership climate" is such that supervisors can readily put to use

---

[24]The following book is of interest in the training of supervisors: Arnold P. Goldstein and Melvin Sorcher, *Changing Supervisor Behavior* (Elmsford, New York: Pergamon Press, 1974).

[25]See Chapter 14, A Contingency Model of Leadership Effectiveness, pp. 334–343.

their newly found skills.[26] Organizational or leadership climate is made up of the attitudes and practices of top management and is reflected by the extent that management practices delegation, the degree that they recognize the organization as a system, and their use of participation as a method of introducing change. Yet the chief advantage gained by a supervisor from the organizational climate created by higher management is increased *influence* or power in relation to immediate subordinates.

Pelz and others of the University of Michigan's Survey Research Center show that a supervisor's influence or power has a great deal to do with productivity and employee satisfaction.[27] In work groups having high production records, promotions recommended by supervisors were generally approved by higher management; or no recommendations were made at all. On the other hand, the supervisors of low-producing groups frequently made recommendations for promotion that were not approved by higher authority. Three factors seem to contribute most to a supervisor's influence: (1) the supervisor's contribution to decisions made by superiors, (2) the freedom and autonomy exercised in the operation of one's own department, and (3) salary, interpreting salary as a measure of responsibility and status within the organization. Note that these conditions determining the amount of supervisory influence are not the direct result of a supervisor's actions within his own department or something that may be asked for and received; these traits are a reflection of the supervisor's position and status in the organization — the result of organizational climate.

Improved Delegation

One of the keys to effective supervision, as measured by productivity and employee satisfaction, is the ability to delegate responsibility to subordinates and to allow as much leeway in the performance of assigned duties as the situation permits. Improvement in delegation requires that the supervisor have a clear perception of the leader's role and that a careful study be made to determine how closely the work of subordinates should be followed. Let us discuss, first, the differentiation of the supervisor's role.

---

[26]Edwin A. Fleishman, Edwin F. Harris, and Harold E. Burtt, "Leadership and Supervision in Industry." Reprinted in Robert A. Sutermeister (ed.), *People and Productivity* (New York: McGraw-Hill Book Co., 1963), pp. 410–425. This reading is a re-edited and up-to-date version of Chapter 9 of *Leadership and Supervision in Industry* (Columbus, Ohio: Bureau of Educational Research, Ohio State University, 1955) by the same three authors.

[27]Donald C. Pelz, "Influence: A Key to Effective Leadership in the First-Line Supervisor," *Personnel*, Vol. 39 (November, 1952), pp. 209–217.

A more recent study by Ronan indicates that direct supervision is significant as a determinant of positive relationships between job satisfaction and behavior on the job. W. W. Ronan, "Individual and Situational Variables Relating to Job Satisfaction," *Journal of Applied Psychology Monograph*, Vol. 54, No. 1 (February, 1970), pp. 1–29.

Differentiating the Supervisor's Role. Drs. Robert L. Kahn and Daniel Katz, in a summary of much of the work of the Survey Research Center of the University of Michigan, report that supervisors of groups with high production records assume a role that is more differentiated from the work of those supervised than the role assumed by the supervisors of low-producing work groups.[28] High-producing supervisors perform those tasks traditionally associated with the managerial functions of planning, organizing, directing, and controlling. The differentiation between the task of the worker and the supervisor begins with the supervisor's self-perception as a member of management and an understanding of the functions of management. At the same time, subordinates have an unusually acute perception of what their supervisor is doing in comparison with what should be done. The supervisory task perceived most readily by subordinates is that of planning the work to be done. Members of high-producing railroad section gangs and departments in a tractor manufacturing company rate their supervisors as superior in planning work, providing materials, and watching or supervising the performance of the work. Supervisors with better than average production records also spend more time than their low-producing counterparts in solving the interpersonal problems arising in the work group. Low-producing supervisors are prone to get lost in paper work and spend too much of their time doing the same type of work performed by subordinates. Supervisory tasks include not only the planning function but also directing on-the-job training.

Closeness of Supervision. The supervisor who spends a large percentage of time performing those tasks normally associated with supervision is delegating authority and assigning responsibility. The supervision of hourly workers is primarily the assignment of responsibility to perform work. However, the delegator still remains accountable for the performance of assigned duties. Close supervision is associated with excessively detailed instructions, constant checking on progress, and insistence that all decisions be approved before being put into effect. However, a careful engineering of the work to be performed and the establishment and exercise of necessary controls to assure proper progress are not considered excessively close supervision; instead, they are part of the normal supervisory function. Closeness of supervision refers primarily to the personal conduct of the supervisor, and when supervision becomes too close, it is a reflection of the supervisor's own insecurity and inability to delegate.

---

[28]Robert L. Kahn and Daniel Katz, "Leadership Practices in Relation to Productivity and Morale," from Dorwin Cartwright and Alvin Zander (eds.), *Group Dynamics*, Research and Theory (2d ed.; Evanston: Row, Peterson & Co., 1961), pp. 554–570.

In studies of clerical workers in an insurance company and production workers manufacturing tractors, it is found that there is an inverse relationship between closeness of supervision and productivity; i.e., the closer the supervision, the lower the productivity. Also, the closeness of supervision has a great deal to do with the three factorial dimensions of employee morale. Employees not closely supervised are more likely to have a high degree of satisfaction with their jobs, their supervisors, and the company than those who are closely supervised. However, there is evidence that closeness of supervision is in many instances a reflection of the type of supervision received by the supervisor. If a superior fully delegates authority, the supervisor is likely to do the same. But when the supervisor is closely supervised, it is difficult for the process of delegation to occur.

A Situational Approach

Much has been written about supervisors being either production-centered or employee-centered with respect to attitudes concerning the work of their departments and their subordinates. Early research in the area of job satisfaction and morale implicitly assumed that the orientation of the supervisor is best described in terms of a continuum with production-centered concepts at one pole and employee-centered concepts at the other extreme. However, later studies, particularly those conducted at the tractor company, cast doubt upon the usefulness of a continuum as a model for describing supervisory orientation. High-producing workers at the tractor company reported, as might be expected, that their supervisor took an interest in them, that they got along well with him, and that he was easy to talk to. Yet, they also stated that production was important to their supervisor and that he supervised them in such a manner that production standards were met — a situation quite impossible to describe on a continuum model.[29]

Dr. Robert L. Kahn suggests that we use a four-celled table to describe the orientation of the supervisor.[30] In one cell are those supervisors who are high in their interest in production and at the same time have a high interest in the welfare of their employees. Another cell would best describe those with a high orientation toward production but low in employee-centered attitudes. The third square would fit those low in production but high in employee-centered interests. The fourth possibility consists of those supervisors with low interests in

---

[29]The following two review articles are recommended as summaries of the literature concerning supervisory style.

Stephen M. Sales, "Supervisory Style and Productivity: Review and Theory," *Personnel Psychology*, Vol. 19, No. 3 (Autumn, 1966), pp. 275–286.

Abraham K. Korman, " 'Consideration,' 'Initiating Structure,' and Organizational Criteria — Review," *Personnel Psychology*, Vol. 19, No. 4 (Winter, 1966), pp. 349–361.

[30]Robert L. Kahn, "Productivity and Job Satisfaction," *Personnel Psychology*, Vol. 13 (Autumn, 1960), pp. 275–287).

both production and employees. In effect, the four-celled table represents a systems orientation, with the most effective supervisor recognizing simultaneously the goals and needs of the organization and its members.

At first glance it may seem quite impossible to be production-centered and employee-centered at one and the same time.[31] Such is not the case provided the supervisor meets the following three requirements. First, the supervisor must make clear that high but realistic and attainable standards of performance are expected. In so doing the tenor of the operation is established. Second, the supervisor must have the power to deliver appropriate rewards or punishment if the stated goals are to mean anything. Third, the supervisor must demonstrate to the satisfaction of subordinates that supervisory power is used effectively. One of the best ways of demonstrating a wise use of power and influence is a willingness to "go to bat" for subordinates when the need arises. But the supervisor does not stand alone in meeting these three conditions. The management that the supervisor represents must create the climate to make possible the exercise of an effective emphasis upon production and at the same time a concern for subordinates.[32]

Participation and Change

Overcoming resistance to change is a problem confronting all levels of supervision. The proposed change in method or content may have little direct effect upon the worker's ability to perform his job, or the change may be of such a nature that the learning of new skills or the transfer of existing skills to a new work situation is required. Regardless of the amount or type of change, there are varying degrees of resistance that are manifested by an extremely long period of time to learn the new job, open expressions of hostility toward management, or an increase in the number of voluntary terminations of employment. One explanation that has been offered for resistance to change is that the rate of learning for the new job is inhibited because of its similarity to the old job. For example, an expert typist might experience greater difficulty initially in learning the finger movements required in playing a piano than one with no skill in typing. However, research indicates that resistance is caused by psychological factors

---

[31]The following articles indicate that initiating structure to meet the goals of the organization and consideration for the members are not mutually exclusive:

Richard W. Beatty, "Supervisory Behavior Related to Job Success of Hard-Core Unemployed over a Two-Year Period," *Journal of Applied Psychology*, Vol. 59, No. 1 (February, 1974), pp. 38–42.

Leopold Gruenfeld and Saleem Kassum, "Supervisory Style and Organizational Effectiveness in a Pediatric Hospital," *Personnel Psychology*, Vol. 26, No. 4 (Winter, 1973), pp. 531–544.

[32]Edwin A. Fleishman and James G. Hunt (eds.), *Current Developments in the Study of Leadership* (Carbondale, Ill.: Southern Illinois University Press, 1973). Of special interest among the articles appearing in this book is the one by Edwin A. Fleishman, "Twenty Years of Consideration and Structure," pp. 1–40.

and may be controlled by using participation when introducing change.[33]

The Coch and French experiments concerning resistance to change were conducted in the Marion, Virginia, plant of the Harwood Manufacturing Company, a garment manufacturer. Harwood's employees are paid on a piece-rate incentive system, with 60 units representing the standard production for one hour. Further, the company normally tries to cushion the effects of change by conducting orientation programs and by paying a special bonus to those affected by change. Despite these efforts, any change in production methods usually results in failure to meet production standards in the same length of time required by a new employee to learn the job, an increase in the number of resignations, and expressions of hostility toward the management of the company.

In the experiments, four groups of employees were studied. Group One, the control group, had the change introduced in the usual fashion, with no participation on the part of employees in the change. However, the reasons for the change were presented to them in a meeting. Group Two elected representatives who participated in developing the change and were trained as "special operators" to work out the details of the change prior to its being adopted by the entire group. In Groups Three and Four, the total participation groups, all employees participated from the very beginning in developing the need for the change and working out the details of how the changed jobs should be performed. Though the changes made in the jobs varied for each group, they were comparable and minor in nature. Group One, pajama pressers, formerly stacked their finished work in lots of one-half dozen on pieces of cardboard. The change required them to stack their finished work in one-half dozen lots in boxes. Group Two had to alter their method of folding pajama coats, while Groups Three and Four, inspectors, were required only to cut certain threads from the garment and inspect all seams instead of cutting all loose threads and inspecting all seams.

Resistance developed in the control group immediately. There was conflict with the methods engineer, grievances were filed, and 17 percent of the group quit during the first 40 days after the change. As a group they did not reach the standard of 60 units an hour. Group Two, the one with elected representation, produced 61 units per hour at the end of 14 days; also, there was only one act of aggression against a supervisor and no layoffs during the first 40 days after the change. The two total participation groups recovered faster than Group Two. There was a slight drop in production the first day of change, but it immediately rose to 14 percent above prechange levels. There were no acts of aggression, nor any quits during the first 40 days. Later the remaining

[33]Lester Coch and John R. P. French, "Overcoming Resistance to Change," *Human Relations*, Vol. I (August, 1948), pp. 512–532. This study contains a discussion of the theoretical aspects of resistance to change as well as the results of the experiments.

members of the control group were reassembled as a unit and a change was introduced in their work; but this time they participated in the change. As expected, they performed in the same way as the total participation group had.

The results of these experiments are clear — participation reduces resistance to change. Yet, two limitations must be presented. Participation in the introduction of change is not decided by the supervisor; it is an expression of organizational climate. Second, at the present time there is no record of a company that has used total participation to introduce change over an extended period of time. Thus, the question arises as to how effective participation would be in overcoming resistance to change if it were normal operating procedure.[34]

Case Problem 17-B, The New Truck Problem, is different from the other cases you have analyzed in that its solution calls for role playing.[35] You may be asked to assume the role of the foreman or one of the repairmen. If you are not a participant, you will be asked to observe and evaluate the decision made by the foreman.

Case Problem 17-B
THE NEW TRUCK PROBLEM

"General Instructions for Crew.

"You are repairmen for a large company and drive to various locations in the city to do your work. Each of you drives a small truck and you take pride in keeping it looking good. You have a possessive feeling about your trucks and like to keep them in good running order. Naturally, you like to have new trucks, too, because a new truck gives you a feeling of pride.

"Here are some of the facts about the trucks and the men in the crews who report to Walt Marshall, the supervisor of repairs.

"George — 17 years with the company, has a 2-year-old Ford truck.

"Bill — 11 years with the company, has a 5-year-old Dodge truck.

"John — 10 years with the company, has a 4-year-old Ford truck.

"Charlie — 5 years with the company, has a 3-year-old Ford truck.

"Hank — 3 years with the company, has a 5-year-old Chevrolet truck.

"Most of you do all your driving in the city, but John and Charlie cover the suburbs.

"In acting your part, accept the facts as given as well as assume the attitudes supplied in your specific role. From this point on let your feelings develop in accordance with the events that transpire in the role playing process. When facts or events arise which are not covered by the roles, make up things which are consistent with the way it might be in a real-life situation."

[34]For an interesting account of how an organizational climate conducive to change was established for two companies brought together as a result of a merger the following is recommended: Alfred J. Marrow, David G. Bowers, and Stanley E. Seashore, *Management by Participation*, Creating a Climate for Personal and Organizational Development (New York: Harper & Row, Publishers, 1967).

[35]Norman R. F. Maier and Lester F. Zerfoss, "MRP: A Technique for Training Large Groups of Supervisors and Its Potential Use in Social Research," *Human Relations*, Vol. 5 (May, 1952), pp. 180–181.

Note to Instructor: Since role playing requires that participants be unaware of hidden motivations of others in the role playing situation, the roles of the crew are not included in the case. They are in the instructor's manual and should be reproduced on separate sheets of paper and distributed prior to the role playing.

1. The supervisor has been described as being "the man in the middle." Is this characterization borne out by the two legal definitions of the supervisor? How?

2. What inferences could you make concerning the organizational climate of a company whose supervisors petitioned for a union of their own? As a member of middle or top management, what action would you recommend upon receiving notification of such a petition?

3. Recognizing that most supervisors are promoted from the hourly ranks, why is there such a cleavage between the hourly worker's self-description and the self-perception of the supervisor?

4. Discuss and give an example showing the significance of each of the dimensions of supervisory performance as described by Peres.

5. What is meant by the "linking-pin" function? How is this function related to the supervisor's position in the organization? Is it of significance in the motivation of employees? How?

6. The Day and Stogdill study reports that male supervisors advance more rapidly than female supervisors even when both have the same degree of leadership effectiveness. Why? Discuss.

7. Comment on the following statement: "You could dispose of almost all of the leadership training courses for supervision in American industry today without anyone knowing the difference."

8. Describe and give an example illustrating the methods commonly used for training in human relations.

9. Define in your own terms the meaning of organizational climate.

10. Evaluate each of the factors that contributes to a supervisor's influence. Which do you believe to be the most important? Relate the concept of influence and the performance of college graduates in training positions.

11. What major factor limits the applicability of participation as a means of introducing change? What is the next step if the employees fail to see the need for change?

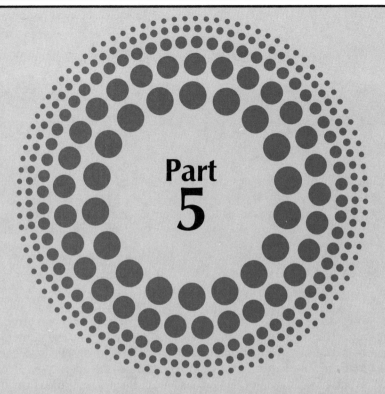

Part 5

The Control Function

The first three chapters of this last section discuss the control function. The last chapter is a summing up of our study of management. The control function is a three-step process of setting standards, measuring current performance against standards, and taking corrective action when necessary to bring performance in line with standards. The characteristics of good control are summarized. Commonly used nonbudgetary controls ranging from personal observation and reports to the more complex break-even and time-event-network techniques are examined. Internal audit programs with emphasis upon the relatively new human resource accounting procedures and ratio analysis are also included among the nonbudgetary controls examined in Chapter 19. A discussion of budgetary controls follows. Types of budgets are discussed and the methods of securing flexibility with budgets are described. The concept of zero-base budgeting is introduced.

The third step of the control process, the taking of corrective action, touches upon the lives of people. The attitudes held toward control are as important as the techniques of control in determining the success of the control function. The last part of Chapter 20 discusses behavioral reactions to all controls, nonbudgetary as well as budgetary. The typical control procedure, a seemingly endless cycle of control, resistance, and more control, is analyzed in terms of its effect upon people. The reasons for resistance to controls and the unfavorable responses to controls are presented in detail. The chapter closes with recommendations for the effective use of controls.

Each of the functions of the management process — planning, organizing, leading, and controlling — has been discussed in sequence; the task remains to integrate these functions. The first part of Chapter 21 reviews the functions of planning and control as a planning-control-planning cycle. Interrelationships between this cycle and the functions of organizing and leading are described. A discussion of management and the systems concept is a means of furthering the concept of management as an integrated process. A hierarchy of systems and the characteristics of open systems are presented in tabular form. Organizations are social systems and as such are open systems. Some of the major characteristics and functions of business organizations are reviewed within the framework of open systems characteristics. A brief discussion of current issues confronting today's managers, to be resolved by the managers of tomorrow, follows. The chapter closes with a brief statement that relates the introductory course in management to subsequent courses in the business administration curriculum.

Chapter 18

The Basis of Control

Case Problem 18-A
A NEED FOR CONTROL

Standard Building Service Company of St. Louis is a 15-year old company that provides janitorial services for office buildings and industrial plants. Standard was purchased five years ago by Leslie Waller and, at the time of the purchase, annual sales were approximately $500,000. In three years she was able to double the sales volume to the present level of $1,000,000, but for the past two years sales volume has remained relatively constant. Waller attributes the lack of growth for the past two years to her being unable to call on new accounts because the business has grown to such an extent that her full energies and time are required in solving the myriad of problems that arise each day. She recognizes that the few new accounts she does obtain do no more than offset the normal turnover of accounts lost each month.

Janitorial services are usually performed after the tenants have left the building for the day; consequently, very few of Standard's employees start work before 6 p.m. Waller has found from experience that in order to keep employees, she must offer them at least 20 hours of work a week. On the other hand, very few people seem willing to work more than 25 hours a week. As a result, the work force of

approximately 275 men and women are part-time employees. Waller also found that by hiring persons presently employed she is assured of stable, motivated employees. However, since her employees are working full-time elsewhere, there is considerable resistance when supervisors expect an above-average amount of work from them.

A recent analysis of the 121 accounts serviced by the company shows that 40 customers require the services of only one person working a maximum of 25 hours a week. Thirty-five accounts require two people with total man-hours ranging from 35 to 50 hours a week. Fifteen accounts require an average of 100 man-hours a week, thus utilizing the services of up to four employees. There is one large industrial plant that requires 500 hours of service each week and approximately 20 workers. The remaining 30 accounts range between 100 and 400 man-hours each week, and require between four and sixteen employees.

Waller is not sure which size job yields the most profit. Jobs are priced on a rule-of-thumb basis and depend upon the type of floor surfaces, the amount of building traffic, number and types of offices, and other similar factors. Waller and one of her two full-time supervisors estimate the man-power requirements for each new job. An analysis of company records shows that for the past five years variable costs — direct labor and materials (waxes, detergents, etc.) — average about 80 to 85 percent of total revenue.

The full-time organization consists of Waller, two supervisors, a secretary, an accountant, and a supply person who also maintains some of the larger pieces of cleaning equipment such as the floor polishers. In addition, there are five part-time supervisors, each of whom supervises 40 to 50 workers in a given geographic area of the city. Most of their time and energy is spent in delivering supplies and materials to the various buildings within a given geographic area of the city. They also reassign personnel as the need arises and collect the weekly time cards. The two full-time supervisors have no specific duties assigned to them nor is either one responsible for the work of any particular part-time supervisor.

At the present time Waller has only two sources of information to guide her in the operation of her business. One of these is customer complaints, which serve as a check on the quality of work. The other source is the weekly payroll, which is prepared by a local bank. Each week time cards are submitted to the bank and from these records payroll checks are prepared. The bank also maintains the necessary social security and income tax records. In addition, a summary is prepared showing the total man-hours per week for each job. At present, no consistent use is made of this information. However, on the occasions when she has examined these weekly reports, Waller has found that the total hours per week run as much as 400 hours in excess of the number of hours used in computing the price of the services. There is no record of the use of supplies for each job.

PROBLEMS

1. Is there a need for control in this company? Why?
2. If controls are needed, what areas of the business are most in need of control?
3. What type of standards are now being used? What kind would you recommend?
4. How can the organization be modified to improve the control function?

The control function is one of the four major functions of the process of management. The usual sequence assigned to these functions places planning first, next is organizing, the third is the human relations function — frequently called leading — and the last function is control. The word, control, and its position in the management process sequence are indicative of the nature of the control function. In this chapter we will first examine the nature of the control function, and second, we will study in detail the steps of the control process. The characteristics of effective controls are then discussed and from this discussion several principles of control are developed.

THE NATURE OF CONTROL

If plans were never in need of revision and were executed flawlessly by a perfectly balanced organization under the direction of an omnipotent leader, there would be no need for control. However, as Robert Burns observed years ago, "The best-laid schemes o' mice an' men gang aft agley."[1] In addition, organizations do not always work smoothly and need revision to meet changing conditions. Also, the effectiveness of leadership is often open to question. It is the purpose of the control function to take the corrective action necessary to assure the fulfillment of organizational objectives. Although control denotes corrective action that may be objective in all respects, the reactions of those subjected to controls may be highly emotionalized and tinged with resentment. The reason for this reaction is that control always touches upon the people who make up organizations, for they are charged with responsibilities and are accountable to their superiors for the performance of these duties. When determining whether or not goals are being met, it is the performance of the people of the organization that is actually being reviewed. One way of developing an understanding of the nature of control is to place the control function in perspective within the framework of a systems concept.

Cybernetics and Control

The study of how dynamic systems maintain a state of equilibrium, or steady state, though subject to changing environmental conditions is called *cybernetics*.[2] Examples of cybernetic systems are numerous and familiar. The thermostat maintains the temperature of a room at a predetermined level by making or breaking an electrical circuit that starts or stops the furnace. The rotating arms of a steam-engine governor rise or fall with changes in centrifugal force, thereby controlling the input of steam into the cylinders of the engine with the result that a constant speed is maintained under varying load conditions. Another example is a photoelectric cell placed in a circuit to turn on lights in the evening when daylight illumination decreases to a predetermined level and to turn off the artificial lighting the next morning when natural illumination is sufficient.

---

[1]The closing stanza of Robert Burns "To A Mouse" is a statement that could be made by many of today's executives:
"Still thou art blest, compared wi' me!
The present only toucheth thee.
But och! I backward cast my e'e
    On prospects drear!
And forward though I cannot see,
    I guess an' fear!"
[2]For a complete discussion of cybernetics, see:
Norbert Wiener, *Cybernetics*, Control and Communication in the Animal and the Machine (New York: John Wiley & Sons, 1949).
Norbert Wiener, *The Human Use of Human Beings*, Cybernetics and Society (2d ed.; New York: Doubleday & Co., 1954.)
For a more recent discussion of the interaction of subsystems the following is suggested: Leroy H. Mantell, "Objectives, Controls and Motivation," *Human Resource Management*, Vol. 12, No. 4 (Winter, 1973), pp. 18–23.

The above examples of cybernetic systems illustrate the major characteristics of such systems. First, there is a predetermined steady state or equilibrium to be maintained. In the first example, a constant temperature is the state of equilibrium to be maintained; the second illustration focuses upon speed as the steady state, and the third example uses a predetermined intensity of light as the state of equilibrium. Second, in all of the above instances there is constant change in the environment within which the system operates, thus forcing adjustments within the system in order to maintain an equilibrium; hence, the term "dynamic system." Third, there is a transfer of information from the external environment to within the system. The "information" that activates the thermostat is a change in temperature; centrifugal force is the information transmitted by the steam-engine governor, and the intensity of light is the information received by the photoelectric cell. Fourth, there is a mechanical device so designed that corrective action is taken, with the result that the equilibrium of the system is maintained. The bimetal of the thermostat makes or breaks the electrical circuit, the moving arms of the governor open and close a valve regulating the flow of steam, and the photoelectric cell responds to the intensity of light by opening or closing the circuit. In each of these instances the control device is engineered to perform the specific function necessary to maintain the system's equilibrium.[3]

All living organisms are by definition cybernetic systems, for they must maintain equilibrium in order to survive. It is useful to apply the concept of cybernetics — the maintenance of a steady state through the interpretation of information and subsequent corrective action — to organizations. The concept of cybernetic systems is not being introduced for the first time in this chapter. The systems concept is first discussed in Chapter 2. In Chapter 5, Figure 5-3 (reproduced here as Figure 18-1) shows how the major business functions of finance, production, marketing, and personnel form a self-correcting system with a feedback loop to the external environment between the marketing department and the external environment, the customer. Feedback loops with outside forces could also be shown between finance and sources of capital, between production and vendors, and between personnel and the labor supply. There is also a continual exchange of information internally between the major functions of an organization.

The Parable of the Spindle, Case Problem 6-A, illustrates how the cook performs a control function by selecting the most efficient combination of orders from information contained on tickets stored on a spindle. Further, the tickets can be used as a control device by the

---

[3]Robert Chin, "The Utility of System Models and Developmental Models for Practicioners," from W. G. Bennis, K. D. Benne, and Robert Chin (eds.), *The Planning of Change*, Readings in the Applied Behavioral Sciences (New York: Holt, Rinehart & Winston, 1961). This article discusses several types of models and their application to business situations.

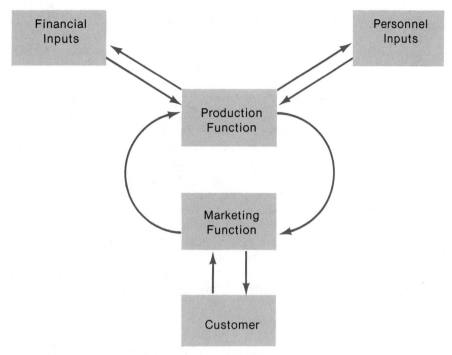

**Figure 18-1
MAJOR BUSINESS
FUNCTIONS AS A
CYBERNETIC
SYSTEM**

waitress and can be checked against the order received. At the close of the day the tickets may also be used as a control measure when compared with cash receipts. The schematic concept of a business as shown in Figure 18-1 and the specific illustration of the experience of a restaurant illustrate that control is the interpretation of information, from both internal and external sources, so that corrective action may be taken in order to reach desired objectives.[4]

Steps in the Control Process

There is agreement among students of management concerning the three steps of the control process:

1. Establishing standards of performance.
2. Measuring current performance in relation to established standards.
3. Taking corrective action.

Let us now interpret these three steps of the control process in the light of what we know about cybernetic systems. The establishment of

[4]For a discussion of interorganizational relationships, especially between buyer and seller, the following is of interest: Raymond G. Hunt and Ira S. Rubin, "Approaches to Managerial Control in Interpenetrating Systems: The Case of Government-Industry Relations," *Academy of Management Journal*, Vol. 16, No. 2 (June, 1973), pp. 296–311.

standards defines the desired state of equilibrium. Standards are definitions of the objectives of an organization, but it must be remembered that objectives can and do change. The second step, measurement of current performance, requires that information be processed and interpreted by someone so that a conclusion can be drawn concerning present position, or performance, relative to the desired position as defined by the standards. The information used in measurement is not limited to financial data reflecting the economic condition of the company; it also includes reports on the quality of the product, the amount of inventory, the morale of personnel, or even the intuitive judgment of a manager that all is not going well. Taking corrective action intended to bring performance in line with predetermined standards requires executive decision making and a realignment of company resources. The person who makes the decision corresponds to the control device of the mechanical cybernetic system.[5]

The next major section of this chapter discusses in greater detail each of the three steps of the control process; first, however, there is one more question to answer for a more complete understanding of the nature of control. Who does the controlling?

Who Controls?

Many students, particularly those majoring in accounting, consider as a personal career objective the position of controller of a business organization. Figure 18-2 presents two typical position descriptions — one, the controller of a large company, and the other, the combined position of treasurer and controller in a medium-size company. In general, the controller is closely associated with the finance function of the company, but may or may not report to the vice-president for finance. If not reporting to the financial officer, the controller reports to the president or chief executive officer of the company. Controllers are usually responsible for designing the systems and procedures necessary for management control; thus, in companies having integrated data processing systems the controller may be responsible for the design and maintenance of such systems. Traditionally the controller's function is concerned with those aspects of the business that can be reduced to dollars and cents; for this reason the controller is usually concerned with the efficiency of production and the cost of sales. Few companies require that the controller secure information concerning morale of employees, the status of innovations in the organization, or

---

[5]For a comprehensive review of the literature concerning control theory from 1900 to 1972, the following provides a summary of the knowledge available to the executive in performing the control function: Giovanni B. Giglioni and Arthur G. Bedeian, "A Conspectus of Management Control Theory: 1900–1972," *Academy of Management Journal*, Vol. 17, No. 2 (June, 1972), pp. 292–305.

FUNCTIONS OF THE CONTROLLER IN THE LARGE COMPANY

Objectives

The Controller (or Comptroller) of Accounts is responsible for the effective financial and cost controls of the company's activities.

Functions

1. Prescription of principles and methods to govern accounting controls throughout the enterprise
2. Provision of adequate protection against loss of the company's money and property
3. Prescription of principles of accounting determining cost of product, and normal volume of production in order to compute costs and install appropriate systems
4. Verification of the propriety of expenditures
5. Providing comparison of capital expenditures and appropriations
6. Preparation of the accounts of the corporation
7. Determination of income and expenditure allocation among plants and departments
8. Proposals regarding the nature of the corporation's financial statements
9. Preparation of the financial statements
10. Preparation of analyses assisting others to improve the earnings of the enterprise
11. Observation of the manner of performing accounting responsibilities

Relationships

The Controller of Accounts reports to the Vice-President for Finance.

FUNCTIONS OF THE TREASURER AND CONTROLLER IN THE MEDIUM-SIZE COMPANY

1. Accountability for the safekeeping and custody of corporate funds, securities owned by the company, and the corporate seal
2. Establishment of a General Accounting Department with the following duties:
   a. Post-audit of plant transactions
   b. Installation and maintenance of primary books of accounts
   c. Setting the policies, procedures, and standards of accounting and cost records and reports
   d. Setting up methods of cash disbursement, accounts receivable, plant and equipment records
   e. Cash management
   f. Preparation of financial statements and reports
   g. Credit approval
3. Establishment of a cost accounting department with a view to:
   a. Prescribing and administering factory timekeeping and payroll procedures
   b. Maintaining inventory controls
   c. Supervision of timekeeping methods
   d. Setting up a cost system in each plant
4. Establishing a budget department to present standards of performance to management with a view to:
   a. Showing the results of operations
   b. Establishing standards of performance
   c. Proposing a budget forecast
   d. Informing executives of variations from the budget
   e. Continuous revision of the budget

Source: Ernest Dale, *Planning and Developing the Company Organization Structure* (New York: American Management Association, Research Report No. 20, 1952), pp. 200–201.

Figure 18-2 FUNCTIONS OF THE CONTROLLER

the quality of management; yet these factors are legitimate areas of control.[6]

We still have not answered the question, who controls? Note in Figure 18-2 there is no statement saying that it is the duty of the controller to control by taking corrective action. Control, the act of taking corrective action, is a function of the line manager. The controller, a member of the staff organization, may design the information system, secure and interpret data concerning performance, and even make recommendations as to what might constitute the most appropriate corrective action. However, the final decision and the request for corrective action are the responsibility of the line manager. Nor is control by the line organization limited to any level of management; indeed, for effective control all levels of management must exercise control over those functions assigned to them. There is much that first-line supervisors can control in their departments that cannot be controlled directly by anyone else in the organization.

THE CONTROL PROCESS

We have described the control process as consisting of the following steps: (1) establishing standards of performance, (2) measuring current performance in relation to the established standards, and (3) taking corrective action. Standards are the basis of the control process, for without adequate standards the subsequent steps of measurement and corrective action are meaningless. Let us examine, first, the nature of standards; then, problems encountered in the measurement of performance; and last, the kind of corrective action that should be taken.

Establishing Standards

The dictionary definition of standards includes two concepts. First, a standard is a rule (unit) for measuring. It is intended to serve as a model or criterion. Second, a standard is established by authority. *Thus, a standard may be defined as a unit of measurement established to serve as a model or criterion.* The 72-stroke par for an 18-hole golf course is an excellent example of a standard. Par is a recognized level of performance or achievement established by authority (custom and the various golfing associations). Second, par demonstrates clearly that a standard is not perfection — many professional golfers consistently exceed, or break, par. Nor is par the average of the level of performance for all golfers; indeed, the average would be considerably higher than 72. Thus, par is a difficult, but attainable, level of performance. It serves as a criterion for comparing the proficiency of one

---

[6]The expanding horizons of the controller's job are discussed in the following: Robert J. Mockler, "The Corporate Control Job: Breaking the Mold," *Business Horizons*, Vol. 13, No. 6 (December, 1970), pp. 73–77.

golfer against that of another in terms of an objective unit of measurement — the number of strokes required to complete the course. Par is analogous to the work standards established by a company for its employees.

Scope of Business Standards. Standards in business organizations are not limited to establishing levels of performance for individual workers; instead, they are applicable to all phases of the operation. Ralph C. Davis suggests that standards be set for all activities that contribute to the primary service objectives of the organization. He recommends establishing standards of service, including the development of criteria for the particular good or service being offered by the organization. Standards of policy and function include an evaluation of the organization structure and its method of operation. Standards should also be determined for the evaluation of the physical facilities of the organization, for determining the characteristics of the kind of personnel required, and for determining the level of performance of personnel.[7]

Another approach to describing the scope of standards is to set standards for each of several key result areas. General Electric uses this approach and establishes standards for each of the following eight key result areas:

1. Profitability
2. Market position
3. Productivity
4. Product leadership
5. Personnel development
6. Employee attitudes
7. Public responsibility
8. Balance between short-range and long-range goals.[8]

Some of the major considerations necessary to establish standards for each of the key result areas are discussed below.

Profitability. The standard for profitability may be expressed by means of the widely used rate of return ratio, percent of profit to sales,

---

[7]Ralph C. Davis, *The Fundamentals of Top Management* (New York: Harper & Brothers, 1951), pp. 28–29. Chapter 2, "Standards and Standardization," pp. 21–42, presents a complete discussion of standards in business organizations.

[8]Robert W. Lewis, "Measurement, Reporting, and Appraising Results of Operations with Reference to Goals, Plans, and Budgets," from the report, *Planning, Managing, and Measuring the Business:* A Case Study of Management Planning and Control at General Electric Company (New York: Controllership Foundation, 1955), pp. 29–41. Lewis discusses the problems inherent in the measurement of performance in each of the eight key result areas.

The student should also review the eight major objectives of an organization described by Peter Drucker and note the similarity between Drucker's objectives and the key result areas of Lewis. Drucker suggests objectives for each of the following eight areas: market standing, innovation, productivity, physical and financial resources, profitability, manager performance and development, worker performance and attitude, and public responsibility. See Chapter 3, "Objectives and Ethics," and the following:

Peter F. Drucker, "The Objectives of a Business," from *The Practice of Management* (New York: Harper & Brothers, 1954).

or total dollar volume.[9] The expression of profit as a ratio between profits earned and capital employed is useful in comparing the contribution of each of several decentralized units with respect to current performance and is also of value in determining which of several alternatives to select for future operations. Deviations from expected profit expressed as a percent of sales may indicate variations in cost or the need for changing the price of the product or service. However, profit expressed as a ratio — either return on investment or percent of sales — is not necessarily a valid measure of the contribution of personnel to the profitability of a given operation. For example, the profit of a retail store expressed as a percent of sales may be a function primarily of the cost of goods sold and the cost of renting physical facilities, factors that may be beyond the control of the manager. The expression of profits in terms of total dollars earned is a measure of the effectiveness of sales effort on the part of store personnel over a period of time. Standards of profitability should reflect the contribution of personnel in controlling costs and expanding volume as well as the utilization of physical and financial resources.

Market Position. The position of a company in a chosen market is a measure of the extent to which its product or service is accepted by the customer and an indication of the effectiveness of its sales-promotion techniques. Standards intended to measure a company's market position must be expressed in terms of the total market. A company may, for example, increase its sales at the rate of two percent a year and be the largest in its field; yet, if the total market for the good or service offered is increasing at the rate of four percent a year, that company's market position is deteriorating.[10]

Productivity. Measures of productivity are immediately associated with the production function, but standards of productivity should be set for administrative and sales functions as well as for production. Typically, productivity is expressed as the relationship between total output, measured with respect to dollar volume or units produced, and units of input — for example, the number of man-hours required for a stated level of output. Standards of productivity should be determined for other units of input as well as for man-hours. Efficiency of production may be expressed in relation to the number of machine hours, and a retail establishment is interested in the dollar volume produced per square foot of floor space. The use of total payroll dollars as an index of input indicates whether or not the rate of productivity is keeping

---

[9]The following article discusses return on investment in relation to planning and control: J. Fred Weston, "ROI Planning and Control," *Business Horizons*, Vol. 15, No. 4 (August, 1972), pp. 35–42.

[10]The following article discusses the effects of competition upon the structure of control. Pradip N. Khandwalla, "Effect of Competition on the Structure of Top Management Control," *Academy of Management Journal* Vol. 16, No. 2 (June, 1973), pp. 285–295.

pace with the increasing cost of labor — sometimes a more significant measure than the number of man-hours employed.

Product Leadership. Standards for profitability, market position, and productivity are not too difficult to express in relatively objective, quantitative units of measurement, but corporate achievement must be measured in areas where the criteria are qualitative in nature rather than quantitative. A company's position with respect to product leadership is difficult to express quantitatively; yet an estimate of position is necessary if it is a company objective to become or remain a leader in its field. A simple count of new products or services introduced is not sufficient. The significance of the new contribution should also be weighed. Standards of quality and performance for current products should be compared with those of competitors. Determination of the significance of research in the development of new products and an evaluation of research effort offer a means of estimating potential leadership capabilities. Customer surveys indicate the degree of product acceptability and may furnish suggestions for product improvement. Finally, a value judgment must be made as to whether the company is meeting its goals of product leadership.[11]

Personnel Development. Standards for measuring the effectiveness of management development programs are also qualitative in nature. Since management development is usually the result of long-range planning and intended to meet future needs, it is difficult to assess the success of any such program on a year-to-year basis. However, an annual reporting of developmental activities establishes a trend in this area, and when compared with projected managerial needs resulting from expected growth, an estimate may be made concerning the need for expanding the management development program. The number of people participating in formal developmental programs, the success of those who have received training compared with those who have not been trained, and the number of managers hired from outside the company should be included in annual reports of personnel development. A current inventory of personnel skills when compared with forecasts for immediate personnel needs may indicate the short-range effectiveness of a management development program.

Employee Attitudes. Although there is some question regarding the existence of a positive relationship between employee attitude and short-range production goals (Chapter 16), there is no doubt that employee attitudes have their effect upon the success of an organization over a long period of time. Attitudes may be measured operationally by an analysis of labor turnover, absenteeism, grievances, and safety

---

[11]Barry M. Richman, "A Rating Scale for Product Innovation," *Business Horizons,* Vol. 5 (Summer, 1962), pp. 37–44. Richman presents a method of screening and selecting new products.

records. Measurement of these factors can be accomplished in an objective, quantitative manner; the difficulty lies in establishing the standard, or criterion, of what is acceptable or desirable. Year-to-year figures and comparisons between different units in the same organization or with industry experience may be used as a guide to determine expected results. Product quality, if within the control of employees, and the number of suggestions for improvements in operating methods may be used as measures of employee attitudes. Attitude surveys conducted at periodic intervals indicate the degree of progress being made in the improvement of employee attitudes. The determination of employee attitudes is significant for the company desirous of maintaining a position of respect and leadership in its community.

Public Responsibility. The fulfillment of goals in the area of public responsibility is highly intangible and difficult to measure. Included are contributions to the life of the community in the form of stable employment, participation in community affairs, and the leadership supplied for community activities. Standards of performance are not readily expressed in quantitative terms; consequently, the results obtained in the area of public responsibility are appraised in terms of their broad contribution to the public.

Balance Between Short-Range and Long-Range Goals. Again, the measure of success is subjective in nature. Implied in this measurement is the existence of long-range goals, say 15 or 20 years from now; and the existence of intermediate and short-range plans to achieve the objectives of those long-range goals. The inclusion of a measurement of the balance between short-range and long-range goals forces a company to review its entire planning process and emphasizes that future success is dependent upon the execution of carefully developed plans.

Methods of Establishing Standards. It is apparent from the number and kinds of the areas for which standards may be established that one method of establishing standards cannot be applied to all areas. There are three methods used to determine the level of expected performance. One is to develop statistical, or normative, data from sources internal and external to the company; another is to appraise results in the light of experience and judgment; and the third method is to develop engineered standards.

Statistical Standards. Statistical standards, sometimes called historical standards, are standards based upon an analysis of past experience. The data used may be drawn from the company's own records or may be a reflection of the experience of several companies. The particular statistic selected for the criterion may be the average or it may be a stated point above or below the midpoint, for example, the upper quartile. While an analysis of past experience may be helpful in setting standards of performance in some areas, the statistical approach has many pitfalls in setting production standards. The following example illustrates the weakness of a historical analysis.

> The accounting department of a rebuilder of automobile parts kept a careful, complete record of the number of labor hours, broken down into direct and indirect labor hours, required to rebuild each of several parts. At the end of each fiscal year, the average number of hours required to rebuild each part was determined. Thus, the average for the past year became the standard for the current year and deviations from the average were reported as above or below standard. Despite the fact that this company was producing parts well within the limits set by its own standards, its labor costs were considerably in excess of those of its competitors. A consultant called in to review the situation discovered that there were many bottlenecks in the production control department and that the output per man-hour was only 70 percent of what could reasonably be expected based upon sound time study standards.

The lesson is clear: meeting standards of past performance is not sufficient, particularly when past performance is only a fraction of potential performance.

Yet, if used as an adjunct to other sources of information, statistical data is not only helpful but sometimes the only guide available. Indexes of profitability vary widely from one industry to another, and an analysis of industry data may prove helpful in setting criteria of profitability. Analysis of the experience of competing firms and one's own historical records of growth aid in setting realistic goals relative to market position. Companies choosing to set standards in the area of employee attitudes may find it useful to analyze the results obtained by other firms using the same attitude or opinion survey. The average contribution to charities and educational institutions may be significant in setting goals of public responsibility. In all of these instances before a final criterion can be set, the information gained from statistical sources is combined with another factor — judgment.

Standards Set by Appraisal. Standards do not have to be expressed in units of measurement accurate to the third decimal place. Some areas of corporate performance are, in the last analysis, appraised primarily in terms of a manager's past experience and judgment. As indicated in our discussion of statistical standards, normative data is a useful adjunct in setting standards of performance with regard to profitability, market position, employee attitudes, and to some extent in the area of public responsibility. However, the final determination of what constitutes a satisfactory level of performance is a judgment based upon management's past experience. Standards set by appraisal are essentially *value* judgments and can be as realistic and attainable as statistical or engineered standards. In the absence of standards determined by formal study and analysis, all managers are expected to appraise the output of their subordinates in terms of what they, as managers, believe to be a satisfactory day's work. In so doing, standards are being set by appraisal.

Engineered Standards. Engineered standards, so called because they are based upon an objective, quantitative analysis of a specific work situation, may be developed for the measurement of machine output and for measuring the output of individual workers. Machine output standards express the production capabilities of a given piece of equipment and are determined by mechanical design factors. Machine capacity figures are developed by the designers of the equipment and represent the optimum output of the equipment in normal production use. Machine capacities are significant in determining output standards in industries using automatic equipment; for example, the metal and glass container industry.

Engineered standards developed to measure the output of individual workers, or groups of workers, are called either *time standards* or *time study* standards. The reason is that time is the element of measurement and is almost always measured by means of a stopwatch.[12] The first time studies in this country were completed by Frederick W. Taylor in 1881 at the Midvale Steel Company.[13] His studies were directed toward an analysis of the productivity of hourly workers in a steel mill. Since then, time study techniques have been applied to all types of production jobs — including material handling and maintenance — clerical positions, and even sales jobs.

In setting time standards the actual time taken to perform a given job is determined. This value is termed the *actual* time. The standard time is the time that should be required to perform the job under certain specified conditions. These conditions are usually defined as an average worker, trained in the skills of the job, working at normal pace (rate of speed), and following the prescribed methods for the job. Determining effort, or pace, is a matter of judgment and is related to the effort expended — and the speed required — to walk three miles an hour on level ground. Standard times are usually developed for a normal eight-hour workday and include allowances for fatigue, unavoidable delays, personal time, and other interruptions of work that occur

---

[12]The student is referred to the following references for a more complete discussion of time study methods:

Marvin E. Mundel, *Motion and Time Study*, Principles and Practice (4th ed.; Englewood Cliffs: Prentice-Hall, 1970).

Claude S. George, Jr., *Management in Industry* (2d ed.; Englewood Cliffs: Prentice-Hall, 1964), pp. 368–390.

Franklin G. Moore, *Production Management* (6th ed.; Homewood: Richard D. Irwin, 1973), pp. 362–383.

Richard N. Owens, *Management of Industrial Enterprises* (4th ed.; Homewood: Richard D. Irwin, 1961), pp. 362–393.

For a point of view that is highly critical of time study methods, the following book is suggested:

William Gomberg, *A Trade Union Analysis of Time Study* (2d ed.; Englewood Cliffs: Prentice-Hall, 1955).

[13]See Chapter 2, page 19.

at predictable intervals. Workers who perform their work according to the standards set for the job are said to be working at 100 percent of standard. The use of the expression, 100 percent of standard, causes much of the initial misunderstandings of time study. The term, 100 percent, normally conveys the idea of perfection, of maximum effort and maximum output. A more acceptable expression would be to use the term, par.

Time study standards are essential if incentive plans are to be installed, but it does not follow that incentives are necessary to make effective use of time study. On the contrary, time standards can be used quite effectively as a means of increasing production without the introduction of incentives. The presence of time standards alone tends to increase production.[14] Time standards also form the basis of standard costs. Standard costs are composed of the cost of labor performing at standard plus standard allowances for materials and allocated overhead.

The need for establishing standards varies widely from one company to another, but any company that has labor costs greater than 30 percent of its total product or service cost should investigate the possibility of establishing time standards to serve as the basis for control when measuring human output.

Measuring Current Performance

There is an intermediate step in the control process between the first step of the process, establishing standards, and the final phase of the process, the taking of corrective action. The middle step is that of measuring current performance. To a degree, the problems of measurements are defined, and sometimes partially solved, by the manner in which standards are defined. Standards of profitability, for example, imply that the measuring unit be one of dollars; but the statement of criteria in the areas of product leadership and public responsibility requires ingenuity in developing satisfactory methods of measurement. The variety and the number of performance factors for which standards may be set make it virtually impossible to discuss problems of measurement by describing units of measurement applicable to all business situations. Nonetheless, there are certain characteristics of effective control measurements to be examined. In addition, further elaboration of the significance of the measurement of current progress to the entire control process is helpful in assessing the worth of measuring devices.

Fundamental to sound control measures is recognition that management control systems are cybernetic systems, defining cybernetics as the processing and the interpretation of information. Thus, control

---

[14]See Chapter 16, pages 375–408.

systems are best regarded as information systems. The appropriateness of corrective action, the end point of the control process, is dependent almost entirely upon the kind of information received. Information intended to measure and describe current performance can be evaluated by seeking answers to the following five questions:

1. Is the information timely?
2. Are the units of measurement appropriate?
3. How reliable is the information received?
4. Is the information valid?
5. Is information being channeled to the proper authority?

Let us discuss each of these questions so that the problems of measuring performance are better understood.

Timeliness of Information. Control information, to be of greatest use, must reflect present position. Typically, managers rely too much on data supplied by the accounting department and as a result fail to develop other sources of information. Accounting statements are prepared at the end of a given time period, for example a calendar month, and, even with efficient procedures, seven to ten working days are required to prepare statements of the preceding month's operations. Though this information may have historical significance and be of value in the preparation of annual reports, it is of little or no value to the manager responsible for the efficiency of day-to-day operations. Ideally, managers of each operating unit should have information presented to them during the course of each working day so that they might have an adequate basis for corrective action. Is such timeliness possible? The following example suggests that it is.

> The manager of a plant producing stamped automobile parts devised the following method of securing information concerning the quantity produced by each of several production departments on an hourly basis. Departments were designated by the operations performed and included the following: shearing, stamping, chrome plating, and buffing and polishing. The manager placed in his office a large blackboard ruled into vertical columns for each production department. Horizontal lines were drawn for each hour of the day. A production clerk checked with the foreman of each production department at the end of each hour, received the quantity produced by each department, and posted the information on the board in the manager's office. In this way the manager became immediately aware of trouble spots and could anticipate future difficulties likely to arise resulting from a shortage of parts or from a breakdown in earlier operations in the production sequence.

Another result of the control procedure described in the above incident is that the foremen of the various departments confer more frequently with each other and with the plant manager to minimize delays in production. Timely control information can be obtained through telephone calls, daily reports, or personal observation without having to wait for information prepared and distributed by formal reporting systems.

Appropriate Units of Measurement. One of the most difficult tasks in measuring current performance is the selection of an appropriate unit of measurement. Occasionally the use of several different units offers a partial solution to this problem. For example, profit is expressed as a percentage of sales, as the percentage return on capital invested, and as total dollars. Similarly, production may be measured and described as a ratio of output to input or as total units produced. Market position is also measured by several different methods. The use of multiple measures to describe performance is sound because each measure serves as a cross check on the information provided by the other measures and at the same time emphasizes one particular aspect of the performance under review.

The measurement of performance against standard for profits, productivity, and sales utilizes quantitative units of measurement. However, much of the evaluation of a company's progress depends on qualitative, rather than quantitative, units of measurement. In the absence of quantitative measures managers drawing upon past experience and their own sets of values, must judge for themselves whether or not standards are being met. Such judgments must be made in the areas of personnel development, public responsibility, and determining the balance between long-range and short-range goals. Attempting to express achievement in these areas by relying solely upon quantitative units can be misleading. For example, measuring personnel development by a head count of the number of persons who have completed a given training program does not answer the question of the effectiveness of the program in improving performance on the job. Even though qualitative measures are difficult to apply and generally unreliable when compared with quantitative units, it is a mistake not to set standards in those areas where measurement must be made in qualitative terms.

Reliability of Information. Reliability of information pertains to its degree of accuracy. It is assumed that the data is free from clerical errors. Thus, the accuracy referred to by the term reliability is with respect to the consistency of data and the extent to which all aspects of the problem are measured. Almost always a compromise must be made between reliability and timeliness. Usually the reliability of information is positively related to its completeness. Computer predictions of election returns illustrate the increasing accuracy of predictions as more and more data is reported and interpreted. However, most managerial interpretations of operations — and the subsequent corrective action — are based upon incomplete information. Sales managers having reports for only the first two weeks of a calendar month may be required to take corrective action even though data is not fully reliable because it is not a complete description of the month's activities. Even so, partial information on recurring time cycles, such as monthly sales and production reports, can be analyzed and related to the entire cycle and provide a relatively accurate basis for analysis and action.

In addition to decreased reliability of information when using data for only a part of the reporting period, there is a marked decrease in the reliability of data covering initial phases of an operation. The reason for this type of loss in reliability is best explained by the adage, "practice makes perfect." At the start of a new operation quality and quantity of performance are at their lowest point; but with time, there is improved individual performance and better methods are usually developed. Graphic representations of improved performance are called *learning curves*. The aircraft industry, constantly faced with changing products, short runs, and the threat of contract cancellation, has developed techniques to predict with considerable accuracy the average level of performance by projecting an improvement or learning curve. Data from the beginning of an operation is not characteristic of the entire operation or its latter phases and is a highly unreliable source of information unless interpreted as part of a learning curve. Though the use of learning curves is most highly developed in the aircraft industry, the same techniques are applicable to the prediction of final performance in maintenance operations, in building heavy equipment, in construction, and in the performance of salespeople introducing a new product. The danger lies not in using the initial data of a new operation but in failing to recognize that there is a predictable improvement factor.[15]

Validity of Information. It is possible for information to be highly reliable, yet not valid. Likewise, the appropriate unit of measurement, either quantitative or qualitative, can be established, and yet the information received may not be valid. The validity of a measurement refers to the degree to which a measurement actually reflects the phenomenon that it is intended to measure. An example of a highly reliable, quantitative measure with virtually no validity is the experience of a printing company in trying to determine the quantity of daily production. The figure used was the total number of pounds of finished materials shipped each day. There are several reasons why the total number of pounds shipped is not a valid measure of the company's productivity. First, the total number of pounds bore no consistent relationship to dollar volume of sales, profitability, or man-hours required for production because of the diversity of product line, which included

---

[15]Winifred R. Hirschmann, "Profit from the Learning Curve," *Harvard Business Review*, Vol. 42 (January-February, 1964), pp. 125–139. Hirschmann's article discusses the characteristics of the learning curve and the reasons why it has not been accepted widely, and suggests some practical applications of the concept.

cellophane and pliofilm packaging materials, lithographed products, foil wrappings, and fiberboard cartons. Second, the pounds shipped bore only an indirect relation to production for any given day since up to 40 percent of the orders shipped on any given day came out of a warehouse and not directly from that day's production. Thus, the number of pounds shipped did not measure what it was intended to measure — the amount of goods produced in a given day.

Another example of a measurement that may or may not be valid is the use of gross sales as an index of profitability. Whenever the performance being reviewed is complex and composed of many different elements, it is extremely difficult to develop one single unit of measurement that adequately portrays what it is intended to portray. In these situations it is best to measure each segment of performance separately rather than use a single indicator that may not be valid.

Channeling Information to Proper Authority. The timeliness of information, the appropriateness of the unit of measurement, and the reliability and validity of control data are directed toward having the right information at the right time. A fifth requirement must be met, the channeling of information to the proper authority. Only then do we have all ingredients of a good information system for control — the right information at the right time and at the right place. What constitutes the proper channel for information flow varies with each company organization structure, the kind of information to be interpreted, and the kind of corrective action required to attain expected standards. Even so, the following generalization can be made: control information should be directed toward the individual assigned responsibility for the operation and at the same time having authority to take corrective action.

There is much discussion concerning the effect of integrated data processing systems upon the flow of information. Some argue that integrated systems encourage centralized control, with the result that the control of an organization ultimately rests in the hands of a few at the top of the organization. Others point out that the speed with which information can be handled and the variety of information processed make it possible to supply control information to first-line supervisors and middle management never available to them before. Although there seems to be a trend toward centralized control, the trend is not necessarily a function of integrated data processing systems. Rather, it may be an expression of a desire to place control information in the hands of those possessing the authority to take action.[16]

---

[16]The following articles discuss problems inherent in the establishment and measurement of control structures. J. Timothy McMahon and G. W. Perritt, "The Control Structure of Organizations: An Empirical Examination," *Academy of Management Journal*, Vol. 14, No. 3 (September, 1971), pp. 327–339. J. Timothy McMahon and G. W. Perritt, "Toward a Contingency Theory of Organizational Control," *Academy of Management Journal*, Vol. 16, No. 4 (December, 1973), pp. 624–635.

In summary, the measurement of organizational performance with respect to stated standards is not precise; yet, measure we must if we are to improve the quality of corrective action. An awareness of the difficulties inherent in measuring current position eventually leads to the development of meaningful control information.

Taking Corrective Action

The third and last step of the control process, taking corrective action, epitomizes the busy, efficient executive. Here is a person making things happen and getting things done. Without action there is no control. The actions taken are the result of executive decisions and as such reflect the personality of the person taking the action as well as being determined by situational, or environmental, factors. Thus, the personality of the person in control has much to do with the kind of control. Before discussing the range of action available to the controlling executive, it is well to examine more closely the influence of personality upon corrective action, to determine who should take corrective action, and to make sure that causes — not symptoms — are being corrected.

Personality and Control. Personality factors, rather than the demands of the situation, are the cause of the extremes in control. One extreme is typified by the Captain Queeg approach to management — too much control. The other extreme might be called the Will Rogers approach to management — too little control.[17] Captain Queeg, as described by Herman Wouk in the *Caine Mutiny*, hewed to the letter of the law and insisted that his men do the same. He had to know every detail of what every man aboard his ship did and rationalized such excessive control as a means of assuring himself, and the Navy, that all regulations were being carried out. The same approach in an industrial organization results in a mass of paper work, so much so that the real work of the organization is neglected.

What motivates a Captain Queeg to check on every last detail? The answer is simple: The same personality that makes it impossible to delegate effectively. When effective delegation is practiced, there is little need for tight control. In Chapter 11, four personality characteristics that interfere with effective delegation are discussed. They are worth recounting at this point. First, there are those who by vocational choice — notably engineers and accountants — are trained to attend to details and as a result find it difficult to delegate effectively when

---

[17]Arnold F. Emch, "Control Means Action," *Harvard Business Review*, Vol. 32 (July-August, 1954), pp. 92–98. Emch uses Captain Queeg and Will Rogers as the extremes in control. His article sets forth rules and guides for effective control and emphasizes good delegation as the key to good control.

placed in a supervisory position. Next there are those managers who want to avoid the major issues and occupy themselves by attention to petty detail. Third, there are those who, for either real or imagined reasons, fear failure; and last, there are those who have a mistrust of others.[18] These are the traits that prevent effective delegation and at the same time result in excessive control over the relatively unimportant. The effect on an organization is stultifying. Initiative, innovation, and creativity on the part of subordinates are stifled.[19]

The other pole in control, the Will Rogers approach, is equally ineffective in achieving organizational goals. Here everything is assumed to be going along just fine, there is no need to check because these are wonderful people in the organization, and things are bound to work out just right in the long run. Also, there is a hesitancy about offending people by questioning them about their performance. The Will Rogers type is a defender of the Theory Y approach to organization. Eventually, however, the manager wants to know more about the operation than the mere fact that there is a certain amount of money in the bank at the end of each month. With no clearly defined organization, the inevitable happens — an "assistant-to" is created to perform the controlling for the manager. It is quite possible that the assistant-to might become another Captain Queeg. But more importantly, the creation of an assistant-to leads us once again to the question, "Who controls?"

Who Controls? The payoff of the control process is not the setting of standards, nor is it the measurement of performance against standards. It is taking the corrective action necessary to bring performance in line with the standards. The logical person to take this action is the manager who has been assigned the responsibility of managing a particular aspect of the business and who has been delegated the authority necessary to fulfill the assigned responsibilities. Thus, effective control is the result of sound organizational structure and the practice of an important organizational process — delegation. Taking corrective action is executive action and as such is in the hands of the line manager. The controller's office may be involved in the setting of standards and almost always participates in the measurement of current position against standard, but the taking of corrective action belongs to the manager of an organizational unit.

---

[18]See Chapter 11, page 242, for a more complete discussion of these personality traits.

[19]For discussions of the relationship between the types of control and certain measures of satisfaction in a large insurance company and in two state agencies, the following articles are recommended: John V. Ivancevich, "An Analysis of Control, Bases of Control, and Satisfaction in an Organizational Setting," *Academy of Management Journal*, Vol. 13, No. 4 (December, 1970), pp. 427–436. William E. Turcotte, "Control Systems, Performance, and Satisfaction in Two State Agencies," *Administrative Science Quarterly*, Vol. 19, No. 1 (March, 1974), pp. 60–73.

Symptoms or Causes? Prior to taking corrective action it is necessary to differentiate between symptoms and causes. Most of us have had the experience of taking an antihistamine drug at the first sign of a cold, and after a day or so we stop taking the medicine. Sometimes, much to our disgust, the sniffling and sneezing return and we discover that we have done an excellent job of treating symptoms but not getting at the cause of the cold. A manager must learn to recognize a symptom for what it is and to devote attention to the cause of the problem. Cost control, or the control of expenses, often falls into the category of treating symptoms rather than causes.

Excessive costs are an indication that something has gone wrong; they are the result of someone's performance and if costs are to be brought in line it is the performance that must be corrected. First, it is wise to examine the standard to determine whether or not the costs in question are in fact excessive. Next, try to determine the contribution of each factor that makes up the total cost. How much of total cost is attributable to direct labor, to materials, and to overhead? Finally, examine each of these factors separately and determine how performance can be improved in each area. The same analytical procedure can be applied to the marketing function. The answer to a declining sales volume is not necessarily more salespeople or better performance on the part of the present sales force; instead, the decline in sales may be the result of a poorly designed product or the failure to meet the challenge of competitors.

The Management Process Cycle. After determining the cause for poor performance, corrective action is in order. It is impossible to formulate a list of actions available to the manager; each situation is unique and calls for its own solution. There is, however, a frame of reference of value to the manager in evaluating a proposed action. That framework is the management process cycle — replanning, reorganizing, redirecting, and continued control since in a going organization all these functions have been performed in one way or another. Failure to meet expected levels of performance is sometimes unavoidable and calls for the development of new plans with the possibility of revised standards of performance. Though there is merit in the adage, "the difficult we do immediately; the impossible we do tomorrow," there are times when one must recognize that the impossible cannot be accomplished in accordance with present plans. Delays in a construction schedule resulting from inclement weather necessitate a revision of plans. Failure to meet a marketing objective may mean allocating more money for advertising or a restatement of expected results.

The present organization may need revising. Is the organization structured in such a manner that there is clear-cut responsibility for each organizational unit, or is there need for the creation of a new unit? What about the people in the organization? Are they performing their assigned duties satisfactorily? A change in either organizational structure or personnel may be necessary to correct the causes of poor performance. Or the difficulty may lie in leadership.[20] Sometimes a restatement of what is expected brings the desired results. Finally, there is the control process itself — it must be exercised continually. The management cycle is not composed of the four discrete steps of planning, organizing, leading, and controlling; instead, it is a continuous process, with control functioning as a catalyst to produce an integrated continuous process.

CHARACTERISTICS OF GOOD CONTROL

In the preceding discussion of the steps of the control process, many of the characteristics of an effective control system are implied and touched upon briefly. Control is an extremely critical factor in the achievement of organizational objectives, with the effectiveness of the control function dependent upon the information received. Control systems, to be of greatest use, must possess certain characteristics. Again, we are unable to describe all control systems since each control situation is unique. Despite this difficulty, there is general agreement that good control has the following characteristics: timeliness, follows organizational lines, strategic, economical, shows both trends and status, and stresses the exception.[21] Each of these characteristics is discussed separately.

Timeliness

Accounting records are relatively precise, detailed statements of a company's activity for a stated period and are historical in nature since they are prepared after the period has closed. Frequently these reports are of great value to the planning process, but they are often inadequate as control reports because they are not timely. Ideally, the optimum form of control information should forecast deviations from standard prior to their occurrence. In practice, such forecasting is seldom achieved, but every effort should be made to report deviations from standard while the event in question is still in process. We mentioned the control device developed by the plant manager of an automobile parts manufacturer that enabled him to keep abreast of the output of each production department at hourly intervals. Supervisors

---

[20]For a discussion of training in order to change the behavior of workers especially the following is suggested. Everett E. Adam, Jr. and William E. Scott, Jr., "The Application of Behavioral Conditioning Procedures to the Problems of Quality Control," *Academy of Management Journal*, Vol. 14, No. 2 (June, 1971), pp. 175–193.

[21]John Richard Curley, "A Tool for Management Control," *Harvard Business Review*, Vol. 29 (March, 1951), pp. 45–86. General characteristics of tools for control based upon the experience of RCA are presented. A brief discussion of accounting controls and their limitations is also included.

of production departments frequently find it necessary to develop control information during the course of the day. One supervisor in a large printing company placed a small blackboard at the end of each press, with the cumulative standard production posted for each hour. He requested the pressmen to post actual production for each hour alongside the posted standard. One immediate result of this procedure was that the pressmen called the supervisor when trouble began to develop, thereby permitting the rescheduling of work to other presses.[22]

Another means of focusing upon timely information is to require unit managers, such as plant managers and sales managers, to prepare monthly forecasts and to submit revisions of these forecasts on either a weekly or a biweekly basis. While it is true that the information used in these forecasts may not be accurate when compared with the accounting records prepared at the close of the period, the process of forecasting and revising forces the manager to develop and rely upon timely information. If a choice must be made between timeliness and accuracy of control information, timeliness should be emphasized for the control of current operations.

Follows Organizational Lines

The excessive control of a Captain Queeg and the hands-off attitude of a Will Rogers, with the eventual inevitability of an assistant-to, reflect the same organizational shortcoming — a failure to delegate. Responsibility is not assigned nor is authority delegated, with the result that clear-cut accountability to superiors in the organization is not established. The control function can in no way substitute for poor organizational practices and structure. Good controls are closely related to organizational structure and reflect organizational structure and processes in their design and function.

Accumulated total product costs are of great significance to the sales department in the pricing of a given product, yet such figures may not be meaningful to manufacturing personnel charged with the responsibility of controlling costs. To be meaningful to manufacturing departments, cost data must reflect the portion of total cost added to the product by each department. Only then is the manager aware of the chargeable departmental costs and in a position to control those costs. Defects in quality should be traced to component parts and reported to the operating department responsible for the production of the defective part. Wage and salary plans can be utilized for control by reporting the average rate paid for each job classification and each salary grade. The information should be prepared for each organizational unit as well as for the entire company. Directing information to

---

[22]For a discussion of what is termed "feedforward" control as it applies to cash planning, inventories, and new products, the following is of interest: Harold Koontz and Robert W. Bradspies, "Managing Through Feedforward Control," *Business Horizons*, Vol. 4, No. 3 (June, 1972), pp. 25–36.

the responsible manager is an effective way of making it possible to exercise control at the lowest possible echelon of the organization.

Strategic Placement

It is impossible to establish controls for every aspect of even a small to medium-size business because of its complexity. Thus, it becomes necessary to establish controls at certain points of the operation selected because of their strategic value. A company whose primary contact with customers is through letters written by the correspondents in the sales order department may experience difficulty in maintaining good customer relations as the result of inconsistencies from the many sources of contact with customers. A strategic control of correspondence is the requirement that all letters be prepared for the signature of the sales manager, a step that permits the manager to sample all outgoing correspondence. Most governmental agencies require the signature of the chief administrator on all outgoing mail.

Quality control programs rely heavily upon the selection of strategic points where inspection approaches the 100-percent level as a means of meeting quality standards. A major appliance, such as a refrigerator, is checked after final assembly by connecting it to a test circuit to see if it cools properly. Also, the components of the compressor are subjected to complete dimensional checks prior to assembly to insure proper fit. Establishing key control points prior to the assembly of a critical component and after final assembly minimizes the likelihood of expensive rework and the possibility of defective products reaching the customer.

A few well-chosen measures of performance are often sufficient for the overall control of medium-size business operations. The owner-manager of a firm manufacturing trays for use in cafeterias and drive-in restaurants received weekly reports containing the following information: the backlog of orders, finished goods inventory, number of units shipped, and total hours of factory labor. A change in the order backlog with the other measures remaining relatively constant indicated the effectiveness of sales effort, and the number of units shipped was closely related to gross sales for the month. Total labor hours when balanced with inventory and units shipped let the manager know something about manufacturing efficiency, and a rising inventory indicated the need for either increasing sales effort or decreasing direct labor hours. To this manager, changes in the interrelationships of these four measures revealed potential trouble spots and enabled immediate corrective action.

Economical Administration

In addition to its stifling effects on human effort, the excessive control of a Captain Queeg can be expensive. The story is often told of a consultant encountering strategic controls similar to those used by the manager of the tray manufacturing company. The consultant suggested that in addition to these overall controls there was a need to control overhead costs. The recommended controls were put into effect. At the end of several months a marked decline in profits was noticed, and the amount of the decline corresponded to the additional costs of administering the new controls. Figure 5-2, page 108, presents a graphic model showing the relationships between total cost, the cost of taking managerial action — for example, quality control — and decreasing costs resulting from managerial action. This model serves well as a means of judging the economic cost of proposed controls.

There is an old saying. "You can inspect yourself out of business." Yet, failure to detect defective products results in the loss of customers. One method of balancing the cost of quality control against the cost of not taking action is the use of sampling techniques where every 10th or 100th item is checked thoroughly. Another area deserving careful attention is the use of incentives as a means of reducing unit labor costs. Although incentives may reduce the cost of direct labor, the indirect costs of maintaining up-to-date time studies by the industrial engineering department may more than counterbalance any savings in direct labor. Some companies have found measured day work — the use of time standards to determine a fair day's work — to be satisfactory since the standards do not have to be maintained with the same degree of accuracy as required when standards are used as the basis for incentive pay. Accuracy of measurement is an important factor in determining the cost of a given set of controls. Sometimes the presence of a deviation from standard and its direction, rather than the precise amount of the deviation, is sufficient for control purposes.

Reveals Trends As Well As Status

Controls that show the current status of a specific phase of an operation are relatively easy to prepare since all that is needed are periodic statements of the particular activity in question. Although such measures show present status, they do not necessarily reveal the trend of performance; i.e., monthly production reports do not show whether production is increasing or decreasing. This limitation of periodic reporting is overcome by using a graphic method of presentation that shows successive measures, thus forming a trend line, or by presenting the data in tabular form and including year-to-date or month-to-date figures. However, establishing and showing the trends of specific business functions do not always provide sufficient control information. It is necessary to include supporting information that is closely related to the primary function under observation. In the case of production, concentration on the number of units produced without the inclusion of a measure of units of input gives no indication of the cost or efficiency of production — an aspect of production that may be more important for control purposes than the total produced.

Interpreting trends in the light of related happenings is of special significance in the development of control information for the measurement of market position. There is the well-known example of a soap manufacturer who recorded continuous gains in the sales of soap, but neglected to focus attention on the increasing share of the home-laundry market claimed by detergents, with the result that the company discovered too late that it was last in the newer and larger market. One of the largest and oldest manufacturers of men's suits measured market position not only with respect to the market for suits but also with respect to the total amount spent for men's outer wear. As a result, the company discovered that an increasing share of the money spent for outer wear was spend on sports clothes and thus established plants for the manufacture of men's sportswear. Control data showing market position should show position in relation to competitive items as well as the position relative to that of competitors.

Stresses the Exception

In Chapter 2, Jethro's recommendations to Moses are presented. The three recommendations are: teach "ordinances and laws" to the people; select leaders and assign them "to be rulers of thousands, and rulers of hundreds, and rulers of fifties, and rulers of ten"; and those rulers should administer all routine matters and bring to Moses only the important questions. The third suggestion is often referred to as the *principle of the exception*. There are two reasons why effective systems of controls stress the exception. First, the amount of information generated in even small organizations is so great that it becomes difficult, if not impossible, to determine the significance of all information. To review every action of subordinates or to consult with them prior to taking action consumes too much of the time and energy of the manager. Second, when information stressing the exception is presented to the manager, attention is directed toward those items that require corrective action.

Examples of control that point up the exception are numerous in all functions of management. The sales data presented to a national sales manager should specify those districts that deviate from predicted standards of performance beyond a predetermined range; for example, those districts that vary more than plus or minus 5 percent. The exceptions must include those areas that exceed expected performance as well as those that fail to meet the standards. It is quite possible that the reasons for successful performance can be applied to those districts where performance is below par. The reporting of the exception is of value in the control of quality, cost, production, or any other measure of performance for which standards have been set. Usually acceptable performance is defined as performance within the limits of a predetermined range, with the breadth of the range varying for each performance factor, rather than satisfactory performance as a point value with no tolerance allowed.

Control by exception is closely related to the process of delegation and is not necessarily the exercise of corrective action after the function in question has been performed. Instead, effective control is exercised by either approving or disapproving the exceptional action prior to its occurrence. When responsibilities are assigned, authority within prescribed limits is delegated in order that these responsibilities may be fulfilled. Occasionally a manager requires greater authority in order to fulfill assigned responsibilities. When need arises, managers may request their respective superiors to recognize the exception and grant additional authority. For instance, the supervisor of a manufacturing department may have the authority to spend $100 for the repair of any one piece of equipment and $1,000 per month for total repairs in the department. Deviations beyond these maintenance cost standards require prior approval from the plant manager. The plant manager, in turn, may be permitted to spend $1,000 on any single item of general plant maintenance and $5,000 in any month. For the expenditure of sums exceeding these limits, the plant manager must secure prior approval from the manufacturing vice-president. Clearly defined limits of authority and the requirement of prior approval to exceed these limitations permit the control of the exception prior to its happening. Thus, the concept of control by exception is used to control deviations from standard before the exception occurs as well as to emphasize those areas in need of corrective action.

Each of the six preceding characteristics of an effective control system — timeliness, following organizational lines, strategic placement, economical administration, showing both trends and status, and stressing the exception — is important to the control of operations. These characteristics are descriptive of two different aspects of the control process and as such can be condensed and stated as two principles of control.[23] The establishment of controls that present information while it is still timely, that reveal information that is of strategic value in the control of operations, and that follow established organizational lines is descriptive of the purposes and structures of the control system. The characteristics of economy of administration and the reporting of trends as well as current status are also a function of the purpose and structure of the control system. The last of the six characteristics, stressing and reporting the exception, leads directly to the essence of control — corrective action. Thus, logically there are two

<hr />

[23]Harold Koontz and Cyril J. O'Donnell, *Principles of Management*, An Analysis of Managerial Functions (5th ed.; New York: McGraw-Hill Book Co., 1972), pp. 672–676. Professors Koontz and O'Donnell present 12 principles of control grouped into three general categories: (1) those reflecting the purpose and nature of control, (2) those emphasizing the structure of control, and (3) those emphasizing the control process. The following reference presents a more complete discussion of control principles:

Harold Koontz, "Management Control: A Suggested Formulation of Principles," *California Management Review*, Vol. 1 (Winter, 1959), pp. 47–55.

fundamental principles of control. The *principle of control design* emphasizes the nature and design of the control system and states:

> Effective control systems are designed to be economical in their administration and to reflect organizational structure. Such systems should provide management with information that is timely, of strategic value, and descriptive of the trends of operations as well as current status.

The *principle of the exception* emphasizes the essence of the control process — taking corrective action:

> The most efficient use of managerial time and energy is possible when control information stresses the exception and focuses attention upon those functions that need corrective action.

Case Problem 18-B describes two widely divergent degrees of control within the same organization and offers an opportunity to determine the proper degree of control that is needed and the methods to be utilized in establishing such control.

Case Problem 18-B
CONTROLLING SALES EXPENSE

Frank Montano, a district manager for Paper Products Company, has been in charge of the Chicago district sales office for two months. Prior to his transfer to Chicago to replace Tom Aderly, who has been in Chicago for 30 years, the last 20 as sales manager, Montano had been assistant manager of the New York sales district. When reviewing his new assignment with the vice-president in charge of sales, Montano was told that the Chicago sales expenses were 50 percent higher than those in New York and that sales volume had not kept pace with the rate of increase shown by other large offices. He was advised that he should first reduce the cost of operating the Chicago office and that as soon as costs were under control he should take steps to increase sales volume.

Montano arrived in Chicago a month prior to Aderly's retirement and had occasion to review with him the operations of the office. Aderly recognized that the Chicago expenses were higher than those for New York but attributed this difference to the size of the district, which covered many more square miles than New York. When Montano asked to see

the records of daily calls made by each sales representative, a list of potential customers, and the names of the new customers for each month, Tom Aderly answered as follows:

"Frank, I don't bother much with things like that. Every morning I visit with each of my eight reps when they come into the office. I've known every one of them since the first day they started to work here. I know that they have the best interests of the company at heart, and I'm sure that they're all doing their very best. I help them when they ask for it, but otherwise I let them follow their own leads. Makes for a nice friendly atmosphere."

After Aderly formally retired, Montano had the opportunity to examine more closely the representatives' expense accounts. He found that the average expense advance was $250 instead of the $100 maximum allowed by company policy, and that one sales representative had drawn a $500 expense advance. Montano realized that, in order to bring expenses and sales volume in line with those of other districts in the company, a radical change in the method of managing the Chicago office was needed. He decided to present these changes in memo form and to discuss the changes in the first of the newly instituted weekly meetings scheduled for Friday afternoons. The following is a copy of the memorandum.

To: Sales Representatives, Chicago District, Paper Products Company.

Re: Expense Control.

You are all aware that the expenses of the Chicago District sales office are much higher than those of offices in other large cities. For example, our expenses are 25 percent higher than those of Los Angeles, a district of comparable size. It is necessary that we get our expenses in line with those of similar offices in the company. The following procedures are effective beginning next Monday.

1. Expense advance will be limited to the $100 per week as outlined in the company sales policy manual. Those of you who have outstanding balances of more than $100 will not be permitted to draw additional advances; further, the amount in excess of $100 must be paid by the end of this month. If not paid by that time, authorization will be asked for to deduct the balance in excess of $100 in three equal monthly installments from your salary.

2. Sales representatives will no longer report to the office each morning; instead, each of you is expected to telephone the office between 9 and 9:30 each morning and give my secretary a schedule of the calls you intend to make that day. You are also asked to call between 1 and 1:30 p.m. so that we may relay messages from customers that have been received during the morning.

3. Each representative is expected to report to this office in person between 4 and 5 p.m. every day to review with me the calls made during the day and arrange appointments for calls on large accounts so that I can make the calls on these customers with you.

4. Daily expense records will be kept and are to be completed each afternoon when you are in the office.

5. Prior approval must be obtained for any entertainment expense exceeding $25.

6. Monthly time and expense reports must be summarized by the 25th of each month, showing total number of sales calls made, total expense, and total dollar volume of orders received. These summaries will then be forwarded to New York. No salary checks will be issued to any representative until monthly time and expense reports have been received by the New York office.

PROBLEMS

1. How would you characterize Mr. Aderly and Mr. Montano with respect to their methods of exercising control?
2. Is there need for stricter controls in the Chicago office? Why?
3. Do you agree that there is need for the controls set forth in Montano's memo? Do you approve of the method he is using in establishing these controls?
4. How would you have handled this situation? Explain.

CHAPTER QUESTIONS FOR STUDY AND DISCUSSION

1. Define in your own terms the meaning of the word "cybernetics." Give an example of a cybernetic system and explain why it is so classified.
2. Comment on the following statement: All dynamic systems involve the transmission of information.
3. Relate the three steps of the control process to the concept of a cybernetic system.
4. What are the major functions of a person holding the title of controller in an organization? In an organization, whose responsibility is it to take the corrective action?

5. Describe the relationship between the controller and the manager of an organizational unit.
6. What are the characteristics of a standard? Does the concept of par, borrowed from the game of golf, provide a good analogy for the understanding of the concept of standard? Why?
7. How are standards and objectives related? Illustrate by example.
8. Evaluate the three methods of establishing standards by indicating which methods are most likely to be appropriate in establishing standards for each of the eight key result areas.
9. Discuss each of the major problems encountered in the measurement of performance.
10. What relationship, if any, exists between the process of delegation and the control process? Explain fully.
11. As a manager, what steps would you take to assure yourself that you were able to distinguish symptoms from causes?
12. If it is true that each control system is unique, how is it possible to develop the characteristics of a good control system? State briefly why each of these characteristics is necessary.
13. How are the principle of control design and the principle of the exception related to the characteristics of a good control system? What are the likely results when these principles are violated?

Chapter 19

Nonbudgetary Control

Case Problem 19-A
IMPROVING OPERATING RATIOS

Margaret von Rolf, long a manager for a Chicago-based national moving and storage company, has recently been assigned the position of manager of a newly acquired company, Sunshine Moving and Storage Company. Sunshine's annual sales are approximately $850,000. Though the company is not as profitable as similar companies in the national system, Sunshine was considered a good buy because it is well located in a West Coast city of one million people, the rolling equipment is relatively new, and the two warehouses are modern and well kept. The parent corporation believes that increased sales efforts should produce an annual sales volume of at least $950,000 and a net profit before taxes of six percent of annual sales.

After studying the operating statement for the previous year, shown in Exhibit 1, von Rolf prepared a summary of the major operating ratios used as guides by the parent company in evaluating the performance of company-owned moving and storage facilities and in advising those privately owned companies that operate under a franchise system. Regarding revenue sources, it is recommended that companies located on the West Coast derive no more than 25 percent of their revenue from long-distance moving, with at least 27 percent of their revenue coming from local moving. It is important to control the ratio between long-distance and local-moving revenues because the direct operating expenses incurred by long-distance moving approximate 80 percent of long-distance revenue, while local-moving operating expenses are about 77 percent of local-moving revenue. It is also recommended that storage and warehousing revenue account for at least 18 percent of total revenue, with 20 percent of total revenue from this source being entirely possible. Similarly, packing and crating revenues should range between 14 and 16 percent of the total, and commissions earned from business booked for vans from other terminals should account for at least 10 percent of total revenue. Commissions are regarded as a particularly valuable source of revenue because little capital equipment is utilized and there is usually additional income resulting from required packing and crating.

Recommended ratios for major expense items are summarized in the figures shown on page 468.

SUNSHINE MOVING & STORAGE COMPANY

Revenue Sources:

1. Long distance	$301,750
2. Local moving	204,850
3. Commissions	85,000
4. Storage & warehousing	128,350
5. Packing and crating	130,050
Total revenue	$850,000

Expense Items:

6. Traffic & sales

Supervision, sales, and clerical salaries	$ 34,000
Advertising	12,750
Other expenses	12,750
Total traffic & sales	$ 59,500

7. Administrative & general expense

Salaries (officers & managers)	$ 42,500
Other administrative salaries	45,900
Other general administrative expense	90,950
Total administrative & general expense	$179,350

8. Trucking expense (includes long distance and local moving)

Equipment maintenance	$ 39,515
Insurance and safety	19,757
Depreciation	20,264
Taxes and licenses	15,705
Transportation — supervisor, wages, fuel oil	331,316
Total trucking expense	$426,557

9. Storage & warehousing expense

Supervision and clerical employees	$ 5,519
Building expense	34,783
Insurance, taxes, maintenance, & supplies	11,423
Wages	25,625
Total storage & warehousing expense	$ 77,350

10. Packing & crating expense

Supervision & office employees	$ 2,601
Depreciation, insurance, taxes	11,835
Materials and supplies	22,499
Wages	41,265
Total packing & crating expense	$ 78,200

Profit or loss:

11. Profit	$ 29,043

**Exhibit I
ANNUAL
OPERATING
STATEMENT**

DEPARTMENT	PERCENTAGE OF TOTAL REVENUE
Traffic and Sales:	
Supervision, sales, and clerical personnel	5.7%
Advertising	3.0
Other expenses	.9
	9.6%
Administrative and General:	
Salaries (officers and managers)	4.5%
Other salaries	5.5
Other general expenses	10.5
	20.5%

DEPARTMENT	PERCENTAGE OF DEPARTMENTAL REVENUE
Trucking Department:	
Equipment and maintenance	6.0%
Insurance and safety	3.5
Depreciation	3.5
Taxes and licenses	2.5
Transportation (including fuel, wages, and subsistence)	62.0
	77.5%
Storage and Warehousing:	
Supervisory and office personnel	4.5%
Building expense	28.0
Depreciation, insurance, and taxes	9.5
Wages	20.0
	62.0%
Packing and Crating:	
Supervision and office personnel	3.1%
Depreciation, insurance, and taxes	9.5
Materials and supplies	15.0
Wages	29.0
	56.6%

PROBLEMS

1. Are company expectations for sales and profits reasonable? What action would you take to increase sales?
2. Analyze each of the operating departments — trucking, storage and warehousing, and packing and crating — with respect to company recommendations for such operations and indicate the steps you would take as manager of Sunshine Moving and Storage Company in order to bring performance in line with expected results.
3. How profitable is each of the four sources of revenue — commissions, trucking, storage and warehousing, and packing and crating — when traffic and sales expense and administrative and general expense are apportioned to each in the same percentage amount that the source is of total sales?

In Chapter 18, it is stated that standards may be set for each of the following key result areas: (1) profitability, (2) market position, (3) productivity, (4) product leadership, (5) personnel development, (6) employee attitudes, (7) public responsibility, and (8) balance between short-range and long-range goals. Since the nature of the goals and the kind of performance required to meet stated objectives in each of these areas are different, it seems highly unlikely that a single control device can be used with equal effectiveness in all areas. Such is the case. Budgets, discussed in Chapter 20, are a very effective means of controlling expense and revenue items; thus, they are particularly useful in controlling performance in the areas of profitability and productivity. However, there are other means of control, conveniently referred to as *nonbudgetary*, that are necessary to establish an effective and complete system of control. These techniques of nonbudgetary control, arranged in order from the simple to the more complex, are as follows: personal observation, reports, audit programs, ratio analysis, break-even analysis, and time-event-network analysis.

PERSONAL OBSERVATION

Personal observation is a means of securing control information applicable to all key result areas and is used by all levels of management. The supervisor in charge of a manufacturing department or a clerical section relies to a great extent upon impressions gained as the result of personal contact with subordinates. Output is judged by observing the pace of subordinates; quality can be evaluated by personally inspecting the work in progress; and an estimate of morale and attitudes results from seeing employees, listening to their spontaneous remarks, and obtaining responses to questions. The plant manager who makes a daily tour of the plant is able to obtain firsthand information concerning conditions in the plant that are not revealed by formal reports. Similarly, many presidents and chief executive officers visit all company installations at least once each year so that the personal impressions thus gained may become a part of the basis for their decisions.

Personal observation as a means of gaining information is time consuming and is often criticized for this reason. Also, there is the possibility that subordinates may misinterpret a superior's visit and consider such action as meddling or failure to delegate. Finally, the value of firsthand information obtained from personal contact is limited by the perceptual skills and interpretative ability of the observer. Even so, personal observations are often the only means of substantiating impressions gained from other sources, and personal contacts almost always have a salutary effect upon subordinates since the presence of one's superior reveals an interest in the operation.

REPORTS

In designing or evaluating control reports, two closely related questions arise: (1) What is the purpose of the report? and (2) Who should receive the report?

Purpose of Control Reports

The primary purpose of control reports is to supply information intended to serve as the basis for corrective action if needed. At the same time, the significance of control reports must be kept in proper perspective. Control reports are only a part of the planning-control-planning information cycle that is necessary for a complete management information system. Refer to Figure 6-1, Anatomy of Management Information, on page 137. Note that control information includes nonfinancial as well as financial data, that it measures performance, and that it isolates variances from standard. Control information also provides feedback so that planning information may be updated and corrected.

An example of a set of relatively simple control reports that contribute to the control process as well as provide a basis for updating the planning process is presented in Chapter 18, page 459. In this illustration the owner of a company manufacturing trays for cafeterias and drive-in restaurants receives reports containing information that shows the current backlog of orders, finished goods inventory, number of units shipped, and total hours of factory labor. A decline in the backlog of current orders, with the other three measures remaining relatively constant, indicates the need for corrective action resulting in increased sales. In this instance, the information provided serves primarily the control function. However, an increase in the order backlog, again with all other measures remaining constant, signals the need for additional planning so that production may be increased to meet the increased demand. Whenever possible, control reports should be designed so that they provide feedback for the planning process as well as provide information of immediate value to the control process.

Distribution of Control Reports

Since the culmination of the control process is the taking of necessary corrective action to bring performance in line with standards, it follows that control information must be directed to the person who is organizationally responsible for taking the required action. Usually the same information, though in a somewhat abbreviated form, is given to the responsible manager's superior. The supervisor of a manufacturing department requires detailed information that describes the performance of equipment and personnel of the department. The plant manager may receive condensed summary statements showing performance in relation to standard, expressed as a percentage, for each of several operating departments. A district sales manager needs a complete daily record of the performance of each salesperson; yet, the report forwarded to the regional sales manager summarizes only the performance of each sales district in the region. In preparing reports for higher echelons of management, summary statements and recommendations for action should appear on the first page; substantiating data, usually the information presented to the person directly responsible for the operation, may be included if needed.

Characteristics of Good Reports

Since control reports are an integral part of a control system, they should incorporate the characteristics of an effective control system as described in Chapter 18, pages 457 to 463. They should be timely, particularly those prepared for a unit supervisor. When reports provide information intended primarily for the purpose of control, they should follow organizational lines. It must be remembered that for the same information to become effective as a basis for additional planning, it is necessary to cross organizational lines. Reports should be prepared to reveal activity in the more sensitive or strategic areas of the business. In organizations where progress depends upon new products, frequent periodic reporting of research and development activities may be required. A firm whose chief concern is manufacturing efficiency may emphasize a detailed reporting of the production process. Reports should be economical, and their costs should be measured in terms of the extent to which they actually contribute to the control process. In preparing reports, sufficient data should be included so that trends as well as current status are reflected. Finally, reports should be prepared so that the exception is emphasized. Summary statements should stress performance that deviates from standard and show clearly both the direction and magnitude of the deviation.

AUDIT PROGRAMS

Traditionally, auditing, an independent appraisal of a company's financial records, seeks to test the reliability and validity of financial records by determining the degree of accuracy and the extent to which financial statements reflect what they purport to represent. As a result, audit programs are often regarded as a means of encouraging honesty on the part of employees and safeguarding the company's financial resources. This concept of auditing, the verification of company financial records, is limited in scope and is associated with *external audits* conducted by outside agencies such as bank examiners or a firm of public accountants. When conducted by a specialized staff made up of company personnel, auditing can be an effective means of control as well as a means of verifying financial records, and is known as the *internal audit*. It is possible also to apply the techniques of auditing as a means of assessing the overall effectiveness of management, an application often referred to as the *management audit*. In addition, *human resource accounting* can be used by companies whose production depends primarily on the creativity of its personnel. Each of these forms of auditing, the external audit, the internal audit, the management audit, and human resource accounting is discussed in turn.

External Auditing

The external audit is usually conducted by a firm of public accountants. Its primary purpose is to determine whether or not company records of financial transactions present a true statement of the company's financial condition. It is essentially a verification of the accuracy of the records and a determination of the consistency of application of accepted accounting procedures. In order to make a summary statement of the financial condition of a company, it is necessary for the auditors to spot check all types of basic financial transactions to determine their accuracy. It is the checking phase of the auditing process that causes many to regard external auditing as a means of encouraging honesty on the part of employees. For example, a review of inventory records, a part of the process of verifying assets, may reveal shortages that may be the result of dishonesty.

The contribution of the external audit to the control process is indirect and limited in its nature. For instance, a company might wish to allocate certain capital expenditures as expense items, but independent auditors will not certify such allocations unless they are consistent with previously established accounting procedures. The same indirect form of control may be exerted if a company attempts to modify its statement of assets by altering established practices of evaluating finished goods or raw material inventories. The value of the external audit as a means of assessing financial position is limited by the appropriateness, or validity, of existing accounting procedures. When the summary information of the audit — usually a verification of the balance sheet items of assets, liabilities, and net worth — is used as a basis for formulating the corrective action of the control process, its worth is no greater than the validity of the accounting techniques used to record the financial condition of the company.

Internal Auditing

As the name implies, the internal audit is conducted by a specialized staff made up of company personnel. Like the external audit conducted by an outside source, the internal audit verifies the accuracy of company records and determines whether or not such records are what they purport to be. However, the purpose of the internal audit is to provide a means of internal control. It seeks to determine the effectiveness of other controls; consequently, the internal audit may be regarded as a master control over all other forms of control.

The potential benefits of an effective internal auditing program are many; however, there are three contributions that stand out above all others. First, internal auditing provides a way of determining whether established procedures and methods are effective in meeting stated company objectives and insuring compliance with stated policies. If, for example, it is the objective of a company to build a product having the highest possible quality, procedures are established to insure that component parts of the product are the best available. In reviewing purchase requisitions, the internal audit team goes beyond the accuracy of the records of the purchasing department and seeks to determine whether or not, in fact, components are of the highest available quality. The determination of the extent to which company policies are observed leads directly to the second major contribution of internal auditing — formulating recommendations for the improvement of policies, procedures, and methods so that they are more effective in the attainment of stated objectives. It may be necessary to modify existing controls, establish new controls, or change present procedures or methods. Deviations from established procedures may arise because someone has discovered a supposed short cut, or there may have been an honest misunderstanding of the procedure due to its complexity. Whatever the reason, it is the task of the internal auditor to recommend those changes necessary to insure compliance, including the recommendation for additional or improved controls.

The third benefit of an internal auditing program may seem paradoxical at first glance. Internal auditing provides a means of providing a greater degree of delegation of authority and, if desirable, a means of facilitating the decentralization of operations. Delegation of authority and its broader organizational counterpart, the decentralization of authority to operating units, do not imply an absence of centralized control. On the contrary, the extent of delegation and decentralization is dependent to a large measure upon the effectiveness of central control. Internal auditing offers a means of continually checking the effectiveness of established controls and recommending needed improvements.

The use of the internal audit as a means of control has been increasing, particularly in large companies. Even though many small and medium-size companies do not have internal auditing departments, the function of internal auditing can still be accomplished to a degree by emphasizing that one of the functions of control is to determine the extent to which procedures and methods are being observed and to recommend improvements.

The success of internal auditing is dependent not only upon the attitude of top management but also upon the degree of acceptance accorded the audit team by lower and middle echelons of management. Acceptance by other members of management is more readily attained when internal auditors perform the functions of consultants and act as special staff advisors concerned with the improvement of all operations rather than appearing as custodians of company resources.

The Management Audit

The external audit is concerned chiefly with verifying the reliability and validity of financial records. Internal auditing goes a step further and determines the degree of compliance with company policies, procedures, and methods, and, if necessary, makes recommendations to insure the observance of established company practices. An even broader form of auditing is the *management audit*, a systematic approach to the appraisal of the overall performance of management.

One of the better known methods of appraising managerial performance is the management audit developed by Jackson Martindell of the American Institute of Management (AIM).[1] The AIM management audit evaluates the performance of a company in relation to the performance of other companies in the same industry and in relation to the performance of outstanding companies in other industries. Some of the information needed for the management audit is a matter of public record, but much of it comes from the answers to a 300-item questionnaire. Point values for the answers given to each question are assigned, with the maximum number of points being 10,000. Managerial performance in each of the following 10 categories is evaluated:[2]

1. Economic Function
2. Corporate Structure
3. Health of Earnings
4. Service to Stockholders
5. Research and Development
6. Directorate Analysis
7. Fiscal Policies
8. Production Efficiency
9. Sales Vigor
10. Executive Evaluation

There has been much criticism of the AIM audit. For many, it is oriented too much toward the investment concept of business management. Of the 10,000 total points, only 500 are allowed for corporate structure; 2,200 for executive evaluation; and 800 for directorate analysis — making a maximum of 3,500 points for these categories. Production efficiency and sales vigor comprise a maximum of 2,000 points; the remaining 4,500 are distributed among the categories of economic function, health of earnings, service to stockholders, research and development, and fiscal policies. Another criticism is that the audit rates past performance too heavily and does not attempt to evaluate future performance.[3] In support of these criticisms, instances are cited of companies with recent ratings of "excellent" that have experienced severe financial difficulties. For example, Douglas Aircraft Company received the rating of "excellently managed" for 1957, 1958, and 1959, and then suffered severe financial reverses during the latter

---

[1]Jackson Martindell, *The Appraisal of Management for Executives and Investors* (New York: Harper & Row, Publishers, 1962). This book is a revised statement of Martindell's original program that was first published under the same title and by the same publisher in 1950.

Jackson Martindell, "Management Audits Simplified," *The Corporate Director*, Special Issue, No. 15 (December, 1951), pp. 1–6.

[2]Jackson Martindell, "The Management Audit," *The Corporate Director*, Vol. 9 (December, 1962), pp. 1–4. This is a paper presented to the Academy of Management at the annual meeting held in Pittsburgh in December, 1962.

[3]Robert B. Buchele, "How to Evaluate a Firm," *California Management Review*, Vol. 5 (Fall, 1962), pp. 5–16. Buchele presents a method for evaluating a firm that attempts to weight the future more than the past.

part of 1959 and 1960. In 1957 Allis Chalmers Manufacturing Company and Olin Mathiesen Chemical Company received "excellently managed" ratings that were soon followed by marked financial problems.[4]

Despite the shortcomings of the management audit, the audit program developed by the American Institute of Management establishes firmly the concept that the performance of management can and should be subject to evaluation as a part of an overall control program. The management audit focuses attention upon many aspects of managerial performance rather than upon one or two easily measured performance areas. Second, the audit emphasizes the measurement of the results of managerial performance rather than appraising the purpose of managerial performance. Third, individual companies that work seriously with the concept of auditing management's performance may develop as the result of experience within their own organization a means of assigning weight to the various performance categories that will prove a valid predictor of future performance.[5]

Human Resource Accounting

An approach that offsets some of the major shortcomings of the AIM management audit, particularly its inability to predict future performance, is human resource accounting. Fundamental to the concept of human resource accounting is the positive relationship that exists between the performance of an organization and the quality and quantity of its human resource capability. The quality of human resources is highly significant for those companies whose product or service relies upon knowledge, research, and creativity. Traditionally the expenditure of funds for recruitment, training and development, and other items associated with the acquisition and upgrading of personnel are treated as expense items. Human resource accounting regards these expenditures as an investment in assets. Conventional accounting practices do not offer a true picture of an organization's effectiveness or potential. For the firm that is building human resources faster than they are being consumed, conventional accounting understates net income; conversely, the firm that is consuming its human resources faster than the replacement rate has an overstatement of its profits. Also, in the budgeting process expenditures for physical facilities are regarded as capital expenditures and are not necessarily justified in terms of revenue for the current year. Yet the manager who wishes to invest in human resources is forced to justify expenditures in this area in terms of additional revenue for the current year since costs

---

[4]The ratings are presented in *Manual of Excellent Managements* (New York: American Institute of Management, 1957).

[5]The following reference may be of interest to small businesses: *Management Audit for Small Retailers* (Washington: Small Business Administration, 1972).

associated with people are considered an expense. Human resource accounting seeks to treat expenditures in human resources as an investment in assets thereby enabling one to predict future performance as the rate of consumption of human resources relative to the rate of replacement of human resources becomes known.[6]

The R. G. Barry Corporation, a leisure footwear manufacturer headquartered in Columbus, Ohio, instituted a plan to develop human resource accounting in conjunction with William C. Pyle, Director of Human Resource Accounting Research of the University of Michigan. As noted by Robert J. Woodruff, Jr., vice president — human resources of R. G. Barry Corporation, the company has a technology comparable to the apparel industry with one of the lowest ratios of capital investment per employee of any industry and with labor representing a significant portion of total product costs. Further, the R. G. Barry Corporation has long had a strong philosophical commitment to the recognition of the importance of people to its operations. The seven functional accounts developed by the R. G. Barry Corporation for use in its human resource accounting are:

1. *Recruiting outlay costs* — costs associated with locating and selecting new (management) personnel. This category includes search fees; advertising; interviewer or interviewee travel expenses; allocations of personnel; and acquiring department time for internal screening, interviewing, testing, and evaluation expenses. Outlay costs for unsuccessful candidates are allocated to the cost of obtaining the candidate hired.

2. *Acquisition costs* — costs incurred in bringing a new man "on board." This category includes placement fees, moving costs, physical examination, allocation of personnel, and acquiring department time in placing a man on the payroll and situating him with the necessary equipment to perform his job.

3. *Formal training and familiarization costs* — costs normally incurred immediately after hire or possible transfer from one location to another. These refer to formal orientation programmes, vestibule training, etc.

4. *Informal training costs* — costs associated with the process of teaching a new person to adapt his existing skills to the specific job requirements of his new job. The costs related to this process are normally salary allocations only and vary with each position depending upon the level of the job in the organization, number of subordinates, interaction patterns outside the department, etc.

5. *Familiarization costs* — costs associated with the very complex process of integrating a new manager into the organization to the

---

[6]William C. Pyle, "Human Resource Accounting," *Financial Analysts Journal*, Vol. 26, No. 5 (September-October, 1970), pp. 69–77.

Rensis Likert, *The Human Organization*, Its Management and Value (New York: McGraw-Hill Book Co., 1967). The reader's attention is directed to Chapter 9, "Human Asset Accounting."

point where he can be a fully effective member. Such costs include learning the company's philosophy, history, policies, objectives, communications patterns, past practices, precedents, understanding of the people with whom the new position-holder will regularly interact. These costs, which can be sizable, depending upon the level and scope of the position, include salary allocations.

6. *Investment building experience costs* — costs associated with investments in on-the-job training which occur after the initial familiarization period and which are expected to have value to the company beyond the current accounting period. Investment building experience is the development of a capability which would not reasonably be expected as a normal part of the person's job.

7. *Development costs* — costs associated with investments in increasing a manager's capabilities in areas beyond the specific technical skills required by the position. In this category are management seminars, university programmes or courses, etc. Costs are collected by means of a "Training & Development Requisition," and are modified by the participant's evaluation of the pertinency of the study.[7]

The R. G. Barry Corporation has since developed a pro forma balance sheet, an income statement that shows the effect of human resource accounting concepts upon the conventional accounting statement.[8] In effect, human resource accounting provides internal control over the long-term management of human resources.[9]

RATIO ANALYSIS

A *ratio* is a way of expressing the proportional relationship that exists between two measures. Ratios may be expressed as:

1. A proportion, by using a colon to separate two measures — 1:2.
2. A fraction — ½.
3. A percentage — ½ × 100 = 50%.

Whatever the method of expression — proportion, fraction, or percentage — a ratio shows the magnitude of the relationship between two measures. The analysis of ratios existing between various measures of organizational performance is a very useful and necessary control technique.

Single measures of organizational performance seldom have much meaning. For example, the statement that a company earned $100,000, after taxes, during the past fiscal year expresses only the dollar volume

---

[7]R. L. Woodruff, Jr., "Human Resource Accounting," *Canadian Chartered Accountant*, Vol. 97, No. 3 (September, 1970), pp. 156–161. The functional accounts are stated on pp. 157–158.

[8]*Annual Report 1968* (Columbus, Ohio: R. G. Barry Corporation).

[9]The following article discusses Likert's "Systems 4" and sets forth the computations used in arriving at dollar estimates concerning the value of personnel: Rensis Likert, "Human Resource Accounting: Building and Assessing Productive Organizations," *Personnel*, Vol. 50, No. 3 (May-June, 1973), pp. 8–24.

of earnings. For a statement of earnings to have more meaning, it is necessary to compare and describe the earnings of a competitor. In a like manner, the fact that a salesperson sold $5,000 worth of goods last month or that a production worker produced 50 units yesterday conveys little information. We have to know the performance standards for salespeople and production workers before drawing conclusions concerning the adequacy of their performance.

Ratio analysis is not new, and much has been written about it as a control technique.[10] It is beyond the scope of this chapter to survey all or even a majority of the ratios used in analyzing and controlling business operations since there are many of them and the usefulness of a given set of ratios varies considerably from one industry to another. However, a few of the most frequently used ratios are presented and discussed briefly. For convenience, the ratios discussed are classified as *financial ratios* — contributing primarily to a greater understanding of the financial condition of a company — and *operating ratios* — providing greater understanding of the operational aspects of a company. Some of the difficulties in interpreting ratios are also presented.

Financial Ratios

Admittedly, financial ratios tell us something about the manner in which a company is operated as well as reveal financial condition. Yet, these ratios may be regarded as primarily financial in nature since much of the basic data is derived from the balance sheet and the information provided by these ratios is descriptive of a company's financial condition. The first and second ratios discussed below are statements of profitability; the last two ratios are statements of liquidity and are of particular significance to creditors.

Profit As a Percentage of Capital Invested. Many consider the relationship between profit (after taxes) and invested capital to be the most important single ratio. In the use of this ratio, profit is expressed as a percentage of invested capital, and when computed annually, a trend line is established. Profit as a percent of invested capital reveals how well the capital resources are being utilized. Comparisons may be made with other companies in the same industry, but the value of such comparisons is limited because the method used in evaluating invested capital varies from one company to another. Although there is no means of determining the optimum level of profitability, a realistic minimum level can be defined. The return on invested capital, after taxes, should be greater than the return guaranteed by other forms of

---

[10]Spencer A. Tucker, *Successful Managerial Control by Ratio-Analysis* (New York: McGraw-Hill Book Co., 1961). Mr. Tucker discusses the relatively simple first-degree ratios obtained by comparing two variables and also reviews the analysis of relationships between more than two variables.

investment — for example, tax-exempt municipal bonds. In addition to the basic rate of return offered by securities, there should be some compensation for risk and managerial effort.

Profit As a Percentage of Sales. Again, it is necessary to compute profitability from year to year so that a trend may be established. Also, comparisons with other companies in the same industry are valuable. Expressing profit as a percentage of sales volume is particularly helpful when analyzing the possible contribution of new product lines or when considering the deletion of current products. The profit-to-sales ratio is of value in measuring managerial effectiveness in the control of variable or controllable costs. For instance, within a retail chain, units of similar sales volume and fixed costs can be compared and differences in profitability may be attributed to the control of variable costs.

Current Ratio. The *current ratio* is of particular significance to creditors because it is an indication of a company's ability to pay its bills promptly. Current ratio is determined by dividing current assets by current liabilities as stated on the balance sheet. Unlike the measures of profit, which are usually expressed as a percentage, current ratio is expressed as a proportion; i.e., 2:1 or 2.5:1. Although there seems to be general agreement that a company should have a current ratio of assets to liabilities of at least 2:1 to insure ability to pay current obligations, the determination of what constitutes a satisfactory ratio is much more complex than it appears to be. Some of the problems encountered in interpreting the current ratio are discussed later under the heading, "Interpreting Ratios."

Quick Ratio. The *quick ratio*, sometimes called the *acid test ratio*, is found by dividing the company's quick assets, usually cash and negotiable securities, by current liabilities. Accounts receivables and inventory, generally a part of current assets and used in computing the current ratio, are excluded since there may be considerable time required to convert these items into cash. A minimum quick ratio of 1:1 indicates that there is sufficient cash to meet maturing obligations.

Operating Ratios

There are several ratios that contribute more to an understanding of the operations of a company than they do to an appreciation of the financial structure of a company; thus, they are referred to as operating ratios. Three of these ratios contribute to our knowledge of the sales function of a company. The fourth ratio is a generalized concept of input-output functions.

Net Sales to Average Inventory. Dividing net sales by average inventory value yields a measure of inventory turnover. For instance, net sales of $600,000 with an average inventory evaluation of $200,000 indicates that the inventory turnover rate is three times a year. If desired, the average number of days required for a complete inventory turnover can be computed as follows: $\dfrac{\text{Average Inventory} \times 365}{\text{Net Sales}}$. In the example above, the average number of days is 121. The net sales to average inventory ratio is an indication of how well the working capital invested in inventory is being utilized; consequently, the ratio should be interpreted in conjunction with profitability expressed as a percentage of sales. A profit of 2 percent on net sales, typical of many retail food operations, does not seem very great; but with an average inventory of $100,000 and an annual inventory turnover rate of 35, the absolute dollar volume of profit is considerable in relation to the amount of capital invested in inventory. The sales to inventory ratio provides the control information that is needed to insure maximum inventory turnover.

Net Sales to Total Market. Expressing net sales as a percentage of the total market — defined either geographically or by product line — indicates whether or not a company is maintaining its share of an ever-changing market potential. Dollar volume of sales does not provide such information since it is quite possible for a company's sales to show an annual increase, yet the rate of increase may be less than the market's rate of growth. Thus, a firm with an annual sales increase of four percent in a market that is expanding at a rate of six percent shows an increasing sales volume and a decreasing share of the potential market.

Selling Expense to Net Sales. Expressing selling expense as a percentage of net sales offers a means of determining the efficiency of the selling function. Selling expense may be broken down into greater detail by specifying the costs of maintaining a sales force, of advertising, or of administrative costs.

Input-Output Ratios. The number and the kind of input-output ratios used as control measures vary a great deal from one company to another. Such ratios are almost always expressed as percentages and are measures of efficiency in the utilization of inputs. Some of the more common measures of inputs and outputs are as follows:

Inputs	*Outputs*
Payroll dollars	Net sales
Man-hours worked	Units produced
Square feet of floor space	Units sold
Advertising costs	

Each input can be paired with any one of the outputs.

Interpreting Ratios

Although ratios are widely used, there are three difficulties encountered in their interpretation that limit their value as a means of providing precise control information. First, a ratio is a quotient obtained by the arithmetic process of dividing a numerator by a denominator. A change in the value of a quotient may result from a change in the value of either the numerator or the denominator. There is no way of determining which member of the fraction changed in value by noting the change in the quotient. An analysis of the current ratio illustrates this point. Assume that a company has current assets of $60,000 and current liabilities of $30,000, thereby producing a comfortable current ratio of 2:1. Do we know what has happened if we read that the company now has a current ratio of 3:1? Fixed assets may have been sold in the amount of $30,000 and added to current assets to yield the 3:1 ratio. Or the amount realized from the sale of assets may have been $10,000 and applied to the reduction of current liabilities, again creating a 3:1 ratio. When changes occur in a ratio, it is necessary to inspect the original data used in arriving at the numeric values of the numerator and the denominator in order to have a sound basis for determining the significance of the change that has occurred.

Second, it must be realized that there is no precise means of determining what constitutes a good or a satisfactory ratio. Ratios should be used over a period of time so that trends may be established. Only then can a determination be made as to which ratios offer significant information for the control process. Occasionally it is helpful to compare ratios with those of similar companies in the same industry. Even so, there must be some assurance that the accounting systems used by the several companies are comparable.

The third danger inherent in the use of ratios is that of inferring causal relationships that are not warranted. A marketing manager may conclude that an increase in selling expense as a percentage of sales indicates a decrease in the number of units sold by the sales force, but the real reason could be due to a decrease in unit price. Most faulty inferences result from a failure to examine closely the direction and magnitude of change in both the numerator and denominator and failure to evaluate the validity and reliability of the data used in computing the ratio.

Despite the difficulties encountered in interpreting ratios, they remain a useful control device when there is a thorough understanding of the manner in which they are developed and when there are several related ratios presented so that the significance of any one ratio may be checked by comparing it with another.

BREAK-EVEN ANALYSIS

Break-even analysis utilizes the same concepts employed in the construction of variable budgets (Chapter 20, pages 500 to 503). There are striking similarities between the break-even chart (Figure 19-1) and the graphic representation of a variable expense budget shown in Figure 20-1, page 501. However, there are two important differences: First, the vertical axis of the break-even chart is designated as a revenue-expense axis rather than being labeled an expense axis; and second, the sales revenue line of the break-even chart shows the expected revenue for each level of sales volume. The point where the revenue line intersects the total cost line is the break-even point.

An understanding of the dynamic relationships existing between the factors included in the break-even chart enables one to forecast and plan for profit. The break-even point and consequently the amount of profit vary with changes in any one of four factors: unit volume, fixed cost, variable cost, and unit selling price. Further, the precise effect upon the break-even point resulting from a change in one or any combination of these variables can be determined by means of the following formula:

$$\text{Break-Even Point} = \frac{\text{Fixed Expense}}{P/V \text{ ratio}}$$

$$\text{when } P/V = \frac{\text{Sales} - \text{Variable Costs}}{\text{Sales}}$$

The ability to predict changes in profits under various operating conditions has obvious applications to the process of planning. A knowledge of the relationship of the factors that influence profit is equally applicable to the control process, a re-emphasis of the continuous nature of

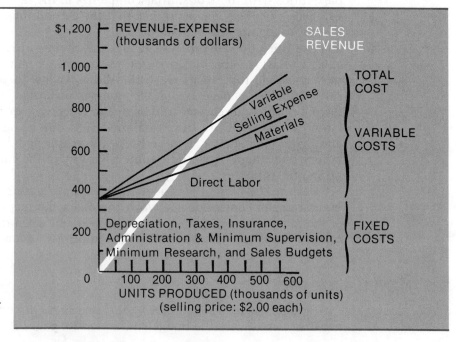

**Figure 19-1
BREAK-EVEN
CHART**

the planning-control-planning cycle. Specifically, break-even analysis provides information that aids in the control of costs and underscores the importance of sales volume.

Cost Control

Break-even charts can be prepared so that they contribute to overall control by showing both fixed and variable costs for the entire company. They can also be prepared for smaller operating units such as manufacturing departments or sales districts. In either case, fixed costs are segregated from variable costs. Fixed costs move slowly and show little variation as the result of changes in sales volume. Variable costs, on the other hand, vary directly as a function of volume. By their very nature, variable costs are subject to some degree of control. By clearly separating these variable costs, attention is directed toward those areas where corrective action is possible. When presented in the graphic form of a break-even chart, deviations from budgeted expenses are readily recognized.

Sales Volume

An analysis of the break-even formula above shows clearly the effect of sales beyond the break-even point upon profit. The *P/V* ratio, the denominator of the fraction on the right side of the equation, expresses the profitability of an operation after the break-even point has been reached. Too many small and medium-sized firms tend to express profitability as a percentage of total sales rather than as a percentage of sales beyond the break-even point. The following operating statement indicates a net profit of 10 percent of total sales:

Revenue from sales		$1,000,000
Variable costs	$500,000	
Fixed costs	400,000	
Total costs		900,000
Net profit		$ 100,000

However, the P/V ratio $\dfrac{\$1,000,000 - \$500,000}{\$1,000,000}$ indicates that the profitability of each unit sold beyond the break-even point is 50 percent. By emphasizing the contribution to profit of additional sales beyond the break-even point, there is greater incentive to stimulate and control sales effort.

TIME-EVENT-NETWORK ANALYSIS

To meet the requirements of what has been called "an age of massive engineering" — in contrast to repetitive production — a number of fairly sophisticated techniques for the analysis of networks have been developed.[11] Two time-event-network analysis techniques were developed separately and published in 1959. The Program Evaluation Review Technique (PERT) was developed by the Special Projects Office of the U. S. Navy Bureau of Ordinance, with the assistance of staff members of the management consulting firm of Booz, Allen, and Hamilton. It was first used in the development of the Polaris Fleet Ballistic Missile.[12] The Critical Path Method (CPM) of network analysis was developed by DuPont to reduce downtime for periodic maintenance.[13] PERT is credited with saving two years in the development of the Polaris missile, while the CPM cut DuPont's downtime for maintenance in the Louisville plant from 125 to 93 hours.[14] Before discussing the relative merits and applications of PERT and CPM, let us review some of the fundamentals of network analysis.[15]

Fundamentals of Network Analysis

In order to use network analysis for purposes of planning and control, several conditions must be met:

1. *A clearly recognizable end point or objective.* One-of-a-kind projects, such as developing and building the first prototype of the Polaris missile or the construction of a shopping center, meet this requirement. The installation of a data processing system, the construction of a highway interchange, or the building of a piece of special machinery all have clearly definable and recognizable end points. In contrast, the 100,000th car from an assembly line is difficult to distinguish from its immediate predecessor or successor.

2. *A series of events.* There should be a series of clearly defined, separate, but interrelated, events leading up to the completion of the final project. In constructing a highway interchange, temporary routes must be built, bridges constructed, drainage facilities installed, service roads prepared, and many other distinct subprojects completed before the interchange is ready for use.

3. *Time for each activity.* The time required for the completion of the work or activity preceding each event must be calculated. Herein lies one of the major differences between PERT and CPM. PERT employs

---

[11]See "Thinking Ahead: The Age of Massive Engineering," *Harvard Business Review*, Vol. 39 (January-February, 1961), p. 138.

[12]Donald G. Malcolm, John H. Rodrboom, Charles E. Clark, and Willard Fazar, "Applications of a Technique for Research and Development Program Evaluation," *Operations Research*, Vol. 7 (September-October, 1959), pp. 646–699.

[13]James E. Kelley, Jr., and Morgan R. Walker, "Critical Path Planning and Scheduling," *Proceedings of the Eastern Joint Computer Conference* (December, 1959).

[14]F. K. Levy, G. L. Thompson, and J. D. Wiest, "The ABCs of the Critical Path Method," *Harvard Business Review*, Vol. 41 (September-October, 1963), p. 100. On pp. 102–103 there is a discussion of how to determine the critical path through the use of a relatively simple algorithm.

[15]The term, review, is used advisedly since network analysis required by PERT and CPM is similar to the analysis of information systems required in the design of an integrated data processing system. See p. 135.

a method of estimating probable time, even though there has been no prior experience to serve as a basis for estimating time. CPM implies some prior experience or knowledge of the time estimated for the completion of activities leading to each event.

4. *A starting point*. There must be a recognizable starting point — the issuance of a sales order for a piece of special machinery, notification from the government to begin the development of a weapons system, or the date of a scheduled plant shutdown as the beginning of an annual maintenance program.

Figure 19-2 is a schematic diagram of a network analysis. Each square in the diagram represents an event. The number that appears in each square except the first is a statement of the amount of work, expressed in days, that must be completed so that the event in question can occur. Events, as such, require no time; they merely serve as milestones. The letter in each square designates the event and in an actual chart would be explained in a legend. The arrows indicate the sequence of events. The length of each arrow has no particular significance. The color arrows represent the *critical path*, the longest route in time from start to finish. If the duration of the project is to be shortened, it must be shortened by reducing the time intervals necessary for the completion of each event along this pathway. To reduce the work time along another path would not reduce the total time required for the project; instead, it would merely create more "slack" — excess time in the other pathways.

Let us assume that the project represented by the network in Figure 19-2 is a piece of special-purpose machinery including both electrical and mechanical components. In charting a network, the analysis of the project commences with the end result, the finished machine, and then works backwards, step by step, until the origin of the project is

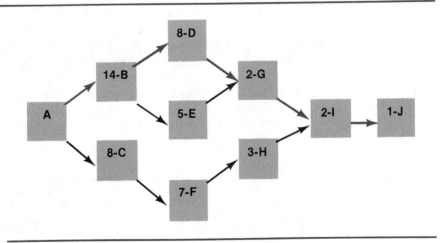

Figure 19-2 SCHEMATIC NETWORK ANALYSIS

reached, the issuance of a sales order. The machine is ready for shipment when it has passed final inspection (J), a process that takes one day after the completion of final assembly (I). Thus, the number 1 and the letter J are entered in the square designating the completion of the project. Final assembly takes two days to complete but cannot be started until the subassembly of all electrical components (H) and all mechanical components (G) is finished. To perform the mechanical subassembly, components must be released by the milling department (D) and the lathe department (E). The largest single requirement for time in this network is the 14 days needed to procure mechanical components (B). The project starts with the issuance of the sales order (A). The same procedure is followed in analyzing the sequence of operations in the production of the electrical components of the manufacturing process.[16]

Two major advantages result from the use of time-event-network analysis techniques. In the first place, breaking a project down into its component events, specifying the time required for the completion of each activity, and designating the sequence of events force a degree of planning that improves any production process. Presenting this information pictorially as a network offers the second advantage — a clear understanding of the interdependence and relationships that exist between the various events. We know that the critical path, by definition, is the longest route in time. In the example discussed, and shown in Figure 19-2, the critical path is 27 days. If the duration of the project is to be shortened, attention and control effort must be directed toward the critical path.

With this introduction to network analysis, let us examine PERT in more detail.

PERT

PERT in its original form stresses the time required to perform the activities necessary for a given event to occur. The unique contribution of PERT as a form of network analysis is that it provides a means of obtaining a probability estimate of the expected time to complete activities that have not been performed previously and, therefore, have not been measured. The building of the Polaris missile, the first application of PERT, is a case in point. None of the activities leading up to the specified events had been performed before; consequently, there were no historical records or time study standards to serve as a basis for estimating expected times.

---

[16]E. T. Alsaker, "The Basic Technique: Network Analysis," in Gabriel N. Stilian *et al.*, *PERT: A New Management Planning and Control Technique* (New York: American Management Association, No. 74, AMA Management Reports, 1962), pp. 37–60. This publication presents in concise form a series of papers on PERT theory, the applications of PERT, and a discussion of related techniques such as the CPM and the Line of Balance system of control.

To determine the probable expected time for activities leading to an event, PERT requires three time estimates. First is the most optimistic time — the time that is required if everything goes right. The probability of a most optimistic set of circumstances occurring is about 1 out of 100. Second, the most likely time is estimated — the time required in the normal course of events. The third time estimate is most pessimistic — the time required if everything that could go wrong does go wrong. Again, the probability for the most pessimistic set of circumstances occurring is 1 out of 100; however, catastrophies such as floods, fires, and strikes are excluded. Designating the most optimistic time as a, the most likely time as m, and the most pessimistic time as b, the expected time, T_e, is found by substituting estimated times in the following formula:

$$T_e = \frac{a + 4m + b}{6}$$

There is also a formula to determine the standard deviation of the expected time, thus making it possible to state a statistical probability that the expected time will fall within a stated range.[17]

CPM

The difference between PERT and CPM (Critical Path Method) is one of degree rather than kind. PERT emphasizes time and provides a way of computing the most probable time; however, CPM emphasizes cost as well as time.[18] CPM differs from PERT in three respects. First, only one time estimate is given for each set of activities leading up to a given event, instead of the three time estimates required by PERT. Second, with CPM, a cost estimate is included along with each estimated time for both *"normal"* and *"crash"* operating conditions. Normal operating conditions are usually defined as the least-cost method for the performance of an activity; and "crash" conditions represent the time and cost incurred in the performance of activities in less than the normal time. For example, under normal operating conditions two persons assigned to the day shift take three days to complete a job. The time can be shortened under "crash" conditions by assigning two persons to each of three consecutive shifts — a reduction in elapsed time but with a resultant increase in cost because the workers on the second

---

[17]There has been much discussion concerning the mathematics of the PERT time estimate. The following report discusses the Beta distribution, a fundamental assumption of the estimated time computation: *PERT Summary Report, Phase I* (Washington: Special Projects Office, Department of the Navy, July, 1958).

A brief description of the mathematics of PERT, along with a discussion of its application, is presented in the following article: Robert W. Miller, "How to Plan and Control with PERT," *Harvard Business Review*, Vol. 40 (March-April, 1962), pp. 93–104.

[18]Levy, Thompson, and Wiest, *op. cit.*, pp. 98–108.

For another discussion of the critical path method, see Walter Cosinuke, "The Critical Path Method," in Stilian *et al., op. cit.*, pp. 147–163.

and the third shifts will receive premium pay. Third, CPM assumes some previous experience with the work necessary for the completion of each event; otherwise, it would be impracticable to state a single time and cost estimate.

These differences explain to a large degree why PERT is used primarily for one-of-a-kind projects involving an extensive amount of research and development prior to the building of a prototype and for similar projects where time is of greater importance than cost. CPM, on the other hand, is widely used in complex construction and maintenance projects where cost is a significant factor and prior experience offers a basis for making a reliable estimate of both time and cost.[19]

Evaluation of PERT and CPM

There are three major benefits to be derived from the use of either PERT or CPM in the planning and control of certain production functions. First, the application of network analysis techniques forces a high degree of planning and results in plans that are objective, structured, and flexible.[20] In so doing, either PERT or CPM approaches the optimum condition summarized in Chapter 4, page 83. The second advantage of network analysis is that the establishment of a network system makes it possible to determine the critical path. The significance of the critical path to the control process is that knowledge of the key elements in a complex production system makes possible the design and administration of a set of forward-looking controls so that corrective action may be taken before serious deviation from schedule occurs. Third, network analysis shows clearly the interrelationships between the various organizational components of a complex production system, thereby making it possible to improve both communications and organizational structure.

Nonetheless, there are two limiting conditions that must be fulfilled before the advantages described above can be realized. First, network analysis is most effective when applied to one-of-a-kind projects that include several subprojects. Further, both the main project and the various subprojects must be fairly well defined and recognizable. They cannot be too nebulous. Examples of activities amenable to network analysis are construction projects, research and development

---

[19]The above discussion refers to PERT in its original form. Since its introduction, there have been many variations of PERT. For this reason the original PERT is often referred to as basic PERT or PERT/Time to differentiate it from later variations such as PERT/Cost. The following article discusses the application of PERT/Cost: Hilliard W. Paige, "How PERT-Cost Helps the General Manager," *Harvard Business Review*, Vol. 41 (November-December, 1963), pp. 87–95.

For a discussion of the application of PERT to the control of production activities see the following: Peter P. Schoderbek and Lester A. Digman, "Third Generation, PERT/LOB," *Harvard Business Review*, Vol. 45, No. 5 (September-October, 1967), pp. 100–110.

[20]The following article emphasizes the importance of PERT/CPM to the planning process: Richard J. Schonberger, "Custom-tailored PERT/CPM Systems," *Business Horizons*, Vol. 15, No. 6 (December, 1972), pp. 64–66.

programs, the installation of an integrated data processing system, the design and construction of a weapon systems, and the design and manufacture of special machinery or equipment. The second factor that limits the effectiveness of network analysis is organizational structure. Experience has shown that a task force or project form of organization is necessary to obtain maximum benefits from either PERT or CPM (See Chapter 10, page 229). Task force organization requires organizational flexibility and highly trained personnel. In summary, both the project and the organization must be appropriate if full benefit is to be realized from the application of either PERT or CPM as a means for planning and control.[21]

Case Problem 19-B offers an opportunity to determine how the critical path in building a house can be shortened. Though a contractor might include more separate events than shown in the case problem, there are sufficient events presented to enable you to see for yourself how CPM points up the interrelationships of the various phases of a complex process.

Case Problem 19-B
SHORTENING THE CRITICAL PATH

Ralph Billings, an independent building contractor, has completed building the fifth house of a projected development of 25 homes in the $30,000 price range. Recently he read of an application of the Critical Path Method to the building of a shopping center and became interested in applying the method to his own business. Currently he employs four carpenters and two laborers. Much of his work, such as excavating, plumbing, grading, cement work, bricklaying, and electrical work, is performed by subcontractors who base their charges on a combination of materials and man-hours required for each job. Billings hopes that the application of CPM to his operation will result in a reduction of the total number of days required to build a house and in better utilization of the labor he now has.

As a first step in applying the Critical Path Method to his own building efforts, Billings determined the average time required for each phase of the building of the first five houses. These values, along with the sequence of each building operation, are shown in Exhibit 1, page 490.

PROBLEMS

1. Using the information presented in Exhibit I, construct a schematic network analysis similar to Figure 19-2 and determine the critical path.
2. What recommendations would you make to shorten the critical path?

---

[21]There have been relatively few reports in the literature concerning the limitations of network techniques and difficulties encountered in their application. The following two studies indicate some of the limitations.

Lawrence S. Hill, "Perspective: Some Possible Pitfalls in the Design and Use of PERT Networking," *Academy of Management Journal*, Vol. 8, No. 2 (June, 1965), pp. 139–145.

Peter P. Schoderbek, "A Study of the Applications of PERT," *Academy of Management Journal*, Vol. 8, No. 3 (September, 1965), pp. 199–209.

Job No.	Description	Immediate Predecessors	Normal Time (Days)
a	Start		0
b	Excavate and Pour Footers	a	4
c	Pour Concrete Foundation	b	2
d	Erect Wooden Frame Including Rough Roof	c	4
e	Lay Brickwork	d	6
f	Install Basement Drains and Plumbing	c	1
g	Pour Basement Floor	f	2
h	Install Rough Plumbing	f	3
i	Install Rough Wiring	d	2
j	Install Heating and Ventilating	d, g	4
k	Fasten Plaster Board and Plaster (including drying)	i, j, h	10
l	Lay Finish Flooring	k	3
m	Install Kitchen Fixtures	l	1
n	Install Finish Plumbing	l	2
o	Finish Carpentry	l	3
p	Finish Roofing and Flashing	e	2
q	Fasten Gutters and Downspouts	p	1
r	Lay Storm Drains for Rain Water	c	1
s	Sand and Varnish Flooring	o, t	2
t	Paint	m, n	3
u	Finish Electrical Work	t	1
v	Finish Grading	q, r	2
w	Pour Walks and Complete Landscaping	v	5
x	Finish	s, u, w	0

**Exhibit I
SEQUENCE AND
TIME
REQUIREMENTS
OF JOBS**

Source: F. K. Levy, G. L. Thompson, and J. D. Wiest, "The ABC's of the Critical Path Method," *Harvard Business Review*, Vol. 41 (September-October, 1963), p. 100. Copyright © 1963 by the President and Fellows of Harvard College; all rights reserved.

CHAPTER QUESTIONS FOR STUDY AND DISCUSSION

1. What factors in the situation and what factors in the manager would tend to either increase or decrease the value of personal observations as a means of securing control information?

2. What points should be considered when designing or using control reports? Develop examples to illustrate both effective and ineffective control reports.

3. Comment on the following statement: Control reports are primarily a part of an information system rather than a control system.

4. Differentiate between internal and external auditing and show by example the strengths and weaknesses of each type of audit.

5. State in your own words the basic assumptions underlying the concept of human resource accounting. Is there a relationship between the technology used by a firm and the potential value that might result from the use of human resource accounting? If so, state the relationship.

6. Give an example of each of the more common forms of operating ratios and financial ratios.

7. How can the difficulties in interpreting ratios be minimized?

8. How do the techniques of break-even analysis contribute to the effectiveness of the control process?

9. In your opinion, do break-even analysis and *P/V* analysis have greater impact in the area of manufacturing through cost control than in the area of sales planning? Why?

10. Under what conditions would you recommend the use of PERT as opposed to CPM?

Case Problem 20-A
DEVELOPING A REVENUE AND EXPENSE BUDGET

Adele Barr suddenly found herself in the retail business as a result of the unexpected death of her father, James O'Leary, who owned and managed The Avenue, a men's clothing and furnishings store. Mrs. Barr was appointed acting manager by the executor of her father's estate and served in that capacity during the peak sales period that normally occurs during the last three months of the calendar year. When the estate was settled in mid-December, Mrs. Barr and her husband, who had recently retired from the Air Force, decided to continue managing the store rather than sell it. The records kept by O'Leary were rather sketchy and incomplete, but they did indicate that net sales had been $200,000 a year for the past three years and that net profit before taxes had varied between 4 and 5½ percent of net sales for the same period.

Mr. Barr had worked with budgets as an officer in the management control section of the Air Force and decided that the development of a revenue and expense budget would serve as a useful guide during the coming year. After studying the information made available to them by the Small Business Administration and the publications of the National Association of Retail Clothiers and Furnishers, the Barrs decided to use the percentages for revenue and expense items as shown in Exhibit I. They considered dividing the total for each of these accounts by 12 to develop a budget for each month, but later decided that the variation in sales volume and advertising costs from month to month was great enough to require that these items be computed on the basis of the variations shown in Exhibit II. Both Exhibit I and Exhibit II are based upon an annual net sales volume of $200,000.

PROBLEMS

1. Develop monthly revenue and expense budgets for a year for the store owned and operated by the Barrs.
2. What additional information would you need to prepare a cash budget? a balance sheet budget?
3. What kind of standards have the Barrs used in determining budgeted performance?
4. Would flexible budgets be of any value in allocating monthly sales volume and advertising expenses?
5. Of what value will this budget be in succeeding years?

ACCOUNT	PERCENTAGE OF NET SALES
Sales:	
1. Gross sales	102.6
2. Customer returns and allowances	2.6
3. Net sales	100.0
Cost of goods sold:	
4. Beginning inventory	30.9
5. Net purchases plus transportation charges paid	66.1
6. Total cost of merchandise handled	97.0
7. Ending inventory	32.3
8. Net cost of merchandise sold	64.7
9. Net busheling (alterations) cost	2.1
10. Total cost of merchandise sold	66.8
11. Gross margin	33.2
Operating expenses:	
12. Payroll:	
A. Salaries of owners	7.3
B. Salaries and wages of employees	9.0
Total payroll	16.3
13. Rent expense	2.9
14. Taxes and license fees (omit real estate, Federal income and sales taxes)	1.1
15. Insurance	.6
16. Depreciation and amortization	.8
17. Repairs	.2
18. Supplies (omit repair materials)	1.0
19. Services purchased	.9
20. Traveling (business trips)	.3
21. Communication (include parcel post)	.4
22. Advertising and publicity	2.8
23. Professional services (outside professional agencies)	.2
24. Unclassified (all expenses not under headings):	
A. Losses from bad debts	.3
B. Other unclassified expenses	.5
Total unclassified expenses	.8
25. Total expenses	28.3
26. Net profit (or loss) before Federal income taxes	4.9

Exhibit I
BUDGETED
OPERATING
REVENUE AND
EXPENSES FOR
ANNUAL NET
SALES OF
$200,000

MONTH	PERCENTAGE OF ANNUAL NET SALES	PERCENTAGE OF ANNUAL ADVERTISING COSTS
January	8%	9%
February	5	7
March	6	6
April	6	7
May	8	7
June	9	8
July	7	7
August	7	8
September	7	9
October	9	8
November	10	10
December	18	14

Exhibit II BUDGETED NET SALES AND ADVERTISING COSTS FOR EACH MONTH

The budget is without doubt the most widely used control device in both business and government; indeed, it is used so extensively that for many people the word budget is synonymous with control. Yet, the preparation of budgets originates as part of the planning process, and the budget itself is the end point of the planning process — the statement of a plan. Some companies, in order to avoid the negative reactions often associated with the concept of control, refer to their budgetary controls as either *profit plans* or *profit paths*.

In our discussion of budgetary controls we shall first examine the nature of budgets and review the types of budgets used most frequently. The success or failure of either budgetary or nonbudgetary controls (discussed in the previous chapter) depends on their acceptance by the people in an organization; consequently, consideration is given to behavioral reactions to control.

THE NATURE OF BUDGETS

A *budget* may be defined as a plan expressed in quantitative terms. However, this overly simplified definition of a budget does not tell us much about the nature of budgets or of budgetary control. The process of preparing a budget is planning in every sense of the word, and the budget itself is the resultant plan. As such, the budget, like any other plan, should possess the characteristics of objectivity, structuralization, and flexibility. The extent to which a budget reflects these characteristics is a measure of its probable success.[1]

Even so, there are certain aspects of budgets that differentiate them from other plans. First, the reason for preparing a budget is to provide a means for controlling operations. Second, as a means of controlling operations effectively, a separate budget is usually prepared for each organizational unit, and individual budgets may be prepared for each of the several functions within an organizational unit. Third, a budget is designed to cover a specific period of time. The fiscal year is the unit of time used most frequently, but this unit may be subdivided into semiannual, quarterly, or monthly periods. Also, budgets may be prepared for periods of time greater than one year; for example, capital expenditure budgets. Finally, budgets are expressed in financial terms since dollars serve well as a common denominator and thereby permit the comparison and coordination of all phases of a company's operations.

Though planning is an essential ingredient in the process of preparing budgets, the preparation of budgets is more closely related to the control process than it is to the planning process. The budget itself is the stated standard of performance. Thus, preparing budgets is, in effect, setting standards — the first step of the control process. The measurement of current performance against standards, the second step in the process of control, is facilitated because the budget expresses standards of performance in quantitative terms — dollars. Deviations from budgeted or expected results are readily identified and show the need for corrective action, the last step in the process of control. Undoubtedly, the preparation of budgets refines the planning process necessary for the establishment of standards, or goals; however, the greater value of budgeting lies in its contribution to improved coordination and control. When budgets are prepared for all organizational units and the various functions performed by these units, a basis is provided for the coordination of the efforts of the organization. At the same time, budgets establish a basis for the corrective action of control since deviations from expected results are more readily identified and measured. Thus, the preparation of budgets may be expected to result in better planning and improved coordination, and to provide a basis for control — the primary purpose for establishing budgets.

Types of Budgets

Virtually every aspect of the operations of an organization can be budgeted. A business firm may prepare budgets for sales, inventory, shipments, production, maintenance, direct labor, and indirect labor.

---

[1]See Chapter 4, pp. 79–83.

Budgets may also be used to forecast the operations of the industrial relations department, the cost of industrial engineering, and the needs for research and development. The list of organizational units and functions susceptible to budgetary control is almost endless. Fortunately, there is a logical framework that provides an easily remembered classification of budgets. This classification follows roughly a time sequence in the operation of a business and results in the following four types of budgets:

1. Revenue and expense budget
2. Cash budget
3. Capital expenditure budget
4. Balance sheet budget

As we shall see, each of these major types of budgets may be further subdivided so that the individual needs of each company may be fully met.

Revenue and Expense Budget. If one were starting a new business or beginning to prepare the initial set of budgets for a going concern, the first need would be a summary statement of the company's operations. The *revenue and expense budget*, sometimes called an *operating budget*, provides a bird's eye view of operations. Since revenue from the sale of products or services is the main source of income, the revenue budget is often referred to as the *sales budget*. All other budgets must be coordinated with the sales forecast since revenue from sales defines the upper limits of expenses and profits.

Sales Budget. In preparing a sales forecast, careful consideration must be given to external environmental factors as well as to conditions within the company itself. General economic conditions, the availability of credit, and the action of competitors are illustrative of the external factors that influence a company's level of sales. Accurate sales forecasts are difficult to achieve, at best, but the experience gained from the preparation of successive annual sales budgets gradually narrows the gap between budgeted and actual sales.

The content and the format of the sales budget vary with each company; however, certain generalizations are possible. For companies with multiple products or services, the expected revenue from each product or service should be stated separately. For large companies, a breakdown of expected sales by territory is essential. Sometimes the forecast should reflect expected sales for each class of customer. Since sales are seldom the same for each month of the year, the expected revenue for each calendar month should be stated to show clearly the seasonal variations. A forecast of revenue by month is necessary for the preparation of cash budgets.

Expense Budget. The second part of the revenue and expense budget is a statement of expected expenses. Two considerations guide the preparation of expense budgets. First is a determination of the classification of items to be included in expense budgets; and second, the allocation of expense items according to organizational unit. Expense budgets may be prepared for every item listed in the expense division of the company's chart of accounts. In manufacturing firms, a manufacturing budget is prepared to show the expenses anticipated in the manufacture of the company's products. Included are the cost of material, the cost of inventory, direct and indirect labor charges, factory overhead including the cost of supervision, and the cost of maintaining equipment and other manufacturing facilities. General administrative costs and the cost of sales are shown separately.

If the budget is to be an effective tool in the control of expenses, a budget must be prepared for each organizational unit and placed in the hands of the managers of those units. Manufacturing budgets are prepared for operating departments and become a statement of expense responsibilities for the manager of each department. Managers of territorial or product divisions of the sales department are charged with the responsibility of keeping the cost of sales within budgeted limits. Difficulties encountered in controlling expenses are often a result of ill-defined organizational structure rather than an unwillingness on the part of departmental managers to cooperate in reducing expenses.

Cash Budget. The *cash budget*, derived from the basic data included in the revenue and expense budget, shows the cash requirements of the business during the budget period. The need for a specific budget detailing cash requirements arises from the fact that rarely does the flow of cash into the firm from sales coincide with the amount and frequency of disbursements necessary to pay expenses. For example, if too little cash is on hand to purchase materials in order to increase inventory levels to meet seasonal sales requirements, it may be necessary to borrow and thereby incur the added cost of interest. Also, having sufficient cash on hand makes it possible to take advantage of cash discounts offered by suppliers. Excess cash may be used for short-term investments, or it may make possible an earlier than expected fulfillment of capital expenditure plans. When the amount of cash falls below budgeted expectations, it may be an early warning that accounts receivable are running too high. Budgeting cash requirements may not alter significantly the amount of profit earned by a firm, but it does help to assure a liquid position and is considered one of the hallmarks of prudent management.

Capital Expenditure Budget. If the planning and control of the revenue and expense budget are successfully managed, revenue should exceed expenses. A part of this balance is reinvested in the company to insure the continued existence and growth of the firm. Since these expenditures produce revenue, they are classed as capital expenditures and are included in the *capital expenditure budget*. Typically, one finds in the capital expenditure budget allotments for the replacement of present facilities, including plant and equipment, and funds for the expansion of facilities for increased production of the present product line or the development and manufacture of a new product.

However, there are expenses other than those for physical facilities and equipment that require the appropriation of fairly large sums of money and the passage of a relatively long period of time before the anticipated results become apparent. Executive development programs, including the recruitment of college graduates, require support on a continuing basis; and it may take many years before the results of such personnel programs can be assessed. The decision to spend a greater than usual amount on advertising in order to develop new markets is another long-range investment of company funds. Research and development plans for new and improved products require continued appropriations for their completion. Institutional advertising intended to establish a desired public image also requires special budgetary appropriations. Consequently, some companies develop a single *appropriation budget* to reflect intended expenditures for capital equipment, personnel development, the development of new markets, research and development programs, and institutional advertising.

Budgeting capital or appropriation expenditures poses some rather difficult problems not directly related to the control of expenses. Since emergency needs in the five areas mentioned above arise infrequently, the control of expenses is relatively easy to achieve — one simply does not spend more than the budgetary allowance. Instead, the difficulty in preparing budgets for special appropriations arises from the long-term nature of these investments and the limited amount of money available for such expenditures. Because these projects are long term, their true worth cannot be computed until completed or until their useful life, in the case of capital equipment, is exhausted. Even then one is not sure that the course selected is of more value than some of the rejected alternate courses of action. But alternate courses must be weighed and choices made since the funds available to a company are never unlimited. Difficult as the appraisal of the results of capital expenditure budgeting may be, there are, nonetheless, several important benefits to be gained from this class of budget. First, capital or appropriation expenditures should be controlled and can be controlled relatively easily once they are budgeted. Second, budgeting the major appropriations forces an improvement of the planning process in each of the functional areas so that a careful weighing of alternate forms of investment may be accomplished. Third, capital expenditures require cash and as a result must be budgeted if the cash budget is to be of maximum value as a control device. Fourth, special appropriations must be included so that the greatest degree of coordination of the company's resources, especially financial, is achieved.

Balance Sheet Budget. The *balance sheet budget* is a forecast of expected financial status as of the last day of the budget period, usually the close of the fiscal year. The balance sheet forecast, a statement of the relationships between assets and liabilities, does not require the preparation of any additional budgets; rather, it is a consolidation of all preceding budgets. Preparing a balance sheet forecast shows what might be expected if performance meets the standards defined in the other budgets. By preparing a forecast of anticipated financial position, management may discover that the other budgets when consolidated do not result in an entirely favorable financial condition as revealed by certain key ratios. For example, the ratio between current assets and current liabilities or expected earnings and current market price per share may be such that the value of the company's stock would be adversely affected. When this happens, the other budgets have to be recast. The balance sheet showing the actual financial position at the close of the budget period serves as a useful check on the accuracy of preparation and the degree to which all other budgets have been met. Also, deviations between the actual and the forecasted balance sheets may show the need for preparation of special budgets to improve control over performance in certain areas; for instance, accounts receivable, accounts payable, or finished goods inventory.

Securing Flexibility with Budgets

Several disadvantages may arise as the result of an overzealous application of budgetary controls. In the administration of budgetary controls, it is all too easy to emphasize conformance to the budgetary goals of the organization. For example, a regional sales manager who is experiencing difficulty in meeting sales objectives may have every reason to believe that a market research study would be of help in solving the problem; yet, it may be impossible to conduct such a study because there is no provision for it in the budget. Another criticism arising from the use of budgets is that the statement of objectives in numeric terms lends a degree of precision and exactness that is seldom warranted. After all, goals stated numerically are no more reliable than the original estimates from which they are drawn. However, the greatest potential danger of budgetary control is that it may lead to inflexibility. Budgets are statements of plans and, like any other plan, if they are to be successful, they must be flexible as well as possess the characteristics of objectivity and structuralization. Flexibility in budgetary control may be achieved by either one of two methods: *periodic budgetary reviews* and *flexible budgets*.

Periodic Budgetary Review. Normally, budgets are prepared in advance for a 12-month period. However, changes in operating conditions may occur that make the attainment of stated budgetary goals a virtual impossibility. Some of the factors frequently subject to change during the course of the budget period are labor costs, selling price, and the predicted volume of business. Periodic budgetary reviews are intended to incorporate and reflect changes in any of the first two factors, while flexible budgets are designed specifically to reflect changes in the anticipated volume of business.

Periodic budgetary reviews may be prepared on a monthly basis, prior to the beginning of the new month. Then, during the third month of the budgetary period, a revised quarterly estimate is prepared. For example, a company whose fiscal year is the same as the calendar year would prepare revised estimates of the budget for the months of January, February, and March prior to the beginning of each of these months. During the month of March, a revised quarterly budget for the second quarter might be prepared in addition to the revised estimate for April. Also, revised quarterly budgets may be prepared for the third and fourth quarters prior to their beginning, along with the usual monthly revisions.

However, there is a danger inherent in the use of periodic budgetary reviews as a means of recognizing changing conditions. If changes are made too frequently and if the magnitude of these changes is too great, it is quite possible for the original budget to become meaningless. Also, the other extreme is possible; that is, periodic reviews of the budget, backed by ample evidence, may show the need for a restatement of budgeted goals but may not be permitted because the original budget is considered inviolate. One way of minimizing the variation between the annual budget and the revised budget resulting from periodic reviews is to anticipate in the preparation of the annual budgets the changes that might reasonably be expected in labor rates, raw materials, and selling prices. Past experience is a good guide in these areas. Changes suggested as the result of periodic reviews must not only be substantiated, but reasons must also be given showing why it was impossible to anticipate these changes in the preparation of the original budget. In this manner the accuracy of the original budget is improved over a period of years.

Flexible Budgets. Periodic budget reviews allow management to compensate for changes in labor costs, selling price, the cost of raw materials, a change in technology, or the method of operation. In many respects the amount of change resulting from these factors is unpredictable, with the result that the extent of their effect on the budget can be determined only after the change has begun. However, the effect of changes in the volume of business of a company upon the revenue and expense budgets can in many instances be predicted in advance. When budgets are prepared for the coming fiscal year, they are prepared on the basis of an assumed or predicted level of revenue or volume — a statement of expected expenses for an expected amount of revenue. Flexible or variable budgets show the effect of changes in the volume of business upon certain expense items in the revenue and expense budget.

From our study of break-even analysis (Chapter 19), we know that some costs regarded as fixed or standby do not vary proportionately with the volume of business and that other costs vary proportionately with changes in volume. Good examples of fixed and variable costs are the costs incurred in operating an automobile. The cost of depreciation, insurance, and garaging the automobile are not a function of the number of miles driven (volume). Rather, these costs are incurred at the time the car is purchased and do not change appreciably as a result of the number of miles driven. For this reason these costs are termed fixed, or standby, costs. On the other hand, the costs of tires, oil, gasoline, and repairs vary directly with the number of miles driven; hence, these costs are called variable costs. Similarly, a company's costs for depreciation, insurance, and administration remain relatively unchanged within wide ranges of volume and are termed fixed costs. Labor costs, the cost of materials, and variable selling expenses such as commissions are representative of those costs that vary directly with changes in volume and are called variable costs.

Figure 20-1 shows in graphic form the relationship between the fixed and the variable expenses of a flexible budget. Determination of the nature of the relationship between variable costs and volume level may be accomplished by (1) a historical analysis of costs incurred at varying levels of volume and (2) the development of standard costs.

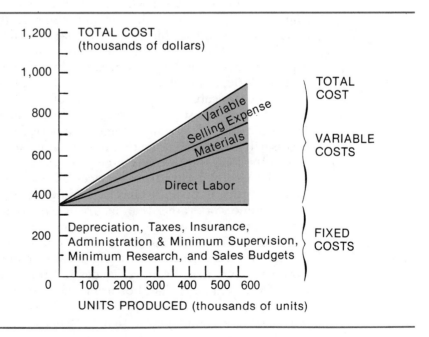

Figure 20-1
GRAPHIC
REPRESENTATION
OF A VARIABLE
EXPENSE
BUDGET

Historical Analysis of Costs. The historical approach is an effective tool for determining the relationship between variable costs and volume when the company's product line is limited to a few products and when each product contributes a relatively constant percentage to total sales volume. In its simplest form, historical analysis may consist of determining actual costs incurred in producing the company's historical maximum volume and the costs incurred for the lowest point of the sales record. These two points, the high and the low, may be plotted on a graph and a straight line drawn to connect them; thus, by interpolation, a prediction may be made concerning expected costs for each level of volume between the historical high and low points. More sophisticated techniques include plotting sales and cost data for each year and determining by the method of least squares the line of best fit. For those companies with diverse product lines, it becomes necessary to analyze the variable costs for each product.

Standard Costs. Standard costs for each product may be developed and may show the predicted cost for labor, materials, and supplies that might be expected for each unit produced. The predicted standard costs become the budgeted amount of variable costs, and the total cost for varying levels of volume can be readily computed.

Evaluation of Flexible Budgets. Variable budgets, particularly those utilizing standard costs, are often criticized as being too costly from the standpoint of both time and money in their preparation. Another criticism of variable budgets is that in practice they are extremely difficult to apply in a manner that results in savings in variable expenses. Part of the difficulty arises from an inability to predict short-term variations in volume. Even when this can be done, it is sometimes impracticable to take advantage of this information. For example, a department supervisor may normally supervise a work force of 15 machinists. A decline in volume for a period of two months does not necessarily result in a reduction in force since it may be more economical in the long run to retain highly skilled employees instead of running the risk of losing their services as a result of a layoff. Also, a sudden upturn in business may be handled more efficiently by assigning overtime work rather than incurring expenses resulting from training new employees. An advantage of variable budgets is that there is a budgeted goal for varying levels of volume without having to rework the entire budget each time a significant change in activity occurs. However, a greater advantage comes not from the variable goals feature of the flexible budget but from the study and analysis necessary for the preparation of a flexible budget. In addition to focusing attention upon the variable costs that contribute to the total cost of each unit, the preparation of flexible budgets requires a closer analysis of all costs in separating fixed and variable costs.[2]

Zero-Base Budgeting

The application of flexible budgets is primarily limited to manufacturing operations and at best offers a means of controlling variable manufacturing and sales costs. The question arises, how does one control the costs of supportive or staff functions? Some states have passed "sunset" laws to control the proliferation of regulatory agencies. These laws provide that a given agency is established for a specified period of years, and then is automatically eliminated at the end of the stated time period. In order to be reestablished the agency must justify its existence to the legislature by showing the benefits received in relation to the costs expended for its services. Business firms and other formal organizations can create their own sunset laws by requiring support functions to start their budgeting process at ground zero at the beginning of each budget period.

Zero-base budgeting is quite simple in concept. First, it is necessary to describe each support activity as a "decision" package. Second, each of the discrete decision packages, or activities, is evaluated and ranked by means of cost-benefit analysis (see Chapter 4, pp. 87–90). Third, the resources of the organization are allocated on the basis of the results of the second step and in accordance with the contribution of each function to the attainment of the goals of the organization.

In the normal budgeting process it is tacitly assumed that the current budget for service functions is necessary. Thus, the question is whether to increase the present budget or to continue it at its present level. Zero-base budgeting requires that one must consider what would happen if the function were eliminated. For example, the zero-base budget of a quality control department or a production control department would be the elimination of both departments entirely. The functions of quality control and production planning could be assigned to the first-line manufacturing supervisor, thereby saving the total cost of the operation of both departments. However, such an operation would place undue burden on manufacturing supervisors and would undoubtedly create many problems and inefficiences due to poor quality and late deliveries that could offset the savings gained by eliminating the departments. Consequently, the proposed budget should contain an alternate form of operation funded at a level below

---

[2]Adolph Matz and Milton F. Usry, *Cost Accounting*, Planning and Control (6th ed.; Cincinnati: South-Western Publishing Co., 1976), pp. 471–576. The three chapters on budgets, Chapters 16, 17, and 18, provide a discussion of the nature of budgets and offer many problems and examples of budgetary controls.

the current level with a statement of the attendant costs and benefits to be derived. The present funding is justified in a similar manner. Perhaps it might be wise to increase the funding if it can be shown that the benefits gained outweigh the costs incurred. Finally, it may be possible to combine similar functions. For example, if sales engineering and manufacturing are both operating a quality assurance program, the activities may be combined and thereby save the cost of at least one departmental manager. Ultimately each support area must be ranked and evaluated by top management at each proposed level of funding so that the final allocation of funds represents the greatest benefits for the organization in relation to the costs incurred.

Admittedly, such decisions are difficult to quantify and many times are based upon judgment. Decisions are especially difficult in such areas as personnel. A zero-base budgeting process applied to a personnel department would probably include interviewers and personnel clerks at the lowest level of funding. The presence or absence of a labor union determines whether or not a separate labor relations function is established in the personnel department. In addition, increasing regulation of the personnel function by outside agencies such as the Equal Employment Opportunity Commission may create the need for increased funding. A personnel department may request increased funds for the employment of an equal employment opportunity specialist. The costs are the additional salaries and expenses. The benefit that may be expected is the avoidance of monetary penalties that might be assessed as the result of an infraction of the EEOC regulations.

Though difficult to apply, zero-base budgeting affords a means of determining periodically whether the costs of given support or staff functions can be justified in terms of the benefits received. Also, analyzing each separate support function offers the possibility of combining some functions thereby offering a means of controlling the ever-increasing costs of support activities.[3]

Advantages of Effective Budgetary Control

Although budgets are one of the most widely used control techniques, it must be remembered that they are but one of several control devices. There are potential dangers as well as distinct advantages resulting from the use of budgets. Oddly enough, one of the strengths of budgets — the conversion of all aspects of organizational performance into a single comparable unit of measurement, dollars — can become its greatest weakness because it may result in measuring only those things that are easy to measure; i.e., those aspects of organizational

---

[3]The above discussion is based upon the application of zero-base budgeting as it is used in Texas Instruments, Inc. See Peter A. Pyhrr, "Zero-Base Budgeting," *Harvard Business Review*, Vol. 48, No. 6 (November-December, 1970), pp. 111–121.

performance readily converted into dollars. Equally important factors, such as manager performance and plans for organizational development, may be ignored because achievement in these areas is not readily convertible into dollar units. Second, there is a danger of identifying symptoms as causes. A decline in revenue from sales does not necessarily call for greater sales effort; instead, the real cause may be a poor product, the action of competitors, or general economic conditions. And finally, there is a danger of autocratic control by the staff organization. The function of the controller or the budget director is to coordinate and guide the development of budgets, but the actual control of performance must remain in the hands of the line managers.

The obvious advantage of budgetary control is that a comparable statement of goals is provided for all organizational units; and since the budget serves as a standard of performance, deviations from this standard are readily measurable and provide the basis for necessary corrective action. However, there are indirect advantages resulting from the proper use of budgets. The consistent and uniform application of budgets results in a more clearly defined organizational structure since budgets measure the performance of organizational units. Second, more meaningful accounting systems and terminology are developed. Traditionally, accounting has a deep preoccupation with the preparation of historical and tax records rather than focusing upon the reporting of current operations and the forecasting of future performance. Third, better planning of all phases of the company's operations results from the use of budgets. Budgets are carefully structured plans and serve to emphasize the continuous nature of the planning-control-planning cycle. Lastly, a clearer statement and understanding of organizational goals comes from the use of budgets because managers are forced to develop and state attainable goals for organizational units. Thus, wishful thinking with respect to organizational objectives is minimized.[4]

BEHAVIORAL REACTIONS TO CONTROL

The application of any control device, whether it is one of the non-budgetary controls (discussed in the preceding chapter) or a budget, bears directly upon the people of an organization. The success or failure of a control program depends to a greater degree on the attitudes of those subjected to control — members of middle management as well as hourly employees — than it does on the accuracy and kind of technique used in its preparation. Attitudes and overt responses to controls vary from open hostility and resentment, through indifference

---

[4]For a discussion of the relationship between information utilized in accounting systems and its effect upon organizational members, the following is of interest. Klaus Macharzina, "On the Integration of Behavioral Science into Accounting Theory," *Management International Review*, Vol. 13, No. 2–3 (1973), pp. 3–14.

and tolerance, to complete understanding and appreciation of the need for controls. Before discussing the commonly observed reasons for resistance to controls and the usual reactions to controls, let us examine a procedure that is usually followed in the establishment and administration of controls.

Typical Control Procedure

All too often the establishment and the administration of controls seemingly follow an endless cycle destined to have little chance of success. Top management determines objectives and sets the standards of performance required to meet these objectives; however, middle management and hourly employees react with attitudes and responses of hostility and resentment or indifference and bare tolerance. Such reactions are interpreted by top management as evidence of the need for additional and firmer controls. Robert Katz describes this cycle of control, resistance, and more control as follows:

1. The predetermined program is implemented. It is characterized by general, nonpersonal rules, division of labor, specialized competencies, and continuous checking to assure compliance.
2. Here the program immediately encounters unsought-for behavior as employees and subordinate managers seek to maintain their feelings of self-worth, their potential for self-determination, and their needs to have others acknowledge these capabilities.
3. Employees' reaction — Management's unilateral imposition of rules and detailed programming of behavior conflicts with employees' needs for self-determination and self-respect.

   Employees feel misunderstood, unappreciated, manipulated. They develop behavior patterns which enable them to resist rigid task pressures and permit some degree of self-regulation through informal social relationships.

   Performance stabilizes at the minimum level tolerated by management. Employees tend to produce well below their capacities, have low involvement in their tasks, show little initiative, do only what they are directed to do.
4. Subordinate manager's reaction — Expected by top management to obtain the employees' compliance in the program without deviation, subordinate managers are likely to feel helpless, asked to do the impossible, and misunderstood. They try to escape their feelings of inadequacy by blaming "unreasonable and uncontrollable" employees or "unreasonable and unsympathetic" superiors.

   Depending on their temperament, individual managers will tend either to (a) insist on more precise performance of the program, instituting closer controls, closer supervision, more rigorous use of rewards and punishments, or (b) abdicate, contacting subordinates as little as possible, giving instructions, and then busying themselves elsewhere.

5. In either case, whether the subordinate manager cracks down or with-draws, his employees tend to react to his response by developing new behavior patterns. These patterns tend to stabilize at a new level of minimal performance and minimal satisfaction so that all of the old problems remain while new anxieties are created.

6. At this point, top management becomes apprehensive and convinced that things are "out of control." Seeing widespread deviation from its predetermined program, top management is likely to respond to its anxieties by replacing the subordinate manager, applying more pressure for compliance, establishing more elaborate controls, or trying to train the subordinate manager in "how to get people to do what he wants them to."

7. Top management's action only serves to heighten the subordinate manager's anxieties and feelings of inadequacy. The proverbial "man in the middle," he finds his superiors expecting that he *should* be able to get his employees to perform strictly according to plan, and his subordinates expecting that he should attend to *their* needs which underlie their deviation.

8. No matter what the subordinate manager does, the likely outcome is that employees will feel more unappreciated and misunderstood than before, the subordinate manager more helpless and insecure, and top management more anxious about its lack of control.

9. Top management responds by devising new predetermined programs, installing new controls, shuffling personnel, but *not* by questioning any of its original assumptions. Thus, the cycle of unanticipated consequences starts all over again.[5]

Obviously something is wrong. The cycle of control, resistance, and more control cannot go on endlessly. Usually a compromise, or more accurately, a stalemate, is reached. Top management settles for standards of performance that fall short of budgeted expectations; and subordinates, including middle management, tacitly recognize but do not wholly accept or understand the need for control. An understanding of the reasons for resistance to controls enables us to prepare and install them in such a manner that the cycle of control, resistance, and more control never begins.

Why Resistance Develops

Seemingly, most of us have a built-in resistance to any form of control; perhaps such reactions are necessary for the preservation of one's own individuality. Nonetheless, as managers, we must learn not only to cope with our own reactions to control but also to meet and minimize the resistance of subordinates to control. The three steps of the control process — setting standards, measuring performance, and

---

[5]Robert L. Katz, "Toward a More Effective Enterprise," *Harvard Business Review*, Vol. 38, No. 5 (September-October, 1960), pp. 86–87. Copyright © 1960 by the President and Fellows of Harvard College; all rights reserved.

taking corrective action — provide a logical outline for our discussion of resistance to controls.

Standards Are Too Tight. A frequent initial reaction to budgets and other forms of control is the complaint that the standard of performance is unreasonable or too tight. There are several reasons why people respond in this manner. There may be no understanding of or desire to meet organizational objectives expressed by the standard. Such reactions occur when standards are imposed without any explanation concerning their need. Unless the reasons for standards can be presented in such a way that they become personal objectives for persons who are expected to meet such standards, complaints that the goals are unreasonable are sure to arise.

Another reason for objecting to standards is that historically they have a way of moving in only one direction — up. Consequently, is it any wonder that the initial reaction to them is the belief that they are unreasonable or too tight? A sales budget may show that a higher dollar volume is expected from each sales representative for the current year; however, the increased volume may be the result of higher prices rather than the result of an increase in the number of units sold. In a like manner, an increase in the number of units expected from a production worker is often the result of improved methods or more efficient production equipment that actually call for less effort on the worker's part. Since budgets are prepared annually and usually show a steady increase in expected performance, it is necessary that those affected by standards understand not only the reasons for the changing objectives but also how the new standards can be met.

The third reason for resistance to standards lies in the way in which they are administered on a day-to-day basis. Regardless of how carefully standards may have been developed, unexpected conditions arise that make their attainment impossible. Materials that fail to meet stated specifications or machine breakdowns lower the output of the production worker. Unexpected product developments by competitors or even unseasonable variations in the weather can affect the performance of a sales representative. In such cases the wise administrator notes the reasons for variances from standards and does not place undue pressure upon subordinates.

Measurements Not Accurate. Many times standards of performance are accepted, but the methods used in measuring performance are considered inaccurate. When control measures are criticized as not being accurate, more often than not factors other than accuracy are involved. The real complaint on the part of a supervisor operating under budgetary controls may be that the information provided is not timely enough to be of use in the operation of the department. Also, a supervisor's superior may criticize control measurements because they are not timely enough to aid in the coordination of the activities of several departments.

The comment is often heard that the measures used are satisfactory as far as they go, but they do not begin to measure all that is being done. The implication is that the measurements being used are not measuring those things that are important. The production foreman may agree that the unit count is an accurate statement of what is produced but reveals nothing about the decline in the number of units rejected by final inspection and the consequent decrease in the cost of rework. A salesperson may readily admit that the dollar volume statement of sales is correct and at the same time complain that the information used to measure sales performance is unfair because it does not reflect the number of new accounts or the miles and travel time required in order to call on customers. Before corrective action is taken, it is well to make sure that all the significant aspects of performance are being measured.

However, the bitterest complaint of all concerning measurements used in the control process is that they do not measure effort. Students may receive a grade of C on an assignment that in their opinion was worth at least a B in terms of the amount of effort expended. Unfortunately, for those whose work is subject to measurement and comparison to standard, the information required for control purposes is an accurate statement of the amount of variance from standard. A good supervisor will note the effort spent in doing a job and should commend a subordinate for such effort. By so doing, one may be able to minimize the normal resistance of subordinates to having their work measured — particularly when performance does not meet expected goals.

Dislike of Corrective Action. In the first paragraph of this section on behavioral reactions to control, it is stated that the administration of controls bears directly upon the people of an organization. Specifically, it is the corrective action taken as the result of failure to meet standards that is disliked and sometimes even feared. Somehow there is the belief that where there are no controls there is always the possibility that poor performance will not be noticed and, if detected, plausible excuses can be offered and will be accepted.

One reason for disliking corrective action, even a mild form of admonition, is that it is a form of criticism directed toward an individual. Criticism of a person can never be completely impersonal even though such criticism might be based upon an objective analysis of all the facts. Consequently, we all have a tendency to reject at least a part of any criticism and to interpret what is said with some degree of animosity.

Another reason for disliking corrective action is that it exposes a person's shortcomings to one's peers and sometimes to subordinates and superiors in the organization as well. Such exposure is practically unavoidable when demotion or discharge is the corrective action taken. It is the dislike and the fear of potential corrective action more than resistance to standards and criticisms of the methods of measurement that lead to most of the undesirable reactions to controls.

Unfavorable Responses to Controls

Our analysis of resistance to controls shows that any of the three steps of the control process may serve as a focal point for resistance. To some observers, resistance is regarded as a reaction to the pressures created by application of controls. Before studying the specific form of resistance demonstrated by either an individual or a group, let us find out why controls are commonly regarded as pressure devices.

Controls As Pressure Devices. There are two major reasons why controls, especially budgets, are commonly regarded as pressure devices. First, controls are standards of performance. Standards, like the 72-stroke par of golf, should be difficult but attainable. It is expected that the amount of effort expended by an individual in attaining a standard is somewhat greater than the amount expended if there were no stated standard. Thus, a certain degree of pressure is inherent and intended in any statement of standards. The second source of pressure arises from the procedures frequently followed in the installation and administration of controls. More often than not, controls are developed solely by top management and imposed upon the middle and the lower echelons of the organization. Supervisors and hourly employees alike cannot help but believe that top management is not entirely satisfied with the usual level of performance. Many times top management affirms their subordinates' view of controls as a means of pressure by pointing to the increases in productivity that occur after the installation of controls. Often the reaction to control imposed from above results in the control, inadequate response, more control cycle described earlier.

Improperly conceived and administered controls can result in serious human relations problems. One writer has summarized what may happen when budgets are improperly applied.

1. Budget pressure tends to unite the employees against management, and tends to place the factory supervisor under tension. This tension may lead to inefficiency, aggression, and perhaps a complete breakdown on the part of the supervisor.
2. The finance staff can obtain feelings of success only by finding fault with factory people. These findings of failure among factory supervisors lead to many human relations problems.
3. The use of budgets as "needlers" by top management tends to make each factory supervisor see only the problem of his own department.

4. Supervisors use budgets as a way of expressing their own patterns of leadership. When this results in people getting hurt, the budget, in itself a neutral thing, often gets blamed.[6]

Note that the pressure of budgets can affect both individuals and groups in an organization.

Effects on Individuals. Unfavorable individual responses to budgets or other controls on the part of supervisors are essentially reactions resulting from their failure either to understand or to meet stated budgetary goals. Occasionally the tensions and pressures created by budgets may result in a supervisor suffering a complete breakdown. Apathy, loss of interest in the job, and compliance to "the letter of the law" are forms of behavior that reflect a withdrawal from an unpleasant situation. Some supervisors respond with overt aggressiveness that is intended to shift the responsibility for failure to meet standards from themselves and their department to other departmental managers or to members of the staff organization.

Budgetary controls always contain the potential threat of disrupting cooperative relationships between members of the line and staff organizations. When imposed from above, the budget is developed and administered by a specialized staff group — usually a part of the controller's office. The measure of success of the budget staff is the extent to which the line managers meet the budgeted goals. Failure to meet these goals is interpreted as failure on the part of the line organization rather than the result of poorly stated or unattainable goals by the budget group. When budgets are fulfilled, ensuing budgets can be tightened so that they are more difficult to attain; thus, the line manager is once again faced with the threat of failure. Under these conditions, it is understandable why the relationships between the line manager and the controller's staff are in a state of perpetual conflict.

The departmental supervisor may generalize the conflict with the controller's staff and attempt to broaden the blame for difficulties arising from controls to other staff groups. The personnel department may be criticized for failure to enforce disciplinary action and for not supplying qualified and sufficient personnel. Quality control may be accused of setting quality specifications that make it impossible to meet budgeted cost and production standards. The production control staff comes under attack for failure to schedule long production runs and for scheduling unreasonable sequences in the production of different

---

[6]Chris Argyris, "Human Problems with Budgets," *Harvard Business Review*, Vol. 31 (January-February, 1953), p. 108. Copyright © 1976 by the President and Fellows of Harvard College; all rights reserved. Argyris' article is a report of a research study undertaken for the Controllership Foundation to determine the effects of budgets on human relationships in an organization and the extent to which budgets accomplish their purpose. Suggestions are given to improve the effectiveness of budgets.

products. Plant maintenance departments receive their share of criticism for not maintaining production equipment and other facilities at peak levels of efficiency.

The reactions discussed so far are descriptive of how the individual supervisor might react when controls are interpreted as a means of exerting pressure. The supervisor may withdraw from the situation through sickness or apathy or by becoming aggressive and striking out in any and all directions. There may be an attempt to shift the blame to other operating departments, to the controller's staff, or to other staff groups. Unfavorable reactions to controls do not remain individual reactions indefinitely; instead, individuals form cohesive groups and the strength of the group is utilized to combat the pressures of control.

Group Reaction to Pressure. Organized group resistance to any kind of external control pressure does not develop immediately, nor is it planned. However, the formation of group resistance is inevitable and follows a consistent evolutionary pattern. Argyris describes this process well:

1. First, the individuals sense an increase in pressure.
2. Then they begin to see definite evidences of the pressure. They not only feel it, they can point to it.
3. Since they feel this pressure is on them personally, they begin to experience tension and general uneasiness.
4. Next they usually "feel out" their fellow workers to see if they too sense the pressure.
5. Finding out that others have noted the pressure, they begin to feel more at ease. It helps to be able to say, "I'm not the only one."
6. Finally, they realize that they can acquire emotional support from each other by becoming a group. Furthermore, they can "blow their top" about this pressure in front of their group.[7]

When leadership crystallizes and emerges, the group is ready to act in unison. Let us see what happens; first, on the hourly level; then, within the ranks of management.

The Hourly Level. Assume that the production of a manufacturing department, or the output of a clerical section, is stabilized at a rate that time study shows to be 65 percent of standard. Certain conditions or forces are holding production at this level. Perhaps supervision is satisfied, and an output of 65 percent of standard may be the most comfortable pace considering the methods used in performing the work. The individual worker has no reason for deviating from this pattern since conformance assures continued membership in the group and enables one to assume the protective coloring of the group. Now, incorporate the time study data into standards and express these standards as part of a budget — unannounced and imposed from above.

---

[7]*Ibid.*, p. 100.

Pressure is felt first by the supervisors, who, in turn, attempt to enforce the newly stated standards by requiring an increased level of production. The development of group cohesiveness as described by Argyris begins. Eventually a static state of balance between the pressures of the budget and the pressures of the group may be reached; a level higher than the original 65 percent but still short of the budgeted 100 percent. These are the *frozen* groups of Zaleznik or the *sick* groups described by Gellerman.[8] When the informal group achieves cohesiveness and adopts the leadership and resources of a formal organization — the union — the groundwork is laid for labor-management strife.

Groups Within Management. The formation of groups whose primary purpose is to combat the pressures exerted by top management is not limited to groups composed of hourly or clerical employees. Informal groups may develop within the ranks of management as well. The first-line supervisors of a plant may feel themselves caught between the pressure of the budget from above and the resistance of their subordinates from below. They are literally caught in the middle and seek the support offered by others who are in the same position. When talking to subordinates, the supervisor blames the "budget people" for the pressures of production. When reporting to a superior, the incompetence and the uncooperativeness of subordinates are offered as the causes for failure to meet budgeted expectations. There are instances of supervisory groups having become so firmly solidified that they eventually became formal unions of supervisors. Many supervisory or management clubs have been formed to nullify the cohesiveness of informal groups of supervisors and forestall their becoming formal union organizations. The labor unions of engineers and scientists, though not directly the result of budgetary controls, are another example of resistance to top management that has led to the formation of groups so that group pressure may be applied in opposition to the pressure exerted by management.

Informal groups may develop within either the line or the staff organization and make it almost impossible to achieve the benefits that might be realized from the application of budgets or other forms of control. When line management unites as a group and opposes the recommendations of the staff organization, one can be sure that the staff, as a group, will oppose any suggested modifications of their programs that come from members of the line organization.

Effective Use of Controls

Our review of those aspects of the control process that cause resistance, the concept of pressure associated with the administration of

---

[8]See Chapter 16, "Motivating Employees," p. 386.

budgets, and the responses of individuals and groups to pressure does not seem to offer much encouragement for the successful application of controls. Fortunately, there are ways to minimize resistance to controls. The following suggestions have been found helpful in making the application of controls more effective.

Establish Proper Attitudes. The attitudes of the members of an organization toward controls depend on the underlying motivation of top management. Controls can be established as a device to goad managers into better performance, or they can be used by the managers themselves as an instrument for measuring and guiding performance. These two divergent uses of controls are analogous to the uses that may be found for two long pieces of wood. At the end of one piece of wood, there is a sharp point. This piece of wood is used as a prod to keep managers in line and moving in the right direction. Another piece of wood — the same length, is divided into 36 equal segments and becomes the familiar yardstick, a tool that can be used to measure progress. For controls to be most effective, they must be regarded as yardsticks developed to measure performance rather than prods intended to keep people in line. The development of proper attitudes towards the goals established by control is most likely to occur when there is participation in the goal-setting process.[9]

Place Controls in the Hands of Managers. One of the best ways top management has of expressing its understanding of controls is by placing the responsibility for their preparation and administration in the hands of departmental managers. True, a well-trained controller's staff is valuable in company-wide consolidation and coordination, but the preparation and administration of controls at the operating level are best accomplished by the responsible manager. In preparing controls, managers should make the first draft; then if revisions are needed, cooperative effort between the controller's office and line management is required to reach a final statement of goals. In order to administer controls properly, managers must have adequate standards of performance, timely information concerning their performance, and freedom to manage. Standards serve as a measure of performance and form the backbone of any control. In manufacturing departments, standards should be developed for labor, materials, supplies, and the maintenance of equipment. Standards of performance and cost can also be determined for administrative and sales units. The controller should

---

[9]See the discussion in Chapter 3 of management by objectives, pp. 45–52.

Also the following two papers support the need for participation in setting budgetary and other control goals. Roger L. M. Dunbar, "Budgeting for Control," *Administrative Science Quarterly*, Vol. 16, No. 1 (March, 1971), pp. 88–96, and D. Gerald Searfoss and Robert M. Monczka, "Perceived Participation in the Budget Process and Motivation to Achieve the Budget," *Academy of Management Journal*, Vol. 16, No. 4 (December, 1973), pp. 541–554.

provide departmental managers with timely information so that necessary corrections may be made and so that performance conforms to budgeted expectations. Controls are not intended to restrict the activities of managers; they must have freedom to manage. So that freedom in operations may be increased, some companies state only the total of the expense items and leave to the discretion of the manager the allocation of the amount to be spent for each item. Finally, procedures must be clearly stated to set forth steps to be followed in securing revisions, and practice must show that such revisions are possible.

Follow Organizational Lines. Fundamental to effective budgetary control is a clear concept of organization structure. Managers of departments must know their immediate superiors and also their immediate subordinates. In addition, the relationships with other departments must be clearly defined. When organizational lines are clearly stated, the budgets become the yardstick capable of measuring performance; however, when organizational lines are fuzzy and ill defined, there is a tendency to use the budget as a prod since there is no means of defining duties and assigning responsibilities. The clarity of organizational definition marks the upper limit of the effectiveness of controls as a determinant of organizational performance.

Case Problem 20-B is a continuation of Case Problem 20-A. All did not go as planned, and now there is need for corrective action. Two points are illustrated in this closing case. First, even though performance did not measure up to expectations, the presence of a budget pinpoints the areas requiring corrective action. Second, each variation from a budget may be small, but the aggregate can sometimes be alarming.

Case Problem 20-B
A NEED FOR CORRECTIVE ACTION

It was the latter part of January before the Barrs completed the proposed revenue and expense budget described in Case Problem 20-A. Only then did they know they would not make a profit during the first quarter of the year and that the best they could expect would be to break even by the end of June. In an attempt to offset the normally slow months of February, March, and April, they decided to increase advertising outlays and to gain a competitive advantage by lowering prices slightly. During the year they hired additional sales personnel to offset their own lack of sales experience and knowledge of the men's clothing business. Also, the lease expired during the year, and a new one was negotiated at a somewhat higher figure. The results of the Barrs' first full year of managing the store are shown in Exhibit III, page 516.

PROBLEMS

1. Are the results shown in Exhibit III attributable to poor budgeting techniques or to poor management? Explain.
2. What corrective action would you take as manager of this store?

THE AVENUE MEN'S STORE

Account	Budgeted % of Net Sales ($200,000)	Actual Dollar Rev./Exp.	Actual Percentage of Budgeted Net Sales ($200,000)
Sales:			
1. Gross sales	102.6	$206,000	103.0
2. Customer ret. & allow.	2.6	5,000	2.5
3. Net sales	100.0	201,000	101.0
Cost of goods sold:			
4. Beginning inventory	30.9	61,800	30.9
5. Net purchases plus transportation charges paid	66.1	137,000	68.5
6. Total cost of merchandise handled	97.0	198,000	99.4
7. Ending inventory	32.3	66,800	33.4
8. Net cost of mdse. sold	64.7	132,000	66.0
9. Net busheling (alterations) cost	2.1	6,000	3.0
10. Total cost of mdse. sold	66.8	138,000	69.0
11. Gross margin	33.2	62,000	31.0
Operating expenses:			
12. Payroll:			
A. Salaries of owners	7.3	14,600	7.3
B. Salaries and wages of employees	9.0	21,000	10.5
Total payroll	16.3	35,600	17.8
13. Rent expense	2.9	6,000	3.0
14. Taxes and license fees (omit real estate, Federal income and sales taxes)	1.1	2,200	1.1
15. Insurance	.6	1,200	.6
16. Depreciation & amort.	.8	1,600	.8
17. Repairs	.2	200	.1
18. Supplies (omit rep. mat'ls.)	1.0	2,400	1.2
19. Services purchased	.9	1,400	.7
20. Traveling (business trips)	.3	400	.2
21. Communications (include parcel post)	.4	1,200	.6
22. Advertising and publicity	2.8	6,400	3.2
23. Professional services (outside professional agencies)	.2	200	.1
24. Unclassified:			
A. Losses from bad debts	.3	800	.4
B. Other unclassified	.5	1,200	.6
Total unclassified expenses	.8	2,000	1.0
25. Total expenses	28.3	60,800	30.4
26. Net profit (before Federal income taxes)	4.9	1,200	.6

**Exhibit III
BUDGETED AND
ACTUAL
PERFORMANCE**

CHAPTER QUESTIONS FOR STUDY AND DISCUSSION

1. How are budgets different from other kinds of business plans? Show why each of these differences is necessary.
2. Are the terms budget and standard synonymous? If so, what type of standards are utilized in the development of the four major types of budgets?
3. Discuss the following statement: Flexible budgets make periodic budgetary reviews unnecessary.
4. What is the purpose of zero-base budgeting? What benefits may be derived from the utilization of the zero-base budgeting concept?
5. Should expense budgets be stated at a lower figure than that actually computed in order that final expenses will not exceed the budgeted amount? Support your answer.
6. Why are budgets or other controls many times regarded as "pressure devices"?
7. Of what worth would a control be if it did not create pressure? Discuss.
8. What are the attitudes essential for the effective use of controls?
9. Describe the steps you would take to offset the usual resistance that develops when controls are installed.
10. Describe the steps you would take in establishing an effective sales budget.

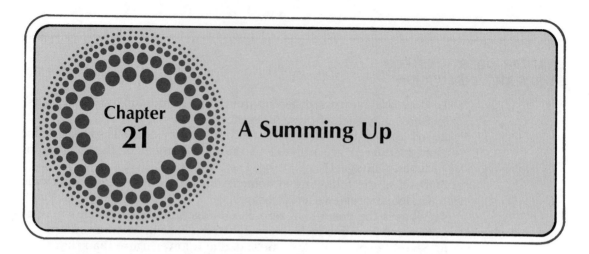

Chapter 21   A Summing Up

The four functions of the management process — planning, organizing, leading, and controlling — are utilized as a broad framework for the study of management. These functions should not be regarded as discrete steps in the management process; instead, they should be regarded as interdependent subsystems with each subsystem contributing its share to the total system of management. In the last paragraph of Chapter 20, the interdependence between the control function and the organizing function is indicated by the statement that clear organization structure is fundamental to effective control. The control function also depends upon sound planning and effective leadership.

The first step in summing up our study of management is an integration of the four functions of the management process. Next, there is a summary of the systems concept and its application to the management of systems. Some of the major issues confronting today's managers, to be resolved by the managers of the future, are presented, and we conclude with a brief epilogue that discusses the introductory course to management in relation to other courses in the business administration curriculum.

INTEGRATING MANAGEMENT FUNCTIONS

A major assumption underlying the management of formal organizations is that such organizations are teleological in nature. The extent of commitment to purpose is in large measure the result of the clarity and manner in which objectives are stated. Without objectives there is no need for a formal organization; and were it possible to create a formal organization without a stated purpose, it would soon deteriorate and dissolve. Similarly, an existing organization that no longer has a goal to fulfill — e.g., one whose product or service is no longer needed or desired by society — must recast its objectives if the organization is to survive. It is axiomatic that without an organization there is no need for managers or the management process. Hence objectives are considered fundamental to the process of management.

Admittedly there are differences of opinion concerning whether the setting of objectives should be considered as part of planning or regarded as an activity distinct from and preceding the planning function. There is no right or wrong answer concerning the inclusion of objectives as a part of planning or the consideration of objectives as a distinct activity. Those who favor the inclusion of objectives as a part of the planning process point out that planning activities are sometimes needed to clearly define an objective and that stated objectives are sometimes modified as the result of undertaking the development of plans for the fulfillment of previously stated goals. Those who view the setting of objectives as being apart from and preceding the planning function do so to add emphasis to the importance of setting objectives and to stress the need for a clear-cut goal before undertaking any activity. Further, objectives may result from individual desires or needs neither related to nor dependent upon planning. In this text objectives are considered apart from the function of planning, yet susceptible to modification as the result of subsequent planning. Regardless of the inclusion or exclusion of the setting of objectives as part of the planning function, it is agreed that objectives are basic to the management process. We now review the functions of that process.

Planning — Control — Planning Cycle

Most introductory textbooks of management discuss the planning function first and follow with a treatment of the functions of organizing and leading in that sequence, then close with a discussion of the control function. However, it is more in keeping with the performance of managerial functions to regard the planning and control functions as a continuous cycle. The chief reason for presenting the functions separately is that such separation provides a convenient framework for organizing the functions of the process of management in a manner that facilitates the analysis of each function. Also, it is difficult to discuss the control function immediately after a discussion of planning since control is dependent so much upon the structure of the organization. Without knowledge of the organizing function and familiarity with the terminology used to describe organizational processes and relationships, the concept of control can be presented only in vague and general terms. In addition, the nature of and the manner in which the leadership function is executed is a major variable in determining the effectiveness of any control procedure. Before discussing the planning-control-planning cycle, let us first examine briefly each function separately.

Planning. Planning is generally accorded a position of primacy among the management functions since logically it is the first function that should be performed. Also, planning is considered pervasive in nature because planning is required to form the organization, to determine the patterns of leadership, and to design the control system. The results of planning are plans that serve as guides for the actions of the members of the organization in the achievement of stated objectives. In addition to those plans that are developed to serve a given project, such as locating and building a new plant, some plans become relatively permanent in nature and are sometimes called standing plans. These plans, depending upon their breadth or scope, are classified as policies, procedures, or methods.

In its simpliest form planning is an activity that can be executed by any member of an organization as illustrated by the planning of one's activities for a day, several days, or a week. As the nature of the problem under consideration becomes more complex, so do the methods of planning. In medium and large organizations the volume of data gathered to be analyzed and evaluated prior to making a final choice has increased significantly with the utilization of electronic data processing in the planning process. Part of the increase in the amount of data evaluated in the planning process is the result of a desire to improve the quality of the final plan by developing and examining many alternative courses of action, and part is due to the capabilities of information processing equipment. Because of virtually unlimited capabilities for storage, retrieval, and processing of data, there is a tendency to examine more data than needed simply because it is available.

Control. The purpose of the control function is to insure the proper execution of plans. Control is accomplished through a three-step process — the determination of expected standards of performance, the measurement of current performance in relation to expected standards, and the taking of corrective action when necessary to insure that standards are met. The sequence of events, the date each event is to be completed, and the organization responsible for the completion of a given event are quite evident when plans are developed in detail and are highly structured. The budget, the instrument most frequently associated with the control function, is a plan for profit that has been converted into dollars to be received, spent, and earned during a specified period of time. Similarly, the time-event-network analysis used as a means of control is a statement of the sequence and timing of activities to be accomplished in order to complete a given project.

The Cycle. The planning and control functions of management are best described as a planning-control-planning cycle since each of these functions is a different aspect of the same continuous management information system. Information for planning is drawn from external environmental sources such as socioeconomic data. Financial and other internal resources available in the form of physical plant and personnel are also utilized in planning. Control relies heavily upon internal data developed as the result of the execution of plans; yet changes in the external environment, for example the actions of competitors and customers, are also significant. More often than not, when corrective action is required the modification of plans is a part of that action. The interlocking nature of the information utilized in the planning and control functions is illustrated in Figure 6-1, page 137.

However, the planning-control-planning cycle is but one phase of the management process. Organizations are required to develop and execute plans, and organizations must be actuated in order to achieve the desired level of effectiveness.

Organizing

The classical approach to the study of organization reveals two major themes. The first is concern for the structuring of work and results in the creation of roles that guide and limit the behavior of people. Closely associated with and a part of the process of structuring is the subsequent arrangement of work into manageable units. The structuring and arranging of work into units is known as departmentation. The arrangement of these units of work under the jurisdiction of a single manager creates a span of management. The second theme that appears in the classical discussions of the organizing function is the concept of authority. There are two major opinions concerning the source of authority — the institutional source which states that authority is derived from society and the subordinate acceptance view which holds that authority is granted by subordinates.

Another facet of authority is its transfer within the organization. Superior-subordinate relationships are referred to as the chain of command, and the process of transferring authority from superior to subordinate is known as the delegation of authority. When the subordinate is a manager of a lower level organizational unit, the process of delegating authority to that manager is known as the decentralization of authority. Although the phrase, decentralization of authority, is used frequently to describe the authority relationships between a plant manager and a vice-president of manufacturing or between a district sales manager and a vice-president of marketing, it is best to reserve the term decentralization for those instances where the decentralized unit is of sufficient scope so that there is a clear responsibility for profits. Such a limitation requires the unit manager to have responsibility for both the production function and the marketing function.

It is apparent that there is an obvious need for an organization — defining an organization as people with assigned and interrelated roles — to execute the planning function. Of equal significance are the benefits obtained for the well-defined organization in executing the control function. A clearly defined organization aids in the flow of information necessary for the measurement of performance. The corrective action of the control function is accomplished by the managers responsible for the variance from expected standards. It is difficult to designate which managers are responsible without a clearly defined organization.

Leading

The leadership function is termed variously as leading, directing, actuating, or motivating. Despite the variation in terminology used to designate the function, it is agreed that the purpose of the function is to elicit desired forms of behavior on the part of the members of the organization. Within the context of independent, intervening, and dependent variables leadership is best regarded as an independent variable — an input into the organization intended to influence behavior. The results of effective leadership are expressed in many ways. The statement of objectives may be an expression of the goals of one person, or it may represent a consensus of the top echelon of the organization. The quality of leadership is reflected in the development and execution of plans, in the clarity and appropriateness of the organizational structure, and in the design and administration of control systems.

Leadership in formal organizations includes not only those characteristics of interpersonal relationships known as leadership style; it also includes all of the actions of a manager necessary for the performance of the managerial functions of planning, organizing, and controlling, as well as the selection of the appropriate style of leadership. Consequently, the concept of managing is broader in scope than the concept of leading. Similarly, the managerial function known as leading is broader than the interpersonal relationships between manager and subordinate. Among the managerial functions associated with the function of leadership are the design and administration of motivational systems, planning and executing formal communication programs, and the staffing and development of the organization on a continuing basis. The performance of these managerial functions is a major contribution to the formation of organizational climate, which in turn becomes a significant determinant of behavior of the members of the organization.

MANAGEMENT AND THE SYSTEMS CONCEPT

Utilization of the systems concept is another means of emphasizing the integrative nature of the management process. In Chapter 2, an integrative view outlining the parts of a system and the processes that link a system is presented. In Chapter 5, the major business functions — finance, marketing, production, and personnel — are examined within the context of a servo system, and in Chapter 8 the parameters of a systems approach to organization theory are presented. The development of information systems is discussed in Chapter 6. The control function and its contribution as a part of a cybernetic system is presented in Chapter 18.

Since the systems concept is utilized as a way of describing the management process, it is helpful to present in summary form two aspects of systems theory that are of particular significance to managers. First is recognition that there is no single system; instead, there is a wide range in the complexity of systems with the result that systems are best regarded as forming a hierarchy. The hierarchical arrangement of systems is shown in Figure 21-1. The second aspect of systems theory significant to managers is an understanding of the characteristics of open systems since managers are concerned primarily with the management of social systems, a form of open system. The characteristics of open systems are shown in Figure 21-2 on page 525.

A Hierarchy of Systems

Boulding's classification of systems into a hierarchy of levels of complexity is in effect a "system of systems."[1] His classification is of value because it is one more step toward a general systems theory intended to unify the many diverse fields of knowledge. It is also useful in that it shows the evolutionary nature of systems as well as the differences and similarities that exist among the many types of systems.[2]

The first systems level, static structure, is descriptive in nature. An accurate descriptive statement of the phenomenon being studied is a necessary first step in the development of knowledge. An accurate description is also necessary to progress to the second level which is an analysis and description of simple dynamic relationships. Simple dynamic systems may evolve into cybernetic systems capable of maintaining a balanced dynamic relationship within specified limits. Although dynamic systems, such as the solar system, maintain a dynamic relationship due to gravitational forces, the cybernetic system marks the beginning of the utilization of information as a means of keeping the system in balance.

The fourth, fifth, sixth, and seventh levels of the systems hierarchy show gradations in the complexity of living organisms. The cell, level number four, clearly marks the beginning of open systems. Open systems must interact with their environment in order to survive. Energy

---

[1] Kenneth E. Boulding, "General Systems Theory — The Skeleton of Science," *Management Science*, Vol. 2, No. 3 (April, 1956), pp. 197–208.

[2] The following papers are recommended for those interested in exploring the concept of a general systems theory.

Ludwig von Bertalanffy, "The History and Status of General Systems Theory," *Academy of Management Journal*, Vol. 15, No. 4 (December, 1972). pp. 407–426.

Newman S. Peery, Jr., "General Systems Theory: An Inquiry Into Its Social Philosophy," *Academy of Management Journal*, Vol. 15, No. 4 (December, 1972), pp. 495–510.

Frederick Thayer, "General System(s) Theory: The Promise That Could Not Be Kept," *Academy of Management Journal*, Vol. 15, No. 4 (December, 1972), pp. 481–493.

1. *Static structure* is a level of *frameworks*; for example, the geography and anatomy of the universe, the pattern of structure of atoms, genes, cells, and the solar system.
2. *Dynamic systems* are known as the level of *clockworks*; machines, ranging from a simple lever to complex steam and gasoline engines, fall into this category.
3. *Cybernetic systems*, known as the level of the *thermostat*, are capable of maintaining a dynamic relationship within specified limits.
4. *Open systems* are the beginning of life and may be termed the level of the *cell*. There are self-maintaining characteristics and the ability to reproduce.
5. *Genetic-societal systems* are the level of the *plant* and are characterized by a division of labor among the cells with differentiated yet dependent parts such as roots, leaves, seeds, etc.
6. *Animal systems* are the next level and are characterized by increased mobility, purposeful behavior, and self-awareness. Also, specialized receptors for receiving outside information are developed.
7. *Human systems* incorporate all of the characteristics of animal systems and in addition there is self-consciousness and the ability to interpret and manipulate symbols.
8. *Social systems* are composed of humans and at this level the concept of values, the development of historical records, and the expression of the arts appear.
9. *Transcendental systems* are in the words of Boulding "the ultimates and absolutes and the inescapable unknowables, and they also exhibit systematic structure and relationship."

Figure 21-1
A HIERARCHY OF SYSTEMS

Source: Kenneth E. Boulding, "General Systems Theory — The Skeleton of Science," *Management Science*, Vol. 2, No. 3 (April, 1956), pp. 202–205.)

is imported from outside; a through-put or conversion of that energy occurs with part of the energy being used by the organism to sustain life itself and part being exported to the environment as an output. One of the outputs of animal life, carbon dioxide, is imported by plant life, and during the through-put is converted then exported as oxygen, to be imported by animal life. Recognition of the symbiotic relationships that exist between the many forms of life is the basis for the current drive to improve the quality of our environment.

Note that social systems are eighth in the hierarchy of complexity. This is the level of greatest interest to students of management because managers manage and are members of social systems. Obviously a human being (also a system) is a component of social systems, yet it is doubtful that people are the unifying aspect of social systems. Instead, it appears that roles — expected and prescribed behavior — are the basis for the continuity and predictability of organizations.

Perhaps the greatest value of Boulding's classification is that it clearly shows the nature of our problem in studying the management of organizations. It is doubtful that there are any thoroughly tested theoretical models beyond level four. We have fairly accurate models of dynamic and cybernetic systems, borrowed from the physical sciences, that we try to apply to level eight, social systems. Such applications have inherent and obvious shortcomings, yet they are all that is available at the present time. With these limitations in mind, let us examine the characteristics of open systems as shown in Figure 21-2.

1. *Importation of Energy*. Open systems import energy from the external environment; for example, the cell imports oxygen, food, and water from the external environment.
2. *The Through-put*. Open systems convert energy into a form that can be utilized, thus within the system work is accomplished with part of the imported energy utilized to maintain the system itself.
3. *The Output*. Open systems export a product or service to the external environment.
4. *Cycles of Events*. Social systems, a form of open systems, are best regarded as cycles of events rather than being considered as things or objects.
5. *Negative Entropy*. Entropy is the tendency for systems to disintegrate or die; in order to survive systems must develop negative entropy.
6. *Feedback*. An open system must maintain a continuing source of information concerning its relationship with the external environment; the feedback of this information to the system enables the system to measure its relationship to the external environment and make necessary corrections in order to survive.
7. *Dynamic Homeostasis*. Open systems maintain a steady state or a condition of homeostasis. Since a homeostatic condition presents a continual energy exchange between inputs and outputs the term dynamic homeostasis is utilized.
8. *Differentiation*. As open systems develop there is a tendency toward differentiation and specialization so that the system may operate in a more efficient manner.
9. *Equifinality*. The concept of equifinality states that a given end condition may be attained from several different starting points and by means of different pathways to the end condition.

Figure 21-2 CHARACTERISTICS OF OPEN SYSTEMS

Source: Daniel Katz and Robert L. Kahn, *The Social Psychology of Organizations* (New York: John Wiley & Sons, 1966), pp. 19–26.

Characteristics of Open Systems

The elements of the basic model of open systems are expressed in the first three open systems characteristics — the importation of energy, the through-put, and the output. The fourth characteristic offers a way of viewing open systems as cycles of events. The next three characteristics — negative entropy, feedback, and dynamic homeostasis — are attributes that contribute to the continuity, or life, of open systems. The remaining characteristics — differentiation and equifinality — are helpful in understanding the functioning of complex social organizations. Each of these three groups of open system characteristics is examined.[3]

The Model. The basic open system model is that of an energetic input-output system. Energy is imported from the external environment; there is a transformation of that energy in the through-put with part of the energy being used to maintain the system itself and part being exported as an output to the external environment. The fourth characteristic is an admonition that it is best to regard the three steps of importation, transformation, and exportation as events rather than objects or things.

For the manufacturing firm the production function is one of creating a product. The product is exported to the external environment where it is exchanged for cash which, in turn, is exchanged for raw materials so that the cycle of procurement, production, and sales begins anew. However, not all of the money realized from the sale of the product is utilized for the purchase of raw materials. Part must be used to maintain the system itself. People must be paid, capital equipment must be maintained and replaced, and the costs of promotional efforts in the selling of the product must be met.

The production function, or through-put, is present in all formal social organizations. For the air transport industry it is the transportation of passengers and freight; for the educational institution it is the education of people; and for the charitable organization it is the distribution of benefits to its recipients. In each case there is a definite sequence of events — importation, transformation, and exportation.

Sustaining Characteristics. Entropy is the tendency for systems to disintegrate and die. Open systems, by importing more energy than required for the conversion process in the through-put and the maintenance of the system, can theoretically arrest entropic processes. To a degree biological systems import more than is required for immediate needs and are able to store energy; however, the quality of the energy imported is not of the type required to forestall entropy indefinitely.

However, formal social organizations have potentially an unlimited duration. Yet few have succeeded in lasting more than a century or so. Among those that have lasted longer are the Roman Catholic Church, Harvard University, and the Hudson Bay Corporation. Maintenance subsystems must be created if social organizations are to arrest entropy. One such subsystem is the financial function of organizations. There must be sufficient monetary inputs so that the system can

---

[3]Daniel Katz and Robert L. Kahn, *The Social Psychology of Organizations* (New York: John Wiley & Sons, 1966). This work is a major theoretical contribution to the study of social organizations as systems. The discussion above is based upon Chapter 2, "Organizations and the System Concept," and Chapter 3, "Defining Characteristics of Social Organizations," pp. 14–70.

perform its production function and have enough energy (money) remaining to bring new people into the organization; to prepare these people to perform necessary organizational roles; and to make these roles so rewarding that the people do not voluntarily leave the organization. When the personnel function is viewed as the development of the characteristic of negative entropy, its importance becomes obvious. The human asset accounting used by the R. G. Barry Corporation (Chapter 19) tacitly recognizes that organization development is the development of negative entropy.

Adaptive systems are necessary to sustain the open system. There must be provision for an informational feedback between the system and its environment and between the subsystems of the total system. The internal feedback of information between the financial, personnel, production, and marketing functions are shown within the context of a servo system in Figure 5-3 (page 118). The marketing function is a part of the feedback loop with the customer. The financial and personnel functions must also maintain informational circuits with organizations outside the system and provide the information necessary for the system to adapt to both internal and external changes. Management information systems are an adaptive mechanism.

Systems must maintain a steady state, or equilibrium, to survive. However, a steady state is not a constant; instead, it is a prescribed range of variation. Hence the term, dynamic homeostasis. Open systems undergo constant change in the process of adapting to internal changes as well as to external changes, yet the change is within prescribed limits and occurs over a period of time with the result that there is seldom a loss of identity. The growth of plants and animals is an example of continuous change with the retention of identity. Formal organizations lose members who must be replaced; products and services are modified to meet the changing needs of customers; and changes must be made within the system itself in respect to both structure and function if it is to survive in an ever changing environment. Market research, product development, and long-range planning are some of the adaptive functions that contribute to the maintenance of a dynamic homeostasis in business firms.

Differentiation and Equifinality. As open systems become more complex there is a differentiation of functions with specialized resources being developed for each function. The one-man hamburger stand is illustrative. In the beginning the one man performs the four functions of the management process; in addition, he performs the business functions of finance, production, sales and personnel. He is an undifferentiated organization. As the business grows, limitations imposed by time and knowledge force the process of differentiation and specialization. The need for a subsystem known as management develops long before the hamburger stand becomes a chain of restaurants.

Plans must be made for the continuity of the business, an organization must be created and directed, and a control function must be established. In this sense, management is a subsystem whose function is to coordinate, control, and direct the activities of the other subsystems.

The concept of equifinality may be paraphrased by the old saying, "there is more than one way of skinning a cat." The process of attaining a stated dollar sales volume offers an example of equifinality in business firms. The stated sales volume may be attained by expanding existing facilities, by developing new products, and by increasing one's share of the market. It is a method often referred to as internal growth or growth from within. The same sales objectives may be reached by the acquisition and merger route. Although there is a measure of equifinality in all organizations, there is some evidence that as the degree of differentiation and specialization of open systems increases there is a corresponding decrease in the characteristic of equifinality.

CURRENT ISSUES IN MANAGEMENT

One of the favorite topics of those writers who popularize management are predictions of what managers of the future will do. Such forecasts are often extrapolated from a superficial examination of one aspect of management and based upon somewhat tenuous assumptions. Rather than predict the future, it seems more prudent to discuss current issues confronting today's managers since these are the issues to be resolved by the managers of tomorrow. Admittedly, not all students of management would select the three issues discussed below; however, these three would in all probability be included in a ranking of the ten most significant issues by serious students of management. The issues discussed are related to information technology, organization development, and the social value issues in business.

Information Technology

With the advent of the computer there has been a change, not only in the method of processing information, but also in the significance of information per se in the management of formal organizations. We have moved from the laborious transcription of data by hand and decisions based largely on intuition and personal experience to electronic data processing and its seemingly limitless capability to process, store, and retrieve information to be used in the decision-making process. Virtually all medium and large business organizations utilize electronic data processing to some degree, and many are well along the way toward the development of a completely integrated data processing system designed to integrate all information necessary for planning and control. Implied in the development of integrated data processing is a centralized information processing function. What effect will the establishment of integrated data processing have on the degree of centralization of authority to make decisions, and what effect will it have on the functions of the middle manager?

Traditionally some positions, such as district sales manager, have considerable authority to make decisions since the manager is the one person in the organization who knows the customers and their needs. When a company installs an information system that permits the customer to order directly through a remote terminal to an information center that processes the order, prepares billing and shipping instructions from the coded input, and notifies the warehouse to ship the item, such procedures are bound to affect the functions of the field sales force. Another typical middle management position, the production control manager, has considerable influence and decision-making authority in many plants. However, when the information system is extended to correct the inventory balance automatically and, when necessary, to notify a plant to replenish the item to a predetermined inventory level, the role of the production control manager is changed significantly.

There is no single criterion that can be used to predict the effect of integrated data processing upon the degree of centralization or decentralization of authority to make decisions within a given company or the effect that it will have upon middle management positions such as those described above. Arguments have been developed that have equal force in predicting either a greater degree of centralization or a greater degree of decentralization of authority to make decisions as the result of integrated data processing. However, two factors seem highly significant in determining the probable effects of integrated data processing within a given company. First is the basic philosophy of the company. If it is the desire of the company to place decision making at the lowest possible level of the organization, information technology can serve as an effective means of placing complete information for the decision-making process in the hands of lower echelon managers. However, if the desire is to centralize decision making as much as possible, information technology can be used for that end. The second factor is the technology of the organization, and that technology may limit the philosophical desires of management. For some organizations, the technology may be such that the need for a high degree of centralization outweighs the philosophical inclinations of management to decentralize. For other companies, technology may be such that decentralization of the authority to make decisions may be realized, provided management has the desire to move in that direction.

Another aspect of information technology, and one seldom treated in discussions of the subject, is its effect upon what may be termed human values or the quality of life. Almost everyone has had the frustrating and discouraging experience of trying to correct a billing error.

As yet there seems to be no effective way for a customer to have a computerized billing error corrected. Another example, and one most students will appreciate, is the tendency to identify people by number rather than by name. Colleges or universities use the student's social security number as a means of identification. The same number is used when opening a bank account, when seeking employment, and when applying for retirement benefits. There is a recent serious proposal that each child entering the first grade be issued a social security number — it could be argued that the number should be issued at birth, thereby assuring the collection of more accurate vital statistics. Surely, such a process of reducing names to numbers has its effect on the quality of life.

Organization Development

Formal development programs are not uncommon in business firms. As a first step many programs utilize color-coded charts as a basis for determining personnel needs arising from anticipated growth and attrition resulting from retirement. In such manner, the managerial needs of the organization may be determined quite accurately. Some companies establish formal training programs that utilize facilities staffed by company personnel; in addition, programs offered outside the company by universities may be used. Also, managers may be encouraged to seek advanced degrees through tuition rebates and other financial incentives. The goals of organization development programs range from the supplying of needed managerial manpower to that of changing the management style of the organization. Despite widespread interest in and support of organization development, it is highly doubtful that many companies define organization development within the context of open system characteristics. Until organization development is viewed as a process of developing the characteristic of negative entropy, the full potential of organization development programs cannot be realized.

Though the phrase, organization development, indicates that it is the organization that is being developed, the actual means of such development is the development of individual members of the organization. Yet, there is a serious question to be resolved concerning the degree of compatibility that exists between the individual and the organization. Written records indicate that humans have always been social creatures and have lived and functioned as members of a group. However, in recent years much has been written concerning conflicts that result from the pressures of the organization and its demands upon the individual and the needs for fulfillment and self-actualization on the part of the individual. Such expressions of doubt concerning the compatibility of the individual and the organization are not confined to the ranks of managers as evidenced by interest in job enrichment and job satisfaction at the hourly level. Thus one of the major issues in organization development is that of striking a balance between the needs of the organization and the needs of the individual; further, it is a problem that exists at all levels of the organization.

Social Value Issues

Perhaps the most significant issues confronting today's corporate managers — to be resolved by the managers of tomorrow — are in the broad area of social values. One issue is size. Is size, defined as a combination of sales volume and number of employees, sufficient grounds for subjecting a corporation to the antitrust divestiture procedure? What is the role of the corporation vis-a-vis community, state, and national government agencies? What responsibility does the corporation have for improving the blighted areas of our cities or for employing and training the disadvantaged? These and similar questions require value judgments in their solution.

As a first step in answering questions requiring value judgments in their solution, it is necessary to develop an appropriate model of the present-day corporation. At one extreme there is the traditional economic model of the corporation. Within this framework the corporation is an instrument that is designed primarily to serve the stockholders. The welfare of employees is, at best, a secondary goal. Customers are included in the model, but in its extreme form the guide for relationships with customers is *caveat emptor*. Using this model the criterion provided for the resolution of social issues is the welfare of the stockholder. The model provides no clearly defined relationship with community, state, or national government. The other extreme is the metrocorporation. Here the managers, not the stockholders, are the decisive group. Managers must consider not only the wishes of the stockholder, but in addition those of the government, employee groups, customers, and the needs of society as a whole. The firm is regarded as a "citizen" of society with obligations to other "citizen groups." Government is accepted in full partnership so that the general welfare of society may be enhanced. If hard choices are to be made between the welfare of the firm and the welfare of society, the number of persons who might benefit would be a dominant consideration in making the decision rather than the welfare of the stockholder.

The shortcomings of either extreme model presented above are obvious. Corporations can no longer — if for that matter they ever did — operate as purely economic institutions. At the same time it is highly doubtful that the extreme form of the metrocorporation could meet the minimal economic requirements necessary for survival. Thus one of the major challenges is the development of a viable corporate model that can both fulfill the economic needs of the corporation and its investors and fulfill the needs of society.

EPILOGUE

The introductory course to any field of study introduces and discusses a broad range of topics. As might be expected neither all students nor all instructors are in complete agreement with the amount of space assigned to each topic by the author. In the field of management the problem of selecting content is compounded by the various approaches (sometimes called schools) to the study of management. The texts of 10 or 15 years ago are representative of the classical approach to management. Presently there are texts with titles that indicate a behavioral approach, a systems approach, or a quantitative approach. One way of lending some order to the diversity of opinion concerning the content and emphasis of the introductory course is to examine the introductory course within the context of the sequence of courses normally taught in the business administration curriculum.

Most authors of management textbooks define management as a process. As a result their books have, in addition to an introductory section, four major sections — planning, organizing, leading or directing, and controlling. The execution of the planning function and the control function rely more heavily upon mathematical techniques than the other two functions of the management process. The development and application of quantitative techniques to the problems of management, primarily related to the functions of planning and controlling, has emerged as an academic field of study known as management science. It is questionable whether it is either desirable or possible for the introductory course to do more than indicate the problems that may be resolved by mathematical techniques. The interested student may explore the quantitative aspects of managerial problem solving and decision making in subsequent management science courses.

The origin of that body of knowledge discussed in the organizing function is lost in antiquity; however, much of it does come from the writings of military leaders. Most introductory courses confine the discussion of the organizing function to the level of description. The chapter titles of the section concerned with organizing in this text are typical of the material presented in most texts. Beyond the introductory course there are advanced courses in organization theory and detailed studies of specific organizational forms such as the bureaucratic model.

The behavioral sciences — especially psychology, sociology, and anthropology — are the academic disciplines that provide the subject matter content to be applied to the leadership function. Most business schools offer additional courses in organization behavior, industrial and organizational psychology, and industrial sociology so that the interested student may explore the behavioral sciences in depth.

The student who is studying the discipline of management is at the same time, in most colleges and universities, specializing in one of the functional areas of business management in order to perform one of the specialized jobs in the business organization. The student may complete a major in accounting, personnel, finance, marketing, or production, or may receive special training for positions in quality control, industrial engineering, or purchasing. Since these are the traditional majors within schools of business administration, they are not explored in depth in the introductory course to management.

When the introductory course to management is viewed as the beginning course within the emerging academic discipline known as management and when it is recognized that the student is acquiring necessary skills and knowledge for performing a specific function within the modern industrial organization, it seems best to adopt an eclectic approach to the study of management. Consequently, the concepts of planning and control that draw heavily upon management science in their more complex applications are introduced in their simpler forms. Systems theory, organization theory, and the major findings of the behavioral sciences are presented in the discussions of the functions of organizing and leading. The breadth of an eclectic approach best meets the needs of those students who will have no additional courses in management and at the same time best prepares students who have opportunity for further study in the field of management.

CHAPTER QUESTIONS FOR STUDY AND DISCUSSION

1. Discuss briefly the reasons for considering the setting of objectives as an action apart from the planning process. What are the reasons for including the setting of objectives as a part of planning? Which position do you prefer? Why?
2. Describe in your own words the interrelationships that exist between the four functions of the management process. Is it possible to rank these functions in order of significance within the management process? Discuss.
3. Comment on the statement in the text that the concept of managing is broader in scope than the concept of leading. Do you agree with this statement? Why?
4. What is meant by an open system? Differentiate between an open and a closed system. Can inanimate; i.e., non-living, systems properly be considered as open systems?
5. Why are social systems considered open systems? Discuss the major implications of considering formal organizations as open social systems.
6. Of the three current issues presented in the text, which do you consider to be the most significant? Why?

7. What are the shortcomings and the strengths of the traditional economic model of the firm? What are the advantages and disadvantages of the metrocorporation model?
8. We hear much concerning the quality of the environment in which we live. To improve it will cost money. Who is to bear this burden — the corporation, the customer, government, or society as a whole? Discuss.

Appendix A

Cues II:
College & University
Environment Scales[1]

DIRECTIONS: Colleges and universities differ from one another in many ways. Some things that are generally true or characteristic of one school may not be characteristic of another. The purpose of the College & University Environment Scales (CUES II) is to help describe the general atmosphere of different colleges. The atmosphere of a campus is a mixture of various features, facilities, rules and procedures, faculty characteristics, courses of study, classroom activities, students' interests, extracurricular programs, informal activities, and other conditions and events.

You are asked to be a reporter about your school. You have lived in its environment, seen its features, participated in its activities, and sensed its attitudes. What kind of a place is it?

There are 160 statements in this booklet. You are to answer them *True* or *False*, using the answer sheet given you for this purpose.[2]

As you read the statements you will find that many cannot be answered True or False in a literal sense. The statements contain qualifying words or phrases, such as "almost always," "frequently," "generally," and "rarely," and are intended to draw out your impression of whether the situation described applies or does not apply to your campus as you know it.

As a reporter about your college you are to indicate whether you think each statement is *generally characteristic*, a condition that exists,

---

[1]C. Robert Pace, *College & University Environment Scales: Technical Manual* (2d ed.; Princeton, N.J.: Educational Testing Service, 1969). Directions and CUES II are copyrighted by C. Robert Pace and are published and distributed by ETS, Princeton, N.J. These materials are reproduced with the permission of the author and publishers. They should not be used in any manner other than as a part of Case Problem 13-A. College and universities desiring to conduct a formal evaluation using CUES II as the measuring instrument should write directly to Institutional Research Program for Higher Education, Educational Testing Service, Princeton, N.J.

[2]Answer sheets for CUES II, form x-2s, are in the *Student Enrichment Activities*.

an event that occurs or might occur, the way people generally act or feel — in short, whether the statement is more nearly True than False; or conversely, whether you think it is *not generally characteristic*, does not exist or occur, is more nearly False than True.

The CUES II is not a test in which there are right or wrong answers; it is more like an opinion poll — a way to find out how much agreement or disagreement there is about the characteristics of a campus environment.

1. Students almost always wait to be called on before speaking in class.
2. The big college events draw a lot of student enthusiasm and support.
3. There is a recognized group of student leaders on this campus.
4. Frequent tests are given in most courses.
5. Students take a great deal of pride in their personal appearance.
6. Education here tends to make students more practical and realistic.
7. The professors regularly check up on the students to make sure that assignments are being carried out properly and on time.
8. It's important socially here to be in the right club or group.
9. Student pep rallies, parades, dances, carnivals, or demonstrations occur very rarely.
10. Anyone who knows the right people in the faculty or administration can get a better break here.
11. The professors really push the students' capacities to the limit.
12. Most of the professors are dedicated scholars in their fields.
13. Most courses require intensive study and preparation out of class.
14. Students set high standards of achievement for themselves.
15. Class discussions are typically vigorous and intense.
16. A lecture by an outstanding scientist would be poorly attended.
17. Careful reasoning and clear logic are valued most highly in grading student papers, reports, or discussions.
18. It is fairly easy to pass most courses without working very hard.
19. The school is outstanding for the emphasis and support it gives to pure scholarship and basic research.
20. Standards set by the professors are not particularly hard to achieve.
21. It is easy to take clear notes in most courses.
22. The school helps everyone get acquainted.
23. Students often run errands or do other personal services for the faculty.
24. The history and traditions of the college are strongly emphasized.
25. The professors go out of their way to help you.
26. There is a great deal of borrowing and sharing among the students.
27. When students run a project or put on a show everybody knows about it.
28. Many upperclassmen play an active role in helping new students adjust to campus life.
29. Students exert considerable pressure on one another to live up to the expected codes of conduct.
30. Graduation is a pretty matter-of-fact, unemotional event.

31. Channels for expressing students' complaints are readily accessible.
32. Students are encouraged to take an active part in social reforms or political programs.
33. Students are actively concerned about national and international affairs.
34. There are a good many colorful and controversial figures on the faculty.
35. There is considerable interest in the analysis of value systems, and the relativity of societies and ethics.
36. Public debates are held frequently.
37. A controversial speaker always stirs up a lot of student discussion.
38. There are many facilities and opportunities for individual creative activity.
39. There is a lot of interest here in poetry, music, painting, sculpture, architecture, etc.
40. Concerts and art exhibits always draw big crowds of students.
41. Students ask permission before deviating from common policies or practices.
42. Most student rooms are pretty messy.
43. People here are always trying to win an argument.
44. Drinking and late parties are generally tolerated, despite regulations.
45. Students occasionally plot some sort of escapade or rebellion.
46. Many students drive sports cars.
47. Students frequently do things on the spur of the moment.
48. Student publications never lampoon dignified people or institutions.
49. The person who is always trying to "help out" is likely to be regarded as a nuisance.
50. Students are conscientious about taking good care of school property.
51. The important people at this school expect others to show proper respect for them.
52. Student elections generate a lot of intense campaigning and strong feeling.
53. Everyone has a lot of fun at this school.
54. In many classes students have an assigned seat.
55. Student organizations are closely supervised to guard against mistakes.
56. Many students try to pattern themselves after people they admire.
57. New fads and phrases are continually springing up among the students.
58. Students must have a written excuse for absence from class.
59. The college offers many really practical courses such as typing, report writing, etc.
60. Student rooms are more likely to be decorated with pennants and pin-ups than with paintings, carvings, mobiles, fabrics, etc.
61. Most of the professors are very thorough teachers and really probe into the fundamentals of their subjects.
62. Most courses are a real intellectual challenge.

63. Students put a lot of energy into everything they do in class and out.
64. Course offerings and faculty in the natural sciences are outstanding.
65. Courses, examinations, and readings are frequently revised.
66. Personality, pull, and bluff get students through many courses.
67. There is very little studying here over the weekends.
68. There is a lot of interest in the philosophy and methods of science.
69. People around here seem to thrive on difficulty — the tougher things get, the harder they work.
70. Students are very serious and purposeful about their work.
71. This school has a reputation for being very friendly.
72. All undergraduates must live in university approved housing.
73. Instructors clearly explain the goals and purposes of their courses.
74. Students have many opportunities to develop skill in organizing and directing the work of others.
75. Most of the faculty are not interested in students' personal problems.
76. Students quickly learn what is done and not done on this campus.
77. It's easy to get a group together for card games, singing, going to the movies, etc.
78. Students commonly share their problems.
79. Faculty members rarely or never call students by their first names.
80. There is a lot of group spirit.
81. Students are encouraged to criticize administrative policies and teaching practices.
82. The expression of strong personal belief or conviction is pretty rare around here.
83. Many students here develop a strong sense of responsibility about their role in contemporary social and political life.
84. There are a number of prominent faculty members who play a significant role in national or local politics.
85. There would be a capacity audience for a lecture by an outstanding philosopher or theologian.
86. Course offerings and faculty in the social sciences are outstanding.
87. Many famous people are brought to the campus for lectures, concerts, student discussions, etc.
88. The school offers many opportunities for students to understand and criticize important works of art, music, and drama.
89. Special museums or collections are important possessions of the college.
90. Modern art and music get little attention here.
91. Students are expected to report any violation of rules and regulations.
92. Student parties are colorful and lively.
93. There always seem to be a lot of little quarrels going on.
94. Students rarely get drunk and disorderly.
95. Most students show a good deal of caution and self-control in their behavior.
96. Bermuda shorts, pin-up pictures, etc. are common on this campus.
97. Students pay little attention to rules and regulations.

98. Dormitory raids, water fights, and other student pranks would be unthinkable.
99. Many students seem to expect other people to adapt to them rather than trying to adapt themselves to others.
100. Rough games and contact sports are an important part of intramural athletics.
101. The vocational value of many courses is emphasized.
102. Most people are aware of the financial status of students' families.
103. Student organizations are required to have a faculty adviser.
104. There are good facilities for learning vocationally useful skills and techniques.
105. Most faculty members really know the regulations and requirements that apply to student programs.
106. There is a well-organized and effective job placement office for the graduating students.
107. Many faculty members are involved in services or consulting activities for outside groups — business, adult education, etc.
108. Professors will sometimes increase a student's grade if they think he has worked especially hard and conscientiously.
109. Most students want to get a degree because of its economic value.
110. Vocational guidance is a main activity of the counseling office.
111. New ideas and theories are encouraged and vigorously debated.
112. Students who don't make passing grades are quickly dropped from school.
113. Students are allowed to help themselves to books in the library stacks.
114. Excellence in scholarship is the dominant feature of this institution.
115. There are lots of quiet and comfortable places for students to study.
116. Even in social groups students are more likely to talk about their studies than about other things.
117. There are many excellent facilities for research on this campus.
118. The main emphasis in most departmental clubs is to promote interest and scholarship in the field.
119. Most students are pretty dissatisfied if they make less than a B grade.
120. The library is one of the outstanding facilities on the campus.
121. The campus design, architecture, and landscaping suggest a friendly atmosphere.
122. Student groups often meet in faculty members' homes.
123. Counseling and guidance services are really personal, patient, and helpful.
124. There are courses which involve students in activities with groups or agencies in the local community.
125. Most of the students here are pretty happy.
126. There are courses or voluntary seminars that deal with problems of marriage and the family.
127. In most classes the atmosphere is very friendly.
128. Groups of students from the college often get together for parties or visits during holidays.
129. Most students seem to have a genuine affection for this school.

130. There are courses or voluntary seminars that deal with problems of social adjustment.
131. There is a regular place on the campus where students can make speeches about controversial issues.
132. Students are free to cut classes at their own discretion.
133. Many faculty members have worked overseas or frequently traveled to other countries.
134. There is a lot of variety and innovation in the way many courses are taught.
135. Many professors permit, and sometimes welcome, class discussion of materials that are outside their field of specialization.
136. Many students are interested in joining the Peace Corps or are planning, somehow, to spend time in another part of the world.
137. Many student groups invite faculty members to lead special discussions.
138. Groups of students sometimes spend all evening listening to classical records.
139. Student chorus, orchestra, and theater groups are really excellent.
140. Students like to browse in book stores.
141. Many professors require students to submit an outline before writing a term paper or report.
142. The Dean of Students office is mainly concerned with disciplinary matters.
143. Faculty members always wear coats and ties on the campus.
144. A major aim of this institution is to produce cultivated men and women.
145. In literature, drama, and music the main emphasis is on the classics.
146. Nearby churches have an active interest in counseling and youth programs.
147. Proper standards and ideals are emphasized in many courses.
148. Most professors think of themselves as no different from other adults in the community.
149. Faculty members are always polite and proper in their relations with students.
150. In most exams the emphasis is on knowing the correct answers rather than on being able to defend a point of view.
151. There are students on many academic and administrative committees.
152. Students have real authority to determine some campus policies and procedures.
153. Some faculty members are active in experimenting with new methods of teaching, new courses, and other innovations.
154. There is much student interest and activity about social issues — such as civil rights, justice, peace.
155. The administration is receptive and active in responding to student proposals for change.
156. There is an "experimental" college or program where a variety of new courses are offered (whether for credit or not).

157. Massive disruption, force, or violence by students would be unthinkable on this campus.
158. The attitude of most college officials about drugs is generally patient, flexible, and tolerant.
159. The response of most college officials toward student sit-ins or other "confrontations" is (or would be) firm, forceful, and unsympathetic.
160. Due process considerations are expected by students who are accused of violating laws or college rules.

Appendix B

Comprehensive Case: Buying and Operating a Motel

The accommodation industry with annual sales in excess of seven billion dollars provides the industrial setting for this comprehensive case study.[1] There are several reasons for selecting a 95-unit motel as the specific setting of the case. First, almost every student has been a guest in a motel; consequently there is some knowledge of the characteristics and services provided. Second, motels and motor hotels are the growth segment of the accommodation industry. Further, the modern motel is a complex operation and offers a career opportunity for the professionally trained manager.

The format of the case parallels the major parts of the text. The first part of the case presents a discussion of the nature of the industry and offers an opportunity to formulate specific internal and external business objectives. The second part examines the planning required to determine whether or not the purchase of the property in question is a sound decision. Next, you are asked to determine the optimum organization necessary for the efficient, long-term operation of the motel. Questions concerning the most effective type of leadership and means of motivating employees are considered. Finally, the controls normally used in the operation of a motel are developed. Each major part of the case may be considered as an integrating case to be studied in conjunction with the corresponding part of the text, or the case may be regarded as a comprehensive case drawing upon all of the functions of the management process. However the case is used, it is suggested

The author wishes to thank the following persons of the Ramada Inn organization who gave generously of their time in supplying information for the preparation of this case: Prentiss R. Moore, Regional Manager; James Daniels, Manager of the Arlington, Texas, Inn; and Charles Steadman, Assistant Director of Training, Management Development Center, Phoenix, Arizona.

[1]*Trends in the Hotel/Motel Business: Thirty-fifth Annual Review* (New York: Harris, Kerr, Forester & Company, 1971). Much of the information concerning the operation of the hotel-motel industry was drawn from this report which was provided by Eric Green, partner, Harris, Kerr, Forester & Company, Certified Public Accountants.

that the student read the entire case before analyzing each of the five parts. Also, the information presented and the experience gained in analyzing the case should enable you to evaluate a motel in your area as either an investment opportunity or for employment as a manager.

THE NATURE OF THE MOTEL BUSINESS

It is axiomatic that if one is to fulfill the accommodation needs of the traveler such facilities must be located so that they are readily accessible. The earliest accommodation facilities established in this country were for those who traveled on foot or horseback and are typified by the colonial inns of New England.[2] As stagecoach routes developed so did the way station and the coffee house. In the mid-nineteenth century the railroad system of this country began its development, and in time the inn, the way station, and the coffee house diminished in importance and were replaced by the downtown hotel. The major hotels of Chicago, New York, St. Louis, and Philadelphia are all located near the rail terminals of these cities. With the advent of the automobile, and highways that make their use possible, the mode and pattern of transportation shifted again. Tourist cabins appeared along the highways to accommodate those who used this mode of transportation.

The development of the tourist cabin, soon followed by the tourist court and the motel, marks the completion of a full circle that began with the New England inn to accommodate the individual traveler, followed by the downtown hotel for those using the mass transportation of the railroads, and back to roadside facilities for the individual traveling by automobile. However, change in the mode and pattern of transportation still continues. The large jet airport, the result of mass air transportation, is located away from the central city and has created the need for a new type of lodging facility readily accessible from the airport.

Types of Facilities

For many years the mainstay of the accommodations industry has been the transient hotel. Although most of these hotels were built prior to 1930, new transient hotels have been built in recent years. These are full service hotels and provide all the services that a traveler needs, whether traveling for business or pleasure, or attending a convention. There are resort hotels which are located in resort areas and characterized by marked seasonal fluctuations in business. In addition, some

---

[2]George O. Podd and John D. Lesure, *Planning and Operating Motels and Motor Hotels* (New York: Ahrens Publishing Co., 1964). Much of the background information of the industry was obtained from this source, which is a comprehensive treatment and analysis of the problems encountered in operating a motel or motor hotel.

hotels are classed as residential since the majority of their guests are permanent residents rather than transients.

The modern motel had its beginnings in the tourist cabin and the tourist court. In the 1920's, mainly in the South, Southwest, and California, roadside tourist cabins made their appearance to serve those who were traveling by automobile. These early facilities were in rural areas and offered minimal services. Private baths, telephone service, food, and linen service were unknown. Tourist cabins soon developed into the tourist court and many services associated with hotels were added. Sometime during the 1930's the descriptive term, motel, made its appearance and was readily accepted. The motel of this period was a relatively modest establishment and did not pose a serious threat to the well-established hotel industry. For the most part there was individual ownership, often husband and wife, who could and did perform all of the work necessary for its operation. The capital investment was small, $2,000 to $3,000 per unit with an average of ten units, and units could be added as desired. Managing a motel became a way of life for many retired persons.

With the development of the interregional highway system and the construction of new airports the characteristics of the motel industry, again adapting to the mode and pattern of transportation, changed significantly. The number of guest rooms increased sharply with the result that motels with 300 units are not unusual. Also, full hotel services, including public meeting rooms and facilities for conventions, made their appearance. One is tempted to describe the modern motel as a horizontal hotel, but that description is not accurate since many so-called motels are multi-story buildings, and some are even located in the central city. If a differentiation must be made between the full service motel and the traditional hotel, it is in the availability and accessibility of parking facilities. Usually the motel has a parking lot or parking garage which is adjacent to and is an integral part of the building complex.

The Tradition of Innkeeping

Since the primary function of the accommodation industry is to provide a service, it may be considered as a part of that broad segment of industry known as the service industry. It is also a part of the retail industry since services are sold to the customer who is also the consumer. However, the accommodations industry differs from other service and retail establishments in that there is a distinguishing relationship between the customer and the seller. It is a relationship that is best described by the terms "guest" and "host." Guests are more than travelers away from home; they are there by invitation. The manager or owner does more than merely provide service; he must, in the tradition of innkeeping, provide the personal attention, warmth, and courtesy that makes the traveler a truly welcomed guest. It is not an easy task. The guest-host relationship is not easily attainable with corporate ownership and professional management, yet the traditional innkeeping relationship of guest and host should be one of the major objectives of any motel.

The Business Aspects

In addition to formulating service objectives within the tradition of innkeeping, there are significant financial considerations in the operation of a motel. A motel is a long-term investment in real estate. The initial land investment is improved with the construction of a special purpose building. If the real estate improvement does not succeed as a motel, the only value that normally remains is the value of the land. Further, the capital investment per room is significant. Construction costs of $15,000 per guest unit are not uncommon. Though the rewards are great, the risk is high. The construction of a new highway, a new airport, the closing of a major industry in the area, or the building of additional rooms by competitors can all spell disaster. Thus the need arises to determine a reasonable rate of return on equity capital invested in an enterprise having a substantial degree of risk which is often due to factors beyond the control of the investor. Return on other investments having a lower degree of risk, such as corporate and tax free municipal bonds, must be examined. For these reasons a rate of return on equity capital of 10 to 12 percent a year is considered to be minimal.

PLANNING TO BUY

The Apex Motel, which is readily accessible and visible from the interstate highway, is located 40 miles from a major city with a population of 850,000. The motel property is within the city limits of a town that has a population of 50,000. The metropolitan area is one of the 10 largest in the United States and ranks sixth with respect to expected population growth. The motel was built eight years ago and opened with 98 guest rooms, an apartment for the manager, a lobby newsstand and sundries shop, and a large swimming pool. At the present time there are 95 rooms available to guests since one of the intended guest rooms is used as an employee's lounge, one for storage, and another is equipped as a maintenance shop. Shortly after opening, a separate restaurant with three public meeting rooms was built adjacent to the motel. The present owner intends to retain and operate this property; however, the purchase agreement includes an option to buy the restaurant in three years. There are adequate parking facilities for both motel and restaurant guests, and the courtyard and pool area are attractively landscaped. The rooms are comfortably furnished and most of the carpeting has been replaced, but there is need for a planned refurnishing of all guest rooms. The present owner is asking $950,000 and is willing to finance 50 percent of this amount for 15 years at an annual rate of 9 percent.

How does one determine a fair price for an existing motel? When building a new motel, the first step is a feasibility study to show immediate and expected market potential, the cost of land and construction, and projected operating revenues and expenses. However, when purchasing an existing property, current operating statements are of primary significance; yet the feasibility study must be updated to obtain a reliable forecast of the future.

Current Operations

The primary source of income for motels without restaurants is almost entirely room sales revenue which should range between 92 and 95 percent of total income.[3] Telephone service (usually operated at a loss) should provide two to five percent of gross sales, and miscellaneous income derived from vending machines and space rentals such as a lobby sundries shop and newsstand usually contributes between one and two percent. The direct costs of operating the rooms — wages for the rooms department employees, linens, cleaning supplies, glassware, and other supplies — and the cost of providing telephone service are deducted from total sales. The result is defined as gross operating income, which should be between 67 and 75 percent of total income. Administrative and general expenses, including the manager's salary and the cost of front office personnel; advertising; heat, light, and power; and the cost of repairs and maintenance are subtracted from gross operating income to determine gross operating profit, an amount that should range between 40 and 50 percent of total income. Fire insurance, approximately one percent of total income, and real estate taxes — from four to nine percent of total income — are deducted from gross operating profit to determine operating profit before other capital expenses. Profit after real estate taxes usually ranges between 35 and 45 percent of total income. The most recent operating statement of Apex Motel is shown in Exhibit I.

An examination of the operating statement shows an operating profit, after real estate taxes but before other capital expenditures, of

---

[3]The classification of accounts used in this discussion and presented in Exhibit I, Table I, and Exhibit II are based upon the following industry sources.

Edward F. Chirhart, Kemper W. Merriam, and Robert W. McIntosh, *Uniform Classification of Accounts for Motels, Motor Hotels, or Highway Lodges* (Temple, Texas: Tourist Court Journal, 1962).

Uniform System of Accounts and Expenses Dictionary for Motels, Motor Hotels, and Small Hotels (New York: American Hotel and Motel Association, 1962). This publication was prepared under the direction of Co-Chairman Thomas J. Hogan, C.P.A., and John D. Lesure, C.P.A., and is approved by the American Hotel and Motel Association.

			Percentage of Total Income
TOTAL SALES & INCOME			
Rooms	$424,768.00		95.0
Telephone	16,200.00		4.0
Other	4,100.00		1.0
Total		$445,068.00	100.0
DEPARTMENTAL EXPENSES			
Rooms Department			
Salaries & Wages	96,304.00		21.7
Payroll Taxes & Employee Benefits	7,223.00		1.6
Laundry	21,730.00		4.9
Other — China, Glass, Cleaning Supplies	21,462.00		4.8
	146,719.00		33.0
Telephone	20,250.00		4.5
Total		166,969.00	37.5
GROSS OPERATING INCOME		$278,099.00	62.5
DEDUCTIONS FROM INCOME			
Administrative & General Expenses			
Salaries & Wages	42,900.00		9.6
Payroll Taxes & Employee Benefits	4,281.00		1.0
Other A & G Expenses	17,019.00		3.8
	64,200.00		14.4
Advertising & Sales Promotion	12,000.00		2.7
Heat, Light & Power	29,560.00		6.7
Repairs & Maintenance	30,184.00		6.8
Total		135,944.00	30.6
GROSS OPERATING PROFIT		$142,155.00	31.9
Fire Insurance & Franchise Taxes	4,850.00		1.1
PROFIT BEFORE REAL ESTATE TAXES & OTHER CAPITAL EXPENSES		$137,305.00	30.8
Real Estate Taxes	29,125.00		6.5
PROFIT AFTER REAL ESTATE TAXES BUT BEFORE OTHER CAPITAL EXPENSES		$108,180.00	24.3

Exhibit I
APEX MOTEL
CURRENT
OPERATING
REPORT FOR
YEAR ENDING
DECEMBER 31,
19--

24.3 percent of total revenue. Though many buyers assume that they have the management skill to improve operating ratios, the prudent buyer makes no such assumption and forecasts net profit based upon current operations and projected capital expenses. Counsel advises that the proposed selling price of $950,000 may be distributed on the following basis expressed as cost per guest room:

Land	$ 1,000.00
Buildings	7,600.00
Pool	200.00
Furnishings	1,200.00
Total	$10,000.00

Counsel indicates that the buildings may be depreciated on a 20-year basis and that the pool and furnishings may be depreciated on an 8-year basis. Both depreciation schedules are computed by the straight-line method. The nine-percent, 15-year mortgage with fixed monthly payments, including payments on principal, results in an interest charge of $42,180.00 and payments on principal of $15,675.00 for the first year. Total debt service is $57,855.00 per year. Proposed capital expenses are shown in Table 1.

Table 1 APEX MOTEL PROPOSED CAPITAL EXPENSES			Percentage of Total Income
	Interest on Mortgage	$42,180.00	9.5
	Depreciation on Buildings & Furnishings	$52,725.00	11.8
	Profit Before Income Taxes	$13,275.00	3.0

When interest on mortgage and depreciation charges, 9.5 percent and 11.8 percent of total income respectively, are deducted from profit after real estate taxes, profit before federal and state income tax is 3.0 percent, a return of 2.8 percent on the equity capital of $475,000.00. It is difficult to project income taxes as each buyer's situation differs; however, assume that Apex is being bought by a newly formed corporation and that there are no other properties. The federal tax of 20 percent on the first $25,000 of corporate earnings amounts to $2,655.00 which must be paid out of the $13,275.00 profit.[4] From the balance, $10,620.00, repayment of principal, $15,675.00, is deducted and results in a net loss of $5,055.00. Any state income tax creates a greater loss.

An obvious first step in determining the reasonableness of a proposed selling price for real estate is to request a professional appraisal.

---

[4]The 1975 Internal Revenue Service Code provides for a 20 percent tax on the first $25,000, 22 percent on the next $25,000, and 48 percent for all profits over $50,000.

Such an appraisal has been made of the Apex Motel, and the report indicates that the asking price is equitable; that is, the appreciation sought by the original owner is in line with similar properties in the area. Further, with proper maintenance, the building is expected to have a useful life of 20 years with minimal risk of obsolescence. Nonetheless, there is a question concerning the true worth of the room furnishings, and the appraiser's report strongly recommends that all room furnishings be replaced within three years. It is estimated that the cost of refurnishing will average $1,500.00 per room.

A motel is more than bricks and mortar on a parcel of land; it is an ongoing business. Rules of thumb have developed and serve as guides in evaluating the worth of a given property. The gross income multiplier is obtained by dividing the selling price by gross income. The normal range of gross income multipliers is three to seven, with four being the average. The net operating profit multiplier is another index. Net operating profit is defined on a cash-flow basis and shows the amount of money available from net profit and depreciation after debt service which includes payments on principal and interest. This value is also termed net spendable and when divided into the equity investment the result is the pay out period for the recovery of equity capital. It is estimated that a buyer should recover equity capital in four to five years.

The Feasibility Study

A remark attributed to Mr. E. M. Statler, founder of the Statler Hotels, states that there are three factors that determine the success of a hotel. They are: location, location, and location. The original feasibility study indicates that the site selected for Apex Motel was the last available motel site within the city limits and that there were no planned changes in either the state highway system or the interregional system. At the request of the present owner of Apex the consultants who did the original feasibility study have recently brought the earlier study up to date. The favorable economic forecast for the entire metropolitan area remains the same. The university in the town where Apex is located has grown and now has an enrollment of 15,000 students. In addition, there are plans for a community college scheduled to open within a year. Four additional manufacturing plants have located within five miles of Apex during the past five years. The nearby major city has built a convention center and now has a National Football League team and a National League baseball team. There are also professional basketball, hockey, and soccer teams. Several seasonal amusement parks, similar to Disneyland, have been established in the last eight years.

The current survey of the occupancy rates of the five motels (there are no hotels) competing directly with Apex is presented by month in

Table 2. The current annual occupancy rate for the area is 70 percent, the same occupancy rate that Apex experienced during the last full year of operation. The consultants believe that Apex could increase its occupancy rate by replacing room furnishings. They also recommend an evaluation of the current rate structure so that the average revenue per room may be increased from the present $17.50 to $18.50 per room, an amount that would put Apex in line with the immediate area. No decrease in occupancy rate is foreseen, provided the rooms are well maintained.

	MONTH	OCCUPANCY RATE	MONTH	OCCUPANCY RATE
	January	55%	July	82%
	February	60	August	85
	March	70	September	68
	April	79	October	76
Table 2	May	78	November	58
AREA	June	80	December	49
OCCUPANCY				
RATES	Annual Occupancy Rate — 70%			

THE ORGANIZATION

The organizing function for small service organizations is primarily a manning problem rather than one of creating a managerial hierarchy. Apex Motel is large enough to warrant the services of a full-time manager who lives on the premises. He is classified as an exempt employee; all others are non-exempt and their base pay is computed on a 40-hour week. Determining an optimum organization is complicated by the need for maintaining a 24-hour day, 7-day week operation and by daily and seasonal fluctuations in the occupancy rate.

It is difficult to set precise manning standards because of variations in physical layout, service objectives, and the availability and quality of labor. Even so, normative data indicate that total payroll costs, excluding payroll taxes, for motels without restaurants range between 22 and 28 percent of total sales and income. The average is 26 percent and results in an annual cost of $924.00 for each available room and $1,273.00 for each occupied room. Payroll costs (excluding the cost of payroll taxes) for the rooms department should be between 14 and 18 percent of room sales. A labor cost of 16 percent is acceptable. The total cost of operating the rooms department, including payroll taxes and the cost of supplies, should be about 25 percent of room sales.

The present manning of the rooms department is considerably above the recommended average and is the result of the present owner's method of allocating motel labor costs. An analysis of the payroll costs, excluding payroll taxes and other benefits, charged to the rooms department shows a total of $96,304.00, or 22 percent of room sales. These costs are distributed as follows:

12 Maids	$57,408.00
1 Housekeeper (working)	5,200.00
1 Houseman	4,992.00
6 Porters	28,704.00
Total	$96,304.00

It is difficult to determine how many maids are required to service a motel effectively. Under normal conditions a maid is expected to clean a room in approximately 30 minutes, and during the course of an eight-hour day she can be expected to clean 14 rooms. In addition to the seasonal variations in occupancy, shown in Table 2, there are variations in the daily occupancy rate with Friday, Saturday, Sunday, and Monday showing a lower rate than the days in the middle of the week. Also, there are the factors of absenteeism and the need to maintain a seven-day week operation. Proposed manning, allowing for these factors, results in a monthly average of eight maids. If labor costs remain constant, $2.30 per hour, total annual projected payroll costs for maid service is $38,272.00. The working housekeeper, who schedules the maids and is responsible for maintaining the cleaning supplies inventory, is expected to be retained at her present rate of $2.50 per hour. The houseman picks up the clean linen and delivers the soiled linen to the local linen service, cleans the hallways, and performs other services as required. His annual pay, at $2.40 an hour, is $4,992.00. Three porters, with an hourly rate of $2.30, earn a total of $14,352.00. The total annual cost of the proposed manning for the rooms department is $62,816.00, excluding payroll taxes.

There are relatively few persons allocated to the administrative and general payroll account. There are four desk clerks, one of whom works as relief and on weekends. Payroll cost for each person is $475.00 per month and the annual cost for desk clerks is $22,800.00. All of the clerks know how to operate the switchboard and can perform the duties of cashier when assigned that duty. The layout of the front office is such that a full-time telephone switchboard operator is not needed. The night auditor, who works from 11:00 p.m. to 7:00 a.m., has agreed to remain at his present monthly salary of $675.00. The manager also indicates that he will continue at his present salary of $12,000.00 per year. It is highly doubtful that any significant changes can be made in the operations of the front office; thus, projected payroll costs shown in Exhibit II, page 552, for A & G personnel are the same as in Exhibit I.

The total payroll costs for maintenance personnel are $14,184.00. The maintenance man is a good mechanic and is capable of handling all minor repairs and painting. The yardman fills in occasionally as a porter and also helps the maintenance man. On a monthly basis the

			Percentage of Total Income
TOTAL SALES & INCOME			
Rooms	$424,768.00		95.0
Telephone	16,200.00		4.0
Other	4,100.00		1.0
Total		$445,068.00	100.0
DEPARTMENTAL EXPENSES			
Rooms	109,719.00		24.7
Telephone	20,250.00		4.5
Total		129,969.00	29.2
GROSS OPERATING INCOME		$315,099.00	70.8
DEDUCTIONS FROM INCOME			
Administrative & General Expenses	64,200.00		14.4
Advertising & Sales Promotion	12,000.00		2.7
Heat, Light & Power	29,560.00		6.7
Repairs & Maintenance	30,184.00		6.8
Total		135,944.00	30.6
GROSS OPERATING PROFIT		$179,155.00	40.2
Fire Insurance & Franchise Tax	4,850.00		1.1
PROFIT BEFORE REAL ESTATE TAXES & OTHER CAPITAL EXPENSES		$174,305.00	39.1
Real Estate Taxes	29,125.00		6.5
PROFIT AFTER REAL ESTATE TAXES BUT BEFORE OTHER CAPITAL EXPENSES		$145,180.00	32.6
Interest on Mortgage	42,180.00		9.5
Depreciation on Building & Furnishings	52,725.00		11.8
		94,905.00	21.3
PROFIT BEFORE FEDERAL INCOME TAX		$ 50,275.00	11.3

Exhibit II PROPOSED BUDGET (ASSUMING NO CHANGE IN OCCUPANCY RATE OR AVERAGE RATE PER ROOM)

payroll cost (including payroll taxes) for the maintenance man is $842.00, and for the yardman the amount is $428.00. Considering the age of the motel and the need for refurnishing all rooms, it seems wise to retain both of these employees. If the number of persons assigned to maintenance and administrative and general expenses remains constant, and if the proposed manning for the rooms department is achieved, total payroll costs at present hourly rates are $128,892.00, including all payroll taxes.

THE PROBLEM OF LEADERSHIP

In Chapter 14 and again in Chapter 21 a differentiation is made between leadership style and leadership behavior. Leadership style pertains to the interpersonal relationships that exist between a leader and the members of the group. Leadership behavior encompasses all of those actions normally associated with the management process and includes formal and informal communications, methods of motivating and compensating employees, and supervisory practices. In addition to those characteristics necessary for effective interpersonal relationships, the manager of a motel must have the ability to establish the guest-host relationship discussed earlier. The purpose of this section of the case is to offer you an opportunity to crystallize your thinking with regard to the leadership function in a motel. The recommendations that you make to the manager of Apex Motel and the standards used to judge his performance as a leader may or may not apply to other forms of business organizations.

Leadership Style

Whether an authoritarian personality, one who is highly directive in his relationship with subordinates, can establish and maintain an optimum guest-host relationship is open to question. If one assumes that it is possible for the authoritarian manager to maintain an effective guest-host relationship, the effect of such a personality upon subordinates must be considered. How effective would their performance be, what attitudes would they demonstrate toward guests, and how would they react to control?

As one moves away from the authoritarian pattern of leadership, there are varying degrees of participative leadership. What is the optimum degree of participation? In discussing the organization structure of a motel it is noted that problems arise in manning a 24-hour day, 7-day week operation with a fluctuating work load. Should work schedules be fixed or should they be rotated? More important, who should make the determination, the manager or the employees? Also, how much should employees participate in setting the standards used for control? Your answers to these and similar questions are indicative of your own leadership style and influence your judgment of the effectiveness of managerial performance.

Leadership Behavior

Now let us consider the formal actions of the manager in determining and administering personnel policies. As noted in Chapter 16, there is marked interest in the measurement of job satisfaction. Although many studies show a consistent, but low, correlation between job satisfaction and performance, a conclusion that there is a causal relationship between job satisfaction and performance is not warranted. Considering these findings and also considering the nature of the motel business, what steps would you take as a manager to determine the level of job satisfaction of your employees?

The present owner of Apex Motel has not formulated any clear statement of personnel policy; however, during preliminary discussions he stated that he believed that the large motel chains with formal policies and retirement plans were able to attract a better quality employee than he did. Thus the question arises concerning the advisability and nature of a formal statement of personnel policy for an independent operation such as Apex Motel.

ESTABLISHING CONTROLS

Exhibit II presents the optimum operating ratios that the group considering the purchase of Apex Motel have developed as a basis for establishing a budget. They believe that these ratios are attainable since they are virtually the same as those presented in Exhibit I. The major difference between Exhibit I and Exhibit II is that the latter reflects a reduced manning in the rooms department.

The proposed budget must be evaluated with respect to the extent to which it fulfills the financial objectives of the purchasers and the probability that it can be attained. If the financial objectives of those desiring to purchase Apex Motel are not fulfilled by the budget proposed in Exhibit II, there are additional steps that may be taken before making a decision to withdraw and invest their capital elsewhere.

Author Index

Dauten, Carl A., 96
Davey, Neil G., 259
Davis, Charles S., 279
Davis, Keith, 358, 365–366
Davis, Louis E., 393
Davis, Ralph C., 79, 443
Day, David R., 417
Dearden, John, 135
DeLeo, Philip J., 405
Dickson, G. W., 138
Dickson, W. J., 32
Digman, Lester A., 488
Donnelly, James H., Jr., 310
Dowling, William F., 308, 328
Drucker, Peter F., 50, 140, 144, 443
Dunbar, Roger L. M., 514
Dunnette, Marvin D., 346, 383, 388, 405

E

Eddy, William B., 182
Emch, Arnold F., 454
England, George W., 55–60, 184, 291

F

Farace, Richard V., 357
Faunce, William A., 364
Fayol, Henri, 25–29, 63
Fazar, Willard, 484
Festinger, Leon, 291, 293
Fiedler, Fred E., 324, 335–343, 347–348
Fisch, Gerald, 227
Fitzpatrick, Susan, 387
Fleishman, Edwin A., 425–426, 429
Flesch, Rudolf, 361
Follett, Mary Parker, 24–25
Forehand, Garlie A., 297
France, R. R., 302
Frederick, William G., 39
French, John R. P., Jr., 281–282, 430
French, Wendell L., 306
Front, Carl F., 182

G

Gallagher, Charles A., 139
Gallagher, James D., 136
Gannon, Martin J., 239, 413
Gardner, B. B., 411
Gatza, James, 282
Gellerman, Saul W., 383, 386, 401, 404, 513
Gemmill, Gary R., 229
George, Claude S., Jr., 448
Georgopoulos, Basil S., 418–419
Ghiselli, Edwin E., 334
Giglioni, Giovanni B., 440
Gilbraith, Jay R., 270
Glueck, William F., 259
Goldstein, Arnold P., 425
Golembiewski, Robert T., 225
Gomberg, William, 448
Gordon, Oakley J., 398
Gordon, William J. J., 160
Graen, George, 341
Graicunas, V. A., 196–198, 249
Grayson, C. Jackson, 153
Greene, Charles N., 310
Greenwood, William T., 40
Grimes, A. J., 182
Grove, B. A., 306
Gruenfeld, Leopold, 429
Guest, Robert H., 394, 418
Guion, Robert M., 397

H

Hage, Jerald, 184
Haire, Mason, 304–306
Hall, Douglas T., 303
Hall, Jay, 162
Hamilton, Ian, 196
Hampton, David R., 52
Haney, William V., 352
Harrell, Thomas W., 276–277
Harris, Edwin F., 426
Harrison, Frank, 390
Hartley, E. L., 304, 399
Hass, George H., 357
Havens, A. Eugene, 183

Hayakawa, Samuel I., 352
Hayden, Spencer, 291
Hellriegel, Don, 297
Hendrick, Hal W., 162
Heneman, Herbert G., Jr., 87, 405
Henning, Dale A., 79, 223
Herold, David M., 76
Herzberg, Frederick, 388, 401
Hettenhouse, George W., 89
Hickson, David J., 182, 184
Higginson, M. Valliant, 77
Hill, Lawrence S., 489
Hinrichs, Harley H., 88
Hirschmann, Winifred R., 452
Hitch, Charles J., 84, 87
Hlavacek, James D., 229
Hollerith, Herman, 130
Holloman, Charles R., 162
House, Robert J., 75–76, 314, 383, 397
Huber, George P., 162
Huberman, John, 423
Hulin, Charles L., 396–398
Hunt, James G., 429
Hunt, Raymond G., 183, 439

I

Ingham, Geoffrey K., 183
Inkson, J. H. K., 182
Ivancevich, John M., 310, 455

J

Jamieson, Bruce D., 52
Jenkins, C. D., 314
Jenkins, David, 393
Jensen, J. Michael, 359
Jerdee, Thomas H., 422
Johnson, D. M., 304
Johnson, Richard A., 128
Jorgenson, Dale O., 405

K

Kahn, Robert L., 308, 311, 398–400, 427–428, 525–526

U

Urwick, Lyndall F., 34, 73, 198–199, 249
Usry, Milton F., 503

V

Veroff, Joanne B., 382
Veroff, Joseph, 382
Viteles, Morris S., 388
von Bertalanffy, Ludwig, 523
von Haller Gilmer, B., 297
Vroom, Victor H., 183, 346, 401, 404

W

Wagner, Harvey M., 36, 149
Walker, C. R., 394
Walker, James W., 260
Walker, Morgan R., 484
Wallace, John, 259
Warner, W. Keith, 183
Waters, L. K., 381
Watson, W. H., 162
Weber, C. Edward, 215
Weick, Karl E., 295
Weiss, E. C., 303
Welshans, Merle, 96
Wernimont, Paul F., 387
Weston, J. Fred, 96, 444
White, Donald D., 52
White, E. B., 357
White, K. K., 259
Whiting, Charles S., 158–159
Whybark, D. Clay, 152
Whyte, William Foote, 122, 384–385, 387, 411
Wicksberg, A. K., 229
Wiener, Norbert, 437
Wiest, J. D., 484, 487, 490
Wigdor, Lawrence A., 397
Wilemon, David L., 229
Withington, Frederic G., 130–131
Wofford, J. C., 333–334, 338
Wolf, S., 315
Wolff, H. G., 315
Wolfson, Alan, 291
Woodruff, Robert J., Jr., 476–477
Woodward, Joan, 184
Worthy, James C., 300, 302
Wray, D. E., 411
Wrege, Charles D., 23

Y

Yoder, Dale, 87, 170, 377
Yuchtman, Ephraim, 182

Z

Zajonc, Robert J., 158
Zaleznik, Abraham, 385–386, 513
Zalkind, Sheldon S., 315, 317–318
Zander, Alvin, 293, 427
Zerfoss, Lester F., 422, 431

Subject Index

A

access, random, 127
accountability, 236; absoluteness of, 238–239; in committees, 205–206
accounting, human resource, 471, 475–477
acid test ratio, 479
advertising, 105
advisory authority, 222–223
affection needs, 380
analysis, 146
appraisal interview, 281–282
appraisals, performance, 278–282
appropriation budget, 498
assets, fixed, 100
assistant manager, 220–222
assistant-to a manager, 220–222
attitude, 298
audit: external, 471–472; internal, 471–473; management, 471, 473–475
audit programs, 471–477
authoritative committee, 206
authority, 27, 213–217; advisory, 222–223; decentralization of, 235, 246–248; defined, 171; delegation of, 234–246; effectiveness of, 216–217; functional, 222–223; line, 218–219; overlapping, 216–217; parity of

responsibility and, 237–238; service, 222–223; sources of, 214–216; staff, 220–223; superior, 216; in Theory X organization, 171; in Theory Y organization, 175–176
authority relationships, 270
automated data processing, 129

B

backward integration, 107
balance sheet budget, 499
behavioral science research methods, 290–296
benefit-cost analysis, 87–90
benefit programs, employee, 391, 393
benevolent autocracy, 328
bonds, 99
brainstorming, 159–160
break-even analysis, 481–483
budget: appropriation, 498; balance sheet, 499; capital expenditure, 497–498; cash, 497; expense, 496–497; flexible, 500–503; flexibility with, 499–503; nature of, 494–505; operating, 496; revenue and expense, 496–497; sales, 496; types of, 495–499; zero-base, 503–504

budgetary control, advantages of, 504–505
budgetary review, periodic, 499–500

C

capital: acquisition of, 99–101; long-term, 99; utilization of, 100–101; working, 100
capital expenditure budget, 497–498
case method of leadership training, 420–421
case problems, analysis of, 11–14
case study, 292
cash budget, 497
chain of command, 172, 218–219
channel of distribution, 103–104
chart: circular, 263; horizontal, 263; organization, 263; vertical, 263
circular chart, 263
classical approach to management, 21–29
climate, organizational, 296–303, 425–426
cluster chain, 365
coaching, 278
coacting group, 335–336
code of ethics, 64

dividends, 101

E

economic effectiveness of planning, 83–87

EDP. *See* electronic data processing

electronic data processing, 129–140; decentralization and, 247–248; design of system, 135–139; development of, 130; evaluation of, 139–140

empathetic listening, 368–371

empirical school of management, 35

employee attitudes, 445–446

employee benefit programs, 116, 391, 393

environment: concept of, 382–383; control over, 384

equifinality, 527–528

esteem needs, 380

ethics, 52–64

exception, principle of the, 461, 463

execution of decision, 148

executive, plural, 208

executive development, 114, 272

expense budget, 496–497

experiment: field, 294–295; laboratory, 295–296; natural, 293–294

experimental studies, 293–296

external audit, 471–472

external data, 81

external objectives, 48–49

F

facility policies, 109–110

field experiment, 294–295

field studies, 291–292

finance function, planning for, 96–101

financial ratio, 478–479

fixed assets, 100

flexibility of plans, 83

flexible budgets, 500–502; evaluation of, 502–503

forced obsolescence, 102

foreman, 410

formal communication, 357–358

formal organization, 37

forward integration, 107

function, as basis of departmentation, 192–193

functional authority, 222–223

functional-teamwork, 227–229

G

game theory, 151–152

general management committee, 206

general systems theory, 39

geographic dispersion, 246

geography, as basis of departmentation, 193

Gordon technique, 159–161

grapevine, 365–366

group: coacting, 335–336; counteracting, 335–336; interacting, 335

group factors in decision making, 157–162

group judgment, 201–202

group-task classification, 338

H

halo effect, 306

Hawthorne Effect, 33

Hawthorne Studies, 32–33

hierarchy of needs, 378–381; variations in, 381–382

historical analysis of costs, 502

horizontal chart, 263

human relations, supervisor's training in, 420–422

human relations approach to management, 29–34, 327

human resource accounting, 471, 475–477

hygienic factor, 388–391

I

identification, 275

incentive plan, 116

incident process method of leadership training, 421

independent variable, organizational climate as, 296–303

individual: change and the, 276–277; as intervening variable, 303–308; in Theory X organization, 174; in Theory Y organization, 179

informal organization, 37

information system: components of, 125–129; defined, 125

information systems, management, 129

information technology, 528–530

input device, 126

institutional source of authority, 214

integrated data processing, 129

integration: backward, 107; forward, 107; vertical, 106–107

interacting group, 335

interface, organizational, 312

internal audit, 471–473

internal data, 81

internalization, 275

internal objectives, 49

interpersonal communications, 358–366

inter-person conflict, 312

inter-role conflict, 311–312

inter-sender conflict, 311

intervening variable, 293; individual as, 303–308

interview, appraisal, 281–282

intra-sender conflict, 311

inventory, 101, 108–109

J

job design, 392–396; current, 393

job enlargement, 394

job enrichment, 394

job satisfaction: other studies of, 398; productivity and, 397–405

L

laboratory, 295

laboratory experiment, 295–296

labor-management relations, 116–117

law of diminishing returns, 84

law of variable returns, 84

leader-member relationship, 337–338

leadership: components of, 329–334; human-relations approach to, 327; patterns of, 267–269; revisionist approach to, 327–329; situational factors in , 331–334; theories of, 325–329; trait approach to, 330–331; work-centered approach to, 326–327

leadership effectiveness: contingency model of, 334–343; determinants of, 346–347; leadership style and, 341–343

leadership style, 338–341; effectiveness and, 341–343; how to select a, 343–347; LPC and, 340–341

leadership training: case method, 420–421; incident process method, 421; problems in, 422–425; role playing method, 421–422

leading, 522

learning curves, 452

least preferred co-worker (LPC), 340

linear programming, 150

line authority, 218–219

line-staff structure, 217–230, 299–300

linking-pin function, 415

longitudinal study, 292

long-range plans, 75

long-term capital, 99

long-term notes, 99

M

maintenance seekers, 391

make-or-buy decision, 107

management: classical approach to, 21–29; current issues in, 528–531; defined, 9; functions of, 5–7; as a group, 7; human relations approach to, 29–34; need for, 5; as a profession, 8; scientific, 23–24, 326–327; span of, 195–200, 269, 300; task force, 229–230

management audit, 471, 473–475

management by objectives, 45–52

management development, 114–272; approaches to, 272–278

management functions, integrating, 518–522

management information, anatomy of, 137

management information systems, defined, 129

management process cycle, 456–457

management science, 36

manager: assistant, 220–222; assistant-to, 220–222

man-machine-system, 38

manual, organization, 263–265

marginal product, 85–86

marketing function, planning for, 101–105

market position, 444

mathematical school of management, 36

measurement, appropriate units of, 451

memory unit, 126

methods, 78

moderating variables, 293

money and motivation, 383–388

Monte Carlo technique, 151

morale, 397–398

mortgages, 99

motivation, 378–383; current theories in, 401–405; in industry, 383–396; money and, 383–388; two-factor theory of, 388–396

motivator, 388–391

N

natural experiment, 293–294

needs: affection, 380; conflicting, 384–387; esteem, 380; hierarchy of, 378–382; physiological, 379; safety, 379–380; self-actualization, 380–381

network analysis, fundamentals of, 484–486

nonauthoritative committee, 206

nonbudgetary control, 469

Non-Linear Systems, Inc., 167–169, 185–187

nonunion employees, treatment of, 117

O

objectives: external, 48–49; internal, 49; management by, 45–52; principle of, 46; statement of, 49–50; value of, 46–48

obsolescence: forced, 102; product, 102–103

on line computer operations, 131

open systems, characteristics of, 525–528

operating budget, 496

operating ratio, 478–480
operational plans, 75
operations analysis, 36
operations research, 36; applications of, 150–153; defined, 149–150; limitations of, 153–154; techniques of, 150–153
order, principle of, 28
organization: change and the, 277–278; contingency approach to, 248–253; defined, 169–170; formal, 37; shape of, 302; size of, 249; task force, 229–230; total, 297, 301–303; undifferentiated, 239
organizational analysis, 259–272; advantages of formal, 266; disadvantages of formal, 266–267; evaluation of formal, 266–267; procedures for, 259–261; tools of, 261–265
organizational behavior, 308–318
organizational climate, 296–303, 425–426
organizational effectiveness, evaluating, 267–272
organizational interface, 312
organization chart, 263; circular, 263; horizontal, 263; vertical, 263
organization development, 114, 272–282, 530–531
organization development program, 278
organization levels, 298–299
organization manual, 263–265
organization questionnaire, 261–262
organization relationships, 211–231
organization structure, 188–208, 269–270; in Theory X organization, 172–173; in Theory Y organization, 176–178

organizing, 521–522
Osborn brainstorming, 159–160
output device, 128–129

P

participative organization, 175
people-centered approach to leadership, 327
perceived, 307
perceiver, 305–307
perception: factors influencing, 305–307; improving, 307–308; nature of, 303–305; of a problem, 154–155
perceptual set, 304
performance: measuring current, 449–454; standards of, 281
performance appraisals, 278–282; improving, 282; purpose of, 280–281
periodic budgetary review, 499–500
personal observation as means of control, 469
personal selling, 104
personal staff, 220–222
personal values in decision-making, 156–157
personnel development, 445
personnel function, planning for, 111–117
person-role conflict, 312
PERT and CPM, evaluation of, 488–489
PERT (Program Evaluation Review Technique), 484, 486–487
physiological needs, 379
plan, 71; classified by function, 76–77; classified by scope, 77–78; classified by time, 75–76; evaluation of, 78–90; long-range, 75; operational, 75; procedural analysis of, 79–83; short-range, 75; standing, 149;

strategic, 75; types of, 74–78
planning: defined, 71; for the finance function, 96–101; for the marketing function, 101–105; overall, 267; for the personnel function, 111–117; pervasiveness of, 73–74; primacy of, 72–73; for the production function, 105–110; purpose of, 72
planning authority, designation of, 80
planning-control-planning cycle, 519–521
plural executive, 208
policies, 77
policy statements, integrating, 117–118
position description, 262–263
position power, 336
preferred stock, 99
pricing, 103
principle of control design, 463
principle of the exception, 461, 463
principle of the objective, 46
probability theory, 152–153
problem solving, 144
procedural analysis of plans, 79–83
procedures, 77–78
process, as basis of departmentation, 193
processing unit, 127–128
product, as basis of departmentation, 193–194
product diversification, 102
production function, planning for, 105–110
productivity, 444; job satisfaction and, 397–405
product leadership, 445
product obsolescence, 102–103
product quality, 103
product selection, 102–103
product standardization, 103

profit, 98; distribution of, 101; as percentage of capital invested, 478–479; as percentage of sales, 479
profitability, 443–444
profit paths, 494
profit plans, 494
programming: linear, 150; quadratic, 150
projection, 306
promotion, 104–105
promotion of personnel, 112
psychosomatic disorder, 314
public responsibility, 446

Q

quadratic programming, 150
quality, product, 103, 107
quantitative aids in decision making, 149–162
questionnaire, organization, 261–262
queuing theory, 150–151
quick ratio, 479

R

random access, 127
rate buster, 387
ratio, 477; acid test, 479; current, 479; financial, 478–479; input-output, 480; interpreting, 481; net sales to average inventory, 479–480; net sales to total market, 480; operating, 478–480; quick, 479; selling expense to net sales, 480
ratio analysis, 477–481
reasoning, 144
received role, 309–310
reciprocity, vendor, 110
reference, 352, 354–355
referent, 352, 354–355
refreezing, 275–276
reinvestment, 101
relationships: cross, 197; direct, 197; group, 197; line and staff, 217–230; organization, 211–231

remuneration, principle of, 28
reports, control, 469–471
research, operations. See operations research
research methods, behavioral science, 290–296
responsibility: assignment of, 235–236; in line-staff relationships, 225–226; parity of authority and, 237–238
restricted committee, 206
revenue and expense budget, 496–497
revisionist approach to leadership, 327–329
role, 38, 307–310; received, 309–310
role ambiguity, 312
role behavior, 310
role conflict of supervisor, 416–417
role expectations, 309
role overload, 312
role playing method of leadership training, 421–422
role sending, 309

S

safety needs, 379–380
sales budget, 496
sales promotion, 105
sales volume, 483
scientific management, 23–24
scientific method, 79
selection of personnel, 112
self, concept of, 382–383
self-actualization needs, 380–381
selling, personal, 104
semantics, 352
sequence, as basis of departmentation, 195
service authority, 222–223
servo system, 117
set, perceptual, 304
short-range plans, 75
short-term capital, 100
signs, 352–354, 356–357

simulation, 81, 151
situational approach to supervisory performance, 428–429
situational factors in leadership, 331–334
social facilitation, 158
social systems school of management, 35
social value issues, 531
somatization reaction, 314
span of control, 195
span of management, 195–200, 269, 300
specialized staff, 222–223
staff: personal, 220–222; specialized, 222–223
staff authority, 220–223
staffing, 112
staff-line structure, 299–300
staff relationships, 240
standard costs, 502
standardization, product, 103, 108
standards: appraisal as means for setting, 447–448; engineered, 448–449; establishing, 442–449; methods of establishing, 446–449; of performance, 281; scope of business, 443–446; statistical, 446–447; time, 448; time study, 448
standing plan, 149
status, 307
stereotyping, 305
stock, 99; common, 99; preferred, 99
storage unit, 126
strategic plans, 75
stress, 312–318; behavioral reactions to, 315–318; physiological reactions to, 313–315
stressor, 312
structure, organization, 188–208, 269–270
study: case, 292; comparative, 292; experimental, 293–296; field, 291–292;

longitudinal, 292; survey, 291–292
subordinate-acceptance source of authority, 214
suborganizational units, 297; properties of, 298–301
subunit, size of, 300–301
superior-subordinate communication, 359–362
supervision: bypassing intermediate, 240; current problems in, 415–418
supervisor, 410; differentiating role of, 427; improving performance of, 425–431; job of, 410–418; legal definition of, 411–412; male vs. female, 417–418; performance of, 413–415; role conflict of, 416–417; self-perception of, 412–413; technical and administrative training of, 419–420; in Theory X organization, 172–174; in Theory Y organization, 178–179; training in human relations for, 420–422; training of, 418–425
survey study, 291–292
symbols, 352–354, 356–357
system, 37; state of, 252–253. *See also* information system

systems: hierarchy of, 523–525; open, 525–528
systems concept, management and, 522–528

T

task force organization, 229–230
task structure, 337
termination of personnel, 113
theory: game, 151–152; probability, 152–153; queuing, 150–151; waiting-line, 150–151
Theory X, 170–174; compared with Theory Y, 179–181
Theory Y, 174–179; compared with Theory X, 179–181
time-event-network analysis, 483–489
time standards, 448
time study standards, 448
total-organization, 297; characteristics of, 301–303; size of, 301–302
training, 113–114; of supervisors, 418–425
trait approach to leadership, 330–331
triangle of meaning, 352–355
two-factor theory of work motivation, 388–396

U

unfreezing, 274–275
unity of command, 239–240; principle of, 27
unity of direction, principle of, 27

V

value systems of managers, 55–60
variable: dependent, 308–318; intervening, 293, 303–308; moderating, 293; organizational climate as independent, 296–303
variable returns, law of, 84
vendors, selection of, 110
vertical chart, 263
vertical integration, 106–107
VIE relationships, 402–405
VIE theories, 401–402
visibility, 307

W

waiting-line theory, 150–151
work-centered approach to leadership, 326–327
working capital, 100

Z

zero-base budgeting, 503–504